Western Civilization

Beyond Boundaries

Western Civilization

BEYOND BOUNDARIES

Sixth Edition VOLUME A: To 1500

Thomas F. X. Noble
University of Notre Dame

Barry Strauss
Cornell University

Duane J. Osheim
University of Virginia

Kristen B. Neuschel
Duke University

Elinor A. Accampo
University of Southern California

David D. Roberts
University of Georgia

William B. Cohen
Late of Indiana University

WADSWORTH
CENGAGE Learning™

Australia • Brazil • Japan • Korea • Mexico • Singapore • Spain • United Kingdom • United States

WADSWORTH
CENGAGE Learning™

Western Civilization: Beyond Boundaries,
Volume A, Sixth Edition
Thomas F. X. Noble, Barry Strauss, Duane J. Osheim, Kristen B. Neuschel, Elinor A. Accampo, David D. Roberts, William B. Cohen

Senior Publisher: Suzanne Jeans

Senior Sponsoring Editor: Nancy Blaine

Associate Editor: Adrienne Zicht

Editorial Assistant: Emma Goehring

Senior Media Editor: Lisa Ciccolo

Executive Marketing Manager:
Diane Wenckebach

Marketing Coordinator: Lorreen Pelletier

Marketing Communications Manager:
Christine Dobberpuhl

Senior Content Project Manager: Jane Lee

Senior Art Director: Cate Rickard Barr

Senior Print Buyer: Judy Inouye

Senior Rights Acquisition Account Manager:
Mollika Basu

Production Service: Elm Street Publishing
Services

Text Designer: Henry Rachlin

Senior Photo Editor: Jennifer Meyer Dare

Cover Designer: Harold Burch

Volume A cover image: Painting on stucco
showing the tomb owner and his wife
ploughing and reaping flax and wheat in
the mythical fields of Iaru from the Tomb of
Sennedjem, Deir el Medina, Tombs of the
Nobles, Thebes, Egypt. Werner Forman/Art
Resource, NY

Compositor: Integra Software Services Pvt. Ltd.

For product information and technology assistance, contact us at
Cengage Learning, Customer & Sales Support, 1-800-354-9706

For permission to use material from this text or product,
submit all requests online at **www.cengage.com/permissions.**
Further permissions questions can be e-mailed to
permissionrequest@cengage.com.

Library of Congress Control Number: 2009934607

ISBN-13: 978-1-424-06958-3
ISBN-10: 1-424-06958-0

Wadsworth
20 Channel Center Street
Boston, MA 02210
USA

Cengage Learning is a leading provider of customized learning solutions with office locations around the globe, including Singapore, the United Kingdom, Australia, Mexico, Brazil, and Japan. Locate your local office at **international.cengage.com/region.**

Cengage Learning products are represented in Canada by Nelson Education, Ltd.

For your course and learning solutions, visit **www.cengage.com.**

Purchase any of our products at your local college store or at our preferred online store **www.ichapters.com.**

Printed in the United States of America
1 2 3 4 5 6 7 13 12 11 10 09

BRIEF CONTENTS

CONTENTS

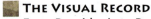

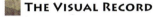

9 The Expansion of Europe in the High Middle Ages, 900–1300   227

10 Medieval Civilization at Its Height, 900–1300   259

11 Crisis and Recovery in Late Medieval Europe, 1300–1500   289

12 The Renaissance 321

MAPS

DOCUMENTS

THE VISUAL RECORD

PREFACE

An old adage says that each generation must write history for itself. If the adage is true, then it would also be true that each generation must teach and learn history for itself. The history, of course, does not change, although new discoveries come to light all the time. What does change is us, each succeeding generation of us. What causes us to change, and thus to experience and understand history in ever new ways, are the great developments of our own times. Think of the world-changing events of the last century: two world wars, the Great Depression, the cold war, nuclear weapons, the civil rights movement, the women's movement, the explosion in scientific knowledge, and the media revolutions involving radio and television, the computer, and the Internet. The pace of change has accelerated in our time, but the process of change always affects people's view of their world.

As we launch the sixth edition of this book we are once again acutely aware of the need to address big questions in ways that make sense to teachers and students right now, in the world we live in today. As these words are being written, the news is full of reports from Afghanistan, Iraq, Iran, Darfur, Somalia, and North Korea. The world's economy is in a perilous state. The United States has elected an African American as its president. In such circumstances we might well ask, What is the West; what is Western? Some believe that we are engaged in a "Clash of Civilizations." Is one of these Western Civilization? If so, who or what is its adversary? The West is sometimes understood geographically and sometimes culturally. For most people, the West means western Europe. And yet western Europe itself is the heir of the peoples and cultures of antiquity, including the Sumerians, Egyptians, Persians, Greeks, Romans, Jews, Christians, and Muslims. In fact, Europe is the heir of even earlier civilizations in Asia and Africa. As a cultural phenomenon, "Western" implies many things: freedom and free, participatory political institutions; economic initiative and opportunity; monotheistic religious faiths (Judaism, Christianity, and Islam); rationalism and ordered thought in the social, political, and philosophical realms; an aesthetic sensibility that aspires to a universal sense of beauty. But the West has felt free to evoke tradition as its guiding light and also to innovate brilliantly, to accommodate slavery and freedom simultaneously, and to esteem original thought and persecute people who deviate from the norm. "Western" indeed has meant many things in various places at different times. This book constantly and explicitly attempts to situate its readers in place, time, and tradition.

Another big question is this: What exactly is civilization? No definition can win universal acceptance, but certain elements of a definition are widely accepted. Civilization is the largest unit within which any person might feel comfortable. It is an organizing principle that implies common institutions, economic systems, social structures, and values that extend over both space and time. Cities are crucial; with cities emerge complex social organizations that involve at least a minimal division of labor. Some people work in the fields, some in the home. Soldiers defend the city, and artisans provide its daily goods. Governing institutions have a wide measure of acceptance and have the ability to enforce their will. Civilizations also develop religious ideas and authorities; literatures and laws that may be oral or written; monumental architecture, especially fortifications, palaces, and temples; and arts such as music, painting, and sculpture. Every civilization enfolds many cultures, a term that may be applied to the full range of expressions of a people in a given place and time. So, for example, the cultures of Egypt, Greece, and Rome were distinctive but all fit under the broad umbrella of Western Civilization.

Western Civilization has had an influence on almost every person alive today. The West deserves to be studied because its tale is compelling, but it demands to be studied because its story has been so central to the development of the world in which we live. Many of the world's dominant institutions are Western in their origin and in their contemporary manifestations—most notably parliamentary democracy. Commercial capitalism, a Western construct, is the world's dominant form of economic organization. The Internet, fast food, and hip-hop music are all western in origin but world-wide in reach today.

Until a generation or so ago, Western Civilization was a staple of college and university curricula and was generally studied in isolation. Although it was, and is, important for us to know who we are, it is also important for us to see that we have changed in dramatic ways and that we can no longer understand ourselves in isolation from the world around us. Accordingly, this book repeatedly sets the experience of the West into its global context. This is not a World History book. But it is a book that sees Western Civilization as one significant segment of the world's history.

BASIC APPROACH

Nearly two decades ago the six original authors of *Western Civilization: Beyond Boundaries* set out to create a textbook for a course that would, as a total effort, inform students about essential developments within a tradition that has powerfully, though not always positively, affected everyone in the contemporary world. Although each of us found something to admire in all of the existing textbooks, none of us was fully happy with any of them. We were disappointed with books that claimed "balance" but actually stressed a single kind of history. We regretted that so many texts were uneven in their command of recent scholarship. Although we were convinced of both the inherent interest of Western Civilization and the importance of teaching the subject, we were disconcerted by the celebratory tone of some books, which portrayed the West as resting on its laurels instead of creatively facing its future.

We decided to produce a book that is balanced and coherent; that addresses the full range of subjects that a Western Civilization book needs to address; that provides the student reader with interesting, timely material; that is up-to-date in terms of scholarship and approach; and that is handsome to look at—in short, a book that helps the instructor to teach and the student to learn. We have kept our common vision fresh through frequent meetings, correspondence, critical mutual readings, and expert editorial guidance. The misfortune of the untimely death of one member of our team has brought us the fortune of a new colleague who has inspired and challenged the rest of us in new ways. Because each of us has focused on his or her own area of specialization, we believe that we have attained a rare blend of competence, confidence, and enthusiasm. Moreover, in moving from plans for a first edition to the preparation of a sixth, we have been able to profit from the experience of using the book, the advice and criticism of dozens of colleagues, and the reactions of thousands of students.

Western Civilization is a story. Therefore, we aimed at a strong chronological narrative line. Our experience as teachers tells us that students appreciate this clear but gentle orientation. Our experience tells us, too, that an approach that is broadly chronological will leave instructors plenty of room to adapt our narrative to their preferred organization, or to supplement our narrative with one of their own.

Although we maintain the familiar, large-scale divisions of a Western Civilization book, we also present some innovative adjustments in arrangement. For instance, we incorporate a single chapter on Late Antiquity, the tumultuous and fascinating period from about A.D 300 to 600 that witnessed the transformation of the Roman Empire into three successors: Byzantine, Islamic, and European. One chapter studies those three successors, thereby permitting careful comparisons. But we also assign chapters to some of the greatest issues in Western Civilization, such as the Renaissance, the age of European exploration and conquest, the Scientific Revolution, and the industrial transformation. Our twentieth-century chapters reflect an understanding of the last century formed in its closing years rather than in its middle decades. What is new in our organization represents adjustments grounded in the best scholarship, and what is old represents time-tested approaches.

In fashioning our picture of the West, we took two unusual steps. First, our West is itself bigger than the one found in most textbooks. We treat the Celtic world, Scandinavia, and the Slavic world as integral parts of the story. We look often at the lands that border the West—Anatolia/Turkey, western Asia, North Africa, the Eurasian steppes—in order to show the to-and-fro of peoples, ideas, technologies, and products. Second, we continually situate the West in its global context. Just as we recognize that the West has influenced the rest of the world, we also carefully acknowledge how the rest of the world has influenced the West. We begin this story of mutual interaction with the Greeks and Romans, carry it through the European Middle Ages, focus on it in the age of European exploration and conquest, and analyze it closely in the modern world of industry, diplomacy, empire, immigration, and questions of citizenship and identity.

Another approach that runs like a ribbon throughout this textbook involves balance and integration. Teachers and students, just like the authors of this book, have their particular interests and emphases. In the large and diverse American academy, that is as it should be. But a textbook, if it is to be helpful and useful, should incorporate as many interests and emphases as possible. For a long time, some said, Western Civilization books devoted excessive coverage to high politics—"the public deeds of great men," as an ancient Greek writer defined the historian's subject. Others felt that high culture—all the Aristotles and Mozarts—was included to the exclusion of supposedly lesser figures and ordinary men and women. In the 1970s, books began to emphasize social history. Some applauded this new emphasis even as they debated fiercely over what to include under this heading.

In this book, we attempt to capture the Western tradition in its full contours, to hear the voices of all those who have made durable contributions. But because we cannot say everything about everybody at every moment, we have had to make choices about how and where to array key topics within our narrative. Above all, we have tried to be integrative. For example, when we talk about government and politics, we present the institutional structures through which power was exercised, the people who possessed power as well as the people who did not, the ideological foundations for the use of power, and the material conditions that fostered or hindered the real or the would-be powerful. In other words, instead of treating old-fashioned "high politics" in abstract and descriptive ways, we take an approach that is organic and analytical: How did things work? Our approach to the history of women is another example. A glance at this book's table of contents and then at its index is revealing. The former reveals very few sections devoted explicitly and exclusively to women. The latter shows that women appear constantly in every section of this book. Is there a contradiction here? Not at all. Women and men have not been historical actors in isolation from one another. Yet gender, which is relational, reciprocal, and mutual, is an important variable that has shaped individual and collective experience. Hence we seek to explain why certain political, economic, or social circumstances had differing impacts on men and women, and how such conditions led them to make different choices.

Similarly, when we talk of great ideas, we describe the antecedent ideas from which seemingly new ones were built up, and we ask about the consequences of those ideas. We explore the social positions of the authors of those ideas to see if this helps us explain the ideas themselves or gauge their influence. We try to understand how ideas in one field of human endeavor prove to be influential in other fields. For instance, gender is viewed as connected to and part of the larger fabric of ideas including power, culture, and piety.

We invite the reader to look at our narrative as if it were a mosaic. Taken as a whole, our narrative contains a coherent picture. Viewed more closely, it is made up of countless tiny bits that may have their individual interest but do not even hint at the larger picture of which they are parts. Finally, just as the viewer of a mosaic may find his or her eye drawn especially to one area, feature, color, or style, so too the reader of this book will find some parts more engaging or compelling than others. But it is only because there is, in this book as in a mosaic, a complete picture that the individual sections make sense, command our attention, excite our interest.

One word sums up our approach in this book: "balance." We tell a good story, but we pause often to reflect on that story, to analyze it. We devote substantial coverage to the typical areas of Greece, Rome, Italy, France, Great Britain, and so forth, but we say more about western Europe's frontiers than any other book. We do not try to disguise our Western Civilization book as a World History book, but we take great pains to locate the West within its global context. And we always assume that context means mutuality and reciprocity. We have high politics and big ideas alongside household management and popular culture. We think that part of the fascination of the past lies in its capacity to suggest understandings of the present and possibilities for the future.

Our subtitle, "Beyond Boundaries," is intended to suggest growth, challenge, and opportunity. The West began in Mesopotamia but soon spread to all of western Asia. Gradually the Greeks entered the scene and disseminated their ideas throughout the Mediterranean world. The Romans, always heirs of the Greeks, carried ideas and institutions from Britain to Mesopotamia. As the Roman order collapsed, Rome's imprint was left on a small segment of Europe lying west of the Rhine and south of the Danube. Europeans then crashed through those boundaries to create a culture that extended from Iceland to the Russian steppes. At the dawn of the modern age Europe entered into a complex set of commercial, colonial, military, and political relations with the rest of the globe. Our contemporary world sees Western influences everywhere. No western "boundary" has ever been more than temporary, provisional.

DISTINCTIVE FEATURES

To make this book as accessible as possible to students, we have constantly been aware of its place in a program of teaching and learning. In the preceding paragraphs something has been said about this book's distinctive substantive features and how, we believe, they will contribute to the attainment of a deeper understanding of Western Civilization, as well as of its importance and place in the wider history of the earth's peoples. Teaching and learning also involve pedagogical techniques and innovations. We have attended conscientiously to pedagogical issues from the start, and we have made some significant changes in this edition.

Our chapters have always begun with a vignette that is directly tied to an accompanying picture. These vignettes alert the reader to one or more of the key aspects of the chapter. Thus the readers have encountered a thematic introduction that evokes interest while pointing clearly and in some detail to what follows.

To make our chapter introductions more effective, which means to give students greater confidence as they proceed through the book, we have taken numerous steps. First, as in past editions, we reviewed and revised our opening vignettes to connect text and picture more closely and to use both to invite the reader into the chapter.

Second, the first page of each chapter contains a succinct Outline that immediately and dramatically tells the reader what he or she is going to encounter in the following pages. Third, the chapter introductions conclude with a list of Focus Questions that both echo the introduction and set the reader off on the right path into the following pages. Fourth, as the student begins to read the chapter proper, a Chronology serves as yet another orientation to the material contained in the chapter. Subject-specific chronologies still appear in various parts of the book, but we felt readers would benefit from a chronological guide at the beginning of each chapter.

In this edition, we have repeated each Focus Question at the head of the section to which it pertains. At the end of each major section, we provide a succinct Section Summary. Each chapter concludes with a Chapter Summary that reiterates the Focus Questions and then briefly answers them once again.

As a complement to text coverage, a ready reference, and a potential study guide, all of the Key Terms have been gathered into a Glossary included in the website that accompanies the book. For this edition, we have also placed definitions on the pages where the Key Terms first appear.

In addition to this fundamental attention to chapter themes and contents, we have sought to improve the book's teachability by adding a pronunciation guide. Whenever we use an unfamiliar name or term, we show the reader how to pronounce it. Instead of using the intricate rules of phonetics, we provide commonsense guides to pronunciation in parentheses directly following the word.

This edition is a bit shorter than its predecessors. Relevance, "teachability," and "learnability" were our guides in streamlining our coverage at many points. Virtually every chapter experienced some slimming in the interest of keeping major points and themes front and center.

Having always been conscious of this book's physical appearance, we have this time adopted a dynamic, single-column design to enhance the reader's experience of the book. Attractively laid-out pages, a handsome full-color design, engaging maps, and beautifully reproduced pictures enhance the book's appearance. In keeping with our desire to integrate the components of the book into a coherent whole, we carefully anchor the maps and pictures into the volume. Our maps, always chosen and conceptualized by the authors, have for the sixth edition been completely redesigned to make them fresher, more attractive, and more informative. Map captions have been carefully written, and revised, to make them effective elements of the book's teaching program. The same is true of the pictures: the authors selected them, worked with the book's designers to place them advantageously (and not just decoratively), and wrote all the captions. For this edition, we paid particular attention to reviewing all the captions and to revising many of them. All of the maps are cross-referenced in the text, some of them several times, and the text often refers directly to the pictures.

From the start, every chapter in this book has had boxed documents, one of which treated a "global" theme, as well as a two-page feature entitled "Weighing the Evidence." For this edition, we thought hard about our features and decided to take some decisive steps to make them work better for teachers and students. First, we reduced the number of features to three per chapter. Second, we introduced a uniform structure and format. One feature, entitled "The Global Record," presents a significant document that sets some aspect of Western Civilization within the global perspective. These documents are substantial, are carefully introduced, and conclude with study questions. Another feature is called "The Written Record." This feature contains a significant document relevant to the text materials then under discussion with a careful introduction and study questions. The third feature is called "The Visual Record." This feature represents a reconceptualization of our former "Weighing the Evidence" feature. Most of those features did focus on visual evidence, but now the Visual Record features all do so. As with the Global Record and Written Record features, the Visual Records have helpful questions. Whereas the Weighing the Evidence features always concluded our chapters, now the Visual Records are placed into the chapters at the most appropriate position. For the fifth edition, we cast a careful eye over all the Visual Record features and prepared eight new ones, and for the sixth edition, we have prepared two new ones. Finally, we took two last steps. We deleted the "Looking Ahead" sections because reviewers suggested that this "telegraphing" of what was to come might confuse the student reader as to what he or she has just read. And we moved the "Suggested Readings" to the book's website.

ORGANIZATION AND CONTENT CHANGES

Throughout the book, the authors have made changes to improve the narrative and to incorporate new ways of talking about particular topics. Chapter 1 has been trimmed by cutting the short section "The First Cities" and by eliminating the larger section "Widening Horizons: The Levant and Anatolia, 2500–1150 B.C." The original subsection "War Abroad, Reform at Home, 1786–1075 B.C." has been divided into two separate sections and the material on the Amarna Archives and the Hittites has been moved to the new "War Abroad" section.

Chapter 2 gained a new main section, "Traders Invent the Alphabet: Canaanites and Phoenicians, ca. 1400–450 B.C.," with new subsections on "The Canaanite City-States, ca. 1400–1200 B.C." and "The Phoenicians, ca. 1050–450 B.C." Material on the Phoenicians, formerly found under "Assyrians and Babylonians," has been moved to the new section. These revisions create sharper focus and clearer organization. A new Visual Record feature, "The Siege of Lachish," has been introduced. The entire main section on "Early Greece" has been moved to Chapter 3, once again in the interest of sharpening the focus.

In Chapter 5, two subsections, "The Roman Household" and "Patrons and Clients," have been combined and shortened into one new section entitled "Families and Patronage." The sections on Roman expansion, both in Italy and in the wider Mediterranean, have been recast as follows: The former section on "The Latin League and Beyond" has been replaced by a section entitled "Keeping the Peace," which has been moved to the section "Republican Expansion: The Conquest of Italy, ca. 509–265 B.C." The sections on "Rome Versus Carthage: The Punic Wars, 264–146 B.C." and "Victories in the Hellenistic East, ca. 200–133 B.C." have been combined into one new section, "Punic Wars and the Conquest of the Greek East." The sections on "The Gracchi" and on "Marius and Sulla" have been recast as "Reformers and Revolutionaries." Chapter 6 has a new Written Record feature on "Boudicca's Revolt."

Chapter 8 has been substantially revised. The long and largely introductory section "Catholic Kingdoms in the West" has been deleted. Its material, much abbreviated, has been recast as the opening subsection, "Medieval Europe takes Shape," under the main section "The Rise of the Carolingian Empire." This main section includes revised and trimmed subsections entitled "The Carolingian Dynasty," "Carolingian Government," "The Carolingian Renaissance," and "The Fragmentation of Charlemagne's Empire." The former subsections "Social Patterns" and "The Experiences of Women" have been combined into a new section, "Social Patterns."

In Chapter 12, the section "Renaissance Court and Society" has been revised as "Politics and Renaissance Culture." In Chapter 14, the map "Reform in Germany, 1517–1555" has been replaced by a new map, "The Global Empire of Charles V." Chapter 15 has been significantly reorganized. The material in the subhead "The Failure of the Invincible Armada" has been moved into the section on "The Formation of the United Provinces." Material from the former subhead "Henry IV and the Fragile Peace" has been moved into the section "Decades of Civil War." The main heading "Religious and Political Conflict in Central and Eastern Europe" has been recast as "The Holy Roman Empire and the Thirty Years' War." The subheads in this main section have been revised, shortened, and renamed. The social and cultural sections of this chapter have been revised and reorganized. One old map 15.4 ("Two Empires in Eastern Europe, ca. 1600") has been deleted. In Chapter 16, material on "The Dutch War" has been moved into the section on "The Burdens of War and the Limits of Power." The section on "Competition Around the Baltic" has been tightened.

Chapter 17 has a new subsection, "Women Scientists and Institutional Constraints," and the former section on "Pierre Bayle" has been revised as "Skepticism and the Spread of Scientific Rationality" to signal the central issues more clearly. Similarly, in Chapter 18, the old section "Adam Smith and David Hume" has been recast as "Economic Thought and the Scottish Enlightenment." Some subsections within the former section on "Monarchy and Constitutional

Government" have been eliminated and the whole section reorganized under "Monarch and Parliament in Great Britain." The subheads in the rest of this chapter have been revised, and two main headings "The Widening World of Commerce" and "Economic Expansion and Social Change" have been eliminated with some of their material reorganized and placed in other sections and other material retained under the new main heading "The Widening World of Trade and Production." Finally, this chapter acquires the new main heading "The Widening World of Warfare" that pulls together military history issues. In Chapter 19, several minor subheads have been shortened and combined into other sections, but a new subhead on "Revolution in the Atlantic World" has been added to the section "The Legacy of Revolution for France and the World" and an old section, "The View from Britain," has been deleted. In general, the revisions in Chapters 15 to 19 aim to gather like with like, to streamline the narrative, and to make topics more explicit.

Two important sections in Chapter 20 have been renamed: "Advances in the Cotton Industry" to "Mass Production" and "Iron, Steam, and Factories" to "New Energy Sources and Their Impacts." Several small, fifth-edition subheads have been incorporated into the larger section on "The Spread of Industry to the Continent." The former subhead "The Working Classes and Their Lot" has been renamed "Social Class and Family Structure," which also gained some material from the deleted section "Industrialization and the Family." This chapter acquired a new Visual Record feature, "St. Giles," while material from the former Visual Record "Collective Action" has been creatively reintegrated into the chapter.

Chapters 21 and 22, which deal with the tangled political history of the nineteenth century, received significant attention in this edition. The first major heading in Chapter 21, "The Congress of Vienna," has been reorganized under a heading entitled "Restoration and Reaction." This move permits new subheads, "The Congress of Vienna," "Restored Monarchs in Western Europe," "Eastern Europe," and "Spain and Its Colonies," to carry the political story effectively down to 1830. Then, the former main heading "Restoration, Reform, and Reaction" has been recast as "The Quest for Reform." In other words, the chapter now establishes Europe's restored regimes and then looks inside them to understand their internal political dynamics. Accordingly, the old heading "Western Europe: From Reaction to Liberalism, 1815–1830" has been deleted because its essential material has already been presented. The chapter does receive a new heading entitled "The Revolution of 1830 and the July Monarchy in France," but a number of smaller subheads have been eliminated and their material redistributed. In Chapter 22, the former main heads "Italian Unification, 1859–1870" and "German Unification, 1850–1871" have been combined into one major section, "Forging New States," that itself contains subsections on the main stages in Italian and German unification subordinated to central themes. The main heading on "The Emergence of New Political Forms in the United States and Canada, 1840–1880" has been eliminated, along with its maps. As in earlier chapters, the aim has been to streamline and focus the narratives in these two as well.

In Chapter 23, some headings received new titles, for instance "The Declining Aristocracy" became "The Adapting Aristocracy," while "The Workers' Lot" shifted to "Improving Conditions Among the Workers and the Poor." The former main heading "Social and Political Initiatives" has been deleted with its most important material, particularly "Educational and Cultural Opportunities," redistributed elsewhere. Old Map 23.1, "European Rails, 1850–1880," has been cut.

Chapter 24 has a new title: "Imperialism and Escalating Tensions, 1880–1914." Its first main heading, "The New Imperialism and the Spread of Europe's Population," has been changed to "The New Imperialism and the Spread of Europe's Influence." This change permitted deletion of the subsection on "Overseas Migration and the Spread of European Values." A new subhead on "Unanticipated Consequences: Rebellion and Colonial War" has been added. Former Map 24.3, "European Migrations," has been replaced by a new map on the Ottoman Empire. In Chapter 25, two maps (25.1 and 25.2) have been combined into one new map called "The War in Europe, 1914–1918," and a new map has been added, "The European Peace Settlement and the Peace in the Middle East." In Chapter 26, one main head, "Weimar Germany and the Trials of New Democracies," has been renamed "The Trials of the New Democracies." In Chapter 28, the main heading "The Victory of Nazi Germany, 1939–1941" received a new title, "German Military Successes, 1939–1941." In Chapter 29, the subhead "The Energy Crisis and the Changing Economic Framework" has been moved under the main heading "Prosperity and Democracy in Western Europe." The subhead "New Nations in Asia" has been deleted with its most important information transferred to "The Varieties of Decolonization."

Our attempt to bring the story up to date means that Chapter 30, as always, received considerable attention. This begins with a new opening photo and vignette on the financial crisis, the meeting of the G-20 in London in April 2009. Several subheads received new titles, for example "Origins of the Union" became "Renewing the Union," "War Crimes Tribunals" became "War Crimes Trials," "Unemployment and Economic Challenges in Western Europe" became "Responding to New Economic Challenges," and "Immigration, Assimilation, and the New Right" became "Immigration, Assimilation, and Citizenship." The subhead "The Post-Communist Experiment" has been expanded with new material on Vladimir Putin and the confrontation between Russia and Georgia. One subhead, "Consensus in the Established Democracies" was deleted. The last section, "The West in the Global Age," has been rewritten, especially the subsection "Questioning the Meaning of the West."

ANCILLARIES

Instructor Resources

PowerLecture CD-ROM with ExamView® and JoinIn® This dual platform, all-in-one multimedia resource includes the Instructor's Resource Manual; Test Bank, revised to reflect the new material in the text by Dolores Grapsas of New River Community College (includes key term identification, multiple-choice, short answer, essay, and map questions); Microsoft® PowerPoint® slides of both lecture outlines and images and maps from the text that can be used as offered, or customized by importing personal lecture slides or other material; and *JoinIn®* PowerPoint® slides with clicker content. Also included is ExamView, an easy-to-use assessment and tutorial system that allows instructors to create, deliver, and customize tests in minutes. Instructors can build tests with as many as 250 questions using up to 12 question types, and using ExamView's complete word-processing capabilities, they can enter an unlimited number of new questions or edit existing ones.

HistoryFinder This searchable online database allows instructors to quickly and easily download thousands of assets, including art, photographs, maps, primary sources, and audio/video clips. Each asset downloads directly into a Microsoft® PowerPoint® slide, allowing instructors to easily create exciting PowerPoint presentations for their classrooms.

Instructor's Resource Manual Prepared by Janusz Duzinkiewicz of Purdue University North Central, the Instructor's Resource Manual has been revised to reflect the new material in the text. This manual has many features, including instructional objectives, chapter outlines and summaries, lecture suggestions, suggested debate and research topics, cooperative learning activities, and suggested readings and resources. The Instructor's Resource Manual is available on the instructor's companion site.

WebTutor™ on Blackboard® With WebTutor's text-specific, pre-formatted content and total flexibility, instructors can easily create and manage their own custom course website. WebTutor's course management tool gives instructors the ability to provide virtual office hours, post syllabi, set up threaded discussions, track student progress with the quizzing material, and much more. For students, WebTutor offers real-time access to a full array of study tools, including animations and videos that bring the book's topics to life, plus chapter outlines, summaries, learning objectives, glossary flashcards (with audio), practice quizzes, and weblinks.

WebTutor™ on WebCT® With WebTutor's text-specific, pre-formatted content and total flexibility, instructors can easily create and manage their own custom course website. WebTutor's course management tool gives instructors the ability to provide virtual office hours, post syllabi, set up threaded discussions, track student progress with the quizzing material, and much more. For students, WebTutor offers real-time access to a full array of study tools, including animations and videos that bring the book's topics to life, plus chapter outlines, summaries, learning objectives, glossary flashcards (with audio), practice quizzes, and weblinks.

Student Resources

Book Companion Site A website for students that features a wide assortment of resources, which have been revised to reflect the new material in the text, to help students master the subject matter. The website, prepared by David Paradis of the University of Colorado, Boulder, includes a glossary, flashcards, crossword puzzles, tutorial quizzes, essay questions, weblinks, and suggested readings.

CL eBook This interactive multimedia eBook links out to rich media assets such as video and MP3 chapter summaries. Through this eBook, students can also access self-test quizzes, chapter outlines, focus questions, chronology and matching exercises, essay and critical thinking questions (for which the answers can be emailed to their instructors), primary source documents with critical thinking questions, and interactive (zoomable) maps. The CL eBook is available on ichapters.

Wadsworth Western Civilization Resource Center Wadsworth's Western Civilization Resource Center gives your students access to a "virtual reader" with hundreds of primary sources including speeches, letters, legal documents and transcripts, poems, maps, simulations, timelines, and additional images that bring history to life, along with interactive assignable exercises. A map feature including Google Earth™ coordinates and exercises will aid in student comprehension of geography and use of maps. Students can compare the traditional textbook map with an aerial view of the location today. It's an ideal resource for study, review, and research. In addition to this map feature, the resource center also provides blank maps for student review and testing.

Rand McNally Historical Atlas of Western Civilization, 2e This valuable resource features over 45 maps, including maps that highlight classical Greece and Rome; maps document European civilization during the Renaissance; follow events in Germany, Russia, and Italy as they lead up to World Wars I and II; show the dissolution of Communism in 1989; document language and religion in the western world; and maps that describe the unification and industrialization of Europe.

Document Exercise Workbook Prepared by Donna Van Raaphorst, Cuyahoga Community College. A collection of exercises based around primary sources. This workbook is available in two volumes.

Music of Western Civilization Available free to adopters, and for a small fee to students, this CD contains many of the musical selections highlighted in the text and provides a broad sampling of the important musical pieces of Western civilization.

Exploring the European Past A collection of documents and readings that give students first-hand insight into the period. Each module also includes rich visual sources that help put the documents into context, helping the students to understand the work of the historian.

Writing for College History, 1e Prepared by Robert M. Frakes, Clarion University. This brief handbook for survey courses in American history, Western Civilization/European history, and world civilization guides students through the various types of writing assignments they encounter in a history class. Providing examples of student writing and candid assessments of student work, this text focuses on the rules and conventions of writing for the college history course.

The History Handbook, 1e Prepared by Carol Berkin of Baruch College, City University of New York and Betty Anderson of Boston University. This book teaches students both basic and history-specific study skills such as how to read primary sources, research historical topics, and correctly cite sources. Substantially less expensive than comparable skill-building texts, *The History Handbook* also offers tips for Internet research and evaluating online sources.

Doing History: Research and Writing in the Digital Age, 1e Prepared by Michael J. Galgano, J. Chris Arndt, and Raymond M. Hyser of James Madison University. Whether you're starting down the path as a history major, or simply looking for a straightforward and systematic guide to writing a successful paper, you'll find this text to be an indispensible handbook to historical research. This text's "soup to nuts" approach to researching and writing about history addresses every step of the process, from locating your sources and gathering information, to writing clearly and making proper use of various citation styles to avoid plagiarism. You'll also learn how to make the most of every tool available to you—especially the technology that helps you conduct the process efficiently and effectively.

The Modern Researcher, 6e Prepared by Jacques Barzun and Henry F. Graff of Columbia University. This classic introduction to the techniques of research and the art of expression is used widely in history courses, but is also appropriate for writing and research methods courses in other departments. Barzun and Graff thoroughly cover every aspect of research, from the selection of a topic through the gathering, analysis, writing, revision, and publication of findings presenting the process not as a set of rules but through actual cases that put the subtleties of research in a useful context. Part One covers the principles and methods of research; Part Two covers writing, speaking, and getting one's work published.

Reader Program Cengage Learning publishes a number of readers, some containing exclusively primary sources, others a combination of primary and secondary sources, and some designed to guide students through the process of historical inquiry. Visit Cengage.com/history for a complete list of readers.

Custom Options Nobody knows your students like you, so why not give them a text that is tailor-fit to their needs? Cengage Learning offers custom solutions for your course—whether it's making a small modification to *Western Civilization: Beyond Boundaries* to match your syllabus or combining multiple sources to create something truly unique. You can pick and choose chapters, include your own material, and add additional map exercises along with the *Rand McNally Atlas* to create a text that fits the way you teach. Ensure that your students get the most out of their textbook dollar by giving them exactly what they need. Contact your Cengage Learning representative to explore custom solutions for your course.

ACKNOWLEDGMENTS

The authors have benefited throughout the process of revision from the acute and helpful criticisms of numerous colleagues. We thank in particular: **Stephen Andrews,** Central New Mexico Community College; **Sascha Auerbach,** Virginia Commonwealth University; **Jonathan Bone,** William Paterson University; **Kathleen Carter,** High Point University; **Edmund Clingan,** Queensborough Community College/CUNY; Gary Cox, Gordon College; **Padhraig Higgins,** Mercer County Community College; **John Kemp,** Meadows Community College; **Michael Khodarkovsky,** Loyola University; **William Paquette,** Tidewater Community College; **David Paradis,** University of Colorado, Boulder; **Sandra Pryor,** Old Dominion University; **Ty Reese,** University of North Dakota; **Michael Saler,** University of California, Davis; **Janette VanBorsch,** Midlands Technical College; and **Matthew Zembo,** Hudson Valley Community College.

Each of us has benefited from the close readings and careful criticisms of our coauthors, although we all assume responsibility for our own chapters. Barry Strauss has written Chapters 1–6; Thomas Noble, 7–10; Duane Osheim, 11–14; Kristen Neuschel, 15–19; and David Roberts, 25–30. Originally written by William Cohen, Chapters 20–24 have been substantially revised and updated by Elinor Accampo.

Many colleagues, friends, and family members have helped us develop this work as well. Thomas Noble continues to be grateful for Linda Noble's patience and good humor. Noble's coauthors and many colleagues have over the years been sources of inspiration and information. He also thanks several dozen teaching assistants and more than 4,000 students who have helped him to think through the Western Civilization experience.

Barry Strauss is grateful to colleagues at Cornell and at other universities who offered advice and encouragement and responded to scholarly questions. He would also like to thank the people at Cornell who provided technical assistance and support. Most important have been the support and forbearance of his family. His daughter, Sylvie; his son, Michael; and, above all, his wife, Marcia, have truly been sources of inspiration.

Duane Osheim thanks family and friends who continue to support and comment on the text. He would especially like to thank colleagues at the University of Virginia who have engaged him in a long and fruitful discussion of Western Civilization and its relationship to other cultures. They make clear the mutual interdependence of the cultures of the wider world. He particularly wishes to thank H. C. Erik Midelfort, Arthur Field, Brian Owensby, Joseph C. Miller, Chris Carlsmith, Beth Plummer, and David D'Andrea for information and clarification on a host of topics.

Kristen Neuschel thanks her colleagues at Duke University for sharing their expertise. She is especially grateful to Sy Mauskopf, Bill Reddy, John Richards, Tom Robisheaux, Alex Roland, Barry Gaspar, and Peter Wood. She also thanks her husband and fellow historian, Alan Williams, for his wisdom about Western Civilization and his support throughout the project, and her children, Jesse and Rachel, for their patience and interest over many years.

Elinor Accampo is deeply indebted to the late Bill Cohen whose chapters in the first four editions offered a model of expertise and prose, and she continues to carry on what he originated with pride and respect. She owes special thanks to Kristen Neuschel and Rachel Fuchs for friendship and advice, to her daughter, Erin Hern, for her expert input as a consumer of college textbooks, and, as always, to her husband Robert Hern for his encouragement and enduring support.

David Roberts wishes to thank Sheila Barnett, Vici Payne, and Brenda Luke for their able assistance and Walter Adamson, Timothy Cleaveland, Karl Friday, Michael Kwass, John Morrow, Miranda Pollard, Judith Rohrer, John Short, William Stuek, and Kirk Willis for sharing their expertise in response to questions. He also thanks Beth Roberts for her constant support and interest and her exceedingly critical eye.

The first plans for this book were laid in 1988, and over the course of twenty-one years there has been remarkable stability in the core group of people responsible for its development. The author team lost a member, Bill Cohen, but Elinor Accampo stepped into Bill's place with such skill and grace that it seemed as though she had been with us from the start. Our original sponsoring editor, Jean Woy, moved up the corporate ladder but never missed an author meeting with us. Through five editions we had the pleasure of working with production editor Christina Horn and photo researcher Carole Frohlich. For this edition Jane Lee and Catherine Schnurr filled those roles, and we are grateful for their efforts. Our sponsoring editor for more than a decade, Nancy Blaine, has been a tower of strength. She believes in us, as we believe in her. We have been fortunate in our editors, Elizabeth Welch, Jennifer Sutherland, Julie Swasey, and Adrienne Zicht. All these kind and skillful people have elicited from us authors a level of achievement that fills us at once with pride and humility.

Thomas F. X. Noble

ABOUT THE AUTHORS

Thomas F. X. Noble   After receiving his Ph.D. from Michigan State University, Thomas Noble taught at Albion College, Michigan State University, Texas Tech University, and the University of Virginia. In 1999 he received the University of Virginia's highest award for teaching excellence and in 2008 Notre Dame's Edmund P. Joyce, C.S.C., Award for Excellence in Undergraduate Teaching. In 2001 he became Robert M. Conway Director of the Medieval Institute at the University of Notre Dame and in 2008 chairperson of Notre Dame's history department. He is the author of *The Republic of St. Peter: The Birth of the Papal State, 680–825; Religion, Culture and Society in the Early Middle Ages; Soldiers of Christ: Saints and Saints' Lives from Late Antiquity and the Early Middle Ages; From Roman Provinces to Medieval Kingdoms; Images, Iconoclasm, and the Carolingians;* and *Charlemagne and Louis the Pious: Five Lives.* He was a member of the Institute for Advanced Study in 1994 and the Netherlands Institute for Advanced Study in 1999–2000. He has been awarded fellowships by the National Endowment for the Humanities (twice) and the American Philosophical Society. He was elected a Fellow of the Medieval Academy of America in 2004.

Barry Strauss   Professor of history and Classics at Cornell University, Barry Strauss holds a Ph.D. from Yale. He has been awarded fellowships by the National Endowment for the Humanities, the American School of Classical Studies at Athens, The MacDowell Colony for the Arts, the Korea Foundation, and the Killam Foundation of Canada. He is the recipient of the Clark Award for excellence in teaching from Cornell. He is Chair of Cornell's Department of History, Director of Cornell's Program on Freedom and Free Societies, and Past Director of Cornell's Peace Studies Program. His many publications include *Athens After the Peloponnesian War: Class, Faction, and Policy, 403–386 B.C.; Fathers and Sons in Athens: Ideology and Society in the Era of the Peloponnesian War; The Anatomy of Error: Ancient Military Disasters and Their Lessons for Modern Strategists* (with Josiah Ober); *Hegemonic Rivalry from Thucydides to the Nuclear Age* (co-edited with R. New Lebow); *War and Democracy: A Comparative Study of the Korean War and the Peloponnesian War* (co-edited with David R. McCann); *Rowing Against the Current: On Learning to Scull at Forty; The Battle of Salamis, the Naval Encounter That Saved Greece – and Western Civilization; The Trojan War: A New History;* and *The Spartacus War.* His books have been translated into six languages. His book *The Battle of Salamis* was named one of the best books of 2004 by the Washington Post.

Duane J. Osheim   A Fellow of the American Academy in Rome with a Ph.D. in History from the University of California at Davis, Duane Osheim is professor of history at the University of Virginia. He has held American Council of Learned Societies, American Philosophical Society, National Endowment for the Humantities and Fulbright Fellowships. He is author and editor of *A Tuscan Monastery and Its Social World; An Italian Lordship: The Bishopric of Lucca in the Late Middle Ages; Beyond Florence: The Contours of Medieval and Early Modern Italy;* and *Chronicling History: Chroniclers and Historians in Medieval and Renaissance Italy.*

Kristen B. Neuschel   After receiving her Ph.D. from Brown University, Kristen Neuschel taught at Denison University and Duke University, where she is currently associate professor of history and Director of the Thompson Writing Program. She is a specialist in early modern French history and is the author of *Word of Honor: Interpreting Noble Culture in Sixteenth-Century France* and articles on French social history and European women's history. She has received grants from the Josiah Charles Trent Memorial Foundation, the National Endowment for the Humanities, and the American Council of Learned Societies. She has also received the Alumni Distinguished Undergraduate Teaching Award, which is awarded annually on the basis of student nominations for excellence in teaching at Duke.

Elinor A. Accampo   Professor of history and gender studies at the University of Southern California, Elinor Accampo completed her Ph.D. at the University of California, Berkeley. Prior to her career at USC, she taught at Colorado College and Denison University. She specializes in modern France and is the author of *Blessed Motherhood; Bitter Fruit: Nelly Roussel and the Politics of Female Pain in Third Republic France;* and *Industrialization, Family, and Class Relations: Saint Chamond, 1815–1914.* She has also published *Gender and the Politics of Social Reform in France* (co-edited with Rachel Fuchs and Mary Lynn Stewart) and articles and book chapters on the history of reproductive rights and birth control movements. She has received fellowships and travel grants from the German Marshall Fund, the Haynes Foundation, the American Council of Learned Societies, and the National Endowment for the Humanities, as well as an award for Innovative Undergraduate Teaching at USC.

David D. Roberts After receiving his Ph.D. in modern European history at the University of California, Berkeley, David Roberts taught at the Universities of Virginia and Rochester before becoming professor of history at the University of Georgia in 1988. At Rochester he chaired the Humanities Department of the Eastman School of Music, and he chaired the History Department at Georgia from 1993 to 1998. A recipient of Woodrow Wilson and Rockefeller Foundation fellowships, he is the author of *The Syndicalist Tradition and Italian Fascism; Benedetto Croce and the Uses of Historicism; Nothing but History: Reconstruction and Extremity After Metaphysics; The Totalitarian Experiment in Twentieth-Century Europe: Rethinking the Poverty of Great Politics;* and *Historicism and Fascism in Modern* Italy, as well as two books in Italian and numerous articles and reviews. He is currently Albert Berry Saye Professor of History *Emeritus* at the University of Georgia.

Western Civilization

BEYOND BOUNDARIES

CHAPTER OUTLINE

Origins, to ca. 3000 B.C.

Mesopotamia, to ca. 1600 B.C.

Egypt, to ca. 1100 B.C.

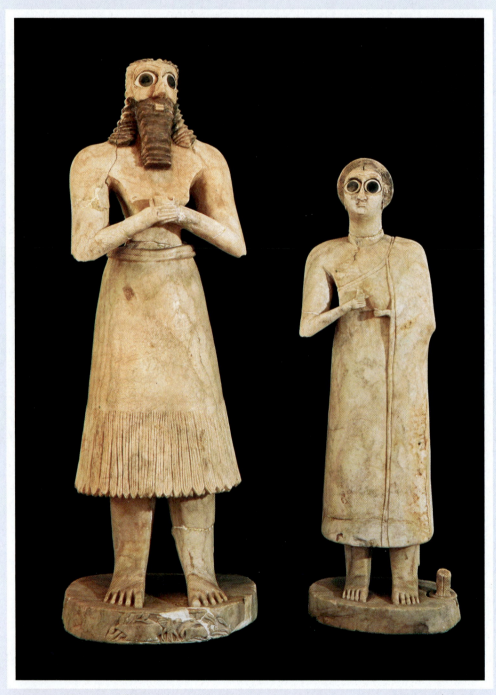

Male and Female Statuettes

Early Dynastic Period, Mesopotamia.   (Iraq Museum, Baghdad/Scala/Art Resource, NY)

The Ancestors of the West

Their huge staring eyes peer out across the centuries. He has long hair, a flowing beard, and a pleated skirt. She has short black hair and wears a simple dress and cloak that go down to her ankles. The man is taller and broader and grabs our attention with his big hair and his hands clasped in prayer. The woman seems modest and may originally have had a child beside her. They represent one of history's oldest couples, dating back to about 2500 B.C.

The powerful gaze of their inlaid alabaster eyes is a way of looking toward heaven. In fact, the couple may have represented gods. Certainly, they did not lack for company, to judge from the dozen other figurines and busts found with them, most of them smaller than the couple and are probably priests and worshipers. One is inscribed with a name, no doubt of an important person. They all come from a temple in the ancient Mesopotamian city of Eshnunna (modern Tell Asmar in Iraq), where they had been placed as an offering to the gods. The statuettes show us that early civilization was religious, artistic, literate, structured by rank and status, and fascinated by the relationship between men and women.

The world of 2500 B.C. had already seen the most momentous inventions in human history. They began approximately 100,000 years ago, when the first modern humans evolved from humanlike ancestors. Human beings wrestled with an often-hostile environment, engaging in a continuing series of experiments, until beginning about 10,000 B.C., they learned how to plant crops and tame animals. The shift from a food-collecting to a food-producing economy dramatically increased the amount of human life that the earth could support. Then between 3500 and 3000 B.C., in parts of what is today the Middle East, human society reached a new stage. These complex societies were marked by inequality and governed by states whose administrators used the first written records. In short, these societies had achieved civilization.

What we call Western civilization, however, was still more than two thousand years away. As a term, *Western civilization* is imprecise, inviting disagreement about its definition and about the lands, peoples, and cultures that it embraces at any given time. In the strictest sense, Western civilization means the "West," and that, in turn, has traditionally meant the lands and peoples of western Europe.

Initially, however, the West embraced the Greek and Roman peoples, plus the foundational monotheistic religions of Judaism and Christianity. These first Westerners, in turn, borrowed many ideas and institutions from the earlier civilizations of western Asia and Egypt. (These civilizations are sometimes referred to as the ancient Near East.) Indeed, civilization began in those lands and came only relatively late to Europe.

Western Asia and Egypt contributed greatly to the cultures of Greece and Rome and to the religious visions of the Jews and Christians. Yet, those earlier civilizations are

FOCUS QUESTIONS

- How did the earliest human beings adapt to their environments and create the first civilizations?
- What were the Mesopotamians' major contributions to government, religion, and art and culture?
- How did the king's power affect various aspects of Egyptian society?

This icon will direct you to additional materials on the website: www.cengage.com/history/noble/westciv6e

See our interactive eBook for map and primary source activities.

sufficiently different from the West and its society, politics, and religion that they are better considered as ancestors or forerunners of the West rather than as its founders. (For a longer discussion of the definition of Western civilization, see the Preface.)

So, after briefly surveying the origins of the human species, the historian of the West must begin with the emergence of civilizations, after 3500 B.C., in two great river valleys: the valley of the Tigris (TY-gris) and Euphrates (yoo-FRAY-tees) in Mesopotamia (today, Iraq and Syria), and the valley of the Nile in Egypt. Impressive in their own right, Mesopotamia and Egypt influenced a wide range of other early civilizations in western Asia and northern Africa, including the Hittites and the Canaanite city-states.

ORIGINS, TO CA. 3000 B.C.

How did the earliest human beings adapt to their environments and create the first civilizations?

The earth is old; modern human beings are young; and civilization is a recent innovation. Scientists have made great strides in explaining human origins, but great disagreement still reigns. We can be more certain about the series of processes, beginning around 10,000 B.C., that led to the emergence of civilization by 3500 to 3000 B.C. The period studied in this chapter includes both prehistory—the term often used for time before the invention of writing—and recorded history. Writing appeared last among the complex of characteristics that marks the emergence of civilization.

Over a period of several thousand years, humans abandoned a mobile existence for a sedentary one. They learned to domesticate animals and to cultivate plants. They shifted from a food-collecting economy to a predominantly food-producing economy. They developed the first towns, from which, over several millennia, the first urban societies slowly evolved. The result—the first civilizations, found in western Asia and Egypt—laid the groundwork on which later would be built the founding civilizations of the West: the Greeks, Romans, and Hebrews.

The First Human Beings

Anatomically modern human beings, *Homo sapiens sapiens*—genus *Homo*, species *sapiens*, subspecies *sapiens*—first appeared about 100,000 years ago, but the human family is much older. Also known as **hominids**, the human family includes many ancient and extinct species.

hominids The primate family *Hominidae*, which includes humans. The modern human being, *Homo sapiens sapiens*, is the only species of this family still in existence.

Africa is the cradle of humanity. The first hominids appeared in Africa's tropics and subtropics over 4 million years ago. By 2.5 million years ago, they had evolved into creatures who invented the first technology, simple stone tools. Prehistory is traditionally referred to as the Stone Age because stone was the primary medium from which hominids made tools. The hominids were migratory: not less than 1.6 million years ago and perhaps much earlier, they appeared in East Asia and the eastern edge of Europe. The next important stage in human evolution is *Homo erectus* ("upright person"), a hominid with a large brain who used more complex stone tools and may have acquired language. The appearance of *Homo erectus* is usually dated to 1.8 million years ago, but a recent discovery in China may date *Homo erectus* as early as 2.25 million years ago.

About 800,000 years ago, another species of early humans lived in Europe. They are sometimes known as *Homo heidelbergensis* ("Heidelberg person") from the discovery spot of a jaw bone near Heidelberg, Germany. Beginning about 400,000 years ago, Europe was home to the ancestors of the best-known archaic people, the Neandertals. Neandertals lived in Europe and western Asia until about 30,000 years ago. They had strong and stocky physiques, perhaps an adaptation to the rugged climate of the Ice Age, the period of fluctuating cycles of warm and cold, beginning about 730,000 years ago and ending only about 10,000 years ago, an era when glaciers ebbed and flowed. Yet, the Neandertals were no brutes, as they are usually imagined to be. They were, for example, among the first people to bury their dead, often with grave offerings—for example, flint, animal bones, or flowers—which suggest they were sensitive enough to mourn their losses. Recent research shows that Neandertals were both clever enough to use tools to attack one another and caring enough to nurse their wounded back to health.

Neandertals, however, were not modern humans. The most recent research suggests that all anatomically modern humans are descended from a single African ancestor. About 89,000 years ago, the *Homo sapiens sapiens*, from whom we are all descended, was born in Africa. About 70,000 years ago, descendants of that person left Africa for the other continents.

Modern humans entered Europe about 35,000 years ago. Within 5,000 years, Neandertals had disappeared—whether through war, disease, or an inability to compete with modern humans, we do not know. The first modern humans tended to be taller and less muscular than Neandertals. They also used their hands more precisely and walked more efficiently, and they lived longer. The modern human skull, with its high forehead and tucked-in face, is distinctive, but differences between the modern and archaic human brain are a matter of scholarly debate. What no one debates, however, is that, with the disappearance of Neandertals, modern humans put into effect a revolution in culture.

The Revolution in Human Culture, ca. 70,000–10,000 B.C.

Before the emergence of modern humans, people had relatively little ability to change the natural environment. Modern humans changed that. They exploited natural resources, largely by means of technology and organization. Thus, they began the process of human manipulation of the environment that—sometimes brilliantly, sometimes disastrously—has remained a leading theme of the human experience ever since. The key to this change was a dramatic increase in the amount and complexity of information being communicated—what might be called the first information revolution. The twin symbols of the revolution are cave paintings and notations made on bone, signs that humans were thinking about their environment and their experiences.

CHRONOLOGY

ca. 4.4 million years ago	Earliest hominids
800,000 years ago	First humans in Europe
ca. 100,000 years ago	*Homo sapiens sapiens*
40,000–10,000 B.C.	Upper Paleolithic era
10,000–2500 B.C.	Neolithic era
3500–3000 B.C.	First civilizations
3500–3100 B.C.	First writing in Mesopotamia
3300–3200 B.C.	First writing in Egypt
ca. 3200 B.C.	Unification of Nile Valley
2800–2350 B.C.	Early Dynastic Period
2695–2160 B.C.	Egyptian Old Kingdom
2500–2350 B.C.	Cuneiform texts from Ebla
2025–1786 B.C.	Egyptian Middle Kingdom
1650–1180 B.C.	Hittite Old, Middle, and New Kingdoms
1550–1075 B.C.	Egyptian New Kingdom
1450–1300 B.C.	First international system
1250–1150 B.C.	Sea Peoples invade

(All dates in this chapter are approximate.)

Chauvet Cave Art This black-painted panel shows horses, rhinoceroses, and wild oxen. The purpose of cave paintings is unknown, but perhaps they served as illustrations of myths or as attempts to control the environment through magic. (Courtesy, Jean Clottes/ Ministère de la Culture)

It was long thought that these dramatic changes began in Europe about 40,000 B.C.* Recently, however, they have been traced to southern Africa, probably more than 70,000 years ago. The discovery there of carefully worked bone tools and stone spearheads pinpoints the dawn of modern human technology. Still, it is not in Africa, but elsewhere, that we can best trace the early evolution of the modern human mind. Europe from about 40,000 to about 10,000 B.C. provides reliable evidence of the life and the culture of early human hunter-gatherer societies, which survived by a food-collecting economy of hunting, fishing, and gathering fruits and nuts. This period is sometimes called the Upper Paleolithic (Greek for "Old Stone") era. Then, around 10,000 B.C., a second revolution began in western Asia: the invention of a food-producing economy through the domestication of animals and the cultivation of crops. The period from about 10,000 to 3000 B.C. is sometimes called the Neolithic (Greek for "New Stone") era.

Archaeology tells us something about early people's way of life. So do analogies from contemporary anthropology, for even today, a few people still live in hunter-gatherer societies in isolated corners of the globe. An educated guess is that early humans lived in small groups, of maybe twenty-five to fifty persons, related by kinship or marriage. Early hunter-gatherers moved from place to place, following the seasonal migration of game, but by the eve of the invention of agriculture, some hunter-gatherers had settled down in villages. Modern cases suggest that work was usually, but not always, divided by sex. Usually, women gathered plants and cared for children and elders, while men went hunting. In some modern cases, however, women hunt as well or better than men, and that might have been the case in Paleolithic times too.

It was probably common for men and women to pair off, have children, and establish a family, much as marriage is a near-universal practice among humans today. Compared with other animals, humans produce extremely dependent infants requiring years of attention. To ensure the survival of the young to adulthood, men as well as women may have needed to play a role in child rearing.

Early people found shelter by building huts or, frequently, by living in caves or rock shelters—hence, our notion of the "caveman." Caves offered shelter, could be heated, and made a naturally good vantage point for observing prey and hostile humans. In the Upper Paleolithic era, about 30,000 years ago, caves were the site of the earliest representational art. The most spectacular Upper Paleolithic paintings discovered so far have been found in caves in southern France (for example, at Lascaux [lass-CO] and at Chauvet [show-VAY] Cave) and in Spain (at Altamira). European cave paintings of animals, such as the bison, horse, reindeer, and woolly mammoth (a huge, extinct member of the elephant family with hairy skin and long, upward-curving tusks), attest to early human artistic skill.

Other early art includes engravings on stone of animals, birds, and stylized human females, as well as female figurines carved from ivory or bone. Usually represented with exaggerated breasts or buttocks, the carvings are called Venus figurines, after Venus, the Roman goddess of love. They may represent an attempt to control fertility through magic.

Upper Paleolithic craftsmanship is as impressive as the art. The early human tool kit included the first utensils in such easily worked materials as antler and ivory. Stone tools became longer and more varied. The first stone and bone spear points, the first bows and arrows, and the first bone needles and awls (probably for sewing animal skins) all appeared.

Hunting was a communal enterprise. Related families probably joined together in clans, which in turn may have formed tribes. Many scholars think of these groups as patriarchal (literally, "ruled by the father"), that is, with the family governed by the father, and the tribe by a male headman or chief. Yet, some later myths (for example, among the ancient Greeks) envision women as the rulers of prehistoric society. Today, some historians see the possibility of matriarchy (literally, "rule by the mother") in the Venus figurines but that is not firm evidence of matriarchy. If chiefs were generally male, as in later periods, some tribes may have had no chief at all, following the decision of the community rather than an individual leader.

hunter-gatherers Food-collecting society in which people live by hunting, fishing, and gathering fruits and nuts, with no crops or livestock being raised for food.

---

* We follow the traditional practice in the West of expressing historical dates in relation to the birth of Jesus Christ (actually, to a now discredited calculation of his birth date, because in fact Jesus was not born in A.D. 1; see page 159). Dates before his birth are labeled B.C. (which stands for "before Christ"), and dates after his birth are labeled A.D. (*anno Domini*, Latin for "in the year of the Lord"). A widely used alternative refers to these dates as B.C.E. ("before the common era") and C.E. ("of the common era").

The Coming of Agriculture, ca. 10,000–5000 B.C.

The human invention of agriculture was dramatic, meriting the name **Neolithic Revolution** that scholars sometimes give it. Yet if dramatic, the invention spread slowly and unevenly. In most areas, hunting and fishing continued to be a major source of food, even though agriculture fed more people. Agriculture was first invented sometime after 10,000 B.C. in western Asia, then discovered again independently in other parts of the world. By 5000 B.C., information about the new practices had spread so widely that farming could be found in many places around the world.

The story begins about 13,000 B.C., when humans began to specialize in the wild plants they collected and the animals they hunted. They had good reason to do so because hunter-gatherer society had become increasingly complex, and in some places, permanent settlements had appeared. There were now probably more mouths to feed, requiring more food. The next step is not surprising: learning how to domesticate plants and animals.

The first animals to be domesticated were probably dogs because they were useful in hunting. Then came sheep, goats, and cattle. Wheat and barley were the first plants that humans learned to grow, followed by legumes (beans). With males occupied in hunting, it may well have been females who first unraveled the secrets of agriculture.

Domestication began in a crescent-shaped zone of land of dependable annual rainfall. The region stretches west to east from what is today southern Jordan to southern Iran: scholars call it the Fertile Crescent (see **MAP 1.1**). With domestication came small agricultural settlements, which were increasingly common after 7000 B.C. Thus was born the farming village, probably the place that most people have called home since the spread of agriculture around the world.

Neolithic Revolution

Human discovery and spread of agriculture, between about 10,000 and 5000 B.C. People first domesticated dogs and other animals and then learned how to cultivate crops.

MAP 1.1—Western Asia

The Neolithic Revolution began after 10,000 B.C. in the Fertile Crescent, an arc-shaped region of dependable annual rainfall. In this area between the Tigris and Euphrates Rivers known as Mesopotamia, the world's first urban civilization took root about 3500 to 3000 B.C.

Scholars once thought of Neolithic villages as simple places devoted to subsistence agriculture, with no craft specialization, and as egalitarian societies lacking social hierarchies. In recent years, new evidence and a rethinking of older information have altered this picture considerably. A Neolithic village site in eastern Anatolia (modern Turkey), for example, provides evidence of metalworking (of copper) and specialization of labor (in beadmaking) from approximately 7000 to 6000 B.C. The site also contains the world's earliest known example of cloth, probably linen, woven around 7000 B.C. Artwork shows men wearing loincloths and headdresses, women wearing pants and halter tops, and both sexes wearing jewelry.

The Neolithic town of Çatal Hüyük (CHAH-tal Her-yerk) in south-central Anatolia (see **Map 1.1**) had six thousand people in 6000 B.C., making it by far the largest settlement in its time. It was probably a trading center and perhaps a religious shrine. Carbonization from fire has preserved many objects showing Çatal Hüyük's sophistication, including woven fabrics, obsidian (a sharp volcanic glass used in tools), mirrors, wooden vessels, and makeup applicators.

Agriculture made human populations richer and more numerous, but it also bred disease and probably increased the scale of war. More men than ever before were available to fight because agriculture proved to be so efficient a source of food that it freed people for specialized labor—including war.

Evidence of war comes from Jericho (JEH-rih-co). Located in Palestine near the Dead Sea (see **Map 1.1**), Jericho may be the oldest continuously settled community on earth. Around 7000 B.C., Jericho was a town surrounded by massive walls 10 feet thick and 13 or more feet high, about 765 yards long, and probably enclosing an area of about 10 acres. The most prominent feature of the walls was a great tower 33 feet in diameter and 28 feet high with an interior stairway. Inside the walls lived a densely packed population of about two thousand people.

This is not to say that war in Neolithic times was sophisticated. Indeed, it was probably more a matter of group skirmishes and sporadic raids than of systematic warfare. Spanish rock art shows a confrontation between two groups of archers, one following what seems to be a leader. The scene may be a ritual rather than a violent conflict, but we have evidence, too, of actual bloodshed. The earliest known evidence of what may have been organized warfare comes from a cemetery in Sudan dating from 12,000 to 4500 B.C. Of fifty-nine human skeletons there, nearly half died violently, including women and children.

Neolithic and Copper Age Europe, 7000–2500 B.C.

Europe was one day to become the center of Western civilization, but the region lagged behind its neighbors at first. Innovations from the east reached Europe after 7000 B.C. and slowly transformed it. At the same time, Europeans developed their own unique culture.

Today, "Europe" has a political meaning, referring to specific countries or to the European Union, but its most basic meaning is geographical. The term **Europe** refers to a vast peninsula of the Eurasian continent with several distinct regions. Southern Europe is made up of a rugged and hilly Mediterranean coastal strip, linked to northern Africa and western Asia by the sea and by similarities in climate and landscape. High mountains are found in the Alps of south-central Europe, from which chains of lower mountains radiate toward the southwest and southeast. Northern Europe, by contrast, consists in large part of a forested plain, indented here and there by great rivers. In the southeast, the plain, or steppe, becomes open and mostly treeless. The eastern boundaries of Europe are, in the north, the Ural Mountains and, in the south, the Caucasus Mountains. Georgia, Armenia, and Azerbaijan are all considered parts of Europe.

Before 7000 B.C., Europeans lived a traditional hunter-gatherer existence. Then came farming, which was introduced in southeastern Europe around 7000 B.C. by migrants from western Asia. Agriculture expanded across Europe between about 6000 and 4500 B.C., but not until 2500 B.C. did the majority of Europeans adopt a food-producing way of life. Yet, Europe was hardly static in the meantime. The era of European prehistory from 4500 to 2500 B.C. is known as the Late Neolithic Age, or the Copper Age, because copper came into use on the Continent during this time, as did gold.

Between about 3500 and 2500 B.C., Copper Age Europe grew in sophistication. The urbanization of Mesopotamia (in modern-day Iraq; see **Map 1.1**) had an impact on southeastern Europe, which supplied raw materials for western Asia. Greece underwent the greatest transformation, to the extent that it developed its own urban civilization by about 2000 B.C. (see Chapter 2). The recent discovery of a Copper Age corpse, preserved in the ice of the Italian Alps, opens a window

Europe The westernmost peninsula of Eurasia, Europe is one of the world's seven continents. Civilization came late to Europe, although the continent was destined to become the center of the West.

into northern Italian society of about 3200 B.C. (See the feature, "The Visual Record: The Iceman and His World.")

On Europe's northern and western edges, people began to set up megaliths—stone tombs and monuments—often of huge blocks. Such monuments may illustrate an awareness of time created by the spread of agriculture, with its seasonal rhythms. In Britain, megalithic architecture reached its peak with Stonehenge, built in stages from about 2800 to 1500 B.C. This famous monument consists of a circle of stones oriented precisely on the rising sun of midsummer—a sign both of early Europeans' interest in the calendar and of their skill in technology.

The Emergence of Civilization, 3500–3000 B.C.

Civilization comes from the Latin word *civitas*, meaning "commonwealth" or "city." Yet, it is not the city but the state that marks the first civilizations, which began in Mesopotamia and Egypt between 3500 and 3000 B.C. Cities played a major role in Mesopotamia but were less important in Egypt. Civilization allowed human beings to think big. A large and specialized labor force, organized by a strong government, made it possible to expand control over nature, improve technology, and trade and compete over ever widening areas. An elite class emerged that was able to pursue ever more ambitious projects in art and thought and to invent systems of writing. In short, the advent of civilization in the fourth millennium B.C. marked a major turning point. Thereafter, the human horizon expanded forever.

Civilization arose in Iraq, in the valley between the Tigris and Euphrates Rivers (see **MAP 1.1**), a region that the Greeks named Mesopotamia (literally, "between the rivers"). At around the same time or shortly afterward, civilization also began in the valley of the Nile River in Egypt. Both Mesopotamia and Egypt are home to valleys containing alluvial land—that is, a relatively flat area where fertile soil is deposited by a river. Although these civilizations each developed largely independently, some borrowing between the two took place.

The first states emerged through a process of action and reaction. In order to feed rulers, priests, and warriors, farmers worked harder, used better techniques, and increased the amount of land under cultivation. Meanwhile, both the number and variety of settlements increased.

Along with states, came writing, which developed between about 3500 and 3100 B.C. in Egypt and Mesopotamia. The growth of writing from simple recordkeeping can be traced step by step. Before writing, Mesopotamian people used tiny clay or stone tokens to represent objects being counted or traded. By 3500 B.C., with 250 different types of tokens in use, the system had grown unwieldy enough for people to start using signs to indicate tokens. It was a short step to dropping

THE DEVELOPMENT OF WRITING

The Maltese Female
The "Sleeping Lady," a terra-cotta statuette of the late fourth millennium B.C. from Malta, shows a reclining woman, perhaps a goddess or priestess. Her double-egg–shaped buttocks are thought to symbolize fertility or regeneration. (Erich Lessing/Art Resource, NY)

The Iceman and His World

On September 19, 1991, a German couple went hiking in the Italian Alps. At 10,530 feet above sea level, in a mountain pass, they thought they had left civilization and its problems behind until they stumbled on an unexpected sight: the body of a dead man lying in the melting ice. Nor was that their only surprise. At first they thought the corpse was the victim of a recent accident. When the authorities arrived, however, the body was discovered to be very old. A helicopter was ordered, and the body was brought to a research institute in Innsbruck, Austria. When the investigators were through, it was clear that the hikers had chanced upon one of the most remarkable archaeological discoveries of the century.*

He was 5,300 years old. The Iceman—as the corpse has become known—is a natural mummy, preserved under the snow: the oldest known remains of human flesh. If that weren't striking enough, consider the clothes and extensive gear that survived with him—they are a window into the European world of about 3200 B.C. The most difficult and most fascinating question is this: Who was the Iceman?

His body offers an introduction. The Iceman stood 5 feet 2 inches tall. He was in his mid-40s and probably had a beard. Genetic testing shows that he was a European, a close relative of modern northern and alpine Europeans. His sinewy frame points to a life of hard work, and scientific tests indicate other difficulties. His growth was arrested by periods of illness, grave hunger, or metal poisoning. His teeth are badly worn, the result perhaps of chewing dried meat or, alternatively, of working leather. He may have undergone a kind of acupuncture; at any rate, he is tattooed, which in some cultures is a medical treatment rather than a form of decoration. He has several broken ribs, which indicates either damage under the ice, mishandling when the body was discovered, or an ancient accident or fight.

The Iceman died violently. The story began in a valley south of the mountains one spring day—pollen analysis specifies the season. There the Iceman ate goat meat and vegetables. Then he decided to climb into the mountains, perhaps to escape after a fight. At least several days before he died, the Iceman received a severe cut on his right hand from a rough blade, which should indicate trouble.

In the mountains the Iceman enjoyed his very last meal, consisting of red deer and some cereals. Soon afterwards he encountered someone who shot him in the shoulder with an arrow. The arrow struck a major artery, which caused the Iceman to bleed to death within minutes. Who killed the Iceman and why? We don't know. Some evidence suggests that as many as four people attacked him but not all scholars agree about that.

Whoever killed the Iceman pulled out the shaft and left the arrowhead in his victim. Nor did the killer take any of the

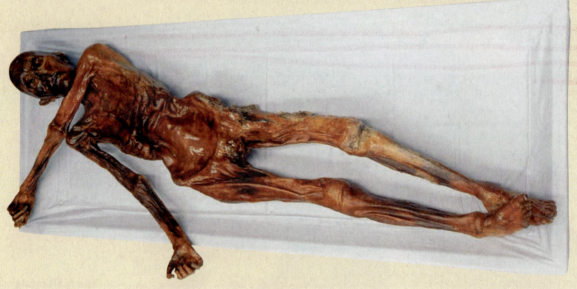

Mummy of Iceman (Copyright Photo Archives, South Tyrol Museum of Archaeology)

cuneiform First writing system in Mesopotamia, consisting of wedge-shaped impressions in soft clay. Named from the Latin word for "wedge-shaped," it was developed about 3500–3100 B.C.

the tokens and placing the signs on a clay tablet by making indentations in the clay with a reed stylus: writing. New words were soon added through pictographs (pictures that stand for particular objects). The pictographs evolved into ideograms—that is, abstract symbols that are no longer recognizable as specific objects and thus can be used to denote ideas as well as things.

In the centuries following its introduction, Mesopotamian writing became standardized. Scholars call the signs **cuneiform**, from the Latin for "wedge-shaped," a good description of what early writing looks like (see **FIGURE 1.1**). In its first centuries, cuneiform was used almost

Iceman's valuable gear, which may suggest that he didn't want to be caught with any of the dead man's property. Today that gear provides tantalizing clues to the Iceman's social status. Look at the artist's drawing. A woven grass or reed cape lies over the Iceman's deerskin coat, which in turn covers a leather loincloth and garter, held in place by a leather belt. A bearskin hat, skin leggings, and calfskin shoes, stuffed with grass for insulation, complete his wardrobe. The Iceman and his contemporaries knew how to dress for the cold weather of the mountains.

The Iceman carries a rich tool kit. Notice his copper ax and 6-foot-long bow, made of yew, the best wood then available for making bows. A quiver (arrow case), two birch-bark containers, a waist pouch, and a frame—probably part of a backpack—hang from his body. Among his items of equipment are flint tools (including a dagger, a retouching tool, and a scraper); a piece of net; two birch-fungus-like "polypores" threaded on a leather thong, probably used as a natural antibiotic; and fourteen arrows, all, oddly, broken. In short, it appears that the Iceman was equipped with a state-of-the-art mountain survival kit of his day. It is not clear why he carried broken arrows, but he would not have had time to change his gear before he fled.

Scholars differ about the Iceman's occupation. Educated guesses range from to a herdsman to a hunter to a trader to a warrior to an outlaw to a shaman (a priest who uses magic). The Iceman's complex weapons and well-made clothing point to a sophisticated culture. The copper ax is the key to that culture and its relationship with the wider world. Similar axes have been found in northern Italian tombs in Remedello, about 240 miles south of the Alps. Before the discovery of the Iceman, archaeologists believed that Italians learned the metalwork technology needed for such an ax from Anatolia, where similar pieces of metalwork are dated to approximately 2700 to 2400 B.C. Hence, the Remedello culture was usually also dated to that period. The discovery of the Iceman means that Remedello must be backdated by about five hundred years. It is clear, then, that by about 3200 B.C., northern Italians not only borrowed from the more advanced eastern Mediterranean areas but also created their own original technology and culture. Thus, a small object (a copper ax), placed within a larger body of evidence (Italian and Anatolian met-

Artist's Rendition of the Iceman   (© Michael Rothman)

alwork), permits broad generalization about the interaction and independence of ancient cultures.

QUESTIONS

1. What do the Iceman's clothing, tools, and weapons tell us about his society?

2. How do modern, scientific tests add to our knowledge of the Iceman?

3. How does the discovery of the Iceman change our understanding of the relationship between Europe and Anatolia about five thousand years ago?

4. How skilled at technology was Copper Age Europe?

5. What role did violence play in prehistoric human relations?

---

* For an introduction to the Iceman, see Brenda Fowler, *Iceman: Uncovering the Life and Times of a Prehistoric Man Found in an Alpine Glacier* (Chicago: University of Chicago Press, 2001); Stephen S. Hall, "Last Hours of the Iceman," *National Geographic* (July 2007), http://ngm.nationalgeographic.com/2007/07/iceman/hall-text/1; James H. Dickson, Klaus Oeggl, and Linda L. Handley, "The Iceman Reconsidered," *Scientific American* (May 2003); and <http://www.mummytombs.com/mummylocator/featured/otzi.htm>.

entirely for economic records or commercial transactions. Then it was used to record offerings to the gods. By 2350 B.C., cuneiform had evolved into a mixed system of about six hundred signs, most of them phonetic (syllabic), with relatively few ideograms.

Egyptian writing developed independently, beginning around 3300 to 3200 B.C.: It was not derived from or related to cuneiform. Whether writing began in Egypt or Mesopotamia, therefore, is an open question. What is clear, however, is that writing was invented to meet economic rather than creative needs. In Egypt, the earliest writing includes records of the delivery of linen

papyrus Paperlike writing material used by the ancient Egyptians, Greeks, and Romans. Made primarily in Egypt from the papyrus plant, it was durable, flexible, and easy to write on.

Uruk IV ca. 3100 B.C.	Sumerian ca. 2500 B.C.	Old Babylonian ca. 1800 B.C.	Neo-Babylonian ca. 600 B.C.	SUMERIAN Babylonian
				APIN epinnu plow
				ŠE še'u grain
				ŠAR kirû orchard
				KUR šadû mountain
				GUD alpu ox
				KU(A) nunu fish
				DUG karpatu jar

■ **FIGURE 1.1—Early Mesopotamian Writing**

The pictographs of early writing evolved into a system of phonetic syllables and abstract symbols. Simplified and standardized, this writing was *cuneiform*, or "wedge-shaped." Over time, it was adapted from Sumerian to Babylonian and other languages throughout western Asia.

(From *Babylon*, by Joan Oates. Published by Thames and Hudson Ltd., 1978. Reprinted by permission of the publisher.)

and oil as taxes to King Scorpion I (ca. 3250 B.C.). The writing consists of early *hieroglyphs* (literally, "sacred carvings"), a system of pictures and abstract signs that represent sounds or ideas, later to become more formal and standardized.

Either Egyptian or a Mesopotamian language called Sumerian was the first written language. They are the earliest known of the many thousands of human languages that have existed in history. Most belong to large groupings of related languages called language families. Egyptian, for instance, is part of the Afro-Asiatic family of languages. Sumerian, in contrast, stands on its own; it cannot be reliably classified into any language family.

Incising cuneiform on clay was much clumsier than writing with pen and ink on **papyrus**, as became possible in Egypt. The papyrus plant grew in the Nile marshes and it was the source of the ancient world's favorite writing material. (Our word *paper* comes from "papyrus," although modern paper comes from a different source, trees.) Nonetheless, cuneiform was flexible enough to be used for poetry as well as for bookkeeping. Moreover, cuneiform became the standard script in western Asia for several thousand years. Clumsy it may have been, but cuneiform was writing, and writing is both a catalyst for change and the historian's best friend. Mesopotamia after 3000 B.C. was dynamic, sophisticated, and, best of all, intelligible to us.

SECTION SUMMARY

- Anatomically modern human beings are called *Homo sapiens sapiens* and first appeared about 100,000 years ago.

- Humans lived by hunting animals and gathering nuts and berries until agriculture was invented shortly after 10,000 B.C. in western Asia.

- Early Europeans were skilled metalworkers and architects, but they lagged behind the more advanced regions, Egypt and Mesopotamia.

- The first civilizations in Mesopotamia and Egypt emerged between 3500 and 3000 B.C. and probably contained the first cities.

- Civilization meant bigger and more complex societies, with specialized labor forces, strong governments, and well-structured armies.

- Along with cities came writing, which developed independently in Egypt and Mesopotamia between about 3500 and about 3100 B.C.

MESOPOTAMIA, TO CA. 1600 B.C.

What were the Mesopotamians' major contributions to government, religion, and art and culture?

After 3000 B.C., the people of Mesopotamia flourished. They experimented in government, in cooperation and conflict among different ethnic groups, in law, and in the working out of class and gender relations. Keenly aware of human limitations and vanity, they sought divine justice, as their literary and religious texts show. Their engineering skill, mathematics, and astronomy set ancient science on an upward path. In later centuries, Western civilization would build on these foundations, and then take off in new directions.

The fertile Tigris-Euphrates plain had to be tamed by would-be farmers. Most of the soil was either so dry or so marshy that agriculture required considerable irrigation and drainage—that is, the use of channels, dikes, or dams to control floodwaters and improve the fertility of the land. Making matters worse, Mesopotamia was also given to extreme heat and scorching winds. Some scholars argue that the very hostility of Mesopotamia's environment generated the cooperation and control that civilization requires.

Archaeologists sometimes refer to the third and second millennia in the eastern Mediterranean and western Asia as the Bronze Age. In this period, people mastered the technology of making bronze, an alloy of copper and tin, and bronze frequently replaced stone as a primary material for everyday use.

The City-States of Sumer

Though their culture is long dead, the Sumerians live on. Whenever someone today counts the minutes, debates politics, or quotes the law, the Sumerians live, for these are all legacies of that ingenious society.

The dominant inhabitants of Mesopotamian civilization in its first flowering are named **Sumerians**. Present in southern Mesopotamia by 3200 B.C., and probably earlier, the Sumerians entered their great age in the third millennium B.C., when their **city-states** enjoyed a proud independence (see **MAP 1.1**).

The formative era of Mesopotamian civilization is known as the Uruk Period (ca. 3800–3200 B.C.), after one of its major archaeological sites. During the Uruk Period, the Sumerians invented the wheel and the plow, planted the first orchards—of dates, figs, or olives—and developed the first sophisticated metal-casting processes. They built some of the first cities, for example, Uruk. They expanded the size of territories and populations, the scale of war, the complexity of society, and the power of government. Finally, as if to cap a period of remarkable change, at the end of the Uruk Period, the Sumerians invented cuneiform writing.

By the period that scholars have named the Early Dynastic Period (2800–2350 B.C.), named for the first royal dynasties (ruling families), large Mesopotamian cities had grown to the point where they might cover 1,000 acres surrounded by more than five miles of walls, within which lived about fifty thousand people. Such cities were part of a network of thirty such city-states. It was a web of culture, commerce, and competition, sometimes leading to war. The system was bigger, more complex, and more technologically advanced than any predecessor. Hence, the city-states of Mesopotamia may be called the first civilization.

It was a land of cooperation and conflict. The Sumerian cities had much in common: language, literature, arts and sciences, and religion. Yet, the cities often quarreled, often over farmland boundaries or water rights. Each city had its own urbanized area and surrounding agricultural land irrigated by canals. Cities traded with one another and with the outside world. The primary political units of southern Mesopotamia for most of the third millennium B.C., Sumerian city-states were an incubator of civilization.

A history of Sumerian government begins in the Early Dynastic Period, because good evidence for earlier times is lacking. Historians once labeled these cities as temple-states, governed by priests, but there is no proof of that. Certainly, the first Sumerian temples were wealthy and powerful. Each city had at least one temple, the house of its patron god and the common symbol of the community.

By the Early Dynastic Period, around 2800 B.C., political power in a Sumerian city rested largely with its Council of Elders, whose members were probably wealthy landowners. Some

Sumerians Dominant inhabitants of Mesopotamia in the third millennium B.C. They established the world's first civilization, thirty flourishing city-states with a common culture, commerce, and tendency to make war on one another.

city-states State consisting of an independent city and the surrounding territory under its control. Early examples were the Sumerian city-states in the third millennium B.C.

scholars argue that the council shared power with a popular assembly, creating, in effect, a bicameral legislature and perhaps even a primitive democracy. But this is just a theory.

Ordinary people enjoyed only limited freedom. Even if they owned their own land, farmers often had to provide forced labor for the state as a kind of taxation—maintaining the vast Mesopotamian irrigation system, for example. There was also apparently a large group of semi-free people who owned no land of their own but worked others' land. Finally, there were slaves—that is, people who could be bought and sold. Slaves were not numerous because there was no policing system to catch runaways. Slaves were usually foreign prisoners of war, but some were local people who had been sold into slavery to pay off a debt; often poor parents sold their own children (especially daughters).

By about 2700 B.C., political power shifted. War between cities became chronic and many felt the times demanded a strong hand. The new ruler was not a Council of Elders but rather a "big man" (*lugal*) or, less often, a "governor" (*ensi*)—that is, a king or, occasionally, a queen. Kings and queens sponsored irrigation works, raised fortification walls, restored temples, and built palaces, but the monarch was first and foremost a warrior.

One of the earliest Sumerian kings, dating from ca. 2700–2600 B.C., was Gilgamesh (GIL-ga-mesh) of Uruk, a hero of epic poetry whom many scholars consider a genuine historical personage. In the cities of Ur and Lagash, the king's wife was often a power in her own right. Kish was ruled by Ku-baba (r. ca. 2450 B.C.), history's first recorded reigning queen.

Though warriors, Sumerian monarchs also recognized a responsibility for promoting justice. History's earliest known reformer of law and society was Uru-inim-gina, king of Lagash around 2400 B.C. Surviving documents describe Lagash as a city in which wealthy landowners interfered with the temples and oppressed the poor, and in which royal administrators mistreated ordinary people. Uru-inim-gina attempted to manage the bureaucracy, protect the property of humble people, and guard the temples. He also put into effect the first known wage and price controls. Uru-inim-gina's proclaimed intention was to promote impartial justice, a goal that he expressed in the formula "[the king] will protect the mother that is in distress, the mighty man shall not oppress the naked and the widow." No doubt he also wanted to weaken independent sources of power threatening royal authority. As it turned out, Lagash was conquered only a few years after Uru-inim-gina's reign. His reforms nonetheless survived as the precedent for a long Mesopotamian tradition of royal lawgiving.

Conquest and Assimilation, ca. 2350–1900 B.C.

The poor and hardy peoples of the desert and the mountains coveted Mesopotamia's wealth. They attacked: some from without, by raising armies and assaulting cities, while others immigrated and climbed to power from within the Sumerian city-states. The attackers were sufficiently impressed by Sumerian culture to adopt a great many Sumerian customs and ideas. The most successful attacker was Sargon (r. 2371–2316 B.C.), who rose from nowhere to a high position under the king of the city of Kish before founding his own capital city, Agade (ah-GAH-day). Notice that Sargon was a native speaker not of Sumerian but of Akkadian.

The Akkadians were originally a seminomadic people who lived as shepherds on the edge of the desert. They had begun settling in the northern cities of southern Mesopotamia by the end of the Uruk Period, in a part of southern Mesopotamia known as Akkad. Their language, Akkadian, belongs to the Semitic group of languages, a subfamily of the Afro-Asiatic language family. Semitic languages include Arabic and Hebrew.

As commander of one of history's first professional armies, Sargon conquered all of Mesopotamia, and his power extended westward along the Euphrates and eastward into Iran. Rather than rule conquered peoples directly, the Akkadians generally were satisfied with loose control, as long as they could monopolize trade. They adopted Sumerian religion and wrote Akkadian in cuneiform.

Akkadian Bronze   This stern-faced, life-size cast-bronze head, with its stylized ringleted beard and carefully arranged hair, shows Mesopotamian craftsmanship at its finest. Thought by some to be Sargon (r. 2371–2316 B.C.) or Naramsin (r. ca. 2250–2220 B.C.), it was deliberately mutilated in ancient times.   (Scalar/Art Resource, NY)

Sargon's son inherited his throne. His dynasty boasted that it reigned over "the peoples of all lands" or "the four quarters of the earth." Sargon proved to be one of western Asia's most influential figures because his ideal of universal rule would continue to inspire future conquerors.

Assimilation was another lasting Akkadian legacy. Although Sargon made Akkadian the language of administration, he made many concessions to Sumerian practices. For instance, his daughter Enkheduanna (en-khe-du-AN-na), whom he appointed high priestess at Ur and Uruk, wrote poetry in Sumerian, is still quoted often in later Sumerian texts. The first known woman poet, Enkheduanna celebrated the union of Sumerians and Akkadians.

As a political reality, Akkadian rule proved short-lived, but assimilation survived as a cultural ideal. Around 2200 B.C., the Akkadian kingdom broke up into a series of smaller successor states. Then, after a century of rule by invaders from the east, the Sumerians returned to power under the Third Dynasty of Ur (2112–2004 B.C.). Far from stripping away Akkadian influence, the new Sumerian rulers spoke of themselves as "kings of Sumer and Akkad." The title would have a long and potent history: For the next fifteen hundred years, many of the great kings of western Asia would use it, in recognition of a common Mesopotamian society.

After renewed turmoil in Mesopotamia around 2000 B.C., a new kingdom emerged in the south under the rule of the Amorites around 1900 B.C. The Amorites were Semitic speakers and shared Mesopotamian culture and traditions. Babylon, northwest of Ur in the central part of Mesopotamia, became the Amorite capital. From Babylon, Amorite kings issued cuneiform decrees that, although written in a Semitic language, drew heavily on Sumerian material.

Hammurabi's Code

The most famous Amorite king, Hammurabi (r. 1792–1750 B.C.) ruled in Babylon about six hundred years after Sargon. Much of his forty-two-year reign was devoted to creating a Mesopotamian empire. He was a careful administrator who ushered in an era of prosperity and cultural flowering. He is most famous for the text known as **Hammurabi's Code**. Although the work was less a "code" than a collection listing various crimes and their punishments—a kind of treatise on justice glorifying Hammurabi's qualities as a judge—we shall use the familiar name. Hammurabi's Code became both a legal and a literary classic, much copied in later times.

Hammurabi's Code offers a portrait of Mesopotamian society. The document contains nearly three hundred rulings in cases ranging from family to commercial law, from wage rates to murder. The administration of justice in Mesopotamia was entirely practical: We find no notion of abstract absolutes or universal principles, not even a word for "law."

Though occasionally less harsh than earlier law codes, which date as far back as around 2100 B.C., Hammurabi's Code was by no means lenient. Whereas earlier codes were satisfied with payment in silver as recompense for crime, Hammurabi's Code was the first to stipulate such ruthless penalties as mutilation, drowning, and impaling. It also introduced the law of retaliation for wounds: "If a man has destroyed the eye of a member of the aristocracy: they shall destroy his eye. If he has broken his limb: they shall break the (same) limb." Moreover, children could be punished for the crimes of their parents.

The code was inscribed in forty-nine vertical columns on a stone stele about 7½ feet high and displayed in a prominent public place. Thus, Hammurabi's Code symbolized the notion that the law belonged to everyone. Although ordinary people could not read, it was possible for them to find a patron who could. Yet, the societies of western Asia and Egypt were anything but egalitarian, and Hammurabi's society was no exception. Punishments were class-based: Crimes against a free person, for example, received harsher treatment than crimes against a slave or a semi-free person. Debt seems to have been a serious and widespread problem, frequently leading to debt slavery. While women could own and inherit property and testify in court, the code tended to enshrine the power of the male head of the family.

Hammurabi's Code
An influential collection of various crimes and punishments, this work was named for the famous Amorite king Hammurabi (r. 1792–1750 B.C.).

Divine Masters

The Sumerians were polytheists—that is, they had many gods—and their gods (like the later gods of Greece) were anthropomorphic, or human in form. Indeed, Sumerian gods were thought to be much like humans, by turns wise and foolish, except that they were immortal and superpowerful. Many Sumerian gods represented the forces of nature: An, the sky-god; Enki, the earth-god and freshwater-god; Enlil, the air-god; Nanna, the moon-god; and Utu (Semitic, Shamash), the sun-god. Other Sumerian gods embodied human passions or notions about the afterlife: Inanna (Semitic, Ishtar), goddess of love and war; and Ereshkigal, goddess of the underworld.

The Sumerians sometimes envisioned their gods holding an assembly, much like a boisterous Sumerian assembly. The Sumerians and Akkadians considered Enlil, city-god of Nippur, to be the chief god. The Babylonians replaced him with Marduk, city-god of Babylon.

Every Mesopotamian city had its main temple complex, the most striking feature of which was a *ziggurat*, or stepped tower. Constructed originally as simple raised terraces, ziggurats eventually became seven-stage structures. Unlike the pyramids of Egypt, ziggurats were not tombs but "stairways" connecting humans and the gods.

The keynote of Mesopotamian religion was pessimism. It is not surprising that the Mesopotamians, living in a difficult natural environment, regarded the gods with fear and awe. Although the gods communicated with humans, their language was mysterious. To understand the divine will, the Mesopotamians engaged in various kinds of divination: They interpreted dreams, examined the entrails of slaughtered animals, and studied the stars (which stimulated great advances in astronomy, as we will see).

Most people expected nothing glorious in the afterlife, merely a shadowy existence. It was thought that with a person's last breath, his or her spirit embarked on a long journey to the Netherworld, a place under the earth. More than one Mesopotamian text describes the Netherworld as the "Land-of-no-return" and "the house wherein the dwellers are bereft of light, / Where dust is their fare and clay their food, / Where they see no light, residing in darkness."[1] The dead resided there permanently, though in some texts their spirits return to earth, often with hostile intent toward the living.

Archaeological evidence indicates a possible shift in such attitudes toward death, at least on the part of the Mesopotamian upper classes, by the late third millennium B.C. The kings and nobles of the Third Dynasty of Ur were buried with rich grave goods and with their servants, who were apparently the victims of human sacrifice following the master's death. Perhaps the rulers now expected to have the opportunity to use their wealth again in a comfortable immortality, possibly influenced by Egyptian ideas (see pages 19–21).

Arts and Sciences

The people of Mesopotamia were deeply inquisitive. They focused on the beginning and the end of things. "How did the world come into being?" and "What happens to us when we die?" are perhaps the two basic questions of their literature. Consider, for example, the Babylonian creation epic, known from its first line as *Enuma Elish* ("When on high"). An epic poem is the story of heroic deeds, in this case, the deeds of the gods of order, who triumphed over the forces of chaos. Another important Babylonian literary form, known as wisdom literature, responded to life's ups and downs with teachings that are sometimes simple, sometimes sophisticated. It proved eventually to influence the wisdom literature of the Hebrew Bible.

Epic of Gilgamesh   The best-known example of Mesopotamian literature, the *Epic of Gilgamesh* is one of the earliest known poems and, in its original form, may date back to the Sumerians ca. 2500 B.C.

The best-known example of Mesopotamian literature is the *Epic of Gilgamesh*. Frequently translated and adapted by various western Asian peoples, *Gilgamesh* might originally have been a Sumerian work dating to about 2500 B.C. Gilgamesh, king of Uruk, was probably a real historical person, but the poem concerns his fictionalized personal life. The main themes are friendship, loss, and the inevitability of death. As king, Gilgamesh is a tyrant; Enkidu arrives and puts him in his place, and then the two become close friends and comrades in arms. Enkidu's untimely death makes Gilgamesh aware of his own mortality. Distraught by his friend's passing, Gilgamesh goes on a vain quest for immortality. The *Epic of Gilgamesh* contains stories that presage the later biblical Eden and Flood narratives; there is little doubt but that those narratives found their way from Mesopotamia to the Hebrew Bible. (See the feature, "The Written Record: Heroism and Death in Mesopotamia.")

Cuneiform spread beyond Mesopotamia to Anatolia and the Levant (le-VANT)—the geographic region consisting today of such countries as Syria, Lebanon, Israel, Palestine, and Jordan. One cultural advance took place at Ebla (EH-bla) (modern Tell Mardikh), in northern Syria, where the world's earliest known dictionaries were written down between 2500 and 2300 B.C. A prosperous city, Ebla was known for commerce and artisanry as well as scholarship.

The Mesopotamians, meanwhile, made advances in mathematics, astronomy, medicine, and engineering. The Sumerians had two systems of numbers: a decimal system (powers of ten) for administration and business and a sexagesimal system (powers of sixty) for weights and mathematical or astronomical calculations. Like the Babylonians, we still divide hours by

Heroism and Death in Mesopotamia

The Epic of Gilgamesh sheds light on notions of gender and power in Mesopotamia. Men such as King Gilgamesh and his friend Enkidu have heroic adventures and risk death. Women lead quieter lives but are wiser and more realistic, as the following excerpts show. Here Gilgamesh, who wanders in his grief over the death of Enkidu, comes to the cottage of the tavernkeeper Siduri.

Who are you? You are no one that I know. / I am Gilgamesh, who killed Humbaba / And the bull of heaven with my friend.

If you are Gilgamesh and did those things, why / Are you so emaciated and your face half-crazed?

I have grieved! Is it so impossible / To believe? He pleaded. / My friend who went through everything with me / Is dead!

No one grieves that much, she said. / Your friend is gone. Forget him. / No one remembers him. He is dead Enkidu. Enkidu. Gilgamesh called out:

Help me. They do not know you as I know you?

Then she took pity on him / And let him enter and lie down and rest. / She gave him her bed to fall into and sleep / And rubbed his back and neck and legs and arms / When he was coming out of sleep, still muttering / About the one "who went with me through everything." / Like those old people who forget their listeners / Have not lived through their past with them, / Mentioning names that no one knows. / Enkidu, whom I loved so much, / Who went through everything with me / He died—like any ordinary man. / I have cried both day and night. / I did not want to put him in a grave. / He will rise, I know, one day. / But then I saw that he *was* dead. / His face collapsed within / After several days, / Like cobwebs I have touched / With my finger.

She wiped his face with a moist cloth / Saying: Yes yes yes yes, / As she made him cooler / Trying to help him forget / By the steady softness of her flesh. / She moved her lips across his chest / And caressed the length of his tired body / And lay over him at night until he slept.

You will never find an end to grief by going on, / She said to the one half sleeping at her side, / Leaning forward to wipe the perspiration from his face. / His eyes were open though his whole self felt asleep / Far off alone in some deep forest / Planted in his flesh / Through which he felt his way in pain / Without the help / Of friends. / She spoke as to a child who could not understand / All the futility that lay ahead / Yet who she knew would go on to repeat / Repeat repeat the things men had to learn. The gods gave death to man and kept life for / Themselves. That is the only way it is. / Cherish your rests; the children you might have; / You are a thing that carries so much tiredness.

QUESTIONS

1. What differences between men and women appear in this excerpt?

2. Why is it so hard for Gilgamesh to accept Enkidu's death?

3. Is Siduri's view of the gods pessimistic or realistic?

Source: Excerpt from *Gilgamesh: A Verse Narrative* by Herbert Mason. Copyright © 1970 by Herbert Mason. Reprinted by permission of Houghton Mifflin Harcourt Publishing Company. All rights reserved.

sixty today. Furthermore, our modern system of numerical place-value notation—for example, the difference between 42 and 24—is derived, through Hindu-Arabic intermediaries, from the Babylonian system. The Babylonians were adept at arithmetic and could solve problems for which we would use algebra. A millennium before the Greek mathematician Pythagoras (who claimed to have studied the Mesopotamian tradition) proved the validity of the theorem that bears his name, they were familiar with the proposition that in a right triangle the square of the longest side is equal to the sum of the squares of the other two sides. In the first millennium B.C., the Babylonians developed a sophisticated mathematical astronomy (see page 34). As early as the seventeenth century B.C., they made systematic, if not always accurate, recordings of the movements of the planet Venus.

In medical matters, they demonstrated considerable critical ability. Physicians made advances in the use of plant products for medicines and in very rudimentary surgery. The Babylonians had a simple pregnancy test of moderate accuracy, for example, and their surgeons were experienced at setting broken bones. When they became ill, however, most people in Mesopotamia set more store by magic and incantations than by surgery or herbal medicine.

SECTION SUMMARY

- Approximately thirty city-states of southern Mesopotamia spoke Sumerian and flourished in the third millennium B.C.

- Sargon, an Akkadian, conquered the Sumerian cities of Mesopotamia and united them in one kingdom.

- Hammurabi's Code (1792–1750 B.C.), one of the earliest collections of laws, reveals the inequality and harshness of Mesopotamian society.

- Mesopotamians were religious, believed in many gods, and expected only a grim and shadowy Netherworld after death.

- Mesopotamia's rich culture excelled in mathematics, astronomy, and epic poetry.

EGYPT, TO CA. 1100 B.C.

How did the king's power affect various aspects of Egyptian society?

From Babylon to the valley of the Nile River was about 750 miles by way of the caravan routes through Syria southward—close enough to exchange goods and customs but far enough for a distinct Egyptian civilization to emerge. As in Sumer, civilization in Egypt arose in a river valley, but Egypt was much earlier than Mesopotamia in becoming a unified kingdom under one ruler. Moreover, ancient Egypt survived as a united and independent kingdom for over two thousand years (to be sure, with some periods of civil war and foreign rule). Egypt made great strides in a variety of areas of human achievement, from the arts to warfare. Western civilization borrowed much from Egypt, especially in technology and religion.

Ancient Egypt is a product of the unique characteristics of the Nile River (see **MAP 1.2**). Yet, most of Egypt is desert. Today, only about 5 percent is habitable by humans, including a few oases, the Nile Delta, and the Nile Valley itself, which extends about 760 miles from Cairo to Egypt's modern southern border: Upper Egypt, a long and narrow valley never more than about 14 miles wide. North of Cairo, in "Lower Egypt," the Nile branches out into the wide, low-lying delta before flowing into the Mediterranean Sea.

Divine Kingship

The fertility of the Nile River gave ancient Egypt a prosperous economy and optimistic culture. The river's annual floods, which took place during late summer and autumn, were generally mild and predictable. With less human effort than was required in Mesopotamia, the floodwaters could be used to irrigate most of the farmland in the Nile Valley. As a result, Egyptian agriculture was one of the wealthiest in the ancient world.

No wonder many Egyptians considered change as undesirable. Even death appeared to be a minor event compared with the eternal regularity of the Nile, which may help explain the prominence in Egyptian religion of belief in the afterlife. In addition, the static outlook helped promote the idea of an absolute, all-powerful, and all-providing king—namely, **pharaoh**.

Agriculture and settled village life emerged in Egypt around 5000 B.C. By 4000 B.C., villages had grown into towns, each controlling a strip of territory. By about 3100 B.C., Egyptian communities up and down the Nile Valley had cleared marshes and expanded the amount of land under cultivation, which in turn could support a larger population. The Nile Valley became one unified kingdom of Egypt, with a capital city perhaps at Memphis.

The new kingdom had monumental architecture, writing, and a king. For several centuries, Egyptians consolidated their institutions. Although few specifics are known about this Archaic Period (3200–2695 B.C.), it clearly laid the groundwork for the next era. Around 2700 B.C., a remarkable, distinctive, and relatively well-documented period of creativity began.

The history of third- and second-millennium B.C. Egypt is usually divided into three distinct eras of great prosperity:

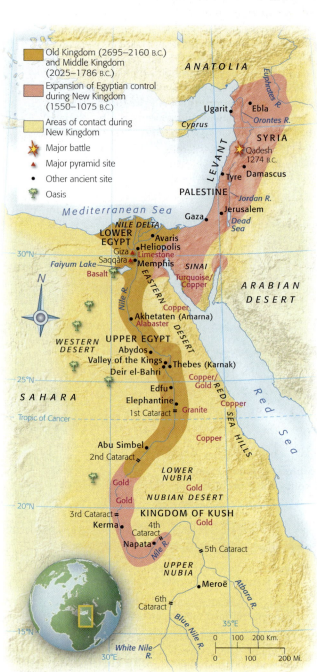

🌐 **MAP 1.2—Ancient Egypt and the Levant**
The unique geography of the Nile Valley and its fertile soil left a stamp on ancient Egypt. Egypt enjoyed trade and cultural contact—and sometimes went to war—with nearby lands such as Nubia and the Levant.

the Old Kingdom (2695–2160 B.C.), the Middle Kingdom (2025–1786 B.C.), and the New Kingdom (1550–1075 B.C.). Each kingdom is subdivided into dynasties, that is, ruling families. Between the kingdoms, central authority broke down in the Intermediate Periods. Broadly speaking, the Old Kingdom was an era of spectacular creativity and originality, symbolized by the building of the Great Pyramids; the Middle Kingdom, an era of introspection and literary production; and the New Kingdom, an era in which Egypt's traditional isolation gave way to international diplomacy and expansion.

Egypt's was the first government in recorded history to govern a large territory. Indeed, a chart of Egypt's power structure would look like a pyramid, with a broad base of laborers and artisans supporting a small commanding elite. The holder of the highest point of power was considered so important that, for centuries, Egyptians referred to the office rather than to the person, calling it "the Great House"—in Egyptian, *per-aa*, or "pharaoh," as the ruler himself (or occasionally herself) was eventually called.

Egyptian kingship was sacred monarchy. In Mesopotamia, the king generally claimed to have been appointed by the gods. In Egypt, pharaoh was deemed to *be* a god. The most dramatic symbol of the king's divinity was a building—or, rather, a series of buildings—the pyramids. The ancients built thirty-five major and many smaller pyramids, of which the best known are the Great Pyramids of Giza—three gigantic, perfectly symmetrical limestone tombs. Now, nearly five thousand years later, the pyramid of King Khufu (r. 2589–2566 B.C., better known by his Greek name, Cheops) is still the largest all-stone building in human history. Near the Great Pyramids stands the Great Sphinx, a human headed lion carved out of a rock outcropping, perhaps representing Khufu's son, King Khafre (r. 2558–2532 B.C.; Greek name, Chephren), for whom the second pyramid at Giza was built.

pharaoh Ancient Egyptians' title for their king, an absolute, all-powerful, and all-providing ruler.

Great Pyramids of Giza Royal funerary monuments of three Egyptian kings of the twenty-sixth century B.C., the pyramids symbolize the power and ambition of the Old Kingdom. The pyramid of King Khufu (or Cheops, rearmost in the photo) is still the largest all-stone building in human history. (Hisham Ibrahim/Photodisc/Getty Images)

The pyramids were not just monuments to an ego, but also temples where the king would continue to be worshiped and served in the afterlife. The structures served a political purpose as well. When the Great Pyramids were constructed, the kingdom of Egypt was still young and fragile. By building a pyramid, the king made a statement of his power—an eloquent, simple, and irrefutable statement. The sheer size of the Great Pyramids demonstrated the king's ability to organize a vast labor force. Indeed, the encampment of workers at Giza may have been the largest gathering of human beings to that date.

In theory, the king owned all the land, but in practice, Egypt's economy was a mixture of private enterprise and centralized control. The king delegated authority to a large group of officials, including governors, mayors, military commanders, judges, treasurers, engineers, agricultural overseers, scribes, and others. The highest official was the vizier, a sort of prime minister who had more day-to-day power than pharaoh himself.

The essence of good government was what the Egyptians called *ma'at*, whose basic meaning is "order"—in government, society, or the universe; *ma'at* can also mean "truth" or "justice." Egypt had a well-functioning system of judges who heard lawsuits, and it probably also had a detailed law code, although few written laws survive.

Life and Afterlife

Egyptian life was full of religious practices, from daily rituals and seasonal festivals to ethical teachings and magic. Egyptian religion tended toward *syncretism*—that is, the blending of mutually opposed beliefs, principles, or practices. For example, Egyptian mythology taught variously that the sky was a cow, was held up by a god or by a post, or was a goddess stretched over the earth. No one was troubled by such inconsistencies, as a modern worshiper might be, because Egyptians believed that a fundamental unity underlay the varieties of nature.

Egypt's religion had many greater and lesser deities, including human, animal, and composite gods. Various animals, from cats and dogs to crocodiles and serpents, were thought to represent the divine. Important deities included Thoth, the moon-god and god of wisdom; Nut, goddess of the sky; Ptah, a creator-god; Osiris, who invented agriculture and became lord of the dead; Horus, son of Osiris, a sky-god imagined as a giant falcon; and Isis, wife of Osiris and mother of Horus, a mother-goddess. Temples were numerous and lavish.

Egyptian religion focused on the afterlife. Unlike the Mesopotamians, the Egyptians believed that death could be a pleasant continuation of life on earth. Hence, they actively sought immortality. The wealthy built tombs that were decorated with paintings and inscriptions and stocked with cherished possessions for use after death. The most cherished possession of all was

Egyptian Book of the Dead   This scene from a lavishly illustrated papyrus shows a dead person's appearance before a divine court of judgment. His heart is being weighed in the balance to determine his fate in the afterlife.   (Courtesy of the Trustees of the British Museum)

the body, and the Egyptians provided for its preservation through their mastery of the science of embalming—thus, the Egyptian mummies.

Reserved for the king and his officials in the Old Kingdom, the afterlife became, as it were, democratized by the Middle Kingdom. By the Middle Kingdom, even ordinary Egyptians believed they could enjoy immortality after death, as gods, as long as they could purchase for their graves funerary texts containing the relevant prayers. The texts emphasize ritual—incantations, magic spells, prayers—as the key to eternal life. Yet, from time to time, we find other texts, especially from the Middle Kingdom, that say that ritual is not enough; ethical behavior also is required. New Kingdom texts describe the details of a dead person's appearance before a divine court for judgment. The sinless are admitted into eternal life in the kingdom of the blessed. The guilty, their heavy hearts devoured by a beast, suffer a second, final death.

Egyptian women did not enjoy equal status with men, but they had more freedom than women in other ancient societies, particularly in legal matters. As in Mesopotamia, so in Egypt, a woman could buy or sell, bequeath or inherit, sue or testify in court, but a married Egyptian woman, unlike her eastern sisters, could do so without a male guardian's approval. A married woman in Egypt remained legally independent. She could own property without her husband's involvement. But how often did women exercise such privileges? Egyptian women worked in agriculture and trade, in the textile and perfume industries, in dining halls, and in entertainment, but they were rarely managers. Women also served as priestesses of various kinds. Yet, in Egypt, as elsewhere, women were expected to make the home the focus of their activities.

War Abroad, 1786–ca. 1150 B.C.

The humane attitudes of the Middle Kingdom were swept away after about 1700 B.C., when Semitic-speaking immigrants from Canaan*—the Hyksos (HICK-sos)—conquered much of Egypt. In many ways gentle conquerors, the Hyksos worshiped Egyptian gods, built and restored Egyptian temples, and intermarried with natives. As foreigners, however, the Hyksos were unpopular. Eventually, a war launched from Upper Egypt, which had retained a loose independence, drove the Hyksos out.

The first restored Egyptian ruler of the New Kingdom was Ahmose I (r. 1550–1525 B.C.). His Egypt proved to be a new Egypt indeed. The Hyksos had brought advanced military technology to Egypt, including the horse-drawn war chariot, new kinds of daggers and swords, and the composite bow. Made of laminated materials, including wood, leather, and horn, the composite bow could hit a target at 600 yards.

Warlike, expansionist, and marked by a daring attempt at religious reform, the New Kingdom's Eighteenth Dynasty (1540–1293 B.C.) has long held a special fascination for historians. One of the dynasty's memorable names is that of Queen Hatshepsut (HAT-shep-soot). Widow of Thutmose II (r. 1491–1479 B.C.), Hatshepsut first served as regent for her young stepson and then assumed the kingship herself (r. 1479–1457 B.C.). Other Egyptian queens had exercised royal power before, but Hatshepsut was the first to call herself king. Although Hatshepsut dispatched Egyptian armies to fight, her reign is best known for peaceful activities: at home, public works and temple rebuilding; abroad, a commercial expedition over the Red Sea to the "Land of Punt" (perhaps modern Somalia, in eastern Africa).

After her death, Hatshepsut was succeeded by her stepson, Thutmose III (r. 1479–1425 B.C.). Late in his reign, he tried to erase his stepmother's memory by having Hatshepsut's statues destroyed and her name expunged from records—an attempt, perhaps, to cut off a claim to the throne by her supporters. A warrior pharaoh, Thutmose III, led his dynasty's armed expansion in western Asia and northern Africa. Thutmose won his greatest victory during his first campaign, at the Battle of Megiddo in Canaan in 1457 B.C. (see **MAP 1.2**), where Egypt's triumph prevented the kingdom of Mitanni from expanding southward. Egypt now ruled an empire with territory in Nubia and Canaan.

The years from about 1450 to about 1300 B.C. marked a period of peace among the great powers from Egypt to Anatolia and Mesopotamia—what historians call the first international system.

---

* Canaan is an ancient name for the lands currently called Israel, Palestine, and coastal Syria and Lebanon.

The arts of peace are illustrated in surviving treaties and letters between monarchs, many of which come from Amarna.

The Amarna Archives (mid-fourteenth century B.C.), written in Akkadian cuneiform, illustrate formal communication among states. Rulers of great powers addressed each other as "brother," while Canaanite princes called pharaoh "my lord and my Sun-god" and assured him that they were "thy servant and the dirt on which thou dost tread." The texts reveal a system of gift exchange and commerce, politeness and formality, alliance and dynastic marriage, subjects and governors, rebels and garrisons. Because of a rough equality of power, no king was likely to defeat the others, so the parties avoided all-out war. They preferred instead to compete by jockeying for allies among the small Canaanite border states.

Sometimes, the competition turned into war. By the late fourteenth century B.C., Egypt had a new rival abroad, the **Hittites,** who had built a great empire in Anatolia. The Hittites were masters of the horse and rank among the leading charioteers of what was the golden age of chariot battle. They made full use of Anatolia's mineral wealth and made a limited number of iron weapons as well as the more usual bronze.

The Hittite state was vibrant if often divided. Hittite kings were powerful, but they had to deal with a strong nobility. Hittite queens and queen mothers often had considerable power. Puduhepa (pu-du-HE-pa), wife of King Hattusilis (hat-tu-SIL-is) III (r. 1278–1250 B.C.), played a memorable role in state affairs. Some of her prayers were written down and survive to this day.

Hittite is the oldest recorded Indo-European language, the language group to which English belongs. Thousands of Hittite texts have survived. They paint a picture of a sophisticated society with rich traditions in law, scholarship, poetry, and religion. One thing that stands out in their texts is the Hittites' vivid sense of history.

During the Hittite New Kingdom (ca. 1380–1180 B.C.), the Hittites' power extended into Syria and northern Mesopotamia (see **MAP 1.3**), which became the arena of conflict with

Hittites Builders of a great empire in Anatolia in the Late Bronze Age, the Hittites fought Egypt to a standstill and made history's first peace treaty between equals. Hittite is the oldest recorded Indo-European language, the language group to which English belongs.

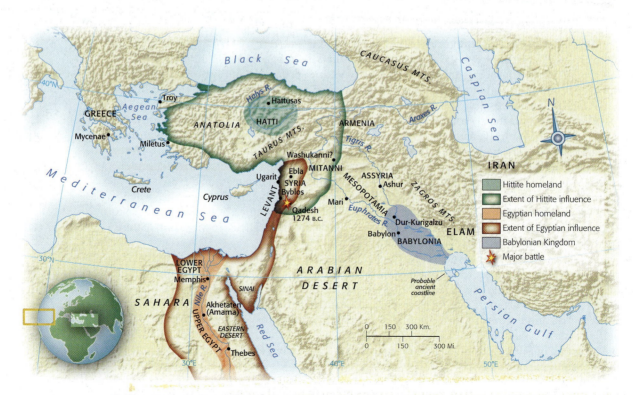

🌐 **MAP 1.3—The International System, ca. 1500–1250 B.C.**
This era of competing kingdoms and city-states witnessed considerable war, especially between Egypt and the Hittites for control of the Canaanite states. Yet it was also a period of international trade, diplomacy, and, from 1450 to 1300 B.C., peace.

Peace and Brotherhood

After the stalemate at Qadesh (1274 B.C.) the kings of Egypt and the Hittites (referred to below as Hatti) agreed to make peace permanently. The result was a landmark of history, the first peace treaty between equals. A copy of this treaty is displayed in the United Nations building in New York City.

Preamble

P1 (A obv. 1–3) [The treaty which] Ramses, [Beloved] of Amon, Great King, King [of Egypt, Hero, concluded] on [a tablet of silver] with Hattusili, [Great King], King of Hatti, his brother, in order to establish [great] peace and great [brotherhood] between them forever....

Purpose of Treaty; Previous Relations

P3 (A obv. 7–13) I have now established good brotherhood and good peace between us forever, in order likewise to establish good peace and good brotherhood in [the relations] of Egypt with Hatti forever. As far as the relations of the Great King, King of Egypt, [and] the Great King, King of Hatti, are concerned, from the beginning of time and forever [by means of a treaty] the god has not allowed the making of war between them....

Future Relations

P4 (A obv. 13–18) And Ramses, Beloved of Amon, Great King, King [of Egypt], has indeed created <it> (the relationship) [on] this [day] by means of a treaty upon a tablet of silver, with [Hattusili], Great King, King of Hatti, his brother, in order to establish good peace and good brotherhood [between them] forever. He is [my] brother, and I am his brother. <He is at peace with me>, and I am at peace with him [forever. And] we will create our brotherhood and our [peace], and they will be better than the former brotherhood and peace of [Egypt with] Hatti. P5 (A obv. 19–21) Ramses, Great King, King of Egypt, is in good peace and good brotherhood with [Hattusili], Great King, King of Hatti. The sons of Ramses, Beloved of Amon, <Great King>, King of Egypt, will be at peace and [brothers with] the sons of Hattusili, Great King, King of Hatti, forever.

And they will remain as in our relationship of brotherhood [and of] peace, so that Egypt will be at peace with Hatti and they will be brothers like us forever.

Non-aggression

P6 (A obv. 22–27) And Ramses, Beloved of Amon, Great King, King of Egypt, for all time shall not open hostilities against Hatti in order to take anything from it. And Hattusili, Great King, King of Hatti, for all time shall not open hostilities against Egypt in order to take [anything] from it. The eternal regulation which the Sun-god and the Storm-god made for Egypt with Hatti is intended <to provide> peace and brotherhood and to prohibit hostilities between them....

Defensive Alliance

P7 (A obv. 27–30) And if someone else, an enemy, comes against Hatti, and Hattusili, [Great King, King of Hatti], sends to me: "Come to me to my aid against him," then [Ramses, Beloved] of Amon, Great King, King of Egypt, must send his infantry and his chariotry and they will defeat [his enemy and] take revenge for Hatti.

P8 (A obv. 31–33) And if Hattusili, Great King, King of Hatti, [becomes angry] with his own [subjects], after they have offended against him, and he sends to Ramses, Great King, King of Egypt, on account of this, then Ramses, Beloved of Amon, must send his infantry and his chariotry, [and] they will destroy all with whom he is angry....

[The next two paragraphs repeat these obligations but with the roles of the two kings reversed.]

Fugitives

... P18 (A obv. 60–64) [And if] a single man flees from [Hatti, or] two men, [or three men, and they come to] Ramses, Beloved [of Amon, Great King, King] of Egypt, his brother, [then Ramses], Beloved of Amon, Great King, [King of Egypt, must seize them and send them] to Hattusili, his brother [...]—for they are brothers. But [they shall not punish them for] their offenses. They shall [not] tear out [their tongues or their eyes]. And [they shall not mutilate(?) their ears or [their] feet. [And they shall not destroy(?) their households, together with their wives] and their sons.

QUESTIONS

1. What does the treaty mean by "good brotherhood and good peace"?
2. In what ways does the treaty display more concern for kings than for their subjects?
3. What punishments were usually given to fugitives from justice?

Source: "Peace and Brotherhood" from Gary Beckman, *Hittite Diplomatic Texts*, 2/e, pp. 96–99. Copyright © 1999. Reprinted by permission of Society of Biblical Literature.

Egypt. The most dramatic episode was the Battle of Qadesh in northern Syria in 1274 B.C., where twenty thousand Egyptian troops faced seventeen thousand Hittites. Qadesh is the first well-documented battle in history. Since neither of the two evenly matched powers managed to conquer the other, they made peace. The treaty between them still survives, and it is the oldest surviving peace treaty between equals. (See the feature, "The Global Record: Peace and Brotherhood.")

However, peace was temporary. Between about 1200 and 1150 B.C., the international system came to a crashing end. From Mesopotamia to Greece, from Anatolia to Egypt, one state after another collapsed. Surviving evidence is fragmentary, but it suggests that both foreign and domestic problems were devastating. Raiders and invaders beset the eastern Mediterranean in this period. Called "Sea Peoples" by the Egyptians, they attacked both on land and at sea. We do not know precisely who they were. In addition, some evidence of regional famine and climatic change indicates that natural causes may have led to disruption and rebellion.

Whatever the cause, what followed would prove to be a different world. Yet the end of the international system did not result in the disappearance of ancient cultures. Although new peoples appeared and old peoples changed, both continued to borrow from the cultures that had flowered before 1200 B.C.

Reform at Home and Its Aftermath, 1352–1075 B.C.

Empire brings power, and power often causes conflict. In imperial Egypt during the fourteenth century B.C., kings and priests struggled over authority. Consider the Amarna (a-MAR-na) reform, named for a major archaeological site at the modern town of Tell el-Amarna.

The **Amarna reform** was carried out by Thutmose III's great-great-grandson, King Amenhotep IV (r. 1352–1336 B.C.). Earlier, the god Amun-Re had become the chief deity of the New Kingdom. As supporters of imperialism, his temple priests had been rewarded with enough land and wealth that their power now rivaled pharaoh's own. Amenhotep IV responded by forbidding the worship of Amun-Re and replacing him with the god Aten, the solar disk. The king changed his own name to Akhenaten ("pleasing to Aten"). He also created a new capital city: Akhetaten (modern Amarna). Akhenaten's wife, Nefertiti, figures prominently in Amarna art, and she too may have played an important role in the reform.

The reformers gained power, but we need not doubt their sincerity. Contemporary literature suggests intense religious conviction in Aten as a benevolent god and one who nurtured not only Egypt but all countries. Although the Aten cult focuses on one god, only Akhenaten and his family were permitted to worship Aten directly; the rest of the Egyptian population was expected to worship the god through pharaoh.

Bold as the reform was, it was too radical to last. After Akhenaten's death, his son-in-law and successor, Tutankhaten (r. 1336–1327 B.C.) restored good relations with the priests of Amun-Re, which he signaled by changing his name to Tutankhamun. The Amun-Re cult was revived, the Aten cult was abolished, and the city of Akhetaten was abandoned.

Egyptian Queen This elegant, red granite statue of the pharaoh Hatshepsut (r. 1479–1457 B.C.) is one of the few to depict her as a woman. She is usually shown as a man, complete with beard, to symbolize her royal power. Centuries later the proportions and carving techniques of Egyptian stone sculpture would influence the Greeks, although Greek artists chose less to copy the Egyptians than to try to outdo them (see the photo on page 64). (Brian Brake/Photo Researchers, Inc.)

Amarna reform Term for the ancient Egyptian king Amenhotep IV's seizure of power from temple priests by replacing the god Amun-Re with Aten and renaming himself Akhenaten.

Arts and Sciences in the New Kingdom

The Egyptians were superb builders, architects, and engineers. In addition to pyramids and irrigation works, they constructed monumental royal tombs, palaces, forts, and temples, and they erected looming obelisks. At their best, Egyptian architects designed buildings in harmony with the unique landscape—one of the reasons for the structures' lasting appeal. Their most original and enduring work was done in stone. Stone temples, for example, culminated in the imposing pillared structures of the New Kingdom. That period also saw the construction of rock-cut temples, the most famous of which is Ramesses II's (r. 1279–1213 B.C.) project at Abu

Hittite God This figurine in gold, standing only 1.5 inches high, represents Hittite art of the Old Kingdom (ca. 1650–1450 B.C.). The clothes, shoes, and conical hat are typical of Hittite depictions of gods. (Louvre, Paris, France/Réunion des Musées Nationaux/Art Resource/NY)

Simbel (see **Map 1.2**). In front of the temples sit four colossal statues of Ramesses, also carved out of rock. Obelisks were slender, tapering pillars carved of a single piece of stone. Inscribed with figures and hieroglyphs, and usually erected in pairs in front of a temple, obelisks were meant to glorify the sun-god.

Throughout history, royal courts have excelled as patrons of the arts; the Egyptian court was one of the first and greatest. Egyptian craftsmen were master goldsmiths, glassmakers, and woodworkers. The major arts are well represented in tombs, which were decorated with rich, multicolored wall paintings, the first narrative depictions.

Sculpture was another art form in which Egyptians excelled. Carved in stone, wood, or metal, Egyptian sculpture is a study in contrasts. The body posture is usually rigid and stiff, the musculature only sketchy; the face, in contrast, is often individualistic, the expression full of character and drawn from life. Statues represent kings and queens, gods and goddesses, husbands and wives, adults and children, officials, priests, scribes, and animals.

Ancient Egyptian literature is notable for its variety. Religious subjects, historical and commemorative records, technical treatises in mathematics and medicine, and secular stories survive alongside business contracts and royal proclamations. Egyptian writing is best known for hieroglyphs. Elaborate and formal, hieroglyphs were generally used after the Archaic Period only for monuments and ornamentation. Two simplified scripts served for everyday use.

The people who built the pyramids had to be skilled at arithmetic and geometry. Egyptians were able to approximate pi (the ratio of the circumference of a circle to its diameter) and to solve equations containing one or two unknowns. The Egyptian calendar was also a remarkable achievement. Based on observation of the star Sirius, the Egyptian calendar, with its 365-day year, approximates the solar calendar. Corrected to 365 1/4 days, it survives to this day as the calendar of Europe, the Americas, and much of the rest of the world.

Egyptian medical doctors were admired in antiquity and in demand abroad. They knew how to set a dislocated shoulder and used a full battery of splints, sutures, adhesive plasters, elementary disinfectants (from tree leaves), and burn treatments (fatty substances). One Egyptian treatise offers something like modern triage, dividing diseases into three categories: treatable, possibly treatable, and untreatable. Egyptian doctors may have done postmortem dissection in order to understand the human body better.

SECTION SUMMARY

- The Nile River, with its dependable annual flooding, gave ancient Egypt fertile soil, economic prosperity, and an optimistic worldview.
- Egypt invented the idea of worshiping the king as a god; eventually, the king became known as pharaoh.
- Egyptians believed in a happy afterlife after death, as long as the gods judged that the dead person had led a life without sin.
- Egypt's New Kingdom was a great military power that expanded into southwest Asia.
- The earliest known Indo-European civilization is that of the Hittites, who established a great kingdom in today's Turkey and left thousands of documents.
- The conflicts between Hittites and Egyptians led to history's first great system of diplomacy, its first well-documented battle (Qadesh), and its first peace treaty between equals.
- The Amarna reform of the 1300s was history's first great struggle between church and state.
- The Egyptians excelled at architecture, such as the pyramids, as well as at sculpture and medicine, and they invented the solar calendar that we still use (in revised form) today.
- We are not sure why, but the great civilizations of the ancient Near East all either declined, split apart, or collapsed not long after 1200 B.C.

CHAPTER SUMMARY

The earliest human beings, probably beginning before 70,000 B.C., invented human culture—that is, they developed communications well enough that people could cooperate and exploit their natural environment by means of technology. Next came the move from a food-collecting to a food-producing economy. After beginning in the Fertile Crescent region of western Asia shortly after 10,000 B.C., food production spread to Europe beginning around 7000 B.C. Over the thousands of years following the invention of agriculture, human society became more complex and won increasing control of the natural environment. The result was the emergence of civilization in Egypt and Mesopotamia after 3500 B.C. The first cities appeared in Mesopotamia about 3500 B.C. and maybe even earlier. Writing was invented independently in Mesopotamia and Egypt between 3500 and 3000 B.C. In Mesopotamia, the Sumerians and Akkadians flourished in city-states, which were eventually conquered and united into a kingdom. The Mesopotamians wrote the first law codes, including the famous Hammurabi's Code (1792–1750 B.C.). Mesopotamians were religious, believed in many gods, and expected only a grim and shadowy Netherworld after death. Mesopotamia's rich culture excelled in mathematics, astronomy, and epic poetry.

Egyptian society and culture was focused on the king. Egypt invented the idea of worshipping the king as a god; eventually, the king became known as pharaoh. Early Egypt was relatively peaceful and inward-looking, but after a period of foreign rule, the newly liberated Egypt of the New Kingdom was a great military power that expanded into southwest Asia. The Egyptians excelled at architecture, such as the pyramids, as well as at sculpture and medicine, and they invented the solar calendar that we still use (in revised form) today.

Our language, English, belongs to the Indo-European language group; the first known Indo-European civilization is that of the Hittites, the dominant power in Anatolia from 1650 to 1180 B.C. The conflicts between Hittites and Egyptians led to history's first great system of diplomacy, its first well-documented battle (Qadesh), and its first peace treaty between equals. The great civilizations of the ancient Near East all either declined, split apart, or collapsed not long after 1200 B.C. Although this destruction is often attributed to the Sea Peoples, the cause is still uncertain.

FOCUS QUESTIONS

- How did the earliest human beings adapt to their environments and create the first civilizations?

- What were the Mesopotamians' major contributions to government, religion, and art and culture?

- How did the king's power affect various aspects of Egyptian society?

 This icon will direct you to additional materials on the website: www.cengage.com/history/noble/westciv6e

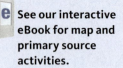 See our interactive eBook for map and primary source activities.

KEY TERMS

hominids (p. 4)
hunter-gatherers (p. 6)
Neolithic Revolution (p. 7)
Europe (p. 8)
cuneiform (p. 10)

papyrus (p. 11)
Sumerians (p. 13)
city-states (p. 13)
Hammurabi's Code (p. 15)

Epic of Gilgamesh (p. 16)
pharaoh (p. 19)
Hittites (p. 22)
Amarna reform (p. 24)

NOTES

1. James B. Pritchard, ed., *Ancient Near Eastern Texts Relating to the Old Testament*, 3d ed., with Supplement (Princeton, N.J.: Princeton University Press, 1969), p. 107.

2

Bull from Ishtar Gate, Babylon
(Bildarchiv Preussischer Kulturbesitz/Art Resource, NY)

The Ship, the Sword, and the Book: Western Asia ca. 1500–400 B.C.

The bull in brick relief shown on the left symbolizes power even today, twenty-six hundred years after it was molded and glazed. About 4 feet high, this bull was one of several dozen figures of bulls and dragons that decorated the massive Ishtar Gate, which led through the inner town wall of Babylon (BAB-eh-lon) into the palace. The gate represents only a small part of a magnificent reconstruction of the city by the Neo-Babylonian kings who ruled western Asia around 600 to 539 B.C.

Imagine the king's surprise had he known that under his nose an obscure prophet—we know him only as "Second Isaiah" (eye-ZAY-ah)—was preaching a bold message to his compatriots, a conquered people living in exile in Babylon. Isaiah reminded them that Yahweh (YAH-way), their god, was a god of justice and mercy—the one and only true god of the entire world—and that Yahweh had chosen the king of mountainous, backward Persia to conquer western Asia and redeem Yahweh's people. The Neo-Babylonian king might have laughed at the idea. Yet the Persians, under Cyrus the Great, conquered Babylon in 539 B.C. and proclaimed the freedom of Yahweh's people—the Jews—to return to Palestine and re-establish the Temple to their god in the city of Jerusalem (juh-ROO-suh-lem). They did so, and around this time, they wrote down their religious and historical traditions in large sections of what would become the Hebrew Bible, or Old Testament.

It was a momentous development, because the Hebrew Bible founded the West's religious tradition. Along with Greece and Rome, ancient Israel may be considered one of the three founders of the West. Greece began the western tradition of philosophy and politics; Rome began Western law and administration. Israel gave the West ethical monotheism, the idea that God is one and that everything he does is good.

In contrast to ancient Israel, the other peoples studied in this chapter are all ancestors of the West: the Phoenicians and other Canaanites, the Neo-Babylonians and the other great empires of the era, the Assyrians and Persians. Traders or conquerors, they came to power through merchant ships or by the sword, but once in power they spread civilization, serving as conduits through which the achievements of earlier civilizations were transmitted. They spread trading networks that brought the alphabet to the Greeks, which would prove essential to preserving the brilliant culture that later developed in Greece. They built great empires whose institutions were eventually transformed into notions of mass citizenship under law and justice in a universal empire by the third founder of the West, Rome.

The first half of the first millennium B.C., therefore, left a divergent legacy to the West. On the one hand, new empires arose that were more systematically organized, fartherflung, and more diverse ethnically than those created before. On the other hand, prophets and poets looked in new and deeper ways into the human soul.

FOCUS QUESTIONS

- Who were the Phoenicians and what did they contribute to Western civilization?

- What made the first-millennium B.C empires of the Assyrians, Neo-Babylonians, and Persians so much more effective than earlier empires?

- What was the religious experience of ancient Israel, and what is its legacy today?

This icon will direct you to additional materials on the website: www .cengage.com/history/ noble/westciv6e

See our interactive eBook for map and primary source activities.

29

In this chapter we look at the deeply influential developments in empire, religion, and thought forged in the first half of the first millennium B.C. At the same time, we consider the peaceful expansion in this era, through trade and colonization, particularly under the Phoenicians. Finally, we examine the material innovation that has earned the period the title "Iron Age."

TRADERS INVENT THE ALPHABET: CANAANITES AND PHOENICIANS, CA. 1400–450 B.C.

Who were the Phoenicians and what did they contribute to Western Civilization?

Canaan (CAY-nan) is an ancient name for the lands currently called Israel, Palestine, Lebanon, and Syria. Often eclipsed by Egypt, Mesopotamia, and the Anatolian kingdoms, the Canaanite (CAY-nan-ites) city-states made important contributions to the West. Not only did they take part in the first international system of states, the era documented by the Amarna Archives ca. 1450–1300 B.C., but they also served as the cradle of Western writing systems. After surviving the invasions of the Sea Peoples, the Canaanite city-states on the coast prospered in the first millennium B.C. Now known as Phoenicians, they were great sailors who planted colonies throughout the Mediterranean and spread the alphabet.

The Canaanite City-States, ca. 1400–1200 B.C.

Canaanite centers thrived both inland and on the Mediterranean coast. The first flowering of Canaanite civilization came in the third millennium B.C. at such sites as Ebla, but Ebla's greatest days were behind it after being conquered around 2000 B.C. To find a much more vibrant city in Syria after 2000 B.C., we need only look at the coast and the city of **Ugarit** (see **MAP 1.3**). Ugarit (OO-ga-rit) was a thriving Mediterranean port, especially around 1400 to 1180 B.C. It was located in what is today Syria, at the modern Ra's Shamrah, near today's port of Latakia. Further south, in what is today Lebanon, other Canaanite cities also existed in the second century B.C., such as Tyre, Sidon, Byblos, and Beirut.

Ugarit A thriving, cosmopolitan Mediterranean port in what is today Syria, whose scribes developed an alphabet in the 1300s B.C.

A multiethnic city, Ugarit's cosmopolitanism made it distinctive among western Asian city-states. As a trading center, it linked ships coming from the eastern Mediterranean island of Cyprus or the Anatolian ports with land caravans heading to Babylonia. The native inhabitants of Ugarit spoke a Semitic language. The merchants of Ugarit, however, were often foreigners, and the bazaars echoed with a multitude of languages. In its heyday, Ugarit housed documents written in at least four different languages.

alphabet A set of letters (written symbols) each of which represents roughly one sound in a spoken language.

Ugarit played an important role in the spread of one of history's most important writing systems: the **alphabet**. Unlike the pictographic or syllabic systems of Mesopotamia, Egypt, and China, in an alphabet each letter—that is, written symbol—stands for one sound in a spoken language or for several closely related sounds such as the "s" in "say" and the "s" in "was." In the 1300s B.C., scribes in Ugarit developed an alphabet. It was not the first alphabet, however. In Egypt, in the desert west of the Nile, limestone inscriptions have recently been found in a Semitic script with Egyptian influences. Dated to about 1900 to 1800 B.C., during the Middle Kingdom, the writing is now recognized as the earliest known example of an alphabet.

We do not know whether that alphabet was invented by Egyptians or by speakers of a Semitic language that were visiting Egypt, nor do we know if that alphabet influenced Ugarit. What is clear is that Ugaritic scribes invented thirty cuneiform signs as an alphabet to write their Semitic language. Later adapted by the Phoenicians and, through them, the Greeks, the Ugaritic alphabet is the source of the Roman alphabet, used today by English and many other languages around the world.

The Phoenicians, ca. 1050–450 B.C.

Ugarit was destroyed by the Sea Peoples ca. 1180 B.C. Most Canaanite cities survived, however. After the invasions of the Sea Peoples and others, the Canaanites' once-large territory was reduced to a narrow strip along the Mediterranean in the area of modern Lebanon and northern Israel (see **MAP 2.2** on page 41). Between 1050 and 750 B.C., the inhabitants of the area flourished;

historians call them, as did the ancient Greeks, "Phoenicians." Their purple-dyed textiles gave the Greeks their word for the color purple: *Phoenician*. Besides textiles, the Phoenicians exported the famous cedars of Lebanon for shipbuilding.

In the Hebrew Bible, the **Phoenicians** (fuh-NEESH-anz) loom large as merchants and seamen, as "traders the world honored" (Isaiah 23:8). Phoenicians were Canaanites, speakers of a Semitic language and heirs to the civilization that had prospered in Ugarit around 1400 B.C. (see page 30).

The Phoenicians were master shipbuilders and sailors. Around 600 B.C., their ships accomplished the first known circumnavigation of Africa. Around 450 B.C., they made the first known commercial sailing trip to the British Isles. Some scholars think they even reached Brazil. The most lasting Phoenician achievement at sea, however, was the planting of colonies in the Mediterranean, probably beginning in the ninth century B.C. Apparently, the colonies left a deep imprint. A recent genetic study shows that as many as 1 in 17 men living today on the coasts of North Africa and southern Europe may be directly descended from the Phoenicians.

Phoenician colonies were located in Cyprus, North Africa, Sicily, Malta, Sardinia, Italy, southern France, and Spain and Portugal. Many of their colonies eventually became independent states. The greatest Phoenician colony was Carthage (CAR-thidge), founded by the city of Tyre around 750 B.C. It was the major port city of the western Mediterranean for much of the next thousand years. There was also a Phoenician colony at the western gateway to the Mediterranean, at Gibraltar.

Phoenician culture was open to outside influences. Phoenician religious art is full of Egyptian sphinxes, coffins that look like mummy cases, and women wearing wigs in the style of Egypt's New Kingdom. But Phoenician art also contains Near Eastern seals and figures out of Greek myths.

Phoenician traders introduced advanced material goods, slaves, and possibly law codes to the Greeks. It was probably from the Phoenicians, whose alphabet derived from Ugarit, that the Greeks adapted their alphabet, probably shortly after 800 B.C.

One aspect of Phoenician culture is less attractive: child sacrifice. The Hebrew Bible, as well as Greek and Roman writers, state that Phoenician and other Canaanite parents sacrificed a child, especially their first-born child, to a god in return for divine favor. Many Phoenician archaeological sites contain an area with large numbers of infant burials. While skeptics consider that evidence only of infant mortality, most scholars hold it as confirmation of the literary record.

Around 750 B.C., the Phoenician city-states lost their independence to the Assyrians, and in later years Neo-Babylonians, Persians, and other foreign conquerors followed. But Phoenician culture survived—at home, in the colonies, and among the many Mediterranean peoples influenced by it. The result, though unintended, was that Phoenician colonists exported the civilization of western Asia to the western Mediterranean.

CHRONOLOGY

ca. 1900–1800 B.C.	Earliest known alphabet
ca. 1400–1180 B.C.	Height of Ugarit
1250–1150 B.C.	Sea Peoples invade the eastern Mediterranean
1180 B.C.	Ugarit destroyed
1075–656 B.C.	Third Intermediate Period in Egypt
ca. 1050–750 B.C.	Height of Phoenician city-states
1004–928 B.C.	Reigns of David and Solomon
722 B.C.	Assyrians conquer kingdom of Israel
612 B.C.	Conquest of Nineveh ends Assyrian power
598 B.C.	Neo-Babylonians conquer kingdom of Judah
559–530 B.C.	Reign of Cyrus the Great
550–330 B.C.	Achaemenid Persian Empire
539 B.C.	Cyrus conquers Babylon; permits Jews to return to Palestine
ca. 425 B.C.	Judean assembly accepts the Torah
701 B.C.	Siege and destruction of Lachish

Phoenicians Canaanites whose civilization flourished about 1050–750 B.C. in present-day coastal Syria, where they established major trading ports. Master sailors, they planted colonies around the Mediterranean, many of which, including Carthage, became independent states.

ASSYRIANS, NEO-BABYLONIANS, AND PERSIANS, CA. 1200–330 B.C.

What made the first-millennium B.C empires of the Assyrians, Neo-Babylonians, and Persians so much more effective than earlier empires?

Ancestors of the West, three great multiethnic empires emerged between the 800s and 500s B.C. Ruthless soldiers, brutal conquerors, and innovative administrators, the Assyrians established an empire in western Asia and Egypt during the ninth through seventh centuries B.C. They were followed in turn by a Neo-Babylonian empire in the late seventh and sixth centuries.

🌐 **MAP 2.1—The Assyrian and Persian Empires**

In the 660s B.C., the Assyrians ruled the largest empire the ancient world had seen, extending from the Tigris to the Nile. The Persian Empire was even greater. Around 500 B.C., it reached from its heartland in southwestern Iran westward to Macedonia and eastward to India.

However, neither of these was as successful or as durable as the empire of the Persians (ca. 550–330 B.C.). At its height, the Persian Empire stretched from central Asia and northwest India in the east to Macedonia and Libya in the west (see **MAP 2.1**). Persia's vast empire was loosely governed by a Persian ruling elite and its native helpers. Unlike the ironfisted Assyrians, the Persians were relatively tolerant and respectful of their subjects' customs. Many of Persia's kings were followers of Zoroastrianism, an ethical and forceful religion. A period of relative peace in most of Persia's domains from the 530s to the 330s B.C. fostered widespread economic prosperity.

The Persians borrowed the administrative methods of the Assyrians and Medes (meedz) and the long-established officialdom of Babylon and built a new and durable imperial government. Their official art stressed the unity of the peoples of the empire under Persian leadership. Persian rule represented the greatest success yet in implementing the notions of universal kingship that dated back to Sargon of Agade (r. 2371–2316 B.C.) (see page 14). In turn, Persia transmitted the idea of absolute kingship to later ambitious rulers, from Alexander the Great to the caesars of Rome and from the Byzantine emperors to the Muslim caliphs.

Assyrians and Neo-Babylonians

Assyrians Warlike people who ruled the ancient Near East during the first millennium B.C. Their innovations included using cavalry as their main striking force and having weapons and armor made of iron.

The **Assyrians** already had a long history as a military and commercial power in the Bronze Age. They lived in what is today northern Iraq and spoke a Semitic language. Around 1200 B.C., their state collapsed during that era of international crisis (see page 24), but they held on to a small homeland of about 5,000 square miles, roughly the size of Connecticut. The toughened survivors emerged with an aggressive, expansionist ideology.

Assyria's greatest successes came in the eighth and seventh centuries. One by one, states large and small fell—Babylonia, Syria, the kingdom of Israel, Cilicia in southern Anatolia, even Egypt (though Assyrian rule there lasted only a generation). Assyria became the first state to rule the two great river valleys of the ancient Near East, the Nile and the Tigris-Euphrates (see **MAP 2.1**).

The Assyrians were warriors. Ashur, their main deity, was a war-god. Theirs was an ideology of power, conquest, and control. The key to Assyria's success was its army—100,000 to 200,000 men strong—which made an unforgettable impression on observers and foes. The Israelite prophet Isaiah of Jerusalem ("First Isaiah") said of Assyrian soldiers: "[Their] arrows are sharpened, and all their bows bent, their horses' hoofs are like flint, their chariot wheels like the whirlwind. Their growling is like that of a lion" (Isaiah 5:28–29). He might have added that Assyrian spearmen, archers, and cavalrymen were equipped with weapons and armor of iron.

Thanks to new heating and cooling techniques, metal smiths in the ancient world produced an alloy of carbon and iron that was harder and more durable than bronze. It was also easier to obtain since iron ore is widespread—unlike tin, an essential element of bronze. Iron tools and weapons were often stronger and cheaper than their bronze predecessors, which opened up new technical and military possibilities.

Adding to its might, Assyria was the first major state to employ regular cavalry units (rather than charioteers) as the main strike force. The Assyrians were also excellent engineers, adept at taking walled cities by siege.

In addition, the Assyrians displayed superb organizational skills. The central standing army was supplemented with draftees conscripted from around the empire. Provinces were kept small to prevent the emergence of separate power bases, and independent-minded nobles were regularly checked by the kings.

To control the restive subjects of their far-flung empire, the Assyrians met rebellion with ferocious reprisals. Disloyal cities were attacked and, if need be, destroyed. Sculptured reliefs and inscriptions were set up to show, often in gruesome detail, the fate awaiting Assyria's enemies. We see or read of cities burned to the ground; of men flayed alive, even though they had surrendered, and walls covered with their skin; and of piles of human skulls. (See the feature, "The Visual Record: The Siege of Lachish" on pages 44–45.)

The Assyrians also engaged in mass deportations. They uprooted the people of a conquered country, resettled them far away—often in Assyria itself—and colonized their land with Assyrian loyalists. The so-called Ten Lost Tribes of Israel—the people of the northern Israelite kingdom (see page 41)—were conquered by Assyria in 722 B.C., and many of them were transported to Mesopotamia, where they disappeared from history. (Those who remained in Israel mixed with colonists, and the new group became known, and scorned, as Samaritans.)

Assyrian policy was the result of careful calculation. The political goal was to punish rebellion; the economic goal was to create a varied labor force. For example, although it is estimated that the Assyrians deported several million people, they deported not whole populations but a carefully chosen cross section of professions. They also deported entire families together, to weaken deportees' emotional ties to their former homes.

Assyria's success also was due in part to the relative weakness of other powers. After a period of great warrior-pharaohs and builder-pharaohs during the Nineteenth Dynasty (ca. 1291–1185 B.C.), Egypt suffered a series of weak kings who lost power to the priests of Amun during the Twentieth Dynasty (ca. 1185–1075 B.C.). When the Twentieth Dynasty ended in 1075 B.C., the New Kingdom ended with it, and regional conflict between the Nile Delta and Upper Egypt broke out.

Egypt was at the mercy of factions and invaders for much of the Third Intermediate Period (1075–656 B.C). Around 950, for example, the kingship came into the hands of Libyan mercenaries. From the eighth century on, their rule was challenged, in turn, by invaders from the south, rulers of a new Nubian kingdom called Kush (see **MAP 1.2** on page 18). Kushite pharaohs governed Egypt

Assyrian Winged Genie   This alabaster relief comes from a temple of the Assyrian king Ashurnasirpal II (r. 883–859 B.C) at his capital of Calah (Nimrud). The figure holds an incense pouch in one hand and a pine cone in the other, perhaps symbols of the tree of life.   (The Metropolitan Museum of Art, Gift of John D. Rockefeller, Jr., 1931 [31.72.1])

Phoenician Ivory This delicately carved plaque of a cow and calf, just 3 inches high, illustrates the wealth of artistic talent at the disposal of the Phoenicians, whose civilization reached its peak between 1050 and 750 B.C. (Iraq Antiquities Department)

Neo-Babylonians Rulers of western Asia between 612 and 539 B.C., who elaborately rebuilt Babylon, creating the famous Hanging Gardens. They destroyed Jerusalem, deporting many Judeans in what is known as the Babylonian Captivity.

Persian Empire Vast, prosperous, and law-abiding West Asian empire, from about 550 to 330 B.C., it represented the greatest success yet of a universal kingship. The Persians also built the first great navy.

from around 719 until 656, when they withdrew back south. It was they who faced the Assyrian attacks in 671 and 667.

The conquest of Egypt marked imperial Assyria's greatest extent—and its overextension (see **MAP 2.1**). A coalition army consisting of soldiers from a new Babylonian kingdom and from the Medes (who had formed a powerful state in Iran) conquered Nineveh (NIN-eh-veh), the Assyrian capital, in 612 B.C. and defeated the remnants of the Assyrian army in battles in 609 and 605. Few of its subjects mourned the empire's passing.

The destruction of Assyria led to revival for Babylon, whose rulers attempted to recapture the glories of Hammurabi's day (see page 15). For a short period, until the Persian conquest in 539 B.C, the **Neo-Babylonian** dynasty (founded in 626 B.C), as it is known today, and the Medes of Iran were the dominant military forces in western Asia. The Neo-Babylonian king Nebuchadrezzar II (neh-boo-khad-REZ-zar) conquered the kingdom of Judah (in southern Palestine) in 598 and destroyed Jerusalem, its capital, in 586. He deported many thousands of Judeans to Babylon, an event remembered by Christians and Jews as the Babylonian Captivity. Most of the rest of western Asia also fell to Nebuchadrezzar's troops. His most enduring achievement was rebuilding Babylon on a grand scale. In addition to the city's numerous temples, shrines, and altars, he created the so-called Hanging Gardens celebrated by later Greek writers. They describe the structure as a large terraced complex that Nebuchadrezzar built for his queen, although it may have been a plant-covered ziggurat.

The Neo-Babylonians and Assyrians both made great strides in astronomy. Their primary motive was not scientific but religious—that is, a belief in astrology (the study of the movements of heavenly bodies in the belief that they influence human affairs). Astrology led to advances in the scientific observation of the heavens. Assyrian priests had produced relatively accurate circular diagrams (astrolabes) that showed the positions of the major constellations, stars, and planets over the course of the year. By 600 B.C., Assyrian and Neo-Babylonian astronomers could predict solstices, equinoxes, and lunar eclipses.

Astronomy in Mesopotamia reached its heights in the centuries after 500 B.C. The zodiac, a diagram showing the movement of the sun and planets relative to the constellations, was invented in Persian-ruled Babylon in the fourth century B.C. In the third and second centuries B.C., when Babylonia was under Hellenistic Greek rule, native scientists made impressive advances in mathematical astronomy, composing tables that could be used to calculate movements of the moon and planets. More sophisticated mathematical astronomy would not be produced in the West until the Scientific Revolution of the sixteenth century A.D.

Building the Persian Empire

A thousand miles east of Phoenicia, a great empire took root. Indo-European–speaking peoples, the Medes and Persians arrived in what is now western Iran, probably around 1500 B.C., but perhaps not until 900 B.C. The two peoples were closely related in language and customs. The Medes lived in the central Zagros Mountains. The Persians made their homeland farther south in Anshan (modern Fars). At first, the Medes ruled the Persians, but in 550 B.C., the tables were turned when the Medes were suddenly conquered by the young Persian king Cyrus the Great (r. 559–530 B.C.).

It took Cyrus only twenty years to conquer most of western Asia and much of central Asia. Within five years of his death in 530 B.C., his son and successor, Cambyses (kam-BYE-seez) (r. 530–525 B.C.), added Egypt and Libya. Cambyses' successor, Darius (dah-RYE-us) (r. 521–486 B.C.), corralled northwestern India and Thrace. The frontier regions, especially Egypt, were often in revolt, and the attempt of Darius and his successor, Xerxes (ZURK-seez) (r. 486–465 B.C.), to extend Persian rule to Greece ended in failure (see pages 69–70). But the Achaemenid **Persian Empire** (named after a legendary founder, Achaemenes) survived for two hundred years, until a Greco-Macedonian army under Alexander the Great, king of Macedon (r. 336–323 B.C.), destroyed it.

why was the Persian Empire successful?

Let us consider several reasons for the success of Achaemenid (ah-KEE-men-id) Persia. The first was military prowess. Persia was ruled by a warrior-aristocracy whose traditional values, according to the Greek historian Herodotus, were "riding, hunting, and telling the truth." The state was able to field a huge army of about 300,000 men, conscripted from the various subject peoples. Although the resultant hodgepodge of soldiers from across the empire did not always fight as a unit, a crack infantry group, called the 10,000 Immortals, provided a solid core. The Persians excelled as bowmen and cavalrymen. Following the Assyrians, they made cavalry into the decisive strike force of the battlefield, assigning a more minor role to chariotry. Persia was even more innovative at sea, where it had its subjects build the first great navy. Although Persians served as marines and sometimes as commanders, the rowers and seamen were usually Phoenicians or Greeks.

The second reason for Persia's success was political. Unlike the Assyrians, the Persians considered generosity and tolerance to be more effective than terrorism and brutality. As Cyrus prepared to attack Babylon, he portrayed himself as the champion of the traditional Babylonian religion, and Babylon surrendered to him without a fight. Cyrus also emphasized his continuity with earlier Mesopotamian history by adopting the traditional title of "King of Sumer and Akkad." He did not hesitate to break with Assyrian and Neo-Babylonian population transfers, as witnessed in his edict permitting the Jewish exiles in Babylon to return to Judea.

The third reason for Persia's success was its skill at administration and organization. Darius played a crucial role in reorganizing the imperial administration and finances. Like the Assyrian Empire, the Persian domain was divided into provinces, called *satrapies* (SAY-truh-peez). Each of the twenty satrapies was a unit of administration and tax collection. For the first time, taxes could be paid with a stable, official coinage: the gold daric (named after Darius) and the silver shekel. Coins had been invented in the kingdom of Lydia in western Asia Minor in the seventh century B.C. Croesus (CREE-sus) (r. 560–547 B.C.), Lydia's king, was known for his wealth—hence, the expression "rich as Croesus"—before Cyrus conquered him in 547 B.C.

The provincial governors, or *satraps,* were powerful, often quasi-independent figures, but the king tried to keep a firm hand on them. Each province had a royal secretary and was visited regularly by traveling inspectors called "the king's eyes." A network of good roads radiated from the capital cities of Susa and Persepolis. The most famous road, the so-called Royal Road, stretched 1,600 miles from western Iran to western Anatolia (see **Map 2.1**). Covering the whole distance took most travelers three months, but the king's relay messenger corps could make the trip in a week, thanks to a series of staging posts furnished with fresh horses.

Another unifying element was a society that was law-abiding and prosperous. Darius proclaimed in an inscription that he had fostered the rule of law: "These countries [of the empire] showed respect toward my law; as was said to them by me, thus it was done." Darius and other Persian kings helped create the conditions for compliance and security by taking an interest in the economy. For example, they opened to commercial traffic Persian roads and a canal connecting the Red Sea and the Nile.

Language, too, built unity. Not Persian, which relatively few people spoke, but Aramaic, the most widespread language of western Asia, became the empire's basic language of commerce and administration. A Semitic language related to Hebrew, Aramaic was first used by the Aramaeans (air-uh-MAY-unz), a nomadic people who settled in northern Syria about 1100 B.C. and ruled an area extending into Mesopotamia before succumbing to Assyrian conquest about 725 B.C. The Aramaeans dominated the overland trade routes, which, combined with the simple and easily learned Aramaic alphabet, contributed to the spread of their language. Aramaic facilitated the development of literacy and recordkeeping. Aramaic would become the common language of western Asia for over a thousand years, until Arabic replaced it; Jesus of Nazareth was to be its most famous native speaker.

The King of Kings

Persia's empire had several weaknesses. First, Cyrus had bequeathed a legacy as a charismatic war leader. Feeling the need to live up to his example, his successors sometimes undertook ambitious and expensive expeditions that failed, such as wars with the

Achaemenid Persian Silver This silver rhyton (drinking vessel) is in the shape of a griffin, a mythological animal that is part lion and part eagle. Persian rulers commanded the talents of western Asia's best artists and craftsmen, silversmiths among them. (Courtesy of the Trustees of the British Museum)

Scythians (a tough nomadic people in Ukraine) and the Greeks. Second, however mild Persian rule, however peaceful and prosperous, it was still ruled by foreigners and it still involved taxation. Persian officials, military garrisons, and colonists were found—and were resented—in every corner of the empire. Native resentment, particularly in Egypt, and the independence of certain satraps led to intermittent provincial revolts.

The exaltation of the Persian king served as a counterweight to rebellious tendencies. From Darius on, the Persian monarch tried to overawe his officials with his majesty and might. The "King of Kings," as the monarch called himself, sat on a high, gold and blue throne, dressed in purple, decked out in gold jewelry, wearing fragrant oils and cosmetics, and attended by corps of slaves and eunuchs (castrated men employed in high positions). Although he was not considered a god, he had to be treated with reverence. Persians spoke of the king's *khvarna,* his "kingly glory," a mysterious aura of power. Anyone who came into the royal presence had to approach him with a bow to the ground, face-down.

Impressive as the court ceremonial was, Persian kings were not all-powerful. They were bound by the rule of law and by the considerable power of Persia's proud nobility, on whom they relied to fill the top administrative positions. Competing factions of ministers, wives, concubines, eunuchs, and sons often brought intrigue and discord to court, especially in the fourth century B.C., a time of frequent rebellion.

Royal authority was symbolized in the decoration of the great palaces at Susa and Persepolis, a project begun by Darius I and completed by his son and successor, Xerxes. The Susa palace, the larger of the two, reflected the universality of the empire in the variety of hands that built it. Craftsmen from east and west took part in the construction. (See the feature, "The Global Record: The Subject Peoples of a Multicultural Empire.") The Persepolis palace, too, displayed the heterogeneity of the empire in its architecture. The palace was placed on a terrace, as in

Frieze at Persepolis   This sculptured relief lines the stairway to the audience hall of King Darius (r. 521–486 B.C.). It depicts Persian nobles, well groomed and formally dressed, carrying flowers for the New Year's feast.   (Ronny Jaques/Photo Researchers)

The Subject Peoples of a Multicultural Empire

The Persian Empire ruled more people than ever before, and the kings were proud of that. This inscription from the capital city of Susa, dated probably about 520 B.C., emphasizes the participation of a variety of peoples, from India to Egypt and the Aegean Sea, in the construction of King Darius's palace.

§2. I am Darius, the Great King, the king of kings, king of the lands, king of this earth, son of Hystaspes, an Achaemenid. And Darius the king says: "Ahura Mazda, who is the greatest of the gods, has created me, has made me king, has given me this kingdom, which is great, and which has good horses and good men. By the favor of Ahura Mazda, my father Hystaspes and Arsames, my grandfather, were both alive when Ahura Mazda made me king on this earth. Thus it was the desire of Ahura Mazda to choose me as his man on this entire earth, he made me king on this earth. I worshipped Ahura Mazda. Ahura Mazda brought me aid. What I ordered (to be done), this he accomplished for me. I achieved all of what I did by the grace of Ahura Mazda.

§3. "This palace which I built at Susa: its materials were brought from afar. The earth was dug down deep, until the rock was reached in the earth. When the excavation had been made, then rubble was packed down, some 40 cubits (ca. 65 feet) deep, another (part) 20 cubits deep. On that rubble the palace was constructed. And that earth, which was dug deep, and that rubble, which was packed down, and the sun dried bricks, which were molded, the Babylonian people—they performed (these tasks).

§4. "The cedar timber was brought from a mountain called Lebanon. The Assyrian people brought it to Babylon. From Babylon the Carians and Ionians brought it to Susa. The sissoo-timber was brought from Gandara and from Carmania. The gold which was worked here was brought from Sardis and from Bactria. The precious stone lapis lazuli and carnelian which was worked here was brought from Sogdiana. The precious stone turquoise, which was worked here, this was brought from Chorasmia. The silver and the ebony were brought from Egypt. The ornamentation with which the wall was adorned was brought from Ionia. The ivory which was worked here was brought from Ethiopia, and from India and from Arachosia. The stone columns which were worked here were brought from a village called Abiradu, in Elam. The stonecutters who worked the stone were Ionians and Sardians. The goldsmiths who worked the gold were Medes and Egyptians. The men who worked the wood were Sardians and Egyptians. The men who worked the baked brick were Babylonians. The men who adorned the wall were Medes and Egyptians."

§5. Darius the king says: "At Susa a very excellent work was ordered, a very excellent work was brought to completion. May Ahura Mazda protect me, and Hystaspes my father and my country."

QUESTIONS

1. What does Darius consider to be special signs that heaven favored him? Why does he choose these signs?

2. List all the different materials in the palace and all the different ethnic groups that brought them to Susa. What do you think was the most valuable material? Least valuable?

3. How does the variety of peoples and materials demonstrate Darius's power?

Source: From *The Persian Empire from Cyrus II to Artaxerxes I* (*LACTOR* 16), translated and edited by Maria Brosius, Copyright 2000 London Association of Classical Teachers. Reprinted by permission of L.A.C.T.

Mesopotamia, but contained columned halls as in Egypt, with Assyrian-style column capitals or tops. In Persepolis, a frieze of sculpted relief panels lining a monumental stairway leading to the palace emphasized the king's vast power. The panels depict an endless procession of the peoples of the world paying homage to the King of Kings: from the nobility to the Immortals, to Median and Persian soldiers, to tribute-bearing subjects from the ends of the earth. The overall feeling of the scene is static, as if the Persian Empire would last forever.

Zoroastrianism

Like ancient Israel, Persia developed a highly ethical religion in the first millennium B.C. From obscure beginnings, Zoroastrianism (zoh-roh-AS-tree-un-izm) became the religion of Persia that persisted until the Muslim conquest in the seventh century A.D. Although largely extinct in today's Iran, an Islamic country, Zoroastrianism still survives in small communities elsewhere, primarily in India. Some scholars argue that Zoroastrian beliefs eventually influenced Judaism and Christianity, as well as Roman paganism and Indian Buddhism.

It is easier to describe ancient Zoroastrianism in broad strokes than in detail, partly because the religion changed radically over the course of its ancient history, and partly because relatively little information survives before A.D. 300. This much is clear: The religion was founded by a great reformer and prophet named Zarathustra (*Zoroaster* in Greek). Zarathustra (zah-ruh-THOOS-truh) lived in

Zoroastrianism Religion founded about 1000–550 B.C. by the Persian prophet Zarathustra (*Zoroaster* in Greek). Zoroastrians believe in a supreme deity and a cosmic contest between good and evil within each individual.

SECTION SUMMARY

- Iron arms and armor, engineering skill, organizing ability, and brutality all helped build Assyria's empire, at its height in the 660s B.C.

- The Neo-Babylonian kingdom (626–539 B.C.) was famous for its Hanging Gardens and astronomers.

- Phoenicia's outstanding sailors spread the alphabet and established the great city of Carthage.

- From their homeland in Iran, the Persians built the ancient world's largest empire yet, the Achaemenid Empire (ca. 550–330 B.C.).

- Rather than try to "Persianize" the empire, the Persian kings emphasized the variety of peoples under their rule.

- Zoroastrianism, an ethical religion emphasizing the struggle between good and evil, flourished in Achaemenid Persia.

eastern Iran. His teachings survive in the *Gathas* ("Songs"), a portion of the Zoroastrian holy book called the *Avesta*. Some scholars date Zarathustra as late as 550 B.C.; others prefer an earlier date, 750 or even 1000 B.C.

Zarathustra's society was dominated by warriors whose religion consisted of blood cults, violent gods, animal sacrifice, and ecstatic rituals in which hallucinogens were eaten. Zarathustra rejected such violent practices in favor of an inward-looking, intellectual, and ethical religion. He favored ceremonies involving fire, considered a symbol of purity. Zarathustra was not a strict monotheist like the Jews, but he did emphasize the power of one god over all people, the supremely good and wise creator of the universe, whom he called Ahura Mazda ("Wise Lord"). Unlike the Jews, Zarathustra considered the problem of evil to be the central question of religion. If god was one, good, and omnipotent, how could evil exist?

Zarathustra's answer might be called *ethical dualism* (dualism is the notion of a grand conflict between good and evil). Ahura Mazda had twin children: the Beneficent Spirit and the Hostile Spirit. Each spirit had made a free choice: one for the "truth" and the other for the "lie"—that is, one for good and the other for evil. Every human being faces a similar choice between good and evil. "Reflect with a clear mind—man by man for himself—upon the two choices of decision, being aware to declare yourselves to Him before the great retribution," says Zarathustra.[1] Indeed, humanity is caught in a great cosmic struggle in which individuals are free to make a momentous choice. Zarathustra distinguished between two states of being: the spiritual and the material. The more a person pursued spiritual purity, the greater was the person's ability to choose good rather than evil.

Zarathustra held a linear conception of history, similar to that in the Hebrew Bible. His religion is marked by a strong *eschatology* (interest in the end of the world) as well as *soteriology* (belief in a savior). He believed that one day, through an ordeal by fire, Ahura Mazda would judge all the people who had ever lived. Those who had chosen good would be rewarded, and those who had chosen evil would be punished. Then would follow a Last Judgment in which the dead would be transfigured and restored to a glorious bodily existence. There would be, Zarathustra promised, "long destruction for the deceitful but salvation for the truthful." The notion of a savior who would initiate the Last Judgment is an early Zoroastrian belief, if perhaps not a doctrine of Zarathustra himself.

In later centuries, Zarathustra's followers eased his uncompromising rejection of Iranian paganism. Under the leadership of priests, known as *magi* (MAY-jye) in western Iran, the religion changed considerably. Lesser deities beneath Ahura Mazda were added to the Zoroastrian pantheon, in part, to suit the religion to the needs of the huge, multicultural Persian Empire.

It is tempting to attribute Cyrus's policy of toleration to the ethical teachings of Zarathustra, but it is uncertain whether Cyrus was Zoroastrian. We are on firmer ground with later Persian kings, particularly Darius I, who had an image of himself alongside Ahura Mazda carved on the face of an Iranian cliff. In an accompanying inscription Darius announces: "For this reason Ahura Mazda bore aid, and the other gods who . . . [exist], because I was not hostile, I was not a Lie-follower, I was not a doer of wrong—neither I nor my family. According to righteousness I conducted myself."[2]

ISRAEL, CA. 1500–400 B.C.

What was the religious experience of ancient Israel, and what is its legacy today?

In the first millennium B.C., a small, often-conquered people turned imperialism on its head. Human achievement is meaningless, they argued; only the power of divinity matters. There is only one god, they said; all other gods are false. The one true god had revealed himself not to the awesome, imperialistic Assyrians, but to the less powerful Hebrews—ancient Jews. They founded the Western tradition of religion. The God of ancient Israel eventually gave rise to the God of Christianity and of Islam, as well as of modern Judaism.

The Hebrews, also known as Israelites, had existed as a people since about 1200 B.C. and perhaps for centuries earlier. They spoke a Semitic language.

The Hebrew Bible as a Historical Record

As literature and as religious teaching, the Bible is the most influential single text in the history of Western civilization. As a source of history, however, it presents difficulties. Many Jews and Christians today believe that God gave the Hebrew Bible (called the Old Testament by Christians) in its entirety to the Jewish people at Mt. Sinai. In addition, Jews believe that unwritten laws were handed down at Sinai as well, and that these laws were preserved via oral tradition across the generations. Scholars argue differently. They believe that the Hebrew Bible is man-made and that it is based on written sources that probably date back at least as far as the early Israelite monarchy of about 1000 B.C. Other parts of the Hebrew Bible are probably the product of an oral tradition, and the nature, antiquity, and reliability of that tradition are the subject of much scholarly debate.

Israelite Seal This seal stone, which shows a roaring lion, was used by a man named Shema, an official of King Jeroboam of Israel. The stone was used to make an impression in hot wax, creating a seal on a document. (Reuben and Edith Hecht Collection, University of Haifa, Israel/Erich Lessing/Art Resource, NY)

Archaeological evidence from the area of ancient Israel; a small number of inscriptions, that is, writings on stone or other durable material (almost all after 800 B.C.); and some information in Greek and Roman literary sources provide an alternative source of information. Yet, little of that alternative evidence sheds light on the period before about 1200 B.C., and it offers only partial insight into the later period. The historian needs both to pay attention to the Bible and to consider its nature.

The Hebrew Bible reached something close to its current form a century or two before the birth of Christ. It consists of three main sections: (1) the **Torah** (TOE-rah), also known as the Pentateuch, or five books of Moses (that is, the first five books of the Bible); (2) the Prophets, that is, the "historical" books of the early prophets (Joshua, Judges, Kings, and Chronicles) and the books of the later prophets (Isaiah, Jeremiah, Ezekiel, and the twelve "minor prophets"); and (3) the Writings, various books of poetry, proverbs, and wisdom literature.

The books of the Hebrew (and Christian) Bible are canonical: one by one, each was accepted by established authority as sacred. Two key dates stand out in the canonization of the Hebrew Bible: 622 B.C. and about 425 B.C. On the first date, Josiah, king of Judah (see page 41), assembled "the entire population, high and low" to swear to obey "the scroll of the covenant which had been discovered in the house of the Lord" (the scroll probably was Deuteronomy, now the fifth book of the Torah). On the second date, a similar assembly of the people, called by the religious leader Ezra, swore to accept the five books of the Torah that had by then been assembled. The introduction of the Torah (literally, "teaching") made its worshipers into what they have been ever since: "a people of the Book," as the Muslims would put it centuries later. The written tradition and literacy became central to the Hebrews.

The Hebrews are the first people we know of to have a single national history book. That book was written not as secular history, but as sacred history. It is the story of the working out of God's pact, or **covenant**, with the Hebrews, his chosen people. All ancient peoples told stories of their semidivine foundation. Only the Hebrews imagined the nation created by an actual treaty between the people and their God.

The central fact of human existence in the Hebrew Bible is God's covenant with the Hebrews. Because of the covenant, history has meaning. History is the story of the success or failure of the Hebrew people in carrying out God's commandments. The focus is on the individual: on individual people taking actions that have not just moral, but military and political consequences that unfold over time.

Many of the themes, narrative details, and styles of writing in the Hebrew Bible derive from earlier cultures. The biblical Flood story, for example, seems to have been modeled on a similar

Torah First five books of the Bible. Accepted as sacred by the Hebrews around 425 B.C., it relates the working out of God's pact, or covenant, with the Hebrews, his chosen people.

covenant As told in the Hebrew Bible, the pact God made with Abraham, the first patriarch of Israel. In return for the land of Canaan and the promise of becoming a great nation, the Israelites agreed to worship no other gods.

flood in the *Epic of Gilgamesh* (see page 17). Biblical poems in praise of God are often similar to Egyptian poems in praise of pagan gods, and biblical wisdom literature (that is, works containing proverbs and rules of conduct) often recalls Egyptian or Babylonian parallels. In spite of such borrowings, the Hebrew Bible is dramatically different from its predecessors because it subordinates everything to one central theme: God's plan for humanity and, in particular, for his chosen people—the Hebrews.

The Emergence of Hebrew Monotheism, ca. 1500–600 B.C.

We first hear of the Hebrews, outside of the Bible, in an inscribed monument of the New Kingdom Egyptian pharaoh Merneptah (r. 1224–1214 B.C.). After a military expedition into Canaan (CAY-nan), pharaoh declared triumphantly that "Israel is laid waste." Most scholars accept this as evidence of an Israelite presence in Canaan, but the question is how did they get there? The Bible says that the **Israelites** settled Palestine by conquering its earlier inhabitants. Most scholars now reject that account. Archaeological evidence suggests, rather, a more complex process. The Israelites, it seems, were a combination of three groups: armed conquerors, shepherds who gradually entered the country and later settled down to farming, and dispossessed and oppressed Canaanites who rebelled against their masters.

From such sources, the Israelites may have emerged. The Bible, however, tells a different story of Israelite origins. Although much of it is credible, none of it is confirmed by nonbiblical sources. Still, the biblical story of Israelite origins has been so influential in later Western culture that we must examine it. If one follows the Bible, Hebrew history began sometime during the period 2000 to 1500 B.C., with the patriarchs, or founding fathers. Abraham, the first patriarch, migrated to Canaan from the city of Haran in northern Mesopotamia. A seminomadic chieftain, Abraham settled on territory north and west of the Dead Sea, where he grazed his herds. Seminomadic clans in the region frequently made long migrations in antiquity, so the biblical account of Abraham and his descendants, Isaac and Jacob, is plausible.

The Bible, however, emphasizes the implausible: Abraham's extraordinary decision to give up Mesopotamian polytheism for belief in one god. This god commanded Abraham to leave Haran; indeed, he made a treaty, or covenant, with Abraham. In return for Abraham's faith, said the god, "As a possession for all time I shall give you and your descendants after you the land in which you are now aliens, the whole of Canaan, and I shall be their God" (Genesis 17:8). Abraham was not a strict monotheist: Although he worshiped only one god, he did not deny the existence of other gods. (See, for a comparison, the discussion of Akhenaten on page 24.) Nevertheless, he took a giant step on the road to pure **monotheism** by coming to believe that only one god rules *all* peoples.

According to the Bible, the next important step took place several hundred years later. In a time of famine in Canaan, many of Abraham's descendants left for prosperous Egypt. At first, they thrived there, but in time, they were enslaved and forced to build cities in the Nile Delta. Eventually, Moses, a divinely appointed leader, released the Hebrews from bondage in Egypt and led them back toward Canaan and freedom.

The Exodus ("journey out," in Greek), as this movement has been called, is a rare example of a successful national liberation movement in antiquity. Among those who accept its historicity, a date in the thirteenth century B.C. is frequently assigned to the Exodus. According to the Bible, the Exodus marked the key moment of another covenant, this time between the god of Abraham and the entire Israelite people. At Mount Sinai (SYE-nye), traditionally located on the rugged Sinai Peninsula between Egypt and Palestine, the Israelites are said to have first accepted as their one god a deity whose name is represented in Hebrew by the letters corresponding to YHWH. YHWH is traditionally rendered in English as "Jehovah," but "Yahweh" is more likely to be accurate. The Israelites accepted Yahweh's laws, summarized by the Ten Commandments. In return for obedience to Yahweh's commandments, they would be God's chosen people, his "special possession; . . . a kingdom of priests, . . . [his] holy nation."

The **Ten Commandments** are both more general and more personal than the laws of Hammurabi's Code. They are addressed to the individual, whom they commit to a universal standard. They emphasize prohibitions, saying more about what one should *not* do than about what one should do. The first three commandments establish Yahweh as the sole god of Israel, prohibit any sculpture or image of God, and forbid misuse of the divine name. The next two commandments are injunctions to observe the seventh day of the week (the Sabbath) as a day free of work and to honor one's parents. The sixth and seventh prohibit destructive or violent acts

Israelites People who settled on the eastern shore of the Mediterranean around 1200 B.C., or perhaps earlier. Their belief in one God directly influenced the faith of Christians, Muslims, and modern Jews.

monotheism Belief that there is only one God. The Hebrew Bible places this belief as originating about 2000–1500 B.C., when God commanded Abraham to give up Mesopotamian polytheism for belief in one God.

Ten Commandments According to the Hebrew Bible, these ten basic ethical and religious rules were given by God to Moses and the Israelites at Mt. Sinai. They have played an immensely influential role in Judaism and Christianity.

against neighbors, in particular adultery and killing. The final three commandments regulate community life by prohibiting stealing, testifying falsely, and coveting another man's wife or goods. In contrast to the starkness of the Ten Commandments, an enormous amount of detailed legal material is also found in the Hebrew Bible.

Many scholars doubt whether Hebrew monotheism emerged as early as the thirteenth century. In any case, the Bible makes clear that many ordinary Hebrews remained unconvinced. For centuries afterward, many Israelite worshipers deemed Yahweh their greatest god but not their only god. Unready for the radical innovation that monotheism represented, they carried out the rituals of various Canaanite deities, whom they worshiped on hilltop altars. Forging a national consensus for monotheism took centuries.

From the thirteenth to the late eleventh century B.C., the Hebrews were governed by a series of tribal leaders, referred to as "judges" in the Bible, but eventually the military threat posed by the Philistines (FILL-uh-steenz) persuaded the tribes to accept a centralized monarchy. The Philistines were one of the Sea Peoples, those raiders and invaders who beset the eastern Mediterranean in the Late Bronze Age. The Philistines had settled on the Palestinian coast where they prospered and eventually, seriously endangered Israel. The first Israelite king, Saul (r. ca. 1020–1004 B.C.), had some success against them but eventually fell in battle along with his son, Jonathan. The next king, David (r. 1004–965 B.C.), a former mercenary captain for the Philistines, defeated them decisively.

A recent discovery may provide archaeological evidence of the early Israelite monarchy. A fortress near Jerusalem provides the earliest example of Hebrew script yet discovered, dating from about 1050–970 B.C. The text contains the words "judge," "slave," and "king." It was written in ink on a piece of pottery. The work of a trained scribe, it might be a legal text, although further study is needed to be sure.

David was Israel's greatest king. He extended the kingdom into parts of modern Jordan, Lebanon, and Syria and conquered the Canaanite city of Jerusalem, which he made Israel's capital. David's son and successor, Solomon (r. 965–928 B.C.), was also a great king, a centralizer who moved from a loose kingship toward a tightly organized monarchy. His most famous accomplishment was the construction of the magnificent Temple in Jerusalem. The Temple priesthood and sacrifices became the focus of the national cult of Yahweh. Previously, that focus had been a humble, movable wooden chest known as the Ark of the Covenant.

Solomon's reign represented the high-water mark of the power of the Israelite monarchy. Under his successors, the monarchy was split into a large northern kingdom of Israel with a capital at Samaria and a smaller southern kingdom of Judah (JOO-duh) centered on Jerusalem (see **Map 2.2**). In 722 B.C., the Assyrians conquered the kingdom of Israel and deported its inhabitants. Judah survived, first as a state controlled by Assyria, and then as an independent power.

The religious history of the period of the two kingdoms (928–722 B.C.) and the Judean survivor-state (722–587 B.C.) is marked by an intense drive toward monotheism. The kings of Judah in the seventh century B.C., especially Hezekiah (r. 715–686 B.C.) and Josiah (r. 640–609 B.C.), aggressively attacked the worship of all gods other than Yahweh and all centers of Yahweh worship other than the Temple in Jerusalem. The kings also began the process of canonizing the Hebrew Bible. Ambitious and independent, Hezekiah

🌐 Map 2.2—Ancient Israel

The Israelites settled in the Canaanite hill country west of the Jordan River and the Dead Sea after 1200 B.C. (*top map*). Control of Israelite territory after 928 B.C. was shared between two monarchies (*bottom map*): the kingdoms of Israel (conquered by the Assyrians in 722 B.C.) and Judah (conquered by the Babylonians in 598 B.C.).

joined in a revolt against Assyria that was brutally suppressed in 701 B.C. and almost cost him his kingdom.

The Judean kings could not have succeeded without the help of the prophets, who were prominent from approximately 900 to 500 B.C. Seers, uttering divinely inspired predictions, were universal figures in ancient religion. No other culture of antiquity, however, has anything like the Hebrew prophets: charismatic, uncompromising, terrible figures who announced God's anger and ultimate forgiveness. The prophets remind us of the most radical spiritual teachings of Israel: absolute monotheism, an insistence on righteousness, contempt for materialism and worldly power, love of the powerless. They often supported the kings but did not shrink from confronting authority and insisting on uncompromising justice. Among them were Amos, a humble shepherd who preached the superiority of righteousness to ritual; Jeremiah, who prophesied the destruction of Jerusalem as punishment for the people's idolatry; and Isaiah, who predicted the coming of a savior who would inaugurate a new day of universal peace and justice.

A characteristic story of the prophets is the confrontation between Elijah, perhaps the most famous prophet, and Ahab, king of Israel (r. 871–852 B.C.). Ahab coveted the vineyard of one Naboth, but Naboth refused Ahab's offer to buy it. Spurred on by his wife, Jezebel, Ahab trumped up charges against Naboth, who was unjustly stoned to death. Ahab then confiscated the vineyard. God sent Elijah to declare to Ahab that, as punishment for committing murder, "dogs will lick [Ahab's] blood" and that of his family (1 Kings 21:19). In a remarkable scene, we witness not only Elijah's courage in confronting the king, but also the king's surrender and repentance before Elijah's spiritual authority. Ahab (though not Jezebel) humbles himself and is spared, but his son and successor, King Ahaziah, who is equally wicked, is punished with a fatal injury. The Western tradition of civil disobedience owes much to the courage of the Hebrew prophets.

Exile and Return, 598–ca. 400 B.C.

The prophets taught the people of Judah how to survive. They correctly predicted ruin and exile and the promise that divine providence would guarantee return. The Judeans clung to this message with remarkable tenacity. Indeed, they had to, for between 598 and 586 B.C., the Neo-Babylonians conquered Judah, destroying Jerusalem and the Temple. The cultural, political, and economic elite was deported eastward to Babylon. Those who could do so fled for safety in the opposite direction, westward to Egypt. The dispirited remnant in Palestine shared their land with colonists from neighboring regions, with whom they intermarried and among whom their religion all but disappeared.

And that, given the usual fate of exiled and uprooted peoples in antiquity, should have been that. Yet, not only did the Judeans in the Babylonian Captivity persevere in their religious loyalty; they actually returned to Palestine in large numbers.

The Neo-Babylonian rulers allowed Judean deportees to continue to practice their religion. Judaeans in Babylon were not slaves; rather they rented land on royal estates, and some became prosperous. Although some Babylonian Judeans assimilated to local ways, many continued a Judean religious life. Communal worship was observed in open places, perhaps with associated buildings. Some scholars argue that synagogues ("gatherings" in Greek), modest centers of prayer and study that have been the focus of Jewish worship ever since, first emerged in Babylon. It is also possible that the exiles put together the Torah in something like its current form. Elders led the community, while prophets continued to speak out: Two examples are Ezekiel, who preached the restoration of the Temple, and the man known to us only as "Second Isaiah" (Isaiah 40–66). Second Isaiah emphasized the universal aspect of the god of Israel, who made empires rise and fall and would bring the exiles home from far-off Babylon.

The Temple in Jerusalem was rebuilt around 515 B.C., only seventy years after its destruction. This remarkable turn of events was possible partly because of the Persians, who conquered Babylon in 539 B.C. and proclaimed the freedom of the Judeans to rebuild their Temple in Jerusalem. Still, Persian benevolence would not have been enough if the Judean elite had not kept the faith burning among the exiles.

Second Isaiah's message points to a second important development among the exiles of Judah. As striking as the return to Palestine was the survival of large numbers of Judeans as an unassimilated people outside of Judah—in other words, as Jews. The terms *Jew* and *Jewish* began to be used in the fifth century B.C. For the first time, membership in a community of worship was divorced from residence. Jewish communities flourished in Babylon, Persia, and Egypt, but the members often chose not to become Babylonians, Persians, or Egyptians. From the sixth century

B.C. on, a majority of Jews were living outside Palestine, and the Jewish Exile, or Diaspora ("dispersion"), became a permanent fact of history.

The People of the Covenant

Equality, limited government, and the rule of law under God were basic Israelite political principles. Eventually, they would become fundamental political ideals for many in the West, and they would be applied not only to Israelites, but to all people.

According to Israelite belief, God made humans in his own image. Thus, all individuals were equal in a fundamental sense; all were bound by God's law. A king who disobeyed this law was illegitimate. Indeed, Israel was ambivalent at best about the institution of kingship, which was tolerated as an evil made necessary only by the country's many armed enemies. God's covenant with the Hebrews was a religious contract with political consequences, rendering God the only true king of Israel. Far from being gods themselves, or even God's representatives, Israel's kings were merely God's humble servants.

Israelite egalitarianism was restricted to men. Israelite women usually could not own or inherit property, as women could in Hammurabi's Babylon; or sue in court, as women could in pharaonic Egypt; or initiate a divorce, as women could in Classical Athens (see page 69). The powerful goddesses of other ancient cultures were absent in Israel. Women participated in the rituals of early Israelite religion and the original Temple (ca. 940–586 B.C.) but were segregated in a separate women's courtyard in the rebuilt Temple (ca. 515 B.C.–A.D. 79) and kept out of Temple ritual. Indeed, the perspective of the Hebrew Bible is predominantly male. Consider just two examples. First, of the 1,426 names in the Hebrew Bible, 1,315 are male; only 111 women's names appear, about 9 percent of the total.[3] Second, only men and boys can bear the sign of the Lord's covenant with Israel—that is, circumcision.

Nevertheless, Israelite women claimed honor as mothers and partners in running the household. The Hebrew Bible states that woman (as exemplified by Eve, the first woman) was created as "a suitable partner" for man (Genesis 2:18, 20). Reproduction and hence motherhood assume great importance in the Hebrew Bible; the Lord enjoins humans to "be fruitful and multiply" (Genesis 1:28). The Bible also commands that children honor both their father and their mother: The two parents are equal in parental authority (Exodus 20:12).

The Hebrew Bible sometimes displays sympathy for and insights into the strategies that women used to counter the abuses of male power. Rebecca, for instance, thwarts her husband Isaac's plan to give his blessing to their son Esau. As the eldest, Esau was entitled to this honor, but Rebecca preferred her younger son Jacob, and she saw to it that he and not Esau obtained her husband's blessing.

Only about a half dozen women in the Hebrew Bible served as leaders of Israel, but that is more than in the literature of most other ancient cultures. Deborah (ca. 1125 B.C.), for example, a charismatic Israelite prophet, organizes an army that destroys the forces of a Canaanite commander. In a later book, Esther, a Hebrew woman, becomes the wife of a Persian king whom the Bible calls Ahasuerus (probably Xerxes, r. 485–465 B.C.). Esther works ferociously at the Persian court to defeat a conspiracy to wipe out her people, and she saves them. The Book of Ruth (date uncertain) tells the story of a selfless and loyal woman, Ruth, who rescues her mother-in-law, Naomi, from ruin and poverty. The Bible celebrates Ruth as Naomi's "devoted daughter-in-law, who has proved better to you [Naomi] than seven sons." (See the feature, "The Written Record: Ruth.")

Israelite culture prized women for their cunning, courage, and perseverance—qualities that allowed the people to survive. Military prowess was highly valued in men, but their inner qualities were appreciated as well. Schooled in defeat and exile, many Israelites came to the conclusion that "wisdom is better than weapons of war" (Ecclesiastes 9:18). Thus, the Hebrew Bible stresses God's primary interest in goodness of soul: "The Lord does not see as man sees; men judge by appearances, but the Lord judges by the heart" (1 Samuel 16:7). The God of Israel prized righteousness above wealth, might, sacrifice, or ritual.

One might say that Israelite law reflected a similar tension between power and righteousness. On the one hand, just as the God of Israel was omnipotent and jealous, so the law of Israel was meant to be comprehensive and forceful. Capital punishment existed for murder, rape, incorrigible rebelliousness of a son against his parents, adultery by a married woman (both she and her lover were to be executed), a woman's loss of her virginity before marriage, and other offenses. Harsh punishment was mandated for Canaanite towns taken by siege: The entire population was to be killed so as not to corrupt Israel with their religious practices.

The Siege of Lachish

From the distance, it looks like one of the foothills that surround it. Up close, though, it can be clearly seen for what it is: Tel Lachish, the mound of the biblical city of Lachish. It is a link in the chain of evidence that tells one of the most remarkable stories in biblical history.*

Lachish was a great city, a royal fortress, and second only to Jerusalem in its importance to the kingdom of Judah (928–587 B.C.). In 701 B.C., the Assyrians under King Sennacherib (r. 704–681 B.C.) besieged Lachish and took it by force. The siege of Lachish is unique in early biblical history for the wealth of independent corroborating sources. In addition to reports in the Hebrew Bible are many Assyrian written documents. Furthermore, Sennacherib commemorated his victory by depicting the siege and recording the spoils in carved reliefs that he erected in his royal palace at Nineveh. Finally, the mound itself has been excavated, allowing a striking comparison of the archaeological and pictorial evidence of a siege in the biblical period.

Originally a Canaanite town, Lachish was fortified by the Israelite kings because of its strategic location. It sits southwest of Jerusalem in the Judean foothills, dominating the road between the Judean hills to the east and the Philistine coast to the west (see **MAP 2.2**). By the reign of King Hezekiah of Judah (r. 715–686 B.C.), one of the most prominent kings of the House of David, Lachish was a large garrison city constructed on a monumental scale. It included inner and outer rings of thick walls, a massive gate complex, many houses and shops, and, in the center, a palace-fort surrounded by earthen ramps.

Having seen Assyria turn the kingdom of Israel into an occupied province, Hezekiah knew that he was facing the greatest power of the region. Nevertheless, he joined Egypt and the Philistine cities in a revolt soon after Sennacherib came to the throne in 704 B.C. Sennacherib responded by attacking the rebels in 701. The Hebrew Bible states: "In the fourteenth year of the reign of Hezekiah, Sennacherib king of Assyria attacked and took all the fortified cities of Judah" (2 Kings 18:13). We can read the results of the campaign in one of Sennacherib's inscriptions:

"As to Hezekiah, the Jew, he did not submit to my yoke. I laid siege to 46 of his strong cities, walled forts and to the countless small villages in their vicinity, and conquered (them) by means of well-stamped (earth-) ramps, and battering-rams brought (thus) near (to the walls) (combined with) the attack by foot-soldiers, (using) mines, breeches as well as sapper work [that is, digging away foundations]." Hezekiah bowed to Assyrian power. He gave up territory (though not Jerusalem) and agreed to an increase in tribute, which now amounted to "30 talents of gold, 800 talents of silver, precious stones, antimony, large cuts of red stone, couches inlaid with ivory, elephant-hides, ebony-wood, boxwood and all kinds of valuable treasures, his own

daughters, concubines, male and female musicians." So the Assyrian inscription records.

The Lachish reliefs (in Sennacherib's palace) offer a vivid picture of the attack on the city. Lachish was well fortified and well defended, but the Assyrians were experts in taking cities by storm. The reliefs show the camp of the attackers, Assyrian archers and slingers advancing on the city, battering rams and siege engines in action against the walls, flaming chariots thrown down by the defenders, and, after the city was taken, captives impaled on sharp stakes.

Look at the artist's reconstruction of an Assyrian assault on the city, based on the archaeological evidence. The soldiers are climbing a massive siege ramp that the Assyrians built against a "vulnerable" point in the city walls. The excavators of Lachish found the ramp, consisting of a level of stones cemented together over a core of boulders. It is the oldest siege ramp so far discovered in the ancient world. In and around the city the excavators found other evidence of the battle: hundreds of arrowheads, many sling stones, a number of pieces of bronze sheet mail used in armor, and what may be the crest of a helmet worn by one of the Assyrian spearmen shown attacking the city walls in the Lachish reliefs. Most dramatic, the excavators discovered about seven hundred skeletons, evidently civilians killed during the Assyrian attack and then buried in mass graves outside the city. Three of the individuals were trepanned—that is, they were operated on before death by removing a portion of their skulls. Perhaps this represents a last attempt, evidently futile, to save the lives of the wounded.

The Lachish reliefs also depict rows of captives and deportees marching toward Sennacherib on his throne. Look at this detail of the relief, showing a large Judean family leaving Lachish for exile. They are allowed to bring cattle with them, and a woman and child are permitted to ride on a wagon. The Assyrians claimed to have deported 200,150 people from Judah, of whom many men ended up as slave laborers working on Sennacherib's palace.

As for Lachish, it was burned to the ground, as the excavations confirm. Sometime in the seventh century the city was restored and refortified. Lachish was destroyed again, however, in 598 B.C., during the first of two military campaigns in Judah by Nebuchadrezzar, the Neo-Babylonian king. The excavators found a group of pottery sherds with ink inscriptions (called *ostraca*) in old Hebrew script, dating to just before that destruction. This unique set of documents in classical Hebrew writing consists of letters to a man named Yaush, the military governor of Lachish. They testify, among other things, to the worship of Yahweh, to the signal system linking the fortresses of Judah, and to the practices of the scribal profession. Once again, the city's misfortune has proved illuminating to students of the past.

Artist's Reconstruction of an Assyrian Assault on Lachish (Drawing by Gert le Grange, from David Ussishkin, *The Conquest of Lachish by Sennacherib* [Tel Aviv: Tel Aviv University, Institute of Archaeology, 1982], p. 123. Reproduced by permission.)

Detail of the Assyrian Conquest of Lachish, a Relief from the Palace of Sennacherib (British Museum/Erich Lessing/Art Resource, NY)

QUESTIONS

1. What makes the evidence for the siege of Lachish unique in biblical history?

2. What are the various sources of evidence for the siege of Lachish?

3. Why was the city of Lachish so important to the kingdom of Judah?

4. What do we learn about the siege of Lachish from the Assyrian Lachish Reliefs?

5. What information about the siege of Lachish does archaeology at Tel Lachish reveal?

---

*In much of what follows about Lachish (LAH-kish), I rely on the discussion in David Ussishkin, *The Conquest of Lachish by Sennacherib* (Tel-Aviv: Tel-Aviv University, Institute of Archaeology, 1982).

Ruth

*S*ome parts of the Hebrew Bible prohibit intermarriage. The Book of Ruth, however, praises marriage between Judean men and women from neighboring Moab (modern Jordan; see **MAP 2.2**). This excerpt illustrates such unions, as it does the problem of food shortages, which were a special burden for widows.

Once, in the time of the Judges when there was a famine in the land, a man [Elimelech] from Bethlehem in Judah went with his wife [Naomi] to live in Moabite territory. . . .

Elimelech died, and Naomi was left a widow with her two sons. The sons married Moabite women, one of whom was called Orpah and the other Ruth. [After ten years the sons died.] . . . Then Naomi, bereaved of her two sons as well as of her husband, got ready to return to her own country with her daughters-in-law, because she had heard in Moab that the Lord had shown his care for his people by giving them food. Accompanied by her two daughters-in-law she left the place where she had been living and they took the road leading back to Judah.

Naomi said to her daughters-in-law, "Go back, both of you, home to your own mothers. May the Lord keep faith with you, as you have kept faith with the dead and with me; and may he grant each of you the security of a home with a new husband." And she kissed them goodbye. They wept aloud and said, "No, we shall return with you to your people." But Naomi insisted, "Go back, my daughters, go; for I am too old to marry again. But if I could say that I had hope of a child, even if I were to be married tonight and were to bear sons, would you, then, wait until they grew up? Would you on their account remain unmarried? No, my daughters! For your sakes I feel bitter that the Lord has inflicted such misfortune on me." At this they wept still more. Then Orpah kissed her mother-in-law and took her leave, but Ruth clung to her.

"Look," said Naomi, "your sister-in-law has gone back to her people and her God. Go, follow her." Ruth answered, "Do not urge me to go back and desert you. Where you go, I shall go, and where you stay, I shall stay. Your people will be my people, and your God my God. Where you die, I shall die, and there be buried. I solemnly declare before the Lord that

nothing but death will part me from you." When Naomi saw that Ruth was determined to go with her, she said no more.

[They returned to Naomi's hometown, Bethlehem, in Judah.]

Naomi had a relative on her husband's side, a prominent and well-to-do . . . [man named] Boaz. One day Ruth the Moabite asked Naomi, "May I go to the harvest fields and glean [collect excess grain] behind anyone who will allow me?" "Yes, go my daughter," she replied. So Ruth went gleaning in the fields behind the reapers. [She met Boaz in his fields.] . . .

Boaz said to Ruth, "Listen, my daughter: do not go to glean in any other field. Do not look any farther, but stay close to my servant-girls. Watch where the men reap, and follow the gleaners; I have told the men not to molest you. Any time you are thirsty, go and drink from the jars they have filled." She bowed to the ground and said, "Why are you so kind as to take notice of me, when I am just a foreigner?" Boaz answered, "I have been told the whole story of what you have done for your mother-in-law since the death of your husband, how you left father and mother and homeland and came among a people you didn't know before. The Lord reward you for what you have done. . . ."

[Eventually, Boaz marries Ruth; their great grandson would be Israel's greatest king, David.]

QUESTIONS

1. In this excerpt, what are the various ways in which people cope with hunger and famine?

2. Why does Ruth, a foreign widow, stay with her mother-in-law and go to Judah?

3. Why does Boaz admire and eventually marry Ruth?

Source: *Revised English Bible* © Oxford University Press and Cambridge University Press, 1989. Reprinted by permission of Cambridge University Press.

SECTION SUMMARY

- The Bible, including the Hebrew Bible (called Old Testament by Christians) and the Christian New Testament, is the single most influential text in Western civilization.

- The central theme of the Hebrew Bible is God's covenant with his chosen people—the Hebrews.

- Hebrew monotheism evolved between the 1200s and 600 B.C. with tribal leaders, kings, and prophets each playing a major role.

- Jews, deported to Babylon after 598 B.C., maintained their religion and some returned home after the Persians conquered Babylon in 539 B.C.

- Equality, limited government, and the rule of law under God were Israelite political notions that have greatly influenced the later West.

On the other hand, by taking intention into account, Israelite law echoed a note already present in Mesopotamia. The so-called Law of the Goring Ox, for instance, allowed a person to go unpunished for owning an ox that gores a person to death, unless the owner knew beforehand that the animal was dangerous. If the owner did know, however, the owner had to be put to death. Israelite law, moreover, demonstrated a belief in the sanctity of human life by prohibiting human sacrifice. An Israelite had to be ready in his or her heart (but *only* in his or her heart) to sacrifice his or her child to Yahweh, as Abraham was willing to sacrifice Isaac when Yahweh so commanded. After ascertaining Abraham's willingness to obey, even to the point of sacrificing his son, Yahweh freed Isaac from the altar and supplied a ram as a substitute offering. Israelite monotheism thus broke with its Canaanite neighbors and rejected human sacrifice, as did the religions later derived from it.

CHAPTER SUMMARY

The first half of the first millennium B.C. witnessed dramatic developments among both the ancestors of the West and its founders. Canaanite city-states, known as the Phoenicians, created trading networks and spread colonies across the entire length of the Mediterranean Sea. The ships of these great sailors circled Africa and reached faraway Britain. Closer to home, they influenced the culture of Greece, to whom they imparted the alphabet. The Greek alphabet, derived from the Phoenician alphabet, in turn, led to the Roman alphabet, the basis of the English alphabet today.

A new form of empire appeared. New military technology, the frank adoption of brutal and inhumane methods, and improvements in administration led to the creation of the Assyrian Empire, stretching from western Iran to Palestine and briefly even to Egypt. After short-lived hegemonies by Neo-Babylonians and Medes, the Persians established an empire that was larger, better organized, and more tolerant than the empire of the Assyrians. Multi-ethnic, far-flung, and claiming to be universal, such an empire would one day be brought into the Western tradition of Rome.

FOCUS QUESTIONS

- Who were the Phoenicians and what did they contribute to Western civilization?

- What made the first-millennium B.C. empires of the Assyrians, Neo-Babylonians, and Persians so much more effective than earlier empires?

- What was the religious experience of ancient Israel, and what is its legacy today?

The most important developments of the era, however, were not in commerce, weaponry, or imperialism, but in new conceptions of the nature and meaning of human life. The Israelites conquered Palestine and, even after losing it, held on to their identity by means of a tenacious belief in one god. They broke with tradition by insisting that their god was merciful and just. Omnipotent, God gave history meaning and direction. The purpose of life, in the Israelite view, was to serve God by acting righteously. The new religion laid the foundation for Judaism as well as Christianity and Islam. The Jews wrote down their religious and historical traditions in a book that, along with the Christian New Testament, proved to be the most influential single text in the history of the West: the Hebrew Bible.

KEY TERMS

Ugarit (p. 30)

alphabet (p. 30)

Phoenicians (p. 31)

Assyrians (p. 32)

Neo-Babylonians (p. 34)

Persian Empire (p. 34)

Zoroastrianism (p. 37)

Torah (p. 39)

covenant (p. 39)

Israelites (p. 40)

monotheism (p. 40)

Ten Commandments (p. 40)

 This icon will direct you to additional materials on the website: www .cengage.com/history/ noble/westciv6e

e See our interactive eBook for map and primary source activities.

NOTES

1. S. Insler, *The Gāthās of Zarathustra: Acta Iranica*, 8 (Leiden: E. J. Brill, 1975), p. 33.

2. Roland G. Kent, *Old Persian: Grammar, Texts, Lexicon* (New Haven, Conn.: American Oriental Society, 1950), p. 132.

3. Carol L. Meyers, "Everyday Life: Women in the Period of the Hebrew Bible," in *The Women's Bible Commentary*, ed. Carol A. Newsom and Sharon H. Ringe (Louisville, Ky.: Westminster/ John Knox Press, 1992), p. 245.

CHAPTER OUTLINE

Before the Polis: Early Greece, to ca. 725 B.C.

Society and Politics in Archaic Greece, ca. 750–500 B.C.

The Culture of Archaic Greece

Classical Greece

The Public Culture of Classical Greece

Athenian Acropolis, with Pnyx Hill in Foreground
(Julia M. Fair)

The Greeks in the Polis to ca. 350 B.C.

It is dawn. The light reveals a hillside in the city of Athens, a natural auditorium. Its rocky slopes, visible in the photograph opposite, would have been covered, beginning about 500 B.C., with wooden benches facing a platform cut into the rock. The six thousand men gathered there constitute a diverse group, ranging from farmers to philosophers, from dockyard workers to aristocrats. As they take their seats, these, the citizens of Athens, watch priests conducting prayers and offering a sacrifice. Then all eyes turn to the individual who mounts the platform—a herald. His booming voice asks the question that marks the start of business: "Who wishes to speak?" Someone rises to address the assembly. It is the first democracy in history—and the central laboratory in this great experiment in participation.

The assembly meeting recalls the defining features of what was, in its era, the characteristic political institution in much of Greece: the *polis* (plural, *poleis*). The polis dominated Greek life between ca. 750 and ca. 350 B.C., an era that is sometimes called the Hellenic Period. By the time the polis emerged, Greece was old. Two great civilizations had already risen and fell in Greek lands, the Minoans and Mycenaeans. Now, several centuries after their fall, the polis appeared, and its dawn was marked by a great cultural achievement. Around 725 B.C., Homer composed his two great epic poems, the *Iliad* and the *Odyssey*. These poems preserved many of the religious and historical traditions of Greece's earlier period. Yet, in their focus on the individual, they also heralded a new era, one that would differ greatly from the palace economies and warrior kingdoms of Bronze Age Greece.

Usually translated as "city-state," the polis is better understood as "citizen-state." The polis was the product of communal activities—whether in the assembly, the military, or the theater—undertaken by its members: its citizens. Not every polis was a democracy, but every polis emphasized cooperative activities whose participants enjoyed at least a measure of equality. Every polis also sought a balance between the group and the individual, be that person the speaker, a military hero, or a freethinker.

Balance is a difficult state to achieve, however, and the equilibrium of the polis was frequently disturbed by tension and exclusion. Greek democracy failed to grant equal rights to women or immigrants, and it depended on slave labor. Relations among poleis were less often a matter of cooperation than of war. Although the Greeks created magnificent religious architecture, a portion of their intellectual elite came to the conclusion that the gods were of little importance in explaining the universe. Whereas one leading polis, Sparta, was a paragon of militarism, obedience, and austerity, scorning the life of the mind, another, Athens, prided itself on freedom and cultural attainments. Yet, the Greeks made the most even of such tensions, exploring them in literary genres—tragedy, comedy, history, and

FOCUS QUESTIONS

- How did early Greece develop before the polis and what light do the Homeric poems shed on its history?

- What was the Greek polis, and how did it develop in Sparta, Athens, and Corinth in Archaic Greece?

- How did Western individualism and rationalism take root in Archaic Greece?

- What was Athenian democracy and how did it clash with Sparta in the Peloponnesian War?

- How did tragedy, comedy, philosophy, and history all begin and develop in the culture of Classical Greece?

This icon will direct you to additional materials on the website: www .cengage.com/history/ noble/westciv6e

See our interactive eBook for map and primary source activities.

philosophy—that focused on the polis as a central theme. Creative tensions also marked Greek achievements in sculpture, painting, and architecture.

The era of the polis proved to be a defining moment in Western history. Although the Greeks of this era borrowed much from neighboring cultures, they were remarkably original. In the mid-first millennium B.C., the monotheistic religious heritage of the West first emerged among the Jews. During that same era, the Greeks founded the Western tradition in a broad range of culture, including politics; philosophy; literary genres, such as comedy, tragedy, and history; and the visual and plastic arts of painting, sculpture, and architecture. The Jews and the Greeks represent two poles of Western culture: the sacred and the worldly, revelation and reason.

BEFORE THE POLIS: EARLY GREECE, TO CA. 725 B.C.

How did early Greece develop before the polis and what light do the Homeric poems shed on its history?

"La Parisienne"   This masterpiece of Minoan art shows a priestess in a long robe, with her hair tied in a special knot. A fresco from Knossos, it was dubbed "the Parisian lady" because of its elegance.   (Erich Lessing/Art Resource, NY)

The ancient Greek genius reached its height in the Classical period (480–323 B.C.), but it is already visible in the *Iliad* (IL-ee-ud) and the *Odyssey* (ODD-uh-see), the epic poems of Homer. Homer's poems shaped Greece's national identity and provided the basis of Greek education. Homer probably lived around 725 B.C., but his works have roots in the civilization that had flourished in Greece a thousand years earlier. Along with the discoveries of archaeologists, Homer's poems provide evidence for the rise and fall of two great civilizations: the Minoans on the island of Crete and the Mycenaeans on the Greek mainland (see **MAP 3.1**).

Minoans and Mycenaeans, 3000–1180 B.C.

Europe's first civilization appeared in what is today Greece, on the Aegean island of Crete (KREET) around 2000 B.C., and soon spread to the Greek mainland. Civilization came relatively late to Greece, but in comparison with Egypt or western Asia, Greece is not a hospitable land. It is mountainous, dry, and contains little cultivable farmland. Yet, it was destined for greatness.

Cretan civilization would influence early Greece considerably, but in 2000 B.C., Crete was not yet a Greek-speaking island. The Cretans of that era were literate and used a syllabary, or a writing system of syllables that form words, known as "Linear A." Although we know its language is not Greek, we do not know what it is. Most of the evidence of Cretan civilization comes from the excavations of the island's palaces—monumental structures that first appeared at various locations on Crete around 2000 B.C. and reached their height between 1800 and 1490 B.C. Scholars call the palace builders and their civilization "**Minoan** (mih-NO-un)," after King Minos of later Greek myth. He was supposed to have ruled a great sea empire from his palace at Knossos (see **MAP 3.1**).

The Minoan palaces were not merely royal residences but centers of administration, religion, and economics. The largest palace, Knossos sprawled across 3 acres. It was built around a large central court, probably used for public ceremonies and surrounded by a mazelike structure of staterooms, residence quarters, storage rooms, workshops, and bathrooms, interconnected by corridors, ramps, and stairways. The Minoans exploited Crete's natural wealth in agriculture and timber and set up a trading network from the Levant to Sicily. A Minoan settlement flourished on the Aegean island of Thera, 70 miles north of Crete (see **MAP 3.1**). This settlement was destroyed sometime in the late 1600s B.C. by one of the most violent volcanic eruptions ever. It might have given rise to the legend of Atlantis, the city that sank beneath the sea.

Peace and prosperity are themes of Minoan culture, yet Minoan civilization came to a violent and relatively sudden end. All of the palaces except Knossos were destroyed around 1490 B.C.; Knossos fell around 1375 B.C. The archaeological evidence strongly supports the notion of an invasion, but by whom? To find the answer, let us look to the Greek mainland.

Around 1700 B.C., the sleepy Greek mainland suddenly appears to have burst into power and prosperity. So, we can conclude from a series of burial sites, especially those found at Mycenae (see **MAP 3.1**), where the tombs of kings and queens contain a treasure house of objects in gold and other precious metals. The inhabitants of Mycenae (my-SEE-ne) were Greek-speakers. They and the wider civilization they represent are called Mycenaean (My-suh-NEE-un). The **Mycenaeans** had arrived in Greece sometime between 2300 and 1700 B.C., either through migration or invasion.

Warriors at heart, the Myceneans went on raids, around the Aegean, aimed at acquiring loot and prestige. Around 1490 B.C., they achieved their greatest feat: the conquest of Crete. The Mycenaeans adopted the Minoans' palace economy and wide trading network.

Mycenaean civilization was at its height between about 1400 and 1180 B.C. A Mycenaean royal household was organized to produce textiles, arms, and armor, with raw materials provided by the common people. Our knowledge of the palace economy comes primarily from thousands of clay tablets inscribed by palace scribes around 1200 B.C. They are written in a script scholars call "Linear B," an early form of Greek consisting of a combination of syllabary and ideograms (a system of symbols that stand for words or ideas).

It appears likely that Mycenaean Greece suffered from a combination of internal weakness and foreign invasion similar to that experienced by most of the eastern Mediterranean around 1250 to 1150 B.C., the era of the Sea Peoples (see page 24). By 1180 B.C., most of the fortified sites had been destroyed. Afterward, only a few people continued to live in the old towns.

Homer and History

The era from the fall of Mycenae to the rise of the Greek city-states is often referred to as the Greek Dark Ages. New archaeological evidence renders the period less dark but no less gloomy: The evidence shows depopulation, poverty, and invasion. Northern Greeks, probably Dorians, came south, driving out or dominating the Mycenaean Greeks. Many Mycenaean refugees migrated eastward around 1000 B.C. to the Aegean coast of Anatolia, which was destined to become an important center of Greek culture.

In spite of its material poverty, Dark Age Greece produced notable painted pottery and preserved an oral tradition of poetry handed down from the Mycenaean era. After 800 B.C., more settled and more prosperous times led to dramatic changes in politics, warfare, and culture. Around 725 B.C., Greece reached a milestone in literary artistry that heralded a new age: the epic poetry of Homer.

Had ancient Greece produced a Bible, the *Iliad* and the *Odyssey* of **Homer** would have been its two Testaments. Only Hesiod (HEE-see-ud), a poet who lived around 700 B.C., had as much influence on later generations, but his poems (*Theogony* and *Works and Days*), though composed in the epic tradition, were shorter than Homer's and less dramatic. Homer's and Hesiod's poems inspired and educated the Greeks—a large part of a Greek boy's education consisted of learning to recite Homer from memory. Homer's poems shaped Greece's national identity by praising its heroes and by looking back toward the glory days of the Mycenaeans.

CHRONOLOGY	
ca. 750 B.C.	Greek colonization of Magna Graecia begins
ca. 725 B.C.	Sparta conquers Messenia
ca. 675 B.C.	Pheidon becomes tyrant of Argos
ca. 625 B.C.	Sappho active as poet
594 B.C.	Solon is archon in Athens
ca. 560 B.C.	Pisistratus becomes tyrant of Athens
508 B.C.	Cleisthenes begins reforms in Athens
499 B.C.	Ionians revolt against Persia
490 B.C.	Battle of Marathon
480–479 B.C.	Persia invades Greece
477 B.C.	Delian League founded
460–429 B.C.	Pericles at peak of power
458 B.C.	Aeschylus's *Oresteia* first performed in Athens
431–404 B.C.	Peloponnesian War
399 B.C.	Trial of Socrates
395–386 B.C.	Corinthian War
371 B.C.	Battle of Leuctra

Minoan Society that flourished between 2000 and 1490 B.C. on the Aegean island of Crete, where Greece's first civilization appeared. Their sophisticated culture and economy were administered from their magnificent palaces.

Mycenaeans Militaristic people from the Greek mainland who conquered the Minoans around 1490–1375 B.C. Mycenaean civilization was a center of Bronze Age culture until its destruction around 1100 B.C.

Homer Greatest ancient Greek poet, credited as the author of the epics *Iliad* and the *Odyssey*, both written during the eighth century B.C. His dramatic stories inspired, moved, and educated the Greeks.

🌐 MAP 3.1—Aegean Greece

The Minoan civilization (height: ca. 1800–1490 B.C.) and Mycenaean civilization (height: ca. 1400–1180 B.C.) flourished in turn in the Aegean region during the second millennium B.C. The center of Minoan civilization was the island of Crete. A mainland people, the Mycenaeans conquered Minoan Crete around 1490 B.C.

The *Iliad* and the *Odyssey* focus on the Trojan War and its aftermath. The *Iliad* is set in the tenth year of the conflict. The long war leads to a quarrel between Greek chieftains: Agamemnon, king of Mycenae and the leader of the expedition, and Achilles (uh-KILeez), the greatest Greek warrior. The most prominent Trojans, King Priam and his eldest son, Hector, are less petty but suffer the greater ruin. The *Odyssey* is the story of the Greek hero Odysseus (oh-DIS-ee-us) and his struggle to return home to his kingdom after a twenty-year absence, ten years at Troy and ten years wandering homeward. It also focuses on the loyalty and ingenuity of Odysseus's wife, Penelope, who saves the household in his absence, and the maturation of their son, Telemachus (te-LEH-muh-kus), who helps his father regain his kingdom.

Homer's poems look back, but did the Trojan War really happen? That is a controversial subject, but both archaeology and the evidence of inscriptions suggest that the answer is probably yes. Troy really existed: It was a big, wealthy city, strategically located near the entrance to the Hellespont (or Dardanelles), the straits that lead toward the Black Sea. The king of Troy was attached politically to the Hittite empire, and his city had strong trading relations with the Mycenaean Greeks. But Mycenaeans turned quickly from trade to war. Troy was destroyed violently in the period 1210–1180 B.C., possibly by Mycenaean warriors.

Homer lived in a Greek city in Ionia (eye-OH-nee-uh), a region of the western coast of Anatolia (see **MAP 3.2**). Although Homer lived centuries after the end of Troy, he resided in an area whose culture had been affected by Troy and its neighbors. Homer could have drawn some of his material from native populations and traditions. Besides, Homer worked in a continuous,

Lion Gate at Mycenae
Carved about 1250 B.C. above the main gate of the citadel's massive walls, the lions—flanking a column, their front paws resting on altars—probably represent royal authority. Inside the walls is Grave Circle B, a royal burial site. (Dmitrios Harissiadis. From the Photographic Archives of the Benaki Museum)

Greek, poetic tradition going back to the Mycenaean Age, that gave him knowledge of a society that was long gone by his day. His poems are a combination of accurate details of Mycenaean palace life, historical fiction, and details of his own, much later society.

Homer focuses on the elite. Homeric men and women hold aristocratic values and tend to look down on ordinary people. But society in Homer's day was more level and egalitarian. Except for a small number of traders and craft specialists who lived in towns, most Greeks lived in villages and hamlets. Most farmed or herded pigs, goats, or sheep, and most were free. The people of each community were called the *demos* (DEE-mus); the leading men, *basileis* (bah-see-LAYS). *Basileis* means "kings," but it is more accurate to understand them as chiefs.

The main activity of Homer's basileis is warfare. The *Iliad* consists largely of a series of battlefield contests. Since women did not take part in battle, they are not presented as men's equals, but Homer's women are neither timid nor helpless. Penelope, for example, personifies female resourcefulness: By refusing to marry until she has finished weaving a shroud for Odysseus's elderly father, and then by unraveling every night what she has woven during the day, she puts the noble suitors off for years. She is as concerned with honor as any Homeric man. By refusing to accept an offer of marriage while Odysseus might still be alive, Penelope does honor to her own good name and to her husband's.

SECTION SUMMARY

- The Minoans built Greece's first civilization, centered on the island of Crete around 2000–1375 B.C.

- Greek-speakers arrived in Greece about 2300–1700 B.C. and established the wealthy and warlike Mycenaean civilization on the mainland, at its height about 1400–1180 B.C.

- From 1100 to 800 B.C., between the fall of Mycenaean civilization and the rise of the city-states, Greece was largely poor and illiterate.

- Homer did not live until 725 B.C. or later, but an oral tradition of poetry, going back to Mycenaean times, means that the *Iliad* and *Odyssey* are based on a kernel of historical truth.

- Homer expresses the heroic and aristocratic values of elite men and women that would influence Greek antiquity for centuries.

arête   Originally meaning "warrior prowess" or "excellence," *arête* was a key term of ancient Greek culture. It evolved over the centuries to apply to politics and philosophy and to women as well as men.

Both in Mycenaean times and in Homer's day, the Greeks were polytheists. The gods figure prominently in early Greek poetry, but they are less powerful than the Hebrew God, less immediate, and less interested in the inner life of men and women. Already emerging at the beginning of the Greek cultural tradition was the belief that became the hallmark of ancient Greece: that "man is the measure of all things," as the thinker Protagoras would declare in the fifth century B.C.

The gods embody the values of a warrior society that put a premium on **arête** (ah-reh-TAY), meaning warrior prowess or excellence. Because they were thought to live on Mount Olympus, a 9,500-foot-high peak in northern Greece (see **MAP 3.1**), the Greek gods were called the Olympians. The "household" of the Olympians—modeled on a noble's household—included Zeus (ZOOS), a sky god and the "father of gods and men," and his consort, Hera; Zeus's brother, Poseidon, god of the sea, earthquakes, and horses; Ares, god of war; and Aphrodite, goddess of love. Also in the "household" were Zeus's children: Athena, goddess of wisdom and cunning; Hephaestus, god of craftsmen; Hermes, god of travelers and thieves; Apollo, god of disease and healing; and Artemis, goddess of the hunt, of maidens, and of childbirth.

Loyalty to the family played an important role in social relations. A person's obligations to kin included the duty to avenge crime or murder. Friendship, cemented by an exchange of gifts, was another important social institution. Even humble peasants prided themselves on hospitality.

Such values served Homeric society well. Although they would survive in later centuries, they would be challenged after 700 B.C. by the increasing emphasis on public life as the Greek city-state evolved.

SOCIETY AND POLITICS IN ARCHAIC GREECE, CA. 750–500 B.C.

What was the Greek polis, and how did it develop in Sparta, Athens, and Corinth in Archaic Greece?

Archaic Greece   Period of ancient Greek history from around 700 to 500 B.C.

Historians usually call the era in Greek history from roughly 750 to 500 B.C. the "Archaic period." **Archaic Greece** was a patchwork of hundreds of separate city-states, tribal leagues, and monarchies (see **MAP 3.2**). Nevertheless, it displayed a distinctive style and outlook, not only in art, but also in politics, military arrangements, technology, economics, literature, and religion.

The Archaic era laid the groundwork for much of lasting importance in Western civilization. Archaic Greece witnessed the simultaneous growth of individualism and a tight community spirit, the emergence of social cohesion despite a continual state of war, and the coexistence of deep religious piety and the West's first nontheistic philosophy. The Archaic period also saw the origin of characteristic Western types of governmental regimes—tyranny, oligarchy, and the first steps toward democracy—and of fundamental Western notions of citizenship and the rule of law.

Agriculture, Trade, Colonization, and Warfare

An observer of ninth century B.C. Greece would hardly have predicted greatness of that poor, illiterate society of small settlements and low-level trade. Yet, everything began to change in Greece in the eighth century B.C. It was out of these changes that a new communal institution emerged: the **polis** (PO-liss).

polis   Term for an ancient Greek city-state, a system that reached its height around 700–300 B.C.

Change was a product of peace, which stimulated a sharp population rise. In response, the economy shifted from herding to farming, a more efficient source of food. Seeking new agricultural land in the rocky Greek peninsula, farmers terraced hillsides and drained marshes. The typical agricultural unit was the family farm. Most farms were small and roughly equal in size, and so served to stimulate social and political equality.

🌐 **MAP 3.2—Archaic and Classical Greece**
The region of the Aegean Sea was the heartland of Greek civilization around 750 to 350 B.C.
The mountainous terrain, rugged coastline, and numerous islands encouraged political
fragmentation.

Greek commerce, too, was expanding. Shortly before 800 B.C., Greeks from the island of
Euboea, perhaps following the example of Phoenician merchants and seafarers who had been
casual traders in Greece for a century (see pages 30–31), established a trading post in Syria at
Al-Mina, at the end of the chief caravan route from Mesopotamia (see **MAP 3.3**). Shortly afterward, Euboeans established another trading post in the west, on an island in the Bay of Naples in
Italy. In both east and west, Greek merchants sought iron and luxury goods. What they offered in
return was probably silver, of which ancient Greece had rich deposits, and slaves.

From commerce, it was but a short step to colonization in order to siphon off the extra mouths
created by population growth. In colonization as in trade, the Greeks may have followed the
Phoenicians, who had begun establishing colonies probably in the ninth century B.C. Between
about 750 and 500 B.C., the Greeks founded colonies throughout the Mediterranean and the Black
Sea, planting nearly as many cities as already existed in Greece (see **MAP 3.3**). Colonization in
Italy and Sicily began in earnest around 750 B.C.; in the northeast Aegean perhaps a generation
later; in the Sea of Marmara (in modern Turkey) about 680 B.C.; in North Africa around 630 B.C.;
and in the Black Sea about 610 B.C. In the far west, Massalia (modern Marseilles, France) was
established about 600 B.C. Southern Italy and Sicily, whose climate and landscape recalled the
Aegean, were especially intense areas of Greek settlement, so much so that the Romans later

🌐 **MAP 3.3—Phoenician and Greek Colonization**
Both the Phoenicians (beginning perhaps after 900 B.C.) and the Greeks (beginning around 750 B.C.) established numerous colonies on the coasts of the Mediterranean and Black Seas.

called the region *Magna Graecia* ("Great Greece"). Greek colonization spread urban civilization westward, especially into Italy.

One important consequence of foreign contact was the introduction to Greece of the alphabet, borrowed from the Phoenicians shortly after 800 B.C. The Greeks made one significant addition to the Phoenician alphabet by adding vowels. Vowels are not essential to reading a Semitic language, but an Indo-European language like Greek would be almost indecipherable without them. The alphabet spread rapidly and widely after 750 B.C. Literacy underlay the achievements in poetry, philosophy, and the law that Archaic Greece has left behind. However, so few people could read and write well that ancient Greece remained primarily an oral culture.

Another consequence of foreign contact was the introduction of new military technology, which the increase in wealth allowed the Greeks to adopt. Social changes, furthermore, fostered new tactics on the battlefield. The result was the **hoplite phalanx** (HOP-lite FAY-lanks), a tightly ordered unit of heavily armed, pike-bearing infantrymen. The phalanx not only became the dominant military force in Archaic Greece, but, with relatively few changes in equipment and tactics, it remained supreme on land in Greece, western Asia, and other Mediterranean regions for centuries, until its defeat by a Roman army in 197 B.C.

hoplite phalanx
Battlefield tactic of Archaic Greece that relied on a tightly ordered unit of heavily armed, pike-bearing infantrymen.

The phalanx emerged through a process of evolution rather than in a revolutionary leap. Before 800 B.C., single combat among the basileis appears to have decided battles. Around 800 to 750 B.C., armies began to include more men, fighting in close formation. Around 700 B.C., came new armaments. The result was the phalanx. The heavily armed infantryman (hoplite) of the fighting unit (phalanx) wore bronze armor on his shins and chest and a bronze helmet with a narrow opening for eyes and mouth. He carried a heavy wooden shield in his left hand. His weapons were a pike—a heavy, wooden, iron-tipped thrusting spear at least 9 feet long—and a short, iron stabbing sword.

The men of the phalanx were arranged in close ranks, normally four to eight deep. Soldiers stood together in line, each man's shield overlapping his neighbor's. Hoplite combat involved set battles—head-to-head, army-against-army, all-or-nothing affairs—rather than individual skirmishes or guerrilla raids. Battle usually consisted of a charge followed by a grueling contest. The men in the front line pounded the enemy with their pikes, while the men in the rear pushed forward. Finally, one side would give way and run. The victors stayed and erected a trophy.

Greek hoplite warfare rested on deep societal roots. Only independent men of means could afford hoplite armor. Thanks to the spread of the family farm, such men were common in Greece by around 700 B.C. Hoplites were amateur soldiers. Most were full-time farmers outside the fighting season, which lasted only for the summer months. The notion of the farmer-soldier, independent and free, would have a lasting impact on Western political thought. So would the warrior values of what became a way of life in Greece.

Unlike in Homer, whose warriors sought aretê mainly for personal and familial honor, hoplites fought for the community. According to the poet Tyrtaeus (ca. 650 B.C.), a good soldier's death brought glory, not only to his father, but also to his city and his countrymen. Although the battlefield remained the favored arena for displays of aretê, the assembly or the council house became increasingly acceptable as an alternative.

Characteristics of the Polis

The polis was both a product of the changes of the eighth century B.C. and a stimulus for change. As an urban settlement, the polis existed as early as the ninth or even the tenth century B.C., but its intense communal spirit did not emerge until around 750–700 B.C.

Polis came to denote not just a city, but the community as a whole, corresponding roughly to a country or nation. One crude gauge of the centrality of the polis is the number, not to mention the significance, of words the Greeks derived from it: among them, *polites* (citizen), *politeia* (constitution), *politeô* (to govern), *ta politika* (politics), and *politikos* (politician).

Most poleis (PO-lays) were small, many less than 100 square miles in size. Athens was one of the largest. Its territory, known as Attica (see **MAP 3.4**), covered 1,000 square miles (approximately the size of Rhode Island). At its height (ca. 430 B.C.), the population of Athens was about 400,000, but a typical polis contained only between 5,000 and 10,000 people. The philosopher Aristotle (AR-is-tot-il) (384–322 B.C.) wrote that an ideal polis should be small enough that the citizens know one another personally.

The polis consisted of two parts: the urban area, which usually was tiny, and the surrounding countryside, where most people lived. From the earliest times, the urban public space included both a defensible hill (preferably with a water supply), called a "high city" (*acropolis* [uh-CROP-uh-liss]), and a "gathering place" (*agora* [AH-go-rah]), used as a marketplace and meeting area.

Hoplites   A detail from a Corinthian vase of 625 to 600 B.C. shows pike-wielding hoplites closed in battle over a fallen comrade. In this image as elsewhere, Greek artists rendered warriors seminude and fighting in small groups, but in reality hoplites went into battle wearing heavy armor and fought in large units.   (Louvre/Réunion des Musées Nationaux/Art Resource, NY)

There was at least one temple. After 500 B.C., stone buildings, including council houses, theaters, covered porticoes, gymnasia, and baths, became increasingly common.

What distinguished the early polis, however, was not its buildings but its spirit. As the poet Alcaeus (b. ca. 630 B.C.) puts it, "Not houses finely roofed or the stones of walls well-built, nay nor canals and dockyards, make the polis, but men able to use their opportunity."

The Greeks came to call the polis a "common thing" (*koinon*). It belonged to its people, not to a few nobles or to a king or a god. As early as about 700 B.C., important public documents were inscribed in stone. Acts of state were attributed not to a personified polis but to the community—for example, not to Thera but to "the Thereans," not to Sybaris but to "the Sybarites." The emphasis is on the plurality.

The emphasis was on equality as well. The polis developed an ethos of moderation. The ideal citizen was thought to be neither rich nor poor but of moderate means. Women were not considered citizens and were excluded from taking part in politics. Yet, women's behavior was considered important to the polis. For example, some poleis passed laws against extravagant jewelry or unrestrained mourning (mourning the dead was considered women's work).

In theory, all citizens were supposed to be roughly similar, but this was not always true in practice, as the politics of the early polis makes clear.

Corinth and Tyranny

Trade and colonization inspired change at home, for one thing, making increasing numbers of Greeks into seafarers and so generating wealth. Centrally located Corinth became a great seaport and the wealthiest city in mainland Greece. And Corinth was in the forefront of political change.

Political change followed economic trends. Although some Greeks shot to the top of the economic ladder, many of these newly rich lacked the status of the elite basileis. In order to claim a share, the newly rich seem to have made common cause with the independent farmers who staffed the hoplite phalanx. The result was tyranny.

Tyrant originally referred not to an arbitrary and oppressive ruler but rather to a champion of the people. Having overthrown a narrow and entrenched aristocracy, tyrants were popular at first. *Tyrant* did not become a negative word before roughly 550 B.C., when the people soured on the second and third generation of tyrants.

Greek tyranny began in Argos, a polis in the northeastern Peloponnesus (pel-uh-puh-NEE-suss), around 675 B.C. (see **Map 3.2**). The first tyrant was an Argive named Pheidon. By 660 B.C., tyranny had spread to nearby Corinth. During the seventh and sixth centuries B.C., all the major Greek poleis except Sparta became tyrannies.

Much of what the tyrants did, especially in the first generation, was popular and progressive. It appears that they had the support of the prosperous farmers who fought in the phalanx. Tyrants stimulated the economy by founding colonies on trade routes, standardizing weights and measures, and encouraging the immigration of skilled craftsmen from other poleis. They built temples and instituted festivals, providing both jobs and leisure-time activities.

When tyrants passed power on to their sons, however, the second generation tended to rule oppressively. Buoyed by the discontent of the demos, the basileis regrouped and tried to take back power. One second-generation tyrant advised accordingly: To maintain power, a tyrant should "lop off the tallest ears of grain"—that is, execute or exile aristocrats in order to deny leaders to the opposition. However, the tide of discontent was not to be stopped. Few tyrannies lasted beyond the third generation, when they were overthrown and replaced by oligarchy (literally, "rule by the few") or, less often, by democracy (literally, "power of the people"). By 500 B.C., tyranny had disappeared from most of Greece.

Sparta

Sparta was located in Laconia, a fertile valley in the south-central Peloponnesus, in the southern part of mainland Greece, and seemed destined by geography for prosperity but not for glory (see **Map 3.2**). Yet Sparta proved to be a powerful model of citizenship and constitutionalism, virtue and community, austerity and militarism.

Sparta was closed and secretive, which makes its history difficult to write. Scholarship has lifted the veil a little, however. For example, Spartans believed that their unique way of life was created all at once by the legendary lawgiver Lycurgus in the 700s B.C. Archaeological evidence, however, suggests gradual innovations in Sparta rather than revolutionary change, beginning around 650 B.C., and it is by no means clear that there ever was a Lycurgus.

The foundations of the Spartan regime were laid around 650 B.C., when a three-part class system emerged. Helots (HEL-uts), unfree laborers who worked the land, were at the lowest level. In the middle ranks were *perioikoi* (roughly, "neighbors"), who were free but under the thumb of the highest class. At the top stood Similars, who were the only full citizens. We do not know the number of helots, but we do know that they vastly outnumbered the other two classes.

GOVERNMENT

Compared with individuals of the other classes, a Similar had a good life. If male and over age 30, he had the right to attend the assembly and to hold public office. Each male Similar, moreover, was given a basic allotment of land worked by helots, which freed him to fight. As the name implies, Similars were alike but not equal. Wealthy Similars owned more land than the basic allotment.

Although Sparta is remembered as a conservative society, the idea of a large group of men sharing power was radical in its day. When the system began around 650 B.C., Similars numbered about nine thousand. What gave them their clout and prestige? The Similars were probably hoplites, the backbone of Sparta's army.

In the mid-seventh century B.C., Sparta depended on its army to keep the helots down. Most helots were Messenians, whose land had been conquered by Sparta in about 725 B.C. Although fellow Greeks, Messenians were forced to work for the conquerors. Sparta profited, but it now faced a security problem. The restive helots had to be policed, and a revolt sometime between 675 and 650 B.C. almost succeeded. To keep Messenia, Sparta needed a crack army; to get that, Sparta made all its hoplites into Similars.

Sparta was no democracy, however. The ancients classified the Spartan government as "mixed" because it combined monarchy, oligarchy (that is, rule by an elite few), and popular government. The assembly of Similars was the popular element, but its powers were limited. Real power was shared among those Similars who were kings, elders, and *ephors* (overseers), men generally belonging to a few wealthy families.

The elite did not lead lives of luxury, however, at least not after around 550 B.C., when austerity became the order of the day. Society was reordered to promote military discipline. For example, the Spartans' diet was famous for its simplicity. The preferred food was a black broth of pork cooked in its own blood and spiced with salt and vinegar. To discourage consumption, Sparta issued no coins; the official "currency" consisted of heavy and clumsy iron skewers. Since the outside world was considered corrupt, Sparta engaged in little trade and admitted few foreigners to its territory—and those who were admitted were subject to periodic expulsion.

SOCIETY

Whereas other poleis offered little or no formal public education, Sparta schooled its sons from childhood to be soldiers—a system known as the *agoge* (ahgo-GAY) ("upbringing"). Limited to male Similars, the agoge created a life cycle unique in Greece. At birth, babies were examined by public inspectors. Those who were considered deformed or unfit were "exposed"—that is, they were abandoned without food or shelter. The victims might die, but they might also be sold into slavery or even secretly adopted. (Other Greeks also practiced exposure of infants, but the choice was a family matter, not public policy.) Surviving children were raised at home up to the age of 7, at which point, boys left the family to be boarded with a "herd" of their age-mates. For the eleven years from age 7 to age 18, a boy went through rigorous training. On the theory that good soldiers should be strong and silent, boys learned only enough reading and writing for practical ends—for example, to transmit messages to and from military headquarters.

Many boys between the ages of 18 and 20 served in the *krypteia* (secret service), living secretly in the hills of Messenia, where they survived by hunting, foraging, and stealing. They spied on the ever rebellious Messenian helots, whom they could kill freely because every year Sparta declared war on helots. By age 20, all Similars had become hoplites, and they continued to serve in the army until age 60. Supported by helot labor, they devoted all their time to fighting and training the next generation.

Sparta offered more opportunities to elite women than did other Greek states. For example, unlike most Greek girls, Spartan girls received a public education—limited, however, to physical training, which was thought to strengthen females for

Spartan Woman   This bronze statuette (4¾ inches tall) from Laconia (ca. 530 B.C.) shows a woman running. Unlike other Greek women, elite Spartan women underwent physical education. Although their personal freedom was limited, women in Sparta suffered fewer restrictions than their counterparts in democratic Athens.   (C.M. Dixon/Ancient Art & Architecture Collection Ltd)

assembly. Probably from early times on, the assembly had, in theory, supreme lawmaking power as well as authority over war and peace, but voting was by shouting, and few people challenged Eupatrid wishes.

By 632 B.C., the aristocrats faced trouble in Athens as elsewhere because of corruption, economic change, and assertive hoplites. A failed attempt that year to establish a tyranny left the forces for change eager. In 621 B.C., a loose coalition opposed to Eupatrid rule forced a codification of the laws, which were then issued in writing. This Code of Draco (DRAY-co), named for its main drafter, was infamous for its harsh provisions (hence, our adjective *draconian*); it was written, a later commentator suggested, "not in ink but blood." Yet, Draco's Code seems only to have whetted an appetite for change. A wealthy non-Eupatrid elite of hoplites was emerging, grown rich exporting olive oil. Some were merchants; most were prosperous farmers. They now wanted political power. As for ordinary Athenians, they typically worked small family farms. Over the years, bad harvests and soil exhaustion had sent many into debt. Those who had pledged their land as collateral became known as *hektemoroi* ("sixth-parters"), probably because they owed one-sixth of their crops to their creditors. Other farmers sank even further into debt and had only themselves or their children as collateral. Some ended up as slaves, sometimes sold abroad. Because both rich and poor Athenians had grievances against the Eupatrids, revolution was in the air.

Enter **Solon** (ca. 630–560 B.C.), who was appointed to the emergency position of sole *archon* (chief officer) for one year, probably 594 B.C. A Eupatrid who had become a merchant, Solon (SO-lun) understood both the old and the new elite, and he was sympathetic to ordinary Athenians as well. As his surviving writings show, Solon was a moderate. He could have become tyrant, but he preferred to be a mediator.

Solon reformed both economics and politics. Many of his measures were aimed at encouraging Athenian trade, and they led to a commercial boom. More important, Solon helped ordinary people by the "shaking off of burdens," measures that abolished the institution of *hektemorage* and probably canceled some debts. He also abolished the practice of making loans on personal surety and set up a fund to redeem Athenians who had been sold into slavery abroad. By freeing the hektemoroi, Solon ensured Athens a large class of independent small farmers.

Solon made fundamental changes in Athenian government, too. He changed qualifications for office from birth to wealth, a boon to the non-Eupatrid elite. He established four census classes based on agricultural production. Most offices were reserved for men of property, but the poorest class, known as *thetes*, could participate in the assembly and courts. Solon probably established the Council of 400, which prepared the assembly's agenda. He is probably also responsible for setting a regular schedule of council and assembly meetings and for replacing the assembly's voice votes with the counting of hands.

Solon's moderation, respect for law, and liberation of the poor and downtrodden are milestones in Greek history. Without his reforms, it is doubtful that democracy could have later taken root in Athens. Yet Solon's work also had an unexpected byproduct: the growth of slavery in Athens. Though booming, the Athenian economy lost its cheap labor when Solon freed debt slaves and hektemoroi. The solution was to buy slaves abroad and import them to Athens. The island city-state of Chios led the way; it was the first Greek polis to organize a slave trade and always had a large slave population (see **MAP 3.2**). After Solon, Athens joined Chios as a society that depended on slave labor. Unlike helots, slaves could be bought and sold and were often uprooted, and the system was better policed than in earlier societies.

In the centuries after Solon, slavery became widespread in Athens. Some slaves served in agriculture, some labored under miserable conditions in Athenian silver mines, and some were engaged in commerce or the military (where some rowers were slaves). Most, however, worked as domestics or in small workshops as, for example, metalworkers or furniture makers. The vast majority of slaves were non-Greek. Most were prisoners of war; some were victims of pirates or debtors from states where, unlike Athens, citizens might end up in debt slavery. Thrace (roughly, modern Bulgaria) and Anatolia were the main sources of slaves, but some slaves came from North Africa and other Mediterranean regions.

Living conditions for slaves were usually poor and those in the silver mines were abysmal. Emancipation, however, was more common in Athens than in the American South before 1865. A few ex-slaves even rose to positions of wealth and power in Athens. A striking and unusual case is that of Pasion (d. 370 B.C.). Originally a slave employee of a banking firm, he bought his freedom and became the wealthiest Athenian banker of his day, as well as an Athenian citizen.

Solon Statesman of early Athens, he transformed Greek society through mediation, moderation, respect for law, and measures that liberated the poor and downtrodden.

If free Athenians had any moral doubts about slavery, they went unrecorded. Yet, there was much dissatisfaction with Solon's reforms, since his middle way satisfied neither Eupatrids nor champions of the free poor. After years of conflict, around 560 B.C., advocates of radical reform established a tyranny under Pisistratus (pie-SIS-trah-tus) (ca. 600–528 B.C.). He and his sons held power for forty of the next fifty years.

Supported by the common people, the Pisistratids exiled many Eupatrids and confiscated and redistributed their land. Pisistratus kept the façade of Solon's reforms while ensuring that loyal supporters held all key offices.

The tyranny was a stable regime that witnessed prosperity at home and the expansion of Athenian influence abroad. Yet, Pisistratus's dynasty lasted only two generations and was deposed in 510 B.C. Athens's elites by birth and wealth were ready to establish an oligarchy, but the way was open for an unexpected development: the emergence of popular government.

SECTION SUMMARY

- Trade, colonization, and the invention of the Greek alphabet and of the hoplite phalanx all contributed to the emergence of the polis around 750–700 B.C.

- The polis was a community of citizens that emphasized participation and equality.

- Corinth is the best example of a polis where new wealth led to the emergence of the first tyrants—originally, popular champions.

- Sparta's austere and militaristic society turned boys into soldiers and trained girls to be tough and assertive wives and mothers.

- Solon's reforms freed the poor, but unintentionally laid the foundations for the growth of slavery.

THE CULTURE OF ARCHAIC GREECE

How did Western individualism and rationalism take root in Archaic Greece?

While one trend in Archaic culture was communal solidarity, as reflected in the hoplite phalanx, another was the opposite: a growing elevation of individualism. Increased prosperity and mobility (social, geographic, and political) during the Archaic period encouraged the breakdown of old ties and left some people with a sense of their uniqueness. Archaic poetry and sculpture both demonstrate this new consciousness of the self.

Meanwhile, although most Archaic Greeks celebrated religion, a small group of thinkers expressed religious doubts. While monumental stone temples and international centers for divination were being erected to honor the pantheon of gods, Greek thinkers began to move away from divine and toward abstract and mechanistic explanations of the universe. Their defection marked the start of the Western philosophical tradition.

Revealing the Self: Lyric Poetry and Sculpture

Between approximately 675 and 500 B.C., the dominant Greek literary form was lyric poetry. This genre consisted of short poems written in a variety of styles but sharing a willingness to experiment, sometimes by revealing private feelings, sometimes by commenting on politics. Epic poetry, by contrast, was longer, grander in theme and tone, and less personal.

Homer never speaks directly about himself, and Hesiod reveals only a few personal details. In contrast, Archilochus (ar-KIL-uh-kus) of Paros (ca. 700–650 B.C.), the earliest known of the lyric poets, flaunts the self. Born on the Cycladic island of Paros, Archilochus was the son, perhaps the illegitimate son, of a noble. He was a mercenary soldier (that is, he fought for pay for a foreign city) and a colonist before returning home and dying in a hoplite battle against a neighboring island. The varied subjects of Archilochus's poetry include love, travel, and war. Much of his poetry is satire, sometimes mocking and ironic, sometimes vicious and abusive. Archilochus takes a cynical and detached view of hoplite ideals, freely admitting that he once tossed away his shield to escape the battlefield: "And that shield, to hell with it! Tomorrow I'll get me another one no worse."[1]

Sappho of Lesbos (ca. 625 B.C.) is also famous as a private poet, one who composed unmatched descriptions of intimate feelings, among them love for other women. Sappho (SAF-foh) is one of the few women poets of antiquity whose work has survived—very little, unfortunately, but enough to show that she was educated, worldly, and versed in politics. Like a modern experimental poet, she uses language self-consciously. Sappho's sensuality comes through in a description of her feelings at seeing a woman whose company she desires talking with a man: her heart shakes, her tongue is stuck, her eyes cannot see, her skin is on fire. "I am greener than grass," Sappho writes. "I feel nearly as if I could die."[2]

Sappho Ancient Greek poet from the island of Lesbos, she wrote odes, wedding songs, and hymns expressing intimate feelings, including love for other women.

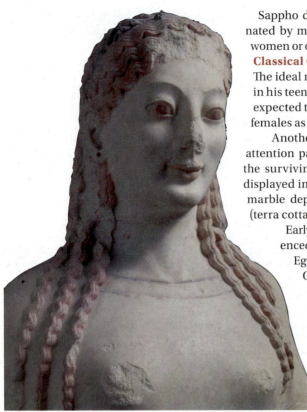

Athenian Kore This statue of a young woman (*kore*) exemplifies Archaic Greek sculpture's interest in the idealized human form. Note the slight smile, the carefully coifed hair, and the elaborate clothes. Influenced by contemporary Egyptian statues, Greek sculptors nonetheless created a new and original style. (Nimatallah/Art Resource, NY)

Classical Greece Period of ancient Greek history from about 480 to 323 B.C.

Sappho discusses female sexuality, a subject that Greek elite culture, dominated by males, tended to ignore. We know little about the sexuality of Greek women or of non-elite males. Among the male elite, romantic love in Archaic and **Classical Greece** was homosexual love or, to be precise, *pederasty* ("boy love"). The ideal relationship was supposed to involve a man in his twenties and a boy in his teens. The male elite was, strictly speaking, bisexual. By age 30, a man was expected to marry and raise a family. Perhaps bisexuality prevailed among elite females as well; Sappho, for example, eventually married and had a child.

Another sign of the interest in the personal in Archaic Greece is the growing attention paid to the depiction of the human body, both in painting (most of the surviving examples are painted pottery) and in sculpture. Archaic artists displayed increasing skill and sensitivity in depicting the human form. The rich marble deposits in Greek soil gave sculptors promising material; baked clay (terra cotta) and bronze were other common sculptural media.

Early Archaic marble sculpture (seventh century B.C.) was strongly influenced by the way Egyptian sculpture represented the human body. Like Egyptian statuary, early Greek sculpture tended to be formal and frontal. Over the course of the seventh and sixth centuries B.C., Greek sculptors experimented with a greater variety of poses and with increasing realism in showing musculature and motion. This realism, however, was expressed within limits, for the favorite subject of Archaic sculptors was not ordinary people but idealized, beautiful youth. The goal was to show people not as they were but as they might be.

Religious Faith and Practice

The Olympian gods who had been worshiped in the Mycenaean era survived in later ages, adapted to fit new political and social conditions. In the Archaic period, accordingly, the Olympian gods became gods of the polis.

Although the Olympians were revered throughout Greece, each polis had its patron deity, as well as its favorite heroes or demigods. Devotees considered it important to build a "house"—that is, a temple—for the local patron god or at least for his or her statue. The first temples were built of wood; the earliest stone temple, a temple of Apollo at Corinth, was built around 550 B.C.

Temples were rectangular structures with long sides on the north and south, short sides on the east and west, a colonnade around all four sides, and a pitched roof. The columns were based loosely on those of Egyptian architecture. Greek temples faced east so sunlight would illuminate the interior, which consisted of two rooms: a small treasury, open to the west, and a larger main chamber, in which a statue of the deity stood. The interior decoration of the temple was simple. Outside, however, brownish red roof tiles, painted sculpture above the colonnade and in the pediments (the area between the gables and the front and rear doorways), and terra-cotta roof ornaments created a festive and lively effect. The bare white ruins seen today are misleading.

The emphasis on exterior decoration reflects the way a Greek temple was used. The main ceremony took place outside. A long altar stood in front of the temple where on feast days temple priests would sacrifice animals (pigs, goats, lambs, and, less often, bulls) on the altar. Only the thighs would be burned for the gods. The rest of the meat would be boiled and distributed to worshipers. Under the tyrants, the number of such days was increased greatly, as a concession to the common people.

As in other ancient cultures, so in Greece, divination was an important element of religion. Divination was institutionalized in *oracles*, places where a god or hero might be consulted for advice. The most famous Greek oracle was that of Apollo at Delphi (DEL-fye) in central Greece. At Delphi, Apollo spoke through the Pythia, a priestess who went into a trance. The utterances of Apollo at Delphi were known for being ambiguous. Because different people might interpret them in different ways, Apollo could not be blamed after the fact if things did not turn out as the listener expected. Politicians and poleis regularly consulted Delphi about public policy.

Archaic thinkers pondered the theme of divine justice. In Archaic literature, we see less of the petty squabbling among the gods than in Homer and more of Zeus's majesty and justice. Although the wicked might seem to prosper, Zeus eventually punishes them or their descendants.

Archaic writers delighted in portraying human emotions, but they had no confidence about the human ability to master emotions. In Archaic literature, people are weak and insignificant; their fortune is uncertain and mutable. Further, the gods are jealous of human success. People who aim too high are guilty of *hubris*—arrogance with overtones of violence and transgression. Hubris inevitably brings *nemesis*, "punishment" or "allotment." The safest course is for a person to be pious and humble.

So, Archaic religion taught a humbling, even pessimistic, lesson. Yet, its teachings were not always heeded. The pages of Archaic history are full of people who aimed high and sought success with seemingly little worry or dire consequences. In Ionia (see **Map 3.2**), one group of Greek thinkers made a radical break with Archaic religion and invented speculative philosophy.

The Origins of Western Philosophy

Abstract, rationalistic, speculative thinking emerged in Greece during the sixth century B.C. The first developments took place in Miletus (my-LEE-tus), an Ionian city. It is often said that the thinkers of Miletus (the Milesians) and their followers in other parts of Ionia invented philosophy. So they did, but we must be precise about what this means.

The Ionians were not the first to ask questions or tell stories about the nature and origins of the universe; virtually every ancient people did so, nor did the Ionians invent science. They conducted no experiments. By 600 B.C., moreover, mathematics, astronomy, medicine, and engineering had been thriving for over two thousand years in Egypt and Mesopotamia, a heritage with which the Ionians were familiar and from which they borrowed.

The real importance of the Ionians is as pioneers of rationalism. They began the movement away from anthropomorphic or divine explanations and toward an abstract and mechanistic explanation of the universe. Later Greek philosophers were rarely (if ever) atheists, but they took for granted what the Ionians labored to establish: the primacy of human reason.

The Ionians saw themselves as students of nature—*physis* (from which the word *physics* is derived). Although they also commented on morality and politics, their interest in natural phenomena is what makes the Ionians significant. In their own day, the Ionians were called "wise men" (*sophoi*); to a later generation, they were "lovers of wisdom," *philosophoi* (from which *philosopher* comes).

Thales (THAY-leez), the first Milesian thinker, made a name for himself by successfully predicting a solar eclipse in 585 B.C. He is credited with founding Greek geometry and astronomy. Little survives of his writings or those of the other Milesians, but it is clear that he created the first general and systematic theory about the nature of the universe. According to Thales, the primary substance, the element from which all of nature was created, was water. He emphasized the mobility of water and its ability to nourish life.

A reply followed soon. Around 550 B.C., Anaximander of Miletus wrote the first known book of prose in Greek, expounding his own philosophy of nature. He attacked Thales for oversimplifying the dynamism of nature. Anaximander accepted Thales' monist assumption—that all matter originated from one primary substance—but he called the substance "the unlimited" or "the undefined" rather than water. A third Milesian, Anaximenes, replied that the primary substance might be unlimited but it was not undefined. It was air, whose properties of condensation and rarefaction symbolized the dynamic and changing nature of things.

Humble as these theories might seem today, they represent a dramatic development: an open and critical debate among thinkers, each of whom was proposing an abstract and rational model of the universe. Many scholars have speculated about the origins of this development. Why Miletus? Why the sixth century B.C.? There are no sure answers, although certain influences have been suggested. Among them are Miletus's contacts on the trade routes with sophisticated Babylon, the proximity of Ionia to non-Greek peoples and the resulting Milesian appreciation of variety and complexity, and the search for law and order in contemporary Greek political life and its extension to the philosophical plane.

In its second generation, early Greek philosophy moved to other Ionian cities and then migrated westward across the Mediterranean. Heraclitus (her-uh-CLY-tus) of Ephesus (ca. 500 B.C.) proposed fire as the primary substance. Although fire was ever changing, it had an underlying coherence. According to Heraclitus, this paradox nicely symbolized the nature of the universe. He summed up the importance of change by the aphorisms "All things flow" and "You cannot step into the same river twice." The universe witnessed a constant struggle of opposites, yet an essential unity and order prevailed. To describe this order, Heracleitus used the term *logos* (LOH-gos). This key concept of Greek philosophy is difficult to translate; among other definitions, *logos* can mean "word," "thought," "reason," "story," or "calculation." The term *logos* embodies the importance of reason in ancient Greek civilization.

Heracleitus's contemporary, Pythagoras (py-THAGuh-russ) of Samos, was both a rationalist and a religious thinker. On the one hand, Pythagoras was a mathematician who discovered the numerical ratios determining the major intervals of the musical scale—that is, the range of sound between high and low. It is less certain if, as tradition has it, he discovered the so-called Pythagorean theorem—that in a right triangle the hypotenuse squared is equal to the sum of the squares of the other two sides.

On the other hand, Pythagoras believed that the purity of mathematics would improve the human soul. Just as he had imposed numerical order on the musical scale, so could philosophers understand the entire universe through number and proportion. The resulting knowledge was no mere academic exercise, but a way of life. Pythagoras devoted himself to "observation" or "contemplation"—to *theoria* (from which *theory* comes).

In Magna Graecia (southern Italy), Pythagoras founded a religious community. Its members observed strict secrecy, but it appears that they abstained from meat because they believed in the kinship of all living things. They also believed in the reincarnation of the human soul, though not necessarily into a human body.

The early Greek philosopher whose work is most fully preserved is Parmenides (par-MEN-uh-deez) of Elea in Magna Graecia. Parmenides (b. ca. 515 B.C.) completely distrusted the senses. He believed that reality was a world of pure being: eternal, unchanging, and indivisible, comparable to a sphere. To Parmenides, change was a mere illusion. Parmenides, therefore, is the first Western philosopher to propose a radical difference between the world of the senses and reality. This fundamental strain of Western thought would be taken up by Plato and his followers and then passed to Christianity.

To sum up, in philosophy, as in so many other endeavors, the Archaic Greeks were great borrowers and even greater innovators who left a profound mark on later ages. By the late sixth century B.C., Archaic Greece was poised on the brink of a revolution that would give birth to the Classical period of Greek civilization.

SECTION SUMMARY

- Lyric poetry and Archaic sculpture display a groundbreaking interest in individual feelings and the human body.
- Archaic Greek religion was pessimistic. It feared human arrogance (*hubris*) and divine punishment (*nemesis*).
- Western philosophy began in Ionia in the 500s B.C.
- The first philosophers were rationalists who offered abstract and mechanistic explanations of nature.

CLASSICAL GREECE

What was Athenian democracy and how did it clash with Sparta in the Peloponnesian War?

demokratia Term coined in Athens in the fifth century B.C. to describe the city's system of direct government.

The word *democracy* comes from the Greek *demokratia* (deh-mo-kra-TEE-uh), coined in Athens early in the fifth century B.C. *Demokratia* literally means "the power (*kratos*) of the people (*demos*)." Modern democracy is characterized by mass citizenship, elections, and representative government. Athenian *demokratia*, in contrast, was a direct democracy in which elections mattered less than direct participation, citizenship was restricted, women were excluded from politics, immigrants could rarely become citizens, and citizens owned slaves and ruled an empire. Modern democracies are big, but Athens encompassed only 1,000 square miles. Modern democracies emphasize individual rights, but Athens placed the community first. Yet Athenian *demokratia* established principles enshrined in democracy today: freedom, equality, citizenship without property qualifications, the right of most citizens to hold office, and the rule of law.

The young democracy's greatest achievement was to spearhead Greece's victory over the Persian invaders in 480 B.C. After that victory, Athens became Greece's leading sea power. Yet Sparta remained the superior land power, and the two poleis were soon locked in a cycle of competition and war. The result nearly destroyed Athenian democracy. Even more serious, it undermined Greece's very independence.

The Development of Demokratia, 508–322 B.C.

In Athens after Pisistratid rule, conditions were ripe for revolution. Solon had left a society of independent small farmers, while the Pisistratids had strengthened the ranks of immigrants and weakened the Eupatrids. Elite leaders nonetheless tried to establish an Athenian oligarchy. We may imagine strong popular opposition.

Ironically, a Eupatrid, Cleisthenes (KLICE-the-neez) (d. ca. 500 B.C.), led the revolution. Originally, Cleisthenes aimed to head the oligarchy, but his rivals shut him out of power. He turned then to the demos, whose leader he became. The watchwords of the day were *equality* and *mixing* (that is, mixing people from different regions of Attica in order to break down local, aristocratic power bases).

Frightened by the assertive populace, the oligarchs called for Spartan military assistance, but to no avail: Cleisthenes rallied the people to victory. The Athenian triumph proved, in Herodotus's opinion, "that equality is an excellent thing, not in one way only but in many. For while they were under a tyranny, [Athenians] were no better at fighting than any of their neighbors, but once they were rid of tyrants they became by far the best."[3]

Cleisthenes extinguished Eupatrid power once and for all by attacking its local bases of support. For example, he abolished the four traditional tribes and apportioned the people among ten new tribes. The tribes formed the basis of a new Council of 500 to replace Solon's Council of 400. The council was divided into ten tribal units, each serving as a kind of executive committee for one of the ten months of the civic year.

The centerpiece of the government was the assembly, some of whose members, emboldened by the new spirit of equality, now spoke up for the first time. The new Council of 500, like its predecessor, prepared the assembly's agenda, but assemblymen felt free to amend it. Only the Areopagus council remained a privileged preserve.

The last and most unusual part of the Cleisthenic system was ostracism, a sort of annual *un*popularity contest that received its name from the pieces of broken pottery (*ostraka*) on which the names of victims were chiseled. The "winner" was forced into ten years of exile, although his property would not be confiscated. Ostracism was meant to protect the regime by defusing factionalism and discouraging tyrants. Judging by Athens's political stability, it worked.

In 508 B.C., the poorest Athenians had relatively little power in Cleisthenic government, but changes by the 450s made Athens even more democratic. During that period, the oldest principle

Greek Trireme *Olympias* is a hypothetical reconstruction of an Athenian war galley of about 400 B.C. Rowed by 170 oarsmen arranged on three decks, the trireme fought by ramming an enemy ship with the bronze ram attached to its bow. (John Coates/Trireme Trust Foundation)

of Greek politics came to the fore: Whoever fights for the state governs it. To counter the Persian threat against Greece in the 480s (see page 70), Athens built a great navy. The standard ship was a trireme (TRY-reem), an oared warship rowed by 170 men on three decks. The core of the rowers consisted of thetes, the poorest free men in Athens. Just as hoplites supported new regimes in Greece after 700 B.C., so rowers supported new regimes in Greece after 500 B.C.

Pericles Leader of fifth century B.C. Athens, he established Athens as a great center of art and literature as well as a great empire.

A second revolution occurred around 461 B.C., when Ephialtes (d. ca. 460 B.C.) and his young associate **Pericles** (ca. 495–429 B.C.) targeted the last bulwark of privilege, the Areopagus. They stripped away the council's long-standing supervisory powers over the regime and redistributed those powers to the Council of 500 and the people's court. The decade of the 450s B.C. saw another innovation: payment for public service, specifically for jurors, who received a half-drachma (perhaps half a day's wages) for a day of jury duty. Eventually, other public servants also received pay. Conservatives complained bitterly because they perceived, rightly, that state pay made political activity by poor people possible. State pay was, an Athenian said, "the glue of demokratia."

Demokratia became closely connected with Pericles (PAIR-ih-kleez), who inherited the constituency of Ephialtes after his assassination around 460 B.C. For much of the next thirty years, Pericles dominated Athenian politics. An aristocrat who respected the common people, an excellent orator who benefited from an education in philosophy, an honest and tireless worker, and a general who led in peace as well as war, Pericles was a political giant. Under his leadership, demokratia became firmly entrenched as the government and way of life in Athens.

Pericles was much influenced by a woman, Aspasia (uh-SPAY-see-uh). She belonged to the small group of noncitizen women called *hetairai*, or courtesans (that is, prostitutes patronized by men of wealth and status). An educated woman from Miletus, Aspasia was Pericles' mistress and bore him a son. Aspasia and Pericles gathered around them a glittering circle of thinkers and artists. Some say that Aspasia even influenced Pericles' political decisions.

Athenian democracy survived, with occasional oligarchic intrusions, for 150 years after Pericles' death. During those years, it became more institutionalized and cautious, but it also became more thoroughly egalitarian.

How Demokratia Worked

Unlike most modern democracies, Athenian demokratia was direct and participatory. Pericles once claimed that in Athens, "people pay attention both to their own household and to politics. Even those occupied with other activities are no less knowledgeable about politics."[4] This is part boast, but only part. Large numbers of ordinary citizens attended the assembly from time to time and held public office or served on the Council of 500 for a year or two.

GOVERNMENT

The central institution was the assembly. Open to all male citizens over age 20, assembly meetings were held in the open air, on a hillside seating several thousand on benches (see the photograph on page 48). In the fourth century B.C., the assembly gathered a minimum of forty times per year, about once every ten days.

The assembly heard the great debates of the day. It made decisions about war and peace, alliance and friendship; it conferred honors and issued condemnations; it passed decrees relating to current issues and set up commissions to revise fundamental laws. In the assembly, top orators addressed the people, but everyone, however humble, was theoretically entitled to speak.

The judicial branch consisted of courts, which, with a few exceptions, were open to all citizens, no matter how poor. Aristotle or a member of his school comments that "when the people have the right to vote in the courts, they control the constitution." Juries were large, commonly consisting of several hundred men chosen by lottery; small juries, it was felt, were easily bribed. After a preliminary hearing, cases were decided in a single day.

The executive consisted of the Council of 500 and some seven hundred public officials (also, under Athens's empire in the fifth century B.C., several hundred others living abroad). All male citizens over age 30 were eligible to serve. Most public officials were chosen by lottery, which put rich and poor, talented and untalented, on an equal footing. To guard against installing incompetents or criminals, all officials had to undergo a scrutiny by the council before taking office and an audit after the term. Most magistracies, moreover, were boards, usually of ten men, so even if a bad man managed to pass this scrutiny, he would be counterbalanced by his colleagues. Only generals and treasurers were chosen by election.

Athens had a weak executive and no president or prime minister. Generals and orators led debates and sometimes exercised great influence, but ordinary people set the agenda and made the decisions by taking votes at each assembly meeting. On the local level, every deme (county) had an annually chosen executive and a deme assembly of all citizens.

So novel and populist a system of government has not been without critics, either in antiquity or today. Some have charged that the Athenian people were uneducated, emotional, and easily swayed by oratorical tricks. Others say that demokratia degenerated into mob rule after the death of Pericles. Still others complain about the lack of a system of formal public education, which denied many citizens equality of opportunity.

Another serious charge against Athenian demokratia is that it was democracy for an elite only. Adult male citizens never amounted to more than one-tenth of the population, approximately 40,000 out of a total population—men, women and children, resident aliens, and slaves—of about 400,000. To become a citizen, a boy at age 18 had to prove that he was the legitimate son of a citizen father and a citizen maternal grandfather. Girls were never officially registered as citizens. Although the term *citizeness* existed, Athenian citizen women were usually referred to as "city women." Resident aliens rarely attained citizenship.

WOMEN AND RESIDENT ALIENS

In the fifth and fourth centuries B.C., Athens had a large population of foreigners. Some were transient. Others were officially registered resident aliens, or *metics* (MEH-tiks). Metics came by the thousands from all over the Greek world and beyond. Some, like Aristotle (a native of a Greek colony in Macedonia [mah-suh-DOE-nee-uh]), were attracted by the city's schools of philosophy, but most came because of its unparalleled economic opportunities. Metics could not own land in Athens, and they had to pay extra taxes and serve in the Athenian military. Nevertheless, they prospered in Athenian commerce and crafts.

Athenian women were excluded from politics and played only a modest role in commerce as small retailers. In legal matters, women were almost always required to be represented by a male guardian. Demokratia also promoted an ideal of the male as master of his household. Women were expected to be obedient and remain indoors.

Practice, however, was another matter. As Aristotle asks rhetorically, "How is it possible to prevent the wives of the poor from going out?" *Poor* is a synonym for *ordinary* in ancient Greek. Ordinary women could not stay at home because they had work to do in the city or fields. Ordinary houses, moreover, were small and cramped, and in the Mediterranean heat, women could not stay inside all the time.

We occasionally get glimpses, sometimes more, of Athenian women resisting or working behind the scenes to correct male mistakes. An inheritance case reveals a woman go-between interceding among her quarreling male relations. Greek comedy shows women mocking male pretensions and establishing sisterly friendships. A woman who brought a large dowry into a marriage could use it and the threat of divorce to influence her husband (the dowry had to be returned to the woman's father or guardian if there was a divorce). In short, Athenian women had some access to the world outside the household and some influence within the household. There existed, nonetheless, a real disparity in power between men and women.

Athenian demokratia lacked many features of modern democracy, including a notion of human rights, the mass naturalization of immigrants, gender equality, the abolition of slavery, and public education. To its small citizen body, however, Athenian demokratia offered freedom, equality, and responsibility, as well as a degree of participation in public life seldom equaled. Demokratia was a model of what democracy could be, but not of who could take part.

The Persian Wars, 499–479 B.C.

In 500 B.C., Sparta, hegemon of the Peloponnesian League, was the most prominent power of the Greek mainland. Across the Aegean Sea in Anatolia, the Greek city-states had been under Persian rule for two generations, since Cyrus the Great's conquest in the 540s B.C. In 499 B.C., however, events began to unfold that not only would revolutionize that balance of power, but also would throw the entire eastern Mediterranean into two hundred years of turmoil.

Led by Miletus, the Ionian Greek city-states rose in revolt against Persia in 499 B.C. Athens sent troops to help, but despite initial successes, Athens reconsidered the alliance and withdrew its forces. The Ionian coalition broke down thereafter and was crushed by Persia. Miletus was besieged and destroyed, but otherwise, Persia was relatively lenient in Ionia.

Upstart Athens, however, could not go unpunished. In 490 B.C., Darius I sent a large naval expedition against Athens. About 25,000 infantrymen and 1,200 cavalrymen (with horses) landed at Marathon, some 24 miles from the city of Athens (see **MAP 3.4**). Athens sent 10,000 men (including 1,000 allies) to defend Marathon, and a great battle ensued.

Persian overconfidence and the superiority of the Greek phalanx over Persia's loosely organized infantrymen won Athens a smashing victory. Persia suffered 6,400 casualties, Athens only 192. (The story, unconfirmed, that a messenger ran from the battlefield to the city of Athens with the news, "Rejoice, we conquer!" is the inspiration for the modern marathon race, a slightly longer distance of about 26 miles.) After the battle, Athens experienced a burst of confidence that propelled it to power and glory.

Meanwhile, Persia sought a rematch. After Darius's death in 486, his son and successor, Xerxes, amassed a huge force of about a thousand ships and several hundred thousand soldiers and rowers. Athens, under the leadership of Themistocles (ca. 525–460 B.C.), prepared by building a fleet of two hundred ships. Athens joined Sparta and twenty-nine other poleis in the Hellenic League of defense, with Sparta in overall command. Most poleis either stayed neutral or, like Thebes and Argos, collaborated with Persia. The Greeks had only three-hundred-plus ships and about fifty thousand infantrymen.

Persia invaded Greece in 480 B.C. and won the opening moves. At the narrow pass of Thermopylae in central Greece (see **MAP 3.2**), the Persians outflanked and crushed a small Spartan army, who died fighting to the last man, including their king, Leonidas. This sacrifice added to the Spartan reputation for courage but left the road south open. Abandoned by its defenders, Athens was sacked.

Amazon Queen   This red-figure Athenian cup (ca. 440 B.C.) shows the Greek warrior Achilles about to slay the Amazon queen Penthesilea during the Trojan War, in which she fought on Troy's side. She was a symbol of feminine courage and beauty.   (Staatliche Antikensammlungen und Glyptothek, Munich)

The tide then turned. The Greeks lured the Persian fleet into the narrow straits between Athens and Salamis. The Persians could not use their numerical superiority in this confined space, and the Greeks had the home advantage. The result was a crushing Persian defeat under the eyes of Xerxes himself, who watched the battle from a throne on a hillside near the shore.

Because their sea links to the Levant had been cut, Xerxes and the remainder of the Persian fleet left for home. Soon afterward, the united Greek army, under Spartan leadership, defeated Persian forces on land at Plataea (just north of Attica; see **MAP 3.2**) in 479 B.C. At about the same time, the Greek fleet defeated a reorganized Persian fleet off the Anatolian coast. The victorious Greeks sailed the coast and liberated the Ionians. Not only did Persia fail to conquer the Greek mainland, but it also lost its eastern Aegean empire.

Greeks did not remember the invader fondly. After 480, they thought of Persians not merely as enemies but as barbarians—that is, cultural inferiors. (See the feature, "The Global Record: The Enemy as Barbarian.") At the same time, Greeks became more conscious of their own common culture.

Struggles to Dominate Greece, 478–362 B.C.

The Greek unity forged by the struggle against Persia was fragile and short-lived. What followed was a constant struggle in diplomacy and war among city-states, usually arranged in leagues under hegemons.

Following the Greek victory over Persia, Athens expanded its power as hegemon of a new security organization. Founded on the island of Delos in the Aegean Sea, the so-called Delian League aimed both at protecting Greek lands and at plundering Persian territory. The number of allies grew from about 150 in 477 B.C. to about 250 in 431 B.C., at the height of the league.

Because they feared entanglement outside the Peloponnesus, most Spartans preferred to leave the Aegean to Athens. Some Spartans, nonetheless, watched with unease and jealousy as Athenian power boomed.

The Enemy as Barbarian

Classical Greeks no longer regarded the enemy as honored rivals, as Homer's heroes had regarded Trojans. Rather, they looked down on the enemy as a barbarian. Greece's archenemies, the Persians, were portrayed as indulgent, effeminate, emotional, slavish, cruel, and dangerous. Consider the contrasting portraits of Persians and Greeks in these excerpts from the historian Herodotus's account of Persia's invasion of Greece in 480 B.C.

The Persians

He [King Xerxes of Persia] then prepared to move forward to Abydos, where a bridge had already been constructed across the Hellespont from Europe to Asia.... It was here not long afterwards that the Greeks under Xanthippus the son of Ariphron took Artayctes the Persian governor of Sestos, and nailed him alive to a plank—he was the man who collected women in the temple of Protesilaus at Elaeus and committed various acts of sacrilege. This headland was the point to which Xerxes' engineers carried their two bridges from Abydos—a distance of seven furlongs.... The work was successfully completed, but a subsequent storm of great violence smashed it up and carried everything away. Xerxes was very angry when he learned of the disaster, and gave orders that the Hellespont should receive three hundred lashes and have a pair of fetters thrown into it. And I have heard before now that he also sent people to brand it with hot irons. He certainly instructed the men with the whips to utter, as they wielded them, the following words: "You salt and bitter stream, your master lays this punishment upon you for injuring him, who never injured you. But Xerxes the King will cross you, with or without your permission. No man sacrifices to you, and you deserve the neglect by your acrid and muddy waters"—a highly presumptuous way of addressing the Hellespont, and typical of a barbarous nation. In addition to punishing the Hellespont Xerxes gave orders that the men responsible for building the bridge should have their heads cut off. This unseemly order was duly carried out . . .

The Greeks

To the Spartan envoys . . . [the Athenians] said: "No doubt it was natural that the Lacedaemonians [Spartans] should dread the possibility of our making terms with Persia; nonetheless it shows a poor estimate of the spirit of Athens. Were we offered all the gold in the world, and the fairest and richest country the earth contains, we should never consent to join the common enemy and bring Greece into submission. There are many compelling reasons to prevent our taking such a course, even if we wish to do so: the first and greatest is the burning of the temples and images of our gods—now mere heaps of rubble. It is our bounden duty to avenge this desecration with all the power we possess—not to clasp in friendship the hand that wrought it. Again, there is the Greek nation—the common blood, the common language; the temples and religious ritual; the whole way of life we understand and share together—indeed, if Athens were to betray all this it would not be well done. We would have you know, therefore, if you did not already know it, that we will never make peace with Xerxes so long as a single Athenian remains alive."

QUESTIONS

1. Find at least three examples in these passages of Persian barbarism.

2. By deciding to make war instead of negotiating peace, are the Athenians barbarians or civilized people?

3. Does Herodotus offer convincing proof that the Persians are more barbarous than the Greeks? Is he fair?

Source: From *The Histories* by Herodotus, translated by Aubrey de Sélincourt, revised with introductory matter and notes by John Marincola (Penguin Classics 1954, Second revised edition 1996). Translation copyright 1954 by Aubrey de Sélincourt. This revised edition copyright ©John Marincola 1996. Reproduced by permission of Penguin Books Ltd.

Afraid of the new titan, the major allied states rebelled, beginning with Thasos in 465 B.C., but Athens crushed each rebellion. Sometimes after surrender, rebels were executed and their wives and children sold into slavery. Allied complaints began to stir Sparta. A conflict loomed between Greece's greatest land power, Sparta, and Greece's greatest sea power, Athens.

The Peloponnesian War, as this conflict is known today, came in 431 B.C. and lasted intermittently until 404 B.C. The war proved bloody and bitter. Battles between huge fleets, economic warfare, protracted sieges, epidemic disease, and ideological struggle produced a devastating war. It was clear that the Greeks could not maintain their unity against Persia; indeed, they appeared to be destroying themselves.

In this era, both democratic Athens and oligarchic Sparta sought to promote their respective ideologies. Some unfortunate states became ideological battlegrounds, often at great cost of life. In Corcyra (modern Corfu; see **Map 3.5**), for example, bloody civil war marked a series of coups and countercoups in the 420s B.C.

Given Spartan supremacy on land and Athenian mastery of the sea, it is not surprising that the Peloponnesian War remained undecided for a decade and a half. The balance of power shifted only after an Athenian blunder, an expedition to conquer Sicily (415–413 B.C.) that became a quagmire and then a disaster, leading to total defeat and thousands of Athenian casualties. In

🌐 **MAP 3.5—Greece in the Peloponnesian War**

During the long and bloody Peloponnesian War (431–404 B.C.), much of the Greek world was divided into two camps: one led by Sparta, the other by Athens.

the aftermath, most of the Athenian empire rose in revolt. Persia re-emerged and intervened on Sparta's side—in return for Sparta's restoration of Ionia to Persia, an ironic counterpoint to Sparta's role in driving Persia from Greece in 479. Athens, nevertheless, was sufficiently wealthy and plucky to hold out until 404 B.C.

Sparta won the Peloponnesian War, but establishing a new Greek order proved beyond its grasp. Spartans were soldiers, not diplomats; infantrymen, not sailors; and commanders, not public speakers. They made poor leaders. Sparta took over Athens's former empire and quickly had a falling-out with its allies: Persia, Corinth, and Thebes.

In addition, Sparta suffered a vast decline in the number of citizens. The original nine thousand Similars of the seventh century B.C. had dropped to only about fifteen hundred in 371 B.C. The main problem seems to have been greed. Rich Spartans preferred to get richer by concentrating wealth in fewer hands, rather than open the elite to new blood. Thousands of men could no longer afford to live as elite soldiers.

The result was military disaster. In 371 B.C., the Boeotian army crushed the Spartans at the Battle of Leuctra, killing a thousand men (including four hundred Similars) and a Spartan king. In the next few years, Boeotia invaded the Peloponnesus, freed the Messenian helots, and restored Messenia to independence, after some 350 years of bondage. It was a fatal blow to Spartan power, but Boeotia, too, was exhausted and its main leaders were dead. None of the Greek city-states had been able to maintain hegemony.

SECTION SUMMARY

- Democracy or "people power" (*demokratia*) began in ancient Greece, and Athens was the most influential Greek democracy.

- Athenian democracy was direct and participatory for adult male citizens, but women, resident aliens, and slaves were all denied citizen rights.

- Persia's massive invasion of mainland Greece in 480–479 B.C. was defeated by a coalition led by Sparta and Athens.

- The Greek *poleis* then turned on each other in a series of wars that lasted about a century.

- Sparta defeated Athens in the most intense phase of these conflicts, known today as the Peloponnesian War (431–404 B.C.).

THE PUBLIC CULTURE OF CLASSICAL GREECE

How did tragedy, comedy, philosophy, and history all begin and develop in the culture of Classical Greece?

The word *classical* means "to set a standard." The culture of Greece between 480 and 322 B.C. proved so influential in the later West that it may justly be called classical. Classical Greek culture was public culture. Poets were not inward-looking or alienated figures. Rather, to quote the Athenian playwright Aristophanes (air-ih-STOF-uh-neez) (ca. 455–385 B.C.), they were "the teachers of men," who commented on contemporary public debate. (As the quotation might also suggest, men, especially citizens, dominated public life.) Dramas were performed in a state theater at state religious festivals. The philosopher Socrates (sock-ruh-TEEZ) (469–399 B.C.) discussed philosophy in marketplaces and gymnasia. It was not private individuals, but the public, that was the major patron of sculpture and architecture.

Public life, accordingly, is the central theme of Classical Greek art and literature. In tragedy, for example, regardless of the particular hero or plot, the same character always looms in the background: the polis. The Classical historians Herodotus, Xenophon, and especially Thucydides focus on public affairs rather than private life. Classical philosophy ranged from biology to metaphysics, but it never forgot politics.

Religion and Art

A hallmark of Classical culture is the tension between the religious heritage of the Archaic period and the worldly spirit of the Classical age. The Classical period was a time of prosperity, political debate, and military conflict. "Wonders are many on earth, and none more wondrous than man,"

The Parthenon   The temple of Athena Parthenos ("the Maiden") on the Athenian Acropolis, the Parthenon was dedicated in 438 B.C. One of the largest and most complex Greek temples, it was built of fine marble. The partially restored ruins symbolize the wealth, power, and greatness of Classical Greece. (William Katz/Photo Researchers)

The Parthenon

The Parthenon, completed in 432 B.C., dominates both the skyline of Athens and the historical imagination of the West. The building's fine marble and Classical proportions symbolize the free, confident, and united society that one might expect of Periclean Athens, the world's first democracy (see the photograph on page 73). A close look, however, suggests a more complex story. The Parthenon's sculpture offers glimpses of the tensions behind the Classical façade.

The temple of Athena Parthenos ("the Maiden"), as the Parthenon is formally known, was a public project of Greece's wealthiest city-state, leading naval power, and premier

Centaur Struggling with Lapith, Parthenon Metope, South Side
(Courtesy of the Trustees of the British Museum)

democracy. Athenians spared no expense on its construction. Sculpture included a gold and ivory statue of the goddess Athena inside the temple and, on the outside, statuary in each pediment (the triangular space under the eaves) and sculptured reliefs running around the building above the exterior and interior colonnades.

So lavish a program of art demonstrated Athenian wealth, but also served an educational purpose: to illustrate basic Athenian values. Because every Athenian male was expected to fight for the city when called on, militant competition is a central theme. Above the exterior colonnade, for example, ninety-two separate panels of relief sculpture depict gods and heroes fighting foes, such as giants and centaurs.

See the detail from the south wall. It shows a fight between a human male and a centaur, a mythological creature who was half-man, half-beast. Both the man and the centaur are powerful, but the centaur is old and ugly, while the man is young and handsome. The man fights fairly, while the centaur makes a savage attack with arm and forelegs. The man belongs to a Greek people known as the Lapiths. According to myth, the centaurs attacked the Lapiths during a wedding celebration, but they were driven off by the Lapith men, led by the bridegroom and his Athenian friend, the hero Theseus.

To a real-life Athenian observer, the triumph of the Lapiths might have symbolized Athens's victory over the Persians. It was easy to make the connection because the Parthenon was in effect a war memorial as well as a temple. When the Persians invaded Athens in 480 B.C., they destroyed the temples on the Acropolis. For forty years after Greece's victory, Athens left the Acropolis empty as a reminder of Persian barbarism. Then Pericles sponsored a building program of new temples, of which the Parthenon was the grandest.

Delian League funds were diverted to pay for the new buildings, which raised controversy. Ironically, democratic Athens used allied money,

said the Athenian tragedian Sophocles (sof-uh-KLEEZ) (ca. 495–406 B.C.). Yet Sophocles was a deeply religious man who also believed that people were doomed to disaster unless they obeyed the laws of the gods.

Classical religion was less sure of itself than its Archaic predecessor. A few people even questioned the very existence of the gods, although most Greeks wanted religion to be adapted to the new age, not discarded altogether. Thus, Athenian religion was tailored to the needs of a democratic and imperial city. In the 440s B.C., under Pericles' leadership, Athens embarked on a vast, ambitious, and expensive temple-building project, using Delian League funds and serving as a large public employment program. Temples were built in and around the city, most notably on the Athenian Acropolis. (See the feature, "The Visual Record: The Parthenon.")

To adapt religion to a new age, new cults also were introduced. The most popular was the worship of Asclipius, god of healing. Traditionally a minor figure, Asclipius became enormously popular beginning in the late fifth century B.C., perhaps in response to the high mortality of the Peloponnesian War. Outside Athens, large shrines to Asclipius became pilgrimage centers in the fourth century B.C. for ailing people in search of a cure.

Four Women in Procession, Parthenon Frieze, East Wall (Louvre/Réunion des Musées Nationaux/Art Resource, NY)

From both of these pieces, we may detect Athenian commonplaces about gender. Young women were expected to be maidenly, reserved, and modest. Their bodies were to be kept private. Young men were expected to be outgoing and assertive. Although men wore clothes in public, they exercised naked in gymnasia, wrestling grounds, and stadiums, competing in a healthy activity considered to be effective preparation for war.

The historian finds subtler messages in the two scenes. For example, however constrained the role of women, their very presence in the frieze is significant. Women were not permitted to attend the Athenian assembly, but they participated in the rituals and festivals that played so large a role in Athenian public life. Notice, for instance, the two girls shown in the back who are carrying ritual vessels.

Scholars disagree about the subject of the procession in the frieze. Most scholars argue that the subject is the Pan-Athenaic procession, held once every four years to honor Athena. The people depicted are said to be the people of Athens—a daring novelty, considering that all previous Greek temple sculpture was restricted to gods, heroes, and mythological figures. Some scholars view the scene as an illustration of a legend from the early history of Athens. In either case, one thing is clear: The Parthenon sculptures depict the Athenians the way they wanted to see themselves—as courageous, pious, and public-spirited.

QUESTIONS

1. In what sense is the Parthenon an example of public education in democratic Athens?

2. What does the Parthenon have to say about gender in Athens?

3. What does the Parthenon have to say about Greek-Persian relations?

earmarked for defense, to glorify itself. Some people considered that oppressive.

The sculpture above the interior colonnade is a continuous band, or frieze, around the four sides of the building, and it illustrates a procession. Warriors aplenty, primarily cavalrymen but also hoplites and charioteers, compose the lineup. Like the Lapith, the cavalrymen are depicted without clothes, and so they embody the ideal of strong bodies in the service of the polis.

Not all of the men in the interior frieze are warriors, though. Women, too, are depicted. See the detail from the east wall. Look at the four women shown here. The women are on foot, clothed and in solemn procession. The heavy folds of their robes, the hands held at their sides, and the expression on the one visible face all suggest calm and decorum.

Women played a major role in Classical Athenian religion. They were priestesses in more than forty major cults. They participated each year in many festivals, including several reserved only for women. One such festival, the Thesmophoria, a celebration of fertility held each autumn, featured a three-day encampment of women on a hillside in the city, right beside the Athenian assembly amphitheater. Women also attended public funeral orations in honor of soldiers who had died in battle. They probably attended plays as well.

In art, Classical sculptors completed the process begun by their Archaic forebears of mastering the accurate representation of the human body. In anatomical precision, Classical Greek sculpture was the most technically proficient sculpture the world had seen. Like Archaic sculpture, it was not, however, an attempt to portray humans "warts and all" but rather an idealization of the human form.

The Sophists and Socrates

Success in democratic politics required knowledge of oratory. This demand was met in the late fifth century B.C. by the arrival in Athens of professional teachers of *rhetoric*, the art of speaking. They

Sophists Professional teachers of rhetoric and other subjects in the mid-fifth century B.C., whose training of ambitious young Athenians challenged the stability of standard values and established institutions. Today, "sophist" has come to mean "twister of words."

were known as **Sophists** (SOF-ists) (from a word meaning "instruct" or "make wise"). Sicilian Greeks invented rhetoric around 465 B.C. by drawing up the rules of argument. For a fee—rarely small and sometimes astronomical—Sophists taught young Athenians the art of speaking. Their curriculum consisted not only of rhetoric, but also of the rudiments of linguistics, ethics, psychology, history, and anthropology—in other words, any aspect of "human nature" that might help an aspiring politician. Within a few years, most ambitious young Athenians of prosperous families were studying with Sophists.

At their best, Sophists sharpened young minds. Athenian tragedians, historians, and philosophers all benefited from sophistic teaching. Protagoras (b. ca. 485 B.C.), perhaps the best-known Sophist, summed up the spirit of the age in his famous dictum, "Man is the measure of all things"—an appropriate credo for the interest in all things human that is apparent in Classical literature and art. There is, however, a more troubling side to the Sophists. As teachers of rhetoric, they taught respect for success, not for truth. Thus, they acquired a reputation as word-twisters who taught men how to make "the weaker argument defeat the stronger."

Much to the distress of conservatives, Sophists drew a distinction between *nomos*, a word that means "law" or "convention," and *physis*, which means "nature." The distinction had revolutionary potential. In general, Sophists had little respect for the established order, or nomos. They considered it mere convention. A great man trained by a Sophist might rise above convention to realize the limitless potential of his nature, or physis. If he used his skill to overturn democracy and establish a tyranny, so much the worse for democracy. Indeed, the Sophists trained both unscrupulous democratic politicians and many of the oligarchs who launched coups d'état against Athenian democracy at the end of the fifth century B.C. As a result, *sophist* became a term of abuse in Athens and remains so to this day.

Classical Greek advances in rhetoric, therefore, were as problematic as they were brilliant. The Sophists influenced many different branches of thought. Consider, for example, the work of the philosopher Democritus (dee-MOCK-ruh-tus) (b. ca. 460 B.C.). Democritus was not a Sophist, but he shared the common Sophistic notion that the reality of nature was far more radical than conventionally thought. He concluded that all things consisted of tiny, indivisible particles, which could be arranged and rearranged in an infinite variety of configurations. He called these particles *atoma*, "uncuttable" (from which the word *atom* is derived).

The physicians of the Aegean island of Cos are known as Hippocratics, from Hippocrates (hih-POKruh-teez) (b. ca. 460 B.C.), the first great thinker of their school. If they were not directly influenced by the Sophists, they shared similar habits of thought. Like the Sophists, the Hippocratics were religious skeptics. They considered disease to be strictly a natural phenomenon in which the gods played no part. Hippocratic medicine was noteworthy for its methodology, which emphasized observation and prognosis (the reasoned prediction of future developments). The Hippocratics were the most rigorously naturalistic physicians to date, although no more successful in healing illness than earlier practitioners.

Socrates Ancient Greek philosopher, he was a founder of the Western philosophical tradition and is credited with the "Socratic method" of learning.

In the fifth century B.C., not all thinkers welcomed the Sophists. Their most notable critic, and the greatest of all fifth century B.C. philosophers, was **Socrates** (469–399 B.C.). Unlike the Sophists, he charged no fees, had no formal students, and did not claim to teach any positive body of knowledge. His main virtue, he believed, was his awareness of his ignorance. Unlike the Sophists, most of whom were metics, Socrates was an Athenian citizen.

Socrates, however, resembled the Sophists in his attention to political theory. Like any good Athenian citizen, Socrates served in the military—as a hoplite during the Peloponnesian War. He had his doubts about democracy, which he considered inefficient and uneducated. He preferred rule by a wise elite. Nonetheless, Socrates was too loyal an Athenian to advocate revolution.

Yet Socrates made many enemies because of his role as a self-styled "gadfly." He stung the pride of Athens's leaders by demonstrating their ignorance. Mistakenly considered a Sophist by the public because of his unconventional opinions, Socrates was tried, convicted, and executed in 399 B.C. by an Athenian court for alleged atheism and "corrupting the young." The Athenian public soon had second thoughts, and the trial of Socrates is usually considered one of history's great miscarriages of justice, as well as one of Athenian democracy's greatest blunders.

Socrates was trained in the Ionian natural philosophy tradition. He went beyond it, as the Roman thinker Cicero later said, by bringing philosophy "down from the heavens into the streets"; he changed the emphasis from the natural world to human ethics. Like most Greeks, Socrates believed that the purpose of life was the pursuit of aretê. Unlike his contemporaries, however, he did not consider aretê to be primarily excellence in battle or in public life, but rather excellence in philosophy. One became good by studying the truth, which is part of what Socrates meant by his saying "Virtue (aretê) is knowledge." He also meant that no one who truly understood goodness would ever choose to do evil.

Teach people well, Socrates says, and they will behave morally. Socrates has gone down in history as an inspiring teacher, despite his protestations of not teaching anything. His emphasis was not on research or writing, and in fact, he refused to write anything down. He believed that truth can be found only in persons, not through books—that philosophy requires a thoughtful verbal exchange. His favorite technique was to ask people difficult questions. Teaching that relies on inquiry is still called the "Socratic method."

Plato and Aristotle

Because Socrates never wrote anything down, we are dependent on others for our knowledge of him. Fortunately for us, he inspired students who committed his words and ideas to paper. Socrates' most distinguished student, and our most important source for his thought, was Plato (427–348 B.C.), who in turn was the teacher of Aristotle (384–322 B.C.). Together, these three men laid the foundations of the Western philosophical tradition. They were thinkers for the ages, but each was also a man of his times.

Socrates grew up in confident Periclean days. **Plato** (PLAY-toe) came of age during the Peloponnesian War, a period culminating in the execution of Socrates. Shocked and disillusioned, Plato turned his back on public life, although he was an Athenian citizen. Instead of discussing philosophy in public, Plato founded a private school in an Athenian suburb, the Academy. Plato held a low opinion of democracy, and when he did intervene in politics, it was not in Athens but in far-off Syracuse (in Sicily). Syracuse was governed by a tyranny, and Plato hoped to educate the tyrant's heir in philosophy—a vain hope, as it turned out.

In an attempt to recapture the stimulating give-and-take of a conversation with Socrates, Plato did not write straightforward philosophical treatises, but instead dialogues or speeches. All of Plato's dialogues have more than one speaker, and in most, the main speaker is named "Socrates." Sometimes this figure is the historical Socrates, sometimes merely a mouthpiece for ideas Plato wished to explore.

Socrates This figure emphasizes the colorful character of one of ancient Greece's greatest philosophers. Note his advanced age, unrefined face, and simple clothing. (Erich Lessing/Art Resource, NY)

A voluminous writer, Plato is not easily summarized. The word that best characterizes his legacy, though, is *idealism*, of which Plato is one of Western philosophy's greatest exponents. Like Parmenides, Plato distrusted the senses. Truth exists, but comes only by training the mind to overcome commonsense evidence. The model for Plato's philosophical method is geometry. Just as geometry deals not with this or that triangle or rectangle but with ideal forms—with a pure triangle, a pure rectangle—so the philosopher could learn to recognize purity. A philosopher would not, say, compare aretê in Athens, Sparta, and Persia; a philosopher would understand the meaning of pure, ideal aretê. No relativist, Plato believed in absolute good and evil.

Philosophy is not for everyone, according to Plato. Only a few people have the necessary intelligence and discipline. In the *Republic*, perhaps his best-known work, Plato displays his idealism and its political consequences. He envisioned a society whose elite would study philosophy and attain enlightenment. They would understand the vanity of political ambition but would accept the responsibility of governing the masses. Plato never makes clear precisely why they should assume this burden. Perhaps he was enough of a traditionalist, in spite of himself, to consider a citizen's responsibility to the polis to be obvious. In any case, Plato's ideal state was one in which philosophers would rule as kings, benevolently and unselfishly.

The ideal state would be like a small polis: self-sufficient and closed to outside corruption like Sparta, but committed to the pursuit of things intellectual like Athens. Society would be divided into three classes—philosophers, soldiers, and farmers—with admission to each class based on merit rather than heredity. Poetry and drama would be censored. Plato advocated public education and toyed with more radical notions: not only gender equality, but also the abolition of the family and private property, which he felt led to disunity and dissension.

Plato's ideas have always been controversial, but rarely ignored. The writings of his great student Aristotle better suited contemporary tastes. Originally from Macedonia, **Aristotle** spent

Plato Ancient Greek philosopher and student of Socrates, he is best known for his work, the *Republic*.

Aristotle Ancient Greek philosopher, student of Plato and tutor of Alexander the Great. His scientific writings were the most influential philosophical classics of Greek and Roman civilization and remained so during the Middle Ages.

most of his life in Athens, first as a student at the Academy, then as founder of his own school, the Lyceum (lie-SEE-um). Like Plato, Aristotle wrote dialogues, but none survive. His main surviving works are treatises, largely compilations by students of his lecture notes. One of the most wide-ranging intellectuals, Aristotle thirsted for knowledge. His writings embrace politics, ethics, poetry, botany, physics, metaphysics, astronomy, rhetoric, zoology, logic, and psychology.

Though influenced by Plato's idealism, Aristotle was a far more practical, down-to-earth thinker. His father had been a doctor, which may account for Aristotle's interest in applied science and in biology and the biological method. Unlike Plato, Aristotle placed great emphasis on observation and fieldwork and on classification and systemization.

Aristotle agreed with Plato about the existence of absolute standards of good and evil, but he emphasized the relevance of such standards to everyday life. Unlike Plato, Aristotle considered the senses important guides. Change, he believed, was not an illusion, but rather an important phenomenon. Aristotle's view of change was teleological—that is, he emphasized the goal (*telos* in Greek) of change. According to Aristotle, every organism changes and grows toward a particular end and is an integral and harmonious part of a larger whole. The entire cosmos is teleological, and each and every one of its parts has a purpose. Behind the cosmos was a principle that Aristotle called "the unmoved mover," the supreme cause of existence.

Aristotle defined an object's aretê as the fulfillment of its inherent function in the cosmos. The aretê of a horse, for example, was to be strong, fast, and obedient; the aretê of a rose was to look beautiful and smell sweet. As for the aretê of a human being, Aristotle agreed with Plato: Only the philosopher achieved true aretê. As a pragmatist, however, Aristotle did not imagine philosophers becoming kings. Even so, he did not advocate democracy, which he considered mob rule. Instead, he advocated a government of wealthy gentlemen who had been trained by philosophers—not the best regime imaginable but, in Aristotle's opinion, the best one possible.

Aristotle believed that men had stronger capacities to make judgments than women and so should rule over them. He condemned states like Sparta that accorded power to women. (See the feature, "The Written Record: Spartan Women," on page 60.) Hence, Aristotle would be cited in later centuries to justify male dominance. Ironically, however, Aristotle was more enlightened on gender issues than most of his contemporaries. For example, he believed that since women played a crucial role in the family, they should receive education in morality.

Aristotle may be the single most influential thinker in Western history. His scientific writings not only were the most influential philosophical classics of Greece, and of Rome as well, but they remained so during the Middle Ages in the Arabic and Latin worlds. It took nearly two thousand years for serious rivals to challenge Aristotle's supremacy.

Athenian Drama

Perhaps the greatest art form that emerged in the polis was drama. Modern comedy and tragedy find distant ancestors in Athens's theater of Dionysus, named for the god of unrestraint, liberation, and wine. Comedy and tragedy began in religious festivals honoring Dionysus (also known as Bacchus) but quickly became an independent forum for comment on public life. Ancient drama was poetry, not prose. Because it highlighted the relation of the individual to the community, drama proved to be the most suitable poetic medium for the ideology of the polis.

tragedy   Serious play with an unhappy ending. Greek tragedy emerged and reached its height in the fifth century B.C. in the works of Aeschylus, Sophocles, and Euripides.

According to ancient tradition, **tragedy** was first presented at the Dionysian festival in Athens by Thespis in the 530s B.C. (hence, the word *thespian* for "actor"). The first surviving tragedy dates from the 470s B.C., the first surviving comedy from the 420s B.C. A play in the fifth century B.C. consisted of a chorus (a group of performers working in unison) and three individual actors, who played all the various individual speaking parts. Plays were performed in an open-air theater on the south hillside of the Acropolis. Enormously popular, drama spread all over Greece, and eventually, most poleis had a theater.

Classical Athenian tragedy was performed at the annual Dionysia in March. Each playwright would submit a trilogy of plays on a central theme, plus a raucous farce to break the tension afterward. Comedies, which were independent plays rather than trilogies, were performed both at the Dionysia and at a separate festival held in winter. Wealthy producers competed to outfit the most lavish and impressive productions. Judges would award prizes for the best plays—a typical reflection of Greek competitiveness.

Tragedy is not easy to define, except generally: a serious play with an unhappy ending. Perhaps a short tag from the playwright Aeschylus (ESS-kih-luhs) can be said to sum up tragedy: *pathos mathei*, "suffering teaches." The essence of tragedy is what has been called the tragic sense of life: the nobility in the spectacle of a great man or woman failing but learning from failure. In *Oedipus the Tyrant* (ca. 428 B.C.) by Sophocles, for example, the hero unknowingly kills his father and

Theater at Delphi Open to the air, an ancient Greek theater contained tiers of stone benches above a circular area where the action took place, behind which backdrops could be erected. The audience often had a view of stirring scenery that, at Delphi, included the temple of Apollo and the valley below. (Vanni/Art Resource, NY)

unknowingly marries his mother. Oedipus cannot escape the consequences of his deeds, but he can react to his fate with dignity and heroism; he can try to understand it. Oedipus loses his power as tyrant and goes into exile, but he retains a degree of honor. He carries out his own punishment by blinding himself. As Aristotle observed, tragedy derives its emotional power from the fear and pity that it evokes and from the purification of the senses (*katharsis*) that it leaves in its aftermath.

The great period of Attic tragedy began and ended in the fifth century B.C. Aeschylus (525–456 B.C.), Sophocles (ca. 495–406 B.C.), and Euripides (ca. 485–406 B.C.) were and are considered the three giant playwrights. Although other tragedians wrote plays, only the works of these three men have survived. Aeschylus was perhaps the most pious of the three. His plays—notably the trilogy of the *Oresteia* (the *Agamemnon*, the *Libation Bearers*, and the *Eumenides*), the only surviving tragic trilogy, dating from 458 B.C.—take as their central question the justice of Zeus. The subject is the myth of the House of Atreus—in particular, the murder of King Agamemnon by his much-wronged wife, Clytemnestra, and her murder in turn by their son, Orestes, avenging his father. Aeschylus casts this primitive saga into an epic of the discovery of justice. In fulfillment of the will of Zeus, Athena puts an end to vengeance killings and institutes the supposed first court of law: the court of the Areopagus in Athens.

Sophocles, too, was interested in divine justice. His tragedies focus on the relationship between the individual and the community. Heroic individuals have a spark of the divine in them, but their towering virtues are threats to ordinary people. In *Antigone* (ca. 442 B.C.), for example, the heroine refuses to compromise with injustice. Her late brother had committed treason, for which his corpse is denied burial—the standard Greek punishment. Antigone, however, insists on following a higher law, Zeus's law, which demands that all bodies be buried. Turmoil, disorder, and death ensue, but Antigone stays true to principle.

Of the three tragedians, Euripides (yoo-RIP-uhdeez) is the least traditional and the most influenced by the Sophists. His plays reflect the disillusionment of the Peloponnesian War era. Euripides was more impressed by divine power than by divine justice. The central gods of Aeschylean drama are Zeus the father and Apollo the lawgiver, while Sophocles focuses on semidivine heroes, but Euripides' major deities are Dionysus and Aphrodite, goddess of erotic passion. In the *Bacchae*

(406 B.C.), for example, an arrogant young king named Pentheus is punished for refusing to recognize the power of Dionysus (Bacchus). When he goes to the hills to spy on drunken women, called "Bacchae," who are worshiping the god, he ends up as their prisoner. Driven to frenzy by Dionysus, the women do not recognize the king. Indeed, Pentheus's own mother, one of the Bacchae, mistakes him for an animal and kills him.

The changes in tragedy from Aeschylus to Euripides reflect the changes in Athens as first imperial arrogance and then the Peloponnesian War took their moral toll. Aeschylus's trust in the community's goodness gives way, first to a focus on the individual struggling to be good, and then to a fundamental doubt about the possibility of goodness. The civic order, celebrated so confidently at the end of the *Oresteia* (458 B.C.), looks less certain in Sophocles' *Oedipus* (ca. 428 B.C.), and by the time of Euripides' *Bacchae* (406 B.C.), seems feeble.

Comedy   Play with a happy ending. Greek comedy emerged and reached its first height in the fifth century B.C. in the works of Aristophanes.

Comedy, too, was invented in Athens in the Classical period. Like tragedy, comedy offers a moral commentary on contemporary Athenian life. Unlike tragedy, which is usually set in the past and takes its characters from mythology, Athenian comedy (the so-called Old Comedy) is set in the present and pokes fun at politicians and public figures.

The greatest writer of comedy in the fifth century B.C. was Aristophanes (ca. 455–385 B.C.). His extant plays are lively, ribald, even scatological, and full of allusions to contemporary politics. Aristophanes loved to show the "little guy" getting the better of the powerful and women deflating the pretensions of men. In *Lysistrata* (411 B.C.), his best-known play, he imagines the women of Greece stopping the Peloponnesian War by going on a sex strike, which forces the men to make peace.

Historical Thought and Writing

Herodotus   Credited, along with Thucydides, of founding history-writing in the West. The word *history* comes from the word *historiai* used by Herodotus.

Thucydides   Ancient Greek historian; with Herodotus, a founder of history-writing in the West.

Like drama, history flourished in the exciting intellectual atmosphere of classical Athens. Indeed, its two greatest historians, **Herodotus** (ca. 485–425 B.C.) and **Thucydides** (ca. 455–397 B.C.), are among the founders of history-writing in the West. This judgment is not meant to discount the contributions of, for example, the Hittites or Hebrews, or the chronicles, inventories, and genealogies of early Greece. Herodotus and Thucydides, however, are more rationalistic than their predecessors, and their subject matter is war, politics, peoples, and customs—what we think of as the stuff of history-writing today. Indeed, the word *history* comes from a word used by Herodotus, *historiai*, meaning "inquiries" or "research."

The works of Herodotus (*The Histories*) and Thucydides (*The Peloponnesian War*) have unifying themes. The thread through *The Histories* is the cyclical rise and fall of empires. Herodotus sees the Persian Wars as merely one episode in a vast historical drama. Again and again, hardy, disciplined peoples conquered their neighbors, grew wealthy, were corrupted by a life of luxury, and were eventually conquered in turn. Success made people arrogant, driving them to commit injustices, which were eventually punished by Zeus. The breadth of Herodotus's vision is noteworthy. A native of Halicarnassus (a polis on the southwestern coast of Anatolia; see **MAP 3.5**), Herodotus traveled widely, eventually settling in Athens. He wrote not only about Greeks, but also about Persians, Egyptians, and a host of other peoples in Europe, Asia, and Africa. (See the feature, "The Global Record: The Enemy as Barbarian," on page 71.)

Only a child at the time of the Persian Wars, Herodotus gathered information by interviewing older people in various countries, as well as by checking what limited written public records existed. Herodotus also wrote about previous centuries and places he had not visited, but with uneven accuracy. He could rarely resist a good story, and alongside solid research are tall tales, unconfirmed accounts, and myths.

Thucydides, by contrast, prided himself on accuracy. He confined himself mainly to writing about an event that he had lived through and participated in: the Peloponnesian War. A failed Athenian general, Thucydides spent most of the Peloponnesian War in exile, carefully observing, taking notes, and writing.

Like Herodotus, Thucydides was influenced by the grandeur of Classical tragedy. He also shows the signs of the Sophist movement, especially in the finely crafted speeches he includes in his writing. Thucydides' great theme is the disastrous effect of war on the human soul. In Thucydides' opinion, Periclean Athens was a high point in the history of civilization. The strain of prolonged war, however, destroyed Athens's moral fiber as well as its empire.

SECTION SUMMARY

- The culture of Greece during 480–322 B.C. is called classical because it has proved influential throughout the history of the West.

- Classical Greek sculpture was the most technically proficient sculpture seen yet, and it set a standard for all future work.

- The Athenian Socrates changed the emphasis of Greek philosophy from nature to human ethics.

- The idealist philosopher Plato and his more practical student, Aristotle, are the most influential philosophers of the West.

- Comedy and tragedy were invented in Athens, flourished in public festivals, and offered a moral commentary on contemporary life.

- Herodotus and Thucydides are among the founders of history-writing in the West.

CHAPTER SUMMARY

Western philosophy, science, politics, sculpture, painting, and literary genres, such as comedy, tragedy, and history, all emerged in Archaic and Classical Greece.

The focus of ancient Greek life between ca. 750 and ca. 350 B.C. was the polis. Trade, colonization, and the invention of the Greek alphabet and of the hoplite phalanx all contributed to the emergence of the polis around 750–700 B.C. Earlier, in the Bronze Age, Minoan and Mycenaean kingdoms had ruled Greek lands. Homer evoked their memory brilliantly in the *Iliad* and *Odyssey* around 725 B.C. but, by then, the spirit of Greek civilization had changed radically. The Bronze Age kingdoms were palace economies, dominated by a noble elite. The polis was a city-state that emphasized participation and equality and invented the idea of the citizen.

Archaic Sparta developed Greece's best citizen-army whose job was to prevent helot uprisings or attacks from abroad. Sparta's stable government and austere culture fostered the idea that public duty is more important than private advantage. Archaic Corinth is the prime example of tyranny, a widespread form of government in Greece in which new wealth led to the emergence of popular champions. Archaic Athens developed, thanks to Solon's reforms, a large class of independent small farmers. They later turned out to be the backbone of democracy. Solon unintentionally created conditions for the growth of slavery.

The culture of Archaic Greece was the seedbed of Western individualism and rationalism. Lyric poetry emphasized individual emotion, and Archaic sculpture focused on the human body. Although Archaic Greece was a religious society, it also gave rise to the first philosophers. They lived in Ionia in the 500s B.C. and offered a nontheological explanation of nature.

Democracy or "people power" (*demokratia*) began in ancient Greece, and the Athenian version is best known. Athenian democracy was direct and participatory but limited to adult males. Classical Greece was a period of intense war. Athens and Sparta united to lead a Greek coalition that defeated Persia's invasion in 480–479 B.C. Afterward, the two poleis turned on each other, most violently in the Peloponnesian War (431–404 B.C.). With its democracy, freedom, and high culture, Athens stands for one aspect of the achievement of the polis; with its hierarchy, militarism, and citizen virtue, Sparta stands for another.

Classical Greek culture has proved influential again and again in the history of the West. Athens became Greece's cultural center. Here, comedy and tragedy were invented, history-writing was founded, sculpture reached a peak of proficiency in showing the human body, and philosophy changed its emphasis from nature to human ethics. The philosophers Socrates, Plato, and Aristotle are among the West's greatest thinkers.

FOCUS QUESTIONS

- How did early Greece develop before the polis and what light do the Homeric poems shed on its history?

- What was the Greek polis, and how did it develop in Sparta, Athens, and Corinth in Archaic Greece?

- How did Western individualism and rationalism take root in Archaic Greece?

- What was Athenian democracy and how did it clash with Sparta in the Peloponnesian War?

- How did tragedy, comedy, philosophy, and history all begin and develop in the culture of Classical Greece?

KEY TERMS

Minoan (p. 51)

Mycenaeans (p. 51)

Homer (p. 51)

arête (p. 54)

Archaic Greece (p. 54)

polis (p. 54)

hoplite phalanx (p. 56)

Solon (p. 62)

Sappho (p. 63)

Classical Greece (p. 64)

demokratia (p. 66)

Pericles (p. 68)

Sophists (p. 76)

Socrates (p. 76)

Plato (p. 77)

Aristotle (p. 77)

tragedy (p. 78)

comedy (p. 80)

Herodotus (p. 80)

Thucydides (p. 80)

This icon will direct you to additional materials on the website: www.cengage.com/history/noble/westciv6e

See our interactive eBook for map and primary source activities.

NOTES

1. Charles Rowan Beye, *Ancient Greek Literature and Society*, 2d ed. (Ithaca, N.Y.: Cornell University Press, 1987), p. 78.

2. Ibid., p. 79.

3. Herodotus, *The Histories*, trans. Barry S. Strauss.

4. Thucydides, *The Peloponnesian War*, trans. Barry S. Strauss.

CHAPTER OUTLINE

Philip and Alexander

The Hellenistic Kingdoms, 323–30 B.C.

Hellenistic Culture

The Turn Inward: New Philosophies, New Faiths

Stag Hunt Pebble mosaic from Pella
(HIP/Art Resource, NY)

Alexander the Great and the Spread of Greek Civilization, ca. 350–30 B.C.

The young men in the pebble mosaic shown opposite wield ax and sword against the stag whom they are hunting. The artist, named Gnosis, was a master at rendering perspective and drama. Clearly, no expense was spared on the work, dated around 325 B.C. Both the vigor of the scene and the quality of the craftsmanship symbolize the spirit of a young man who was born in Pella, the Macedonian (mah-seh-DOE-nee-un) capital where the mosaic was displayed: That man was Alexander the Great. Alexander was a fearless warrior and one of the most brilliant generals in the history of the world. In just twelve years, he conquered all the territory between Greece and India, as well as Egypt.

Alexander created new realities of power as king of Macedon (r. 336–323 B.C.). A northeastern Greek kingdom that had previously been only a fringe power, Macedon rose meteorically under Alexander's father, Philip II (r. 359–336 B.C.), to become the leading military power in Greece. Philip was a brilliant and ambitious general, but Alexander outstripped him.

Alexander laid the foundations of a new Greek world: the world of the Hellenistic (hel-len-IS-tik) period (323–30 B.C.), in which Hellenic, or Greek, language and civilization spread and were transformed. This era was distinct in many ways from the preceding Hellenic period (ca. 750–323 B.C.). In Hellenistic times, Macedonians and Greeks replaced Persians as the ruling people of Egypt and western Asia. Large numbers of Greek-speaking colonists moved south and east. Governed by Macedonian dynasties, Egypt and the Levant became integral parts of the Greek world and remained so until the Arab conquest in the seventh century A.D. Greek-speaking kingdoms thrived briefly as far east as modern Afghanistan and Pakistan.

Conquest put huge amounts of wealth into Greek hands. Alexander and his successors built great new cities: Antioch (AN-tee-ock) in Syria, Pergamum in Anatolia, Seleucia (seh-LOO-she-uh) in Mesopotamia, and, greatest of all, Alexandria in Egypt. Trade increased and expanded southward and eastward. In political life, individual cities continued to be important, but federal leagues (that is, unions of city-states) and monarchies ruled most of the Greek-speaking world.

Material and political expansion led to unanticipated cultural changes, which may be summarized as a turn inward. Frequently finding themselves among strange peoples, the Greeks sought comfort in new philosophies, religions, and modes of literary and artistic

FOCUS QUESTIONS

- How did Macedon under Philip and Alexander conquer both the Greek city-states and the Persian Empire?

- What new states emerged as a result of Alexander's conquests and how did they integrate Greek settlers with native peoples?

- How did Greek civilization spread during the Hellenistic era, and what were the main trends in literature, science, and art?

- What new philosophies and religions emerged in the Hellenistic period?

 This icon will direct you to additional materials on the website: www .cengage.com/ history/noble/ westciv6e

e **See our interactive eBook for map and primary source activities.**

Virtues and Vices of Alexander the Great

Writing in the second century A.D., four centuries after Alexander's death, the historian Arrian composed from earlier accounts what is now the best surviving history of Alexander. A military man himself, Arrian appreciated Alexander's skills but was not blind to his flaws.

Alexander died in the 114th Olympiad, in the archon ship of Hegesias at Athens [June 323 B.C.]. He lived, as Aristobulus tells us, thirty-two years and eight months, and reigned twelve years and eight months. He had great personal beauty, invincible power of endurance, and a keen intellect; he was brave and adventurous, strict in the observance of his religious duties, and hungry for fame. Most temperate in the pleasures of the body, his passion was for glory only, and in that he was insatiable. He had an uncanny instinct for the right course in a difficult and complex situation, and was most happy in his deductions from observed facts. In arming and equipping troops and in his military dispositions he was always masterly. Noble indeed was his power of inspiring his men, of filling them with confidence, and, in the moment of danger, of sweeping away their fear by the spectacle of his own fearlessness. When risks had to be taken, he took them with the utmost boldness, and his ability to seize the moment for a swift blow, before the enemy had any suspicion of what was coming, was beyond praise. No cheat or liar ever caught him off guard, and both his word and his bond were inviolable. Spending but little on his own pleasures, he poured out his money without stint for the benefit of his friends.

Doubtless, in the passion of the moment Alexander sometimes erred; it is true he took some steps towards the pomp and arrogance of the Asiatic kings: but I, at least, cannot feel that such errors were very heinous, if the circumstances are taken fairly into consideration. For, after all, he was young; the chain of his successes was unbroken, and, like all kings, past, present, and to come, he was surrounded by courtiers who spoke to please, regardless of what evil their word might do. On the other hand, I do indeed know that Alexander, of all the monarchs of old, was the only one who had the nobility of heart to be sorry for his mistakes.... In the course of this book I have, admittedly, found fault with some of the things which Alexander did, but of the man himself I am not ashamed to express ungrudging admiration.

QUESTIONS

1. What are Alexander's main virtues, according to Arrian?
2. In what way does Arrian find fault with Alexander?
3. For Arrian, what is the "bottom line" about Alexander?

Source: From *The Campaigns of Alexander* by Arrian, translated Aubrey de Sélincourt, revised with an introduction and notes by J. R. Hamilton (Penguin Classics, 1958, revised edition 1971). Copyright © the Estate of Aubrey de Sélincourt, 1958. Introduction and Notes copyright © J. R. Hamilton, 1971. Reproduced by permission of Penguin Books Ltd.

Alexander Mosaic   This detail of a Roman-era mosaic from Pompeii shows Alexander the Great in battle, probably at Issus. Shining in his battle armor, Alexander is bareheaded, with a wide-eyed, intense gaze betokening his power. The larger scene includes the Persian king Darius, fleeing in his chariot.   (Scala/Art Resource, NY)

THE HELLENISTIC KINGDOMS, 323–30 B.C.

What new states emerged as a result of Alexander's conquests and how did they integrate Greek settlers with native peoples?

Variety, flexibility, and the creation of a new elite to transmit Greek culture compose the Hellenistic political legacy. Hellenistic political units ranged from multiethnic kingdoms to small, ethnically homogeneous city-states (see **Map 4.2**). The Greek peninsula saw both a monarchy, with republican leanings, as well as experiments in federalism and social revolution. In Asia and Egypt, a new ruling elite emerged, consisting both of Greeks and Macedonians and of natives. Although the first group tended to dominate high office, natives were by no means excluded. The immigrants wanted land, wealth, or adventure. Their paths were smoothed by a new ideology that identified being Greek less with loyalty to an individual city than with participation in a common Greek civilization.

Although the Hellenistic world became relatively peaceful after 275 B.C., conflict among the kingdoms continued. Generally waged at a low level of intensity, with bribes and diplomacy as weapons, the conflict nonetheless sometimes broke out into major battles. A number of small states emerged in Anatolia, notably Pergamum, whose wealthy rulers were patrons of literature and art, and Galatia (guh-LAY-shuh), carved out by Celtic invaders from Europe.

Colonialism, Greek Style

Many Greeks and Macedonians emigrated during the fourth and third centuries B.C., but we do not know how many. The few available statistics indicate a significant migration but not a mass exodus. By the second century B.C., the colonizing impulse had diminished in Greece and Macedon, but a large number of Jews left war-torn Judea, particularly for Egypt. Ptolemaic Egypt and the Seleucid realm were also the most common destinations for Greek and Macedonian migrants.

Greek migrants could take advantage of a new definition of being Greek that had begun to emerge even before Alexander's conquests. Isocrates (eye-SOCK-rah-teez) (428–338 B.C.), an Athenian thinker, redefined Greek identity by promoting the idea that Greece was not a collection of city-states but a civilization. "The people we call Hellenes"—that is, Greeks—he wrote, "are those who have the same culture as us, not the same blood."[1]

The ideal of Greek culture made it easier for the migrants to maintain a Greek identity. For that matter, it was now possible for foreigners to become Greek by learning the Greek language and literature. The number of Hellenized foreigners was relatively small, yet their very existence marked a break from the Classical polis, where even a resident genius, such as Aristotle, could not obtain Athenian citizenship because he was not of Athenian descent.

The Greek language also served as a common denominator, along with Aramaic, both of which became the languages of trade in the eastern Mediterranean. To get a sense of the importance of Isocrates' redefinition of **Hellenism**, consider that one of the most famous Greek-speakers of all antiquity was Paul, the Christian apostle who was born a Jew in Tarsus, a city in southern Anatolia.

Hellenism Term used to designate ancient Greece's language, culture, and civilization.

Immigrants sought to realize dreams of prosperity or adventure. Although agriculture was the main economic pursuit, trade, industry, finance, administration, and military service also offered opportunities.

In the Ptolemaic and Seleucid realms, administration was a joint effort of both immigrants and natives. The upper ranks of government were dominated by Greeks and Macedonians, while native elites usually held low- or mid-level government positions. Especially after about 200 B.C., some natives even reached high office. Others worked in the traditional native administrative structures that survived largely intact in the new kingdoms—for example, as judges or village headmen or priests.

To create a hereditary military group in the countryside, Ptolemy (TOL-eh-mee) I settled his soldiers on land grants there. Native Egyptians were excluded from the army at first, although they served as policemen, but by the second century B.C., the dynasty needed native

Egyptians too as soldiers. In return, natives now received land, tax breaks, and the right to call themselves Hellenes. Their Hellenism sometimes just scratched the surface, but other times it went deeper.

An Egyptian named Plenis, a villager in Middle Egypt in the late second century B.C., is a good example. Plenis was a tenant farmer on a royal estate and a priest in a local Egyptian cult. Like his father before him, Plenis served as a soldier in the Ptolemaic army. Plenis could write Greek as well as Egyptian, and he even used a Greek name: Dionysius, son of Kephalas.

Temples, which often administered large estates, represented important sources of local power. Because priests shaped local opinion, they demanded royal patronage. Both **Ptolemies** and **Seleucids** complied: from Babylon to Edfu, money poured into temple-building and renovation.

The Seleucids addressed the security needs of their far-flung realms by establishing over seventy colonies extending to central Asia. Some colonies were civilian, but most were military, composed of retired or reserve soldiers, mostly Greeks or Macedonians, but also Jews and other non-Greek peoples. Colonists received land allotments. Greek-style public buildings were erected, and some cities were laid out according to a rectilinear grid reminiscent of the Classical polis. The gymnasium attained a great practical and symbolic importance as both the center of Greek culture and the preparatory school for entry into the elite. The Hellenistic gymnasium offered education in literature, philosophy, and oratory as well as athletics.

Some Seleucid colonies developed into flourishing Greek cities, particularly in Anatolia and on the coast of Syria. Greek urbanization should not create the false impression, however, that the Seleucids were motivated by some civilizing mission. They were not. They established colonies to increase their power.

Economic Expansion

Immigration and colonization were not the only sources of new economic opportunities. At the beginning of the Hellenistic era, Alexander turned the huge gold and silver reserves of Persia into coinage and released it onto the market virtually all at once. The result was about seventy-five years of inflation, but also a commercial boom. In particular, money largely replaced barter in Egypt, which increased production and trade, helping to render Egypt an economic powerhouse. Another stimulus to trade was the creation of thriving new Hellenistic cities, especially Alexandria with its great harbors, canals, marketplaces, and infrastructure of banks, inns, courts, and shipbuilding facilities.

During Hellenistic times, commerce tended to shift from Greece proper to Anatolia and Egypt (see **MAP 4.3**). The island of Rhodes, located off the southwest tip of Anatolia, grew into a major trading center, especially for grain. The Rhodian aristocracy grew rich off taxes and duties, wisely reinvesting a portion of the profits in naval infrastructure (such as arsenals and dockyards) and in campaigns against pirates. Egypt, too, had many products to trade. Grain was the most important, but textiles, glass, papyrus, and luxury goods were also significant. A network of canals connecting Alexandria to the Nile and the Red Sea beyond made trading possible with Sudan, Arabia, and India.

The Seleucid kingdoms controlled trade routes to the east. Commerce benefited from good roads, safe sea travel between the Persian Gulf and India, and a unified royal coinage. The Seleucids traded agricultural goods and manufactured products for spices from India and Arabia. In the first century B.C., they even imported silk from China. The kingdom of Pergamum, which stretched inland from Anatolia's northwest coast, exported its rich agricultural products, as well as the local gray-blue building stone and, as an alternative to Egyptian papyrus, parchment.

Slavery was an important part of the Hellenistic social and economic scene. Although war and piracy were the main sources of enslavement, some people were born into slavery. In Sicily and southern Italy, slaves worked huge plantations, but eastern Mediterranean slaves were commonly found in the household or in administration, and in cities rather than in the countryside. Many unfree laborers worked on farms in Egypt and western Asia. Following the pre-Greek traditions of those regions, they were generally tenant farmers tied to kings or potentates rather than outright slaves.

Ptolemies Dynasty founded by Ptolemy I and ruled by Egyptian kings; it was the wealthiest, most sophisticated, and longest lasting of the Hellenistic kingdoms.

Seleucids Dynasty founded by Seleucus and governed by rulers of Anatolia from 312 to 64 B.C., it established seventy colonies throughout the Near East.

🌐 **MAP 4.3—The Eastern Mediterranean, ca. 200 B.C.**

The great Hellenistic powers contended for control of this vibrant, turbulent, and prosperous region. Conflict centered on Palestine and the Aegean islands, the rulership of which frequently changed hands.

On some plantations, conditions for slaves were harsh enough to lead to mass uprisings. It was not unusual, however, for domestic or administrative slaves to buy their freedom, sometimes using savings they were allowed to keep, sometimes borrowing money from the master or from friends. Greeks enslaved fellow Greeks, but often, it seems, with guilty consciences; they frequently made special efforts to help Greek slaves win their freedom. Even in bondage, therefore, Greeks had special privileges.

Macedon and Greece

Macedon was the last of the three great Hellenistic kingdoms to emerge from civil war after Alexander's death. Not until 276 B.C. was Antigonus Gonatas, grandson of Alexander's general Antigonus the One-Eyed, established firmly on the throne. His Antigonid (an-TIG-on-id) dynasty lasted about a century, when the Romans conquered Macedon.

True to the traditions of Macedon, the **Antigonids** projected an image of simplicity and toughness. As a young man, Antigonus had studied the new school of Stoic philosophy in Athens (see pages 103–104). As king, he devoted himself to the Stoic dictates of duty, describing his office as "noble servitude" and his diadem as a mere "rag." Antigonus shared the traditional Macedonian ambition to dominate the Greek city-states, but he faced rival powers. Besides Ptolemaic Egypt, there was the kingdom of Epirus in northwestern Greece and two new federal leagues in the south, the Aetolians (ay-TOL-ee-unz) (north of the Corinthian Gulf) and the Achaeans (uh-KEE-unz) (in the Peloponnesus; see **MAP 4.3**).

The new leagues were dominated by the wealthy; they were not democracies. Yet, the leagues interest us as models of federalism that would one day influence the founders of the

Antigonids Dynasty founded by Antigonus Gonatas in 276 B.C. and governed by Macedonian rulers for about 140 years, until the Roman conquest.

United States. The Achaeans, for example, successfully balanced local and federal authorities. Affiliated cities kept their own constitutions while recognizing federal jurisdiction. The federal government consisted of a governing general (both president and commander-in-chief) and ten subordinate magistrates, an executive council, and a general assembly.

Extremes of wealth and poverty, problems of debt, and class conflict challenged Hellenistic Greece. Athens remained a vibrant democracy until the late third century B.C., when the oligarchic upper classes finally won the upper hand for good. The wealthy now contributed less to the public good in taxes and amassed private fortunes instead. Still, they usually made just enough concessions to avoid full-scale revolution.

Sparta was an exception. In the late third century B.C., a social revolution was launched from above by Agis and Cleomenes, two Spartan kings working together. After defeat in the fourth century B.C., Sparta had become impoverished (see page 72). The reformers now offered debt relief, redistribution of land, and restoration of Classical Spartan austerity and equality. Popular in Sparta, the revolution threatened to spread elsewhere. Peloponnesian oligarchs called in Macedonian forces, which crushed Sparta in 222 B.C. and ended the revolution.

Ptolemaic Egypt

The wealthiest, most sophisticated, and longest-lasting Hellenistic kingdom was Ptolemaic Egypt. One of Alexander's great generals, Ptolemy (d. 283 B.C.), founded a dynasty that lasted until Rome annexed Egypt in 30 B.C., after the suicide of the last ruler of the line, Queen Cleopatra (see pages 133–134). By then, Rome had already conquered or annexed all the other Hellenistic kingdoms.

Unlike the Antigonids, the Ptolemies gloried in wealth and grandeur. Ptolemy I showed the way to his successors when he had Alexander's funeral procession hijacked on its way to Macedonia and established a tomb and then a cult in the capital city, **Alexandria**—a Greek hero-shrine in the land of the pyramids. Ptolemy I made arrangements to have himself proclaimed "savior god" after his death; his successors, less reticent, took divine honors while still alive.

Like the pharaohs, the Ptolemies intervened in the Egyptian economy on a massive scale. Putting to use the science of the Museum, the great institute in Alexandria (see pages 96–97), the Ptolemies sponsored irrigation and land reclamation projects, the introduction of new crops (for example, new varieties of wheat), and the greatly expanded cultivation of old ones (such as grapes for wine).

Most of the people of Egypt made their living in agriculture, either as independent small farmers or as tenants on large estates. Government enriched itself through taxes, rents, demands for compulsory labor, state monopolies (on such diverse items as oils, textiles, and beer), and various internal tolls and customs duties. The result was boom times under strong kings and queens in the third century B.C. Egypt became the most prosperous part of the Hellenistic world, and Alexandria became the wealthiest, most populous city in the Mediterranean, as well as its literary capital (see **MAP 4.3**). In the second century B.C., however, continued economic prosperity was derailed by decline, which created conditions for revolt.

To defeat the Seleucids at the Battle of Raphia in Gaza in 217 B.C., the Ptolemies had to enroll thousands of Egyptians in the Macedonian phalanx, because of a shortage of Greek mercenaries. Emboldened by their new military power, people in Upper Egypt soon broke into armed revolt against the government in far-off Alexandria. Rival kings appeared in the south, and unrest continued for about a century.

To advance their cause, the rebels inflamed anti-Greek sentiment. High taxes and regional rivalries, however, probably carried

Tanagra Figurine A terra-cotta (baked clay) statuette of around 320 B.C. shows a modestly dressed woman wearing a hat and carrying a fan. Named for its place of manufacture in Greece, this popular style of figure demonstrates the Hellenistic taste for ordinary, household themes. (Bildarchiv Preussischer Kulturbesitz/Art Resource, NY)

Egyptians Versus Greeks in a Temple

This second-century B.C. papyrus, a petition to the authorities from a Greek worshiper of Serapis, provides insight into relations between Greeks and Egyptians in Hellenistic Egypt. It shows how Greeks lived in the temple at Memphis in order to worship Serapis, a Hellenized Egyptian god (see page 105). It also depicts violence and hostility across ethnic lines.

To Dionysius, general and one of the "friends" [of the king], from Ptolemy son of Glaucias, a Macedonian, one of those "held in detention" [that is, on a voluntary, religious retreat] for twelve years in the great Temple of Serapis in Memphis. As I have suffered grave injustice and my life has been frequently endangered by the temple cleaners whose names are listed below, I am taking refuge with you in the belief that in this way I would best secure justice. For on ... [November 9, 161 B.C.] they came to the temple of Astarte, which is in the sanctuary, and in which I have been living "in detention" for the number of years mentioned above; some of them had stones in their hand and others sticks, and they tried to force their way in, in order to seize the opportunity to plunder the temple and to put me to death because I am a Greek, like men laying a plot against my life. But when I anticipated them and shut the door of the temple, and shouted to them to withdraw in peace, they did not go away even so. When Diphilus, one of the worshipers held "in detention" by Serapis besides me, expressed indignation at their

conduct in such a temple, they pushed him back, handled him very roughly and beat him up, so that their lawless brutality was clear for all to see. When these same men treated me in the same way in....[November 163 B.C.], I immediately addressed a petition to you, but as I had no one to look after the matter further, they were let off scot-free and became even more arrogant. I therefore ask you, if you please, to order them to be brought before you, so that they may receive the punishment they deserve for all these misdeeds. Farewell.

QUESTIONS

1. What is the complaint of Ptolemy, son of Glaucias, about? Is this the first time he has made such a complaint?

2. Why was Ptolemy unable to get justice before? What does this tell us about the way petitions were handled by the government?

3. Why were Ptolemy and Diphilus attacked? What does the attack indicate about Greek-Egyptian relations in second century B.C. Egypt?

Source: Adapted from M. M. Austin, *The Hellenistic World from Alexander, to the Roman Conquest: A Selection of Ancient Sources in Translation,* 2/e, 2006, p.536. Reprinted with the permission of Cambridge University Press.

---

more weight than nationalism in the minds of most people. Although friction between immigrants and natives sparked from time to time, most Egyptians accepted the Ptolemies as pharaohs as long as they brought peace and prosperity. (See the feature, "The Global Record: Egyptians Versus Greeks in a Temple.")

And the Ptolemies reasserted their power. In 196 B.C., for example, Ptolemy V Epiphanes celebrated his coronation in full pharaonic ceremonial in Memphis. Egyptian priests commemorated the occasion in a decree written in Egypt's traditional language of kingship in a trilingual inscription (Greek, hieroglyphic, and demotic—ordinary—Egyptian). This inscription, discovered by French soldiers in 1799 and dubbed the Rosetta stone (named for the place where it was found), led to the modern European deciphering of hieroglyphics.

Despite the frictions, evidence points to native settler cooperation, especially in the countryside, where intermarriage and bilingualism became common. Many an ordinary Greek became fully assimilated to Egyptian ways, and even wealthy, sophisticated, urban Greeks adopted a smattering of Egyptian customs. By 98 B.C., assimilation was evident in the cultural hybrid of a group of 18- and 19-year-old male youths who received traditional Greek military and literary training but prayed to Egypt's crocodile-god.

Alexandria Thriving Hellenistic city in northern Egypt founded by Alexander the Great in 332 B.C.

Western Asia

The kingdom founded by Alexander's general Seleucus (suh-LOO-kus) (ca. 358–281 B.C.) experienced shifting borders and inhabitants. The Seleucid kingdom began when Seleucus took Babylon in 312 B.C. and ended in 64 B.C. when Syria became a Roman province. Many territorial changes occurred in between. The first three kings ruled a domain stretching from the Aegean to Bactria (BACK-tree-uh) (modern Afghanistan), but by the early second century B.C., most of the Iranian Plateau and lands eastward had been lost. At its height, in the third century B.C., the Seleucid kingdom had three nerve centers: Ionia (in western Anatolia), with a capital at Sardis; Syria, with a capital at Antioch; and Babylonia, whose capital was Seleucia-on-the-Tigris (near modern Baghdad; see **Map 4.2**).

The far-flung and multiethnic Seleucid lands presented an enormous administrative challenge. The kings took over the Persian system of satraps (provincial governors), taxes, and royal roads and post (see page 35), to which they added a Macedonian-style army, a common coinage, and a Hellenistic ruler cult. The chief Seleucid innovation was the establishment of colonies. Greek and Macedonian soldiers and administrators dominated, but natives also filled bureaucratic slots.

The greatest Seleucid city was **Antioch**, which became one of the wealthiest and most luxurious of all eastern Mediterranean cities; only Ptolemaic Alexandria outstripped it. The intellectual and artistic capital of Greek Asia in Hellenistic times, however, was not Antioch but Pergamum, in northwestern Anatolia (see **Map 4.3**).

The rulers of Pergamum, the Attalid dynasty of kings, carved out a small kingdom that became independent of the Seleucids in 263 B.C. and fell into Roman hands in 133 B.C. The Attalids made Pergamum into a showplace of Greek civilization, a would-be second Athens. As in Athens, public building was focused on a steep acropolis. The upper city of Pergamum

Antioch   Located near the present-day Turkish-Syrian border, it was the greatest of the cities founded by Seleucus, a general of Alexander the Great.

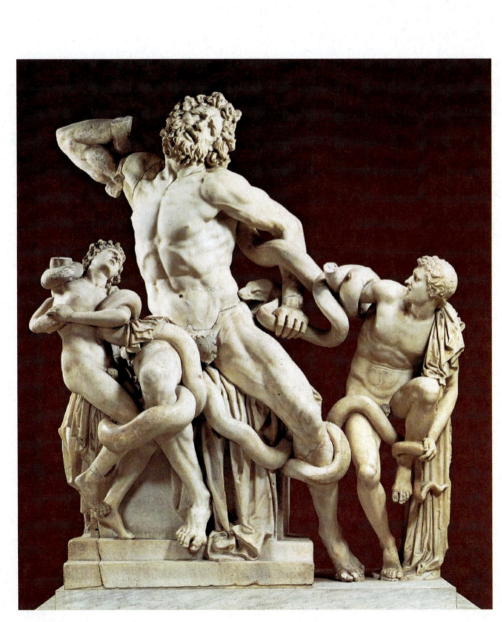

Laocoön   This famous statue group of the second or first century B.C. shows the Trojan priest Laocoön and his sons being strangled by snakes sent by the gods. The scene's emphasis on extreme emotion is typical of Hellenistic art. (Scala/Art Resource, NY)

was laid out on hillside terraces, rising to a palace and fortified citadel. One of the terraces housed the famous Pergamum Altar, a huge monument to an Attalid victory over the Celts, who first invaded Anatolia in 278 B.C. and whose advance the Attalids checked. They could not, however, stop the Celts from settling in central Anatolia, where they created their kingdom of Galatia.

Pergamum was famous for its sculptors and for a library second only to Alexandria's. Pergamene writers focused on scholarship, to the exclusion of poetry, perhaps as a result of the influence of Stoic philosophers, who disapproved of poetry's emotionalism.

The Greco-Indian Interaction

The Seleucids' hold on Alexander's vast eastern domains turned out to be temporary. A new Persian dynasty, the Parthians (PAR-thee-unz), achieved independence in the mid-third century B.C. and over the next century, extended westward into Mesopotamia. But to the east, Bactria remained Greek, if not Seleucid. From the mid-third century B.C., an independent Greek **Bactria** prospered (see **MAP 4.2**).

Vivid evidence of Greek colonization in Bactria comes from the site of Aï Khanum (its ancient name is unknown) in northern Afghanistan. This prosperous and populous city contained many reminders of Greece, among them a gymnasium, theater, and library. A pillar in the gymnasium was inscribed in the mid-third century B.C., with 140 moral maxims from Delphi in Greece, over 3,000 miles away.

In the second century B.C., Bactrian kings extended their rule into the Indus River valley and the Punjab, a region with a modest Greek presence since the fifth century B.C., when the Persians settled Greek mercenaries there. Virtually no literary evidence survives, but monuments and, particularly, coins demonstrate Greco-Indian cultural interaction. For example, some coins from the second century B.C. show bilingual inscriptions in Greek and Indian languages. Their designs include a variety of Indian religious motifs, such as the lotus plant, symbol of Lakshmi, goddess of wealth and good fortune. Indians admired Hellenistic astronomy; one text goes so far as to say that Greek scientists should be "reverenced like gods."

The Hellenistic world seems to have intrigued King Asoka (uh-SO-kuh) (r. ca. 270–230 B.C.), who ruled almost the entire Indian subcontinent. Asoka is best remembered as a religious reformer. A convert to Buddhism, he played a major role in its spread, which proceeded under the slogan of *dhamma*— that is, "morality" or "righteousness." One of his inscriptions apparently records embassies, aimed at spreading Buddhism, to the Hellenistic kingdoms.[2]

The envoys apparently found few converts, for it is difficult to find any trace of Buddhism in Hellenistic Greek culture, at least outside the Greco-Indian kingdoms. There, one of the most powerful Greek rulers, Menander Soter Dikaios (r. ca. 155–130 B.C.), may have converted to Buddhism in the mid-second century B.C. But certain aspects of Indian religion—especially India's powerful currents of asceticism, mysticism, and monasticism—interested Greek intellectuals around the Mediterranean in Hellenistic and Roman times. Observers on Alexander's expedition, Hellenistic envoys, merchants, and philosophers in search of Eastern wisdom all served as conduits between East and West. One of the most influential was Megasthenes, a Seleucid ambassador to the court of Asoka's grandfather, who published his *Indika*, a description of India, around 300 B.C.

Bactria   Bactria flourished as an independent Greek-ruled state in what is today Afghanistan, beginning in the mid-third century B.C., and expanded into what is today India and Pakistan.

A Greek-Influenced Indian Statue   This figure of a *bodhisattva* ("enlightened one") belongs to the Gandharan school, which was heavily influenced by Hellenistic sculpture. The statue's proportions, facial features, and draped clothing particularly recall Hellenistic motifs, suggesting that it may be the work of a Greek sculptor.   (Photograph courtesy of the Royal Ontario Museum, © ROM)

SECTION SUMMARY

- Greek and Macedonian colonists and their descendants dominated the army and administration in the Ptolemaic and Seleucid kingdoms, but natives played a role as well.

- Greek culture made only a small impact in the multiethnic kingdoms of the Ptolemies and Seleucids; native cultures flourished.

- The Antigonid dynasty of Macedon and federal leagues joined city-states as prominent features of Hellenistic Greek political life.

- Ptolemaic Egypt, with its capital of Alexandria, was the wealthiest, most sophisticated, and longest lasting Hellenistic kingdom.

- Seleucid Antioch and Attalid Pergamum were new and thriving cities of Hellenistic southwest Asia.

- Hellenistic Greek kingdoms prospered for centuries in parts of Afghanistan, India, and Pakistan.

Yet, the degree to which this interest influenced Greek and Roman culture is debatable. Although ancient writers mention Greek or Roman philosophers who were attracted by Indian culture, modern scholars tend to be cautious. The ancients had a weakness for tall tales and exotic stories. For example, the great Neo-Platonic philosopher Plotinus (A.D. 235–270) is reported to have traveled with the Roman emperor Gordian's army eastward, hoping in vain to reach India. Some scholars see Indian influence in Plotinus's mysticism and pantheism, but others dismiss the idea.

Central Asian nomads overran Bactria in the late second century B.C. The Hellenistic kingdoms of India and Pakistan, however, survived until about the time of Christ, and some Greek communities lasted until the fifth century A.D. The Gandharan sculptors who flourished in a formerly Greek-ruled region in about A.D. 200 used Greek artistic techniques to depict Buddhist subjects, which might suggest the impact of Indian culture on the remaining Greek population.

HELLENISTIC CULTURE

How did Greek civilization spread during the Hellenistic era, and what were the main trends in literature, science, and art?

The capital of Egypt, Alexandria, was also the main laboratory for transforming Hellenistic Greek culture and so facilitating its spread. By the first century B.C., Alexandria was a city of half a million or more inhabitants. It was one of the largest and wealthiest cities in the world. The bulk of the people were Egyptian, but Greeks and Jews made up large minorities, and no one would have been surprised, in this cosmopolitan center, to see an Indian or a Celt, an Italian or a Persian.

Archaeologists today, looking for submerged parts of the city in Alexandria harbor, have found Egyptian sphinxes and obelisks, as well as Greek statues. Written sources portray a picture of social change in the elite, an increase in leisure time, a growth in educational opportunities for both sexes, royal patronage of culture, and the value of even a limited knowledge of Greek literature as the ticket to advancement.

Athens and Alexandria

In 294 B.C., King Ptolemy I invited the deposed tyrant of Athens, Demetrius of Phalerum, to found an institution of culture in Alexandria. Demetrius had studied with Aristotle's successor at the Lyceum, Theophrastus (the-uh-FRAS-tus) (ca. 370–288 B.C.), a practical man interested in compiling and cataloging knowledge.

Museum Literally "House of the Muses," the Museum was Alexandria's most important scholarly and scientific center. It included the Library, which housed the world's largest collection of Greek writing.

The new institution was called the **Museum** (literally, "House of the Muses," or the home of the female deities who inspired creativity). The Museum was a residence, study, and lecture hall for scholars, scientists, and poets. It was also a research center to keep the king's engineers up to date on new technology for warfare and agriculture. One of the Museum's key components was the Library, in its day, the largest collection of Greek writing in the world. In the third century B.C.—at the height of the Ptolemaic kingdom—the Library contained 700,000 papyrus rolls, the equivalent of roughly 50,000 modern books. Its nearest competitor, at Pergamum, contained less than a third as many rolls. The Library reflects the growth of the Hellenistic reading and writing public. The names of over a thousand writers of the Hellenistic era survive, and after 300 B.C., anthologies, abridgments, and school texts multiplied.

Though modeled on Athens's Lyceum, the Museum represented a break from the public culture of the Classical period. The residents of the Museum were an elite, dependent on royal patronage and self-consciously Greek and not Egyptian. One wit dismissed them as pedants and "fatted fowls that quarrel without end in the hen coop of the Muses."

The background to Alexandrian literature is Hellenistic Athenian literature, which diverged sharply from its Classical roots. The greatest Hellenistic Athenian writer, a man famous throughout the ancient world, was Menander (ca. 342–292 B.C.). He was the master of a style of comedy called "New Comedy," as distinguished from the "Old Comedy" of Aristophanes, which had flourished a century earlier (see page 80). Where Old Comedy was raucous and ribald, New Comedy was restrained; where Old Comedy focused on public matters such as war and politics, New Comedy was domestic and private. New Comedy was typical of the turn away from public life in Hellenistic times.

Menander wrote over seventy plays, but only one complete work has survived, *Dyskolos* (*The Grouch*). There are also large excerpts from several other comedies, as well as Roman imitations. Menander favored stock plots and stock characters: the boastful soldier, the clever slave, the dashing but inept young man, the sweet maiden, and the old miser. Within those limitations, Menander created realistic and idiosyncratic characters. As a Hellenistic critic asked rhetorically: "O Menander and Life, which of you imitated the other?"

Like Menander, Alexandrian writers spurned public themes, but in Alexandria, the characteristic literary figure was not the playwright but the critic: a professional man of letters. Adopted by the Romans, Alexandrian critical standards have influenced the West to this day.

Of the three greatest Alexandrian writers, two—Callimachus (305–240 B.C.) and Apollonius of Rhodes (b. ca. 295 B.C.)—worked at the Library; the third, Theocritus (ca. 300–260 B.C.), probably lived on a stipend from the Ptolemies. Popular for centuries, Callimachus was probably the most influential, the complete Hellenistic poet. A native of Cyrene (see **Map 4.2**) who came to Alexandria as a schoolteacher, Callimachus worked in the Library to compose a virtually universal history of all recorded Greek (and much non-Greek) knowledge.

Callimachus was a prolific writer, but he aimed at brevity: "Big book, big evil" was his maxim. While earlier Greek poets were usually austere and public-minded, Callimachus preferred the private, the light, and the exotic. "Don't expect from me a big-sounding poem," he writes. "Zeus thunders, not I."[3] Callimachus was an expert at the pithy statement in verse—the epigram.

Another major Alexandrian writer was Callimachus's student Apollonius of Rhodes. His major work was the epic poem *Argonautica* (ar-go-NAW-tih-kuh) (*Voyage of the Argo*). The subject is the legend of Jason and the heroes who travel on the ship *Argo* to the Black Sea, in pursuit of the Golden Fleece (the skin of a winged ram). With the help of the princess Medea, who falls in love with Jason, the heroes succeed and return home safely after numerous adventures.

The most striking thing about Apollonius is his doubt about the very possibility of heroism. Apollonius's Jason is no hero of old. Whereas Homer describes Odysseus as "never at a loss," Apollonius describes Jason as "helpless." Men move the action in the *Iliad* and the *Odyssey*; Jason depends on a woman, Medea, for his success. Indeed, much of the *Argonautica* focuses on Medea and her love for Jason. All in all, the *Argonautica* is less a traditional epic than a romance.

Theocritus, a native of Syracuse, composed thirty-one subtle and refined poems, conventionally known as idylls. The best known poems focus on country life. They are the first known pastoral poems; indeed, Theocritus probably invented the genre. Through his Roman admirers, Theocritus's love of nature has exerted a powerful hold on the Western literary imagination.

Outside the Museum, Alexandria had a lively popular culture, much of it Egyptian or influenced by Egyptian models. A glimpse of this culture is offered in the seven surviving mimes, or farces, of an obscure writer named Herondas or Herodas. Though written in literary Greek, they discuss commonplace subjects—shopping for shoes, tourism, lawsuits, and beatings at school—and titillating themes, such as adultery and prostitution.

Advances in Science and Medicine

The Ptolemies not only reaped practical benefits in military and agricultural technology from their Museum, but also became the patrons of a flourishing period in the history of pure scientific inquiry. They unwittingly promoted a split between philosophy and science that has

Street Musicians　The lively scene of a mixed group of young and old, male and female, recalls the jaunty mimes popular with the Hellenistic public. A mosaic from about 100 B.C., the artwork comes from a private villa in the Greco-Italian city of Pompeii.　(Museo Archeologico Nazionale, Naples, Italy/Erich Lessing/Art Resource, NY)

characterized much of Western culture since. Antigonid patronage of ethical and political philosophy helped keep Athens preeminent in those fields. In contrast, the study of science tended to shift to Alexandria and to Pergamum in Anatolia and, far to the west, Syracuse, a flourishing Hellenistic city in Sicily. Hellenistic science benefited from several factors, including the era's wealth, improved communications and literacy, continued warfare, and cross-fertilization between Greek and non-Greek traditions.

MATHEMATICS

Some of the best-known figures of Hellenistic science were mathematicians. In his *Elements*, the Alexandrian Euclid (active ca. 300 B.C.) produced a systematic study of geometry that was hugely influential in both Western and Islamic civilizations.

Archimedes　The greatest ancient Greek mathematician, Archimedes of Syracuse (287–212 B.C.) calculated the approximate value of pi (the ratio of a circle's circumference to its diameter) and invented the water snail (also known as Archimedes' screw).

But the greatest mathematician of Greek antiquity was a Sicilian Greek, **Archimedes** (ar-kuh-MEE-deez) of Syracuse (287–212 B.C.). Among other things, Archimedes calculated the approximate value of pi (the ratio of a circle's circumference to its diameter) and made important discoveries in astronomy, engineering, optics, and other fields. Although Archimedes looked down on practical things as "ignoble and vulgar," he was a notable inventor. His most important invention was the water snail, also known as Archimedes' screw—a device to raise water for irrigation. Created by Archimedes during a stay in Egypt, the screw made it possible to irrigate previously barren land, as did the ox-driven water wheel, another innovation of this period.

Advances in mathematics promoted advances in astronomy. Aristarchus of Samos (active ca. 275 B.C.) is known for his heliocentric hypothesis, which confounded tradition by having the earth revolve around the sun, instead of the sun around the earth. He was right, but Hellenistic astronomy lacked the data to prove his theory, so its rejection was not unreasonable at the time. Eratosthenes (er-uh-TOSS-the-neez) of Cyrene (active ca. 225 B.C.) was saddled with the frustrating nickname of "Beta" (the second letter of the Greek alphabet) because he was considered second best in every branch of study. This "second best" nonetheless calculated through simple geometry an extraordinarily accurate measurement of the earth's circumference.

MEDICINE

Hellenistic medicine thrived in Alexandria. Both Greece and Egypt had long-established medical traditions, but the key to medical advance was the dissection of human cadavers in Alexandria, a first in the history of science. In Greece, as in many ancient societies, religious tradition demanded that dead bodies not be mutilated. But in the frontier atmosphere of early Alexandria, this traditional taboo lost much of its force. Although Egyptians did not practice dissection, they did practice embalming, which may have helped Alexandrian Greeks overcome the prohibition against cutting open the human body.

The leading scientific beneficiary was Herophilus (her-AH-fih-lus) of Chalcedon (ca. 320–250 B.C.), a practicing physician in Alexandria. Among his achievements was the recognition (against Aristotle) that the brain is the center of the nervous system, a careful dissection of the eye, the discovery of the ovaries, and the description of the duodenum, which he named (*duodenum* is a Latin translation of a Greek word meaning "twelve fingers," describing the organ's length). In addition, Herophilus developed a detailed theory of the diagnostic value of measuring pulse rates.

ENGINEERING

Hellenistic technology has long fascinated and frustrated scholars. The great engineers invented both numerous engines of war and various "wonderworks" to amuse the royal court. Among the latter were mechanical puppets and steam-run toys. Given these advances, why did the Greeks achieve neither a scientific revolution, along the lines of the one begun in the early modern era by thinkers such as Copernicus and Galileo, nor an industrial transformation, such as was ushered in by the steam engine around A.D. 1800? Historians are not entirely sure but can venture a guess. Greek machine-making technology was not as sophisticated as that of eighteenth-century Europe. The prevalence of slavery in antiquity discouraged laborsaving machines; steam was used only for playthings and gadgets.

Perhaps the most important point is the Greek attitude toward nature. Whereas Jews and Christians learned from the Bible that human beings have dominion over nature, thereby making possible the conclusion that it is appropriate to conquer nature, the Greeks thought in more restricted terms. They believed that nature set limits, that a virtuous person tried to follow nature, not subdue it. Thus, Greek engineers were not inclined to make the revolutionary changes that their modern counterparts have promoted.

Men and Women in Art and Society

Like Hellenistic literature, Hellenistic art attests to changing male attitudes toward women and toward gender issues. The portrait of Jason and Medea in Apollonius's *Argonautica* makes fun of masculine pretensions and celebrates the triumph of female intelligence. It also presents a sympathetic portrait of a woman's romantic desire for a man, as does Theocritus's work. In the Classical period, depictions of romantic love were generally restricted to relationships between males. Accordingly, statues of naked males were common, but women were almost always depicted clothed. Hellenistic sculpture, by contrast, affords many erotic examples of the female nude.

There are indications that the Hellenistic Greek male of the elite was much more willing than his Classical predecessor to see lovemaking as a matter of mutuality and respect. Classical vase-painting often depicts heterosexual lovemaking with a lusty and explicit mood. In contrast, in Hellenistic vase-painting, the emphasis is more often on tenderness and domesticity. Hellenistic men wrote with sensitivity about satisfying a woman's needs and desires. The vogue for representations of Hermaphrodite (her-MAF-ro-dyte), the mythical creature who was half-female and half-male, may suggest a belief that the feminine was as important a part of human nature as the masculine.

Many a Hellenistic artist or writer seems to be as interested in emotion as in action and to focus on the inner as much as on the outer life. Hellenistic art often depicts women, children, and

Images of Cleopatra

"Cleopatra's nose: if it had been shorter, the whole face of the earth would have changed," wrote the French Blaise Pascal (1623-1662). He does Cleopatra an injustice. It was not a pretty face and classical features that enabled her to win the throne of Egypt (r. 51–30 B.C.), to obtain first Julius Caesar and then Mark Antony as ally and lover, and finally to come close to gaining control of the Roman Empire. Intelligence, daring, charm, and extraordinary diplomatic skill account for Cleopatra's success.

Let us consider the queen's manipulation of her public image—no mean task, given the fragility of Ptolemaic power in the first century B.C. Within Egypt, the monarch had to satisfy several different ethnic groups. Most important were the Greeks and Macedonians—who dominated government, the military, and the economy—and the native Egyptian majority. Daughter of Ptolemy XII (r. 80–51 B.C.), Cleopatra was supposed to rule jointly with her brother, but they had a falling-out. She grabbed the throne from him and then from another brother and thus had to assert her legitimacy. Also, Ptolemaic Egypt had to project an image of unity to the Romans, who were threatening to annex it as they had the other Hellenistic monarchies.

Bronze Coin of Cleopatra   (Courtesy of the Trustees of the British Museum)

Cleopatra, like earlier Ptolemaic monarchs, met these challenges by presenting two faces to the world. To the Greeks and Romans, she was a Hellenistic monarch; to the Egyptians, she was an ancient pharaonic queen. Look first at the bronze coin of Cleopatra issued at Alexandria probably in the 30s B.C. The queen is shown as a young woman. Her hair, tied in a bun at the nape of her neck, is in the so-called melon style often seen in Hellenistic female portraits. She wears a diadem (royal headband), its ends hanging behind her neck. More commonly worn by Hellenistic kings than by queens, the diadem signifies Cleopatra's claim to authority.

So does the queen's profile. She is portrayed with a prominent chin, a large mouth, and a rugged nose. These features may not be the standard attributes of beauty, but they are precisely the features that mark coin portraits of Cleopatra's father. By emphasizing Cleopatra's physical similarity to her father, the portrait artist perhaps subtly suggests her right to sit on his throne.

The side of the coin not shown here is far from subtle: Its legend states clearly in Greek, "Queen Cleopatra." The illustration is of an eagle and thunderbolt and a double cornucopia (horn of plenty) entwined with a diadem. The eagle and thunderbolt recall the Greek god Zeus, and the two cornucopias suggest fertility and prosperity. All are recurrent symbols of Ptolemaic royalty. The coin thus portrays Cleopatra as a Greek monarch, the worthy heir of her father. It would have been an effective image in Alexandria, a city dominated by Greeks and visited by Romans, but not in the countryside, especially south of the Nile Delta, in Upper Egypt, an area that was primarily Egyptian. Following dynastic custom, Cleopatra changed her image there.

In Upper Egypt, earlier Ptolemies frequently had been represented in stone in traditional pharaonic style, and they were great restorers of ancient Egyptian temples and builders of new ones. Look at the sculptural relief from the temple of the Egyptian cow-goddess Hathor at Dendera in Upper Egypt. The temple was a monumental structure initiated and underwritten by Ptolemy XII. Cleopatra, his daughter, added an enormous relief on the outside of the rear wall. Carved into the stone are two persons carrying offerings for Egyptian deities. The persons are Cleopatra (*left*) and her son Ptolemy XV Caesar, who ruled with his mother from 44 to 30 B.C. Alleged to be the illegitimate son of Julius Caesar, Ptolemy XV was commonly known as

domestic scenes. Representations of warriors are as likely to focus on their unrestrained emotions as on their soldierly self-control.

Hellenistic women enjoyed small improvements in political and legal status and bigger improvements in economic and ideological status. Greek women, particularly in the elite, benefited from the spread of monarchy. Queens and princesses had more power than female commoners in city-states. Also, in the new cities, as in many a frontier society, women were permitted to inherit and use property more often than in old Greece.

Relief of Cleopatra and Caesarion (Erich Lessing/Art Resource, NY)

horn of Amon. Caesarion is shown as a pharaoh, wearing the double crown of Upper and Lower Egypt. Mother and son offer incense to the local deities. The small figure between Caesarion and Cleopatra is his *ka*, or soul.

Cleopatra's face is in profile, but otherwise has very little in common with her portrait on the Alexandrian coin. Although the features are stylized pharaonic commonplaces, the shape of her head perhaps echoes the elegant and graceful relief portraits of Hatshepsut (r. 1479–1457 B.C.), the most famous female pharaoh before Cleopatra. Cleopatra commissioned other artworks and monuments in the native style in the Nile Valley. This was the custom of her dynasty, and Cleopatra had absorbed its traditions, but she stands second to none of the Ptolemies in shrewdness and subtlety. She was the only Ptolemaic monarch to learn to speak Egyptian, and she was the only one to come even close to gaining the upper hand over Rome. As the artifacts shown here indicate, she was able to put on an Egyptian face as easily as a Greek one, but she never lost sight of her true interests.

Caesarion, or "little Caesar." At Dendera, however, he and his mother are shown neither as Romans nor as Greeks but as Egyptians.

Look closely at Cleopatra. She wears a long body-hugging robe. On her head is a royal headdress with symbols of the Egyptian gods: the lyre-shaped cow horns and sun-disk of Hathor, the tall plumes of Isis, and the ram's

QUESTIONS

1. Why did Cleopatra need to show two faces to the world?
2. Does Cleopatra's coin emphasize her good looks? Why or why not?
3. What image of herself does Cleopatra present at the Temple of Hathor at Dendera? Why?

It was an era of powerful queens: Olympias, Alexander the Great's mother, played kingmaker after her son's death. Arsinoe II Philadelphus was coruler of Egypt with her husband (who was also her brother) for five years at the height of Ptolemaic prosperity around 275 B.C. The most famous Hellenistic woman, Cleopatra VII, was queen of Egypt from 51 to 30 B.C. Although she was the lover of two of the most powerful men in the world, the Romans Julius Caesar and Mark Antony, Cleopatra was no exotic plaything. Rather, she was a brilliant and ambitious strategist who nearly succeeded in winning a world empire for her family. (See the feature, "The Visual Record: Images of Cleopatra.")

Writers in the new Hellenistic cities often described freedom of movement for women. Theocritus and Herondas, for example, show women visiting a temple or a show. In Hellenistic Athens, aristocratic fathers put up inscriptions in honor of their daughters who had participated in the cult of Athena. Although women generally continued to need a male guardian to represent them in public, in some situations, at least in Egypt (where the evidence is most plentiful), a woman could represent herself. A woman could petition the government on her own behalf. Widows and mothers of illegitimate children could give their daughters in marriage or apprentice their sons. A few cities granted women citizenship and even permitted them to hold public office.

Some Hellenistic cities admitted women to the gymnasium, previously a male preserve. Heretofore, only Sparta had promoted physical education for women, but by the first century A.D., women were even competing in the great Pan-Hellenic games. Gymnasia were also centers of education in music and reading. One consequence of growing literacy was the re-emergence of women poets and the first appearance of women philosophers in the West. Before dying at age 19, Erinna, who lived on the Aegean island of Telos during the late fourth century B.C., wrote the *Distaff*, a poem in memory of her childhood friend Baucis. This three-hundred line poem, famous in antiquity, describes the shared experiences of girlhood. Hipparchia (hih-PAR-kee-uh) of Maroneia (b. ca. 350 B.C.), like her husband, Crates of Thebes, studied Cynic philosophy. The Cynics, like another philosophical school, the Epicureans, supported a measure of equality between women and men. Hipparchia and Crates led an itinerant life as popular teachers and the Hellenistic equivalent of counselors or psychologists.

Much of the explanation for the relative freedom of elite women lies in the new economic power of this group. The new cities generally imposed fewer restrictions on women's economic roles than had Classical poleis such as Athens. In many cities, women could sell land, borrow money, and decide whether their husbands could make loans or contracts on the strength of their dowries. Free women could manumit slaves as well.

Hellenistic women never attained the equality that sometimes exists between men and women today, but they did enjoy genuine improvements in status. Men and women played new roles in a changed, complex world. The new Hellenistic philosophies and religions attempted to address that complexity.

Aphrodite of Cnidos   This 7½-foot-tall marble statue is a Roman copy of an original by Praxiteles (ca. 350–330 B.C.). Perhaps the most famous of Hellenistic female nudes, the statue was housed in a special shrine where it could be viewed in the round to accommodate all the interest it generated.   (Nimatallah/Art Resource, NY)

SECTION SUMMARY

- Alexandria's Museum (a research institute) and Library were the focal point of much of Hellenistic literature and science.

- The playwright Menander and the poets Callimachus, Apollonius of Rhodes, and Theocritus represent the Hellenistic era's turn away from civic and heroic themes.

- Mathematics, astronomy, and medicine are all fields in which notable advances were made in the Hellenistic era, thanks in part to royal patronage.

- Philosophy and science first became separate disciplines, as they are today.

- Hellenistic women experienced real, though limited, improvements in status and power.

THE TURN INWARD: NEW PHILOSOPHIES, NEW FAITHS

What new philosophies and religions emerged in the Hellenistic period?

The events of the Hellenistic era—emigration, a trend from independent city-states to monarchies and federal leagues, new extremes of wealth and poverty, and contact with foreign peoples and customs—all generated uncertainty. In response, Greek culture was spread and transformed. As literacy expanded, more Greeks than ever before could participate in cultural debate. New philosophies and religions arose to meet new spiritual concerns, generating ideas that would be influential for centuries.

The meeting of Jews and Greeks proved to be just as significant. Challenged by Greek conquest, Greek colonization, and their own migration to Greek lands, Jews alternately embraced Hellenism and engaged in resistance, both cultural and armed. In the process, first Judaism and then Hellenism were changed forever.

Hellenistic Philosophy

Although the polis lost its military and political preeminence in the fourth century B.C., philosophy continued to thrive. It was, however, much changed. With the city-state losing significance as a focus of loyalty, and with the Greek-reading public growing in size and geographic extent, Hellenistic philosophy paid less and less attention to politics. Since Hellenistic science tended to become a separate discipline from philosophy, philosophers focused on ethics, the discovery of the best way to live. The essence of the good life, most philosophers agreed, was peace of mind, or freedom from troubles. Hellenistic philosophy won a wide following; indeed, for many people, primarily in the elite, philosophy became a way of life, even a religion.

CYNICISM

Several competing philosophical schools emerged, beginning with Cynicism (SIN-uh-sizm). Never a widespread philosophy, Cynicism is nonetheless important as a precursor of the two most popular doctrines, Stoicism and Epicureanism. Skepticism rejected the main philosophies and proposed instead a commonsense attitude toward ethics.

The first Cynic was Diogenes (dye-AH-juh-neez) of Sinope (ca. 400–325 B.C.). An exile in Athens, Diogenes developed a philosophy that rejected all conventions. People find happiness, he decided, by satisfying their natural needs with simplicity. Accordingly, Diogenes chose a life of poverty. A beggar in rags, he delighted in shocking conventional morality. Famous for wit and shamelessness, he was nicknamed "Dog" (*kuon*) because the Greeks considered dogs to be shameless animals; his followers were called "Doglike" (*kunikoi*, whence the name *Cynic*).

STOICISM

Although he founded no school, Diogenes cast a wide shadow. Among those whom he indirectly influenced was Zeno (ZEE-no) (335–263 B.C.), who began one of the most important philosophical systems of antiquity: Stoicism (STO-ih-sizm). Zeno came to Athens in 313 B.C. from Citium in Cyprus, a multiethnic city; he was possibly of Phoenician origin. Influenced by both Cynicism and Socratic philosophy, Zeno developed his own doctrines, which he taught in the *Stoa Poikile* ("Painted Porch," hence the name *Stoic*), a public building.

Like Plato and Aristotle, Zeno sought an absolute standard of good on which to base philosophical decisions. He found it in the divine reason (*logos*), which he considered the principle of the universe and the guide to human behavior. The best life was spent in pursuit of wisdom—that is, a life of philosophy. Only that rare and forbidding figure, the Sage, could truly attain wisdom; ordinary people could merely progress toward it through study and the attempt to be free from all passion.

Stoicism may seem harsh. It is not surprising that *stoical* has come to describe austere indifference to pain. In some ways, however, Stoicism was comforting. The **Stoics** were empiricists—that is, they trusted the evidence of the senses, an attitude that they thought would inspire confidence and security. They believed in human brotherhood—led, to be sure, by a Greek-speaking elite. Since brothers have a duty to one another, the Stoics argued that a good person should play an active role in public life.

Stoics Believers in a philosophical system begun in Athens by Zeno, which emphasized the pursuit of wisdom, the reliability of sensory experience, and freedom from all passion.

The Stoics emphasized the inner life. They believed that intentions matter. This was an important departure from Greek tradition, which tended to emphasize the outcome of an action, not its motivation. Stoicism also departed from traditional Greek localism, embracing a more cosmopolitan outlook. "This world is a great city, [and] has one constitution and one law," wrote Philo of Alexandria (30 B.C.–A.D. 45), a Stoic and a Jew. Many Stoics believed in a natural law or law of nations—that is, that overarching and common principles governed international relations.

With its emphasis on duty and order, Stoicism became popular with Greek ruling elites, and eventually with the Romans, who used its concept of a universal state to justify their empire. Many Stoic principles were later embraced by early Christian writers.

EPICUREANISM

Epicureans Adherents of the Athenian philosopher Epicurus, they emphasized the avoidance of pain and the pursuit of intellectual pleasure.

Epicurus (341–270 B.C.), an Athenian citizen, founded his philosophical school at around the same time as Zeno founded Stoicism. There were other similarities: Both schools were empiricist and materialist (that is, they tended to trust the evidence of the senses), both sought peace of mind, and both inspired widespread followings. Epicurus, however, taught not in a public place but in a private garden. Whereas the Stoics encouraged political participation, the **Epicureans** counseled withdrawal from the rough-and-tumble of public life. "Calm" and "Live in hiding" are famous Epicurean (eh-pi-kyuh-REE-un) maxims.

Epicurus's materialism is based on the atomic theory of Democritus (see page 76). It envisions a thoroughly mechanistic universe in which the gods exist but play no active role in events. Individuals need fear neither fickle deities nor an unhappy afterlife because the soul is merely a combination of atoms that ceases to exist after death. The purpose of life was the avoidance of pain and the pursuit of pleasure. The latter was called hedonism (from *hedone*, Greek for "pleasure"), but not, as the word has come to mean today, indulgence in food, drink, or sex. Instead, Epicureans meant intellectual pleasure. Friendship and fraternity were Epicurean ideals—the private analogs, as it were, of Stoic brotherhood.

The Epicureans raised eyebrows and sometimes ire, occasionally suffering persecution by the state. They were accused of atheism and sensuality. Classical Greek philosophy defined virtue as the highest good. The Epicurean emphasis on pleasure, even spiritual pleasure, seemed perverse to some. Yet, Epicureanism was simple, sure of itself, and practical, and it offered both friendship and a sense of community. It became a popular philosophy, especially among the wealthy.

SKEPTICISM

Skepticism (SKEP-tih-sizm) was founded by Pyrrho of Elis (ca. 360–270 B.C.), a Greek who traveled with Alexander to India. Like Stoics and Epicureans, Skeptics sought peace of mind. They rejected those thinkers' conclusions, however, on the grounds that they were dogmatic—that is, based not on positive proof but merely on opinion (*doxa*). Considering the senses unreliable, Skeptics rejected the commonsense approach of Stoics and Epicureans. They preferred to suspend judgment on the great philosophical questions (hence, our term *skepticism* for a doubting state of mind). Whoever was able to do so could accept the customs of the community, avoid politics, and thereby obtain peace of mind.

The Mystery Religions

mystery religions Popular Hellenistic cults, featuring the initiation of worshipers into secret doctrines, they replaced the traditional Greek religion of the Olympian gods.

The name "mystery religion" comes from the Greek word for "secret." A mystery religion initiated worshipers into secret teachings. Long a feature of Greek religion, the **mystery religions**—there were several different ones—grew very popular in Hellenistic times. They offered relief similar to that of the philosophical schools: ethical guidance, comfort, release from worries, reassurance about death, and a sense of unity. The rise of the mystery religions went along with the decline of the traditional Greek religion of the Olympian gods.

The old Greek gods came under attack on every front in the Hellenistic era. The newly divinized kings stole their spotlight, while philosophers criticized the Olympians as primitive and immoral. Scholarship got into the act as well. Around 300 B.C., Euhemerus of Messene wrote that Zeus and others were not gods, but merely great kings of the past who were rewarded with deification, much as a Hellenistic monarch might be.

The Olympians retained their temples, but the rituals seemed hollow and antiquarian. What was to replace them? Of the several new religious movements that marked the age, three stand out: the divinization of kings, the cult of Tyche (Fortune), and the mystery religions.

Under the Ptolemies and Seleucids, ruler-worship became standard procedure. Some no doubt considered it just a patriotic formality, while others prayed to the god-king or god-queen to intercede for them in heaven. Meanwhile, the old Greek city-states, especially democracies, bristled. "To transfer to men the honor due to the gods," said one Athenian playwright, "is to dissolve the democracy."

He might have said as much about the Hellenistic cult of Tyche (TOO-kay) (Fortune or Luck), often worshiped as a goddess, sometimes as the protector of a particular city. The most famous example was the Tyche of Antioch, personified as a statue of a woman wearing the battlements of the city on her head as a kind of crown—a very popular statue, to judge by the many copies found around the Hellenistic world.

Various mystery religions flourished. In Athens, the cult of Demeter, goddess of fertility, had long been celebrated in the suburb of Eleusis, and it grew in popularity. Those who took part in the ceremonies received promises of life after death.

New mystery religions from outside Greece grew even more popular, particularly the Hellenized Egyptian cults of Serapis and of Isis. Created under Ptolemy I, Serapis (SEH-ruh-pis) was meant to combine Osiris, the Egyptian god of the afterlife, with Apis, the god of the Nile flood. Serapis also suggested Pluto, the Greek god of the underworld. Hence, it is an early example of the common Hellenistic practice of religious syncretism, or fusion. Despite its roots, Serapis-worship had little appeal to native Egyptians, but the god became popular in the Greek world as the patron of healing and sailing.

Another traditional Egyptian deity, Osiris's wife, Isis (EYE-sis), also became a popular Greek and, later, Roman goddess. Called the Goddess of Ten Thousand Names, Isis was said to symbolize all the female deities of antiquity. Hers was a cult of the afterlife and of the suffering but tender and loving mother; she was particularly popular among women. Thus, under Ptolemaic sponsorship, ancient Egyptian cults were reworked and spread throughout the Greek-speaking world, circulating such notions as the suffering mother, the Last Judgment, and blessed eternal life after death. Early Christianity was much influenced by such Greco-Egyptian religious notions, but it was more directly the product of debate and ferment within Hellenistic Judaism.

A Cretan Dream Interpreter in Egypt A painted stele (ca. 200 B.C.) advertises the services of a Greek in Memphis near the Temple of Serapis, a Greco-Egyptian god. The inscription and pediment are Greek, while the pilasters, women, and sacred bull (facing an altar) are Egyptian. (Egyptian Museum, Cairo)

Hellenistic Judaism

Few consequences of Alexander's conquests had so lasting an impact as the mixing of Greeks and Jews. When Alexander conquered it in 332 B.C., Judea had been a Persian province for 200 years. Now, the fates of Greeks and Jews grew intertwined.

Jewish responses to Greek culture varied. At one extreme stood the Hellenizers, who admired Greek culture and wanted to assimilate to it. At the other extreme were traditionalists, who defended Jewish law as interpreted by scholars and rabbis. Their disagreement led to war, which broke out as follows.

After Alexander's death, Hellenistic Judea was governed first by the Ptolemies until 200 B.C., then by the Seleucids, until the establishment of an independent Jewish state in 142 B.C., which came in turn under Roman control in 63 B.C. The Greeks were not absentee rulers. Rather, they established a large number of Greek colonies in and around Judea, especially under the Seleucids. Many Jews, especially wealthy ones, adopted some degree of Greek culture. Some Hellenizers gave up Jewish customs altogether for the Greek gymnasium, theater, and political institutions. With the help of the Seleucid king Antiochus IV Epiphanes (r. 175–163 B.C.), Jewish Hellenizers in 175 B.C. had Jerusalem proclaimed a Greek polis; they built a gymnasium at the foot of the Temple Mount. They looted the Temple's treasury. In 167 B.C., they attacked the essence of Judaism by outlawing

Bronze Coin with Menorah This issue of Mattathias Antigone (r. 40–37 B.C.), the last Hasmonean king, is an early example of the use of the seven-branched candelabrum as the symbol of the Jewish people. A similar candelabrum was used in the Temple of Jerusalem. (Erich Lessing/Art Resource, NY)

Maccabees Traditionalist Jews led by the Hasmonean family, who, in 167 B.C., revolted against Hellenizing laws and influences.

Sabbath observance, prohibiting circumcision, and rededicating the Temple to Olympian Zeus, to whom they sacrificed pigs.

The traditionalists, however, rallied the Jewish masses into opposition. Soon a guerrilla revolt began in the countryside, led by the Hasmonean family, also known as the **Maccabees**, whose successes are celebrated today by Jews during the holiday of Hanukkah. The guerrilla movement developed into a disciplined armed uprising, which restored all Jewish religious practices and rededicated the Temple. The revolt also forced the Seleucids to tolerate an independent state under the Hasmonean dynasty. Jewish independence lasted from 142 B.C., until the Roman conquest in 63 B.C.

During the struggle over Hellenism, new elements of lasting significance became part of Judaism. First, the Jews developed a literature of spiritual resistance to the foreigner. This literature was apocalyptic—that is, it claimed to reveal dramatic, heretofore secret truths. Drawing on both biblical and Mesopotamian traditions, Jewish apocalyptic writing predicted a future cataclysm, when a royal redeemer would evict the foreigner and establish a new kingdom of Israel. The redeemer was often identified with another notion that first became popular in this era: the Messiah (literally, "anointed one"), someone anointed with oil signifying his election as king, a descendant of King David, who would save Israel. Another new aspect of Hellenistic Judaism was martyrdom, the notion of the holy sacrifice of one's life for a religious cause. There was also a growing belief in a final Judgment Day and resurrection, when God would raise the meritorious dead to live again on earth in their own bodies.

Hellenistic Judaism was diverse. Various sects each proposed its own version of Judaism. Among these sects were the Sadducees (SAJ-oo-seez) (the disciples of one Tzadok), a wealthy establishment group for whom the rituals of the Temple in Jerusalem were the heart of Judaism. Their opponents were the Pharisees (FAIR-ih-seez) (from the Hebrew *perushim*, "those who separate themselves," that is, in order to observe the laws of ritual purity). The Pharisees believed that the written law of the Hebrew Bible needed to be supplemented by an oral tradition that they traced back to Moses and Mt. Sinai. They saw themselves as the only true interpreters of that tradition. They proposed a kind of guided democratization of Judaism, emphasizing study and prayer in small groups under their leadership. Eventually, after several centuries, the Pharisees prevailed: they are the ancestors of modern Judaism. A third group was the Essenes (EH-seenz), generally identified with the Qumran (koom-RAHN) community in the Judean desert (see page 160).

Most Jews of the Hellenistic era lived outside Judea. Some had left voluntarily in search of wealth or adventure, while others had been taken captive in various wars. The Diaspora had spread into (among other places) Syria, Anatolia, the Greek mainland, Babylon, and Egypt, where a strong Jewish presence during the Persian period grew even stronger, particularly in Alexandria. Jews served the Ptolemies as soldiers, generals, bureaucrats, and tax collectors. They also prospered in private enterprise. Hostility to Jews by some Greeks and Egyptians spawned the first anti-Semitic literature. Sporadic violence at times broke into riots and persecution. Yet, there was also considerable admiration among Greek intellectuals for what they saw as Jewish virtue and antiquity.

Greek was the common tongue of Diaspora Jews. Between around 300 and 100 B.C. in Alexandria, the Hebrew Bible was translated into Greek. Known as the Septuagint, or Seventy, from the number of translators who, legend has it, labored on the project, this text made the Bible accessible to a Jewish community increasingly unable to understand Hebrew or Aramaic. In later centuries, the Septuagint became the Old Testament of Greek-speaking Christians.

Foreign conversions and immigration into the Diaspora began to change the meaning of the word *Jew*. The word came to mean less "inhabitant of Judea" than "practitioner of Judaism."

SECTION SUMMARY

- Philosophy changed its emphasis from politics to ethics and won a wide following in the Greek-speaking elite.

- Stoicism, austere and public-spirited, and Epicureanism, which called for withdrawal into private life, were the most popular Hellenistic philosophies.

- The traditional Olympian religion of Greece declined, while so-called mystery religions, which offered secret teachings, grew popular.

- While some Jews adopted the Greek customs of their Seleucid rulers, traditionalists revolted and reestablished an independent Jewish state in Palestine.

- Most Jews in the Hellenistic era lived outside Palestine, in the Diaspora, where they had frequent contacts with other peoples.

CHAPTER SUMMARY

As king, Philip built a state and an army that allowed Macedon to conquer the Greek city-states and prepared to invade the Persian Empire. Upon Philip's assassination, his son Alexander replaced him and led an army of invasion. Although outnumbered and outspent by Persia, the Macedonians won because of their army. As Alexander's empire stretched into India, he became despotic and he planned a fusion of Greeks and Persians. His conquests laid the foundation of the Hellenistic age.

After fifty years of war following Alexander's death, several new states emerged: The most important were Macedonia under the Antigonid dynasty, Egypt under the Ptolemies, and western Asia under the Seleucids. Hellenistic Greek kingdoms were founded in lands as far away as Afghanistan, Pakistan, and India, and they lasted for centuries. Greek and Macedonian colonists to the Ptolemaic and Seleucid kingdoms dominated the army and administration, but there was some room for natives. But few natives adopted Greek ways, and native culture thrived in these multiethnic empires. New cities, such as Alexandria, Antioch, and Pergamum, were flourishing centers of commerce and culture.

Under royal patronage, the Museum (a research institute) and Library were founded in Alexandria and became a focus of Hellenistic literature and science. Hellenistic writers turned away from civic life and heroic themes toward private life and ordinary events. Hellenistic science flourished and there were great achievements in mathematics, astronomy, and medicine. Hellenistic women made small gains in status and power, compared to earlier Greek women.

New beliefs emerged as faith in the Olympian gods declined. Ethics replaced politics as the focus of philosophy. The two most popular new philosophical schools were Stoicism and Epicureanism, the first austere and public-spirited, the second emphasizing withdrawal into private life. So-called mystery religions, which offered secret teachings, drew a wide public. Greeks and Jews came into increasing contact, both in the Diaspora and in Palestine, where Ptolemaic and Seleucid kings ruled in turn. Jews were divided into various schools of thought, with Hellenizers and traditionalists representing the two poles of opinion.

FOCUS QUESTIONS

- How did Macedon under Philip and Alexander conquer both the Greek city-states and the Persian Empire?

- What new states emerged as a result of Alexander's conquests and how did they integrate Greek settlers with native peoples?

- How did Greek civilization spread during the Hellenistic era, and what were the main trends in literature, science, and art?

- What new philosophies and religions emerged in the Hellenistic period?

KEY TERMS

Macedon (p. 84)

Philip II (p. 84)

Alexander the Great (p. 85)

Hellenism (p. 89)

Ptolemies (p. 90)

Seleucids (p. 90)

Antigonids (p. 91)

Alexandria (p. 93)

Antioch (p. 94)

Bactria (p. 95)

Museum (p. 96)

Archimedes (p. 98)

Stoics (p. 103)

Epicureans (p. 104)

mystery religions (p. 104)

Maccabees (p. 106)

This icon will direct you to additional materials on the website: www.cengage.com/history/noble/westciv6e

See our interactive eBook for map and primary source activities.

NOTES

1. Isocrates, "Panegyricus," trans. H. I. Marrou, in *A History of Education in Antiquity*, trans. George Lamb (New York: Mentor Books/New American Library, 1956), p. 130.

2. Romila Thapar, *Aśoka and the Decline of the Mauryas* (Oxford: Oxford University Press, 1961), p. 256.

3. Quoted in Charles Rowan Beye, *Ancient Greek Literature and Society*, 2d ed. (Ithaca, N.Y.: Cornell University Press, 1987), p. 265.

checks and balances that tended toward consensus. The result was efficiency and, for centuries, stability.

Roman politicians sought to control ordinary citizens, but in some ways were more flexible than Greek democrats. Unlike Greece, Rome extended its citizenship to a large population, first throughout Italy and then across its entire empire. The modern nation-state with its mass citizenship owes much to Rome. Indeed, although Rome was not democratic, modern democracy—that is, popular government with a large population, whose officials are elected by the people—has roots in the Roman Republic as well as in the Greek city-state.

Fueled by fear, ambition, and greed, Roman expansion generated its own momentum. Rome's arrogance matched its success: In consolidating power over huge territories, the Romans committed atrocities, enslaved whole peoples, and destroyed cities with little provocation. Ironically, military success slowly undermined both Rome's political stability at home and the socioeconomic basis of its army. Meanwhile, the Romans showed great open-mindedness in borrowing from other societies, in particular, from the Greeks, to whom the Republic owed great cultural debts. Also fascinating is the shrewdness and generosity with which the Romans shared their citizenship with the elites whom they had conquered, thereby winning their loyalty and strengthening Rome's grip on their territories.

Historians conventionally divide the Republic into three periods: Early (509–287 B.C.), Middle (287–133 B.C.), and Late (133–31 B.C.). This chapter begins with the origins of the city of Rome in the early first millennium B.C. and then traces the Republic from its foundation to its imperial conquests to its collapse under their weight. Success spoiled Rome. The unintended consequences of conquest on Rome's society, politics, and culture led to a revolution that, in the century beginning in 133 B.C., saw the Republic's downfall.

BEFORE THE REPUBLIC, 753–509 B.C.

What was early Rome like and how was it shaped by relations with its neighbors?

Romulus Legendary founder of Rome in 753 B.C., whose name supplies a convenient etymology for the city, he may have really existed, as archaeology suggests.

The ancient Romans believed that their city was founded on April 21, 753 B.C., by **Romulus**, a descendant of refugees from the Trojan War. Although the name "Romulus" supplies a convenient origin for "Rome," we cannot take the story at face value. Nevertheless, archaeology shows that by the eighth century B.C. Rome was already on its way to being a city and it had a king. Archaeologists have recently discovered a palace in the Forum from this era. They have also found traces of sanctuaries and a defensive wall. Nearby stands the Palatine Hill, one of the seven hills on which Rome would cluster and the place where tradition puts the settlement of 753 (see inset, **MAP 5.2**, on page 122). Archaeologists have recently found fortification walls on the Palatine from ca. 750 B.C., which lends support to tradition. They have also found an underground chamber there that some would identify with the cave where, according to legend, Romulus was nursed by a she-wolf. In any case, the first settlers on the hills of Rome came even earlier, around 1000 B.C., as pottery and graves show.

Archaeological evidence raises some basic questions: What were Rome's origins, and how did it grow? Are seeds of Roman greatness visible in its early history? By examining the data of archaeology and of those elements in ancient historiography that seem to be based on accurate tradition, we can answer these questions, at least in outline.

The First Romans and Their Neighbors

Italy is a long peninsula, shaped roughly like a boot, extending about 750 miles from the Alps into the Mediterranean (see **MAP 5.1**). In the far north, the high Alps provide a barrier to the rest of

Europe. To the east, the Adriatic Sea separates Italy from modern Slovenia and Croatia; to the west, the Tyrrhenian Sea faces the large islands of Sardinia and Corsica (and the smaller but iron-rich island of Elba) and, beyond, the coasts of France and Spain. Off the "toe" of the Italian boot, and separated from the mainland by a narrow, 3-mile strait of water, is the large island of Sicily, rich farm country in ancient times. Sicily is only 90 miles from North Africa. In short, Italy is centrally located in the Mediterranean. It was both a target for conquerors and a springboard for conquest.

Italy contained some of the ancient Mediterranean's most fertile and metal-rich land. From the watershed of the Po and Adige Rivers in the north, the agriculturally rich plains of Etruria (modern Tuscany), Latium (the region of Rome), and Campania (the region of Naples) unfold southward down Italy's west coast. Although the Apennine (AP-puh-nine) mountains run north-south along most of the Italian peninsula, they are low compared with the Alps and contain many passes, permitting the movement of armies.

A sensational recent archaeological discovery opens a window into second millennium B.C. Italy. Poggiomarino is a prehistoric village consisting of houses that were built on oak pilings and separated by canals. The village, located on a river near Naples, was inhabited from around the 1500s B.C. to around 700 B.C. A masterpiece of prehistoric engineering, the village covered at least 7 acres and was a center of bronze production.

In the first millennium B.C., Italy was a hodgepodge of peoples and languages. They included the Etruscans in the north, Greek colonists in southern Italy and in Sicily, and such mountain peoples as the Sabines and the Samnites. The Samnites spoke Oscan, an Indo-European language, as did the Campanians, who lived around Naples, and the Lucanians, who lived in south-central Italy. Both the Samnites and the Lucanians were warlike peoples who conquered their neighbors before finally being conquered by Rome. (See the feature, "The Visual Record: From Poseidonia to Paestum.")

Latium (LAY-shum) was home to a number of small Latin-speaking towns, one of them Rome. In the fifth century B.C., another important people arrived on the Italian scene: Celts (called Gauls by the Romans), large numbers of whom crossed the Alps and settled in northern Italy after roughly 500 B.C. Most of these various peoples spoke Indo-European languages, of which **Latin**, the language of the Romans (as well as other peoples of Latium), was one.

Rome's location in Italy was central and protected. Located 15 miles inland on the Tiber (TY-ber), the largest river on Italy's west coast, Rome had access to the sea. A midstream island makes Rome the first crossing place upstream from the Tiber's mouth, which offered the Romans freedom of movement north and south. Yet strategically, Rome was protected. It was far enough from the sea to be safe from raiders and pirates. And its seven hills offered a natural defense—from nature as well as humans, because the Tiber often flooded its banks.

In the eighth century B.C., Archaic Rome (as the pre-Republican period is called) began to change from a large village into a city. By the sixth century B.C., Rome had streets, walls, drains, temples, and a racetrack. What caused the transformation? Perhaps the key factor was contact with Magna Graecia (MAG-nuh GREE-shuh), the Greek colonies to the south (see **MAP 5.1**). Established in the eighth and seventh centuries B.C., the colonies transported westward the sophisticated urban civilization of the eastern Mediterranean (see pages 55–56).

Latin Indo-European language of ancient Rome and its empire, from which today's Romance languages developed.

CHRONOLOGY

753–509 B.C.	Monarchy (traditional dates)
509–287 B.C.	Early Republic
449 B.C.	Law of the Twelve Tables
338 B.C.	Latin League dissolved; Roman citizenship extended
289 B.C.	First Roman coinage (traditional date)
287–133 B.C.	Middle Republic
264–146 B.C.	Punic Wars
240 B.C.	First play produced at Rome
197 B.C.	Rome defeats Macedonian phalanx
146 B.C.	Rome destroys Carthage and Corinth
133–31 B.C.	Late Republic
133–121 B.C.	The Gracchi
107–78 B.C.	Marius and Sulla
73–71 B.C.	Spartacus's revolt
66–62 B.C.	Pompey's eastern campaigns
63 B.C.	Consulship of Cicero
58–51 B.C.	Caesar conquers Gaul
44 B.C.	Caesar assassinated
31 B.C.	Antony defeated at Actium; Octavian in power

🌐 **Map 5.1—Early Italy and Region of City of Rome**

Early Italy comprised a variety of terrain and peoples. Rome is located in the central Italian region of Latium. The Alps separate Italy from northern Europe. The Apennine mountain range runs almost the entire length of the Italian peninsula. Much of the rest of Italy is fertile plain.

Etruscans Inhabitants of twelve loosely confederated city-states north of Rome; they were conquered by the Romans by the early third century B.C.

Less well understood is the impact on early Rome of its neighbors to the north, the **Etruscans** (ee-TRUS-kunz). The twelve Etruscan city-states were organized in a loose confederation centered in Etruria (ee-TROO-ree-uh). They grew rich from the mining of iron, copper, and silver, from piracy, from trade, and from a network of influential Etruscan emigrants throughout central Italy, probably including Rome's last three kings (traditionally dated 616–509 B.C.).

The Etruscans were brilliant, wealthy, and warlike. We know less about them than we would like, from their language, which is only partly understood, to their origins, which probably lay in Italy but possibly in Anatolia. Etruscan power extended to many places in central, northern, and even southern Italy. Many scholars argue that the Etruscans conquered pre-Republican Rome, but the evidence does not support that theory. Rather, an Etruscan nobleman, Lucius

Etruscan Tomb Painting This wall painting from Tarquinia shows a married aristocratic couple at a banquet. The style of the figures is derived from Greek art, but the depiction of husband and wife dining on the same couch is characteristically Etruscan. (National Museum, Tarquinia/Scala/Art Resource, NY)

Tarquinius Priscus, migrated to Rome and was eventually elected king. Under him and his son (or perhaps grandson), Lucius Tarquinius Superbus, who was Rome's last king, Etruscan culture left an impact on Rome. For example, the Tarquins sponsored several building projects in Rome, including the great Temple of Jupiter on the Capitoline Hill in the center of Rome. But scholars disagree as to whether the Etruscan impact on Roman culture was superficial or deep.

At least we can be sure that the Etruscans were great artists and architects and very religious. They believed that it was possible to learn the will of the gods by interpreting the sight and sound of lightning and thunder and by carefully examining the internal organs, especially the liver, of sacrificial animals. Etruscan elite women had high status compared with their Greek or Roman counterparts. Etruscan women kept their own names, and Etruscan children bore the names of both parents. In addition, Etruscan elite women were permitted to attend athletic contests in spite of the presence of naked male athletes.

The Roman Monarchy

Tradition says that Rome was ruled by seven kings before the foundation of the Republic. Although the number of kings may be a later invention, their existence is undoubted. In addition to traces of the monarchy in Republican institutions, there is archaeological proof: A form of the Latin word *rex* ("king"), for example, has been found inscribed on a Roman monument from the early sixth century B.C. The king's power, called *imperium* (from *imperare*, "to command"), was very great, embracing religious, military, and judicial affairs.

The king was advised by a council of elders, called the "fathers" (*patres* in Latin) or the "senate" (*senatus*, from *senex*, "old man"). In theory, the senate was primarily an advisory body, but in practice, it was very powerful. Senators were the heads of the most important families in Rome, so the king rejected their advice at his peril. Romans spoke of the senate's *auctoritas* (from which our word "authority" comes), a quasi-religious prestige.

From Poseidonia to Paestum

etween them, the elegant Greek painting and the rough Roman bronze statue shown here sum up the history of the ancient city of Paestum. Paestum is located in southern Italy, about 200 miles south of Rome. It was a port and commercial center in a rich farming region on the Gulf of Salerno. Founded as the Greek colony of Poseidonia around 600 B.C., Paestum ended up as a thriving Roman city after being conquered by the Romans in 273 B.C. In between (410–273 B.C.), Paestum was overrun and ruled by the Oscan-speaking Lucanian warriors of southern Italy. Somehow, no matter who ruled it or what it was called, Paestum managed to flourish. Its remains present a picture of the wealth, high civilization, and ethnic diversity of first millennium B.C. Italy.

Look first at the painting from Greek-era Poseidonia of the man reclining on a couch. He wears a wreath and is holding a lyre in his right hand. He is one of ten men, in a series of paintings, shown participating in a *sumposion*, or "wine party," a typical gathering of aristocratic Greek culture. (Ironically, we get our word *symposium*, or "academic

meeting," from this ancient, alcoholic merrymaking.) His manicured beard and trim physique identify him as a member of the leisure class.

A superb example of ancient painting, it was discovered on the outskirts of Paestum in 1968 and dates to 480/470 B.C. It is part of one of five tomb paintings from the Tomb of the Diver, named after the painting, on the lid of the tomb, of a young man in the act of diving, perhaps a symbol of the journey into the underworld.

The artistic style, the clothing, and the sumposion are all Greek. Yet the practice of painting a tomb and the use of diving as a symbol of death are Etruscan in origin. Thus, the paintings demonstrate the cultural mix of Greek Italy.

This sums up the experience of Poseidonia well, because the city grew rich as a commercial center between the Etruscans and the Greeks farther south. Poseidonia's Greekness is underlined by its excellent Doric temples; the ruins of these are among the best such ruins in the world today. Also of note is the Greek-style rectangular

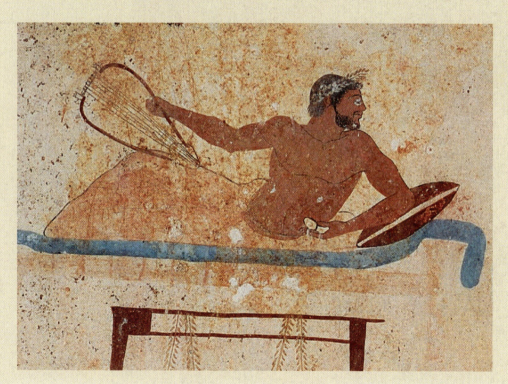

A Guest Holding a Lyre (painting from Tomb of the Diver, Paestum) (Scala/Art Resource, NY)

orders An order is a social class whose members share a common rank.

Most senators were patricians (puh-TRIH-shunz), as early Rome's hereditary aristocracy was known. The rest of the people, the bulk of Roman society, were called plebeians (pleh-BEE-unz). Plebeians were free; most were ordinary people, though some were wealthy. Patricians monopolized the senate and priesthoods, and they did not intermarry with plebeians. The Romans called these two social classes **orders**. Both in the monarchy and, later, in the Republic, most wealthy Romans were landowners.

Marsyas (bronze statue, Paestum) (Scala/Art Resource, NY)

the local elite. Many non-elite inhabitants of Paestum no doubt lost land to the settlers.

Meanwhile, both the landscape and the politics of the city were transformed. The agora of Poseidonia became the forum of Paestum, on whose sides were built Roman-style buildings, including a council hall and a temple of Jupiter (like the temple on Rome's Capitoline Hill). Eventually, Paestum would acquire an amphitheater and Roman baths.

Paestum also acquired a copy of a famous Roman work of art, the bronze statue of Marsyas, which is reproduced here. This statue dates to the mid-third century B.C. It was cast in imitation of a well-known statue of Marsyas in Rome and erected at the center of Paestum on the west side of the forum.

For the Romans, Marsyas symbolized liberty. He was a character from Greek mythology and had been adopted by the prominent plebeian family of Marcius Rutilus to symbolize the victory of the plebeians in their struggle with the patricians.

The statue's right hand would have been raised in a gesture of authority. His calves are ringed by metal bands, like the legs of a slave, except that the chains of slavery have been broken off. For the citizens of Paestum, the statue celebrated their identification with Rome, their liberation from Lucanian rule, their privileged status as Latin colonists, and perhaps their freedom from economic need as landholders in a fertile territory.

The statue of Marsyas is considered today to be one of the most important works of the new culture of an Italy dominated by Rome. But it is many other things as well: It symbolizes the combined plebeian-patrician elite of Rome and its success in extending Roman power throughout the peninsula. It demonstrates the continued importance of Greek culture, since Marsyas was a Greek character, but it also shows the flexibility with which the Roman elite adapted Greek symbols for its own purposes. And it reminds us of the willingness of the Romans to trample on local customs and impose Roman culture throughout Italy.

QUESTIONS

1. How does the history of Paestum illustrate the ethnic diversity of first millennium B.C. Italy?

2. What light on the life of a Greek colony is shed by the Tomb of the Diver?

3. What does the statue of Marsyas symbolize about Roman rule in Italy?

public space, with its central agora, three broad avenues, and thirty-two cross streets, as well as the strong walls.

Under the Lucanian conquerors, Poseidonia continued the traditions of tomb painting and cultural interchange. Many Lucanian tomb paintings from the town survive, and they illustrate a lively mix of Greek and Italic styles.

After Poseidonia was conquered by Rome in 273 B.C., it became known as Paestum and acquired the status of a Latin colony. As soldiers and sailors, the citizens of Paestum defended Roman interests in southern Italy. In return, and because they were Latin colonists, they enjoyed the privileges of free trade with Rome and intermarriage with Romans, as well as the more theoretical possibility of becoming Roman citizens by moving to Rome (but only after leaving a son in the colony). The citizens consisted of around five thousand Roman and Latin settlers, as well as

The whole people, probably both patricians and plebeians, met in an assembly organized in thirty local units, or *curiae*, hence, the name *curiate assembly*. Although the assembly's numbers were large, its powers were limited. Before becoming law, resolutions of the assembly required approval by the senate.

Early Rome was a class-based society, but it was open to foreigners. Among others, Etruscans, Sabines, and Latins—as the inhabitants of other Latin-speaking towns are called—came to settle

SECTION SUMMARY

- Rome was first settled as a village around 1000 B.C. and added a palace and sanctuaries in the 700s B.C.

- Rome borrowed much from the more advanced culture of the Greek colonies in southern Italy and Sicily.

- The twelve Etruscan city-states, north of Rome, were rich, powerful, and sophisticated. Rome's last three kings were probably Etruscan immigrants who added Etruscan elements to Roman culture.

- Early Rome was a class-based society with a monarchy and a sharp division between patricians (aristocrats) and plebeians (commoners).

in Rome. Foreigners, at first, had low status, but they gained equality around 550 B.C., for pragmatic purposes. Rome needed soldiers to fight its wars; in order to expand the body of loyal infantrymen, the immigrants were granted citizenship—a reform traditionally associated with King Servius Tullius (578–535 B.C.).

Servius probably introduced to Rome the hoplite phalanx (see page 56), with immigrants included in its ranks. The changes in the army contributed to the process that, within several generations of Servius's reform, took Rome from monarchy to republic.

THE EARLY AND MIDDLE REPUBLIC AT HOME, CA. 509–133 B.C.

How was the Roman Republic governed, and how did that government shape the Western political tradition?

Tradition says that the Roman Republic was established in 509 B.C., when the kings were overthrown. Nowadays, scholars envision a long process rather than a single, dramatic upheaval. In either case, the Republic differed from the monarchy in two basic ways. First, the Republic stood for liberty, which for the Romans meant both freedom from the arbitrary power of a king and freedom to participate in public affairs. Second, the Republic was a commonwealth, in Latin, **res publica** (rays POO-blee-kuh), literally "public thing," as opposed to *res privata*, "private thing," as the Romans characterized monarchy. As a kingdom, Rome belonged to the royal family, but as a republic, it belonged to the Roman people. In theory, the Roman people were sovereign—that is, the people ruled the state.

But which people? This is a key question because the Romans did *not* embrace another principle that might seem to follow from liberty: equality. Rather, they believed in order, balance, and competition, all of which are central themes of Roman Republican history. Roman society and culture, moreover, were conservative. Once the young Republic had its new values in place, it tried to maintain those values over the centuries, with little change.

We know relatively little about the Early Republic (509–287 B.C.) but enough to know that it witnessed centuries of social and political conflict. The Middle Republic (287–133 B.C.) was a shorter and better documented period of relative consensus at home and massive expansion abroad. Social and political conflict broke out again with a vengeance in the Late Republic (133–31 B.C.), ultimately rendering the Republic a deathblow.

res publica Latin for "public thing," it was the Romans' concept of their republic, which uniquely influenced Western political institutions.

Political Institutions

The best and most even-handed ancient analyst of Roman politics is the historian Polybius (po-LIH-bee-us) (ca. 200–118 B.C.). A Greek and former hostage who lived in Rome, Polybius observed his adopted city with an outsider's careful eye. Polybius argued that in the Middle Republic of his day, Rome was a "mixed constitution," balancing the power of the masses with the authority of the elite. The result was a strong and stable state.

Polybius divides Roman political institutions into three branches: executive, deliberative, and legislative. The American founders adopted a similar division, but they combined the legislative and deliberative functions and added a judicial branch. In Rome the executive branch also administered justice. Rome's executive branch was made up of magistrates—that is, public officials; the deliberative branch consisted of the Roman senate; and the legislative branch was composed of four different assemblies of the people.

senate In the ancient Roman Republic and Empire, the influential and powerful council of elders.

Executive power lay in the hands of Rome's powerful magistrates. They were elected and not chosen by lottery, as in Greek democracy. Election required campaigning, which in turn took money and connections. Magistracies were time-consuming jobs but offered no salary, unlike in Greek democracy. Thus, only a wealthy few could afford to hold public office in Rome.

Eager for strong magistrates, but afraid that power corrupts, Romans imposed the principles of *collegiality* and *annuality* on their officials. Every magistrate had one or more colleagues and held office for only one year. The chief magistrates were eventually called consuls, of which there were two. Each consul had the power to veto the other's actions. Like the former king, each consul had *imperium*, the power to issue commands and order punishments, including execution.

From about 500 B.C. to about 300 B.C., other public offices were created to help the consuls as administration grew more complex. In addition, the Romans elected two censors, older men chosen once every few years for eighteen month terms. At first, their job was to supervise the census, the military register of citizens that recorded each man's property class. Later, the censors became, as it were, supervisors of public morals, since they could punish "bad" citizens.

The Republic's government adapted flexibly to trying circumstances. In times of emergency, for example, the Republic turned power over to a single magistrate. The dictator, as he was called, made binding decisions, but he held office for only six months.

The Roman **senate** guided and advised the magistrates. During most of the Republic, the senate consisted of three hundred men, all former magistrates and each of whom served for life. Senators possessed great authority. They supervised public expenditures and were, for all practical purposes, in charge of foreign policy.

Only the assemblies of the people could make laws. There were four assemblies: the curiate assembly, the centuriate assembly, the council of the plebs, and the tribal assembly. Roman assemblies combined democratic and nondemocratic features. On the one hand, all decisions were made by majority vote, and only after speeches or campaigning. Assembly meetings were often preceded by public meetings, typically in the Forum, which featured lively debate. Women, free noncitizens, and even slaves could attend. On the other hand, voting took place by groups, and those groups were unrepresentative. Furthermore, in contrast to Greece, assembly participants stood rather than sat down and received no salary for attendance.

Although the curiate assembly of the monarchy survived, in the Republic, it had a largely ceremonial role. The centuriate assembly held real power: It elected magistrates, voted on laws and treaties, accepted declarations of war and peace, and acted as a court in cases of treason, homicide, and appeals of the magistrates' decisions. But this assembly was dominated by wealthy men, especially the equestrians, or cavalrymen. The poorest men, known as *proletarii* ("breeders"), often did not have even the chance to vote.

The two other assemblies were the council of the plebs and the tribal assembly. The tribal assembly eventually replaced the plebs and, in fact, became Rome's main legislative body in the third century B.C., outstripping the centuriate assembly in making laws. To understand the evolution and workings of the tribal assembly, we turn now to the class conflicts in Rome during the fifth through third centuries B.C.

A Clear Sign of Power   The lictor, or official, depicted in this bronze statuette (ca. first century A.D.) accompanied Roman magistrates, who had *imperium*, the power to issue punishments resulting in execution. That power is visible in the fasces—an ax in a bundle of wooden rods bound with straps—that he holds.   (Courtesy of the Trustees of the British Museum)

Conflict of the Orders, 494–287 B.C.

Social and political conflict between the patricians and plebeians severely tested the Roman state in the fifth century. There were only 136 patrician families in 509 B.C., but they dominated the Early Republic. The plebs, in contrast, comprised masses of peasants and a tiny number of men who, though prosperous, were not patricians. Plebeian artisans, traders, and shopkeepers made up only a small part of the population. The various plebeian groups each wanted to break patrician power. Wealthy plebeians wanted access to high office, from which they had been largely excluded. Ordinary plebeians demanded relief from debt, redistribution of land, and codification and publication of the law. For a century and a half, the two groups of plebeians worked together, writing an important chapter in the history of political resistance.

Debt and hunger loomed large as concerns of ordinary plebeians. If a free man could not repay a loan, he had to work off what he owed, often for the rest of his life. Plebeians wanted this harsh system abolished. The average farm was too small to feed a family, so most peasants depended on public land for farming and grazing. Time and again throughout Republican history, however, public land was taken by the wealthy, who denied access to the poor. The only plebeian hope was to change the system.

The plebeians organized themselves as a kind of state within the state, complete with their own assembly (the council of the plebs) and officials (the tribunes of the plebs). The decisions of the council of the plebs, called *plebiscita* (from which *plebiscite* comes), were binding only on the plebs; they did not receive the full force of law for over two hundred years. Yet, the plebs did not retreat. On several occasions during the Early Republic, they resorted to secession: The plebs, as a whole, left the city, often for the Aventine Hill, where they stayed until their grievances were addressed (see inset, **MAP 5.2**).

The ten tribunes (TRIB-yoonz), elected annually by the plebs, were the people's champions. A tribune's house stood open to any plebeian who needed him, and he could not leave the city limits. Inside the city of Rome, a tribune also had the right to veto any act of the magistrates, assembly, or senate that harmed plebeians. In return, the plebs swore to treat the tribunes as sacrosanct and to lynch anyone who harmed them.

But the patricians struck back. They controlled important priesthoods and had many supporters in the military. Furthermore, the new tribal assembly, created around the same time as the council of the plebs, used a system of representation that heavily favored landowners, such as patricians. The tribal assembly elected lower magistrates and, like the centuriate assembly, voted on laws and acted as a court of appeals.

Still, the plebeians pressed onward and forced concessions from the patricians, until finally the patricians retreated. They decided to neutralize the poor by meeting the main demands of the plebeian elite. The outcome was a new nobility that combined patricians and well-to-do plebeians. The patricians had decided to compromise to keep most of their privileges. The personnel changed, but the elite maintained power in Rome.

A key moment came in 449 B.C., with publication of the law code known as the "Twelve Tables," eventually, if not at first, on twelve bronze tablets in the Forum. By modern standards, the code was tough and primitive, but its very existence was a plebeian victory because published law was accessible and dependable. Unfortunately, the complex legal procedure remained a secret of the priests for another 150 years, which meant that no poor man could go to court without the help of a rich patron.

Continued plebeian pressure slowly yielded other gains through the fourth century B.C. Around 445 B.C., the patricians accepted patrician-plebeian intermarriage, but it took nearly another eighty years, until 367 B.C., until they agreed to plebeian consuls. That same year saw a debt-relief law, and further debt relief came in 326 B.C.

Finally, in 287 B.C., the patrician and plebeian **orders** were formally merged, and a law called the "lex Hortensia" made decisions of the council of the plebs and the tribal assembly binding on the whole community, including patricians. Rome's new, combined patrician-plebeian elite was based on wealth, not heredity. Most Romans were non-elite, but at least they had won something: debt relief, access to the published laws, increased power for their assembly, and, most important, protection from arbitrary power.

Families and Patronage

The family was the basic unit of Roman society and a model of political authority, both foreign and domestic. Elite Roman families stuck together and wielded great power.

The Latin word *familia* is broader in meaning than the English word *family*. Better translated as "household," it connotes slaves, animals, and property, as well as the members of a nuclear family and their ancestors or descendants. In theory, though not always in practice, the Roman household was an authoritarian institution governed by a male; thus, the familia is an example of patriarchy.

The legal head of the familia was the ***paterfamilias*** (pah-ter-fah-MIL-ee-us)—the oldest living male, usually the father. Roman respect for the paterfamilias stemmed from Roman esteem for ancestors, who were more important than in Greek culture. All patricians and some plebeians belonged to a *gens* (plural, *gentes*), a kinship group that traced its ancestry back to a purported common ancestor. All Roman males had a personal and a family name, and patricians and elite plebeians also had a third (middle) name, indicating their gens—for example, Gaius Julius Caesar, whose personal name "Gaius" was followed by the gens name "Julius" and the familia name "Caesar."

According to Roman law, the paterfamilias had supreme power within the household. He had the right to sell family members into slavery. A son, no matter how old, was always legally subject to the authority of a living paterfamilias. However, practice was more complex than theory. Roman fathers rarely used their power to kill an errant wife or child. The sources are full of fathers who showed affection, love, and even indulgence toward their children. Moreover, Roman women usually married in their late teens and men in their late twenties. Given the low life expectancies, it was common for a man of 25 to have already buried his father. Many, perhaps even most, adult males were independent of a paterfamilias.

Unlike men, Roman women never became legally independent, even on the death of a paterfamilias. Instead of receiving a personal name, a daughter was called by the name of her father's gens. For example, Gaius Julius Caesar's daughter was called Julia; if Caesar had had a second daughter, she would have been Julia Secunda ("Julia the Second"). Although fathers were expected to support all male children, they had to support only the first of their daughters. In other words, they were free to "expose" additional daughters—that is, leave them in the open to die or, as was perhaps more likely, to be adopted or raised as a slave. A father also arranged a daughter's marriage and provided her with a dowry. In theory, again, the customs suggest a most severe relationship, but the evidence shows considerable father-daughter affection, including married daughters who sought advice or aid from their fathers.

Most women in early Rome married *cum manu* (kum MAN-oo) (literally, "with hand"); that is, they were "handed over" to their husbands, who became their new paterfamilias. Even so, Roman wives and mothers had more prestige and freedom than their counterparts in Classical Greece. Legends of early Rome mention some elite women of influence who were peacemakers, negotiators, or catalysts of quarrels among men. Roman women regularly shared meals and social activities with their parents and were expected to take an interest in their husbands' political lives.

Roman society was modeled on the hierarchy of the Roman family. At the center of things stood patrons and clients. *Patron* (derived from *pater*, "father") means "defender" or "protector." *Client* means "dependent." Roman society consisted of pyramidal and hereditary patron-client networks. Most patrons were in turn clients of someone more powerful; only a few men stood at the top of the pyramid. Various paths led to the status of client. A peasant in need of help on his farm might ask a wealthy neighbor to become his patron. A freed slave became the client of his former owner. A conquered foe became the client of the victorious general.

Patron and client helped each other in various ways. A patron might provide a client with food, with property for a dowry, or with legal assistance.

paterfamilias Oldest living male in an ancient Roman family, who had supreme legal power within the household.

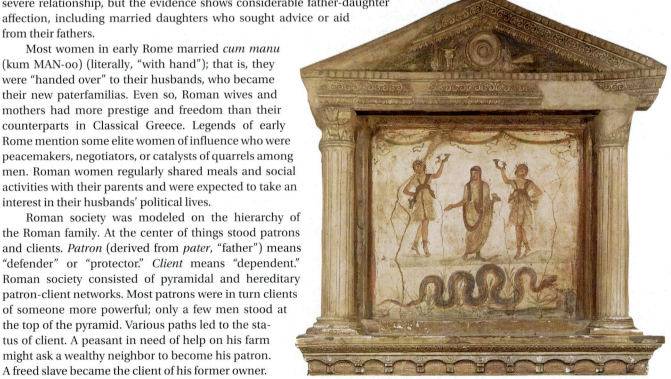

Shrine of a Wealthy Household This painting from Pompeii shows the spirit of the paterfamilias in a toga, which is wrapped around his head in keeping with the Roman procedures of sacrifice. He is flanked by the spirits of departed ancestors. A snake symbolizes fertility. (Alinari/Art Resource, NY)

In return, a client owed his patron his vote and his presence in public on important occasions—possession of a large clientele signified prestige and power.

Cloaked in an elaborate language of goodwill, the patron-client relationship was considered a matter of *fides* (FEE-days) ("good faith" or "trustworthiness"). Romans spoke not of a client submitting to a patron's power, but rather of a client "commending himself" to the patron's fides. A patron spoke not of his clients, but of his "friends," especially if they were men of standing or substance.

Patronage played an important role in domestic politics and in foreign affairs. Experience as patrons schooled Roman leaders in treating the peoples they conquered as clients, often as personal clients. Moreover, the Roman state sometimes took foreign countries into its collective "fides"—much as a patron did a client—thus, allowing Rome to extend its influence without the constraints of a formal alliance.

Religion and Worldview

If we knew nothing about early Roman religion, we could deduce much about it from the familia and patronage. We could expect to find an emphasis on powerful fathers and binding agreements, and both are indeed present. The task of a Roman priest, whether an official of the state or an individual paterfamilias, was to establish what the Romans called the "peace of the gods." Roman cults aimed at obtaining the gods' agreement to human requests, at "binding" the gods—the Latin term for which is *religio*.

The earliest Roman religion was animistic—that is, it centered on the spirits that, the Romans believed, haunted the household and the fields and forests and determined the weather. The spirit of the hearth was Vesta; of the door, Janus; of the rain and sun, Jupiter (later identified with the Greek sky-god and the father-god Zeus), and of the crops and vegetation Mars (later identified with the Greek war-god Ares). The Romans believed that these spirits needed to be appeased—hence, the contractual nature of their prayers and offerings. Over the years, as a result of Greek influence, anthropomorphism (that is, the worship of humanlike gods and goddesses) replaced Roman animism.

Roman state religion grew out of house religion. Vesta, the hearth-goddess, became goddess of the civic hearth; Janus, the door-god, became god of the city's gates; Jupiter became the general overseer of the gods; and Mars became the god of war. When trade and conquest brought the Romans into contact with foreign religions, the Romans tended to absorb them. The senate screened and sometimes rejected new gods, but by and large, Roman religion was tolerant and inclusive.

The Republic sponsored numerous priestly committees, or colleges, to secure the peace of the gods. Originally restricted to patricians, most of the highest priesthoods were opened to plebeians by law in 300 B.C. Although some priesthoods were full-time jobs, most left the officeholder free to pursue a parallel career as a magistrate or a senator. The two most important priestly colleges were the augurs (AW-gers), who were in charge of foretelling the future from omens and other signs, and the pontiffs, who exercised a general supervision of Roman religion. The chief pontiff, the *pontifex maximus* (PON-tih-fex MAX-ih-mus), was the head of the state clergy. He was chosen by election. The pontiffs alone controlled the interpretation of the law until the fourth century B.C. The Romans allowed priests to interpret the law on the theory that an offense against humans was also an offense against the gods.

There were also two colleges of priestesses: those of Ceres, goddess of fertility and death, and those of the Vestal Virgins. The six Vestals tended the civic hearth and made sure that its fire never went out. They served, as it were, as wives of the whole community, as guardians of the civil household. The Vestals were the only Roman women not under the authority of a paterfamilias. Chosen between the ages of 6 and 10 by the pontifex maximus, they had to remain virgins while they served or face death, but enjoyed honorable retirement after thirty years.

Roman ideology promoted simple and austere farmers' virtues—discipline, hard work, frugality, temperance, and the avoidance of public displays of affection, even between spouses. Such virtues underlined the difference between the Republic and the kings, with their luxury and sophistication. At the same time, these virtues papered over class distinctions between rich and poor and so promoted stability.

Other Roman ideals included the supreme virtue of the household, *pietas*—devotion and loyalty to the familia, the gods, and the state. Household duties and gender obligations were defined clearly. Women were to be modest, upright, and practical. Men were to project *gravitas* ("weight" or "seriousness"), never lightness or levity. A serious man would display self-control and constancy, the ability to persevere against difficult odds. The masculine ideal was *virtus* (literally, "manliness"), which indicated excellence in war and government.

Roman men who attained virtus considered themselves entitled to the reward of *dignitas*, meaning not only public esteem, but the tangible possession of a dignified position and official rank—in short, public office. The ultimate test of virtus, however, was in battle. Rome's wars supplied ample occasion to display it.

SECTION SUMMARY

- Republican government consisted of three branches: executive, deliberative, and legislative.
- The magistrates, the senate, and the assemblies were Rome's three main political institutions.
- The Conflict of the Orders led to debt relief for the poor and a combined patrician-plebeian nobility for the rich.
- The Roman household, headed by the *paterfamilias*, was a model of political authority.
- Roman society was made up of networks of patrons and clients.
- Romans idealized *pietas*, that is, loyalty to household, the gods, and the Republic.

THE EARLY AND MIDDLE REPUBLIC ABROAD, CA. 509–133 B.C.

How did Rome conquer an empire?

At the beginning of the Republic (ca. 509 B.C.), Roman territory comprised about 500 square miles. By 338 B.C., Rome controlled the 2,000 square miles of Latium and was moving north into Etruria and south into Samnite country. Three-quarters of a century later, in 265 B.C., Rome controlled all of the Italian peninsula south of an imaginary line from Pisae (modern Pisa) to Ariminum (modern Rimini), an area of about 50,000 square miles (see **Map 5.2**). By 146 B.C., Roman provinces included Sicily, Cisalpine Gaul (northernmost Italy), Sardinia, Corsica, and Spain (divided into two provinces). Once great Carthage was the Roman province of Africa (roughly, modern Tunisia), and once-mighty Macedon was the province of Macedonia, whose governor was also effectively in charge of Greece. The Seleucid kingdom was free but fatally weakened. Rome was the supreme power between Gibraltar and the Levant. It was the greatest empire of the ancient West. How and why had Rome, from its humble beginnings as a local power, reached this breathtaking height?

Republican Expansion: The Conquest of Italy, ca. 509–265 B.C.

Romans maintain that they conquered an empire without ever committing an act of aggression. When war was declared, a special college of priests informed the gods that Rome was merely retaliating for foreign injury. True, the Romans were frequently attacked by others, but often only after provocative behavior by Rome had left its rivals little choice.

Rome's early conquests reveal many of its lasting motives for expansion. No doubt, lust for conquest played a part, as did fear and hatred of outsiders, but self-control and shrewdness were stronger Roman characteristics. Greed, particularly land-hunger, was a perennial theme. Sometimes a domestic political motive was at work, for foreign adventure was a convenient way of deflecting plebeian energies. Perhaps the most significant factors, however, were the personal ambitions of a warrior elite and the presence of conflict in early Italy.

WHY ROME FOUGHT

Victory in battle promised both prestige and booty and the political success that might follow. Military achievement brought unique acclaim. For example, certain victorious generals were allowed to celebrate a **triumph**; no such ceremony rewarded the feats of peacemakers or distinguished judges or other public benefactors. The triumphant general rode a chariot through the city to the Temple of Jupiter on the Capitoline Hill. He was accompanied by his troops, by the spoils of victory, including famous captives, and by the magistrates and senators.

triumph Elaborate procession through the streets of ancient Rome to salute a general's victory over a foreign army.

🌐 **Map 5.3—Roman Expansion, 264–44 B.C.**
Wars against Carthage, the major Greco-Macedonian powers, Gauls, Germans, North Africans, and other peoples brought Rome an empire on three continents.

former territory was annexed as the province of Africa). Exhausted as it was, Rome immediately leaped into a long conflict in Greece and Anatolia. The king of Macedon, Philip V (r. 221–179 B.C.), had made an alliance with Hannibal after Cannae, which left Rome with a score to settle. Rome won a relatively quick and easy victory when, in 197 B.C., the legions crushed the Macedonian phalanx at Cynoscephalae in central Greece (see **Map 5.3**). The age of the phalanx was over; the legion had defeated it decisively.

Rome had hoped to impose a patron-client relationship on Greece and Macedon, thereby avoiding having to sustain a permanent military presence, but the independent-minded Greeks refused to submit to Roman domination. Several years of tension followed, only to lead to renewed wars. First the Seleucids, under the ambitious king Antiochus III (r. 223–187 B.C.), moved into the Greek peninsula and challenged Rome for hegemony. It was in this war that Hannibal took a small, doomed part. Roman forces made short work of the enemy. Driven out not only from Greece, but from Anatolia as well, the Seleucids in effect recognized Roman supremacy in the Mediterranean (188 B.C.).

Then came another two rounds of war that pitted Rome against a resurgent Macedon and various Greek states (171–167 and 150–146 B.C.). Victorious in both wars, Rome deprived the Greeks and Macedonians of their independence. Wherever democracy had survived in Greece, it was replaced with oligarchy. In 146 B.C., Rome destroyed Corinth, one of Greece's wealthiest cities, as a warning against further rebellion. For the next two centuries, Rome would pay little attention to its Greek province except to tax it.

By annexing Carthage, Macedon, and Greece in the mid-second century B.C., Rome created a dynamic for expansion around the entire Mediterranean. Before the century was over, southern Gaul was annexed, and Rome had gained a foothold in Asia. The kingdom of Pergamum (northwestern Anatolia) had supported Rome throughout Rome's wars in the east. When Attalus III of Pergamum died without an heir in 133 B.C., he surrendered his kingdom to the Roman people, who made it into a province of Asia.

Two great Hellenistic states remained independent: the Seleucid kingdom, that is, Syria, and Ptolemaic Egypt. Rome frequently interfered in their affairs, however, and no one was surprised when, in the first century B.C., they too were annexed.

The Socioeconomic Consequences of Expansion

Expansion led to big and unintended changes in Rome's society, economy, and culture. Already wealthy, the Roman elite now came into fabulous riches. Huge profits awaited the generals, patrons, diplomats, magistrates, tax collectors, and businessmen who followed Rome's armies. In Italy, most profits were in the form of land; the provinces offered not only land, but also in slaves, booty, and graft. One of the worst grafters, Gaius Verres, governor of Sicily from 73 to 71 B.C., was prosecuted by Cicero (see page 135) for allegedly extorting tens of thousands of pounds of silver from his province. However, even Cicero skimmed off several thousand pounds of silver as governor of the province of Cilicia (southern Anatolia) from 51 to 50 B.C.

The first Roman coinage, traditionally dated to 289 B.C., facilitated commercial transactions. Previously, the Romans had made do with barter, uncoined bronze, and cast bronze bars, but now they imitated the workmanship and style of Greek coins. Equally prominent in the homes of wealthy Romans were Greek metalwork, jewelry, art objects, and other luxury goods. Conservatives bemoaned the decline of Roman austerity, but they fought a rear-guard action.

Ordinary Romans needed no reminder of the virtues of austerity, for they did not share in the elite's profit from Roman expansion. Indeed, a century of warfare—from the outbreak of the Punic Wars in 264 B.C. to the destruction of Carthage and Corinth in 146 B.C.—pushed the Roman people to the breaking point. Hannibal's invasion ruined much of the farmland of southern Italy and reduced Italian manpower considerably. Yet, most people would have soon rebounded from these problems if they had not faced other serious troubles.

Conscription had become the norm. The average term of military service, between ages 17 and 46, was six years; the maximum term was twenty years. Because experienced legionnaires were at a premium, commanders did not want to release them from service. But the longer a man served, the harder it was for his wife and children to keep the family farm running. A patron might have helped, but most patrons, in fact, added to the problem through the introduction to Italy of large-scale agricultural entrepreneurship.

A revolution in the Italian countryside brought ruin on the free peasantry of Italy. Wealthy Romans wanted to invest in large landed estates, or *latifundia* (lat-uh-FUN-dee-uh), worked by slaves. These estates were either mixed farms (most often devoted to cultivating vines, olives, and grain) or ranches (establishments where animals were raised for meat, milk, and wool). One devotee of the latter was the prominent conservative Marcus Porcius Cato (KAY-toe) (234–149 B.C.), known as **Cato the Censor**. Cato argued that there were only three ways to get rich: "pasturage, pasturage, and pasturage." All a would-be entrepreneur needed was land, which Rome had conquered a huge amount of in Italy. Called public land, Rome's new territory belonged to the Roman people, but an individual was legally entitled to claim about 320 acres as his own. Many entrepreneurs flouted the law, however, and grabbed much more than their fair share of public land. In addition, they often forced families of absent soldiers off private land, either by debt foreclosure or by outright violence. Sometimes, families would leave the land for the city, but usually they stayed as tenants.

The last two centuries B.C. witnessed the transformation of Roman rural society from one of independent farmers to one in which slave labor played a major role. By the end of the first century B.C., Italy's slave population was estimated at two million, about a third of the peninsula's total. Prisoners of war and conquered civilians provided a ready supply of slaves. Most worked in agriculture or mining, and their treatment was often abominable; the fewer house slaves were usually better off.

There were few escape routes from poverty. Before about 170 B.C., poor Romans were sometimes able to find land in colonies, but by 170 B.C., Rome had established all the colonies in Italy that its security demanded. A displaced farmer who wanted to compete in the labor market would have found it difficult to underbid cheap slave labor. In any case, Roman ideology frowned on wage labor by citizens. Nor was it practical for a poor farmer to sue a wealthy patron who seized his land, because a plaintiff himself had to bring the accused into court.

The situation of the Italian peasantry was becoming increasingly miserable by the mid-second century B.C. As one modern scholar has put it, "In conquering what they were pleased to call the world, the Romans ruined a great part of the Italian people."[2]

Cato the Censor Name given to Marcus Porcius Cato, a Roman general and statesman. He was the first Roman historian to write in Latin.

The Impact of Greece on Rome and Its Empire

Rome learned much from its new encounters with foreign peoples—and from none more than the Greeks. Wealthy Romans cultivated interests in Greek art, literature, rhetoric, and speculative thought; poor and rich alike enjoyed Greek drama. Before the mid-third century B.C., Roman literature was virtually nonexistent. An oral tradition of songs, ballads, and funeral oratory kept alive the deeds of the famous, for writing was generally restricted to commercial and government records and inscriptions. In short, the Romans conquered Italy without writing about it.

Contact with the Greek cities brought changes. Large numbers of Roman soldiers in Magna Graecia (southern Italy and Sicily) were introduced to comedy, tragedy, mimes, and sophisticated song lyrics, and many developed a permanent taste for them. It is no accident that the first production of a drama at Rome took place in 240 B.C., the year after the end of the First Punic War. Afterward, the annual production of such dramas became standard procedure.

No one could accuse the Romans of rushing headlong into a new age, however. The authorities continued to look down on theater as emotional and corrupt. They did not allow the building of a permanent theater in Rome until 55 B.C., nor did the Roman elite readily become playwrights or poets. The first gentleman poet in Rome, Lucilius (180–102 B.C.), did not arrive until the second century B.C., and he was a Latin, not a Roman. His predecessors, the founders of Latin literature, were all of low social status; little of their work survives.

The two great early Latin playwrights are Titus Maccius Plautus (ca. 254–184 B.C.) and Publius Terentius Afer, today known as Terence (ca. 195–159 B.C.). Both of them wrote comedies on the model of the great Greek playwright Menander (see page 97). Plautus was a poor man from northern Italy who learned his Latin in Rome; Terence was a North African slave, educated and freed in Rome. Twenty-one plays by Plautus and six by Terence survive. Plautus's plays are generally slapstick farces. They are set in Greece, not Rome, in part, out of escapism (many were written during the Second Punic War), in part, out of the censorial demands of the Roman authorities. They nonetheless reveal much about Roman society. Terence's plays are more subtle than Plautus's, indicating the growing sophistication of Roman theatergoers.

Latin prose developed more slowly than did poetry and drama. The first histories by Romans, composed after the Second Punic War, were written in Greek, for Latin lacked the vocabulary or the audience for history. Cato the Censor was the first historian of Rome to write in Latin. His *Origines*, of which we have only remnants, recounted Roman history from the origin of the city to about 150 B.C. The earliest surviving Latin prose work is Cato's *On Agriculture*.

In the traditional education of a Roman aristocrat, parents and close family friends played the primary role. Although this practice continued, wealthy Romans in the second century B.C. began acquiring Greek slaves to educate their sons in the Greek language and Greek literature. Soon Greek freedmen began setting up schools offering the same subjects. Before long, similar Latin grammar schools also opened.

One of the forms of Greek literature that appealed most to the practical-minded Romans was rhetoric. Roman orators studied Greek models, and many would say that they eventually outdid the Greeks. Cato was the first Roman to publish his speeches, and he also wrote a book on rhetoric. Both gave impetus to the spread of sophisticated rhetoric in Rome.

Scipio Aemilianus, conqueror of Carthage in 146 B.C., not only had a distinguished political and military career; he also served as patron of a group of prominent statesmen and soldiers who shared his love of Hellenism. Among the writers whom they supported were the playwright Terence, the poet Lucilius, the historian Polybius, and the Stoic philosopher Panaetius (ca. 185–109 B.C.). The Stoic emphases on duty, wisdom, and world brotherhood appealed both to Rome's traditional ideology and to its more recent acquisition of empire. Yet, not all Romans shared Scipio's admiration of Greek culture; Cato, for example, was famously ambivalent.

Luxurious Earrings   A wealthy Roman woman might have been proud to wear these refined and expensive gold earrings, produced in a Greek city of southern Italy in the second century B.C. Only 2 inches long, each earring shows a dove standing on a small, garland-trimmed base.   (Pair of earrings with pendant doves, Greek, Hellenistic period, 150–100 B.C.; gold, garnet, and glass paste; L. 5.2 cm. Courtesy of the Museum of Fine Arts, Boston, Harriet Otis Cruft Fund, 68.5a.b)

Cornelia, Scipio Aemilianus's mother-in-law, is an example of the political importance of elite women. She was an educated lover of Hellenism who wrote letters that existed several hundred years later as examples of elegant Latin prose. Her villa in the resort of Misenum on the Bay of Naples was well known for the distinguished guests whom she received there. When her husband, an outstanding statesman and general, died, Cornelia chose to remain a widow. One of the men who tried to change her mind was no less a figure than the king of Egypt. The widow spent her time managing her own estate and supervising the education of her two sons, the future tribunes Tiberius and Gaius Gracchus.

Although Cornelia's privileges were extraordinary, she is nonetheless a reminder of the opportunities that imperial expansion offered to wealthy Roman women. Marriage practices are one example of change. Few women were married *cum manu* anymore—that is, handed over by their fathers to their husbands. A woman's father or nearest male relative, not her husband, was most likely to be her paterfamilias, which meant that a husband's control over his wife's dowry was limited. The result was more freedom, at least for wealthy women.

SECTION SUMMARY

- The flexible infantry formation, known as the legion, was the key to Roman success in battle.

- Rome consolidated its control of Italy by wisely treating its allies with a mixture of firmness and generosity, including the extension of Roman citizenship.

- The strength of Rome's alliance led to success in the Punic Wars with Carthage and then drew Rome into conquering all the Hellenistic Greek states.

- Military expansion brought fabulous riches to the Roman elite, brought misery to the peasants of Italy, and established a slave system of two million people.

- Conquest of and contact with Greek civilization led to the rise of Latin literature.

Cornelia Mother of the Gracchi, Cornelia was an influential elite woman whose letters served as models of Latin prose style.

THE LATE REPUBLIC AND ITS COLLAPSE, 133–31 B.C.

How did the unintended consequences of conquest on Rome lead to a revolution that destroyed the Republic?

A citizen of the Roman Republic in the mid-second century B.C. might have looked forward to a long and happy future for his country, unaware that the Republic—after 350 years of expansion—was about to begin a century of domestic and foreign unrest that would bring down the whole system. Why and how did the Republic collapse? More than a century of warfare weighed heavily on the ordinary people of Italy—the Romans and allied peasants whose farms were ruined while they were off fighting. The Roman elite was bitterly divided over what to do about the problems of the peasants. One group wanted to redistribute land on behalf of the poor; another group had no sympathy for them.

By the Late Republic, the city of Rome was crowded: Scholars estimate the number of inhabitants to have reached one million by the end of the first century B.C. The government had to take charge of the grain supply. But elite politicians exploited the issue for partisan purposes. Once before, during the struggle between the patrician and plebeian orders in the Early Republic, the elite had been similarly divided and had resolved its differences through compromise (see page 118). In the Late Republic, however, ambitious nobles were no longer willing to subordinate themselves to the community. It was not long before competing armies of land-hungry peasants, thwarted from above, were marching across Italy.

Reformers and Revolutionaries

Many Romans fretted over the military dimension of the agrarian crisis. In modern societies, draftees are often the poorest people. In Rome, military service was a prestigious activity, so a property qualification was imposed and the poor were not drafted. As fewer and fewer potential soldiers could afford to own property, however, during the second century, it became necessary to reduce the property qualification several times. If the free peasantry continued its decline, Rome would either have to drop the property qualification for the military altogether or stop fielding armies. Clearly, something had to be done.

Gracchi Led by Tiberius Sempronius Gracchus and later his brother Gaius, this ancient Roman faction challenged the conservative senate on behalf of the poor.

Into the breach stepped Tiberius Sempronius Gracchus (GRAK-us) (d. 133 B.C.), one of the ten tribunes for the year 133 B.C. The son of Cornelia, and a distinguished general and ambassador (also named Tiberius), Tiberius belonged to the eminent **Gracchi** (GRAK-eye) family. He seemed an excellent spokesperson for a group of prominent senators who backed land reform to restore Rome's peasant soldiers.

Tiberius's proposed law restored the roughly 320-acre limit to the amount of public land a person could own (plus an exception for a man with two sons, who was allowed to hold about 667 acres). A commission was to be set up to redistribute land to the poor, in small lots that were to be inalienable—that is, the wealthy could not buy them back. The former landowners would be reimbursed for improvements they had made, such as buildings or plantings.

The proposal was moderate, but wealthy landowners repudiated it outright. Many senators suspected that Tiberius wanted to set himself up as a kind of superpatron, buoyed by peasant supporters. Senators also disliked his pushy and heavy-handed legislative tactics. Finally, Tiberius broke with custom by running for a second consecutive term as tribune. While the tribal assembly prepared to vote on the new tribunes, some senators led a mob to the Forum and had Tiberius and three hundred of his followers clubbed to death.

This shocking event marked the first time in the Republic that a political debate was settled by bloodshed in Rome itself. Tiberius's killers had not merely committed murder, but had attacked the traditional inviolability of the tribunes. The ancient sources agree that it was the beginning of a century of revolution. Over the next hundred years, violence grew as a weapon of politics in the Republic.

The land commission went ahead with its work, even without Tiberius. His younger brother, Gaius (GUY-us) (d. 121 B.C.) became tribune himself in 123 B.C. Gaius expanded Tiberius's coalition, adding to it supporters from the equestrian order and the urban populace, mainly composed of slaves and freedmen. He gave the plebs cheap grain at subsidized prices. The equestrians were wealthy landowners, similar to senators in most respects except for their failure to have reached the senate; they yearned for political power. A small but important group of equestrians was engaged in commerce and tax collection in the provinces. The senate regulated their activities through the so-called extortion courts, which tried corruption cases. Gaius staffed those courts with equestrians. Alluding to the new equestrian power, Gaius remarked, "I have left a sword in the ribs of the senate."

Gaius sponsored an extension of his brother's agrarian law, new colonies, public works, and relief for poor soldiers. Eventually, he ran aground on a plan to include the Italian allies as beneficiaries of reform—a farsighted notion, but one unpopular with the Roman people, who were jealous of their privileges. A riot by his supporters led the senate to pass a declaration of public emergency, empowering officials to use any means necessary to protect the state.

One of the consuls had Gaius and 250 of his followers killed. Another 3,000 Gracchans were executed soon thereafter. The Gracchan land commission gave land to approximately 75,000 citizens. The law, however, was amended to permit the resale of redistributed land, and the commission itself was abolished. With the wealthy poised to buy land back, the settlers' future was uncertain. The senatorial oligarchy was back in control.

Or so it seemed. In fact, Roman politics had become an unstable brew. In time, it became clear that the Gracchi had divided the political community into two loose groupings. On one side were the *optimates* (op-tee-MAH-tayz) ("the best people"; singular, *optimas*), conservatives who asserted the rule of the senate against popular tribunes and the maintenance of the estates of the wealthy in spite of the agrarian crisis. On the other side were the *populares* (pah-poo-LAH-rayz) ("men of the people"; singular, *popularis*), who challenged the rule of the senate in the name of relief of the poor. The populares were not democrats. Like the optimates, they were Roman nobles who believed in hierarchy, but, like the Gracchi, they advocated the redistribution of wealth and power as a way of restoring stability and strengthening the military.

By 100 B.C., Rome's agrarian crisis had become a full-scale military crisis, too. Roman armies under senatorial commanders fared poorly, both in Numidia (modern North Africa) and in southern Gaul against Germanic invaders (see **MAP 5.3**). The situation was saved by an outsider to established privilege, an equestrian named Gaius Marius (157–86 B.C.), the first member of his family to be elected consul, for 107 B.C. This "new man" proved to be a military reformer and a populairs. Marius made several moves to streamline and strengthen the Roman army: Camp followers were reduced in number, and individual soldiers were made to carry their own equipment. To meet the Germans, who attacked in overwhelming waves, maniples—the tactical subunits of a legion—were reorganized and combined into larger units called cohorts, rendering the army firmer and more cohesive. Most important, Marius abandoned altogether the property qualification for the military. As a result, Roman soldiers were no longer peasants doing part-time military service, but rather landless men making a profession of the military.

Politically, they became a force to be reckoned with. As an indispensable general, Marius demanded and won six elections to the consulship, unconstitutional though that was. Furthermore, after gaining victories in North Africa and Gaul, Marius championed his soldiers. In 100 B.C., he asked that land be distributed to them. The senate refused, but its triumph was temporary. The poor recognized that only military leaders, such as Marius, would give them land. As a result, ordinary Romans, who were all now eligible for the army, transferred their loyalty from the senate to their commanders.

Two new wars weakened the Republic further. First, its Italian allies rose against Rome in a bloody and bitter struggle from 91 to 89 B.C., known as the "Social War," that is, war with the *socii* ("allies"). The allies fought hard, and Rome, in order to prevail, had to concede to them what they had demanded at the outset: full Roman citizenship. The other conflict of this period pitted Rome against Mithridates (120–63 B.C.), a rebellious king in northern Anatolia with great ambitions. Mithridates conquered Roman territory in western Anatolia and slaughtered the numerous Italian businessmen and tax collectors there. He invaded Thrace and Greece, where he found great support. Once again a military man rose to save the day for Rome: Marius's former lieutenant, Lucius Cornelius Sulla Felix (ca. 138–78 B.C.), consul for the year 88 B.C.

Sulla was as ambitious as Marius, but he came from the opposite political camp: He was a patrician and an optimas. The two became deadly rivals. The two men's troops fought over the issue of the command against Mithridates. Sulla's forces won the first round by marching on Rome, but after they left for the east, Marius's men retook the city and settled scores. Victorious over Mithridates, Sulla returned to Italy in 83 B.C. and engaged in all-out civil war. Sulla defeated Marius's men in battle (minus Marius himself, who had died in 86), then sealed his victory by executing his political opponents, as many as two thousand men. Their land was confiscated and sold to Sulla's friends. Sulla also confiscated the land of any Italian community that had opposed him and gave it to his veterans, about eighty thousand men.

Having assumed the long-dormant office of dictator—but without a time limit on his tenure—Sulla attempted to restore the senatorial rule of pre-Gracchan days. To do this, he greatly weakened the tribunate and strengthened the senate, whose size he doubled, from about three hundred to about six hundred members.

Sulla retired in 79 B.C. and died a year later. His hope of restoring law and order under the senate died with him. The populares soon regained enough strength to restore the old powers of the tribunes. Discontent smoldered among the men whose land Sulla had confiscated. Equally serious, many senators, aspiring to what Sulla had done and not to what he had said, pursued personal power, not the collective interests of the senate.

Caesar

At first, the dominant leader after Sulla was the optimas Pompey the Great (106–48 B.C.), a brilliant general and a supporter of Sulla. Young Pompey (POM-pee) went from command to command: He put down an agrarian rebellion in Italy and a rebellion in Spain, cleared the Mediterranean of pirates, defeated Mithridates again after that able king started another war, and added rich conquests to the empire in Anatolia, Syria, Phoenicia, and Palestine. In the fifties B.C., however, the tide began turning in favor of Gaius Julius **Caesar** (100–44 B.C.), an even more gifted general and politician—indeed, perhaps one of history's greatest. A popularis, Caesar (SEE-zer) had family connections to Marius. Caesar's career depended on his oratory, his boldness, and his sheer talent at war and politics. Caesar conquered Gaul, gained a foothold in Britain, and laid the foundations of Roman rule in Egypt (see **MAP 5.3**).

Caesar Roman general gifted at war and politics, he was named dictator in 49 B.C. and was later assassinated by the members of the senate in 44 B.C.

While the elite of the Late Republic struggled to maintain order and secure power, ordinary people struggled for survival. Violence had become a way of life in rural Italy. Many once-prosperous farmers, dispossessed peasants, and runaway slaves ended up as robbers or bandits. It was also an era of slave revolts, the most serious of which lasted from 73 to 71 B.C., under the leadership of Spartacus, a Thracian gladiator who had once served as a Roman allied soldier. An able commander, Spartacus beat nine separate Roman armies in two years before finally

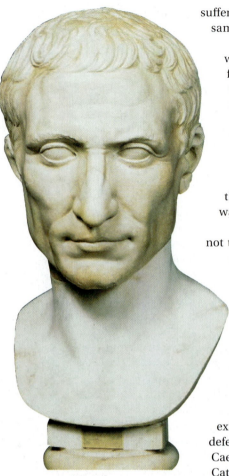

Bust of Julius Caesar This marble sculpture accurately conveys the conqueror's firmness of expression and perhaps his intelligence—but not his looks, since Caesar was bald. (Vatican Museums/Scala/ Art Resource, NY)

suffering defeat. (See the feature, "The Written Record: Spartacus's Slave Revolt.") At the same time, Rome also faced major wars in its provinces.

Pompey and Caesar sought alliances with other families by marrying influential women or by becoming their lovers. In 80 B.C., for example, Pompey divorced his first wife to advance his career by marrying Aemilia, Sulla's stepdaughter. Aemilia was not only married at the time, but pregnant by her first husband. Soon after her divorce and remarriage, she died in childbirth. Caesar had many lovers, among whom, there was the queen of Egypt, Cleopatra (see pages 100–101). Caesar had a penchant for certain Egyptian institutions, such as the Egyptian calendar, and he toyed with becoming a monarch himself, an inclination that Cleopatra perhaps encouraged.

Another of Caesar's lovers was Servilia, stepsister of Marcus Porcius Cato (Cato the Younger, 95–46 B.C.), great-grandson of the famous censor (see page 127). She was also the mother of Brutus, the man who would eventually help murder Caesar.

Pompey was an optimas, Caesar a popularis, but the two of them agreed that they, not the senate or the assemblies, should dominate Rome. Each man's ambition was more important to him than any political principles. In 60 B.C., they entered into a pact with a third ambitious noble, Marcus Licinius Crassus (d. 53 B.C.). Known today as the "First Triumvirate," this coalition amounted to a conspiracy to run the state. Their individual ambitions rebuffed by the senate, each man had an agenda that could be achieved by pooling resources in the triumvirate: for Pompey, ratification of his acts in the east and land for his veterans; for Caesar, who became consul for 59 B.C., a long period of command in Gaul and a free hand in his behavior there; for Crassus, a rebate for the tax collectors of Roman Asia, whom he championed, and eventually, a command in Syria to make war on Parthia (the new Persian Empire).

Having achieved its goal, the triumvirate did not long survive, but its very existence shows how little the Republic now meant. Crassus died in an inglorious defeat against the Parthians at Carrhae in Syria in 53 B.C. (see **MAP 5.3**). Frightened by Caesar's stunning victories in Gaul, Pompey returned to the senatorial fold, now led by Cato the Younger. Cato and his supporters stood for the traditional rule of the senatorial oligarchy. In 49 B.C., they ordered Caesar to give up his command in Gaul, but instead, Caesar marched on Italy with his army. Italy's northern boundary was marked by a tiny stream called the Rubicon; when Caesar defiantly crossed it, he declared, "The die is cast." Indeed it was, for civil war. Caesar swept to victory against the senate's army, led by Pompey, at Pharsalus in Greece in 48 B.C. Pompey fled but was assassinated. The complete destruction of the senate's forces took until 45 B.C.

The years of civil war took Caesar from Spain to Anatolia. During the fighting, he showed the qualities that made him great: He was fast, tough, smart, adaptable, and a risk-taker. He was a diplomat, too, offering mercy to any of his enemies who joined him. A talented writer, Caesar published two books about his military campaigns—*On the Gallic War* and *On the Civil War*—the latter appearing after his death. These works glorified Caesar's conquests and defended his decision to wage civil war. (See the feature, "The Global Record: Caesar on the Gauls.")

Back in Rome, Caesar sponsored a huge number of reforms. His political goal was to elevate Italians and others at the expense of old Roman families. To achieve this, Caesar conferred Roman citizenship liberally, on all of Cisalpine Gaul (northernmost Italy), as well as on certain provincial towns. He enlarged the senate from six hundred to nine hundred, adding his supporters, including some Gauls, to the membership. Caesar sponsored social and economic reforms, too, including reducing debt and founding the first colonies outside Italy, where veterans and poor citizens were settled. He undertook a grand public building program in the city of Rome. Caesar's most long-lasting act was to introduce the calendar of 365¼ days, on January 1, 45 B.C. Derived from the calendar of Egypt, it is known as the Julian calendar.

Caesar did not hide his contempt for Republican constitutional formalities. By accepting a dictatorship for life, he offended conservatives; by flirting with the title of king, he infuriated them. His career ended abruptly on March 15, 44 B.C. (the Ides of March by the Roman calendar), when sixty senators stabbed him to death. The assassination took place in the portico attached to the Theater of Pompey, in front of a statue of Pompey himself, where the senate was meeting that day. It had been eighty-nine years since the murder of Tiberius Gracchus.

Spartacus's Slave Revolt

Spartacus's revolt was the third and most famous of three great slave rebellions that rocked Italy and Sicily between 135 and 71 B.C. The revolt itself was not a success; all of the slaves were either imprisoned or killed. But Spartacus terrified the Roman elite and became a powerful symbol of the struggle for freedom to all who were oppressed. This account, by the ancient writer Appian, illustrates his fight.

At about this same time, at the city of Capua in Italy, gladiators were being trained to fight in spectacles. Spartacus, a Thracian whom the Romans had imprisoned and then sold to be trained as a gladiator, had once fought as a soldier for the Roman army. He persuaded about seventy of the enslaved men to risk a break for freedom rather than to allow themselves to be put on display for the entertainment of others. Using force to overcome their guards, the men made their escape. The fugitives armed themselves with wooden clubs and daggers that they seized from travelers on the roads nearby, and then rushed to take refuge on Mount Vesuvius. Many fugitive slaves and even some free men from the surrounding countryside came to this place to join Spartacus. They began to stage bandit raids on nearby settlements. Spartacus had his fellow gladiators Oenomaus and Crixus as his two subordinate commanders. Since Spartacus divided the profits of his raiding into equal shares, he soon attracted a very large number of followers . . .

[Spartacus wins victories in southern and northern Italy.] With the 120,000 men under his command, he began a march on Rome. So that traveling would be as light as possible, he torched all unnecessary supplies, killed all prisoners of war, and slaughtered all pack animals. Many deserters from the Roman army came to him, but he accepted none of them. The consuls made a stand against him in a place in the land of Picenum. Another great armed struggle took place here and the Romans were defeated again. Spartacus changed his mind about an attack on Rome. He decided that he was not ready for an all-out battle and that his whole army was not yet properly armed for regular warfare. Moreover, so far no city had come over to his side, but only slaves, deserters, and the flotsam and jetsam of humanity . . .

[After many successes and some defeats, Spartacus is forced into a final battle with a Roman army led by Crassus.] Since so many tens of thousands of desperate men were involved, the result was a protracted battle of epic proportions. Spartacus took a spear wound in his thigh. Collapsing on one knee, he held his shield up in front of him and fought off those who were attacking him, until he and the large number of men around him were finally surrounded and cut down. The rest of his army was thrown into disarray and confusion and was slaughtered in large numbers. The killing was on such a scale that it was not possible to count the dead. The Romans lost about a thousand men. The body of Spartacus was never found. When the survivors among Spartacus's men, who were still a large number, fled from the battle, they went up into the mountains, where they were pursued by Crassus's forces. Splitting themselves into four groups, they continued to fight until all of them had perished—all, that is, except six thousand of them, who were taken prisoner and crucified along the whole length of the highway that ran from Capua to Rome.

QUESTIONS

1. Why do you think Spartacus attracted so many followers?

2. Why do you think Spartacus was able to defeat the Romans time and again? Why do you think he finally failed?

3. What evidence does the passage offer to show that Spartacus and his men were brave and determined?

Source: *Spartacus' Slave Revolt from Spartacus and the Slave Wars: A Brief History with Documents.* Translated, edited and with an Introduction by Brent D. Shaw. Copyright © 2001 by Bedford/St. Martin's. Used with permission of Bedford/St. Martin's.

The assassins called themselves Liberators, believing that they were freeing themselves from tyranny just as the founders of the Republic had done centuries before. Indeed, one of the chief conspirators, Marcus Junius Brutus (ca. 85–42 B.C.), claimed descent from Lucius Junius Brutus, traditional leader of the revolt against the Tarquins that was thought to have established the Republic. Like his co-conspirator, Gaius Longinus Cassius (d. 42 B.C.), Brutus had been a magistrate, military officer, and provincial administrator.

The assassination of Caesar threw Rome back into turmoil. Civil war followed for the next thirteen years. The Liberators and Caesar's partisans fought to settle whether the Senate or a dictator would rule Rome. Then, after they defeated the Senate, the two leading Caesarians struggled over power. The final conflict pitted Mark Antony (Marcus Antonius, ca. 83–30 B.C.), Caesar's chief lieutenant and the man who inherited his love affair with Cleopatra, against Octavian (Gaius Julius Caesar Octavianus, 63 B.C.–A.D. 14), Caesar's grandnephew and adopted son and heir to Caesar's name and his huge fortune. At first, it looked as if Antony had the upper hand

Caesar on the Gauls

Julius Caesar (ca. 100–44 B.C.) advertised his achievements in conquering Gaul (58–51 B.C.) in his Commentaries on the Gallic War. The book focuses on battles and negotiations, but here Caesar discusses the society of the Gauls (also known as Celts). He depicts the inhabitants as superstitious and warlike.

In the whole of Gaul two types of men are counted as being of worth and distinction. The ordinary people are considered almost as slaves: they dare do nothing on their own account and are not called to counsels. When the majority are oppressed by debt or heavy tribute, or harmed by powerful men, they swear themselves away into slavery to the aristocracy, who then have the same rights over them as masters do over their slaves. Of the two types of men of distinction, however, the first is made up of the druids (priests), and the other of the knights.

The druids are involved in matters of religion. They manage public and private sacrifices and interpret religious customs and ceremonies. Young men flock to them in large numbers to gain instruction, and they hold the druids in great esteem. For they decide almost all disputes, both public and private: if some crime has been committed, if there has been murder done, if there is a dispute over an inheritance or over territory, they decide the issue and settle the rewards and penalties. If any individual or group of people does not abide by their decision, the druids ban them from sacrifices. This is their most severe punishment. Those who are banned in this way are counted among the wicked and criminal: everyone shuns them and avoids approaching or talking to them, so as not to suffer any harm from contact with them. . . .

Druids are not accustomed to take part in war, nor do they pay taxes like the rest of the people. . . . The principal doctrine they attempt to impart is that souls do not die but after death cross from one person to another. Because the fear of death is thereby set aside, they consider this a strong inducement to physical courage. Besides this, they debate many subjects and teach them to their young men—for example, the stars and their movements, the size of the universe and the earth, the nature of things, and the strength and power of the immortal gods.

The second class is that composed of the knights. When necessity arises and some war flares up—which before Caesar's arrival used to happen almost every year, so that they were either on the offensive themselves or fending off attacks—they are all involved in the campaign. Each man has as many retainers and dependents about him as is appropriate to his status in terms of his birth and resources. This is the sole form of power and influence they know.

The whole of the Gallic nation is much given to religious practices. For this reason those who are afflicted with serious illnesses and those who are involved in battles and danger either offer human sacrifice or vow that they will do so, and employ the druids to manage these sacrifices. For they believe that unless one human life is offered for another, the power and presence of the immortal gods cannot be propitiated.

QUESTIONS

1. According to Caesar, who were the druids, and what did they do? How did they help the Gauls succeed as warriors? How did the druids differ from the knights?

2. What was the status of ordinary people in Gaul?

3. What do you think Caesar and his readers thought of the Gauls' practice of human sacrifice?

Source: Caesar on the Gauls from *Julius Ceasar, Seven Commentaries on the Gallic War with an Eighth Commentary by Aulus Hirtius,* translated by Carolyn Hammong. Copyright © 1996 Oxford University Press. By permission of Oxford University Press.

because Octavian was young and inexperienced, was not a general, and was cursed with poor health. Octavian was, however, a man of unusual cunning and prudence. His forces defeated Antony and Cleopatra at the naval battle of Actium (off northwestern Greece) in 31 B.C.; their suicides followed shortly. The Roman world held its breath to see how Octavian would govern it.

The World of Cicero

Cicero Philosopher, writer, and statesman who was Rome's greatest orator.

Marcus Tullius **Cicero** (106–43 B.C.) is one of the best known figures of all antiquity. His enormous body of writings provides a vivid, detailed, and sometimes damning picture of Roman life at the end of the Republic. They demonstrate both Rome's genius for flexibility and its limits.

Like Marius, Cicero (SIS-er-o) was a wealthy equestrian from the central Italian town of Arpinum who, as consul (in 63 B.C.), became a "new man." Unlike Marius, Cicero was an optimas and defender of the senate. He was, however, ready for compromise with the equestrians, from whose ranks he himself had arisen. He made his name by successfully leading the opposition to Lucius Sergius Catilina, a down-and-out patrician who organized a debtors' revolt in Etruria; the army smashed the rebellion.

Young Cicero studied philosophy and oratory in Greece. As an adult, he produced writings that made the Latin language a vessel for the heritage of Greek thought, even if he never equaled the originality of Plato or Aristotle. Cicero produced over a hundred speeches, of which about sixty survive; several works on speech-writing; philosophical works; poetry, of which little survives; and numerous letters. After his death in 43 B.C., his immense correspondence was published, with little censored.

POLITICS, SOCIETY, AND LAW

Politics in the Late Republic was loud and boisterous. The elite prided itself on free speech and open debate. In senate deliberations, court cases, and public meetings in the Forum that preceded assembly votes, oratory—sometimes great oratory—was common.

Elite women benefited from increased freedom and greater educational opportunities in the Late Republic, which made it possible for women, as well as men, to study oratory. Private tutors were common among the aristocracy, and girls often received lessons alongside their brothers. Girls sometimes also profited from a father's expertise. A particularly dramatic case is that of Hortensia, daughter of Quintus Hortensius Hortalus (114–50 B.C.), a famous orator and rival of Cicero. An excellent speaker herself, Hortensia defied tradition by arguing successfully in the Roman Forum, in 42 B.C., against a proposed war tax on wealthy women.

Ordinary people lacked the education and freedom to express themselves in the manner of a woman like Hortensia, but a less civilized means of expression was open to them: the political gang. Brawls and violence between the rival groups of Clodius, a supporter of Caesar, and Milo, a supporter of the senate, became increasingly common in the fifties B.C. As dictator, Caesar abolished the gangs.

Cicero's works provide evidence of a key development in the practice of Roman law. Often unheralded, what Cicero's contemporaries did was invent the notion of the legal expert, a person devoted to explaining and interpreting the law. Roman law needed interpretation because it was complex and intricate. Much of it was the work not of legislators, but of magistrates, who issued annual statements setting forth how their courts would work. The unsystematic and sometimes contradictory result cried out for someone to make sense of it. Enter the jurisconsults, legal interpreters who emerged in the third and second centuries B.C. At first, they had no special standing, but in the first century B.C., they became true jurists; their interpretations began to be considered authoritative. No earlier Mediterranean society had a professional class of legal experts, but no earlier society had faced issues as complicated and turbulent, or had grown to three million citizens, as the Roman Republic did in the mid-first century B.C. The Western tradition of legal science has its roots in Rome.

A NEW ELITE?

Rome's political system, unlike its legal system, did not adapt flexibly to changing circumstances. The disenfranchised of the Late Republic had reasonable goals: land for those who had fought for their country and admission to the senate of a wider group. Yet the old elite resisted both. Cicero's solution was to build on Sulla's reforms by uniting the senatorial and equestrian orders and by widening the Roman ruling class to include the elite of all Italy. The expanded ruling class could close ranks and establish *otium cum dignitate*, "peace with respect for rank." Cicero's proposed new order was distinctly hierarchical.

In the turbulent times of the Late Republic, the Roman elite often turned to the Hellenistic philosophers. The poet Lucretius (loo-CREE-shus) (ca. 94–55 B.C.) describes the Epicurean ideal of withdrawal into the contemplative life in a long didactic epic called *On the Nature of Things*. Most elite Romans, however, including Cicero, preferred the activist philosophy of Stoicism (see pages 103–104). Cicero put forth a generous view of human brotherhood. He argued that all people share a spark of divinity and are protected by natural law. Consequently, all persons have value and importance and should treat others generously. Such ideas would be influential in the new Roman Empire when, under the leadership of Augustus, fair treatment of provincials was a major theme. For Cicero, however, these ideas existed more as theory than as practice.

Cicero did not hide his lack of sympathy for his fellow citizens who were poor. In one speech, he castigated "artisans and shopkeepers and all that kind of scum"; in a letter, he complained about "the wretched half-starved populace, which attends mass meetings and sucks the blood of the treasury." Cicero also made his disdain for democracy clear: "The greatest number," he said, "should not have the greatest power."

Elitist as Cicero's views were, they were by no means extremist. Cassius, Brutus, and the other Liberators had little interest in even Cicero's limited compromises. Their stubbornness proved successors brought peace and prosperity after a century of disasters under the Late Republic. The Augustan period enjoyed affluence, especially in Italy; the other provinces caught up with Italy by the second century A.D. Agriculture flourished with the end of civil war. Italian industries became leaders in exports. Italian glass bowls and windowpanes, iron arms and tools, fancy silver eating utensils and candlesticks, and bronze statues and pots circulated from Britain to central Asia.

The city of Rome's urban poor, many of them freedmen, enjoyed a more efficient system of free grain distribution under Augustus and a large increase in games and public entertainment—the imperial policy of "bread and circuses" designed to content the masses. Augustus also set up a major public works program, which provided jobs for the poor. He prided himself on having found Rome "a city of brick" and having left it "a city of marble."

The perennial problem of the Late Republic had been land-hunger, which drove peasants into the arms of ambitious generals. Augustus kept his troops happy by compensating 300,000 veterans with land, money, or both, often in new overseas colonies. At first, he paid from his own private sources; after A.D. 6, he made the rich pay via new taxes. The result kept the peace, but many nonsoldiers in Italy remained poor, as of course, did the huge number of slaves.

As for the renegade commanders who had bedeviled the Late Republic, Augustus cut their potential power base by reducing the size of the army, gradually cutting the number of legions from over sixty to twenty-eight. The total size of the army, including light infantry and cavalry, was about 300,000. This reduction lightened Rome's tax burden but left Augustus with little room to expand the empire. In A.D. 9, Rome lost three legions to a native revolt against Rome's plan to extend its rule in Germany as far east as the Elbe River. Short of manpower, Augustus had to accept the Rhine River as Rome's new German frontier (see **Map 6.1**).

Imperial defense remained a major issue. Strong Roman armies were a necessity along the hostile European frontier. On the friendlier border in western Asia and northern Africa, Augustus and his immediate successors set up client kingdoms, such as Judea and Armenia, to protect Roman territory.

To promote his ideology of renewal, Augustus sponsored social legislation embodying the old Republican virtues. He passed a series of laws encouraging marriage and childbearing and discouraging promiscuity and adultery. Such legislation was so flagrantly disobeyed that in 2 B.C., Augustus made an example of his own daughter, Julia (39 B.C.–A.D. 14), his only child, whose adulteries were the talk of Rome. As punishment, she was banished to a barren islet.

Augustus's era marks the beginning of the classical period of Roman jurisprudence, during which the professionalism that had begun to mark Roman law in the Late Republic became a permanent fact. It was probably Augustus who established the practice, followed by later emperors, of granting a few distinguished jurists the exclusive right to issue legal opinions "on behalf of the princeps." He ensured, therefore, that experts guided the administration of justice. The first law school was opened in Rome under Augustus. Roman jurists adapted Roman law to the practices of the provinces. Although various local legal systems remained in use, the international system of Roman law was also used widely in the provinces.

In religion, too, Augustus was a legislator and reformer. He restored once-neglected cults and temples in order to appear as Rome's savior. He would probably have approved when, after his death, he was deified, just as Julius Caesar had been. Even while he was still alive, Augustus was worshiped in the provinces as a god—in both the East, where the cult of Roma and Augustus grew in popularity, and the West, where centers of emperor-worship were established at the sites of Lyon and Cologne (see **Map 6.1**). The imperial cult, an important part of state propaganda until the empire became Christian in the fourth century A.D., was well underway.

Deification, whether formal or informal, was a heady brew, but Augustus deserved it more than most. He not only ended the Late Republican era of civil wars, but established the Roman Empire on a completely new footing. Republican freedom was gone, but the emperor and bureaucrats brought stability. The peace of the Augustan Principate would last, with few interruptions, for two hundred years. Few people in history have created order so successfully.

The Culture of The Augustan Age

Like *Periclean*, the adjective *Augustan* (aw-GUS-tin) has come to signify an era of literary and artistic flowering. In both periods, strong elements of classicism shaped the arts—that is, an attempt to project heroic and idealized values, the values that the rulers of each epoch wished to promote. Both prose and poetry flourished under Augustus. The emperor and his close adviser Maecenas (d. 8 B.C.) were patrons of a number of important poets, chief among them Virgil (70–19 B.C.) and Horace (65–8 B.C.). The historian Livy (59 B.C.–A.D. 17), who wrote his history of Rome from the founding of the city to 9 B.C. under Augustus, also elicited the princeps's interest. All three writers contributed to the Augustan renewal and rededication of Rome.

In many ways, **Virgil** (VER-jill) speaks for his contemporaries. In the *Eclogues*—poems that, following an Alexandrian model (see page 97), have rustic settings—Virgil describes the miseries of the civil wars and the blessings of peace under Augustus. "A god created this peace for us; for he will always be a god to me," one character says. In the Fourth Eclogue, Virgil speaks of the birth of a child to usher in a restored Golden Age. At the Council of Nicaea in A.D. 325 (see page 175) and later, this poem was given a Christian interpretation. In the *Georgics*, Virgil describes the glories of Italian agriculture, which, thanks to Augustus, could be practiced peacefully again.

Virgil's masterpiece is an epic poem, the *Aeneid* (ee-NEE-id), "the story of Aeneas," the legendary Trojan founder of Rome, or at least of the Latin town from which Rome's founders eventually came. Legend also makes Aeneas the ancestor of Augustus. Thus, the *Aeneid* indirectly celebrates Augustus, often considered Rome's second founder. The poem explores the pain and burden, as well as the glory, of empire.

If Virgil's work has the grandeur of marble, Horace's poems—*Odes, Epodes, Satires, Epistles*, and *Ars Poetica* (*Art of Poetry*)—are more like finely cut gems. They tend to be polished, complex, and detached. Like Virgil, Horace explores the themes of war and peace and praises Augustus. "With Caesar [Augustus] holding the lands, I shall fear neither turmoil nor violent death," declares one of the *Odes*. Both Horace and Virgil successfully adapted Greek models and, in the process, created something new. Few writers have had a greater influence on the later Western literary tradition.

Only 35 of the original 142 books of Livy's ambitious history have survived. Livy (LIV-ee) is both a master storyteller and a superb ironist. His anecdotes of Roman history are vivid and told in a grand rhetorical style. Livy is our major source for the Roman monarchy and Early Republic,

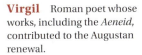

Virgil Roman poet whose works, including the *Aeneid*, contributed to the Augustan renewal.

Mosaic of the Doves
This exquisite mosaic shows a number of doves drinking from or positioned around a gilded bronze basin on a marble pedestal. Derived from a Hellenistic work from Pergamum, this mosaic comes from a wealthy house in Pompeii.
(Scala/Art Resource, NY)

Agrippina the Younger This statue shows the mother of the emperor Nero praying. It is carved in basanite, a stone whose use is typical of the imperial Roman taste for art objects in exotic materials. (Courtesy, Mondadori Electa S.P.A.)

rebuilding program, including a 300-room villa for himself, and was accused of having started the fire. He found a scapegoat for the fire in the members of a small religious sect, the Christians, whom he persecuted. Ordinary Romans supported Nero because he gave them good government. He was unpopular with the senators and, more serious, with the army, because he failed to pay all his troops promptly. Confronted with a major revolt in 68, Nero committed suicide.

The next year, 69, witnessed Rome's first civil war in about a century. Three men claimed the imperial purple after Nero. A fourth, Vespasian (ves-PAY-zhun) (Titus Flavius Vespasianus, r. 69–79), commander of the army quelling a revolt in the province of Judea, was able to make his claim stick. Peace was restored, but not the rule of Augustus's family. Vespasian founded a new dynasty, the Flavians (r. 69–96), which was followed in turn by the Nervo-Trajanic (r. 96–138) and Antonine (r. 138–192) dynasties. The ultimate tribute to Augustus may be that his regime was stable enough to survive the extinction of his family.

SECTION SUMMARY

- Augustus, Rome's first emperor, shared a degree of power with the senate, while keeping the armies firmly under his control.
- Augustus gave Rome its first civil service and first police force; he gave Italy prosperity; he began to raise the status of the provinces.
- Augustus reduced military spending and compromised with Rome's enemies in order to stabilize the frontiers.
- The poets Virgil and Horace and the historian Livy are among the great writers of the flourishing culture of Augustan Rome.
- Although they included such scandalous figures as Nero, the Julio-Claudian emperors (A.D. 14–68) delivered peaceful and effective government.

THE ROMAN PEACE AND ITS COLLAPSE, A.D. 69–284

What was life like in the era of the Roman peace? Why did peace end during the third century A.D.?

Much about Rome in the second century A.D. appears attractive today. Within the multiethnic empire, opportunities for inhabitants to become part of the elite were increasing. The central government was on its way to granting Roman citizenship to nearly every free person in the empire, a process completed in the year 212. The emperors emphasized sharing prosperity and spreading it through the provinces. Italy was no longer the tyrant of the Mediterranean, but merely first among equals. To be sure, rebellions were crushed, but few people rebelled. This period, known as the **pax Romana**, or "Roman peace," seems particularly golden in contrast with what followed: the disastrous and disordered third century A.D., in which the empire came close to collapse, but survived because of a radical and rigid transformation.

pax Romana Latin for "Roman peace," the term refers to the period of peace and prosperity in the Roman Empire from A.D. 69 to 180.

The Flavians and the "Good Emperors"

The **Flavian** dynasty of Vespasian (r. 69–79) and his sons Titus (r. 79–81) and Domitian (r. 81–96) provided good government, and their successors built on their achievements. Unlike the Julio-Claudians, Vespasian hailed not from the old Roman nobility, but from an equestrian family from an Italian town. A man of rough-and-ready character, Vespasian is supposed to have replied when Titus complained that a new latrine tax was beneath the dignity of the Roman government, "Son, money has no smell." Unlike his father and brother, Domitian reverted to frequent treason trials and persecution of the aristocracy, which earned him assassination in 96, although the empire as a whole enjoyed peace and sound administration under his reign.

Flavian Dynasty of the Roman emperors Vespasian, Titus, and Domitian, whose rule was a time of relative peace and good government.

The so-called Five Good Emperors are Nerva (r. 96–98), Trajan (r. 98–117), Hadrian (r. 117–138), and the first two Antonines, Antoninus Pius (r. 138–161) and Marcus Aurelius (r. 161–180). They exemplify the principle of merit. Trajan, a Roman citizen born in Spain, was Rome's first emperor from outside Italy. Hadrian and Marcus Aurelius also came from Spain, and Antoninus Pius from Gaul. Each of the Five Good Emperors, except Marcus Aurelius, adopted the most competent person, rather than the closest relative, as his son and successor, thus elevating duty over sentiment. Marcus Aurelius, a deeply committed Stoic, gave full vent to his sense of duty in his *Meditations*, which he wrote in Greek while living in a tent on the Danube frontier, where he fought long and hard against German raids. Antoninus was surnamed "Pius" (Dutiful) because he was devoted to his country, the gods, and his adoptive father, Hadrian.

The Five Good Emperors made humaneness and generosity the themes of their reigns. Trajan, for example, founded a program of financial aid for the poor children of Italy. They also went to great lengths to care for the provinces. These emperors not only commonly received petitions from cities, associations, and individuals in far-off provinces, but answered them. Yet, humaneness does not mean softness. Hadrian, for instance, ordered a revolt in Judea (132–135) to be suppressed with great brutality.

Like the Julio-Claudians, the Five Good Emperors advertised their wives to the world as exemplars of traditional modesty, self-effacement, and domesticity. In fact, they were often worldly, educated, and influential. Trajan's wife, Plotina, for example (d. 121 or 123), acted as patron of the Epicurean school at Athens, whose philosophy she claimed to follow. She advised her husband on provincial administration as well as dynastic matchmaking. Hadrian's wife, Sabina, traveled in her husband's entourage to Egypt (130), where her aristocratic Greek friend, Julia Balbilla, commemorated the trip by writing Greek poetry, which she had inscribed alongside other tourists' writings on the leg of one of two statues of Amenhotep III at Thebes.

A darker side of the second century empire was the problem of border defense. Augustus and the Julio-Claudians had established client kingdoms where possible, to avoid the expense and political dangers of raising armies. The emperors of the day tended to be more aggressive on the borders than their predecessors. They moved from client kingdoms to a new border policy of stationary frontier defense. Expensive fortification systems of walls, watchtowers, and trenches were built along the perimeter of the empire's border and manned with guards. A prominent example is Hadrian's Wall, which separated Roman Britain from the enemy tribes to the north. Stretching 80 miles, the wall required fifteen thousand defense troops.

The most ambitious frontier policy was that of Trajan, who crossed the Danube to carve out the new province of Dacia (modern Romania) and who used an excuse to invade Parthian Mesopotamia. He won battles as far away as the Persian Gulf, but he lost the war. As soon as his army left, Mesopotamia rose in revolt, followed by Germany. Trajan's reign marked the empire's greatest geographic extent, but Trajan had overextended Rome's resources. When he died, his successor, Hadrian, had to abandon Trajan's province of Mesopotamia (see **Map 6.1**).

Gladiators

Historians and novelists write about them, filmmakers portray them, revolutionaries salute them, and a few years ago, television athletes claimed to be American updates of them. They are gladiators, literally men who carried a gladius, or sword. They fought to the death as entertainment, and they enraptured the Roman Empire.

Gladiators took part in so-called games or combat before large crowds. Armed with various specialized weapons, they fought each other and sometimes wild animals. Some unfortunates were thrust into fights with no weapons at all. The audience, seated in rank order, ranged from slaves to senators to the emperor himself. There was nothing tame about what they had come to see. Consider the word *arena*, referring to the site of the games. It literally means "sand," which is what covered the floor—and soaked up the blood.

Our fascination with the gladiator is nothing compared to the Romans'. Everybody in Rome talked about gladiators. At **Pompeii**, graffiti celebrated a star of the arena whom "all the girls sigh for." Jokes poked fun at gladiators, philosophers pondered their meaning, and literature is full of references to them.

Gladiatorial images decorated art around the empire, from mosaics to household lamps. Look at this mosaic from a Roman villa in Germany, one of several mosaic panels on the floor of the building's entrance hall, depicting scenes from the arena. The illustration shows a *retiarius*, or net-and-trident bearer, fighting a better-armed *secutor*, literally "pursuer," under the watchful eyes of a *lanista*, or trainer. As was typical, the retiarius wears no armor except for a shoulder piece protecting his left side. To defend himself against the dagger wielded by the secutor (in the mosaic, hidden behind the shield), the retiarius had to be fit enough to be able to keep moving. The difference between various types of gladiators would have been as obvious to a Roman as the difference between a catcher and a pitcher is to a baseball fan today.

As for the amphitheaters where gladiatorial combats took place, they were as common in Italy and the Roman Empire as skyscrapers are in a modern city. Look, for example, at this photograph of the amphitheater in the city of El Djem in modern Tunisia (the Roman province of Africa). Built of high-quality local stone in the third century A.D., the structure was meant to have sixty-four arches, but it was never

Roman Amphitheater, El Djem, Tunisia   (Adina Tovy/Robert Harding World Imagery)

completed. The openings in the floor permitted animals to be released into the arena. A large amphitheater like this one held at least thirty thousand spectators, and the largest amphitheater of all, the Flavian Amphitheater—or Colosseum—at Rome, seated around fifty thousand. Amphitheaters were less common in the east, but the fans there also were loyal, so the games went on—in theaters.

Most gladiators were condemned criminals, prisoners of war, or slaves bought for the purpose. The most famous slave gladiator was Spartacus, a Thracian. Along with seventy-seven other gladiators in the Italian city of Capua, Spartacus instigated a slave rebellion that attracted thousands and shook Italy for two years (73–71 B.C.).

Yet, some gladiators were free men who volunteered for a limited term of service. Once even the emperor Commodus (r. 180–192) served, to the disgust of other Roman nobles, who found the arena fascinating but low-class. The gladiator was part warrior, part athlete, part showman, and part butcher. Yet, there was something of the pagan priest in the gladiator, too, for his was a solemn profession. Every gladiator took an oath to endure being burned, bound, beaten, and killed by the sword. They began each combat by greeting the official in charge (in Rome, the emperor) in this way: "We who are about to die salute you."

Students of the Romans find it hard to believe that they adored such a murderous sport, in which dozens and occasionally hundreds of men might die in a single day, to the roar of the crowds. Yet, perhaps the arena makes us uncomfortable not so much because it is foreign, but because it is familiar. Although we no longer flock to games in which men kill each other, we do go in droves to blood sports such as boxing, and we pack hockey rinks to watch men regularly give each other concussions. Modern people no longer kill animals in the arena for sport, but we hunt, fish, go on big-game safaris, watch cockfights, and, in Spain, kill bulls and occasionally get killed by them.

Besides, perhaps our discomfort reflects our instinctive understanding of the symbolism of the arena. The games were brutal, but so was the empire. Rome had brought peace to three continents, but it had done so by brandishing a sword, and it kept the peace by its readiness to fight. The arena kept Romans tough and warlike, or so an intellectual could argue, as does Pliny the Younger, who describes gladiatorial games:

[The games] inspired a glory in wounds and a contempt of death, since the love of praise and desire for victory could be seen, even in the bodies of slaves and criminals. (*Panegyric* 33)

Arguably, the arena also contributed to public order. This was no small achievement, since the imperial army could not police a population of 50 million to 100 million, and few places had even the elementary police force that the city of Rome did. The violence that bloodied the amphitheater stepped into the breach by reminding criminals—or those defined as criminals—what punishment awaited

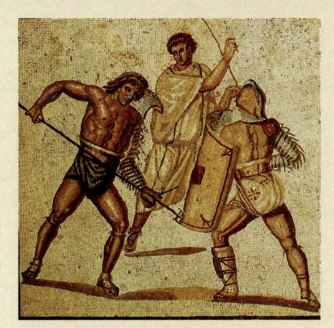

Gladiator Mosaic, Nennig, Germany (Bildarchive Preussischer Kulturbesitz/Art Resource, NY)

them. Rob or kill, and you might end up in the arena. Refuse to worship the emperor, and you might be fed to the lions, as Christians were from time to time. Rebel against Rome, and you might find yourself on a chain gang building a new amphitheater, as tradition says thirty thousand prisoners of the First Jewish Revolt (A.D. 66–70) did. The result was the Colosseum.*

Occasionally pagan, as well as Christian, writers condemned gladiatorial games. Seneca the Younger (ca. 4 B.C.–A.D. 65), for example, criticized them for inciting greed, aggression, and cruelty. Yet, so popular was Rome's theater of power that gladiators and their games were not abolished until around A.D. 400.

QUESTIONS

1. What does the scene on the mosaic show, and what does it indicate about the Roman public's interest in gladiators?

2. What were the main features of the amphitheater at El Djem?

3. How might gladiatorial games have contributed to public order in the Roman Empire?

---

* The preceding two paragraphs lean heavily on the fine discussion in Colin Wells, *The Roman Empire*, 2d ed. (Cambridge, Mass.: Harvard University Press, 1995), pp. 248–255.

Pompeii Italian city destroyed in a volcanic eruption in A.D. 79, the ruins of Pompeii offer the best evidence of life in a Roman city in the era of the Roman Peace.

class distinctions: the division between *honestiores* (in general, the curial order) and *humiliores* (everyone else). Previously, Roman citizens enjoyed certain privileges, such as exemption from flogging by officials, but now citizens who were *humiliores* tended to lose those privileges.

The most basic legal distinction was that between free and slave—and the empire contained millions of slaves. A third category, ex-slaves or freedmen, also became increasingly important. Freedmen owed service to their former masters, who became their patrons. A few freedmen grew rich in commerce or wielded enough power in imperial administration to lord it over even Roman aristocrats. The result was strong elite hostility toward freedmen, which is often reflected in Roman literature. Witness the stereotype of the vulgar freedman, embodied in Trimalchio in the *Satyricon* (suh-TEER-uh-con), a novel by Petronius (first century A.D.). Trimalchio had more estates than he could remember and so much money that his wife counted it by the bushel-load.

As regards marriage, Roman family law was strict and severe in principle. In practice, however, it often proved pragmatic and even humane, as demonstrated by three cases: elite marriages, slave marriages, and soldiers' marriages.

As in the Late Republic, so in the Early Empire, most Roman women married without legally becoming members of their husbands' families—or their children's. This gave women a degree of freedom from their husbands, but it left elite women, who owned property, with a problem: Technically that property was controlled by their fathers or brothers. Yet, society recognized a woman's wish to leave her property to her children, and imperial law increasingly made it possible for her to do so—although the conservative Romans waited until the sixth century A.D. before abolishing completely the rights of greedy uncles. Another case is a mother's right to have a say in her children's choice of marriage partner. This maternal prerogative became accepted social practice, even though Roman law gave women no such right.

Roman slaves married and had children, but they had to do so in the face of both legal and practical obstacles. Roman law gave slaves no right to marry, and it made slave children the property of the owner of the slave mother. Owners could and did break up slave families by sale. Even if a slave was freed, the law expressed far more concern with the continuing obligations

Roman Slaves This first-century A.D. wall-painting from Herculaneum, Italy shows Roman ladies with their slave hairdressers. Note the elaborate hairstyle of the seated woman. (Erich Lessing/Art Resource, NY)

of freedmen to their former masters than with the rights of slave families. Yet, during the Early Empire, cracks appeared in the wall of law that allowed slave families to slip through.

For example, although the law insisted that a slave be age 30 before being freed, it made an exception for an owner who wished to free a female slave younger than 30 in order to marry her. To take another example, the law conceded that slave children owed devotion and loyalty (*pietas*) to their slave parents.

Career soldiers, from at least the time of Augustus on, could not marry, probably on the grounds of military discipline. Yet, many soldiers cohabited anyhow, often with noncitizen women in the areas where they served, and frequently, children were the result. Not until the reign of Septimius Severus (SEH-ver-us) (r. 193–211) were soldiers permitted to marry formally, and then, only after twenty-five years of service. Yet, commanders had permitted cohabitation for two centuries, and the law too made concessions now and then. For example, the Flavians gave soldiers a degree of freedom to make wills, which could allow them to leave property to illegitimate children. Various emperors gave soldiers the privilege, on discharge, to legalize a marriage with a noncitizen, which ordinary Romans were not permitted to do.[2]

The Culture of the Roman Peace

In Latin poetry, the century or so after the death of Augustus (roughly A.D. 18–133) is often referred to as the "Silver Age," a term sometimes applied to prose as well. The implication is that this period, though productive, fell short of the golden Augustan era. It might be fairer to say that the self-confidence of the Augustan writers did not last. As the permanence of monarchy became clear, many in the elite looked back to the Republic with nostalgia and bitterness. Silver Age writing often takes refuge in satire or rhetorical flourish.

The Silver Age was an era of interest in antiquities and in compiling handbooks and encyclopedias; it was also an era of self-consciousness and literary criticism. In the first two centuries A.D., Roman writers came from an ever greater diversity of backgrounds and wrote for an ever wider audience, as prosperity and educational opportunities increased.

Many writers of the era pursued public careers, which offered access to patronage. The historian **Tacitus**, for instance, became governor of the province of Asia. Prominent literary families emerged, such as that of Pliny (PLIH-nee) the Elder (A.D. 23–79), an encyclopedic author on natural science, geography, history, and art; and his nephew, Pliny the Younger (ca. A.D. 62–ca. 113), an orator and letter writer. The most notable literary family is that of Seneca the Elder (ca. 55 B.C.–A.D. 40), a historian and scholar of rhetoric; his son, Seneca the Younger (ca. 4 B.C.–A.D. 65); and Seneca the Younger's nephew, the epic poet Lucan (A.D. 39–65).

Tacitus Roman historian of the "Silver Age," his greatest works were *The Histories* and *The Annals*.

Born in Cordoba, Spain, the younger Seneca moved at an early age to Rome, where he became a successful lawyer and investor. He was banished in A.D. 41 for alleged adultery with a sister of Caligula. Recalled in 49, he was tutor to the young Nero. When Nero became emperor in 54, Seneca became one of his chief advisers and helped bring good government to the empire. Seneca eventually fell out of favor, however, and was forced first into retirement and then, in A.D. 65, into suicide. He had been the major literary figure of his age, a jack-of-all-trades: playwright, essayist, pamphleteer, student of science, and noted Stoic philosopher.

A literary career was safer under the Five Good Emperors. Consider Tacitus and his contemporary, the poet Juvenal (JOO-veh-nal) (ca. A.D. 55–130). Juvenal's *Satires* are bitter and brilliant poems offering social commentary. He laments the past, when poverty and war had supposedly kept Romans chaste and virtuous. Amid "the woes of long peace," he says, luxury and foreign ways had corrupted Rome. Like many a critic who blames society's troubles on marginal groups, Juvenal launches harsh attacks on women and foreigners. Tacitus, too, is sometimes scornful of women.

Yet, if he is biased on matters of gender, Tacitus is far from ethnocentric. Few historians have expressed graver doubts about the value of their country's alleged success. For example, Tacitus highlighted the simple virtues of the Germanic tribes, so different from the sophisticated decadence of contemporary Rome. Nostalgia for the Republic pervades his two greatest works, *The Histories*, which covers the civil wars of A.D. 69, and *The Annals* (only parts of which survive), chronicling the emperors from Tiberius through Nero. A masterpiece of irony and pithiness, Tacitus's style makes an unforgettable impression on the reader.

Plutarch (PLOO-tark) (ca. A.D. 50–120), whose *Parallel Lives of Noble Greeks and Romans* later captured the imagination of Shakespeare, is probably the best-known pagan writer of the first two centuries A.D. Plutarch was a Roman citizen from Greece who wrote in Greek. Like Livy, Plutarch emphasizes the moral and political lessons of history. A careful scholar, Plutarch found his true calling in rhetorical craftsmanship—polished speeches and carefully chosen anecdotes. As in Rome, rhetoric was the basis of much of Greek literary culture in this period.

Another star of Greek culture at this time was the physician Galen of Pergamum (A.D. 129–?199). In his many writings, Galen (GAY-len) was to medicine what Aristotle had been to philosophy: a brilliant systematizer and an original thinker. He excelled in anatomy and physiology and proved that the arteries, as well as the veins, carry blood. He was destined to have a dominant influence on European medicine in the Middle Ages.

The Crisis of the Third Century, A.D. 235–284

Leaving the relative calm of the second century A.D. behind, the third century Roman Empire descended into crisis. Barbarian invasions, domestic economic woes, plague, assassinations, brigandage, urban decline—the list of Rome's problems is dramatic. The empire went "from a kingdom of gold to one of iron and rust," as one writer put it, summing up Roman history after the death of Marcus Aurelius in 180, when the seeds of the **third-century crisis** were sown.

Stability first began to slip away during the reign of the last of the Antonines, Marcus Aurelius's birth son, Commodus (KOM-uh-dus) (r. 180–192), a man with Nero's taste for decadence and penchant for terrorizing the senatorial elite. His predictable assassination led to civil war, after which Septimius Severus, commander of the Danube armies, emerged as the unchallenged emperor (r. 193–211). He founded the Severan dynasty, which survived until 235.

Severan reformers attempted to reestablish the empire on a firmer footing, but they only brought the day of crisis nearer. The main theme of Septimius's reign was the transfer of power—from the senate to the army and from Italy to the provinces. To extend the Roman frontier in North Africa and western Asia, Septimius expanded the army and improved the pay and conditions of service. These measures might have been necessary, but Septimius went too far by indulging in war with Parthia (197–199)—unnecessary war, because the crumbling Parthian

third-century crisis Period from A.D. 235 to 284, when the Roman Empire suffered barbarian invasions, domestic economic problems, plague, assassinations, and urban decline.

Hadrian's Wall   Built in A.D. 122–126, this extensive structure protected Roman England from raids by the tribes of Scotland. It represents the strategy of stationary frontier defense. (Roy Rainford/Robert Harding World Imagery)

Syria Between Rome and Persia

Rome and Persia fought three great battles in western Asia in A.D. 244, 252, and 260, all resounding victories for Persia under King Shapur I (r. ca. 241–272). In the first selection Shapur celebrates his success in an inscription carved in rock near Persepolis. The second selection provides a Greek view of what Syria's inhabitants endured when Shapur "burned, ruined and pillaged" in A.D. 252. It comes from the Thirteenth Sibylline Oracle, a verse commentary on contemporary events, purporting to be ancient prophecy.

The Persian Inscription

I, the Mazda worshipping lord Shapur, king of kings of Iran and non-Iran, whose lineage is from the Gods....

When at first we had become established in the empire, Gordian Caesar raised in all of the Roman Empire a force from the Goth and German realms and marched on Babylonia against the Empire of Iran and against us. On the border of Babylonia at Misikhe, a great "frontal" battle occurred. Gordian Caesar was killed and the Roman force was destroyed. And the Romans made Philip Caesar. Then Philip Caesar came to us for terms, and to ransom their lives, gave us 500,000 denars, and became tributary to us....

And Caesar lied again and did wrong to Armenia. Then we attacked the Roman Empire and annihilated at Barbalissos a Roman force of 60,000 and Syria and the environs of Syria we burned, ruined and pillaged all. In this one campaign we conquered of the Roman Empire fortresses and towns ... a total of 37 towns with surroundings.

In the third campaign when we attacked Carrhae and Urhai [Edessa] and were besieging Carrhae and Edessa Valerian Caesar marched against us. He had with him a force of 70,000....

And beyond Carrhae and Edessa we had a great battle with Valerian Caesar. We made prisoner ourselves with our own hands Valerian Caesar and the others, chiefs of that army, the praetorian prefect, senators; we made all prisoners and deported them to Persis.

And Syria, Cilicia and Cappadocia we burned, ruined and pillaged....

And men of the Roman Empire, of non-Iranians, we deported. We settled them in the Empire of Iran....

We searched out for conquest many other lands, and we acquired fame for heroism, which we have not engraved here, except for the preceding. We ordered it written so that whoever comes after us may know this fame, heroism, and power of us.

The Sibylline Oracle

... the evil Persians....

... the Persians, arrogant men....

... the arrow-shooting Persians ... Now for you, wretched Syria, I have lately been piteously lamenting; a blow will befall you from the arrow-shooting men, terrible, which you never thought would come to you. The fugitive of Rome will come, waving a great spear; crossing the Euphrates with many myriads, he will burn you, he will dispose all things evilly. Alas, Antioch, they will never call you a city when you have fallen under the spear in your folly; he will leave you entirely ruined and naked, houseless, uninhabited; anyone seeing you will suddenly break out weeping....

Alas ... they will leave ruin as far as the borders of Asia, stripping the cities, taking the statues of all and razing the temples down to the all-nourishing earth.

QUESTIONS

1. According to Shapur's inscription, what were Rome's misdeeds toward Persia? According to the *Sibylline Oracle*, what were Persia's misdeeds toward Rome?

2. How did Persia retaliate, according to Shapur's inscription and according to the *Sibylline Oracle*? How and why do the two accounts differ?

3. Which account do you find more convincing? Why?

Source: Inscription: Richard N. Frye, trans., *History of Ancient Iran* (Munich: C. H. Beck's che Verlagsbuchhandlung, 1984), pp. 371–372. Reprinted by permission of Richard N. Frye. Oracle: D. S. Potter, trans., *Prophecy and History in the Crisis of the Roman Empire* (Oxford: Clarendon Press, 1990), p. 175.

kingdom was too weak to threaten Rome. What the war did accomplish, however, was to inspire the enemy's rejuvenation under a new Eastern dynasty, the **Sassanids** (SASS-uh-nids).

The Sassanid Persians spearheaded increased pressure on Rome's frontiers. The Sassanids overran Rome's eastern provinces and captured the emperor Valerian himself in 260. (See the feature, "The Global Record: Syria Between Rome and Persia.") The caravan city of Palmyra (in Syria) took advantage of Rome's weakness to establish independence; its most famous leader was the queen Zenobia. Meanwhile, three Germanic tribes, the Alamanni, the Franks, and the Goths, hammered the empire from the north.

Fending off invasions at opposite fronts stretched Rome to the breaking point. To pay for defense, the emperors devalued the currency, but the result was massive inflation. As if this were not bad enough, a plague broke out in Egypt at midcentury and raged through the empire for fifteen years, compounding Rome's military manpower problems.

Sassanids A Persian dynasty (A.D. 224–651) that greatly strengthened Persian power and threatened Roman rule in western Asia.

Assassinations and civil wars shook the stability of the government. Between 235—when the last Severan emperor, Severus Alexander, was murdered—and 284, twenty men were emperor, however briefly in some cases. Civilians suffered in the resulting disorder.

SECTION SUMMARY

- The Flavian dynasty (A.D. 69–96) and the so-called Five Good Emperors (96–180) brought Rome a long era of stability and good government.

- A modest prosperity, an upturn in trade, and a flourishing city life all characterized the Roman Empire of the first two centuries A.D.

- Most of the empire's 50–100 million inhabitants lived in the countryside and had little contact with Rome, but the urban elite often adopted Roman ways.

- Pragmatic, orderly, and relatively fair, Roman law is one of antiquity's great legacies.

- The historian Tacitus, the poet Juvenal, the essayist and scholar Plutarch, and the man of letters and philosophy Seneca the Younger are among the great writers of Rome's so-called Silver Age.

- Invasions, plague, inflation, crime, and political assassination were among the many woes that made the third century A.D. a period of crisis for the Roman Empire.

Yet, the empire rebounded, which is a tribute to Roman resilience as well as a sign of the disunity and lack of staying power among the empire's enemies. Recovery began during the reign of Gallienus (r. 253–268), who instituted a series of reforms. Gallienus excluded senators from high military commands and replaced them with professionals. Moreover, he began a new, more modest policy of border defense. The Romans now conceded much of the frontier to the enemy and shifted to a defensive mode: Fortified cities near the frontier served as bases from which to prevent deeper enemy penetration into Roman territory. They also concentrated mobile armies at strategic points in the rear, moving them where needed. Thanks to his new policies, Gallienus inflicted defeats on the Alamanni and the Goths. By 275, Aurelian (r. 270–275) had checked the Goths decisively and reconquered the eastern provinces, including Palmyra.

Gallienus's new military and border policies pointed the way to imperial reorganization, but they remained to be completed by the two great reforming emperors at the end of the third century and the beginning of the fourth: Diocletian (r. 284–305) and Constantine (r. 306–337), subjects of the next chapter. When their work was done, the new Roman Empire of Late Antiquity might have been barely recognizable to a citizen of the Principate.

EARLY CHRISTIANITY

What were the origins of Christianity, and how did it fare among the other religions of the Roman world?

Increasing contact between Rome and its western provinces served to plant Roman cities, Roman law, and the Latin language (or its derivatives) in western Europe. As Rome, in turn, owed much to other Mediterranean peoples, so the Roman Empire transported ancient Mediterranean civilization to northern and western Europe. No feature of that civilization was to have a greater historical impact than the religion born in Tiberius's reign: Christianity.

Christianity began in the provincial backwater of Palestine among the Jews, whose language, Aramaic, was understood by few in Rome. It immediately spread to speakers of the two main languages of the empire, Greek and Latin, and the new movement addressed the common spiritual needs of the Roman world. By the reign of Diocletian, Christians had grown from Jesus's twelve original followers to perhaps millions, despite government persecution (see **MAP 6.2** on page 159). In the fourth century A.D., Christianity unexpectedly became the official religion of the entire Roman Empire, replacing polytheism—one of the most momentous changes in Mediterranean history. We turn to that change in the next chapter; here we consider the career of Jesus and the early spread of the Christian Gospel (literally, "Good Tidings"). But first, to set the stage, we look at other religions of the Roman Empire.

Mystery Religions

The Romans were polytheists. They did not try to impose one religion on the empire. Instead, Romans were usually willing to accept new gods, as long as their worshipers took part in the patriotic emperor cult. New religions spread widely during the first three centuries A.D. Besides Christianity and Judaism, the most important religions were Greek mystery cults, the cults of Isis and Mithras, and Manichaeism. These religions displayed a tendency toward syncretism, often borrowing rites, doctrines, and symbols from one another.

Greek mystery cults included the cults of Dionysus, the god of wine, and of Demeter, the goddess of grain, who was worshiped at annual ceremonies at Eleusis, a town outside Athens. The "mystery" consisted of secret rites revealed only to initiates. In the case of Demeter, the rites apparently had something to do with the promise of eternal life.

The cult of Isis derived from the ancient Egyptians' worship of Isis (see page 105), her brother and husband, Osiris, and their son, Horus. Like the cult of Demeter, its central theme was eternal life, through resurrection achieved by moral behavior in this life. Isis, the "Goddess of Ten Thousand Names," was portrayed as a loving mother, and elements of Isis were later syncretized in the cult of the Virgin Mary. Isis's followers marched in colorful, and at times terrifying, parades through Roman streets, flagellating themselves as a sign of penitence.

Although men joined in the worship of Isis, the cult appealed particularly to women. The goddess's popularity crossed class lines; devotees ranged from slaves to one Julia Felix, whose estate at Pompeii included a garden shrine to Isis and Egyptian statuettes. By contrast, the worship of Mithras (MYTH-rus) was dominated by men, and especially by soldiers. Mithras, a heroic Persian god of light and truth, also promised eternal life. His worshipers believed that Mithras had captured and killed a sacred bull, whose blood and body were the source of life. Accordingly, Mithraism focused on bull sacrifice carried out in a vaulted, cavelike temple called a *Mithraeum*. Initiates were baptized with bull blood and participated in various other rituals, among them a sacramental meal. Their moral code advised imitating the life of their hero.

Manichaeism (MAN-ih-kee-izm) also originated in Persia, but later, in the third century A.D. Its founder, the Persian priest Mani, was martyred by conservative religious authorities. Manichaeism attempted to be the true synthesis of the religious beliefs of the period, recognizing not only Jesus, but also Zoroaster and Buddha, as prophets. The main tenet of Manichaeism was philosophical dualism, which emphasized the universal struggle between good (Light) and evil (Darkness). According to believers, the world had been corrupted by Darkness, but eventually the Light would return. In the meantime, good Manichaeans were to attempt to lead pure lives. Manichaeism was a powerful religious force for two centuries, and its believers were spread as far as India. The great theologian Augustine even flirted with it before becoming a Christian.

A new philosophy that developed in the same intellectual world as these Roman religions was Neo-Platonism (nee-oh-PLAY-ton-ism), which was founded by Plotinus (ploh-TIE-nus) (A.D. 209–270). Using the works of Plato as a starting point, Plotinus developed a philosophy in which the individual could first seek inner unity and then achieve oneness with the supreme unity of what Plotinus called the One or the Good. By this, he meant an intangible and impersonal force that is the source of all values. Like the mystery cults, Plotinus's philosophy promised a kind of salvation. Neo-Platonism was destined to have a great influence on Western thought.

Jesus of Nazareth

Christianity begins with **Jesus of Nazareth**. For all its historical importance, Jesus' life is poorly documented. The main source of information about it is the New Testament books of Matthew, Mark, Luke, and John. Jesus left no writings of his own. Early Christians, however, wrote a great deal. Between the second and fourth centuries A.D., Christians settled on a holy book consisting of both the Hebrew Bible, called the "Old Testament" by Christians, and a collection of writings about Jesus and his followers, called the "New Testament." The four **Gospels** provide commanding accounts, but they do not agree on all details. The Gospel according to Mark, probably the earliest Gospel, was most likely written about forty years after Jesus' crucifixion; several of the letters written by Paul of Tarsus (see pages 161–162) date from the 40s A.D.; and the earliest non-Christian sources are later in date and are scanty.

No personality has generated as much discussion among Western scholars as has Jesus. Many would distinguish the Jesus of theology, the object of faith, from the Jesus of history, the man who really lived in first century Palestine. Recent work argues that the historical Jesus must be understood within the Judaism of his day—or rather the Judaisms, because it was an era of debate and disagreement about how to be a Jew. Within two centuries, the lines hardened. By A.D. 200, two new religions had emerged: Orthodox Christianity and **rabbinic Judaism**. The

Jesus of Nazareth
Founder of Christianity. To his followers, he was Christ, "the anointed one," foretold in the Hebrew Bible as the redeemer of Israel who would initiate the kingdom of heaven.

Gospels   One of the four canonical, that is, authoritative books of the New Testament that describes the birth, life, ministry, crucifixion, and resurrection of Jesus.

rabbinic Judaism
Main form of Judaism, which emerged during the first century A.D. under the leadership of the rabbis. It clarified Jewish practice, elevated the oral law to equal authority with the written Torah, and enabled Judaism to evolve flexibly.

Emperors, Bishops, and Heretics

heresy An opinion that goes against religious or political doctrine and beliefs.

Arianism A term for the teaching of Arius and the beliefs of his followers, who believed that Jesus Christ, as "the first born of all creation," was generated by the Father, not coeternal with him. Their teachings challenged the doctrine of the Trinity.

Constantine discovered that his support of the church drew him into heated disputes over doctrine and **heresy**. *Heresy* comes from a Greek word meaning "to choose." Heretics are persons who choose teachings or practices that religious or state authorities deem wrong. The two greatest and most difficult heresies of Late Antiquity involved the central doctrines of Christianity: the deity of Jesus Christ himself and the relationship between his divine and human natures.

Christian belief holds that there is one God, who exists as three distinct but equal persons: Father, Son, and Holy Spirit. But around 320, a priest of Alexandria, Arius (AIR-ee-us) (ca. 250–336), began teaching that Jesus was the "first born of all creation." Christians had long been stung by the charge that their monotheism was a sham, that they really worshiped three gods. **Arianism**, as the faith of Arius and his followers is called, preserved monotheism by making Jesus slightly subordinate to the Father. Arianism won many adherents.

Constantine was scandalized by disagreements over Christian teachings and distressed by riotous quarrels among competing Christian factions. He dealt with religious controversies by summoning individual theologians to guide him and by assembling church councils to debate controversies and reach solutions. In 325, at Nicaea (Ny-SEE-uh), near Constantinople (see **MAP 7.2**),

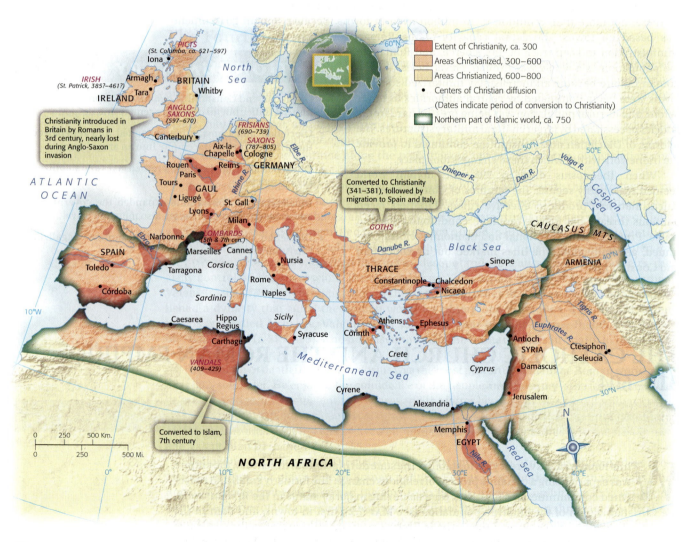

🌐 **MAP 7.2—The Spread of Christianity to A.D. 600**

From its beginnings in Palestine (see **MAP 6.2** on page 159), Christianity, while still illegal, spread mainly in heavily urbanized regions. After Constantine legalized Christianity, the faith spread into every corner of the Roman world.

the emperor convened a council of more than two hundred bishops, the largest council that had met up to that date. The **Council of Nicaea** condemned Arius and his teachings. The bishops issued a creed, or statement of beliefs, which maintained that Christ was "one in being with the Father," coequal and coeternal.

Religious unity remained elusive, however. The Council of Nicaea's attempt to eliminate Arianism was unsuccessful in the short term. Constantius II (r. 337–361), Constantine's son and successor in the eastern half of the empire, was an avowed Arian, as were some later emperors. For more than forty years, Rome's rulers occasionally embraced a faith that had been declared heretical. It was during this time that the Visigothic priest Ulfilas entered the empire, was converted to Arian Christianity, and returned to spread this faith among his people. Arian Christianity spread widely among the barbarian peoples living along the empire's frontiers. By the time those people began to enter the empire in significant numbers (see pages 179–180), catholic Christianity, universal (for that is what *catholicos* means) Christianity proclaimed by councils and emperors, had triumphed over Arianism, leaving the barbarians as heretics.

One emperor—Constantine's nephew Julian—made a last-ditch attempt to restore paganism during his short reign. He did not resort to persecution but forbade Christians to hold most government or military positions or to teach in any school. Although Christianity had been legalized only in 313, by the 360s, it was too well entrenched to be barred from the public sphere, and Julian's pagan revival died with him.

In the fifth century, Monophysitism (literally one-nature-ism) emerged as a result of bitter quarrels between Christian thinkers in Alexandria and Antioch. Theologians were struggling to find a way to talk about the divine and human natures in Christ. Some emphasized one nature, some the other. In 451, an emperor called a new council at Chalcedon (KAL-see-dun) to deal with the issue of Monophysitism. At Chalcedon, the theologians condemned the Monophysites, who emphasized Christ's divine nature, and pronounced that Jesus Christ was true God and true man—that he had two authentic natures. By 451, the Roman world had a large Catholic majority that derived its teachings from Nicaea and Chalcedon and heretical minorities who believed themselves to be the true Catholics.

Council of Nicaea The first "ecumenical" or "all-the-world council." Several more ecumenical councils would meet in Late Antiquity to deal with major heresies.

The Institutional Development of the Catholic Church, ca. 300–600

The earliest Christian communities were urban and had three kinds of officials, whose customary titles in English are *bishop, priest*, and *deacon*. Deacons were responsible for charitable works and for arranging meetings. Bishops and priests presided at celebrations—most prominently the Eucharist (or Holy Communion, as it came to be called)—preached, and taught. Distinctions between bishops and priests developed over time. Towns often had many independent Christian groups, each headed by a priest. By about 200, as a sign of unity and authority, the eldest priest came to be called "overseer," the literal meaning of *bishop*. As more people converted, as the church acquired property, and as doctrinal quarrels began to cause divisions among the faithful, bishops began to be influential local officials. By the late fourth century, the bishops in the major cities of the empire were called *metropolitan bishops*, or sometimes *archbishops*, and they had responsibility for territories often called *dioceses*. The church was adapting to its own purposes the administrative geography of the Roman Empire—another sign of change and continuity in Late Antiquity. (See the feature, "The Global Record: Christianity Arrives in Nubia.")

From its earliest days, the Christian community had espoused the doctrine of *apostolic succession*. In other words, just as Jesus had charged his apostles with continuing his earthly ministry, that ministry was passed on to succeeding generations of Christian bishops and priests through the ceremony of ordination. When one or more bishops laid their hands on the head of a new priest or bishop, they were continuing an unbroken line of clerics that reached back through the apostles to Jesus himself. The bishops of Rome coupled this general notion of apostolic succession with a particular emphasis on the original primacy of Peter, in tradition, the leader of the apostles and the first bishop of Rome. The theory of "Petrine Primacy" was based on Matthew's Gospel (16:16–18), where Jesus founded his church on Peter, "the Rock," and conferred upon him the keys to the kingdom of heaven. The theory held that just as Peter had been the leader of the apostles, so the successors to Peter, the bishops of Rome, continued to be the leaders of the

THE EMERGENCE OF THE ROMAN PAPACY

Christianity Arrives in Nubia

In *the early fifth century, a Constantinopolitan lawyer, Socrates Scholasticus (389–450), wrote an Ecclesiastical History, drawing upon many earlier sources. In the following passage, he recounts the introduction of Christianity into "India," by which he means Nubia, or what is basically today Ethiopia. This document presents the first evidence for Christianity in Africa.*

A certain philosopher, Meropius, was determined to acquaint himself with the country of the Indians. Having taken with him therefore two youths to whom he was related…Meropius reached the country by ship;…he touched at a certain place which had a safe harbor, for the purpose of procuring some necessaries. It so happened that a little before that time the treaty between the Romans and Indians had been violated. The Indians, therefore, having seized the philosopher and those who sailed with him, killed them all except his two youthful kinsmen; but sparing them from compassion for their tender age, they sent them as a gift to the king of the Indians. He, pleased with the personal appearance of the youths, made one of them, whose name was Edesius, cup-bearer at his table; the other, named Frumentius, he entrusted with the care of the royal records. The king dying soon after, left them free, the government devolving on his wife and infant son. Now the queen seeing her son thus left in his minority, begged the young men to undertake the charge of him, until he should become of adult age. The youths accepted the task, and entered on the administration of the kingdom. Frumentius controlled all things and made it a task to enquire whether among the Roman merchants trafficking with that country, there were any Christians to be found: and having discovered some, he informed them who he was, and exhorted them to select and occupy some appropriate places for the celebration of Christian worship. In the course of a little while he built a house of prayer; and having instructed some of the Indians in the principles of Christianity, they fitted them for participation in the worship. On the young king's reaching

maturity, Frumentius and his associates resigned to him the administration of public affairs … and sought permission to return to their own country. Both the king and his mother entreated them to remain; but being desirous of revisiting their native place, they could not be prevailed on, and consequently departed. Edesius for his part hastened to Tyre to see his parents and kindred; but Frumentius arriving at Alexandria, reported the affair to Athanasius, who had recently been made bishop, and acquainted him with his wanderings and the hopes Indians had of receiving Christianity. He also begged him to send a bishop and clergy there, and by no means to neglect those who might thus be brought to salvation. Athanasius … requested Frumentius himself to accept the bishopric, declaring that he could appoint no one more suitable than he was. Accordingly this was done; Frumentius invested with episcopal authority, returned to India and became there a preacher of the Gospel, built several churches, and aided by divine grace, he performed various miracles, healing with the souls also the bodily diseases of many.

QUESTIONS

1. By what routes would a person be likely to sail to Nubia, and how would Frumentius have traveled from Nubia to Alexandria?

2. What impressions does this text give you of the knowledge possessed by Romans of the peoples outside the empire?

3. Do Frumentius and Edesius remind you of Moses?

4. What techniques did Frumentius use to institute Christianity in Nubia?

Source: Socrates Scholasticus, *The Ecclesiastical History*, Book 1, chapter 19, in Philip Schaff and Henry Wace, eds., *A Select Library of Nicene and Post-Nicene Fathers of the Christian Church*, Second Series, Volume 2, 1978. By kind permission of Continuum International Publishing Group.

church as a whole. By the late fourth century, the bishop of Rome was usually addressed as *papa*, or "pope" in English. The growing authority of the bishop of Rome within the church is the most striking organizational process of the fourth and fifth centuries.

Growing numbers of Christians, the increasing prominence of the clergy, and doctrinal quarrels drew emperors more deeply into the public life of the church. Between 378 and 381, Theodosius virtually outlawed the pagan cults, thereby making Christianity and Judaism the only legal religions, and required all Christians to believe as the bishop of Rome did, in the hope of imposing religious unity. Unity under Roman leadership was essential, Theodosius said, because Peter had transmitted the unblemished faith directly to Rome, and Peter's successors had preserved it there. The bishops of Rome took an ambivalent view of Theodosius's laws. They were glad to have the emperor's support but they did not wish for their authority or teaching to rest on imperial decrees. Theodosius's actions reflect the growing power of the bishop of Rome and demonstrate the degree to which the state and the church were becoming intertwined. The decrees themselves failed to achieve the unity Theodosius desired.

Ever since Nicaea, councils, with active participation by the emperors, had settled major disagreements in the church. Pope Leo I (r. 440–461) began to assert papal prerogatives. He had sent representatives to the Council of Chalcedon bearing his doctrinal formulation. Leo insisted that, as the bishop of Rome, he had full authority to make decisions in doctrinal controversies. The emperor skillfully steered Leo's "Tome" to acceptance by the council, but to appease many Eastern bishops, who felt that too much authority was being claimed by the pope, the emperor also encouraged the council to assert that the bishop of Constantinople (or patriarch, as he was often called) was second in eminence and power to the bishop of Rome. Leo, the greatest exponent of "Petrine Primacy" though not its originator, objected strenuously to the Council of Chalcedon's procedures. He disliked the prominent role of the emperor, complained that Eastern bishops had no right to challenge his doctrinal authority, and particularly opposed the elevation of Constantinople's status.

A generation later, Pope Gelasius I (r. 492–496) sent a sharply worded letter to the emperor Anastasius (r. 491–518), who had intervened in a quarrel between the Catholics and the still-numerous Monophysites. Gelasius protested the emperor's intervention. He told the emperor that the world was governed by the "power" of kings and by the "authority" of priests. Ordinarily, the pope said, the jurisdictions of kings and priests are distinct. In a controversy between them, however, priestly authority must have precedence, because priests are concerned with the salvation of immortal souls, whereas kings rule only mortal bodies. Gelasius was telling the emperor to stay out of theology, but he was implying much more. His opposition of the words *power*—meaning mere police power, the application of brute force—and *authority*—legitimacy, superior right—was of great importance. Gelasius elevated the church, with the pope at its head, above the whole secular regime, with the emperor at its head. But Gelasius had no means of coercing emperors. Moreover, many clergy in the eastern Mediterranean refused to accept the idea that the pope had supreme authority in either doctrine or church government.

Pope Gregory I "the Great" (r. 590–604) exemplifies the position of the papacy as Late Antiquity drew to a close. Gregory was the scion of an old senatorial family. He had risen through several important positions in the Roman administration, but then decided to abandon public life, sell off his family's property, and pursue a life of spiritual retreat. Soon, however, the Roman people elected him pope. His reputation for holiness was important to his election, but so too were his impeccable social credentials and wide political connections. Rome was threatened by the Lombards (a barbarian group that had entered Italy in the 560s), the local economy was in a shambles, and relations with the imperial government had been strained. Gregory did not wish to be elected pope, but given his conventional Roman sense of duty and obligation, he had little choice but to accept the office. Immediately, he undertook dangerous diplomatic measures to ward off the Lombard threat, sought improved relations with the emperor, and put the local economy on surer footing. He reorganized the vast estates of the church to place their products and revenues at the disposal of the Romans. In the absence of effective imperial administration in and around Rome, Gregory also began to attend to urban services and amenities, such as streets, aqueducts, and baths.

THE ROLE OF THE ELITE

The rise of the pope in the church as a whole was paralleled by the rise of bishops throughout the empire. By the year 400, members of the social elite were everywhere entering the clergy and rising to its highest offices. This capture of the elite was the final, decisive factor in the triumph of Christianity.

The clergy was an outlet for the talents and ambitions of the elite. For some time, senators had been excluded from military offices and reduced in civilian influence, and decurions were growing dissatisfied with public service. The *episcopal* office (that is, the office of bishop) was desirable to prominent men for many reasons. It was prestigious. Bishops wore distinctive clothing when officiating and were addressed by special titles—traditional Roman marks of respect. They had opportunities to control patronage in the way that prominent Romans always had done. They could intervene on behalf of individuals at the imperial court. They controlled vast wealth, as the generosity of pious Christians put more resources at their disposal. By the middle of the fifth century, the dominant person in most towns was the bishop, not a civilian official. The bishops, however, were the same persons, from the same families, who had once dominated local society through civic service. The overall effect of these social changes was dramatic in the long run, but it happened very gradually.

The change from a secular to an ecclesiastical elite in Roman cities even led to alterations of the topography of the cities themselves. The elite usually financed local building projects, such as temples, basilicas, forums, and amphitheaters. Such benefactions declined sharply during the tumultuous third century. The fourth century at first saw little building on private initiative, but then came the construction of Christian cathedrals (a bishop's church, from *cathedra*, the chair or seat of the bishop's authority), episcopal residences, and other churches. Such buildings, as a rule, were not placed in the old city centers, which had associations with the pagan past. Instead, they were placed on the edges of populated districts. In the future, these Christian centers served as poles around which ancient towns were reconfigured. The Roman elites built to show pride in their cities and to promote themselves. This did not change in Late Antiquity, but this time, the elites were bishops or rich Christians, and the buildings were religious—look again at Santa Maria Maggiore on page 170.

The Rise of Christian Monasticism

monasticism A way of life involving the renunciation of worldly pleasures and the embrace of a life of prayer and solitude. Monasticism arose in fourth-century Egypt and spread all over the Roman world.

For some men and women, the call of the Gospel was radical. They yearned to escape the world and everything that might come between them and God. To do so, many of them embraced a new way of life—**monasticism**. Christian monks and nuns developed a theology and an institution that were among the most creative and long-lived achievements of Late Antiquity.

The practice of rigorous self-denial (*askesis*) was common to several religious and philosophical sects in antiquity—for example, the Pythagoreans and the Stoics—and was well known among the Jews in the time of Christ, as the Essenes show (see page 160). Ascetics believed that if they could conquer the desires of the body, they could commune with the supernatural beings who were greater and purer than humans, encumbered by lust for food, drink, knowledge, sex, and adventure. Sometimes ascetic practices were adopted by tightly knit groups, sometimes by heroic solitaries.

The founder of Christian monasticism was a young Egyptian layman, named Anthony (d. 356). At age 19, Anthony gave away all his possessions and took up, in the Egyptian desert, a life of prayer and renunciation. His spiritual quest became famous, and many disciples flocked to him. Finally, he decided to organize these seekers into a very loose community. His followers remained in solitude except for worship and meals. Anthony's form of monasticism is called *eremitic*, from the Greek *heremos*, or "desert," hence, the word *hermit*.

eremitic monasticism An especially austere, solitary form of asceticism.

Pachomius (pack-OH-mee-us) (290–346) created a more communal form of monastic life. A former Roman soldier, he was baptized a Christian in 313 and retired to the Egyptian desert, where he studied with a hermit. Eventually Pachomius founded a community, which before long had grown to thousands of members. Perhaps because of his military background, or because his religious instincts favored order and unity, Pachomius wrote the first Rule, or code for daily living, for a monastic community. He organized most aspects of his community by designing a common life based on routines of private prayer, group worship, and work. By the time of his death, Pachomius led nine male and two female communities. Pachomius's pattern of monasticism is called *cenobitic* (sen-oh-BIT-ik), from the Greek for "common life." People living this common life were called *monks*, and the place where they lived was called a *monastery*. The head of the community was designated the *abbot*, a word meaning "father." In later times, the term *abbess*, meaning "mother," was coined for the woman who led a female community.

cenobitic monasticism From the Greek *koinos bios*, common life, this form of monasticism was communal.

Monasticism spread from Egypt by means of texts, such as the *Life of Anthony* (a late antique "best seller"), collections of the wise sayings of famous desert abbots, and books written by persons who went to Egypt seeking a more perfect life—among whom were several prominent women. One attraction of monasticism among the devout was that it seemed to be a purer form of Christian life, uncorrupted by the wealth, power, and controversy of the hierarchical church. Many pious women embraced monasticism at least partly because they could not be ordained priests. Positions in monasteries, including that of abbess, provided responsible roles for talented women. Monasticism gave women a chance to choose a kind of family life different from the one available in households dominated by fathers and husbands.

Eremitic monasticism was prominent in Palestine and Syria and eventually throughout the Greek-speaking world. Eastern monasticism produced a great legislator in Basil (330–379), whose Rule was the most influential in the Orthodox Church (see page 193). Generally, these monks assembled only for weekly worship and otherwise ate, prayed, and worked alone.

Eremitic monasticism arrived in the West in the person of Martin of Tours (336–397). Like Pachomius, Martin was a Roman soldier who, after his military service, embraced both

Christianity and asceticism. Even though he was elected bishop of Tours, Martin kept to his rigid ascetic life. Martin's form of monasticism influenced many in the western regions of the Roman world, but set especially deep roots in Ireland. There, the whole organization of the church was based on monasteries. At Kildare, the abbess Brigid (d. 523) had more authority than the local bishop.

In the West, cenobitic monasticism became the dominant pattern. Benedict of Nursia (480–545) abandoned his secular career to pursue a life of solitary prayer in a mountain cave. Benedict's piety attracted a crowd of followers, and in about 520, he established a monastery at Monte Cassino, 80 miles south of Rome. The Rule he drafted for his new community is marked by shrewd insights into the human personality. It emphasizes the bond of mutual love among the monks and obedience to the abbot. The Rule assigns the abbot wide powers but exhorts him to exercise them gently. The Rule allows monks a reasonable diet and decent, though modest, clothing. Although providing for discipline and punishment, the Rule prefers loving correction. In later centuries, Benedict's Rule dominated monastic life.

Monasticism was a conscious alternative and an explicit challenge to the civic world of classical antiquity. Monks and nuns did not seek to give their lives meaning by serving the state or urban communities. They went into remote places to serve God and one another. They sought not to acquire, but to abandon. Spiritual wisdom was more important to them than secular learning, and they yearned for acknowledgment of their holiness, not recognition of their social status. Still, monasticism was sometimes controversial. Whereas many people admired and emulated these holy men and women, others disputed their claims to elite spiritual status.

At the dawn of Late Antiquity, the church was persecuted and struggling. By the end of the period, the church was rich and powerful, its leaders were prominent and prestigious, and in the monasteries, at least, its spiritual fervor was deep. This change was gradual but fundamental.

SECTION SUMMARY

- Imperial legislation and church councils imposed a universal, a catholic, form of Christianity.
- The church developed a hierarchy of officers over which the bishops of Rome gradually achieved preeminence.
- Christians disagreed strongly on basic teachings, such as the Trinity (God is Father, Son, and Holy Spirit) and the divine and human natures of Jesus Christ.
- Some men and women rejected the values of the late antique world and embraced the monastic life of prayer and renunciation, achieving in the process a new kind of status: holiness.

THE RISE OF GERMANIC KINGDOMS IN THE WEST, CA. 370–530

Who were the "barbarians," and what kinds of relations did Romans and barbarians have in Late Antiquity?

The years from the 370s to the 530s were decisive in the history of the Roman Empire in the West. This period saw the transformation of Rome's western provinces into several Germanic kingdoms, most of which maintained some formal relationship with the eastern Roman Empire. Roman encounters with the barbarians took many different forms, ranging from violent conflict to peaceful accommodation. The key point to understand is that although the barbarians supplanted Roman rule in the West, they did so slowly and often with Roman permission and assistance.

Invasions and Migrations

Individual groups of barbarians did invade the empire in various places at different times, but there was never a single, coordinated barbarian invasion of the Roman world that had well-formulated objectives. The Romans and barbarians did not face one another as declared enemies. Indeed, peaceful encounters outnumbered violent confrontations in the history of Romano-barbarian relations. The Romans had long traded with the barbarian peoples, carried out complicated diplomacy with them, and recruited them into their armies. Barbarian veterans were settled in most provinces of the empire.

If we cannot label one grand movement as "the barbarian invasions," we must also avoid the idea that the barbarians were naturally nomadic and migratory. Holding this view would tempt us to see the entry of the barbarians into the empire as one stage in a long process of human movement. Archaeological evidence collected to date makes it clear that the barbarians were settled agriculturists. They lived in villages, farmed the surrounding country, and raised livestock. If barbarians moved from one place to another, their movement must be explained with reference to specific developments and cannot be attributed to migratory habits.

Few images of the ancient world are more fixed in the popular imagination than the overrunning of the Roman Empire by hordes of barbarians who ushered in a dark age. The Romans inherited the word *barbarian* from the Greeks, who had divided the world between those who spoke Greek and those who did not. Barbarians were literally babblers, foreigners who spoke an unknown language.

Who were the barbarians? Linguists classify them as speakers of Germanic languages. The Germanic peoples can be differentiated from the Celts and Slavs with whom they shared much of central and eastern Europe, but apart from some minor linguistic variations, it is difficult to distinguish one Germanic group from another.

What are we to make of the profusion of names offered to us by our sources: Franks, Saxons, Vandals, Visigoths, Ostrogoths, Lombards, Burgundians? The Romans referred to the Germanic peoples as tribes, but that does not mean that they were actually groups of related people. Every Germanic "tribe" was a confederation, and these confederations formed, dissolved, and reformed many times. The confederations were formed either by powerful leaders who coerced less powerful people to join them or by groups of villages that banded together to protect themselves from aggressive neighbors. As a tribe was forming, its constituent peoples would intermarry and adopt the language, law, and lifestyle of the dominant group.

Incorporating the Barbarians

The transformation of the western Roman Empire began as a result of an unexpected set of events involving the Huns, nomadic warriors from the central Asian steppes. (See the feature, "The Written Record: Two Views of the Huns.") After plundering the frontiers of Persia and China for centuries, they turned west in search of booty and tribute. In 374 or 375, they fell on the Ostrogoths, who lived near the Black Sea, and frightened the **Visigoths**, who requested permission to cross the Danube and enter the empire.

Visigoths A "West" Germanic people who coalesced along the Danube frontier in the fourth century, allied with the Romans, eventually entered the empire, sacked Rome in 410, and finally established a kingdom in Gaul.

Because of dynastic quarrels and military challenges, the Romans delayed responding to the Visigoth request. Fearful of the Huns, the Visigoths crossed the Danube on their own and then asked if they might settle in the Balkans. Reluctantly, Valens (VAY-lenz) (r. 364–378) agreed but postponed permanent arrangements. While the government considered how to deal with the Visigoths, local authorities sold them food at exorbitant prices and even traded dog meat for Gothic children, who were then enslaved. When the Visigoths revolted, Valens foolishly marched north to meet them with a small force. The Visigoths defeated his army and killed him at Adrianople in 378.

The history of the Visigoths presents an instructive example of Romano-Germanic relations. They had served as auxiliary troops entrusted with defending a stretch of the Danube frontier for a long time when they requested permission to enter the empire in 376. They did not cross the border as part of a massive invasion but because they were sorely threatened. In 382, Theodosius marched east to pacify the situation. He agreed to grant the Visigoths what they had been demanding: land to settle on and a Roman military title—that is, official status—for their king. A spokesman for Theodosius explained the emperor's motives: "Which is better: To fill Thrace with corpses or with farmers? To fill it with graves or with people? To travel through wilderness or cultivated land? To count those who have perished or those who are ploughing?"

For about thirty years, the Visigoths struggled to improve the terms of their settlements in the Balkans. Alaric (AL-uh-rik), the Visigothic king after 395, grew tired of unfulfilled promises and forced matters by attacking Italy. In 410, the Visigoths sacked Rome. The taking of the city for the first time in eight hundred years shocked the entire Roman world and has loomed large for centuries in people's ideas about the "fall" of the Roman Empire. Actually, it was a ploy by Alaric to improve the terms of his already official status. Alaric died in 410, and his brother led

Two Views of the Huns

The dread and disgust inspired by the Huns is well captured in the first passage, from the Roman historian Ammianus Marcellinus. The second passage, from a surviving fragment of the history of Priscus, shows the Huns in quite a different light. Only rarely can we contrast two different views, and these documents permit us to do so.

(a)

From the moment of their birth they make deep gashes in their children's cheeks, so that when in due course hair appears its growth is checked by the wrinkled scars; as they grow older this gives them the unlovely appearance of beardless eunuchs. They have squat bodies, strong limbs, and thick necks, and are so prodigiously ugly and bent that they might be two-legged animals. Their shape, however disagreeable, is human. They have no use for seasoned food, but live on the roots of wild plants and the half-raw flesh of any animal, which they warm a little by placing it between their thighs and the backs of their horses. They have no buildings to shelter them. They wear garments of linen or of the skins of field-mice stitched together. Once they have put their necks into some dingy shirt they never take it off or change it until it rots and falls to pieces. They have round caps of fur on their heads, and protect their hairy legs with goatskins. They are ill-fitted to fight on foot, and remain glued to their horses, hardy but ugly beasts, on which they sometimes sit like women to perform their everyday business and they even bow forward over their beasts' narrow necks to enjoy a deep and dreamy sleep.

(b)

[The Roman ambassadors] came upon a very large village in which the dwelling of Attila was said to be more notable than those elsewhere. It had been fitted together with highly polished timbers and encircled with a wooden palisade, conceived not for safety but for beauty. Next to the king's dwelling that of Onegisus [chief minister to Attila] was outstanding, and it also had a circuit of timbers but was not embellished with towers in the same way as Attila's. Not far from the enclosure was a large bath. . . . Maidens came to meet Attila as he entered this village, advancing before him in rows under fine white linen cloths stretched out to such a length that under each cloth, which was held up by the hands of the women along either side, seven or even more girls walked. There were many such formations of women under the linen cloths, and they sang Scythian songs. When he [Attila] came near the house of Onegisus, the wife of Onegisus came out with a host of servants, some bearing dainties and others wine, greeted him and asked him to partake of the food which she had brought for him with friendly hospitality. To gratify the wife of his intimate friend, he ate sitting on his horse, the barbarians accompanying him having raised the silver platter up to him. Having also tasted the wine, he went on to the palace, which was higher than the other houses and situated on a high place.

QUESTIONS

1. How do these two accounts differ in tone, emphasis, and details?

2. Leaving aside the question of whether these accounts are true, what impressions do you think they would have made on the Romans? What impressions were they intended to make?

3. How do the public rituals of the Huns compare with those of the Romans?

Sources: Excerpt (a): Ammianus Marcellinus, *The Later Roman Empire (A.D. 354–378)*, 31.2, ed. and trans. Walter Hamilton (Harmondsworth, U.K.: Penguin, 1986), pp. 411–412. Excerpt (b): Priscus, Fragment 8, in C. D. Gordon, *The Age of Attila: Fifth-Century Byzantium and the Barbarians* (Ann Arbor: University of Michigan Press, 1961), pp. 84–85.

the Visigoths north into southern Gaul. For good measure, the new Visigothic king captured the Western emperor's sister, Galla Placidia, and forced her to marry him. However objectionable this act must seem, the Visigoths viewed it as a further demonstration of their loyalty to Rome and their determination to effect a satisfactory new treaty.

In 418, the Roman government gave in. A treaty permitted the Visigoths to settle in southern Gaul, with Toulouse as their base of operations. They were assigned the task of protecting the area from marauding bands of brigands. In return for their service, the Visigoths were given land allotments and a portion of Roman tax receipts as pay.

The Visigoths' treaty with Rome made theirs the first Germanic kingdom on Roman soil. From 418 to 451, the Visigoths served Rome loyally and earned the respect of the Gallo-Roman aristocrats among whom they ruled. Between 466 and 484, the Visigothic kingdom in Gaul reached its high point and continued to receive official recognition from Roman rulers. Southern

Gaul, one of Rome's oldest provinces, gradually passed from the hands of the Roman bureaucracy and the local nobility into the control of the Visigoths.

While they were dealing with the Visigoths, the Roman authorities realized that the Huns, who had settled in the Danube basin after driving the Visigoths into the empire, were a serious menace. They raided the Balkans, preyed on trade routes that crossed the region, and demanded tribute from the Eastern emperor. In 434, the fearsome warrior Attila murdered his brother and became sole ruler of the Huns. In return for a huge imperial subsidy, he agreed to cease raiding the Balkans. At the same time, a Roman general in Gaul concluded an alliance with the Huns in an attempt to use them to check the expansion of the Burgundians, an allied people who lived in the central Rhineland.

Together, Attila and the Romans routed the Burgundians, but Attila realized the weakness of the Roman position in the West. He attacked Gaul in 451 and was stopped only by a combined effort of Romans, Visigoths, Burgundians, and Franks. The soldiers who defeated the Huns were all called "Romans."

More Kingdoms: The End of Direct Roman Rule in the West

To meet threats in Gaul and elsewhere, the Romans had begun pulling troops out of Britain in the fourth century and abandoned the island to its own defense in 410. Thereafter, raiding parties from Scotland and Ireland, as well as seaborne attackers—called "Saxons" by contemporaries because some of them came from Saxony in northern Germany—ravaged Britain. The British continually appealed to the military authorities in Gaul for aid, but to no avail. Between 450 and 600, much of southern and eastern Britain was taken over by diverse peoples whom we call the "Anglo-Saxons." The newcomers jostled for position with the Celtic Britons, who were increasingly confined to the north and west of the island. Amid these struggles was born the legend of King Arthur, a Briton who defended his people and led them to victory. Gradually, several small kingdoms emerged. Although Britain retained contacts with Gaul, the island had virtually no Roman political or institutional inheritance.

Valentinian III (r. 425–455) was born in 419 and became emperor of the West as a 6-year-old. Even when he came of age, his court was weakened by factional strife, and his regime was dominated by military men. After Valentinian, the western empire saw a succession of nonentities, the last of whom was deposed by a Germanic general in 476. Ruling in Italy, he simply sent the imperial regalia to Constantinople and declared that the West no longer needed an emperor. This is all that happened in 476, the traditional date for the "fall" of the Roman Empire.

After the vast coalition defeated the Huns in Gaul in 451, the remaining Roman authorities in the Paris region discovered that the Visigoths were expanding north of the Loire River into central Gaul. To check this advance, the Roman commander in Paris forged an alliance with the Franks. The Franks, long Roman allies, had been expanding their settlements from the mouth of the Rhine southward across modern Holland and Belgium since the third century.

The fortunes of the Frankish kingdom, indeed of all of Gaul, rested with Clovis. He became king of one group of Franks in 481 and spent the years until his death in 511 subjecting all the other bands of Franks to his rule. He gained the allegiance of the Frankish people by leading them to constant military victories that brought territorial gains, plunder, and tribute. The greatest of Clovis's successes came in 507, when he defeated the Visigoths and drove them over the Pyrenees into Spain.

Clovis was popular, not only with the Franks, but also with the Gallo-Roman population, for three reasons. First, Clovis and the Romans had common enemies: Germanic peoples still living beyond the Rhine and pirates who raided the coast of Gaul. Second, whereas most of the Germanic peoples were Arian Christians, the majority of the Franks passed directly from paganism to Catholicism. Thus, Clovis and the Gallo-Romans had a shared faith that permitted Clovis to portray his war against the Visigoths as a kind of crusade against heresy. Third, Clovis eagerly sought from Constantinople formal recognition and titles, appeared publicly in the dress of a Roman official, and practiced such imperial rituals as distributing gold coins while riding through crowds. The Frankish kingdom under Clovis's family—called "Merovingian," from the name of one of his semilegendary ancestors—became the most successful of all the Germanic realms.

Several early Germanic kingdoms were short-lived. The Burgundian kingdom, which had once prompted the Romans to ally with the Huns, was swallowed up by the Franks in the 530s. The Vandals, who crossed the Rhine in 406 and headed for Spain, crossed to North Africa in 429 (see **MAP 7.3**). They were ardent Arians, who persecuted the Catholic population. They refused imperial offers of a treaty on terms similar to those accepted by other Germanic peoples, and they constantly plundered the islands of the western Mediterranean and the Italian coast, even sacking Rome in 455. Roman forces from Constantinople eliminated the Vandals in 534.

The Ostrogoths, who had been living in Pannonia since the 370s as subjects of the Huns, began to pose a threat to the eastern empire after Attila's death. In 493, the emperor decided to send them to Italy to recover that area for the imperial government. The government at Constantinople was familiar with the Ostrogoths' king, Theodoric, because he had been a hostage there for several years

Theodoric conquered Italy quickly and set up his capital in Ravenna, the swamp-surrounded and virtually impregnable city that had sheltered the imperial administration for much of the fifth century. Through the force of his personality, and by a series of marriage alliances, Theodoric became the dominant ruler in western Europe. In Italy, he promoted peace, stability, and good

🌐 **MAP 7.3—The Germanic Kingdoms, ca. 530**

By 530, the western provinces of the Roman Empire (compare **MAP 6.1** on page 140) had evolved into Germanic kingdoms. Just as Roman provincial boundaries had changed numerous times, the existence and extent of Germanic kingdoms were also impermanent.

the kinds of literary contacts that the thousands of surviving letters from Late Antiquity reveal. Friendship also could mean patronage. The doorstep of every noble household was crowded every morning with hangers-on who awaited their patron's small offerings and any commands as to how they might do his will. *Officium*, "duty," was the sense of civic obligation that Roman rulers communicated to the provincial upper classes.

Aristocrats governed in both public and private ways. Though gradually excluded from key military and administrative posts, nobles did not lose their influence. They used their wealth to win or reward followers, bribe officials, and buy verdicts. In towns, decurions controlled local market privileges, building trades, police forces, fire brigades, and charitable associations. Their public and private means of persuasion and intimidation were immense. In the West, in the growing absence of an imperial administration, Roman public power did not so much "decline and fall" as find itself privatized and localized. Patronage and clientage in Roman society had a benevolent dimension, but they also revealed the raw realities of power.

In Roman society, power was everything, and those who lacked power were considered "poor," regardless of their financial status. On this reckoning, much of the urban population was poor because they lacked access to the official means of coercion and security that the notables enjoyed. Merchants, artisans, teachers, and others were always vulnerable because their social, political, or economic positions could change at a moment's notice. They lacked the influence to protect themselves.

Most citizens of the late antique world can be classed as farmers, but this categorization is misleading because it lumps together the greatest landowners and the poorest peasants. Late Antiquity saw a trend in the countryside that continued into the Middle Ages: Freedom and slavery declined simultaneously. In uncertain times, many small farmers handed over their possessions to local notables and received them back in return for rents in money or in kind. They became *coloni*, "tenants." Their patrons promised to protect them from lawsuits and from severe economic hardship. More and more, these coloni were bound to their places of residence and forced to perform services or pay fees that marked their status as less than fully free. At the same time, many landlords who could no longer afford to house, feed, and equip slaves gave them their freedom and elevated them to the status of coloni. Probably, the day-to-day lives of the great mass of the rural population and their position at the bottom of the social hierarchy changed very little.

Women's lives are not as well known to us as men's. "Nature produced women for this very purpose," says a Roman legal text, "that they might bear children and this is their greatest desire." Ancient philosophy held that women were intellectually inferior to men, science said they were physically weaker, and law maintained that they were naturally dependent. In the Roman world, women could not enter professions, and they had limited rights in legal matters. Christianity offered women opposing models. There was Eve, the eternal temptress through whom sin had fallen on humanity, and then there was Mary, the virginal mother of God. The Bible also presented readers with powerful, active women, such as Deborah and Ruth, and loyal, steadfast ones, such as Jesus' female disciples.

Girls usually did not choose their marriage partners. Betrothals could take place as early as age 7 and lawful marriages at 12. Most marriages took place when the girl was around 16; husbands were several years older. A daughter could reject her father's choice only if the intended man was unworthy in status and behavior. Women could inherit property from their fathers and retained some control over their marital dowries. Divorce was possible but only in restricted cases. A divorced woman who had lost the financial security provided by her husband and father was at a distinct disadvantage legally and economically unless she had great wealth.

Christianity brought some interesting changes in marriage practices. Since the new faith prized virginity and celibacy, women now had the option of declining marriage. The church at Antioch supported three thousand virgins and widows. Christian writers tried to attract women to the celibate life by emphasizing that housework was drudgery. Christianity required both men and women to be faithful in marriage, whereas Roman custom had permitted men, but not women, to have lovers, prostitutes, and concubines. Christianity increased the number of days when men and women had to abstain from sex. Ancient cultures often prohibited sexual intercourse during menstruation and pregnancy, but Christianity added Sundays and many feast days as forbidden times. Further, Christianity disapproved of divorce, which may have accorded women greater financial and social security, although, at the cost of staying with abusive or unloved husbands.

Traditionally women were not permitted to teach in the ancient world, although we do hear of women teachers, such as Hypatia of Alexandria (355–415), renowned for her knowledge of philosophy and mathematics. Until at least the sixth century, the Christian church had deaconesses who had important responsibilities in the instruction of women and girls. Medical knowledge was often the preserve of women, particularly in areas such as childbirth, sexual problems, and "female complaints."

Christianity also affected daily life. Churchmen were concerned that women not be seen as sex objects. They told women to clothe their flesh, veil their hair, and use jewelry and cosmetics in moderation. Pious women no longer used public baths and latrines. Male or female, Christians thought and lived in distinctive new ways. All Christians were sinners, and so all were equal in God's eyes and equally in need of God's grace. Neither birth, wealth, nor status was supposed to matter in this democracy of sin. Theological equality did not, however, translate into social equality.

The church also introduced some new status distinctions. Holiness became a badge of honor, and holy men and women became Late Antiquity's greatest celebrities. After their death, they were venerated as saints. Sanctuaries were dedicated to them, and people made pilgrimages to their tombs to pray and seek healing from physical and spiritual ailments. Thus, in some ways, Christianity produced a society the likes of which the ancient world had never known, a society in which the living and the dead jockeyed for a place in a hierarchy that was at once earthly and celestial. But in other ways, Christianity reoriented traditional Roman patron-client relations so that client sinners in this world were linked to sanctified patrons in heaven.

The Quest for a Catholic Tradition

By the middle of the fifth century, the Nicene Creed, first spelled out in 325, had taken definitive shape; it is still recited regularly in many Christian churches. With the Council of Nicaea, we see the first clear evidence that people were striving for a *catholic*, a universal, form of Christianity. Strictly speaking, catholic Christianity would be the one form professed by all believers. It is no accident that the Catholic Church grew up in a Roman world steeped in ideas of universality. The most deeply held tenet of Roman ideology was that Rome's mission was to civilize the world and bend it to Roman ways. As we have seen, however, it proved impossible to attain or impose a single set of beliefs.

One intriguing development in Late Antiquity is the emergence of several Christian communities claiming fidelity to a universal, or catholic, tradition. The Latin Christian church in the West clung tightly to the doctrinal formulations of Nicaea and Chalcedon and took its bearings from Latin church writers. In the eastern Mediterranean, writers tended to use the word *Orthodox*, which means "right believing" but also carries clear implications of catholicism, or "universality." The Orthodox Church centered primarily on the emperors and patriarchs, used Greek, and followed Greek Christian writers. The Coptic Church in Egypt was Monophysite, followed the teachings of the patriarchs of Alexandria, and used the Coptic language. The Jacobite Church, mildly Monophysite, was originally strong in Syria, from which it spread to Mesopotamia and beyond. Each of these churches produced a literature, art, and way of life that marked its members as a distinct community. These traditions did not reflect the emergence of something new in Late Antiquity so much as a Christian reinterpretation of very old cultures and ideals. Each of these traditions exists today.

Christianity drew much from the pagan and Jewish environments within which it grew, but its fundamental inspiration was the collection of writings called in modern times the Bible. It was understood to be a collection of sacred writings, and the individual items in that collection had different meanings. From the second century, Christian writers began trying to define a canon, a definitive list of genuine Old and New Testament scriptures. It was widely recognized that without an official, standardized set of Christian writings, there could be no uniformity of Christian belief. This process of determining authentic Scripture was not completed until the middle of the fifth century.

While the search was underway for an authoritative list of books, it was also necessary to try to get uniform versions of the books that were being pronounced canonical. The Greek East used the Greek version of the Old Testament and the Greek New Testament. But that version was unsuitable in the West, where Latin was the principal tongue. Late in the fourth century, Pope Damasus (DAM-uh-sus) commissioned Jerome (331–420), a man who had renounced his wealth for a life of monasticism and scholarship, to prepare a Latin version based on a new translation of the Hebrew Scriptures and Greek New Testament. Jerome's version was called the **Vulgate Bible** because it was the Bible for the "people" (*vulgus*), who knew Latin.

Vulgate Bible   Prepared by Jerome in the late fourth century, it was a Latin translation of the Hebrew Scriptures (Old Testament) and the Greek New Testament.

Sarcophagus of Junius Bassus Junius Bassus, prefect of Rome, died in 359 and was laid to rest in this splendid sarcophagus (from the Greek "body eater"). Three points are important: First, as members of the Roman elite became Christian, they could afford to employ the finest craftsmen. Second, as Christianity became legal, it could search for artistic expression. Third, these Old and New Testament scenes proclaim Christ's divinity but, in an age of intense theological quarrels, glide over his humanity. Compare Santa Maria Maggiore on page 170. (Scala/Art Resource, NY)

The development of a scriptural canon paralleled the elaboration of a creedal statement that would set down precisely what Christians believed. As we have seen, the Councils of Nicaea and Constantinople defined the nature of the Trinity, and Chalcedon formulated the relationship between the human and divine natures of Christ. There were also debates about the nature of the priesthood, the structure and authority of the church, and the problem of human free will. Practical questions came up, too. How could Christians fulfill the moral demands of their faith while living in a world whose values were often at odds with church teachings?

Answers to these kinds of questions were provided by a group of Greek and Latin writers who are called the "Church Fathers" and whose era is called "patristic" (from *patres*, the Latin word for "fathers"). In versatility and sheer output, they have few rivals at any time. Their intellectual breadth was matched by their elegant style and trenchant reasoning.

Many Christian writers addressed the problems of moral living in the world. In his treatise, *On Duties*, Ambrose of Milan (339–397) attempted to Christianize the public ethos that Cicero had spelled out many years before in his book of the same name. Cicero talked of citizens' obligations to one another and to the law and the need for those in power to be above reproach in the conduct of their personal lives. Ambrose reinterpreted these obligations as duties that Christians owed to one another because of their common worship of God.

Pope Gregory I wrote *The Pastoral Rule* to reformulate Cicero's and Ambrose's ideas in ways that made them relevant to society's Christian leaders, the clergy. John Chrysostom (KRIH-sus-tum) (347–407), a patriarch of Constantinople and one of the most popular and gifted preachers of Late Antiquity (his name means "golden tongued"), bitterly castigated the immorality of the imperial court and aristocracy: By setting a bad example, they endangered the souls of their subjects.

Boethius (bow-EE-thee-us) (480–524) illustrates contemporary themes well. Descended from one of Rome's oldest families, he held high offices but eventually earned the enmity of Theodoric the Ostrogoth, who imprisoned and executed him. He was a prolific writer, whose Latin translations of Greek philosophical texts bequeathed those writings to the Middle Ages. In his most famous book, *The Consolation of Philosophy*, written while he was in prison, Boethius describes how the soul could rise through philosophy to a knowledge of God. Once again, we see the classical and the Christian blended in a new synthesis.

Saint Augustine and the Christian Tradition

The most influential Christian thinker after Saint Paul was **Augustine of Hippo** (354–430). Augustine was born in North Africa to a pagan father and a Christian mother. His family was of modest means, but at great sacrifice, they arranged for him to receive the best education available. He embarked on a career as a professor of rhetoric. Augustine fell under the spell of Ambrose and embraced the Christianity that his mother, Monica, had been urging on him throughout his life. Later, Augustine chronicled his quest for truth and spiritual fulfillment in his *Confessions*, a classic of Western literature. In 395, Augustine became a bishop and, until his death, served the wider Christian world, with a torrent of writings.

Not a systematic thinker, Augustine never set out to provide a comprehensive exposition of the whole of Christian doctrine. Instead, he responded to problems as they arose. Crucial among these were the relationship between God and humans, the nature of the church, and the overall plan of God's creation.

In the early fifth century, some people believed that they could achieve salvation by the unaided operation of their own will. Augustine responded that although God did indeed endow humankind with free will, Adam and Eve had abused their will to rebel against God. Ever since that first act of rebellion, a taint, called by theologians "original sin," predisposed all humans to continual rebellion, or sin, against God. Only divine grace can overcome sin, and only by calling on God can people receive grace. Here was a decisive break with the classical idea of humanity as good in itself and capable of self-improvement, perhaps even perfection, in this world.

Some North African heretics taught that sacraments celebrated by unworthy priests are invalid. Augustine believed that the validity of the church's sacraments—those ritual celebrations that are considered to be channels for the communication of grace, of God's special aid and comfort to the faithful—does not depend on the personal merit of the minister. They depended on the grace of God. To Augustine, God alone is perfect. Clergy, rulers, and churches are all human institutions, all more or less good in particular circumstances.

To many adherents of the traditional Roman religion, the sack of Rome by the Visigoths in 410 was repayment for Rome's abandonment of its traditional gods. To refute them, Augustine wrote the most brilliant and difficult of all his works, *The City of God*. This book is a theology of history. Augustine sees time not as cyclical—the traditional classical view—but as linear. Since the creation of the world, a plan has been in operation—God's plan—and that plan will govern all human activity until the end of time. History is the struggle between those who call on divine grace, who are redeemed, who are citizens of the City of God, and those who keep to the ways of the world, who persist in sin, who live in the earthly city. One may observe the unfolding of the divine plan by seeing how much of the earthly city has been redeemed at any given time.

Even though the Roman Empire was officially Christian, Augustine refused to identify his City of God with it. Nor would he say that the church and the City of God were identical. What he did say was that the sack of Rome was a great irrelevance because many kingdoms and empires had come and gone and would continue to do so, but only the kingdom of God was eternal and, in the long run, important. To a Roman people whose most cherished belief held that the world would last exactly as long as Rome's dominion, Augustine's dismissal of Rome's destiny sounded the death knell of the classical worldview.

Augustine also addressed the problem of education. He regarded salvation as the goal of life but realized that people have to carry on with their ordinary occupations. He also knew that almost the entire educational establishment was pagan in design and content. Education was confined mainly to the elite, who sought schooling partly to orient themselves within their cultural tradition and partly to gain employment, often in the imperial or urban service. This education had three mainstays. Latin or Greek grammar—rarely both—was the first. Augustine, for instance, knew little Greek, and by the sixth century, few people in the East knew Latin. The second mainstay of education was rhetoric, once the art of public speaking but now, increasingly, literary criticism. The third was dialectic, or the art of right reasoning. In Late Antiquity, public schools were fast disappearing as the need for them slipped away. But the church still needed educated persons, so it provided schools in cathedrals and monasteries.

In a treatise entitled *On Christian Doctrine*, Augustine expressed some ideas about education that proved influential for a millennium. He argued that everything a person needs to know to achieve salvation is contained in the Bible. But the Bible, written in learned language, is full of difficult images and allusions. How is an ordinary person to learn what he or she needs to know

Augustine of Hippo
North African bishop and influential Christian thinker, he authored the *Confessions* and *The City of God*.

SECTION SUMMARY

- Despite dramatic political changes, Late Antiquity witnessed relatively little social or economic change.

- Christianity did, however, introduce many changes in morals and values.

- Late Antiquity presents us with the paradox of multiple "Catholic" traditions, that is, different Christian groups who believed that their tradition was universal.

- In the Latin and Greek churches, a catholic tradition was built upon a canon of sacred writings, a creed, and the writings of the Church Fathers.

- The greatest intellectual of Late Antiquity was Saint Augustine, who wrote on theology, history, and education.

in order to master this great book of life? Only by getting some schooling, and that education would inevitably be in the classical languages and literatures. Augustine's attitude toward classical learning was that it was useful only to the extent that it equipped individuals to read the Bible, to understand it, and to seek salvation. Classical culture had no intrinsic merit. It might give pleasure, but it was equally likely to be a distraction or a temptation to immorality.

The Italian writer Cassiodorus (ca. 485–580) gave this Augustinian interpretation of the classical heritage its definitive statement in his treatise, *On Divine and Human Readings*. His treatise served as a kind of annotated bibliography and curriculum of the major writings on school subjects, such as grammar, rhetoric, and dialectic, and on biblical commentary. For centuries, schools organized on Augustine's and Cassiodorus's model did an estimable job of preparing the clergy to carry out their functions.

CHAPTER SUMMARY

When the late antique period opened, Rome's vast and diverse empire was beset with innumerable political, military, and economic problems. The classical culture that had evolved over centuries in the Mediterranean world seemed to have lost much of its vigor and appeal. But energetic rulers, such as Diocletian and Constantine, undertook half a century of intense military, economic, and administrative reform. On religious issues, the rulers differed—Diocletian persecuted Christians while Constantine legalized the new faith. Their reforms put the empire on firm footing while simultaneously changing forever the basic nature of the Roman state.

The fourth century was a period of religious change for the empire. Church officials attempted to resolve disagreements over Christian teachings with ecumenical councils, but religious unity was never fully achieved. Further attempts to resolve controversies strengthened the power of the bishops and created the new role of the papacy. As the power of the pope increased, so too did the role of the elite. However, some men and women yearned to escape the trappings of the world and turned toward a new way of life—monasticism.

In 300, barbarians were a worrisome threat along the northern frontiers of the empire. By 600, barbarians had created, from Britain to Spain, a succession of kingdoms, the most successful of which owed great debts to Rome. The barbarians did not appear suddenly in Late Antiquity. Rome knew these people and had traded, fought, and allied with them for centuries. The barbarians did not come to destroy Rome but to join it, to benefit from it, to learn its ways. The creation of the barbarian kingdoms was, in many ways, one of Rome's most creative political acts.

In the eastern empire, Constantinople rose to become a truly imperial city under the emperors Theodosius and Justinian. Justinian's code, which collected and organized Roman law, is the most influential legal collection in history. Equally impressive was the construction of a new Christian church, the Hagia Sophia. Yet despite these achievements, Justinian had to deal with new enemies, expensive military campaigns, and a devastating plague.

FOCUS QUESTIONS

- What were the most important reforms of Diocletian, Constantine, and their successors, and what roles did those reforms play in saving and transforming the empire?

- How and why did a Roman and Catholic Church emerge in Late Antiquity?

- Who were the "barbarians," and what kinds of relations did Romans and barbarians have in Late Antiquity?

- What challenges did the eastern empire face and what were some of its major contributions?

- How did women and men, elites and ordinary people, urban dwellers and farmers experience continuity and change in Late Antiquity?

While these centuries were a period of great political and religious change, the daily lives of men and women stayed remarkably unchanged. Society was hierarchical and most of the population was categorized as poor. Christianity brought some changes to social practices, such as marriage and relationships between men and women. Believers strived for a universal, or catholic, form of Christianity and this led to the development of a scriptural canon. New writings on Christianity, from Saint Augustine and others, also helped to shape beliefs.

KEY TERMS

tetrarchy   (p. 168)

Edict of Milan   (p. 171)

heresy   (p. 174)

Arianism   (p. 174)

Council of Nicaea   (p. 175)

monasticism   (p. 178)

eremitic monasticism   (p. 178)

cenobitic monasticism   (p. 178)

Visigoths   (p. 180)

Justinian   (p. 186)

Hagia Sophia   (p. 191)

Vulgate Bible   (p. 193)

Augustine of Hippo   (p. 195)

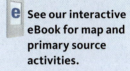 **This icon will direct you to additional materials on the website: www .cengage.com/history/ noble/westciv6e.**

e **See our interactive eBook for map and primary source activities.**

The Great Mosque of Cordoba
(Christopher Rennie/Robert Harding World Imagery)

Early Medieval Civilizations, 600–900

This chapter treats three areas and histories: the Islamic East, the Byzantine Empire, and the Latin West. For each, the seventh century was an era of dramatic change, the eighth century a period of reform and consolidation, and the ninth century a time of upheaval. A new imperial tradition developed in all three areas. Muslims, Orthodox Christians, and Catholics all believed themselves to be chosen by God, and their rulers defined themselves as God's earthly agents. In all three realms, the interaction of local traditions and the Roman past produced new forms of central government that would prove influential for centuries. Commercial ties began to transform the Mediterranean world into a community of peoples who needed to balance mutual interests with bitter rivalries.

The Great Mosque of Cordoba, erected by Abd ar-Rahman in 786–787, at first glance, appears much like a late antique building: elegant columns, arches arranged in arcades, rectangular space. But this is a *mosque*, an Islamic house of worship, and it was built in Spain, one of Rome's oldest provinces. We saw in Chapter 7 that Spain had fallen to the Visigoths in the sixth century and that Justinian had been unable to reconquer the region. Between 711 and 716, an army of Arabs and North African tribesmen overwhelmed Spain and inaugurated seven centuries of Islamic rule on the Iberian Peninsula. A time traveler transported to the Mediterranean world of 600 would almost certainly have predicted only two heirs to Rome: the eastern empire and the kingdoms of the barbarian West. It is extremely unlikely that our intrepid wanderer would have foreseen one of the most dramatic developments in the history of Western civilization: the rise of the Arabs and their Islamic faith.

The Great Mosque serves as a remarkable reminder of how much changed—and how much remained the same—in the early Middle Ages. Arches and arcades graced classical architecture for more than a millennium. But Cordoba's arches are horseshoe shaped, a minor innovation. The arches incorporate alternating bands of red and cream-colored stone. These shapes and colors may be local traditions, an imitation of the Roman aqueduct at Mérida, Byzantine imports, or Syrian characteristics. The building is basilican in shape. In a basilica, the space is oriented to the area where officials presided—to an altar when the basilica is a church. In a mosque, the space is oriented to the *qibla* wall—the wall facing Mecca, the birthplace of Muhammad and Islam. The elements of the Great Mosque were old, but the overall effect was new.

The period from 600 to 900 is commonly called the "early Middle Ages." What does this term mean? In the seventeenth century, a Dutch scholar wrote of the *Medii Aevi*, the "Middle Times" that lay between antiquity and the dawning modern world. The name stuck.

FOCUS QUESTIONS

- What were the most important factors in the rise of the Arab peoples and the Islamic faith?

- Why did a distinctive civilization that can be called "Byzantine" emerge?

- What were the greatest achievements of the Carolingians and why were they so successful compared to the other states that survived Rome's collapse in the West?

- What were the chief similarities and differences among the early medieval civilizations?

This icon will direct you to additional materials on the website: www .cengage.com/history/ noble/westciv6e.

See our interactive eBook for map and primary source activities.

As a label for the post-Roman world, "Middle Ages" (whose adjectival form is "medieval") has become traditional. The fact that we no longer talk of an abrupt and catastrophic "fall" of the Roman Empire means that we no longer use the word *medieval* in negative ways.

THE ISLAMIC EAST

What were the most important factors in the rise of the Arab peoples and the Islamic faith?

Muhammad Prophet and founder of Islam. He began receiving revelations to preach about Allah in around 610. Before his death, he had converted most of Arabia.

Ancient writers took little notice of the Arabs, who inhabited the Arabian peninsula and lands to the north. Around 600, the prophet **Muhammad** (570–632) appeared among them preaching a faith old in its basic elements but new in its formulation. With unprecedented spiritual and military fervor, converts to that new faith conquered territories from Spain to the frontiers of China. Slowly, they built an imperial system with a coherent government and ideology. At the same time, cultural elites began forging a new civilization out of the ethnic, religious, and historical diversity of that vast realm.

Arabia Before Muhammad

The Arab world in 600 was large and turbulent. Long dominated by the Roman and Persian Empires, the region had no large-scale political entities. People belonged to close-knit clans, or extended families, that formed tribes. In theory, tribes were groups of people tracing descent from a known ancestor; in reality—and in this, Arab and Germanic peoples were alike—tribes were complex groups of relatives, allies, and political or economic clients.

The Arab East was also economically intricate and fragile. Bedouins (Arabs who were nomadic pastoralists) provided for their own needs from their herds of sheep and goats, from small-scale trading in towns, and from regular raids on one another and on caravans. Some farmers worked the land, but in many areas, soils were too poor and rain was too infrequent to support agriculture. Cities supported traders who carried luxury goods, such as spices, incense, and perfumes, from the Indian Ocean region and southern Arabia along caravan routes to the cities of the eastern Mediterranean. These traders formed the economic and political elite of Arabia, and they led the tribes. Mecca, dominated by the powerful Quraysh (KOOR-aysh) tribe, was the foremost city of Arabia.

A solution to the competition among tribes and towns for control of trade routes was the institution of *harams* (HAR-ahms), or sanctuaries—places where contending parties could settle disputes peacefully. Mecca was one of the chief harams in Arabia, and its founding was attributed to the Israelite patriarch Abraham and one of his sons, Ishmael. The focus of the sanctuary was the black stone shrine known as the Kaaba (KAH-bah), founded by Abraham, according to Arab tradition. For centuries, people from all over Arabia had made pilgrimages to Mecca, to the Kaaba, supposedly following Abraham's example.

The region's ethnic and religious composition was complicated, too. The Roman world was overwhelmingly Christian, although there were many kinds of Christians. The Persian realm was officially Zoroastrian, but it had Jewish, Christian, Manichaean, and Buddhist minorities. The Arabs themselves were generally pagans, but Arabia had Jewish and Christian minorities.

The Prophet and His Faith

Muhammad was born in 570 to a respectable, though not wealthy or powerful, clan of the Quraysh tribe. His father died before he was born, his mother shortly afterward, leaving Muhammad under the care of his grandparents and an uncle. Like many young Meccans, he entered the caravan trade. By the time he was 20, Muhammad had such a reputation for competence and moral uprightness that he became financial adviser to a wealthy Quraysh widow, Khadija (KAH-dee-ah) (555–619). Though older than Muhammad, she became his wife in 595, and they had a loving marriage until her death.

In 610, Muhammad received the first of many revelations that commanded him to teach all people a new faith that called for an unquestioned belief in one god, Allah, and a deep commitment to social justice for believers. Muhammad began teaching in Mecca, but he converted few people outside his own circle; his wife was his first convert. Some Meccans were envious of Muhammad. Others feared that his new faith and new god might call into question the legitimacy of the shrines in Mecca and jeopardize the traditional pilgrimages to the Kaaba and the trade that accompanied them. By 619, Muhammad's well-connected wife and uncle were dead, and his position was precarious.

At this juncture, citizens from Medina, a smaller trading community wracked by dissension among pagan Arabs, Jews, and followers of Muhammad, asked Muhammad to establish a haram there. In the summer of 622, small groups of Muhammad's disciples made their way to Medina, and, in September, Muhammad joined them. His journey from Mecca to Medina, the *hijra* (HEEZH-rah), marks the beginning of a new era, symbolized to this day in the Arab world by a calendar that dates "In the year of the Hijra."

Although Muhammad was fully in control in Medina, Mecca retained his attention. In addition to his sentimental attachment to Mecca, its political and economic importance was critical to his emerging desire to convert all of Arabia. His followers began attacking Meccan caravans and battled with the Meccans several times in the 620s. In 630, Muhammad and many of his followers returned to Mecca in triumph. Muhammad left the Quraysh in control, and he retained the Kaaba as a focus of piety. After making local arrangements, he returned to Medina and set about winning over the bedouins of the Arabian desert. By the time Muhammad died in 632, he had converted most of Arabia (see **MAP 8.1**).

To what exactly had Muhammad and his followers converted? At the most basic level, people were asked to surrender completely to Allah, the one true God—that is, they were asked to make *al-Islam*, "the surrender." Those who surrendered became *Muslims* and joined the *umma muslima* (OO-mah MOOSE-lee-mah), a completely new kind of community in which membership depended only on belief in Allah and acceptance of Muhammad as Allah's prophet. No longer were one's bonds confined to a particular clan, tribe, or town. All members of the umma were understood to have personal and communal responsibility for all other members. Because of the experience of the hijra, Islam was a religion of exile, of separation from the ordinary world, and of reliance on God.

The basic teachings of Islam are traditionally described as **Five Pillars**: (1) the profession of faith, "There is no God but Allah and Muhammad is His Prophet"; (2) individual prayer five times daily, plus group prayer at noon on Friday in a *mosque*, a Muslim house of prayer; (3) the sunup-to-sundown fast for one month per year; (4) the donation of generous alms to the poor; and (5) a pilgrimage to Mecca at least once in a person's lifetime. These pillars are still the central requirements of Islam.

In the early decades the pillars sustained a faith that stressed strict monotheism and practices that affirmed Islam and built up a sense of community. At certain times of the day, all Muslims everywhere bowed in prayer, with their heads facing toward Mecca. Everyone paid alms, creating thereby a feeling of solidarity among all members of the umma. Mecca itself and the experience of pilgrimage were central to all Muslims.

Originally, there was no elaborate theology, intricate doctrinal mysteries, creed, or clergy. Men called *imams* led the Friday prayers in the mosque and usually offered sermons that applied Muslim teaching to the issues of the day, but Islam involved no ordained priesthood, as in Judaism or Christianity, and no hierarchy, as in the Christian churches.

Muhammad always insisted that he transmitted a direct, verbal revelation, not his own interpretations. That revelation came in the form of "recitations" that make up the **Quran** (koo-RAHN), the Scriptures of Islam. Not long after Muhammad's death, his closest followers arranged

CHRONOLOGY

570–632	Life of Muhammad
597	Pope Gregory I sends missionaries to England
610–641	Reign of Heraclius in Byzantium
622	Hijra
632–733	Muslim conquests
661–750	Umayyad caliphate
664	Council of Whitby
711–716	Muslim conquest of Spain
726–787, 815–842	Byzantine iconoclasm
750	Founding of Abbasid caliphate
751	Lombard conquest of Ravenna
755–756	Foundation of Papal States
755–774	Frankish conquest of Lombards
757–796	Reign of Offa of Mercia
768–814	Reign of Charlemagne
780s–860s	Carolingian Renaissance
786–809	Reign of Harun al-Rashid
800	Imperial coronation of Charlemagne
843	Treaty of Verdun creates three Frankish kingdoms
867–886	Reign of Basil I

Five Pillars The basic beliefs and practices of Islam.

Quran Containing Allah's revelations to Muhammad, it constitutes the scriptures of Islam.

🌐 **MAP 8.1—Arab Conquests to 733**

This map vividly illustrates the spectacular gains by the Arabs in the time of Muhammad, under the first caliphs, and under the Umayyads. Later slow, steady gains in Africa, central Asia, and India expanded the empire even farther. Muslim conquest did not at first mean widespread conversion to Islam; Egypt, for example, was not majority Muslim before the tenth century.

the recitations into 114 *Suras*, or chapters. The Quran contains legal and wisdom literature, like the Hebrew Scriptures, and moral teaching, like the Christian New Testament. It also prescribes regulations for diet and for personal conduct.

For example, the Quran forbids alcohol and gambling, censures luxury and ostentation, and imposes strict sexual restraints on both men and women. (See the feature, "The Written Record: The Message of the Quran.") The Quran permitted a man to have up to four wives if he could care for them and would treat them equitably. A Muslim woman, however, was given her dowry outright, and multiple marriages may have meant that relatively more Muslim women could gain a measure of security.

Initially, the Quran was interpreted rather freely within the umma, doubtless because there was no clergy to impose a uniform interpretation. After the Prophet's death, some people felt the need for an authoritative teaching—as early Christians had felt the need for a canon of Christian scripture and teaching—and their efforts resulted in the collections called the *sunna*, which means roughly "good practice"—that is, the words and customs of Muhammad himself. Crucial in the development of the sunna were the *hadith*, the "sayings" of the Prophet, the comments he sometimes made about how God's revelation was to be understood and applied. Extant compilations of the sunna date from the ninth century, and scholars are not sure what portion of them derives authentically from the age of the Prophet.

The Arab Conquests

Muhammad's death brought a crisis. Who or what was to succeed him? In 632, the Meccan elite chose Abu Bakr as *caliph* (KAY-lif), or "successor to the Prophet." Abu Bakr was elderly, an early convert to Islam, and a former secretary to Muhammad. He and his three successors down to 661 (Umar, Uthman, and Ali) were all Meccans, relatives of the Prophet by marriage, and early converts. Islamic tradition calls them the "Rightly Guided Caliphs."

The Message of the Quran

The Quran consists of 114 Suras, literally the "steps" (we might say chapters) by which one rises to knowledge of Allah. The earliest versions of the Quran were equipped with a running commentary. The first four extracts here illustrate the simplicity and elegance of Muslim prayer and the absolute transcendence of Allah. The last two extracts demonstrate the profound sense of religious continuity that marked Muhammad's teaching.

Sura 1

In the name of Allah, Most Gracious, Most Merciful. / Praise be to Allah, the Cherisher and Sustainer of worlds; / Most Gracious, Most Merciful. / Master of the Day of Judgment. / Thee do we worship and Thine aid we seek. Show us the straight way, the way of those on whom Thou hast bestowed Thy grace, Thou whose portion is not wrath, and who do not go astray.

Sura 4.171

O People of the Book! Commit no excesses in your religion, nor say of Allah anything but truth. Christ Jesus the son of Mary was a messenger of Allah … so believe in Allah and in His messengers. Say not "Trinity" … for Allah is One God. Glory be to Him for He is exalted above having a son. To Him belong all things in the heavens and on earth.

Sura 3.84

Say ye: We believe in Allah, and the revelation given to us, and to Abraham, Ismail, Isaac, Jacob and the descendants (children of Jacob), and that given to Moses and to Jesus and that given to all prophets from their Lord, but we make no difference between one and another of them, and we bow to Allah.

Sura 2.87

We gave Moses the book and followed him up with a succession of messengers; We gave Jesus the son of Mary clear signs and strengthened him with the Holy Spirit.

Sura 48

If the People of the Book rely upon Abraham, let them study his history. His posterity included both Israel and Ismail. Abraham was a righteous man of Allah, a Muslim, and so were his children. Abraham and Ismail built the Kaaba as the house of Allah and purified it, to be a centre of worship for all the world: For Allah is the God of all peoples.

Sura 56

God's truth is continuous, and His prophets from Adam, through Noah and Abraham, down to the last of the prophets, Muhammad, form one brotherhood. Of Imran father of Moses and Aaron sprang a woman, who devoted her unborn offspring to Allah. That child was Mary the mother of Jesus. Her cousin was the wife of the priest Zakariya, who took charge of Mary. To Zakariya, in his old age, was born a son Yahya, amid prodigies: Yahya was the herald of Jesus the son of Mary and was known as John the Baptist.

QUESTIONS

1. What can you discern from these suras about the similarities and differences among Islam, Christianity, and Judaism?

2. Who are the "people of the book"? Why do you think they matter?

3. How is Allah portrayed in these suras?

Source: *The Meaning of the Holy Qur'an*, new edition with revised translation, commentary, and newly compiled comprehensive index by Abdullah Yusuf Ali. Amana Publications, 1988.

Abu Bakr left his successor, Umar, a united Arabia (see **MAP 8.1**), no small feat in that fractious world. Umar began the lightning conquests by the Arabs of much of the Roman and Persian Empires. He initiated the policy of granting choice positions in the expanding **caliphate**, the Arab empire, to old converts and of ranking them according to precedence in conversion. As the old elite divided up the new provinces of the caliphate, some of them became *emirs* (governors), and others became lower administrators. Arab administrators then collected from all conquered people personal taxes and land taxes. Converts to Islam paid only land taxes. Arab settlers paid no taxes and received salaries from the taxes paid by others.

Umar was murdered by a slave in 644, leaving his successor, Uthman, a huge empire to administer. A great centralizer, Uthman chose emirs, regulated the finances of the provinces, and authorized the preparation of the definitive text of the Quran. In attempting to preserve the advantages of the old Meccan elite, Uthman alienated many people, particularly in Egypt, Syria, and Iraq, who had benefited from conquest and who guarded jealously their newfound local wealth and power. Uthman was murdered in 656 and replaced by Ali, Muhammad's son-in-law, whose goal was to create a truly Islamic government by emphasizing the religious side of

caliphate The name for the territory conquered by Muhammad's successors and for the governmental regime they established.

the caliph's office as the leader of the umma. Ali was in turn killed by a disillusioned follower in 661. Years later, some Muslims looked back to Ali as the true model for the caliph. These Muslims formed the *Shi'a*, the "Party of Ali."

When Ali was killed, the caliphate passed to Mu'awiya (MOO-ah-wee-uh), a Meccan who was the governor of Syria and commander of the finest army in the Arab world. That army ensured Mu'awiya's position. From 661 to 750, the Umayyads (OO-my-ahdz), as Mu'awiya's family is called, built many of the caliphate's institutions.

The Umayyads instituted greater centralization. This involved the introduction of a unified coinage, the Arabization of the administration (granting all key positions to Arabs), and taking tight control of provincial government and taxation. The Umayyads moved the capital of the caliphate to Damascus in their own power base of Syria, more centrally located than the old towns of Mecca and Medina and closer to the militarily active zones in eastern Iran and along the Byzantine frontier in Syria. In addition, the Umayyads presided over the final territorial expansion of the caliphate (see **Map 8.1**).

Rome's empire expanded for 350 years, but the caliphate reached its zenith in scarcely 100. How can we account for the astonishingly rapid creation of such a vast empire? Byzantium and Persia had financially and militarily weakened themselves in a series of wars that ended just as the caliphate of Umar commenced. Moreover, the Byzantine and Persian states were exceedingly diverse, and the Arab armies dismantled them piecemeal. Both old empires, but especially the Byzantine, had deep religious divisions. The Byzantines and Persians tended to depend on static frontier garrisons and large armies that could not be quickly mobilized and moved long distances. The Arabs rarely risked great pitched battles. They preferred a gradually expanding military frontier gained by numerous lightning strikes.

The Prophet himself had believed firmly in the need to expand the faith, and his successors shared that belief. Muslim ideology divided the world into the "House of Islam" and the "House of War." In the House of Islam, the justice of Allah reigned supreme. In the House of War, *jihad*, or holy war, was the rule. Christians and Jews, as fellow "Peoples of the Book"—sharers in a scriptural tradition reaching back to Abraham—were spared the choice of conversion or death, but "infidels" were expected to submit and convert. The Arab conquests were carefully planned and directed to channel violence out of Arabia, to populate much of western Asia with loyal Muslims, and to reward members of the umma.

The Abbasid Revolution

Despite their military and administrative successes, the Umayyads were not popular. Many people resented their bureaucratic centralization. Such resentment was acute in areas heavily populated by recent converts, who had always disliked the old Arabian elites, and in frontier provinces, where Arab immigrants along with local converts desired autonomy. The secular nature of Umayyad rule also offended those pious Muslims who expected a high standard of personal morality from their rulers. The opposition came to a head in a series of rebellions that culminated in the naming of a rival caliph, Abu'l Abbas, in 749. In 750, he defeated his Umayyad opponent.

The Abbasids (uh-BASS-idz) reigned until the thirteenth century. Initially, they brought the Islamic world its first golden age. Harun's reign was marked by political stability, economic prosperity, and cultural achievements.

With their frontier origins, the Abbasids were sympathetic to the caliphate's provincial populations. Thus, they created a more international regime. Non-Arabs and recent converts felt toward Islam, the Prophet, and the Prophet's family a loyalty that they would not grant to the old Arabian potentates who had led and initially benefited from the Arab conquests. The Abbasid polity was based on the idea of the fundamental equality of all believers. Local persons got more choice positions than Meccan or Syrian aristocrats. The capital of the caliphate was moved from Syria to Iraq, but to avoid favoring any existing group or region, the Abbasids built a new city, Baghdad, which they called "the navel of the universe." By addressing regional and ethnic sensitivities in an effective way, they were able to maintain, even extend, the centralized state of the Umayyad period.

The first caliphs chose administrators from loyal Arabs and from experienced Christian subjects. Under the Umayyads, the regime was Arabized. Under the Abbasids, the government became international, professional, and hereditary. The chief agency of government was the treasury, which had separate branches dealing with Muslim alms, land and poll taxes paid

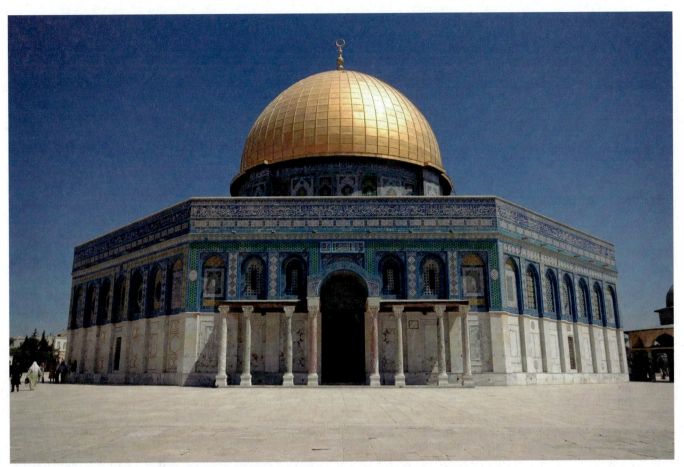

Dome of the Rock   This magnificent mosque in Jerusalem (built in 691–692) is the third-holiest shrine of Islam—after the Kaaba in Mecca and the Prophet's mosque in Medina. Muslims believe that Muhammad ascended to heaven from this spot.   (tamir niv/Used under license from Shutterstock.com)

by subjects, and land taxes paid by converts. Alone among early medieval governments, the caliphate could draw up annual budgets. Alongside the treasury in exerting power was a prestigious group of palace servants. They did not hold major offices, but their informal influence on the caliph and his family was great. The army was another prominent body within the state.

The central government had several links to the provinces. In addition to controlling the army and provincial governorships, the caliph employed a network of regular envoys and spies. The court, especially under the Abbasids, drew able young men from all over into the service of the caliph and created hopes among provincial elites that they, too, might be chosen. In every district and city, there were judges, or *qadi* (KAH-dee), to oversee the application of Islamic law. Qadi were under the authority of the caliph.

The ninth century was a troubled time. Intense family rivalries touched both the succession to the caliphate and the possession of key provincial positions. The bureaucracy became an increasingly influential pressure group, and the palace servants began to foment intrigues. The army became more and more a professional body comprising non-Arabs, especially Turks, hired from the frontiers and beyond because Arabs, enjoying their salaries, declined to serve. The parallel with the Germanization of the late Roman army is striking. The army, the bureaucracy, and the courtiers all had different and conflicting interests and did not hesitate to press their own advantages. Religious divisions persisted, even intensified. Many felt that the Abbasids had not gone far enough in erecting a truly Islamic regime, but some felt that the caliphs had gone too far in claiming both the political and religious authority of the Prophet. After the early tenth century, the Abbasid caliphs had little effective power.

The Emergence of Islamic Culture

Two currents are apparent in the culture of the Islamic East: One is the elaboration of religious thought; the other is the assimilation of multiple cultural heritages. Both were influenced by the spread of Islam that mixed Greek, North African, Iranian, Turkish, and even Hindu elements into a culture already rich with Arab, Christian, and Jewish ingredients.

Muslims assembled for prayer in mosques, the often beautiful buildings usually modeled on the original mosque in Medina. The worshipers—with men and women in separate areas—arrayed themselves in parallel rows and were led in prayer by an imam. Muslim judges began to issue opinions on how the Quran and sunna might be applied to the daily lives of believers. Teachers in mosque schools also were influential. Together, these authority figures, collectively the *ulama*, developed a body of religious thought.

The late ninth and early tenth centuries saw the emergence of a religious split in the Islamic world that persists to this day. The opposing groups are Shi'ite and Sunni Muslims. Shi'ites believe that caliphs should be chosen only according to strict standards of moral and spiritual worthiness. Further, they insist that the only way to ensure such worthiness is to choose caliphs from the line of Ali, the fifth caliph, husband of Muhammad's daughter Fatima and, in 661, a victim of assassination. Moreover, they believe that the whole ulama should measure up to Shi'ite standards. Sunni Muslims, always the vast majority, proclaim that only they adhere to the sunna, the "good practice," of Muhammad himself. Sunnis accept the legitimacy of the whole line of Umayyad and Abbasid caliphs and the teachings of the ulama.

In 832, an Abbasid caliph endowed the "House of Wisdom," an academy for scholars in Baghdad (compare Charlemagne's palace school; see pages 218–219), and from this point on, Muslim scholars had the leisure and wherewithal to begin tackling the corpus of Greek thought, especially the scientific writers. Greek, Persian, and Indian works were collected and translated, manuscripts were copied, and libraries were built.

Was the Islamic caliphate part of the West or not? From the vantage point of 900, the answer we might give to those questions—"largely Western"—differs from the answer we might give today—"largely Eastern." In later chapters, we will see how the Islamic world became less Western and more Eastern.

SECTION SUMMARY

- Muhammad was a great teacher who emphasized *al-Islam*, surrender to Allah.
- The Islamic faith may be summarized in the "Five Pillars."
- Internal and external factors contributed to the lightning conquests of Islam in the century after Muhammad's death.
- Islamic culture was rooted in the religious teachings of the *ulama* and in the scholarship of those who tackled Greek and Persian learning.

THE BYZANTINE EMPIRE

Why did a distinctive civilization that can be called "Byzantine" emerge?

The century after Justinian's death in 565 was difficult for the eastern Roman Empire. Attacks by Persians, Bulgars, and Muslims; riots and rebellions; plagues and famines; and some weak rulers imperiled the empire. Two fundamental changes transformed the eastern Roman Empire into a new civilization that is called "Byzantine" from "Byzantium," the ancient Greek name for the capital city, Constantinople. The empire experienced a sharp geographic contraction until it stabilized into the shape it would hold into the thirteenth century and the empire changed both its basic administrative structures and its cultural orientation.

Shifting Frontiers

In 600, the empire still laid claim, along the southern and eastern shores of the Mediterranean, to most of the lands that Rome had ruled for centuries. But in the East, the empire had been suffering recurrent losses to Persia. In 610, Heraclius (her-ACK-lee-us), a gifted ruler, ascended the throne. Between 622 and 629, Heraclius campaigned brilliantly and defeated the Persians. But he faced a cruel irony. When the Arab expansion began, Heraclius's empire was militarily and financially exhausted. As the seventh century wore on, Arabs captured Syria, Palestine, and Mesopotamia and began a centuries-long push into Anatolia. Eventually, they threatened Constantinople.

In the Balkans, Heraclius and his successors fought constant battles, with mixed results. They checked the advance of the Slavic peoples, who had been expanding southward. The Slavic advance was partly generated by social and political forces among the Slavs themselves and partly a result of pressure from the Avars and Bulgars. These peoples, who were related to the Huns, had begun penetrating into the Danube basin in the late sixth century. The empire tried hard to check their forward march.

Where the West was concerned, Heraclius and his successors were powerless to stop the Arab advance in North Africa and Spain. In Italy, imperial control was confined to a few outposts around Rome, Ravenna, and Sicily. Italy was too far away and strategically insignificant to attract much attention from the imperial government.

By around 700, the empire was assuming the basic geographic shape it would hold for centuries. In contrast to the vast lands once ruled by Rome, the empire was now confined to the eastern Balkans and western Anatolia. In 717, Leo III became emperor in a moment of acute crisis. Arab armies had seized much of Anatolia and had laid siege to Constantinople. Leo repulsed the attack and then ruled successfully until 741. He was followed by his able and charismatic son, Constantine V (r. 741–775). Constantine held the line in Anatolia and enjoyed decades of military success along the Balkan frontier.

In Italy alone, Byzantine (BIZZ-un-teen) policy was unsuccessful. When Justinian reconquered Italy from the Ostrogoths (see page 187), his armies devastated the region and left it poor and weak. Into the gap stepped the Lombards, who gradually built a kingdom in the north of Italy—Lombardy still bears their name—and set up a series of duchies in the center and south of Italy. The Byzantines prudently dedicated their resources to holding their Balkan and Anatolian frontiers, but this strategy left their subjects in Italy clamoring for aid. Eventually, the popes put themselves at the head of a movement in Italy that turned to the Franks for protection. In 755 and 756, the Frankish king marched to Italy, defeated the Lombards, and donated the territories he seized from them to the pope. This inaugurated the **Papal States**, the ever-changing set of lands in Italy whose current remnant is Vatican City, and put an end to effective Byzantine control

Papal States The lands in central Italy ruled by the popes, initially with Frankish help, from the eighth century to 1870.

Greek Fire Invented in the seventh century by Callimachus, a Syrian engineer, Greek fire was a mixture formed from petroleum, sulfur, saltpeter, and lime that ignited on contact with water. It was first used to repel the Muslim siege of Constantinople in 678. (Institut Amatller d'Art Hispanic)

Coin of Empress Irene   This gold *nomisma* of the empress Irene was struck between 797 and 802. The text reads "Irene, Empress." Note the craftsmanship of the Byzantine moneyers.   (Courtesy of the Trustees of the British Museum)

in Italy, except for the areas around Naples and Sicily. In 827, Muslims seized Sicily, and in the ensuing decades, they subjected southern Italy to continuous raids and occasional conquests.

After Constantine V's death, unsettled conditions prevailed until Irene (ca. 752–803) succeeded in 780, first as regent for her son and then as empress—the only woman to rule Byzantium in her own right. Irene was a skilled politician, but under her, the army grew restive because she preferred to make treaties, sometimes on unfavorable terms, than to send troops into the field. She did not trust the military's loyalty. Moreover, Irene had to contend with a foolish son who spent his time trysting with ladies of the court rather than attending to his official duties. In 797, Irene had him blinded, ironically in the very palace chamber where she had given birth to him. This was not a barbaric act in the Byzantine way of thinking. By mutilating Constantine VI, she merely rendered him unfit to rule: Roman ideology held that only a physically perfect person could reign; the alternative would have been to murder him. In any case, Irene's credibility sank to nothing, and in 802, she was deposed by a wily old soldier, Nicephorus (nye-SEFF-for-us) (r. 802–811).

For two generations, Byzantium suffered through short reigns, usurpations, political unrest, and military reverses. In 867, a rough soldier, Basil I (r. 867–886), seized the throne and, like Heraclius and Leo III before him, reversed the fortunes of the state. He established a new dynasty, the "Macedonian," and for the first time in years won important military victories. This dynasty ruled effectively until the eleventh century.

New Forms of Government

Even as its territory was shrinking, Byzantium undertook military and administrative reforms, revised its laws, and refocused its culture, particularly its religious practices. In the early Middle Ages, a distinctive "Byzantium" emerged in place of Rome.

Leo III and Constantine V are reminiscent of Diocletian and Constantine, or of Justinian. They energetically brought to completion military reforms that had been pursued intermittently since the late sixth century. These reforms amounted to a major administrative change. For centuries, Rome had recruited, trained, and paid professional troops out of tax revenues; they even used tax revenues to settle barbarian soldiers in their midst. Leo and Constantine put the finishing touches on a new "theme" system.

Men from frontier regions were now recruited and settled on farms in military districts called *themes*. All themes, whether land-based army ones or sea-based naval ones, were under the command of a leader who was simultaneously the civil and military chief of his theme. The farmer-soldiers did not pay taxes on their farms but discharged their obligation to the state by personal service. Henceforth, the thematic armies (see **MAP 8.2**) formed the backbone of the Roman system. The new system demanded less tax revenue and fewer bureaucrats. The empire was smaller than in the past and needed a different kind of army: Smaller squadrons concentrated near the threatened frontier regions in Anatolia and the Balkans rather than large armies that were expensive to maintain and cumbersome to transport over long distances.

There were other reforms, too. Leo issued the *Ecloga* (ECK-low-guh), the first major revision and updating of Roman law since Justinian's. Leo and Constantine also instituted far-reaching reforms in imperial administration, which had changed little in centuries. Roman bureaucracy had consisted of a few large departments headed by officials with immense responsibilities and power. The revised Byzantine system was characterized by a profusion of departments under officers who had little real power. The emperor neutralized the bureaucrats by drawing them from all social classes, paying them well, and giving them pompous titles and lots of public recognition, all the while dividing their responsibilities, curbing their influence, and making them dependent on himself.

The Birth of Byzantine Culture

Byzantine culture came to be increasingly defined by the church. The massive Arab conquests that stripped Byzantium of so much territory also removed the ancient patriarchates of

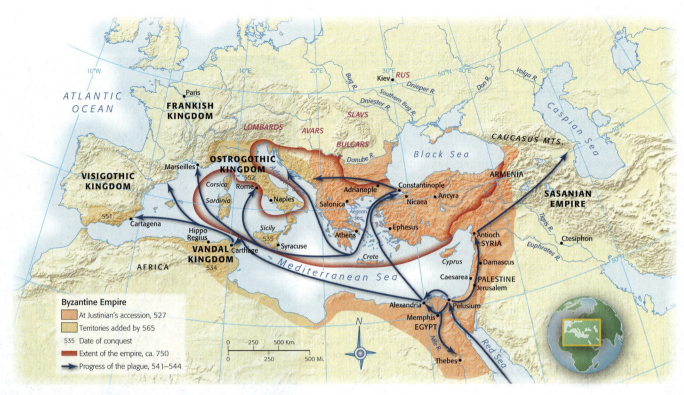

🌐 Map 8.2—The Byzantine Empire in the Eighth and Ninth Centuries

After suffering tremendous territorial losses to the barbarians and Arabs, the Byzantine Empire transformed its military, institutional, and cultural structures to create a regime that lasted until it was conquered by Crusaders in 1204. This map shows the Byzantium's major institutional innovation.

Alexandria, Jerusalem, and Antioch from effective contact with Constantinople. Often, in the past, the empire had been disturbed by severe theological quarrels generated by the differing views held in the several patriarchates. These disputes had been disruptive, but they had also prompted a great deal of learned religious writing. Now, deprived of this stimulus, Byzantium turned inward.

Monasticism gradually assumed a more prominent place in religious life. So many members of elite families sought to become monks that some emperors actually tried to limit entry into the religious life. Byzantine monks tended to be deeply learned, intensely critical of the patriarchs of Constantinople—whom they regarded as worldly and political—and opposed to imperial interference in the church.

In 726, Emperor Leo III embarked on a bold new religious policy: **iconoclasm**. For centuries, a beautiful and inspiring religious art had been emerging that troubled the emperor. Leo, a man of simple but fervent piety, believed that the presence of religious images, called "icons," in churches and public places was offensive to God. Moreover, Leo was convinced that the military disasters suffered by the empire in recent years were attributable to divine displeasure at the violation of Moses' prohibition of "graven images." Accordingly, he and his son banned religious images. They and some of their more enthusiastic followers even destroyed a few of them. Hence, they were called "iconoclasts," which means "image breakers." Iconoclasm was officially proclaimed by a church council in 754, repudiated by another council in 787, proclaimed again in 815, and then definitively rejected in 843.

Iconoclasm had several important consequences in its own time and reveals important aspects of emerging Byzantium to the modern observer. Iconoclasm was categorically rejected as heretical by the popes. This difference drove a sharp wedge between Eastern and Western Catholics. The debates over iconoclasm finally sharpened Byzantine thinking on the role and function of art in religious life. To this day, the icon plays a more prominent role in religious devotion in the East than in the West. (See the feature, "The Visual Record: Icons.") Moreover, the battle over iconoclasm evoked some of the most sophisticated Greek religious writing since Late Antiquity. Writers produced learned treatises in defense of religious art that drew on Greek

iconoclasm Literally means "image breaking"; it describes the rejection or destruction of religious pictures called "icons."

🌐 **MAP 8.3—The Carolingian World**

The territory over which Charlemagne exerted direct or indirect control was vast. The areas beyond the Rhine and Danube, never part of the Roman Empire, became under the Carolingians a permanent part of Western civilization. The Treaty of Verdun (see inset), signed by Charlemagne's grandsons in 843, was the first and most important of many divisions of the Carolingian Empire that eventually led to the emergence of France and Germany.

one another's expense, and drew local aristocracies into their battles. Nevertheless, the *idea* of a single kingdom of the Franks persisted. Kings and aristocrats in the small kingdoms competed for leadership of the realm as a whole. The flourishing culture of late antique Gaul was largely gone, but a creative Christian monastic culture was growing up in all parts of the Frankish kingdom. The seventh century, in other words, was a time when the late antique regime was slowly changing into the medieval regime.

The Carolingian family appeared in history just after 600 and thereafter monopolized the office of mayor of the palace (sort of a prime minister) to the king in Austrasia (the easternmost kingdom; see **MAP 8.3**). The Carolingians were the boldest and wealthiest family in Austrasia (aw-STRAY-zhuh), perhaps in the Frankish world. Within two generations, they unified the Frankish realm and increased their own power.

The Carolingians formed alliances with powerful noble families in many regions. They waged war against the enemies of the Franks to restore the territorial integrity of the kingdom. Charles Martel (d. 741), Charlemagne's grandfather, led the Frankish forces that put an end to Arab raiding in Gaul, defeating a large force near Poitiers in 733. With booty from their wars, tribute from conquered peoples, spoils taken from recalcitrant opponents, and even lands seized from the church, the Carolingians attracted and rewarded more and more followers until no one was a match for them. The Carolingians also allied themselves very early with leading churchmen, both episcopal and monastic. They aided missionaries in the work of converting central Germany, thereby expanding Frankish influence in that area.

For years, the Carolingians were content with the office of mayor of the palace. Then in 749, Pippin III (son of Charles Martel) decided to send envoys to the pope to ask whether it was right that the person who had all the power in the land of the Franks was not the king. The pope responded that this situation ran counter to the divine plan. Accordingly, in 751, the last Merovingian king was deposed, and Pippin was elected in his place (r. 751–768). Pippin had prepared his usurpation very carefully with his Frankish supporters, but he appealed to the pope to make it appear that he had become king with divine approval and not by crude seizure. Three years later, the pope visited the Frankish kingdom, where he crowned and anointed Pippin and his sons, including Charlemagne. (The practice of anointing the head of a ruler with holy oil, which renders the recipient sacred, dates back to the kings of Israel. The head and hands of Catholic bishops also were anointed. The anointing of rulers and churchmen persisted throughout the Middle Ages and into the modern world.) The pope also forbade the Franks ever to choose a king from a family other than the Carolingians and received from their new favorites a promise of aid in Italy.

Charlemagne (Carolus Magnus, "Charles the Great" in Latin) was a huge man, and his stature has grown in European history and legend. Like all great leaders, Charlemagne (r. 768–814) was complex. He spoke and read Frankish, Latin, and some Greek but never learned to write. He promoted Christian morality but perpetrated unspeakable brutalities on his enemies and enjoyed several concubines. Many battles were fought in his name, but he rarely accompanied his armies and fought no campaigns that are remembered for strategic brilliance. Determination and organization were the hallmarks of his forty-six-year reign.

Charlemagne's first major achievement was the articulation of a new ruling ideology in the Latin West. In capitularies (kuh-PITCH-u-lar-eez)—royal executive orders—of 789, Charlemagne required all males to swear an oath of allegiance to him, and he compared himself to a biblical king in his responsibility to admonish, to teach, and to set an example for his people. He referred to the people of his realm as a "New Israel," a new chosen people. Interestingly, this chosen people was not exclusively Frankish. No distinctions were to be made among Franks or Bavarians or Saxons. Everyone was to be equal in allegiance to the king and in membership in a sort of Augustinian City of God.

Einhard (ca. 770–840), Charlemagne's friend and biographer, reports that Augustine's *City of God* (see page 195) was the king's favorite book. The king understood it to mean that two opposing domains contended for power on earth: a City of God consisting of all right-thinking Christians—the "New Israel"—and a City of Man consisting of pagans, heretics, and infidels. This idea is similar to the Islamic umma (see page 201). To Charlemagne and his advisers, it was obvious that as God was the sole legitimate ruler in heaven, Charlemagne was the sole legitimate and divinely appointed ruler on earth.

Modern readers may think that Charlemagne had crossed a boundary between church and state. It is crucial to understand that to Charlemagne, as to his Muslim and Byzantine contemporaries, no such boundary existed. Church (or religion) and state were complementary attributes of a polity whose end was eternal salvation, not military security or personal fulfillment. Charlemagne's ideological legacy was twofold: It created possibilities for bitter struggles later in the Middle Ages between secular rulers and ecclesiastical powers about the leadership of Christian society and it made it hard to define the state and its essential purposes in other than religious terms.

The most disputed event in the reign of Charlemagne was his imperial coronation in Rome on Christmas Day in 800. It is important to separate how this event happened from what it meant to the participants. In April 799, some disgruntled papal bureaucrats and their supporters attacked Pope Leo III (r. 795–816) in an attempt to depose him. Leo escaped and then traveled all the way to Saxony, where the king was camped with his army. Charlemagne agreed to restore the pope to Rome and, as his ally and protector, to investigate those who had attacked him. No real offenses could be proved against the pope, who appeared publicly in Rome to swear that he had done nothing wrong. Everything was handled to avoid any hint that the pope had been put on trial. When Charlemagne went to Saint Peter's Basilica on Christmas, he prayed before the main altar. As he rose from prayer, Pope Leo placed a crown on his head, and the assembled Romans acclaimed him as emperor.

Debate over this coronation arises from a remark of Einhard, who said that if Charlemagne had known what was going to happen, he would not have gone to church that day, even though it was Christmas. Einhard's point was not that Charlemagne did not wish to be emperor. For at least fifteen years, prominent people at the Carolingian court had been addressing Charlemagne in imperial terms in letters, treatises, and poems. Moreover, some were saying that because of

Charlemagne The greatest ruler of the early Middle Ages and a major figure in European lore and legend.

The most durable consequence of this political restructuring along the eastern frontier of the Frankish world was religious. In 863, on an invitation from Moravia and in hopes of countering the Franks, the Byzantine emperor sent the missionaries Cyril (826–869) and Methodius (805–884) into eastern Europe. The emperor hoped to erect an Orthodox union of his own realm, the southern Slavs, and the newly converted Bulgarians. Likewise, he was seeking a diplomatic bulwark between the Bulgarians in the East and the Franks in the West. Unfortunately for Byzantium, Cyril and Methodius agreed with the pope to introduce Roman Catholic Christianity in return for the pope's permission to use the Slavonic language in worship. Cyril and Methodius were formidable linguists who created a religious literature in "Church Slavonic" that went far toward creating a new cultural realm in central Europe.

Finally, a new wave of attacks and invasions contributed decisively to the fragmentation of the Carolingian Empire. In the middle decades of the ninth century, Muslims, Vikings, and Magyars wreaked havoc on the Franks.

Based in North Africa and the islands of the western Mediterranean, Muslims attacked Italy and southern France. The Byzantines lost Sicily to raiders from North Africa in 827 and found themselves seriously challenged in southern Italy. In the 840s, Muslims raided the city of Rome. These same brigands preyed on trade in the western Mediterranean and even set up camps in the Alps to rob traders passing back and forth over the mountains.

"From the fury of the Northmen, O Lord, deliver us," was a plaintive cry heard often in ninth-century Europe. Those Northmen were Vikings, mainly Danes and Norwegians, seeking booty, glory, and political opportunity. Most Viking bands were formed by leaders who had lost out in the dawning institutional consolidation of the northern world. Some were opportunists who sought to profit from the weakness of Carolingian, Anglo-Saxon, and Irish rule. Vikings even began settling and initiated their own state-building activities in Ireland, England, northwestern France ("Normandy"—the region of the Northmen), and Rus (early "Russia").

Magyars, relatives of the Huns and Avars who had preceded them into eastern Europe, were accomplished horsemen whose lightning raids, beginning in 889, hit Italy, Germany, and even France. East Frankish Carolingians tried to use the Magyars as mercenaries against the troublesome Moravians. In the end, the Magyars destroyed the incipient Moravian state and raided with impunity.

All of these attacks were unpredictable and caused local regions to fall back on their own resources rather than look to the central government. Commerce was disrupted everywhere. Schools, based in ecclesiastical institutions, suffered severe decline. The raids represented a thousand pinpricks, not a single deadly sword stroke.

Even though the Carolingian Empire itself disintegrated, the idea of Europe as "Christendom," as a single political-cultural entity, persisted. The Latin Christian culture, promoted by Carolingian schools and rulers, set the tone for intellectual life until the twelfth century. Likewise, Carolingian governing structures were inherited and adapted by all of the successor states that emerged in the ninth and tenth centuries. In these respects, the Carolingian experience paralleled the Roman, and the Islamic and Byzantine, too. A potent, centralizing regime disappeared but left a profound imprint on its heirs. For hundreds of years, Western civilization would be played out inside the lands that had been Charlemagne's empire and between those lands and their Byzantine and Muslim neighbors.

SECTION SUMMARY

- The Carolingian family rose steadily to power, first as mayors of the palace, then as kings, and finally, as emperors.

- Charlemagne instituted far-reaching governmental innovations and reforms intended to make his power effective and to unify the lands under his rule.

- Carolingian rulers launched a cultural revival, called the Carolingian Renaissance, which aimed to master and then communicate basic Christian teachings.

- The Carolingian Empire broke down because of geographic diversity, political disunity, and new waves of invasion.

EARLY MEDIEVAL ECONOMIES AND SOCIETIES

What were the chief similarities and differences among the early medieval civilizations?

The economic and social history of the early Middle Ages provides additional evidence of the similarities among the three early medieval civilizations, while also revealing differences. Overall, the world remained rural, society was hierarchical, and women were excluded from public power. Although broad political frameworks changed, the lives of most people changed rather little.

Trade and Commerce

In the simplest terms, trade is a mechanism for exchanging goods from one person or group to another. There are many such exchange mechanisms. The Roman government, for example, moved large amounts of goods from the center of the empire to the frontiers to supply its armies. Roman, Byzantine, and Islamic governments raised taxes in one place, bought goods in another, and then consumed their purchases someplace else. Tribute and plunder were also effective exchange mechanisms, as were diplomatic gifts: A caliph, for example, sent Charlemagne an elephant.

The most common exchanges were intensely local, but several major trading networks operated during the early Middle Ages. In the East, Mesopotamia was linked by rivers to the Persian Gulf, East Africa, and southern Asia; by land and sea to Byzantium; and by land and rivers to the Black Sea region, Slavic Europe, and the Baltic. Byzantines traded mainly by sea. The whole Mediterranean was open to them, and from the Black Sea, they received the products of the Danube basin. The Muslim world was fundamentally a land empire that had relatively poor roads and primitive wheeled vehicles, so transport considerations were crucial: A caravan of some five hundred camels could move only one-fourth to one-half the cargo of a normal Byzantine ship.

The West had many trade routes. The Rhône-Saône river system carried goods, as did the land routes through the Alpine passes. The North and Baltic Seas were the hubs of a network that linked the British Isles, the whole of the Frankish north (by means of its rivers), the Rhineland, Slavic Europe, Byzantium, and the Muslim world. The Danube was also a major highway. The major trade networks intersected at many points. Despite religious and ideological differences, Rome's three heirs regularly traded with one another. Recent research has documented hundreds of east-west and north-south contacts across the early medieval period.

Food and other bulk goods never traveled very far because the cost was prohibitive. Most towns were supplied with foodstuffs by their immediate hinterlands, so the goods that traveled long distances were portable and valuable. Cotton and raw silk were transported to the

Oseberg Ship   Discovered in 1880, the Oseberg ship was buried in Norway in (probably) the tenth century. The ship may have belonged to a king and contained the remains of Queen Asa. It is 70 feet long and 16 feet wide. Its crew would have been thirty to forty men. (Christophe Boisvieux/Terrra/Corbis)

Mediterranean, where they were made into cloth in, respectively, Egypt and Byzantium. Paper and pottery were transported around the caliphate. Asian spices and perfumes were avidly sought everywhere. The Byzantines traded in silk cloth, fine ivories, delicate products of the gold- and silversmiths' art, slaves, and naval stores. Byzantium, with its large fleet, usually controlled the Black and Mediterranean Seas. Reduced in prosperity, the empire could no longer dictate trade terms to subject peoples and competed badly with the Muslims. Trade in the West was partly in high-value luxury goods, but mainly in ordinary items, such as plain pottery, raw wool, wool cloth, millstones, weapons, and slaves. Some Anglo-Saxon nuns owned ships and invested in commercial activities to support their convents. Almost all aspects of the cloth industry were in women's hands.

Town and Countryside

To think of the ancient world is to think of cities, but to think of the medieval world is to envision forests and fields. Actually, 80 to 90 percent of people in antiquity lived in rural settings, and in the early Middle Ages, the percentage was not much higher. What changed was the place occupied by towns in the totality of human life. Fewer government functions were based in towns, cultural life was less bound to the urban environment, and trade in luxuries, which depended on towns, declined.

Towns in the West often survived as focal points of royal or, more often, ecclesiastical administration. A cathedral church required a large corps of administrators. Western towns were everywhere attracting *burgs*, new settlements of merchants, just outside their centers. Few Western towns were impressive in size or population. Rome may have numbered a million people in the time of Augustus, but only about thirty thousand lived there in 800. Paris had perhaps twenty thousand inhabitants at that time. These were the largest cities by far in Catholic Europe.

In the Byzantine East, apart from Constantinople, the empire had a more rural aspect after the Muslims took control of the heavily urbanized regions of Syria, Egypt, and parts of Anatolia in the seventh century. The weakening of the caliphate in the second half of the ninth century was a spur to renewed urban growth in the Byzantine Empire. In provincial cities, population growth and urban reconstruction depended heavily on military conditions: Cities threatened by Arabs or Bulgarians declined.

The Arabs were great city-builders. Baghdad—four times larger in area than Constantinople, with a million residents to the latter's 400,000—was created from scratch. The most magnificent city in the West was Cordoba, the capital of Muslim Spain. Its population may have reached 400,000, and its Great Mosque, begun in 786, held 5,500 worshipers, more than any Latin church except Saint Peter's. The city had 900 baths, 1,600 mosques (Rome had about 200 churches), 60,000 mansions, and perhaps 100,000 shops. Its libraries held thousands of books, while the largest Carolingian book collections numbered a few hundred.

Agriculture nevertheless remained the most important element in the economy and in the daily lives of most people in all three realms. Farming meant primarily the production of cereal grains, which provided diet staples such as bread, porridge, and beer. Regions tended to specialize in the crops that grew most abundantly in local circumstances. For example, olives and grapes were common in the Mediterranean area, whereas cereals predominated around the Black Sea and in central Gaul. Animal husbandry was always a major part of the rural regime. English sheep provided wool and meat. In Frankish and Byzantine regions, pigs, which were cheap to raise, supplied meat, but for religious reasons, pork was almost absent in the Muslim East—Islam adopted the Jewish prohibition against it.

manor A common term for an agricultural estate that typically had its lands divided between the manor's lord and dependent peasants.

A key development in the Frankish West was the appearance of a bipartite estate, sometimes called a **manor**. On a bipartite estate, one part of the land was set aside as *demesne* [duh-MEEN]), and the rest was divided into tenancies. The demesne, consuming from one-quarter to one-half of the total territory of the estate, was exploited directly for the benefit of the landlord. The tenancies were generally worked by the peasants for their own support. The bipartite estate provided the aristocrats with a livelihood, while freeing them for military and government service.

Estates were run in different ways. A landlord might hire laborers to farm his reserve, paying them with money exacted as fees from his tenants. Or he might require the tenants to work a certain number of days per week or weeks per year in his fields. The produce of the estate might be gathered into barns and consumed locally or hauled to local markets. The reserve might be a separate part of the estate, a proportion of common fields, or a percentage of the harvest. The tenants might have individual farms or work in common fields. Although the manor is one of the most familiar aspects of European life throughout the Middle Ages, large estates with dependent tenants also were evolving in the Byzantine and Islamic worlds.

Social Patterns

Most of the surviving medieval records were written by elite members of society and reveal little about the middle and lower orders of society. Nevertheless, certain similarities are evident in the social structures of all levels in all three societies. The elites tended to be large landholders, to control dependent populations, and to have access to government offices. There were regional differences, too. Scholars ranked higher in Byzantium and the caliphate than in the West; churchmen, especially bishops, were powerful in Christian societies but had no counterparts in Muslim ones. Literature, surely reflecting social realities, portrays the cultivated Muslim gentleman in the Abbasid period. This social type, marked by learning, good manners, and a taste for finery, does not appear in Byzantium or in the West until the twelfth century.

Women were bound to the same social hierarchies as men. Predictably enough, women had few formal, public roles to play. Their influence, however great, tended to function in the private sphere, rarely revealed to us by sources that stem from the public realm of powerful men. Aristocratic women had opportunities and power that were denied ordinary women. Irene ruled at Byzantium as empress. Frankish and Anglo-Saxon queens were formidable figures in their realms. Carolingian queens managed the landed patrimony of the dynasty—dozens of huge estates with tens of thousands of dependents. The combination of a lack of evidence and the rigorous exclusion of women from public life in the Islamic world means that virtually no Muslim women emerge as distinct personalities in the early Middle Ages.

One example of the problems in the evidence concerning women relates to church roles. Women could not hold priestly office, and although deaconesses served at Hagia Sophia in the sixth century, they disappeared soon after and had long before vanished in the West. Religious power could come from personal sanctity as well as holding office. One study of some 2,200 saints from the early Middle Ages finds only about 300 females. It was hard for women to gain recognition as saints. And if a woman became a saint, her holiness was inevitably described either as "manly"—an extreme ascetic was praised for having the strength and courage of a man—or as beautiful, virginal, and domestic—in other words, with female stereotypes.

The middling classes show some disparities among the regions. Merchants, for example, often rose through the social ranks to become great aristocrats in Muslim society. Islamic society often evinced great mobility because of its restless, expanding nature and because Islamic ideology rejected distinctions in the umma. In Byzantium, traditional Roman prejudices against merchants and moneymaking activities persisted. Thus, rich merchants whose wealth gave them private influence frequently lacked public power and recognition. In the West, merchants were neither numerous nor powerful in the Carolingian period. In some towns, moreover, commerce was in the hands of Jews, always outsiders in a militantly Christian society.

Merchants were not the only people occupying the middle rungs of the social ladder. All three societies, in fact, possessed both central elites and provincial elites. Service at the Carolingian, Byzantine, or Abbasid court counted for more than service in a provincial outpost. It was one thing to be abbot of a great monastery and quite a different thing to preside over a poor, tiny house. The thematic generals in Byzantium were lofty personages; their subordinates held inferior positions. The vassals of a Carolingian king formed a real aristocracy, but vassals were of decidedly lower rank.

Degrees of freedom and local economic and political conditions shaped the lives of peasants. In all three societies, some farmers were personally free and owed no cash or labor services to anyone but the central government. In areas such as Abbasid Iraq, ordinary free farmers led a comfortable life. In the Frankish world, most peasants existed outside the dawning manorial system. They were free, and if they lived in areas of good land and political security, such as the Paris basin, their lives most likely were congenial. Byzantine peasants, though free, often lived in areas of military danger, and in some parts of the Balkans, they eked out a living from poor soils. Highly taxed and perpetually endangered, they may have viewed their freedom as small compensation for their economic and personal insecurity. All peasants were alike in their subjection to political forces over which they had no control.

At the bottom of the social scale everywhere were slaves. Christianity did not object to slavery in general but forbade the enslavement of Christians. Islam likewise prohibited Muslims from enslaving other Muslims. Slaves, therefore, tended to be most common in pagan societies—Scandinavia, for example—or in frontier regions where neighboring pagans could be captured and sold. There were more slaves in the Muslim world than in Byzantium, which had, in turn, more than the West.

The domestic sphere is a difficult realm to enter. In Byzantium and the West, families rarely arranged marriages for more than one or two daughters. Others remained single or entered convents. Women at all social levels tended to pass from the tutelage of their fathers to that of their husbands. In antiquity, a suitor usually paid a fee, or "bride price," to his prospective wife's father and then endowed his wife with a "morning gift," money or possessions of her own. Gradually, this practice changed to a system whereby a bride's father paid a dowry to her future husband. Thus, a wife who was cast aside could be left impoverished, for in most places, the law did not permit her to inherit land if she had brothers. Females were such valuable property in the marriage market that rape was an offense not against a girl but against her father. A man could divorce, even kill, his wife for adultery, witchcraft, or grave robbing and then marry again. A woman could usually gain a divorce only for adultery, and she could not remarry. For the vast majority of women, daily life was hedged about with legal limitations and personal indignities.

SECTION SUMMARY

- The early Middle Ages witnessed the elaboration of several major trading networks that made ordinary and luxury goods available over long distances.
- Cities continued to play important roles in the life of the Islamic and Byzantine worlds but played comparatively little role in western Europe.
- Arab, Byzantine, and European societies were elitist and hierarchical. Merchants were less important in Europe than elsewhere. Agriculture was dominant everywhere.
- Women played important political, social, and economic roles in all societies, but women's lives were hedged with restrictions.

CHAPTER SUMMARY

We have traced three parallel histories in the development of early medieval civilizations: that of the Arabs and Islam; that of the Byzantines; and that of Western Europe and the Carolingians. Muhammad was a great teacher who emphasized *al-Islam*, surrender to Allah. He taught a faith that may be summarized in the "Five Pillars" of Islam. Both internal and external factors contributed to the lightning conquests of Islam in the century after Muhammad's death, spreading Islam and Arab rule from Spain to the frontiers of China. Islamic culture was rooted in the religious teachings of the *ulama* and in the scholarship of those who tackled Greek and Persian learning.

FOCUS QUESTIONS

- What were the most important factors in the rise of the Arab peoples and the Islamic faith?
- Why did a distinctive civilization that can be called "Byzantine" emerge?
- What were the greatest achievements of the Carolingians and why were they so successful?
- What were the chief similarities and differences among the early medieval civilizations?

The Byzantine Empire faced hard challenges from Persians and then Muslims in the east, from Slavs, Avars, and Bulgars in the Balkans, and from Lombards in Italy. The Byzantine Empire in the early Middle Ages was much smaller than the Roman Empire that preceded it. The "theme" system was a comprehensive and effective revision of the empire's traditional governmental structure. A distinctive Byzantine culture was based on the Greek language, the Greek Church Fathers, Orthodox religious traditions, and distinctive local practices.

Visigothic Spain suffered from religious, political, and military disunity, while Italy developed three stable regions: a Lombard and then Frankish north; a papal center; and a Byzantine and then Muslim south. In the British Isles, the conversion to Catholic Christianity and the development of ecclesiastical organization were forces for unity and cultural achievement. In the British Isles, political development in the Celtic regions was slow, but England began emerging as a coherent political entity under ambitious and effective kings.

The Carolingian family rose steadily to power, first as mayors of the palace, then as kings, and finally as emperors. The greatest Carolingian, Charlemagne, instituted far-reaching governmental innovations and reforms intended to make his power effective and to unify the lands under his rule. Carolingian rulers launched a cultural revival, called the Carolingian Renaissance, which aimed to master and then communicate basic Christian teachings. The Carolingian Empire broke down because of geographic diversity, political disunity, and new waves of invasion.

The early Middle Ages witnessed the elaboration of several major trading networks that made ordinary and luxury goods available over long distances. Cities continued to play important roles in the life of the Islamic and Byzantine worlds but played comparatively little role in western Europe except as ecclesiastical centers. Arab, Byzantine, and European societies were elitist and hierarchical. Merchants were less important in Europe than elsewhere. Agriculture was dominant everywhere. Women played important political, social, and economic roles in all societies, but women's lives were hedged by legal limitations, social conventions, and religious restrictions.

KEY TERMS

Muhammad (p. 200)

Five Pillars (p. 201)

Quran (p. 201)

caliphate (p. 203)

Papal States (p. 207)

iconoclasm (p. 209)

Orthodox (p. 211)

Charlemagne (p. 215)

vassals (p. 216)

Carolingian Renaissance (p. 218)

manor (p. 222)

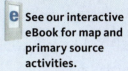

This icon will direct you to additional materials on the website: www.cengage.com/history/noble/westciv6e.

See our interactive eBook for map and primary source activities.

9

Bayeux Tapestry
The tapestry (ca. 1077) depicts the fleet of William the Conqueror of Normandy sailing
to England in 1066.   (Erich Lessing/Art Resource, NY)

The Expansion of Europe in the High Middle Ages, 900–1300

The picture to the left represents one small section of the Bayeux Tapestry, a narrative account—in words and illustrations—of the conquest of England in 1066 by Duke William of Normandy. This scene is an apt introduction to the central theme of this chapter: expansion.

This section of the 230-foot-long tapestry depicts William setting sail for England. Already successful in Normandy, William was about to claim the throne of England. He gathered soldiers from all over western France and boldly crossed the English Channel. Leaving nothing to chance, he transported horses, too, as you can see in the picture.

One group of Normans conquered England, while another seized control of southern Italy. Still other Normans played a decisive role in the period's most prominent manifestation of expansion: the Crusades. Meanwhile, certain Scandinavians settled Iceland and Greenland to the west, while others founded the first state on Russian soil. Spanish Christians pushed back the Muslims in Iberia. From the Baltic to the Balkans, Slavic rulers founded new states and pressed hard against their neighbors. German rulers crossed the Alps into Italy, French kings reached the Pyrenees, and English monarchs pushed into Wales, Scotland, and Ireland. Seldom has Europe's political geography expanded so dramatically as during the High Middle Ages.

Between 900 and 1300, Europe's population began one of its longest periods of sustained growth. People brought more land under cultivation, introduced new crops, and made agriculture more efficient. Villages, towns, and cities grew in number and size. Trade expanded in every material and in every direction.

Europe witnessed the reemergence of centralizing monarchies in France, England, and Spain. Some new realms, such as Denmark and Hungary, built strong central governments. And an explosion of new states occurred along the frontiers of the old Carolingian Empire.

The "West" began taking on a more *western European* character. The Crusades complicated relations between Christian Europeans and Muslims, and both the Crusades and increasing religious differences alienated western Europe from Byzantium, and Roman Catholics from Orthodox believers. The center of Western civilization became more and more anchored to northwestern Europe. And that same western Europe was expanding to influence lands in Scandinavia and the Slavic world that had played no role at all in the West's classical, Mediterranean phase. The High Middle Ages repeatedly posed the question: Where is the West?

FOCUS QUESTIONS

- In how many different realms of life do you see signs of growth and innovation, of expansion?

- What did Germany, Italy, and France owe to the Carolingian past? How alike and different were these areas by 1300?

- What were the chief dynamics in the development of medieval Britain?

- How did new states emerge in Spain, Scandinavia, and the Slavic world, and how do those states compare with their western neighbors?

- What basic factors contributed to the rise, persistence, and eventual decline of the crusading movement?

 This icon will direct you to additional materials on the website: www.cengage.com/history/noble/westciv6e.

e **See our interactive eBook for map and primary source activities.**

ECONOMIC EXPANSION

In how many different realms of life do you see signs of growth and innovation, of expansion?

The economic expansion of Europe is manifest in many kinds of evidence that are more often qualitative than quantitative. Medieval people did not keep the kinds of records of births, deaths, population, or business activity that modern states routinely accumulate. After about 1000, every available indicator points to a growing population and an expanding scale and sophistication of economic activity.

The Growing Population

The population of Europe began rising slowly in the Carolingian period and may have doubled between 1000 and 1200 to 60 million. In regions where family size can be estimated, fertile marriages were producing on the average 3.5 children in the tenth century and from 6 to 7 in the twelfth. People were also living longer than their forebears. Studies of aristocrats, high clergy, and soldiers show that a surprising 40 percent of them were over 40 years old. Male life expectancy was surely longer than female because of the dangers of childbirth, always the great killer of women in the premodern world. The general trend is clear: more babies being born, more infants living into adulthood, more adults living longer.

Everywhere in Europe new land was brought into cultivation. More than half of the French documents relating to land in the twelfth century show new land being brought under the plow. Thousands of acres of forest were cut down. Marshes were reclaimed from the sea. Some 380,000 acres were drained along the western coast of France and probably twice that amount in both Flanders and England. This activity is inexplicable without assuming a growing number of mouths to feed.

Agriculture benefited from a warmer and drier climate through this whole period. Not a single vegetable blight was recorded. Food was more abundant and more nutritious. Animals were increasingly reared for their meat, and higher meat consumption meant more protein in the diet. Beans and other legumes, also rich in protein, were more widely cultivated. People of every class and region were almost certainly eating better and living longer and healthier lives.

Technological Gains

The eleventh century was a decisive period in the spread of new technologies in Europe. Innovations occurred in agriculture, transportation, mining, and manufacturing. Agricultural changes came first as a rising population created an increased demand for food that could be met only by new practices. By the late twelfth century, an acre of farmland in a fertile region was probably yielding a crop three to four times larger than in the Carolingian era. Given the combination of more land under cultivation and more yield per acre, the overall gains in the food supply were enormous.

The increases can be accounted for in several ways. Horses were more frequently used as draft animals. They did, in a day, a third or half again as much work, hauling loads farther and faster than oxen. Thus, fewer people could, with horses, cultivate more land than their predecessors managed with oxen. In addition, they could cultivate the land more frequently and increase yields because more seed would fall on more finely plowed soil. The dissemination of the horse collar made possible the expanded use of horses—older forms of harnesses suitable for the low-slung, broad-shouldered ox would have choked a horse.

Plows, too, were improved. The light wooden scratch plow used by the Romans was satisfactory for the thin soils of the Mediterranean region but barely disturbed the heavy soils of northern Europe. The invention of a heavy wheeled plow with an iron plowshare and a moldboard was a real breakthrough. The iron plowshare cut deep furrows, and then the moldboard turned and aerated the soil. This heavy plow allowed farmers to exploit good soils more fully without exhausting the ground too rapidly. Perhaps introduced into Carolingian Europe from the Slavic world, this plow was widely adopted from the eleventh century.

Wider adoption of nitrogen-fixing crops, such as peas and some kinds of beans, retarded soil exhaustion and also put more protein in the diet. Leaving land fallow also avoided soil exhaustion. In the early Middle Ages, this meant setting aside about half of the arable land every year (the two-field system) or working the land intensively for a few years and then moving on. By the twelfth century, three-field schemes of crop rotation were common. Under the three-field system, two-thirds of the arable land saw nearly constant use. The amount of an estate under cultivation rose from 50 to 67 percent.

Surplus produce was intended mainly for the growing towns. To supply that market, improvements in transportation were necessary. Kings often passed laws to secure the safety of highways, and popes three times (in 1097, 1132, and 1179) threatened highwaymen—robbers who preyed on travelers—with excommunication. Landlords required their dependents to maintain roads and bridges. Many stone bridges were constructed in France between 1130 and 1170 because wooden bridges were so vulnerable to fire. Indeed, fire destroyed the bridge at Angers (in western France) five times between 1032 and 1167.

Transport improved not only because of safer roads, but also thanks to better vehicles. The old two-wheeled cart, drawn by oxen, began giving way to the sturdy four-wheeled, horse-drawn wagon. Because greater quantities of foodstuffs could be moved farther and faster, urban communities could be supplied from larger areas. This was a crucial factor in enabling cities to grow and in providing urban residents with a predictable and diverse range of foods.

Seaborne trade expanded, too. The stern rudder, better sails, the compass (in use by 1180), and better navigational charts facilitated sea travel, as did the growing use of larger ships. An Italian fleet sailed to Flanders in 1277, and within a few years the old overland trade routes began a decline that was not reversed until the invention of the railroad in the nineteenth century.

At any time of year, travel was difficult and costly. Few dared to venture across the Alps in the winter, and the northern seas, especially the passage around Denmark, were treacherous in cold weather. Even in the relatively calm Mediterranean, the Venetians refused to send out their trading fleet between November and March. Overland trade was impeded by snow, rain, mud, and highwaymen, who would rob travelers on the road. Governments tried to restrain robbers, but no one could change the weather.

CHRONOLOGY	
862	Founding of Kiev
870–930	Settlement of Iceland
962	Imperial coronation of Otto I
987	Accession of Hugh Capet in France
988	Kievan Rus accept Orthodox Christianity
1016	Conquest of England by Cnut
1066	Norman Conquest of England
1073–1085	Pontificate of Gregory VII
1078	Decree against lay investiture
1085	Spanish reconquest of Toledo
1086	*Domesday Book*
1096–1099	First Crusade
1122	Concordat of Worms
1171	Henry II of England invades Ireland
1176	Battle of Legnano
1198–1216	Pontificate of Innocent III
1202–1204	French drive English out of Normandy
1203	Fourth Crusade
1212, 1214	Battles of Las Navas de Tolosa and Bouvines
1215	Magna Carta
1265	First Parliament in England
1294–1303	Quarrel between Boniface VIII and Philip IV
1295	Model Parliament

There were notable improvements in both the quarrying of stone and the mining of metals. Mines were not deep because people lacked the means to keep the shafts and galleries free of water. Still, the exploitation of surface veins of ore—principally iron, but also tin and silver—intensified, to supply the increased demand for plowshares, tools, weapons, construction fittings, and coins. Stone quarrying, the most common form of mining in the Middle Ages, benefited directly from more efficient stone saws and indirectly from improvements in transport. Better techniques in stonecutting, construction, and conveyance help to explain, for example, the increase in the number of England's stone religious buildings from sixty to nearly five hundred in the century after 1050.

Forms of Enterprise

Agricultural specialization became common. People began to cultivate intensively those crops that were best suited to local conditions. The area around Toulouse, for example, concentrated on herbs from which blue and yellow dyes were made. The central regions of France focused on cereal grains, while the Bordeaux and Burgundy regions emphasized the grapes that produced wine. Northern Germany specialized in cattle raising; northern England favored sheep.

Agricultural specialization helps to explain the growth in trade everywhere (see **MAP 9.1**). For certain commodities, local trade continued to flourish. Italian wines and olive oil, for example, only moved from countryside to town within a region. The same was true of French or English grains. However, French wines were much prized throughout Europe, especially in England, and certain

Heavy Wheeled Plow The improved plow, the horse collar, and the cooperative labors of many peasants in preparing the fields led to an agricultural boom in the European countryside. (Bibliothèque nationale de France)

products, such as English wool and Flemish cloth, were carried far and wide. Salt fish from the Baltic found its way all over the continent. Lumber traveled across the Mediterranean to the wood-poor Muslim world. Spain produced warhorses. Southern Europe supplied the northern demand for spices, oranges, raisins, figs, almonds, and other exotic foodstuffs. Caen, in Normandy, sent shiploads of its beautifully colored and textured stone to England for the construction of churches and monasteries. Rising population, higher productivity, and greater prosperity added up to a larger volume of goods moving farther and more frequently.

Whether for fuel, or for ships and buildings, the demand for wood grew steadily. Wood exemplifies the expansion and interconnectedness of the medieval economy and society. Forests were essential to daily life, providing the wood for houses, fences, and fuel in villages and towns. Animals, especially pigs, were grazed at the edges of the forest to permit as much land as possible to be dedicated to food crops. Wild animals were hunted in the forest. For aristocrats, hunting was as much for sport as for food. For poorer rural people, however, wild game made up a significant part of the regular diet. The forest was also a plentiful source of fruits, nuts, and honey. Thus, the decision to cut down a stand of trees was a serious one.

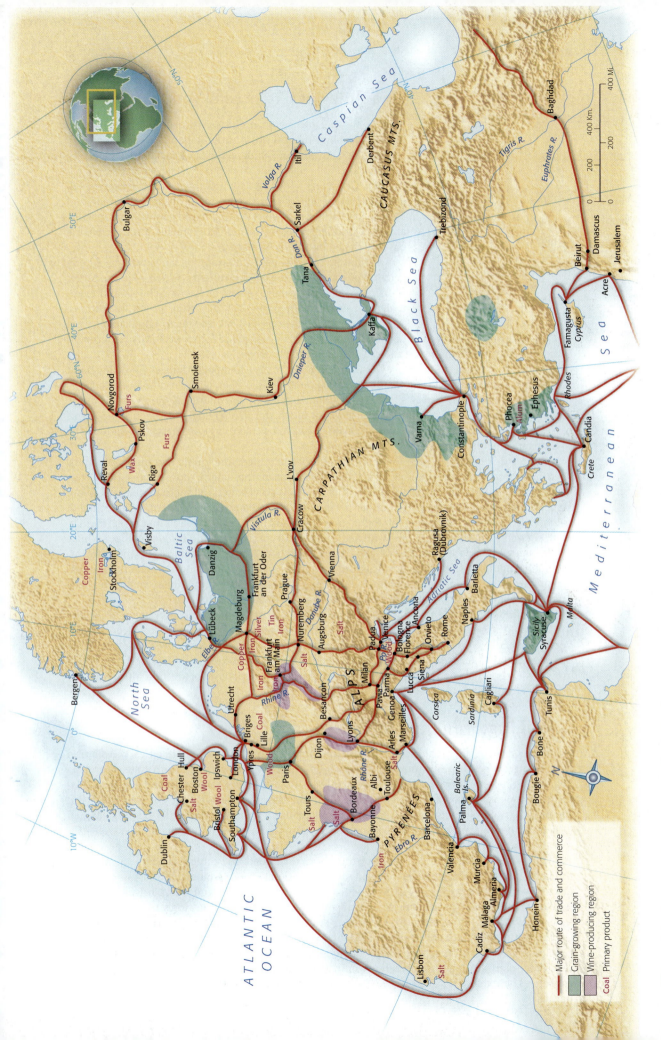

🌐 **MAP 9.1—European Resources and Trade Routes, ca. 1100**

In an age of expansion, some products were consumed locally, but many others were transported over longer and longer distances. Commercial connections expanded, too, creating several interlocking networks.

Legend:
- Major route of trade and commerce
- Grain-growing region
- Wine-producing region
- Coal — Primary product

Labels on map include: Baghdad, Damascus, Jerusalem, Acre, Beirut, Famagusta, Cyprus, Candia, Crete, Rhodes, Ephesus, Phocea, Alum, Constantinople, Varna, Kaffa, Trebizond, Derbent, Itil, Sarkel, Tana, Bulgar, Novgorod, Pskov, Reval, Riga, Smolensk, Kiev, Lvov, Cracow, Danzig, Visby, Stockholm, Bergen, Hull, Chester, Boston, Ipswich, London, Bristol, Southampton, Dublin, Lisbon, Cadiz, Málaga, Almería, Honein, Murcia, Valencia, Barcelona, Palma, Bayonne, Bordeaux, Albi, Toulouse, Tours, Paris, Dijon, Lyons, Besançon, Arles, Marseilles, Genoa, Pavia, Milan, Parma, Lucca, Siena, Florence, Bologna, Venice, Padua, Orvieto, Rome, Naples, Barletta, Ancona, Ragusa (Dubrovnik), Tunis, Bone, Bougie, Malta, Sicily, Syracuse, Cagliari, Sardinia, Corsica, Lübeck, Magdeburg, Frankfurt an der Oder, Prague, Vienna, Nuremberg, Augsburg, Frankfurt am Main, Utrecht, Bruges, Lille, Ypres, Brugge

Regions/Seas: Caspian Sea, Black Sea, Mediterranean Sea, Adriatic Sea, Baltic Sea, North Sea, Atlantic Ocean, Caucasus Mts., Carpathian Mts., Alps, Pyrenees, Volga R., Don R., Dnieper R., Vistula R., Danube R., Rhine R., Rhône R., Ebro R., Tigris R., Euphrates R.

Primary products labeled: Furs, Wax, Copper, Iron, Salt, Tin, Silver, Wood, Coal, Wool

TABLE 9.1
Population Increases In Italian Cities, 1200–1300

City	1200	1300	Percentage Increase
Florence	15,000	96,000	+640%
Siena	19,000	52,000	+274%
Pisa	20,000	38,000	+190%

guilds Voluntary associations of people who shared common crafts or trades.

The Roles of Cities and Towns

All over Europe, towns grew impressively in size and importance. **TABLE 9.1** shows the growth of three Italian cities. Such growth also occurred in cities in Flanders, such as Bruges and Ghent, and in Paris, London, and other cities that were becoming national capitals. Ghent expanded its city walls five times between 1160 and 1300, a sure sign of growth even in the absence of population figures. Similar forces were operating in the countryside. In 1100, about 11 fortified villages surrounded Florence, but by 1200, the city was ringed by 205 such villages.

For the first time since Late Antiquity, cities were becoming centers for many activities. Governments, which required larger staffs of trained personnel, settled in towns. Schools and eventually universities (see pages 280–282) were urban institutions. Mercantile, industrial, ecclesiastical, and legal organizations were located in towns. Towns began to compete with royal and aristocratic courts as literary centers, and cathedrals, the great buildings of the age, were exclusively urban.

A novelty of the twelfth century was the emergence of the Champagne fairs as a meeting point for the commerce of north and south. Since the early Middle Ages, a few locations hosted permanent fairs, and many places sponsored occasional fairs. By the middle of the twelfth century, however, the spices, silks, and dyes of the Mediterranean, the wool of England, the furs and linens of Germany, and the leather products of Spain began to be sold in a series of six fairs held in the Champagne region of France from spring to autumn.

One distinctive urban phenomenon was the rise of **guilds**. The guilds had many functions. Their main purpose was economic: to regulate standards of production, to fix prices, and to control membership in their respective trades. But as towns grew larger and more impersonal, these associations of people engaged in similar occupations fostered a sense of belonging, a feeling of community. Members tended to live in the same areas and to worship together in a parish church. Growing wealth in general, coupled with fierce local pride, produced building competitions whose results are still visible in the huge neighborhood churches that survive in most European towns. The guilds indulged in elaborate festivals and celebrations, which sometimes turned into drunken debauches despite being held to honor saints. The guilds also assisted members who fell on hard times, saw to their funeral expenses, and provided for widows and orphans.

The guilds had a damaging impact on women. As more economic activity came under the umbrella of the guild structures, women were more systematically excluded from guild membership. Usually, women could become guild members only as wives or widows. They could not open economic enterprises of their own, although they were workers in many trades. Despite a growing, diversifying economy, women were increasingly denied opportunities, although later centuries would find women establishing their own guilds.

Changing Economic Attitudes

As medieval society generated more wealth and populations concentrated in cities, people who were relatively well-off became more conscious of those who were less fortunate. Moralists began to argue that the poor were a special gift of God to the rich, who could redeem their own souls by generous charitable benefactions. Most towns established schemes of poor relief. But the numbers of poor people grew so rapidly, particularly in large towns, that helping seemed hopeless, and some gave up trying. Hospitals, for example, began to refuse abandoned babies for fear that they would be deluged with them.

Efforts to alleviate the condition of the poor constituted one ethical concern of medieval thinkers, but two issues attracted even more attention. First, theologians and lawyers alike discussed the "just price," the price at which goods should be bought and sold. Christian teaching had long held that it was immoral to hoard food during a famine or knowingly to sell a damaged item. But what was the correct price in ordinary circumstances? A theological view, often dismissed as unrealistic, held that items could be sold for only the cost of the materials in them and the labor absolutely necessary to produce them. A commercial view, often dismissed as immoral, insisted that a fair price was whatever the market would bear, regardless of costs or consequences. A working consensus held that a just price was one arrived at by bargaining between free and knowledgeable parties.

The other ethical issue concerned usury, the lending of money at interest. Christian writers were always hostile to commercial enterprise, and they had plenty of biblical warrant for their view. Psalm 15 warned that no one can be blameless "who lends his money at usury." Luke's Gospel admonished Christians to "give without expecting to be repaid in full." Luke actually forbade the profit that makes most commercial enterprises possible. In the twelfth century, churchmen began to be much more assiduous in their condemnations of usury, a practice that had been winked at for centuries. Gradually, thinkers began to defend usury on the grounds that a person who lent money incurred a risk and deserved to be compensated for that risk.

Investment demands credit, and credit requires some payback for the lender. Even in the face of deep hostility, credit mechanisms spread in thirteenth-century Europe. They were held up to minute scrutiny by theologians and popular preachers and were found to be evidence of man's sinfulness, acquisitiveness, and greed. But all these practices persisted, fueled by the expansion of the European economy, and began putting individual profit alongside community interest at the heart of social and economic thought.

SECTION SUMMARY

- Europe's population grew dramatically until the late 1200s, owing to better diets and more plentiful foods.
- Technological gains came with wider use of horses, improved plows, and more productive farming techniques.
- Many regions began to specialize in growing or manufacturing products, and this local specialization prompted larger-scale trade.
- Economic growth widened the gap between rich and poor and induced theologians to write about the just price and usury.

THE HEIRS OF THE CAROLINGIAN EMPIRE: GERMANY, ITALY, AND FRANCE

What did Germany, Italy, and France owe to the Carolingian past? How alike and different were these areas by 1300?

The scope of political and institutional life expanded everywhere between 900 and 1300. In 900, the Carolingian Empire was collapsing. By 1300, France had emerged as a large, stable kingdom, and Italy had turned into several reasonably coherent regional entities. The most surprising political development within the old Carolingian lands, indeed within Europe as a whole, was Germany's rise to a premier position in the tenth century and then its long, slow decline. The states that evolved out of the Carolingian Empire faced common challenges: the achievement of territorial integrity; the growing responsibility of the central government; complicated political relations among kings, aristocrats, and churchmen; and the elaboration of new ideas about the state and its responsibilities.

Germany and the Empire, 911–1272

From the ninth century to the present, no state in Europe has been less stable territorially and politically than Germany and the German Empire. Two issues are paramount: the role of dynastic and territorial instability in German history and German rulers' complex, contentious relations with the leaders of the church.

The Treaty of Verdun (see page 219) created something essentially new in 843: an East Frankish kingdom. Frankish rulers had long claimed authority over some of the lands that eventually became Germany, but before 843, no unified kingdom had ever existed in the territories east of the Rhine River (see **Map 9.2**). The lands had no tradition of common or unified rule and there was no single "German" people. Roman culture had barely penetrated into German lands, and Christian culture was recent. "Germany" had—has—no natural frontiers.

After the last East Frankish Carolingian died in 911, the dukes, or leaders, of Germany's major regions chose one of their number as king. Under varying circumstances, the dukes chose kings from different families several times: Saxons (or Ottonians) in 919; Salians in 1024; and Staufer in 1138. This record of frequent dynastic change might be contrasted with the situation in France (see pages 244–245), where one family reigned from 987 to 1328.

At the beginning of Saxon rule, Germany comprised five duchies: Saxony, Franconia, Lorraine, Swabia, and Bavaria. German romantic tradition regarded the dukes as the heroic leaders of distinct

GERMANY'S LAND AND RULERS

🌐 **MAP 9.2—Germany and Its Duchies, ca. 1000–1200**
The chief political dynamic in Germany was a contest for power between the kings and the dukes. The duchies emerged in the ninth and tenth centuries and outlived one dynasty of kings after another.

ethnic communities, the so-called Tribal Duchies. The dukes were actually the descendants of local rulers introduced by the Carolingians. They were wealthy and powerful; they contested with kings for control of the bishops and abbots in their duchies; and sometimes they managed to make vassals out of the lower ranks of the aristocracy in their territories, effectively denying kings connections with these people. In sum, the dukes were extremely jealous of their independence.

When the Saxons came to power, they attempted to control one or more of these duchies. Hoping to win new territories and distract troublesome aristocrats, the Saxons began Germany's centuries-long drive to the east, into Slavic Europe. In 955, Otto I gained power and prestige when he led a combined German force to victory against the Magyars at Lechfeld.

The Saxons also tried to control the church, especially bishops and abbots, to gain the allegiance of powerful and articulate allies. In 962, Otto I, who had begun expanding into Italy in 952, was crowned emperor in Rome by the pope. The imperial title conferred two benefits on the German kings: It gave them immense prestige and power that owed nothing to the dukes, and it raised the possibility of securing huge material resources in Italy, where, as emperors, they did not have to share power the way they did in Germany. The marriage of Otto II to a Byzantine princess was a sign of Germany's growing stature. Their son, Otto III, sponsored a brilliant court, patronizing writers and painters. When he died in 1002, Germany was the preeminent land in Europe.

After 1002, dynastic instability plagued Germany. For example, when Henry III, died in 1056, he left behind a 6-year-old heir and a decade of civil war. Military expansion virtually ceased, and powerful aristocrats struggled with one another and with their kings. Chief among these aristocrats were the dukes, who had chafed under Saxon and Salian efforts to control them. When Henry IV came of age in 1066, he faced opposition on all sides, controlled no duchies, was not yet emperor, and had lost much of his father's control of the church. When he tried to make church appointments in the traditional way, he encountered the fierce opposition of the newly reformed papacy in the person of Pope Gregory VII (r. 1073–1085). Their battles inaugurated the so-called investiture controversy, which lingered on until 1122, when both of the original foes were long dead.

In the twelfth century, the Salian dynasty died out. With the accession of Frederick Barbarossa ("Red Beard") in 1152, a new family, the Staufer, consolidated its hold on the German throne. Frederick, based in Swabia, patiently worked to get other dukes to recognize his overlordship, even though he was powerless to demand payments or services from them. His plan was slowly to build up the idea that the king was the highest lord in the land (a plan that his French and English contemporaries used effectively). In 1158, Frederick summoned representatives of the major Italian cities to demand full recognition of his regalian, or ruler's, rights. These included military service; control of roads, ports, and waterways; administration of tolls, mints, fines, vacant fiefs, and confiscated properties; appointment of magistrates; construction of palaces; and control of mines, fisheries, and saltworks. Frederick's attempts to control northern Italy resulted in the creation of the Lombard League, a union of Italian cities that inflicted a humiliating defeat on German forces at Legnano (len-YAN-oh) in 1176.

Frederick also struggled for more than twenty years to get the popes to recognize his claim to the imperial office, which he viewed as a source of prestige and as a legitimation of his right to rule Italy. When he spoke of his "Holy Roman Empire," he meant that his power came from God himself and from the Romans via Charlemagne. The handsome, energetic, and athletic Frederick accomplished much, and he might have done more had he not drowned in Anatolia in 1190, while on his way to the Third Crusade.

In 1197, Germany's heir was an infant, Frederick II (r. 1212–1250), who had been born in Sicily. His mother, Constance, had no standing in Germany and little influence in Italy. Accordingly, she placed her son under the tutelage of Pope Innocent III (r. 1198–1216). By the time Frederick came of age, he so despaired of governing Germany that he conceded the "Statute in Favor of the Princes," which lodged royal power in ducal hands in return for a vague acknowledgment of his overlordship. Frederick concentrated his own efforts in Italy. Although he made good progress, he faced constant opposition from the popes, who were unwilling to trade a German ruler with interests in Italy for an essentially Italian ruler with interests in Germany. When Frederick II died in 1250, effective central authority in both Germany and Italy collapsed.

A long-lived dynasty might have made a difference. Germany did have great rulers: Otto I, Otto III, Frederick Barbarossa, and even Frederick II were the equals of any contemporary ruler. But repeated changes of ruling family in the context of a fragile political regime provided repeated opportunities for fragmentation. The German monarchy had a very limited territorial base and unimpressive government institutions. The Saxons were based in the north, the Salians in the center, and the Staufer in the south. Thus, continuity of rule was constantly threatened by huge dynastic, institutional, and geographical challenges. Germany's involvement with Italy and quest for the imperial title have occasioned no end of controversy. To some, royal involvement in Italy signals a failure to deal imaginatively with Germany itself. To others, the quest for prestige, power, and money in Italy was actually a creative solution to the monarchy's relative impotence in Germany.

Rulers of Medieval Germany
Saxons
Henry I (919–936)
Otto I (936–973)
Otto II (973–983)
Otto III (983–1002)
Henry II (1002–1024)
Salians
Conrad II (1024–1039)
Henry III (1039–1056)
Henry IV (1056–1106)
Henry V (1106–1125)
Staufer
Conrad III (1138–1152)
Frederick Barbarossa (1152–1190)
Henry VI (1190–1197)
Frederick II (1212–1250)

The key issue in the relations between Germany's rulers and the church is the investiture controversy. In the middle of the eleventh century, a group of ardent church reformers, who were committed to improving the moral and intellectual caliber of the clergy all over Europe, targeted the chief

THE INVESTITURE CONTROVERSY

🌐 MAP 9.3—The Communal Movement in Italy

Beginning in the late eleventh century, many towns in northern Italy, some in the central regions, and a very few in the south erected communal forms of government. This distribution reflects the relative wealth of north and south and the power of the popes in the center. North of the Alps, only Flanders and northern France experienced comparable communal movements.

called *consuls*—a deliberate attempt to evoke the Roman past. Usually elected for a single year, the consuls varied in number from four to twenty in different cities. The consuls proposed matters to an assembly for ratification. By the 1140s, every significant city in northern and central Italy had a commune. One by one, cities either refused to recognize papal or imperial overlordship or else renegotiated the terms under which they would acknowledge the rule of their historic masters. The working out of this ongoing relationship was a major development in the history of the Italian cities in the twelfth century.

By the late twelfth century, the consular communes were still governed by oligarchies of men whose wealth and power came from land, trade, and industry. Guild interests, however, gained in prominence at the expense of the landed groups among whom the communal movement had arisen, and ordinary workers began to clamor for participation. The communes were becoming increasingly volatile and violent.

One solution to this potential crisis was the introduction of the *podestà* (poe-des-TAH), a sort of city manager chosen by the local oligarchy. The podestà often came from the outside, served for a set period (usually six months or a year), and underwent a careful scrutiny at the conclusion of his term. He was expected to police the city as well as defend it. Normally, he could not be a property owner in the town, marry into local society, or dine privately with any citizen. By the middle of the thirteenth century, some podestàs were becoming virtual professional administrators. One man, for example, was elected sixteen times in nine cities over a period of thirty-four years, four times in Bologna alone.

The Italian commune was a radical political experiment. Everywhere else in medieval Europe, power was thought to radiate downward—from God, the clergy, the emperor, the king. In a commune, power radiated upward from the popolo to its leaders. For several centuries, the Italian city was arguably the most creative institution in the Western world.

The key power in central Italy was the papacy, and the main political entity was the Papal States. In the political turmoil of the tenth and eleventh centuries, the papacy lost a great deal of territory. Throughout the twelfth and thirteenth centuries, therefore, a basic objective of papal policy was to recover lost lands and rights. This quest to restore the territorial basis for papal power and income helps explain why the popes so resolutely opposed German imperial influence in Italy.

The most striking development pertaining to the papacy is the expansion of its institutions. The **Papal Monarchy** is meant to characterize a church whose power was increasingly centralized in the hands of the popes. In Rome, the pope presided over the *curia*, the papal court. The College of Cardinals, potentially fifty-three in number, formed a kind of senate for the church. They elected the popes (by majority after 1059 and by a two-thirds majority after 1179), served as key advisers, headed the growing financial and judicial branches of the papal government, and often served as legates, papal envoys. Lateran Councils met often and gathered the clergy from all over Europe to legislate for the church as a whole. The hierarchical structure of the church became more visible as ecclesiastical business tended to accumulate in Rome.

High medieval popes also reserved to themselves certain jurisdictional and coercive prerogatives. Popes could excommunicate persons—that is, exclude them from the sacraments of the church and the community of Christians. This was a form of social death in that excommunicated persons could not eat, converse, or socialize with others. Popes could lay a territory under interdict. This decree forbade all religious services except baptisms and burials and was designed to bring maximum pressure to bear on a particular individual. Finally, popes could invoke the inquisition. Despite horror stories about the inquisition, this was a judicial mechanism fully rooted in Roman law and widely used in the medieval West. Basically, an inquisition involved churchmen taking sworn testimony in an attempt to discover heresy.

THE FATE OF SOUTHERN ITALY

From the ninth century on, the region south of Rome was contested among Byzantines, North African Muslims, and local potentates. In 1026, Norman pilgrims, bound for the Holy Land, landed in southern Italy, where local people enlisted them in the fight against the Muslims. Initially opposed to the Normans, the papacy later allied with their leader as a counterweight against the Germans.

From his capital at Palermo, Roger II "the Great" (r. 1130–1154), ruled a complex state that blended Byzantine, Lombard, and Norman structures. Perched advantageously at the juncture

THE PAPAL MONARCHY

Papal Monarchy
A term meant to signify the enlarged and centralized papal government beginning in the twelfth century.

Important Popes During the High Middle Ages
Gregory VII (1073–1085)
Urban II (1088–1099)
Innocent III (1198–1216)
Boniface VIII (1294–1303)

Coronation of Roger II in Sicily, 1130 Roger's coronation by Jesus Christ makes a powerful ideological statement: He owes his office to no earthly power. The cultural crosscurrents of Sicily are visible: Roger is depicted more like a Byzantine emperor than a Western king. The inscriptions above his head ("Rogerios Rex") and next to Christ's are in Greek, not Latin. Beside Christ's head are the customary Greek abbreviations **IC** (the first and last letters of **I**esu**S**) and **XP**, for **ChR**istos. (The original surely contains the full XP symbol.) (Scala/Art Resource, NY)

of the Latin, Greek, and Arab worlds, the Norman court was more advanced in finance and bureaucratic administration than any of its European contemporaries. No one forgot for a moment, however, that the Normans were primarily great warriors. A chronicler said of the Normans, "They delight in arms and horses."

Once the popes had defeated Frederick II, they decided to look for more pliant allies in the south. They invited a succession of French and Spanish princes to assume the Crown, thus touching off long-standing rivalries in the area. A profusion of outsiders always dominated southern Italy.

Capetian France, 987–1314

When the Treaty of Verdun created the West Frankish Kingdom in 843, no one knew what the future of France might be. Referring to France's tremendous diversity, the twentieth-century French leader Charles de Gaulle once quipped, "It is impossible to govern a country with 325 kinds of cheese." During the late ninth century and much of the tenth, the area suffered cruelly from constant waves of Viking attacks and from repeated failures of the Carolingian family to produce adult heirs to the throne. At the end of the tenth century, however, the Carolingians were replaced by the Capetians (kuh-PEE-shunz), the family of Hugh Capet (r. 987–996). The Capetians ruled France for more than three hundred years—an impressive achievement in light of the repeated failure of German dynasties.

CAPETIAN PRESTIGE

From the very beginning, the Capetian kings of France sought to preserve the royal office, increase its prestige, and consolidate its political base. Hugh Capet inaugurated the tradition of crowning his son as his successor during his own lifetime. This meant that when the old king died, a new king was already in place and the nobility could not easily meddle in the succession. Robert II (r. 996–1031) displayed the "royal touch," a ceremony in which the king was believed to be able to cure people of scrofula (a common respiratory ailment) by touching them. No French nobleman ever laid claim to such miraculous powers. Capetian kings capitalized on their control of the old, rich, prestigious, and centrally located city of Paris. The kings promoted the shrine of Saint Denis, the legendary first bishop of Paris, as a kind of "national" shrine for France. Louis VII (r. 1137–1180) began to make elegant tours of the country to put himself, his office, and his sparkling entourage on display. In Louis IX (r. 1226–1270), the Capetian family actually produced a saint of the Catholic Church—Saint Louis.

BUILDING THE CAPETIAN KINGDOM

The Capetians initially controlled no more than Paris and its immediate region. They contested for control of this region with a number of ambitious and aggressive families, finally ground them down, and made the Île-de-France one of the best-governed regions in all of France. The kings also controlled about two dozen bishoprics and some fifty monasteries in northern France. This power base gave the kings unrivaled opportunities to extend their influence and, in turn, to build up a cadre of loyal and articulate supporters. Although French kings provoked a few battles with the papacy, France experienced no investiture controversy.

France's territorial expansion was tightly connected to military success. The background to French military success is complicated. The counts of Anjou (see **MAP 9.4**), through war and marriage, secured control of almost two-thirds of France. Decisive was the marriage of Henry of Anjou to Eleanor of Aquitaine. To make things even more complicated, in 1154, Henry became king of England through his mother, a granddaughter of William the Conqueror (see below). For two generations, the king of France hammered away at this "Angevin Empire." In 1204, Philip II of France (r. 1180–1223) defeated King John of England (r. 1199–1216) and laid claim to the French holdings of the Angevins—but not to England.

Southeastern France was gained by wars of a different kind. In the last decades of the twelfth century, much of the south became a hotbed of the Albigensian (al-buh-JEN-see-un) heresy—an important religious movement (see page 267). Some Catholic locals and many churchmen urged the kings to undertake military action against the heretics. The French kings bided their time until they had the resources to deal with this turbulent region. Under Louis VIII (r. 1223–1226) and Louis IX, the French monarchy finally extended its authority to France's Mediterranean coast.

The Capetian Kings of France

Hugh Capet (987–996)	Philip II (1180–1223)
Robert II (996–1031)	Louis VIII (1223–1226)
Henry I (1031–1060)	Louis IX (1226–1270)
Philip I (1060–1108)	Philip III (1270–1285)
Louis VI (1108–1137)	Philip IV (1285–1314)
Louis VII (1137–1180)	

🌐 **MAP 9.4—French Territorial Principalities, ca. 1200**
As the Carolingian West Frankish Kingdom (see **MAP 8.3** on page 214) broke down and feudal
bonds proliferated, many territories arose under counts and dukes. Their struggles
to impose control locally and to fight off royal supervision animated French history.

The chief political dynamic in France was the contest for power between the kings and the
territorial princes (see **MAP 9.4**). At stake was the monarchy's ability to introduce effective rule
into the lands won in all those battles. The territorial princes were locally powerful magnates,
rather like the German dukes. But whereas Germany comprised five major duchies, France had
a dozen or more territorial principalities.

    The territorial princes also faced localized rivalries for power and influence. Countless indi-
viduals built castles (see the feature, "The Visual Record: The Medieval Castle"), brutally subjected local peasants, and became lords. Sometimes these individuals were the vassals of the
territorial princes—say, the dukes of Normandy or the counts of Anjou—and sometimes they
had vassals of their own. In the Carolingian world, the number of vassals was small, their fidelity reasonably solid, and their services reliable. By 1100, the number of vassals was immense,
their fidelity was constantly shifting, and they tended to provide only local military service.
Scholars call this shift from effective Carolingian government to myriad local lordships a **feudal
revolution**. For the kings of France to re-create central government, they had to overcome the
disruptive tendencies of this revolution and then consolidate institutions.

    In the twelfth and thirteenth centuries, the Capetians followed a few basic policies to increase
their ability to govern. They circumvented the local lords as much as possible. When they won
military victories, the kings did not dole out the seized lands to lords as new fiefs but instead kept
them in their own hands, or in the hands of family members. The kings introduced into these lands
new officials, called bailiffs or provosts, who were of modest social background, had no personal
ties to their assigned regions, often had some schooling in law, and were intensely loyal to the kings.
By the time of Louis IX, officials called *enqueteurs* (on-KEH-tur) were sent around the country to

**STRATEGIES
OF CAPETIAN
GOVERNMENT**

feudal revolution   A term
that refers to the proliferation
of lord-vassal bonds as key
elements of governmental and
social control.

By the time this three-part view of society was fully established in the West, it had begun to fit social realities less well. It excluded townspeople, who were becoming ever more important. Town residents worked for a living, of course, but only farmers were considered "workers." Alfred and the bishops did not speak about women, and they consciously excluded minorities, chiefly Jews.

Those Who Pray: The Clergy

As the church promoted its own vision of the three-part ordering of society, it assigned primacy to the prayers—its own leaders. Within the clergy, however, sharp disagreements arose over whether the leading prayers were the monks in the monasteries or the bishops in their cathedrals. Whereas in the Carolingian world the clergy served occasionally as an avenue of upward social mobility for talented outsiders, in the High Middle Ages, church offices were usually reserved for the younger sons of the nobility.

Cluny A monastery in France that became a model for religious reform.

In the aftermath of the Carolingian collapse, a great spiritual reform swept Europe. It began in 910 when Duke William of Aquitaine founded the monastery of **Cluny** (CLUE-nee) in Burgundy on land that he donated (see **Map 9.4** on page 290). At a time when powerful local families dominated almost all monasteries, Cluny was a rarity because it was free of all lay and episcopal control and because it was under the direct authority of the pope. Cluny's abbots were among the greatest European statesmen of their day and became influential advisers to popes, French kings, German emperors, and aristocratic families.

Cluny placed great emphasis on liturgical prayer. The monks spent long hours in solemn devotions and did little manual work. Because Cluniac prayer was thought to be especially effective, nobles all over Europe donated land to Cluny and placed local monasteries under Cluniac control. Many independent monasteries also appealed to Cluny for spiritual reform. By the twelfth century hundreds of monasteries had joined in a Cluniac order. Individual houses were under the authority of the abbot of Cluny, and their priors had to attend an annual assembly. Although the majority of houses reformed by Cluny were male, many convents of nuns also adopted Cluniac practices.

Cluny promoted two powerful ideas. One was that the role of the church was to pray for the world, not to be implicated deeply in it. The other was that freedom from lay control was essential if churches were to concentrate on their spiritual tasks.

The same spiritual forces that motivated the Cluniacs inspired Bishop Adalbero of Metz in 933 to promote the restoration of Benedictine practices in the dilapidated Lorraine monastery of Gorze (GORTZ-eh). Customs at Gorze resembled those at Cluny, and they spread widely in Lorraine, Germany, and England. The Gorze reform was well received by kings and nobles; its aim was not so much to withdraw from the world as to improve it. Monks from the Gorze and Cluniac traditions bitterly condemned clerical immorality and inappropriate lay interference in the church. They preached against clerical marriage and simony, the buying and selling of church offices.

Reformers in the more ascetic eremitic tradition (see pages 178–179) desired more profound changes. They criticized the monastery at Cluny, saying that it had become too opulent and successful, and the monastery at Gorze because it seemed too immersed in worldly affairs. A desire to build new communities according to their vision of the apostolic church, featuring a life of poverty, self-denial, and seclusion, captivated the ascetics. Thus, the eleventh and early twelfth centuries saw a proliferation of both male and female experiments in eremitic monasticism. Other Europeans believed that the apostolic calling demanded not only an austere regimen of personal renunciation, but also an active life of Christian ministry. Cathedral clergy, called canons, adapted the Rule of Saint Augustine so that they could live a communal life and also carry out priestly duties.

The greatest critics of the Cluniac tradition, and the real monastic elite of the early twelfth century, were the Cistercians. In 1098, Abbot Robert left his Burgundian monastery of Molesme (MOE-lem) because he believed it had abandoned the strict teachings of Saint Benedict. He founded a new monastery at Cîteaux (SEE-toe) in Burgundy. This house was to follow the Benedictine Rule literally and to refuse all secular entanglements: lands, rents, and servile dependents. So rigorous and poor was the community that it struggled until a charismatic young Burgundian nobleman named Bernard (1090–1153) joined in 1112. Through his writing, preaching, and personal example, Bernard dominated the religious life of Europe in his lifetime. By the end of the twelfth century, there were about five hundred Cistercian (from the Latin for *Cîteaux*) monasteries in Europe. Initially, the Cistercians wished to be an order of adult men. They successfully avoided admitting young boys, but by 1200, they had authorized about one hundred convents of Cistercian nuns.

And it was not just the Cistercians and the traditional Benedictines who attracted women. The twelfth century saw many new communities of women from England to eastern Europe. The age's growing prosperity and population contributed both potential nuns and healthy endowments, but the key factor was that women were responding to the spiritual forces of the age in the same way men were.

With the monastic clergy gaining so much in prestige and visibility, the episcopal clergy countered with its own view of society. Surely, the bishops agreed, spiritual, moral, and intellectual improvement were desirable. Likewise, it was time to end the grossest examples of lay interference in the church. But precisely because so many bishops came from great families and were so well connected, they were less inclined to be rigid about the line of demarcation between lay and clerical responsibilities. In Germany, for example, the king's chapel recruited young noblemen to train them as clerics and to inculcate in them the policies and ethos of the court. Many of these chaplains were appointed to bishoprics and then advanced the king's interests in their new ecclesiastical areas of authority. They were often men of spiritual depth and resented what they regarded as monastic carping about their worldliness.

It was the special responsibility of the clergy to look after the moral order of society. In the turbulent world of gentlemen warriors, the church had its own ideas about what a perfect "fighter" should do. The English bishop and scholar John of Salisbury (d. 1180), reflecting on knighthood in the twelfth century, concluded that it existed "to protect the church, to attack infidelity, to reverence the priesthood, to protect the poor, to keep the peace, to shed one's blood and, if necessary, to lay down one's life for one's brethren."

Turning large numbers of violent young men into servants of the church was a tall order for the clergy, and they had only limited success. One strategy that worked was the creation of military orders. The Palestine-based Knights of St. John, or Hospitallers, and Knights of the Temple, or Templars, are the major examples. The Hospitallers started near Jerusalem as a foundation under Benedictine auspices dedicated to charitable works and care of the sick. They evolved into a monastic order using a version of the Rule of Saint Benedict and devoted themselves to the defense of pilgrims to the Holy Land. The Templars were men living under religious rule and sworn to protect the small states created by the Crusaders (see pages 255–256). These military orders measured up very well to the clergy's idea of what a perfect knight should be.

The clergy could also regulate disputes in society. For example, when a community was divided by a difficult conflict that demanded resolution, it might turn to the *ordeal*—a judicial procedure that sought divine judgment by subjecting the accused to a physically painful or dangerous test. An accused person might walk a certain distance carrying hot iron or plunge a hand into a boiling cauldron to pluck out a pebble. The resulting wounds would be bandaged for a set time and then examined. If they were healing, the person was considered innocent; if they were festering, the person was considered guilty. The clergy officiated at ordeals until the papacy forbade their participation in 1215.

Those Who Fight: The Nobility

In recent years, scholars have spilled a sea of ink trying to define the medieval nobility. The matter is important because even though the nobility constituted only a small minority of the total population, nobles were the ruling class. To appreciate their crucial role, we need to consider the nobles' lifestyle and ethos.

CHRONOLOGY

ca. 900	*Beowulf*
910	Foundation of Cluny
940–1003	Gerbert of Aurillac
960–1028	Fulbert of Chartres
d. 970	Roswitha of Gandersheim
1000–1088	Berengar of Tours
ca. 1033–1109	Anselm of Canterbury
ca. 1050–1150	Maturation of the Romanesque
1079–1142	Peter Abelard
1090–1153	Bernard of Clairvaux
1098	Foundation of Cîteaux
1098–1179	Hildegard of Bingen
ca. 1100	*Song of Roland*
1135–1183	Chrétien de Troyes
1170–1221	Dominic de Guzman
ca. 1177–1213	Mary of Oignies
1181–1226	Francis of Assisi
1184	Waldensians declared heretics
1194–1253	Clare of Assisi
1208	Albigensian Crusade launched
1210–1280	Mechtild of Magdeburg
1225–1274	Thomas Aquinas
1265–1321	Dante Alighieri

Reconstruction of Cluny A view of the monastic complex at Cluny in the early twelfth century. Note the basilica (the largest church in Europe until the sixteenth century), the cloister (to the left, actually south, of the basilica, with its dormitory in the foreground and refectory opposite the basilica), and the workshops. (Based on a drawing from *Cluny des Églises et la Maison du Chef d'Ordre*, by R. J. Conant. Courtesy, Medieval Academy of America)

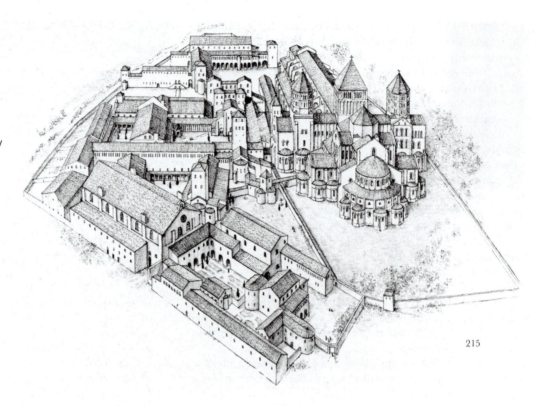

215

In English, the word *noble* can be either an adjective or a noun. More commonly, it is an adjective, as in a "noble sentiment" or a "noble deed." Before the twelfth century, the Latin *nobilis* was almost exclusively an adjective. The word pertained to certain desirable personal qualities. Then, gradually, the word became a noun and pertained to a certain kind of person.

In the ideal case, a noble was a well-born, cultivated, office-holding soldier. In the earlier Middle Ages, many men held offices without necessarily being considered noble. Virtually all free men were expected to be soldiers, but few of them ranked as nobles. It was in the century or so following the feudal revolution (see page 240–241) that these distinct elements were fused into a single social order.

In a world in which lords were everywhere extending their power, military prowess became more valuable. At the same time, the need for horses and for more expensive arms and armor made it almost impossible for ordinary freemen to be soldiers. Likewise, ambitious lords who wished to expand their influence were looking for ways to use their resources to gain followers. These trends came together as lords granted to their followers either military gear or lands, which would generate the income necessary to obtain arms and horses. We call those followers "vassals" and the lands they obtained "fiefs." Vassalage became a widespread institution all over Europe, and fief-holding became a normal accompaniment to vassalage.

Vassals and fiefs bring to mind the concept of *feudalism* or the term *feudal system*. As we saw in Chapter 9, England, France, and, to a lesser degree, Germany and Italy were in some respects feudal realms. That is, lords, right up to the king, secured some personal and political services from vassals in return for material rewards, often landed estates called fiefs. Today, historians are reluctant to use the term *feudal system* because across Europe, and through many centuries, there was nothing systematic about how services were obtained or discharged.

Contemporary sources often call vassals "knights." Knights rarely boasted high birth or venerable ancestry, nor were they initially officeholders appointed by kings or emperors. Moreover, they were not wealthy and did not enjoy the lavish lifestyle that one might expect from nobles. Across the eleventh and twelfth centuries, knights saw their status change, in part because they mimicked the behavior of the nobles, who themselves accepted the necessity of military ability.

All over Europe, especially where royal power was ineffective, both knights and nobles secured tighter control of peasant labor. This process provided knights and nobles with the money to build castles and to acquire fine possessions. As governments expanded their competence, these nobles and knights often held high offices, or if they did not, they pressured kings to concede such offices to them. Lords also tended to gather their lands into coherent blocks and to name themselves after the castles they built on their lands. Families also began to produce genealogies tracing their ancestry to relatives in the distant past and to kings if at all possible. At the same time, families began to practice primogeniture—that is, reserving their lands, castles, and titles to the *primus genitus*, or "firstborn" son.

This allotment of the choicest inheritances to a shrinking group turned loose a large number of younger sons. Many of them entered the clergy, a tendency that helps to explain the rising aristocratic character of the church. This was not a punishment. Sons were not "dumped" on the church. Clerical careers were prestigious and relatively comfortable. But more numerous than clerics were the young men who were without an estate and who lacked the means to secure a bride and to form a family of their own. These men traipsed about Europe looking for fame and fortune, or failing that, a lord to serve. Many of these "young" men were 30 or 40 years old. They were called young because they had not yet established themselves.

By 1200, the nobility was a group identified by the profession of arms, the holding of office, a consciousness of family traditions, and an elevated lifestyle. A specific ethos—chivalry—belonged to the nobility. Today, chivalry is often thought of as either an elaborate code of conduct regulating relations between the sexes or the value system behind the literary image of dashing knights in shining armor saving damsels in distress from fire-breathing dragons. Actually, its very name derives from *cheval*, French for "horse," the classic conveyance of a knight. Chivalry began as the code of conduct for mounted warriors.

Chivalry highly esteemed certain masculine, militant qualities. Military prowess was the greatest of chivalric virtues. A knight who was not a great warrior was useless. Literature of the time exalts the knight who slays fearsome beasts or the hero who single-handedly overwhelms impossible numbers of the enemy. Openhanded generosity was another key virtue. The truly noble person engaged in sumptuous display to manifest his power, to show concern for his dependents, and to enlarge his entourage. Medieval literature is full of rich banquets and stunning presents. Knights were obsessed with their honor, their reputations. They sought glory, the better to win a lord or a bride or, if a lord already, to attract followers. Chivalry also emphasized loyalty, the glue that held feudal society together.

What role was left to noblewomen in a world of chivalry and lordship? By the late eleventh century, three developments adversely affected the position of aristocratic women. First, the elaboration of the chivalric ethos defined most key social and political roles as military and "manly" and thereby excluded women. By the middle of the twelfth century, it was rare for a woman to hold a castle and unheard of for one to ride to arms. Second, the consolidation of lineages by aristocratic families accompanied a moral campaign by the church to promote monogamous, unbreakable marriages. This situation subordinated women's freedom in the marriage market to the dynastic and patrimonial demands of great families. Third, the spread of lordship, with its intricate network of personal and proprietary relationships based on military service, tended to deprive women of independent rights over land.

But every rule has its exceptions. As noble families married off fewer of their daughters to noblemen, "extra" daughters accounted in part for the dramatic increase in the number and size of convents. Convents of aristocratic nuns were places where women could be highly educated and almost entirely in control of their own affairs. Matilda, daughter of the German empress Adelaide, was abbess of Quedlinburg, mistress of vast estates in northern Germany, and a dominant figure in German politics. But knights looking for brides would often marry the younger daughters of noblemen, because if they could establish a household, any children born of that marriage could lay claim to the noble lineage of their maternal grandfathers.

Less predictably, Gaita, wife of a Norman prince in Italy, fought in helmet and armor alongside her husband, as did Duchess Agnes of Burgundy. And let us reflect on the career of Adela of Blois (ca. 1067–1137). She was the daughter of William the Conqueror, the wife of a powerful French count, and the mother of King Stephen I of England. In addition to regularly accompanying her husband as he administered his county, Adela founded monasteries, promoted religious reform, hosted Pope Paschal II, helped to reconcile her brother Henry I with the archbishop of Canterbury (thus averting an English investiture controversy), issued formal legal judgments, held fairs, and skillfully negotiated the aristocratic politics of western France after her husband's death. Adela is unusual because we know so much about her. In other words, noblewomen in high medieval society may often have led interesting, active lives, but there are few surviving records to document this.

Those Who Work: The Peasants

The peasants were the "workers" in the three-part model. An extremely diverse segment of society, "peasants" ranged from slaves to free persons of some means. Except in frontier zones, where victims were available and religious scruples diminished, slaves declined dramatically in numbers during the tenth and eleventh centuries (as illustrated by the shift in meaning of the classical Latin *servus* from "slave" to "serf"). Serfs, persons bound to the soil, constituted the majority of the peasants, although their legal and social statuses differed considerably from place to place. In the twelfth century, serfdom was disappearing in France, even as its terms were hardening in central and eastern Europe. Serfdom was a mixture of economic, legal, and personal statuses. The serf could be flogged in public, could be set upon by dogs, was excluded from many judicial proceedings, required approval to contract a marriage, and was denied the right to bear arms.

The tenth and eleventh centuries were decisive in the reshaping of rural society. As lordships of all kinds and sizes formed in the countryside, they drew communities of people. Castles were critical. Powerful men generally sited their castles in close proximity to wood, water, and iron. (See the feature, "The Visual Record: The Medieval Castle" on pages 242–243 in Chapter 9.) People from a fairly wide area settled in the vicinity of the castle. Many, originally free, commended themselves to the local lord by handing over their properties and receiving them back in return for rents or personal services. Other people fell into dependent status through military or economic misfortune. What eventually emerged was the manor, an institution best described as a powerful lord controlling the lives of an often large number of dependents. He required payments and services from them and regulated their ordinary disputes. His control was simultaneously public and private.

A minor castellan, or lord of a castle, might control only a small manor and would probably be the vassal of a great lord. A powerful landed lord, on the other hand, would generally control many manors and would often give some of them to retainers as fiefs. In other words, the reorganization of the countryside affected the nobility and the peasantry and created parallel sets of vertical bonds of association: feudal lords and vassals entered into political bonds; lords and peasants entered into economic bonds.

The structure of individual manors, and the dues owed by peasants, varied tremendously across Europe. Certain trends were fairly consistent, however. As the economy expanded, as trade brought more and different products into Europe, and as a more consciously aristocratic lifestyle spread, the nobility began to want disposable cash. Thus, in many places corvées (KOR-vay) (labor services) were commuted into cash payments. Peasants were required to pay rent from their own holdings instead of working on the lord's lands. But lords still needed provisions, so they sometimes split peasant payments into cash and kind. The lord could also extract money from his peasants by requiring them to use his mill and oven and then charging them gristing and baking fees.

The trend everywhere, however, was for labor services to diminish. In one region in northern France, twelfth-century peasants owed only three corvées of two days each per year for harvesting and haymaking. Elsewhere, peasants might still be required to haul crops to market or to keep roads, bridges, and buildings in repair. On many estates where the menfolk had been largely freed from corvées, the women might still have to work in the lord's house washing laundry, sewing, plucking fowl, cooking, minding dogs, and tending to other household chores.

In the expanding economy of the eleventh and twelfth centuries, the peasants grew more prosperous, and their lords constantly sought new ways to extract the fruits of that prosperity. Peasants thus began to band together to demand that "customs" be observed. These customs were more or less formal agreements spelling out the terms under which work and fees would be arranged. In general, life improved for the peasants in terms of both legal status and living conditions.

The European village was a key product of the tenth and eleventh centuries. People who originally gathered together around a castle for security and livelihood began to form a durable human community. Their church and graveyard helped to reinforce the community by tying together the living and the dead and by giving the village a sense of memory and continuity. Peasants generally worked only 250 to 270 days per year, so they had a good deal of time for festivals and celebrations. Births, baptisms, betrothals, and deaths provided opportunities for the community to come together and affirm its mutual ties. Market days and sessions of the lord's court also assembled the village. Villagers needed to cooperate in many of the operations of daily life. They shared tools, plow teams, and wagons. They performed their corvées together. The peasants experienced much less social differentiation than the nobility, and so, less tension.

The status of women in peasant society tended to be, in legal theory and in daily reality, the same as that of men at a time when the status of aristocratic women was fragile. Marriage contracts from northern Italy show that brides often entered marriages with a complement of valuable tools. This suggests that peasant women retained some control over their own personal property and also reminds us that the huge gains in rural productivity were almost certainly attributable in part to the work and ingenuity of women.

Those Left Out: Townspeople and Jews

The three-part model excluded two important groups of people. The first neglected group consisted of the increasingly numerous citizens of Europe's growing towns. Obviously, people in towns worked, but the prejudices of the aristocracy were rural, so the only "workers" deemed necessary to the smooth functioning of the social order were farmers. In the second group were Europe's principal religious minority, the Jews. Jews could be found almost everywhere, although they constituted only about 1 percent of the population as a whole and, outside of Rome and parts of Spain, formed no single community numbering more than 1,500 to 2,000.

The central factor in the growth of towns was the rise in the productivity and profitability of medieval agriculture. For the first time in history, a regular and substantial farm surplus could support an urban population that did not produce its own food. Increased local exchange, coupled with the relentless growth of a money economy, meant there were fortunes to be made and cash to be spent. Some of that cash was spent on luxury and exotic products that increasingly became the objects of far-flung commercial networks. A good part of the cash was spent by rural nobles, who earned it from rents, booty, and the profits of the private exercise of public power. When those nobles moved into towns, they created opportunities for merchants, craftsmen, day laborers, domestic servants, and professional people, such as notaries and lawyers. This was particularly true in Europe's most heavily urbanized regions: Flanders, southern France, and northern Italy. The key point is that the growth of the medieval city and of its human community began in the medieval countryside.

Town society was hierarchical, but its structures were new, ill-defined, and flexible. Rich men built up bands of followers who supported them in urban politics, protected their neighborhoods, and occasionally raided the houses of their enemies in the next neighborhood. Relatives, friends, neighbors, people from a common rural district, or those engaged in similar trades tended to worship together in particular churches, observe certain festivals, and look after one another's families.

San Gimignano The towers of this Tuscan city reveal the concentrated and competitive nature of power in the Italian communes. Most of these towers date from around 1300. (Scala/Art Resource, NY)

In the rapidly changing world of the tenth and eleventh centuries, towns provided numerous opportunities for women. In urban industries, such as clothmaking, tanning, laundering, and brewing, women sometimes managed and even owned enterprises. Apart, perhaps, from finance and the law, distinctions between male and female roles were not as sharp in towns as in rural areas.

If urban men and all women stood in an ambiguous relationship to the ideals of the male, rural, aristocratic elite, we can hardly imagine what it must have been like for Jews. Jewish communities had existed in most European towns since antiquity. Then, because the Byzantine and Islamic worlds vacillated between persecution and toleration, many Jews migrated to western Europe, with the largest numbers settling in northern France and the German Rhineland. Paris had northern Europe's largest Jewish community, perhaps two thousand people in the twelfth century. Many cities had Jewish populations numbering two hundred to three hundred, but groups of forty to fifty were common. Although some Jews in Italy, Spain, and Germany owned farms and vineyards, most Jews settled in cities, where they could live and worship in community with other Jews. Urban clusters also provided strength in numbers for people who could at any moment fall victim to persecution and whose power was not based on landholding.

Three of the most important developments in high medieval Europe were disastrous for Jews. First, the growth of the European economy, with its attendant urban and commercial expansion, brought countless Christians into the practice of trade, an occupation dominated by Jews since Late Antiquity. As Jews were excluded from commercial opportunities, they were more and more confined to moneylending. Jews had been moneylenders before the economic surge of the High Middle Ages, but the expanding economy made financial operations more widespread than ever before. Given that, as we saw in Chapter 9, Christian moralists considered handling money to be the Devil's work, the visibility of Jews as moneylenders brought them much criticism, although they were never alone in this practice.

The second phenomenon that adversely affected Jews was the reform of the church. With so much attention being paid to the proper Christian life and the correct organization of the church, it was inevitable that more attention would be directed to the one prominent group in Western society that was not Christian.

Third, the Crusades unleashed vicious attacks on Jews. As crusading armies headed east in 1096, they visited unspeakable massacres on the Jewish communities of several German towns. This awful process was repeated on the eve of the Second Crusade in 1146–1147 and again just before the third in 1189. Popular frenzy identified the Jews as Christ-killers and equated them with Muslims as the enemies of Christianity. In fact, and despite grotesque and groundless stories about Jews kidnapping and ritually killing Christian children, Jews everywhere wished to live in peace with their Christian neighbors and to be left alone to observe their distinctive religious, dietary, and social customs.

The Jews were not without sympathetic champions, however. From the time of Gregory I (r. 590–604), the papacy urged peaceful coexistence and prayers for Jewish conversion. In the twelfth and thirteenth centuries, popes forcefully reminded Christians that while converting Jews was highly desirable, Jews were to be tolerated and left in peace. The Carolingians protected the Jews, and some kings in succeeding centuries repeated or even expanded upon Carolingian legislation.

Jews were vulnerable to attack at almost any time from people who simply disliked them or who owed them money. In 1181, Philip II of France, always on the lookout for income, had his henchmen arrest Jews and confiscate their possessions. In 1182, he expelled them from royal lands. Across the thirteenth century, French kings accorded the Jews less and less protection and often abused them financially. In 1306, Philip IV expelled the Jews from France after confiscating their goods. In England, the story is much the same. The ever-needy Henry II laid crushing taxes on the Jews in 1171. In 1189 in London and in 1190 in York, massive riots stirred by false rumors raged against the Jewish populations. In 1290, Edward I seized Jewish possessions and expelled Jews from the country. Royal protection of German Jews was reasonably effective until the death of Frederick II in 1250, after which time local princes often repudiated debts to Jewish lenders and appropriated Jewish property.

SECTION SUMMARY

- Among the elite, society was divided into "those who pray," "those who fight," and "those who work."

- Constant waves of monastic reform modeled good spiritual behavior.

- Warrior-nobles were the governing class, marked by chivalry, their distinctive ethos.

- Peasants did much of the "work" in medieval society and generally found their lives improving.

- Townspeople enjoyed expanding opportunities but always suffered under the prejudices of landholding elites.

- In religious life, urban occupations, and rural pursuits, women experienced some improvements in their conditions of life.

- The condition of Europe's Jews grew progressively dangerous.

SOCIAL AND RELIGIOUS MOVEMENTS, CA. 1100–1300

Why did some spiritual movements result in heresy, while others ended in new religious orders?

Twelfth- and thirteenth-century Europe witnessed several social movements unlike any that had occurred before. Spurred by increasingly intrusive governments, economic dislocation, and spiritual turmoil, they involved large numbers of people; cut across lines of gender, wealth, status, and occupation; and appeared in many places. Most of these movements had cohesive beliefs, even ideologies, and well-determined goals. They are the first large-scale social movements in European history.

Heretics and Dissidents

The canon lawyer Gratian (see page 267) defined *heresy* as a situation in which "each man chooses for himself the teaching he believes to be the better one"—that is, he ignores official doctrines. For Gratian and his like-minded contemporaries, faith was not an individual matter. Unity of belief was crucial in a catholic ("universal") Christian Europe. In the twelfth century, the church reacted ever more strictly to challenges to its teachings or to its exclusive right to teach. The effort by the church to define its law, theology, and bureaucratic procedures with greater precision drew lines more sharply than ever before between what was and was not acceptable.

Heretics did not see themselves as secessionists from the true church. They saw themselves as its only representatives. Church teachings always encountered a degree of popular skepticism. Not everyone believed, for example, that Jesus was born of a virgin or that he was true God and true man. But such doubts had not previously led to mass defections. Before the middle of the twelfth century, challenges to the church came from men—as far as we can tell, the ringleaders were all men—who saw themselves as inspired reformers.

Tanchelm (TANK-elm) of Antwerp preached between 1100 and 1115 in the Netherlands. He scandalized the mainstream by calling churches brothels and clerics whores. He rejected the sacraments and the payment of tithes. Although Tanchelm was radical and pugnacious, his ideas constituted a fairly coherent program of criticism. Like many others, he was concerned about the immorality and wealth of the church. But Tanchelm and his followers went even further. The heretic distributed his nail and hair clippings as relics of a sort, and in a bizarre public ceremony he "married" a statue of the Virgin Mary.

Coherent movements of much larger proportions emerged later in the century. In 1173, Waldo, a rich merchant of Lyon, decided to sell all his property, give the proceeds to the poor, and embrace a life of poverty and preaching. Waldo was motivated by the same quest for the apostolic life that had animated the eremitic movement of the eleventh century. But there was a difference: He was a layman. Waldo attracted many followers (known as Waldensians), and in 1179, Pope Alexander III (r. 1159–1181) scrutinized him closely, found his beliefs to be essentially correct, and approved his vow of poverty. But the pope commanded Waldo to preach only when invited to do so by bishops. The bishops, jealous about their own power, extended no such invitations.

Waldo and his "Poor Men of Lyon" went right on preaching and in 1184 were formally declared heretics. Until this point it was not their ideas so much as their appropriation of a clerical duty, preaching, that had set the church against them. From this time on, however, the Waldensians became more radical in their attacks. Waldensian communities exist to this day.

The most serious of the popular heretical movements was Catharism (from the Greek *katharos*, meaning "pure"). Because there were numerous Cathars near the southern French town of Albi, the whole movement is sometimes called "Albigensian." In fact, Cathars could be found all over Europe, although they did cluster in northern Italy and southern France. Cathars were the religious descendants of Mani (see page 157), a third-century Persian who taught an extreme dualism that featured polarities in almost all things: good-evil, love-hate, flesh-spirit. Extreme Cathars abstained from flesh in all ways: They were vegetarians and renounced sexual intercourse so as not to produce offspring—that is, more flesh. Cathar ideas had spread widely in the West by the 1140s. Catharism attracted many converts when Nicetas, the Cathar bishop of Constantinople, visited northern Italy and southern France between 1166 and 1176. People of every station joined the new church, which, in its own view, was the only true church.

The Catholic Church sent isolated preachers against the Cathars, but with little success. In 1198 and 1203, Pope Innocent III organized systematic preaching tours in southern France, but these, too, lacked solid results, and in 1208, the pope's legate was murdered by a man who was sympathetic to the Cathars. The killing led to the launching of the Albigensian Crusade, a loosely structured military action that lasted into the 1260s. Although the crusade itself was largely over by the 1220s, violence against Albigensians sputtered for decades: a massacre in 1244 and inquisitorial campaigns in 1246 and again in 1256 to 1257. Isolated resisters struggled on into the fourteenth century.

Albigensians denounced the clergy of their day as rich and corrupt. These teachings attracted urban dwellers who resented the wealth and pretensions of the clergy—the same people who followed Waldo. Nobles may have been drawn to the movement because it gave them opportunities to take possession of extensive tracts of church lands, something the investiture controversy had denied them. In addition, embracing Catharism may have been a way for nobles to resist the increasing encroachment of the government of far-off Paris. The Albigensians also attracted many women. Unlike the Catholic Church, which denied clerical, preaching, and teaching offices to women, the heretical sects tended to permit women to hold leading roles.

The Albigensians, like the Waldensians, were driven by the same spiritual zeal and desire for ecclesiastical reform that moved many of their contemporaries. They differed from other would-be reformers in that they did not seek to reform the Catholic Church from within but departed from it or insisted that they alone represented it. Thus, these heretical movements marked the first serious challenge to the ideology of a uniformly "catholic" Christendom since Late Antiquity.

Reform From Within: The Mendicant Orders

Traditional monastic orders continued to win adherents, but their interpretation of the apostolic life meant ascetic withdrawal from the world, not pastoral work and preaching. Laymen who wished both to embrace poverty and to preach fell under the suspicion of the ecclesiastical authorities. Early in the thirteenth century, a new movement arose, the mendicants (literally, beggars). Mendicants were men who aimed to preach, to be poor, and to create formal but noncloistered religious orders. Though similar to the heretics in many ways, they submitted willingly to ecclesiastical authority.

Francis of Assisi An Italian layman who renounced his wealth and founded a religious order dedicated to charitable works.

The mendicant phenomenon began when **Francis of Assisi** (1181–1226), the son of a rich Italian merchant, decided to renounce the wealth and status that were his birthright. He carried out his renunciation in a most public display before the bishop of Assisi (uh-SEE-zee) in 1206. Francis had gradually grown tired of a life of ease and luxury, but he also experienced a blinding moment of spiritual insight when, by chance, his eyes fell on the passage in the Scriptures in which Christ commanded the rich young ruler, "Go, sell all you have, and follow me." Francis stripped himself naked so that "naked he might follow the naked Christ."

For a few years, Francis wandered about Italy begging for his meager sustenance, repairing churches, caring for the sick, and preaching repentance to all who would listen. By 1210, he had attracted many followers, and together, they set out to see Innocent III to win approval. After considering the matter for a while, Innocent decided to approve the new order of friars (that is, "brothers," from the Latin *fratres*) as long as they would accept monastic tonsure—a ritual haircut signifying submission—profess obedience to the pope, and swear obedience to Francis. The pope was genuinely won over by Francis himself, but he also sensed that by permitting the formation of the Franciscan order, he could create a legitimate and controllable repository for the explosive spiritual forces of the age.

Francis prepared a simple Rule based on his understanding of the scriptural ideals of poverty, preaching, and service. Alarmed by the vagueness of the first Rule and by the extraordinary influx of new members, the papal curia in 1223 prevailed on Francis to submit a revision that stressed order, a hierarchy of officials, and a novitiate—a regularized period of training for new members. Somewhat disappointed by this regulated formality, Francis withdrew more and more from the world and lived reclusively in the hills near Assisi.

After Francis died, the issues of property, power, education, and ordination provoked deep controversies within his order. Usually called "Franciscan," Francis's order is technically the "Friars Minor." The movement had begun among laymen, but over time, more Franciscan brothers became ordained priests. Franciscans established schools in most great cities, and by the middle of the thirteenth century, some of Europe's greatest intellects were Franciscans.

In the 1230s, papal legislation had alleviated strict poverty by permitting the order to acquire property to support its work. Nevertheless, the issue of property continued to spark controversy among the Franciscans.

The other major mendicant order was the Dominican, a product of very different experiences than the Franciscan. Its founder, **Dominic de Guzman** (1170–1221), was the son of a Spanish nobleman. He became a priest and later a cathedral canon. While traveling, he saw firsthand the Albigensian heresy in southern France, and in 1206, he went to Rome to seek permission to preach against the heretics. The Albigensian Crusade began in 1208, but Dominic's methods were those of persuasion, not coercion.

Albigensian criticisms of the ignorance, indifference, and personal failings of the clergy could never be applied to Dominic and his fellow preachers. Dominic and his followers were supported enthusiastically by the bishop of Toulouse, who saw how useful these zealous preachers of unblemished lives could be. In 1215, Dominic, with his bishop's assistance, attempted to form a new order, but by that time, Rome had forbidden the creation of new orders for fear of heresy or uncontrollable diversity. Thus, Dominic's "Order of Preachers" (the proper name for the "Dominicans") adopted the Rule of Saint Augustine, which many communities of cathedral canons had been using since the eleventh century.

In 1217, Dominic presided at the first general meeting of the order. The Dominicans decided to disperse, some going to Paris, some (including Dominic) to Rome, and some to other cities in Europe. Henceforth, the order saw its mission as serving the whole church. Dominican schools were set up all over Europe, and the order acquired a reputation for learning and scholarship. The Dominicans were voluntarily poor, but the order was never rent by a controversy over property as the Franciscans were.

Both the Franciscan and Dominican orders reflected a widespread desire to emulate the apostolic life of the early church by poverty and preaching. Both submitted to legitimate authority. Francis's religious vision of charity and service was the product of a heartfelt need for repentance and renewal. This concern for the soul often caused Franciscans to serve as missionaries. Dominic set out to save the church from its enemies. He desired preachers who were sufficiently learned that they could combat the errors of heretics. Both men saw the need for exemplary lives. Francis was a more charismatic figure than Dominic, and his apostolate to the urban poor was more compelling. By 1300, Franciscan houses outnumbered Dominican by 3 to 1. The mendicants were the greatest spiritual force in high medieval Europe.

Dominic de Guzman
A Spanish nobleman who preached against Albigensian heretics and founded a religious order dedicated to preaching.

Communities of Women

The religious forces that attracted men drew women as well. Traditional orders, however, tended to be hostile toward women. Cluniacs and Cistercians struggled to keep women out of their ranks. The wandering preachers of the twelfth century, without exception, acquired women as followers, but the usual results were either segregation of the women in cloisters or condemnation of the whole movement.

In 1212, Francis attracted the aristocrat Clare of Assisi (1194–1253), who was fleeing from an arranged marriage. She wanted to live the friars' life of poverty and preaching, and Francis wanted to assist her. Aware that the sight of women begging or preaching would be shocking, in 1215, he gave Clare and his other female followers their own rule. Clare became abbess of the first community of the "Poor Clares." Though cloistered and forbidden to preach, the Clares lived lives of exemplary austerity and attracted many adherents.

Beguines (BAY-geenz) were communities of women who lived together, devoted themselves to charitable works, but did not take vows as nuns. The Beguine movement grew from the work in Nivelles, near Liège (lee-EZHE), of Mary of Oignies (ca. 1177–1213). She was drawn to the ideals of voluntary poverty and service to others. So strong was the pull that she renounced her marriage, gave away all her goods, worked for a while in a leper colony, and thought of preaching against the Cathars. Instead, she formed a community.

Groups of Beguines appeared all over the Low Countries, western Germany, and northern France. This was the first exclusively women's movement in the history of Christianity. Beguines sometimes vowed poverty and sometimes did not. They sometimes cloistered themselves into communities and sometimes taught and served the poor and outcast. They neither challenged the officials and teachings of the church nor demanded a right to preach. As laywomen, they did not give rise to scandal as noncloistered nuns would have. They were content to have power over their own lives and communities but not seek a voice in the wider world around them.

The Parting of Mary from the Apostles Duccio di Buoninsegna lived from the middle of the thirteenth century to 1318 or 1319. He did his finest work in Siena, including a huge altarpiece, one of whose panels depicts the touching scene of Mary taking leave of the apostles just before her death. Note the clever way Duccio has arranged the figures and how he balances Saint Paul, standing in the doorway, with Mary, reclining on the bed. (Scala/Art Resource, NY)

Thirteenth-century Europe knew more female than male mystics, and female mysticism tended to focus on Jesus, especially on His presence in the Eucharist. This is the first religious devotion that can be shown to have been more common to women than to men. Most of the mystics were either nuns or Beguines. As the clergy was defining its own prerogatives more tightly, and excluding women more absolutely from the exercise of formal public power, female communities provided a different locus for women's activity.

Women who spent their lives in community with other women reveal, in their writings, none of the sense of moral and intellectual inferiority that was routinely attributed to women by men and often by women themselves. Women who were in direct spiritual communion with God acquired, as teachers, mediators, and counselors in their communities, power that they simply could not have had outside those settings.

SECTION SUMMARY

- Some men and women who opposed the wealth and immorality of some clerics, and who wished to preach and teach, veered off into heresy.

- The Mendicants—Franciscans and Dominicans, chiefly—led holy lives, worked among the poor or preached against heretics, and always had the approval of the papacy.

- Several religious movements were especially popular among women and constituted the first women's movements in the history of Christianity.

LATIN CULTURE: FROM SCHOOLS TO UNIVERSITIES

What signs do you find of an expanding intellectual climate in high medieval Europe?

As in the late antique and Carolingian periods, courts and churches were the greatest patrons of artists and authors. But in this age of expansion, the number and geographic spread of such patrons increased dramatically. By 1150, the church comprised 50 percent more bishoprics and about three times as many monasteries as it had in 900. In 1300, monarchies reigned in many places—Scandinavia and the Slavic world, for example—where none had existed in 900 (see **MAP 10.1**). In addition to an increase in the sheer amount of cultural activity,

🌐 MAP 10.1—Europe, ca. 1230
By the early thirteenth century, the European states that would exist into modern times were clearly visible, although each would continue to undergo changes. To gain a sense of the evolution of Europe, compare this map with **MAPS 6.1, 7.3,** and **8.3.**

the years between 900 and 1300 also witnessed innovations. Logic replaced grammar at the heart of the school curriculum. Latin letters remained ascendant, but literature in many vernacular (native) languages began to appear in quantity and quality. Romanesque art and architecture were fresh and original interpretations of their Carolingian ancestors. Europe's incipient urbanization produced the first stirrings of a distinctively urban culture. In one of those cities, Paris, a new kind of academic institution emerged—the university—which was arguably the period's greatest legacy to the modern world.

The Carolingian Legacy

Political dislocation and constant attacks in the ninth and tenth centuries initially deprived schools and masters of the Carolingian patronage that they had enjoyed for a century or more. The Carolingians left firm enough foundations in a few centers for intellectual life to continue, but the scale of activity between 900 and 1050 was smaller than before. Three examples serve to capture the spirit of the age that set the stage for the High Middle Ages.

Gerbert of Aurillac (DJAIR-bear of OR-ee-ak) (940–1003) was the most distinguished intellect of his age. He left his home in Aquitaine to study in Spain and Italy before settling in Reims, in northern France, where he was a teacher and then briefly a bishop. He attracted the attention of the emperor Otto III and spent some time at the German court, earning appointments as abbot of Bobbio, bishop of Ravenna, and, finally, pope. Gerbert followed Carolingian tradition in being a collector of manuscripts and critic of texts, but he departed from older traditions in his interest in mathematics and in his study of logic—the formal rules of reasoning that, in the Western tradition, trace back over many thinkers to Aristotle (see page 77–78).

Fulbert of Chartres (FULL-bear of SHART), Gerbert's finest pupil, elevated the cathedral school of Chartres to the paramount place in academic Europe. Fulbert (960–1028) wrote letters in elegant Latin and composed fine poems. He carried on his master's literary interests more than his scientific ones, and well into the twelfth century, Chartres remained a major center of literary studies.

Another figure of interest is the aristocratic German nun Roswitha of Gandersheim (d. 970). She wrote poems on saints and martyrs, as well as a story about a priest who sold his soul to the Devil. In her mature years, Roswitha wrote Latin plays in rhymed verse based on the Roman writer Terence. In these plays, she refashioned tales from Roman and biblical history to convey moral truths.

The Study of Law

Law was a field of major innovation. The increasing sophistication of urban life demanded a better understanding of law. The growing responsibilities of the church called for orderly rules, and the church's frequent quarrels with secular rulers demanded careful delineations of rights and responsibilities. Governments issued more laws and regulations than at any time since antiquity.

In Bologna, Irnerius (d. ca. 1130), a transplanted German and protégé of Emperor Henry V, began teaching Roman law from the Code of Justinian (see pages 186–187). This legal work culminated in the publication in 1140 of the *Decretum* of the Bolognese monk Gratian (GRAY-shun). The most comprehensive and systematic book of **canon law** yet written, Gratian's work remained authoritative for centuries.

> **canon law**　The law of the church (as distinguished from civil law). It is based on papal decrees and the rulings of church councils.

Throughout the twelfth century, canon lawyers studied and wrote commentaries on Gratian's *Decretum*. These legists are called "decretists." Gratian had systematically collected earlier papal *decretals* (official pronouncements), but popes continued to issue them. Several collections of these new decretals were prepared in the thirteenth century, and the scholars who studied these later decrees are called "decretalists." The church thus produced a vast corpus of law and legal commentary.

England was precocious in creating a common law, a single law applied uniformly in its courts. But English law was based on the careful accumulation of legal decisions—or precedents—and not on the routine application of the provisions of a law code. There were many law codes elsewhere. Alfonso X of Castile issued the *Siete Partidas*, a comprehensive law code largely reliant on Roman law. Prince Iaroslav (d. 1054) is reputed to have issued the first version of the laws of Kievan Rus. Byzantine law was revised under the Macedonian dynasty.

Greek, Arab, and Jewish Contributions

Norman and German settlement in southern Italy and Sicily, the Reconquista in Spain, the Crusades, and the creation of Italian communities in many Mediterranean cities brought European thinkers face-to-face with the intellectual traditions of Classical Greece, Islam, and medieval Judaism. Between 1100 and 1270, almost the whole corpus of Aristotle's writings, virtually unknown in the West for a millennium, became available. Arab commentaries on Aristotle, as well as Jewish philosophical and theological works, began to circulate. The presence of all these texts and currents of thought was decisive in expanding the range and raising the level of Western thought.

Prior to about 1100, only a few of Aristotle's writings, primarily some of his early writings on logic, had been available in the West. Gradually, scholars recovered Aristotle's full treatment of logic, then his scientific writings, and finally his studies of ethics and politics. Aristotle's books posed a number of problems for Christian scholars. What relationship exists between the Christian faith and reason? Aristotle taught that the universe is eternal and mechanistic. His thought left no room for creation or for the continuing role of a Creator. For Christian thinkers, Aristotle asked questions that demanded answers: Were the Scriptures true? Did God create the world as Genesis said? Did God continue to intervene in this world?

Two major Arab thinkers were particularly influenced by the vast Aristotelian corpus. Ibn-Sina (980–1037), called Avicenna (ah-vih-SENN-uh) in the West, was drawn to the fundamental problem of how to understand the relationship between objects that exist in the world and the knowledge of those objects that is formed and held in the human mind. (See the feature, "The Global Record: The Making of an Arab Scholar.") Ibn Rushd (1126–1198), called Averroes (uh-VERR-oheese), wrote no fewer than thirty-eight commentaries on the works of Aristotle, and at least fifteen of these were translated into Latin in the thirteenth century. Among many contributions, Averroes particularly tried to clarify the relationship between truths acquired through the exercise of reason and truths that depend on divine revelation. His contemporaries and many later scholars understood him to teach the "double truth": Truths about the natural world are more or less accessible to everyone depending on a person's intellectual ability. Revealed truths, however, are available only to the most enlightened.

Spain and northern France were both important centers of Jewish thought. In Spain, some Jewish thinkers also grappled with Aristotle. Solomon ibn Gebirol (1021–1070), called Avicebron, wrote *The Fountain of Life*, a treatise that attempted to reconcile Aristotle with the Jewish faith by finding a role for God in communicating knowledge to every human mind. The greatest of all medieval Jewish thinkers, Moses ben Maimon (1135–1204), called Maimonides (my-MON-uh-deez), wrote *A Guide for the Perplexed*. The perplexed he had in mind were those who had trouble reconciling the seemingly opposed claims of reason and faith. Maimonides taught a doctrine very close to Averroes's double truth.

Solomon ben Isaac (1040–1105), called Rashi, was educated in Jewish schools in the Rhineland and then set up his own school in Troyes (TWAH). He became the most learned biblical and Talmudic scholar of his time, indeed one of the wisest ever. The Talmud was a detailed and erudite commentary on the scriptural studies of the ancient rabbis. Christian scholars who wished to know the exact meaning of passages in the Bible sometimes consulted Rashi and his successors.

From Persia to Spain to France, then, countless thinkers were engaged in serious reflection on the mechanics of knowing, the nature of reality, the relationship between reason and faith, and the meaning and significance of revelation. In the years just around 1100, Latin Christian scholars began to encounter this torrent of thought and writing.

Muslim Scholars in a Garden From a thirteenth-century Iraqi manuscript, this picture shows literary men in a pleasure garden. Beasts are driving a water wheel to refresh them, and a lute player accompanies their poetry with music. (Bibliothèque nationale de France)

The Development of Western Theology

Carolingian schools had focused on grammar—that is, on the basic foundations of language. Gradually, logic supplanted grammar at the center of both intellectual interests and school curricula. Eventually, the wider application of logic produced a new intellectual style and also evoked bitter criticisms.

Berengar (ca. 1000–1088), master of the school of Tours, wrote a treatise that denied Christ's presence in the Eucharist—the Communion bread and wine received by Catholics and Orthodox Christians in the celebration of the mass. This position was heretical. Ordinarily, churchmen would have refuted Berengar simply by quoting various passages from the Scriptures or from the writings of the Church Fathers, along with conciliar pronouncements about the consecrated elements. Berengar's claim was finally proved false, at least to the satisfaction of his opponents, by Archbishop Lanfranc of Canterbury (1010–1089) who used Aristotelian logical argumentation to dispose of Berengar's heretical arguments.

Anselm (ca. 1033–1109), Lanfranc's successor as archbishop of Canterbury, developed an ingenious logical proof for the existence of God. The French theologian and philosopher Peter

The Making of an Arab Scholar

These excerpts from the engaging life of Avicenna (980–1037) reveal not only his remarkable intellectual attainments but also his ongoing encounter with Greek thought. Avicenna was deeply influenced by Aristotle, and, in turn, his writings influenced Jewish and Christian writers who were also coming to grips with the greatest of Greek philosophers. His writings on medicine were authoritative until the seventeenth century.

My father was from Balkh and moved from there to Bukhārā [now Turkmenistan]…where I was given teachers of the Quran and polite letters [literature, especially poetry]. By the time I was ten years old I had mastered the Quran and so much of polite letters as to provoke wonderment. My father decided to send me to a certain grocer who knew Indian arithmetic so that I could learn it from him. Then Abu Abdallah al-Natili, who claimed to be a philosopher, came to Bukhara. My father lodged him in our house in the hope that I would learn something from him. Before he came I was studying jurisprudence…and I was one of the best pupils. Then, under the guidance of al-Natili, I began to study the *Isagoge* [a commentary on some of Aristotle's works]. Thus I learned from him the broad principles of logic, but he knew nothing of the subtleties. Then I began to read books and study commentaries on my own until I mastered logic. I also read the geometry of Euclid. Then I passed on to the *Almagest* [Ptolemy's second-century astronomical treatise]. Eventually I busied myself with the study of the [treatises] and other commentaries on physics and metaphysics [subjects treated at great length by Aristotle and by Avicenna's Arab predecessors, especially al-Farabi], and the doors of knowledge opened before me. Then I took up medicine and began to read books written on this subject. Medicine is not one of the difficult sciences, and in a very short time I undoubtedly excelled in it, so that physicians of merit studied under me. At the same time I carried on debates and controversies in jurisprudence. At this point I was sixteen years old.

I resumed the study of logic and all parts of philosophy. During this time I never slept a whole night through and I did nothing but study all day long. Whenever I was puzzled by a problem…I would go to the mosque, pray, and ask the Creator of All to reveal to me that which was hidden from me and to make easy for me that which was difficult. Then at night I would return home, put a lamp in front of me, and set to work reading and writing.

I returned to the study of divine science. I read the book called *Metaphysics* [by Aristotle], but could not understand it, the aim of its author remaining obscure for me. I read the book forty times, until I knew it by heart, but I still could not understand its meaning or its purpose. Then one afternoon I happened to be in the market of the booksellers, and a crier was holding a volume in his hand and shouting the price. I bought it and found that it was Abu'l Nasr al-Farabi's book explaining the meaning of the *Metaphysics*. I returned to my house and made haste to read it. Immediately the purposes of this book became clear to me because I already knew it by heart. I was very happy at this, and the next day I gave much alms to the poor in thanksgiving to Almighty God.

In my neighborhood there lived a man who asked me to write him an encyclopedic work on all the sciences. I compiled the *Majmu* for him and named it after him. In it I dealt with all sciences other than mathematics. I was then twenty-one years old.

QUESTIONS

1. In what academic subjects was Avicenna particularly interested?

2. In what ways was Avicenna's education like and unlike that received by students in Europe?

3. How did faith and reason play complementary roles in Avicenna's education?

Source: Bernard Lewis, ed., *Islam: From the Prophet Muhammad to the Capture of Constantinople*, vol. 2, 1974, pp. 177–181. Reprinted by permission of Oxford University Press.

Abelard (1079–1142) used logic to reconcile apparent contradictions in the Scriptures and in the writings of the Church Fathers. Anselm and Abelard were not skeptics. Anselm's motto was "Faith seeking understanding."

For conservatives, such as **Bernard of Clairvaux** (see page 260) and **Hildegard of Bingen** (1098–1179), however, faith and immediate divine inspiration were primary. To them, logical approaches to divine truth were the height of arrogance. Hildegard—well educated, musically gifted, and knowledgeable in medical matters—was perhaps the most profound psychological thinker of her age. More than anyone before her, Hildegard opened up for discussion the feminine aspects of divinity. She, like Bernard, believed that God was to be found deep within the human spirit, not in books full of academic wrangling.

The future lay with Anselm and Abelard, however. Anselm was the most gifted Christian thinker since Augustine. He wrote distinguished works on logic, and his theological treatise, *Why God Became Man* (ca. 1100), served for three hundred years as the definitive philosophical and theological explanation of the incarnation of Christ, the central mystery of the Christian faith.

Bernard of Clairvaux
A church reformer, adviser to rulers, and conservative intellectual who opposed the wide application of logic.

Hildegard of Bingen
A German Benedictine abbess and prolific author.

Peter Abelard was a more colorful figure. He argued rudely and violently with all his teachers, though in the end, he was probably more intelligent than any of them. He rose to a keener understanding of Aristotle than anyone in centuries, and he developed a sharper sense of both the power and the limitations of language than anyone since the Greeks. He concerned himself with ethics, too, and was one of the first writers to see intention as more important than simple action.

Abelard seduced and then secretly married Heloise, one of his pupils and the daughter of an influential Paris churchman. Heloise's relatives castrated Abelard for his refusal to live openly with his wife. Abelard then arranged for Heloise to enter a convent, and he joined a monastic community, where he continued writing and teaching. The two carried on a voluminous correspondence that reveals Heloise as a first-rate philosophical thinker and one of her age's most knowledgeable connoisseurs of Classical literature. Some of Abelard's more imaginative ideas earned him formal ecclesiastical condemnations in 1121 and 1140. He popularized the schools of Paris, however, and attracted to them promising scholars from all over Europe.

Abelard and several of his contemporaries engaged in one of the first widespread intellectual debates in Western history, the quarrel over "universals." *Universal* is the philosophical name for a concept that applies to more than one seemingly related object. To illustrate: May we agree that you are reading a book right now? May we further agree that the book you are reading is not identical to any other book on your bookshelf? And may we go one step further and agree that no book on your bookshelf is exactly like any other book on that shelf? So, why do we call all of these objects books? "Book" is here the universal that we are trying to understand.

A medieval "realist," whose thought may be traced back to Plato, would say that there is a concept, let us call it "bookness," that exists in our minds before we ever encounter any particular object that we label a book. Just as no book is ever identical to any other, so too, no specific book is a perfect representation of that concept "bookness." The concept is fully real, and all representations of it in the world are mere hints, suggestions of a more perfect reality.

A medieval "nominalist," on the contrary, would say that "book" is merely a name (*nomen* in Latin, whence nominalism) that we apply to objects that we deem to bear sufficient similarity to one another that they can be adequately captured by one name. But only each particular book is fully real.

With the emergence of the problem of universals, we enter fully into a new intellectual approach that has long been called "Scholasticism." This word has come to have many different meanings, but at the most basic level, it describes a movement that attempted to show that Christian theology is inherently rational, that faith and reason need not be contradictory or antithetical. Scholasticism also implies a certain systematization of thought. Gratian's attempt to organize all of canon law rationally and systematically was a Scholastic exercise. Twelfth-century biblical scholars tried to produce a single, systematic commentary on the Bible. In 1160, Peter Lombard produced the *Four Books of Sentences*, a comprehensive treatment of all of Christian theology.

Thomas Aquinas (1225–1274) was the greatest of the Scholastics, the most sensitive to Greek and Arab thought, and the most prolific medieval philosopher. A Dominican friar, Thomas was educated at Naples, Cologne, and Paris. Apart from brief service at the papal court, he spent the years after 1252 teaching and writing in Paris. His two most famous works are the *Summa Contra Gentiles* and the *Summa Theologiae*. A *summa* is an encyclopedic compendium of carefully arrayed knowledge on a particular subject. One might think of Gratian's and Peter Lombard's works as precursors to the great summas of the thirteenth century. Thomas's first summa addresses natural truth—that is, the kinds of things that any person can know through the operation of reason. His second summa is a summation of the revealed truths of the Christian faith.

Thomas's works are distinctive for two reasons. First, no one before him had so rigorously followed the dialectical method of reasoning through a whole field of knowledge, not just a particular problem. For thousands of pages, Thomas poses a question, suggests answers, confronts the answers with objections, refutes the objections, and then draws a conclusion. Then, he repeats the process. Second, Thomas carefully distinguishes between two kinds of truths. On the one hand are *natural truths*, truths (even theological ones) that anyone can know (or so Thomas thought)—for example, that God exists. On the other hand are *revealed truths*, truths that can be known (if not understood) only through faith in God's revelation—for example, the Trinity or the incarnation of Christ. Thomas maintains that natural and revealed truths simply cannot contradict one another because God is ultimately the source of both. If a natural truth—for example,

Thomas Aquinas
A Dominican theologian and the greatest of the Scholastics.

summa A compendium of knowledge within a particular field.

Aristotle's contention that the world is eternal—appears to contradict a revealed truth, the natural truth is wrong. Thomas was accused by some contemporaries of applying reason too widely, and after his death some of his ideas were condemned by the church. But he actually steered a middle path between intellectual extremes. In this respect, Thomas was like Maimonides and Averroes.

The University

In the early decades of the twelfth century, students gathered wherever famous teachers might be found. Such teachers—figures like Peter Abelard—clustered in a few centers, and the students congregated there as well. The last decades of the twelfth century saw a swarm of masters and students in Paris. Like members of secular guilds (see page 232), the masters organized. The University of Paris was the result of their efforts. By 1300, universities had formed elsewhere in France, as well as in Italy, England, and western Germany.

Several forces drove masters to organize. They wanted to negotiate with the bishop's chancellor, the traditional head of all schools in an episcopal city. They wanted to regulate the curriculum that students followed and to prescribe the requirements for entry into their own ranks. They also desired to set the fees to be charged for instruction. By 1209, the bishop of Paris, the pope, and the king of France had granted formal recognition to the university.

In Bologna, the university developed a little differently. Here the students came primarily to study law, after already acquiring a basic education. These law students were usually older and more affluent than students elsewhere, and foreign to

The Triumph of St. Thomas This painting by Benozzo Gozzoli (1349) for the church of Santa Caterina in Pisa, Italy, is idealized but still reveals much that is true. Above Thomas are four evangelists and two church fathers; to Thomas's right and left stand Plato and Aristotle; at Thomas's feet Averroes crouches, vanquished. Thomas was seen as the great synthesizer of philosophical and theological knowledge. (Scala/Art Resource, NY)

Bologna. Consequently, in Bologna, the university arose from a guild of students who united to set standards in fees and studies and to protect themselves against unscrupulous masters.

Women and Medicine in Twelfth-Century Salerno

Late in the twelfth century, an anonymous author compiled three lengthy medical texts into one that came to be called the "Trotula." The second of these treatises, "On the Cures of Women," was almost certainly written by a woman named Trota. For centuries, scholars argued that a woman could not have written the widely disseminated Trotula because women could neither study nor teach in the Salerno schools. Absolutely nothing is known about Trota herself, but her text presents an intriguing question: How was she able to acquire vast learning in the Greek, Arab, and Persian medical traditions? Perhaps Trota "practiced" medicine. Whatever the case, most of her text involves either physical appearance or problems connected with menstruation and childbirth. Trota's treatise put her ahead of her time, but just maybe there were other women like her, concealed by ignorance and prejudice.

There are some women who, when they come to their time of menstruation, have either no or very few menses. For these, we proceed thus. Take root of the red willow with which large wine jars are tied and clean them well of the exterior bark, and, having pulverized them, mix them with wine or water and cook them, and in the morning give them in a potion when it has become lukewarm.

To those giving birth with difficulty we give aid in this manner. We should prepare a bath and we put the woman in it, and after she leaves let there be a fumigation of spikenard and similar aromatic substances. For strengthening and for opening the birth canal, let there be sternutatives [substances that induce sneezing] of white hellebore well ground into a powder. For just as Copho [a twelfth-century Salerno medical teacher] says, the organs are shaken and the uterus ruptures and thus the fetus is brought out and comes out.

For making the face red, take root of red and white bryony and clean it and chop it finely and dry it. Afterward, powder it and mix it with rose water, and with cotton or a very fine cloth we anoint the face and it induces redness.

For the woman having a naturally white complexion, we make a red color if she lacks redness, so that with a kind of fake or cloaked whiteness a red color will appear as if it were natural.

For freckles of the face which appear by accident, take root of bistort and reduce it to powder, and cuttlefish bones and frankincense, and from all these things make a powder. And mix with a little water and smear it, rubbing, on the (face) in the morning…until you have removed the freckles.

An ointment for whitening the face. Take two ounces of the very best white lead, let them be ground; afterward let them be sifted through a cloth, and that which remains in the cloth, let it be thrown out. Let it be mixed in with rainwater and let it cook until the consumption of the water, which can be recognized when we see it almost completely dried out. Then let it be cooled. And when it is dried out and cooled, let rose water be added, and again boil it until it becomes hard and thick, so that from it very small pills can be formed. And when you wish to be anointed, take one pill and liquefy it in the hand with water and then rub it well on the face, so that the face will be dried. Then let it be washed with pure water, and this will last for eight days.

QUESTIONS

1. Does it make sense that a medical treatise by a woman would emphasize issues of particular concern to women?

2. Why do you suppose that scholars long refused to believe that a woman could have written this book?

3. Do you detect in Trota's writing evidence of experimental, empirical science?

Source: Monica H. Green, ed. and trans., *The Trotula: A Medieval Compendium of Women's Medicine* (Philadelphia: University of Pennsylvania Press, 2001), pp. 117–119, 139, 141, 163. Reprinted by permission of the University of Pennsylvania Press.

Universities were known for certain specializations: Paris for arts and theology, Bologna for law, Salerno in Italy and Montpellier in France for medicine, Oxford for mathematical and scientific subjects. Still, the basic course of study was similar. At Paris, a young scholar came to the city, found lodgings where he could, and attempted to find a master who would guide him through the arts curriculum. These boys might be in their early teens or several years older, depending on their earlier education and financial resources. The arts course, which was the prerequisite to all higher faculties, usually lasted from four to six years. The bachelor's degree was a license to teach, but a bachelor who wished to teach in a university needed to go on for a master's degree. The master's degree required at least eight years of study (including the baccalaureate years), which culminated in a public oral examination. Some masters went on to become doctors in theology, law, or medicine. A doctorate required ten to fifteen years of study.

Student life was difficult. In many ways, students were always foreigners. Although their presence in a town enhanced its prestige, townspeople exploited them by charging exorbitant prices for food and rent. Students' own behavior was not always above reproach. There was surely some truth in the frequently lodged charge that students were noisy, quarrelsome, given to drinking, and excessively fond of prostitutes. England's Oxford and Cambridge were unique in always providing residential colleges for students; Paris got one later, and the mendicants often established houses of study. Typically, though, students were on their own.

Students had to work very hard. The arts curriculum demanded a thorough acquaintance with all the famous texts of grammar, logic, and rhetoric. Higher studies added more Aristotle, particularly his philosophical writings. In theology, the students had to master the Scriptures, the principal biblical commentaries from patristic times to the present, and the *Four Books of Sentences*. In medicine, the ancient writings of Galen and Hippocrates were supplemented by Arab texts as well as by observation and experimentation.

The basic method of teaching provides yet another definition of Scholasticism—that is, the method of studying in the schools. The teacher started by reciting a short piece of a set text, carried on with the presentation and discussion of many authoritative commentaries on that text, and concluded with his own explanations. The teacher then presented another passage of the set text and repeated the whole process. This education focused on standard books and accepted opinions and required students to remember large amounts of material.

SECTION SUMMARY

- Latin studies in literature, law, theology, and philosophy remained important.

- Europe's expansion brought scholars into increasing contact with ancient Greek, Jewish, and Arab thought.

- The increasing prominence of logic drove theology and philosophy to the center of the curriculum and led to the production of majestic summas.

- Formed as guilds of either masters or students, universities were among the most original and durable medieval achievements.

In principle, universities were open to free men, but in practice, they were restricted to those who had the means to attend them. Women were not accepted at universities, either as students or as teachers. It was generally thought, by men, that learning made women insubordinate. Lacking the required education, women were denied entry into the learned professions of theology, law, and medicine, despite the fact that many rural and some urban medical practitioners were women. Nevertheless, women commonly possessed and transmitted knowledge of both folk remedies and scientific medicine. Trota of Salerno, who probably lived in the twelfth century, wrote a knowledgeable treatise, *On the Care of Women*. (See the feature, "The Written Record: Women and Medicine in Twelfth-Century Salerno.") Documents from medieval Naples record the names of twenty-four women surgeons between 1273 and 1410. How these women were educated is utterly unknown.

THE VERNACULAR ACHIEVEMENT

What were the hallmarks of vernacular culture?

A major achievement of high medieval civilization, from Iceland to Kievan Rus, was the appearance of rich literatures in native tongues. Vernacular, from the Latin *vernaculus*, meaning "home-born" or "domestic," is the name for the languages other than Latin—say, English or French. Although Latin remained the language of the clerical elite, writers of vernacular prose and poetry produced some of the greatest works in Western literature.

Literatures and Languages

The number of people who commanded Latin was always a minority in western Europe, just as native Greek-speakers were a minority in Byzantium. As Latin, beginning in Late Antiquity, slowly evolved into the Romance (from Roman) languages, people who used what eventually became French, Italian, and Spanish had some advantages over the people in Celtic, Germanic, or Slavic lands, where the languages bore no obvious relationship to Latin. Persons who spoke Old French in their towns and villages would have had an easier time learning Latin than people who spoke Irish or Polish. Nevertheless, vernacular literatures began to appear at roughly the same time all over Europe, between about 800 and 1000.

Many writers continued to use Latin for several centuries. University scholars continued to compose their learned treatises in the ancient tongue, but now often in a style that was less ornate than before. Most law books and public documents were still in Latin, but in a "vulgar" Latin that was reasonably close to the vernacular in areas where Romance languages were spoken. Technical manuals—on farming and animal husbandry, on warfare and armaments, or on law and government—were prepared in Latin, too, but again in a style that was far more accessible than that of their ancient models. Popular literature—poetry, history and biography, and romance and adventure—was still often written in Latin. Some of this material was serious, but some breathed a light and carefree spirit. The anonymous German known as the Archpoet (d. 1165) wrote poems about drinking and womanizing. These lines are typical of his work:

In the public house to die
Is my resolution;
Let wine to my lips be nigh
At life's dissolution:
That will make the angels cry,
With glad elocution
"Grant this drunkard, God on high,
Grace and Absolution!"[1]

No less insouciant were the authors of biting satires, such as the anonymous *The Gospel According to the Silver Marks*, which parodies the wealth and greed of the papal curia.

The literary masterpieces of the High Middle Ages are almost entirely written in vernacular languages. The epic poem *Beowulf* is the first classic of English literature. We do not know who wrote it or when it was written. Scholars now usually place it in the ninth or possibly the tenth century. The story focuses on three great battles fought by the hero, Beowulf. The first two are against the monster Grendel and Grendel's mother, who have been harrying the kingdom of an old ally of Beowulf's family; the third is against a dragon. *Beowulf* is a poem of adventure and heroism, of loyalty and treachery. It treats lordship, friendship, and kinship. Themes of good and evil resound throughout. The poem is barely Christian, but nevertheless, deeply moral. It speaks, in a mature, vigorous, and moving language, to and for the heart of a warrior society.

Beowulf is the best-known Anglo-Saxon work but by no means the only one. Several volumes of elegiac and lyric poetry, mostly on religious themes, also survive. And Anglo-Saxon writers produced chronicles, legal materials and charters, and at least one large collection of homilies.

Some fragments of poetry in Old French survive from the ninth century, but the great *chansons de geste* ("songs of deeds," or celebrations of the great) appeared in the eleventh century. Undoubtedly, they were transmitted orally for a long time before they were written down. The best is the *Song of Roland*, written around 1100. In 778, as Charlemagne's army was returning from Spain, Basques raided the baggage train and killed Count Roland. By 1100, this obscure event, long kept alive in oral traditions, had been transformed into a heroic struggle between Charlemagne and his retinue and an army of countless thousands of "paynim," who are crude caricatures of Muslims.

Like *Beowulf*, the *Song of Roland* is a story about loyalty and treachery, bravery in the face of insuperable odds, and the kindness and generosity of leaders. Both take us into a man's chivalric world, where females are all but absent. The two works do not show us personal hopes, fears, or motivations. What pours forth is the communal ethos and the dominant values of the elite, male social group. Although *Beowulf* is lightly clothed in Christianity, the *Song of Roland* is thickly vested in the faith.

Southern France, in the middle and late twelfth century, added something new to Western literature: the love lyrics of the troubadours. This poetry, composed by both men and women, profoundly influenced an age and created the literary movement that has long been called "courtly love." **Chivalry** was initially a code for men interacting with other men. In the world of courtly love, chivalry became an elaborate set of rules governing relations between men and women.

Courtly love had several sources. The classical poet Ovid (43 B.C.–A.D. 17?), who wrote *The Art of Love*, a manual of seduction, was one. Another was the lyrical poetry of Muslim Spain. Ironically, feudal values such as loyalty and service played a critical role as men became, in effect, love vassals. Platonic ideas made some contribution, too, particularly the notion that

chivalry Beginning as the dominant ethos of the warrior-nobility, it changed into rules governing relations between men and women.

any love in this world could be only a pale imitation of real love. The courtly poets sang of *fin' amours*, a pure love in contrast to the mere lust of the masses. A lover cherished an unattainable lady. He would do anything for the merest display of pleasure or gratitude on her part, as we see in these lines from Bernart de Ventadorn, court poet of the counts of Toulouse in the late twelfth century:

> *Down there, around Ventadorn, all my friends*
> *have lost me, because my lady does not love me;*
> *and so, it is right that I never go back there again,*
> *because always she is wild and morose with me.*
> *Now here is why the face she shows me is gloomy and full of anger:*
> *because my pleasure is in loving her and I have settled down to it.*
> *She is resentful and complains for no other reason.*[2]

Male troubadours placed women on pedestals and, in ballads, worshiped them from afar. Women troubadours took a different line. Women's poems were more realistic, human, and emotionally satisfying. Castellozza (KAHS-teh-lohtz-eh) (b. ca. 1200), the southern French wife of a Crusader, idealized not at all when she wrote these lines:

> *Friend, if you had shown consideration,*
> *meekness, candor and humanity,*
> *I'd have loved you without hesitation,*
> *but you were mean and sly and villainous.*

And she did not assign the active role exclusively to the man:

> *Handsome friend, as a lover true*
> *I loved you, for you pleased me*
> *But now I see I was a fool*
> *for I've barely seen you since.*[3]

Count William IX of Poitou (1071–1127) was among the first of the troubadours, and his daughter, Eleanor of Aquitaine, brought the conventions of this poetry and point of view to the French and Angevin courts. She and her daughters were the greatest literary patrons of the late twelfth century. The wives of kings and nobles, who were frequently away from home, maintained stunning courts and cultivated vernacular literature.

The courtly literature of northern France broke new ground in both forms and content. The romance and the lay were the chief new forms. Both drew on Classical literature, the heroic Germanic past, and the Arthurian legends of the Celtic world to create stories of love and adventure. The romance usually develops a complex narrative involving several major characters over a long time. The lay is brief and focuses on a single incident. The most famous twelfth-century writer of romance was Chrétien de Troyes (1135–1183), the court writer of Marie of Champagne, the daughter of Eleanor of Aquitaine. The greatest writer of lays was Marie de France, who wrote at the Angevin court in the 1170s.

The romances and lays explore the contradictions and tensions in a variety of human relationships. Loyalty and honor make frequent appearances. Lancelot, a paragon of knightly virtue, desperately loves his lord Arthur's wife, Guinevere. What is he to do? How can he be loyal to his lord, to his love, and to himself? What will he do when a single course of action brings both honor and dishonor? In the epics, speeches are made to swords, to horses, or sometimes to no one in particular; the points being made are universalized. In the romances, credible human beings struggle to resolve powerful and conflicting emotional and moral dilemmas.

France led the way in the production of vernacular literature, but French models did not inspire slavish imitation. This is seen most clearly in the work of the master of all vernacular writers, Dante Alighieri (DAHN-tay ah-lih-GYAIR-ee). Dante (1265–1321) began as a poet in *la dolce stil nuova*, "the sweet new style," which came from France and captivated Italians. But he moved beyond it in many ways. Dante was a man of extraordinarily wide learning and reading. He is best known for one of the masterpieces of world literature, *The Divine Comedy*.

The secret of the *Comedy*'s success is not easy to grasp. It is a long and difficult poem, but it is also humorous, instructive, and moving. In an exquisitely beautiful Italian, Dante took the most advanced theology and philosophy of his time, the richest poetic traditions, a huge hoard of stories, many contemporary events, and a lot of common sense and wove them into an allegorical presentation of the journey of the whole human race and of the individual lives of all people.

Accompanied by the Roman poet Virgil (see page 143), Dante travels through Hell and Purgatory, commenting along the way on the condition of the people he meets. Then, because Virgil is a pagan and only Dante's true love can accompany Dante into Paradise, Beatrice, the love of Dante's youth, joins him for a visit to Heaven. The poet's central metaphor is love; the love he feels for Beatrice symbolizes the love God feels for the world. Dante canvasses humanity from the pits of Hell, which he reserved for traitors, to the summit of Paradise, where a man inspired by pure love might, despite his sinfulness, dare to look into the face of God.

Although the romances and lays were by no means the exclusive preserve of the elite, very little is known about popular literature. Two exceptions are the mystery play and women's devotional writing. Mystery plays made their first appearance in the eleventh century. The liturgy of the church, which formally reenacted the life of Christ, was confined to the clergy. But this limitation did not prevent troupes of actors from staging, on church porches or village greens, scenes from the life of Christ in simple, direct language. Such plays served as both a form of popular entertainment and a device for teaching elementary Christian ideas. The female religious movements of the age gave rise to works in the vernacular. Mechtild of Magdeburg (1210–1280), a German Beguine, wrote *The Flowering Light of Divinity*, a mystical, allegorical account of the marriage between God and a spiritual woman. The vernaculars opened avenues of expression to women, who were normally denied Latin learning.

Innovations in Architecture

Romanesque, "in the Roman style," is a term that was coined in the nineteenth century to characterize the architecture and, to a lesser extent, the painting of the period between the waning of Carolingian art and the full emergence of **Gothic** art in the late twelfth century. Today, scholars view the Romanesque style as a transition between Carolingian and Gothic.

At several places in Ottonian Germany, a return of political stability led to the construction of churches. Ducal dynasties and women of the imperial family were among the most generous patrons. The Germans developed a distinctive architectural style marked by very thick walls, alternating piers and columns in the nave, and galleries. As this architectural style spread all over Europe in the eleventh century, it produced true Romanesque, a style that differed from Roman and Carolingian styles, mainly in the greater internal height and space made possible by vaulting (see **FIGURE 10.1**). To the rectangular elegance of the classical basilica and the height of the Carolingian westworks (see page 219), Romanesque builders added a refined verticality. Among the distinctive features of Romanesque churches were their wall paintings and frescoes, sculpture, reliquaries, pulpits, and baptisteries—in short, their exuberant decoration and ornament.

It is surely no coincidence that Gothic art and architecture emerged just as the West was absorbing the rediscovery of Euclid's mathematical writings and applying the intensely ordered logic of Aristotle to everything from legal problems to theological mysteries. One of the most familiar images of the Middle Ages is the inspiringly beautiful Gothic cathedral. It is thus ironic that the word *Gothic* first appeared in the sixteenth century as a term of derision for what was then regarded as an outmoded style so ugly that only the horrible conquerors of Rome, the Goths, could have been responsible for it. The name stuck, but today, it simply identifies a period in European architecture, sculpture, and painting that began in the middle of the twelfth century and that in some places lasted until the early sixteenth century.

Gothic is a French invention. It was Abbot Suger (SOO-jhay) (1085–1151) of Saint-Denis, a monastery outside Paris, who, in rebuilding his basilica beginning in 1135, consciously sought a new style. He desired to achieve effects of lightness, almost weightlessness, in the stonework of his church and to admit large amounts of light to create a dazzling and mysterious aura on the inside. The

Romanesque The name assigned to architecture "in the Roman style" that dominated the period from about 900 to 1150.

Gothic The name assigned to the architecture that emerged in twelfth-century France, spread all over Europe, and dominated construction until the fifteenth century.

 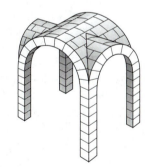

Barrel vault **Groin vault**

■ **FIGURE 10.1—The Structure of Romanesque Architecture**

The basic structural element of Romanesque architecture was the barrel vault, which, when two were joined at right angles, formed a groin vault. These vaults produced great height and strength but gave buildings a massive, fortresslike appearance.

(Source: Anne Shaver-Crandell, *The Middle Ages*. Copyright © 1982 Cambridge University Press. Reprinted with permission of Cambridge University Press.)

Romanesque Interior, Saint Sernin, Toulouse The interior space of Saint Sernin is elegant, high, and well-ordered. But its typical Romanesque effect—from "barrel" vaulting—is that of a tunnel. Massive piers support the gallery and roofing above. (Éditions Gaud)

Bible often uses images of light to refer to God, and Suger wished to give expression to those images in the house of God for which he was responsible.

Suger produced something startlingly original by combining a number of elements that had long been in use—three in particular: A *pointed arch* is more elegant than a round one; it also permits the joining of two arches of identical height but different widths, which, in turn, permits complex shapes and sizes (see **FIGURE 10.2**). The *ribbed vault* is lighter and more graceful than the barrel and groin vaults characteristic of Romanesque architecture; it also exerts less stress and facilitates experimentation with shapes. Finally, *point support*—basically, the support of structural elements at only certain points—permits the replacement of heavy, stress-bearing walls with curtains of stained glass. (See the feature, "The Visual Record: Stained Glass.")

The points of support might be massive internal piers or intricate skeletal frameworks, called *buttresses*, on the outside of the church. These three elements—pointed arch, ribbed vault, and point support—produce a building that is characterized by verticality and translucency. The desired effect is one of harmony, order, and mathematical precision.

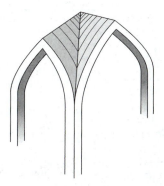

■ FIGURE 10.2—The Structure of Gothic Architecture

The adoption of pointed arches, an import from the Islamic world, let Gothic builders join structures of identical height but different widths (something that barrel and groin vaulting could not do; see Figure 10.1 on page 281). The resulting structures were high, light, airy, and visually interesting.

(Source: Anne Shaver-Crandell, *The Middle Ages.* Copyright © 1982 Cambridge University Press. Reprinted with permission of Cambridge University Press.)

Gothic Interior, Chartres Cathedral   Looking down the early-thirteenth-century nave of Chartres Cathedral provides an opportunity to visualize each of the major building components of Gothic architecture: pointed arch, ribbed vault, point support. The desired verticality is evident.   (Éditions Gaud)

Stained Glass

To walk into one of Europe's great churches is to enter a realm of mystery and beauty produced by the play of light—the brilliant light of the morning sun, the softer glow of the evening sun, the muted tones of a cloudy day—on thousands of square feet of colored glass. This mystery and beauty were created intentionally in Europe in the High Middle Ages. But the magnificent surviving medieval windows are not important solely for their beauty. Their images provide unique and crucial insights into religious and secular life.

Pictured here are two thirteenth-century cathedral windows. The one from Canterbury depicts that city's great bishop and martyr, Thomas Becket. A large window at Chartres depicts Saint Lubin, a sixth-century bishop of the city who was the patron saint of the town's inn and tavern keepers, and Noah, according to the Bible the first planter of grapevines. Here, in a window donated by the vintners guild, we see barrels of wine being hauled to market.

Many of Canterbury's windows represent aspects of the life of the murdered archbishop. The one pictured here shows Thomas as a bishop, not as a martyr. He is wearing a miter, the traditional headgear of a bishop. He also wears a *pallium*, a white wool band sent to a new archbishop by the pope. Becket's vestments are green, the most common liturgical color of the religious year (others were white, purple, and red). This window, then, would have served to remind people of their beloved bishop as he was in life, not martyrdom.

In Chartres, wine was important to the church because of its use in mass, and it was also a staple of the local economy. Accordingly, the vintners are portrayed in twenty-three of this window's forty-one panels. By comparison, most guilds are depicted only once in the windows they donated. These windows remind us, as they reminded contemporaries, of how these magnificent buildings fitted into the daily life of their communities. Religious devotions and secular preoccupations blended in one spot.

Glass is made by heating silica, found naturally in sand, flint, and quartz, to a very high temperature and then fusing the molten silicate with a borate or phosphate, often obtained from ashes produced by burning natural substances. Colored glass was made by adding metal oxides to the molten mixture. Iron oxide produced red, copper oxide produced green, and cobalt produced blue. Such glass, called "pot glass," tended to be opaque, obviously unsuitable for windows. To achieve greater translucency, glassmakers made "flashed glass" by fusing at low temperatures a layer of colored liquid to the

Canterbury, Thirteenth-Century Window: Thomas Becket (Sonia Halliday Photographs)

surface of a panel of clear glass. Although fine glass vessels were made in a number of places, notably in Venice and the Rhineland, the large sheets of colored glass used for church windows were commonly manufactured in Lorraine and Normandy.

To make a stained glass window, a master glazier first drew a cartoon—a sort of rough draft—on a flat board, or perhaps on a piece of parchment. He then cut pieces of

Chartres, Thirteenth-Century Window: Story of Saint Lubin (© Clive Hicks)

colored glass into various irregular shapes according to his design. To produce facial features, folds in garments, or other details, the glazier painted the inner sides of the colored glass pieces with dark-colored paints and then fired them at low temperatures to produce an enamel-like effect. You can see this patina on Thomas's face. Once the glazier had all his pieces cut and placed, he joined them together by means of lead strips that were H shaped. If you look closely, you can see the pieces of glass, lead stripping, and painted details in the images on these pages. The whole picture was then fitted into a metal frame and mounted in a window opening.

Documents first mention the use of glass in church windows in the sixth century. The oldest surviving fragments of stained glass date from the ninth century, and the oldest complete windows from around 1100. With large Romanesque churches, and even more with the huge Gothic churches, came opportunities to use more and more glass. First, the greater height of Romanesque buildings meant that tall windows could be placed high up in the nave walls. Then, the structural innovations of Gothic architecture that removed stress, and hence stone, from the walls permitted them to become vast expanses of glass. Chartres Cathedral has 176 windows. Many high medieval churches had windows more than 50 feet high.

So far, we have looked at *how* medieval Europeans created stained glass and incorporated it into their greatest churches. But *why* did they undertake such time-consuming and costly decoration? Suger, the scholarly twelfth-century abbot of Saint-Denis outside Paris who rebuilt his basilica in the Gothic style, spoke of the spiritual force of his new glass windows:

> When…the loveliness of the many-colored gems has called me away from external cares…then it seems to me that I see myself dwelling in some strange region of the universe which neither exists entirely in the slime of the earth nor entirely in the purity of heaven; and that, by the grace of God, I can be transported from this inferior to that higher world.*

In the Greek philosophers, the Bible, and the Church Fathers, light always represents one way of imagining the unimaginable reality of God. For Suger and his contemporaries, the luminous effect of stained glass suggested the very presence of God. Earthquakes, fires, and wars have destroyed most of the glass that was installed in the Middle Ages. Today's visitor to Europe views more or less valid nineteenth-century reconstructions, except at Canterbury in England and Chartres in France, where almost all of the original glass survives. Usually medieval churches were laid out on an east-west axis. The western façade was normally pierced by tall "lancet" windows and by a single "rose" window. These windows typically portrayed scenes from the life of Christ and/or the Virgin Mary. The northern aisle windows usually contained Old Testament scenes, the southern windows New Testament scenes.

Stained glass played a key role, alongside sculpture, preaching, and churchyard dramas, in communicating the faith to ordinary people. Seldom has a teaching tool been so beautiful. Scholars also speak of stained glass as "painting with glass." Indeed, the art form most like stained glass is painting, especially the painting of illuminations on the pages of manuscripts.

QUESTIONS

1. How was stained glass made and assembled into windows?
2. What kinds of subjects were depicted on stained glass windows?
3. Who was the audience for stained glass windows?

---

*Suger, *De rebus in administratione sua gestis*, ed. E. Panofsky, 2d ed. (Princeton, N.J.: Princeton University Press, 1979), pp. 63–65.

SECTION SUMMARY

- Vernacular literature spread quickly and widely in high medieval Europe.

- Vernacular literature produced *chansons de geste*, romances, lays, sagas, and poetry.

- The High Middle Ages saw the full flowering of Romanesque architecture and then its eclipse by the Gothic style.

The thirteenth century was the most mature period for French Gothic architecture and also the time when Gothic spread most widely throughout Europe. Its popularity may be attributed to the superiority of French masons and stonecutters and also to the tremendous prestige of French culture. By 1300, distinctive Gothic traditions shaped the urban landscape in almost all parts of Europe from Iceland to Poland.

CHAPTER SUMMARY

Comparisons between the Europe of 900 and the Europe of 1300 are instructive both as reminders of what had happened and as suggestions of what was to come. In 900, Carolingian Europe was being attacked on every side. By 1300, Europe was vastly larger than in Carolingian times; not only was its geography greater, but it also had expanded in economic, political, military, and cultural terms.

FOCUS QUESTIONS

- Into what principal social groups were the people of high medieval Europe organized?

- Why did some spiritual movements result in heresy, while others ended in new religious orders?

- What signs do you find of an expanding intellectual climate in high medieval Europe?

- What were the hallmarks of vernacular culture?

At least among the elite, society was divided into "those who pray," "those who fight," and "those who work." Constant waves of monastic reform modeled good spiritual behavior, and monks thought of themselves as society's natural leaders. Bishops embraced reform, too, but as they were often nobles, their views were more flexible than those held by monks. They also saw themselves as leaders. Warrior-nobles *were* the governing class, marked by chivalry, their distinctive ethos that emphasized prowess, courage, loyalty, and generosity. Peasants did much of the "work" in medieval society and generally found the conditions of their lives improving. Townspeople enjoyed expanding opportunities but always suffered under the prejudices of landholding elites. In religious life, urban occupations, and rural pursuits, women experienced some improvements in their conditions of life but always faced legal and social prejudices. The condition of Europe's Jews grew progressively dangerous.

The High Middle Ages saw the birth of powerful religious movements. Some men and women who opposed the wealth and immorality of some clerics, and who wished to preach and teach, veered off into heresy. The Mendicants—Franciscans and Dominicans, chiefly—led holy and blameless lives, worked among the poor or preached against heretics, and always had the approval of the papacy. Several religious movements were especially popular among women and constituted the first exclusively women's movements in the history of Christianity.

Latin studies in literature, law, theology, and philosophy remained important. Europe's expansion brought scholars into increasing contact with ancient Greek, Jewish, and Arab thought, which spurred new research and opened new questions. The increasing prominence of logic drove theology and philosophy to the center of the curriculum and led to the production of majestic summas, compendiums of knowledge in various fields. Formed as guilds of either masters or students, universities were among the most original and durable medieval achievements.

Vernacular literature, literature in "native" languages, spread quickly and widely in high medieval Europe, achieving visibility and prominence everywhere. Vernacular literature was written in many genres: *chansons de geste*, romances, lays, sagas, and poetry. The High Middle Ages saw the full flowering of Romanesque architecture and then its eclipse by Gothic. Magnificent cathedrals are testimony to the prosperity and pride of high medieval Europe.

KEY TERMS

Cluny (p. 260)

Francis of Assisi (p. 268)

Dominic de Guzman
 (p. 269)

canon law (p. 272)

Bernard of Clairvaux
 (p. 274)

Hildegard of Bingen
 (p. 274)

Thomas Aquinas (p. 275)

summa (p. 275)

chivalry (p. 279)

Romanesque (p. 281)

Gothic (p. 281)

 This icon will direct you to additional materials on the website: www .cengage.com/history/ noble/westciv6e.

e **See our interactive eBook for map and primary source activities.**

NOTES

1. John Addington Symonds, *Wine, Women and Song: Medieval Latin Students' Songs* (reprint, New York: Cooper Square, 1966), p. 69.

2. From *Lyrics of the Troubadours and Trouvères,* translated by Frederick Goldin, copyright © 1973 by Frederick Goldin. Used by permission of Doubleday, a division of Random House, Inc

3. From lyrics by Castellozza in *The Women Troubadeurs* by Meg Bogin, (W.W. Norton, 1976). Copyright © 1976 by Magda Bogin. Reprinted by permission of Magda Bogin.

11

A Time of Judgment

On this cover for a fifteenth-century government account book, symbols of death—arrows, a scythe, and a horse—carry the angel of death from place to place. (Bildarchiv Preussischer Kulturbesitz/Art Resource, NY)

Crisis and Recovery in Late Medieval Europe, 1300–1500

In the fourteenth century, Europeans sang an old Franciscan hymn, "Day of Wrath, Day of Burning." Its verses described the fear and disorder that would accompany the end of the world and God's judgment of the saved and the damned. That hymn could well have been in the mind of the painter of the facing illustration. When countless Europeans, such as these poor souls beneath the winged angel of death, fell victim to epidemic disease, many people thought they knew why. The illustrator seems to believe it was God's judgment against sinners, including these gamblers sickened by the angel's plague-tipped arrows. The flood, fire, and pestilence that ravaged late medieval Europe were thought to be premonitions of the breakdown of the world and a time of judgment.

FOCUS QUESTIONS

- How did the Great Schism change the church and the papacy?

- What forces limited the political power of rulers in England, France, and Italy?

- How were economic and social structures changed by plague and economic crisis?

- How did the political makeup of Europe in 1500 differ from that in 1300?

The late Middle Ages (ca. 1300–1500) are often described as a period of continued crisis and decline that put an end to the growth and expansion of the previous three centuries. In truth, however, the years of crisis in the fourteenth and early fifteenth centuries gave way to a dramatic economic, social, and political recovery in the fifteenth century. The cultural and intellectual changes that accompanied the crisis and recovery are the focus of Chapter 12, "The Renaissance."

Military, political, religious, economic, and social crises burdened Europe in the fourteenth and early fifteenth centuries. Between 1337 and 1453, France and England fought a war that touched most of the states of western Europe. The Hundred Years' War, as it has come to be known, was fought primarily over English claims to traditionally French lands. Aristocrats in many parts of Europe challenged the hereditary rights of their rulers. In the towns of Germany and Italy, patrician classes moved to reduce the influence of artisans and laborers in government, instituting oligarchies or even aristocratic lordships in place of more democratic governments.

Questions of power and representation also affected the Christian church as ecclesiastical claims to authority came under attack. Secular governments challenged church jurisdictions. Disputed papal elections led to the so-called Great Schism, a split between rival centers of control in Rome and Avignon (a city in what is now the south of France). In the aftermath of the crisis, the papacy was forced to redefine its place in both the religious life and the political life of Europe.

A series of economic and demographic shocks worsened these political and religious difficulties. Part of the problem was structural: The population of Europe had grown too large to be supported by the resources available. Famine and the return of the plague in 1348 sent the economy into long-term decline. In almost every aspect of political, religious,

This icon will direct you to additional materials on the website: www.cengage.com/history/noble/westciv6e.

See our interactive eBook for map and primary source activities.

and social life, then, the fourteenth and early fifteenth centuries marked a pause in the growth and consolidation that had characterized the earlier medieval period.

Yet, out of the crises, a number of significant changes emerged. By 1500, the European population and economy were again expanding. England and France emerged strengthened by military and political conflicts, and the consolidation of the Spanish kingdoms, the Ottoman Empire, and the states of eastern Europe altered the political and social makeup of Europe. None of the transformations could have been predicted in 1300, as Europe entered a religious, political, and social whirlwind.

THE CRISIS OF THE WESTERN CHRISTIAN CHURCH

How did the Great Schism change the church and the papacy?

Early in the fourteenth century, the king of France attempted to kidnap the pope. His act initiated a series of crises that challenged traditional ideas about church government and the role of the church in the various countries of Europe. First, the popes and their entourages abandoned their traditional residences in central Italy and moved to Avignon, an imperial enclave in the south of modern France. Then, in the wake of a disputed election, two and later three rivals claimed the papal throne. Simultaneously, the church hierarchy faced challenges from radical reformers who wished to change it. At various times, all the European powers became entangled in the problems of the church. In the wake of the crisis, the papacy realized that it needed a stronger, independent base. Papal recovery in the fifteenth century was predicated on political autonomy in central Italy.

The Babylonian Captivity, 1309–1377

The Christian church was in turmoil as a result of an attack on Pope Boniface VIII (r. 1294–1303) by King Philip IV (r. 1285–1314) of France. The king attempted to kidnap Boniface, intending to try him for heresy because of the pope's challenges to the king's authority within his own kingdom. The outstanding issues revolved around the powers of the pope and the responsibilities of the clergy to political leaders. It was, in fact, largely because of tensions with the northern kingdoms that the French archbishop of Bordeaux (bor-DOE) was elected Pope Clement V (r. 1305–1314). Clement chose to remain north of the Alps in order to seek an end to warfare between France and England and to protect, to the extent possible, the wealthy religious order of the Knights of the Temple, or Templars (see page 261), which Philip was in the process of suppressing. After the death of Boniface, it was clear that the governments of Europe had no intention of recognizing papal political authority as absolute.

Clement's pontificate marked the beginning of the so-called Babylonian Captivity, a period from 1309 to 1378, when popes resided almost continuously outside of Italy. In 1309, Clement moved the papal court to Avignon, on the Rhône River in a region that was still part of the Holy Roman Empire—the name that, by the fourteenth century, was given to the medieval empire whose origin reached back to Charlemagne.

The papacy and its new residence in Avignon became a major religious, diplomatic, and commercial center. The size of the court changed as dramatically as its venue: Although the thirteenth-century papal administration required only two hundred or so officials, the bureaucracy in Avignon grew to about six hundred. It was not just the pope's immediate circle that expanded the population of Avignon. Artists, writers, lawyers, and merchants from across Europe were drawn to the new center of administration and hub of patronage. Papal administrators intervened actively in local ecclesiastical affairs, and the pope's revenues from annates (generally a portion of the first year's revenues from an ecclesiastical office granted by papal letter), court fees, and provisioning charges continued to grow.

Not everyone approved of this situation. It was the Italian poet and philosopher Francesco Petrarch (1304–1374) who first referred to the Avignon move as a **Babylonian Captivity of the Papacy**.

Babylonian Captivity of the Papacy Term used to describe the period from 1309 to 1378 when popes resided outside of Italy, relating the pontificate's move to the period when the tribes of Israel lived in exile.

Recalling the account in the Hebrew Bible of the exile of the Israelites and New Testament images of Babylon as the center of sin and immorality, he complained of

> [an] unholy Babylon, Hell on Earth, a sink of iniquity, the cesspool of the world. There is neither faith, nor charity, nor religion. . . . [1]

Two of the most vigorous critics were Saint Catherine of Siena (1347–1380) and Saint Bridget of Sweden (1303–1373). They were part of a remarkable flowering of religious feeling among women who were strong moral critics within their communities. Unlike others, Catherine and Bridget left their homes and neighborhoods and led the call for religious reform and a return of the papacy to Rome.

The Great Schism, 1378–1417

In 1377, Pope Gregory XI (r. 1370–1378) bowed to critics' pressure and did return to Rome. He was shocked by what he found: churches and palaces in ruin and the city violent and dangerous. By the end of 1377, he had resolved to retreat to Avignon, but he died before he could flee Rome. During a tumultuous election, the Roman populace entered the Vatican Palace and threatened to break into the conclave itself, demanding that there be an Italian pope. The subsequent election of the archbishop of Bari, Urban VI (r. 1378–1389), was soon challenged by dissidents who then elected a French cardinal who took the name Clement VII (r. 1378–1394). The church now had two popes.

After some hesitation, Western Christians divided into two camps, initiating the **Great Schism** (SKIZ-em), a period of almost forty years during which no one knew for sure who was the true pope. This was a deadly serious issue for all. The true pope had the right to appoint church officials, decide important moral and legal issues, and allow or forbid taxation of the clergy by the state.

The crisis gave impetus to new discussions about church government: Should the pope be considered the sole head of the church? Debates within the church followed lines of thought already expressed in the towns and kingdoms of Europe. Representative bodies—the English Parliament, the French Estates General, the Swedish Riksdag (RIX-dog)—already claimed the right to act for the realm, and in the city-states of Italy, ultimate authority was thought to reside in the body of citizens. Canon lawyers and theologians similarly argued that authority resided in the whole church, which had the right and duty to come together in council to correct and reform the church hierarchy. Even the most conservative of these **conciliarists** agreed that the "universal church" had the right to respond in periods of heresy or schism. More radical conciliarists argued that the pope as bishop of Rome was merely the first among equals in the church hierarchy and that he, like any other bishop, could be corrected by a gathering of his peers—that is, by an ecumenical council.

The rival popes resisted international pressure to end the schism. In exasperation, the cardinals, the main ecclesiastical supporters of the rival popes, called a general council in Pisa, which deposed both popes and elected a new one. Since the council lacked the power to force the rivals to accept deposition, the result was that three men now claimed to be the rightful successor of Saint Peter. Conciliarists, by themselves, could not mend the split in the church.

Resolution finally came when the Holy Roman emperor Sigismund (r. 1411–1437) forced the diplomatically isolated third papal claimant, John XXIII (r. 1410–1415), to call a general council of the church. The council, which met from 1414 to 1418 in the German imperial city of Constance, could never have succeeded without Sigismund's support. At one point, he forced the council to remain in session even after Pope John had fled the city in an attempt to end deliberations.

CHRONOLOGY	
1303	Pope Boniface VIII attacked at Anagni and dies
1305	Election of Pope Clement V
1309	Clement V moves papal court to Avignon; beginning of Babylonian Captivity
1337	Beginning of Hundred Years' War between England and France
1348–1351	Black Death
1356	German emperor issues Golden Bull
1378	Great Schism
1381	English Rising
1397	Union of Kalmar unites Denmark, Norway, and Sweden
1410	Battle of Tannenberg
1414–1418	Council of Constance
1415	Battle of Agincourt
1420	Treaty of Troyes
1431	Execution of Joan of Arc
1438	Pragmatic Sanction of Bourges
1453	End of the Hundred Years' War Ottoman Turks conquer Constantinople
1469	Marriage of Ferdinand and Isabella unites kingdoms of Aragon and Castile
1480	Ivan III ends Tatar overlordship of Moscow
1485	Tudor dynasty established in England
1492	Spanish conquest of Granada Jews expelled from Spanish lands Columbus commissioned to discover new lands
1494	Charles VIII invades Italy

Great Schism The period from 1378 to 1417 when there were two and eventually three claimants to the papal throne.

conciliarists People who argued that the pope was merely "the first among equals" and that therefore a council of church leaders could correct or discipline a pope.

Gregory XI Returns to Rome   This highly stylized painting conveys the hopes of European Christians when Gregory XI returned from Avignon in 1377. Saint Catherine of Siena, who had pleaded for the pope's return, is seen in the foreground.   (Scala/Art Resource, NY)

Heresy and the Council of Constance, 1414–1418

Sigismund hoped that a council could help him heal deep religious and civil divisions in Bohemia, the most important part of his family's traditional lands (see **Map 11.3**). Far from healing religious division, however, the actions of the council exacerbated tensions in central Europe and created a climate of religious distrust that poisoned relations for more than a century. Bohemia and its capital, Prague, were Czech-speaking. Prague was also the seat of the Luxemburg dynasty of German emperors and the site of the first university in German or Slavic lands. Religious and theological questions quickly became entangled with the competing claims of Czech and German factions. The preaching and teaching of the Czech reformer **Jan Hus** (ca. 1370–1415) were at the center of the debate. As preacher in the Bethlehem Chapel in Prague from 1402 and eventually as rector of the university, Hus was the natural spokesman for the non-German townspeople in Prague and the Czech faction at the university. His criticisms of the

Jan Hus   Czech reformer who attacked clerical privileges and advocated church reform. He was executed as a heretic at the Council of Constance in 1415.

church hierarchy, which in Prague was primarily German, fanned into flames the smoldering embers of Czech national feeling. It was Sigismund's hope that a council might clarify the orthodoxy of Hus's teachings and heal the rift within the church of Bohemia.

The council's response to the theological crisis was based on the church's experience with heresy over the previous forty years, primarily the teachings of John Wyclif (1329–1384). In the 1370s, Wyclif, an Oxford theologian and parish priest, began to criticize in increasingly angry terms the state of the clergy and the abuses of the church hierarchy. By 1387, his ideas had been declared heretical and his followers were hunted out. Wyclif believed that the church could be at once a divine institution and an earthly gathering of individuals. Thus, in his opinion, individual Christians need not unquestioningly obey the pronouncements of the church hierarchy. Final authority lay only in the Scriptures, insisted Wyclif, who sponsored the first translations of the Bible into English. He gathered about himself followers called "Lollards," who emphasized Bible reading and popular piety; some even supported public preaching by women. According to one disciple, "Every true man and woman being in charity is a priest."[2]

Wyclif's influence continued on the Continent, especially in the circle of Jan Hus and the Czech reformers. By 1403, the German majority in the university had condemned Hus's teaching as Wycliffite, thus initiating almost a decade of struggle between Czechs and Germans, Hussites and Catholics. This was the impasse that Sigismund hoped the **Council of Constance** could settle. Accordingly, he offered a suspicious Hus a safe conduct pass to attend the council. The council, however, revoked the pledge of safe conduct and ordered Hus to recant his beliefs. He refused and the council condemned him as a heretic and burned him at the stake on July 6, 1415.

Far from ending Sigismund's problems with the Bohemians, the actions of the council provided the Czechs with a martyr and hero. The execution of Hus provoked a firestorm of revolution in Prague. Czech forces roundly defeated an imperial army sent in to restore order. The Hussite movement gathered strength and spread throughout Bohemia. Moderate Hussites continued Hus's campaign against clerical abuses and claimed the right to receive both the bread and the wine during the sacrament of Communion. Radical Hussites argued that the true church was the community of spiritual men and women; they had no use for ecclesiastical hierarchy of any kind. The German emperors were unable to defeat a united Hussite movement. In 1433, a new church council and moderate Hussites negotiated an agreement that allowed the Hussites to continue some of their practices, including receiving both bread and wine at Communion, while returning to the church. Radical Hussites refused the compromise, and the war dragged on until 1436. Bohemia remained a center of religious dissent, and the memory of Hus's execution at a church council would have a chilling effect on discussions of church reform during the Reformation in the sixteenth century.

Council of Constance
General council of the church convened by the Holy Roman emperor to deal with schism and church reform. It elected Pope Martin V to end the Great Schism.

The Execution of Jan Hus
Stripped of the signs of ecclesiastical office, Jan Hus was forced to wear a paper hat indicating he was a heresiarch, the leader of heretics. This and similar images were meant to show the legitimacy of his execution, but in Bohemia he was revered as a martyred saint. (The Art Archive/University Library Prague/Gianni Dagli Orti/Picture Desk)

The Reunion and Reform of the Papacy, 1415–1513

To most of the delegates at the Council of Constance, the reunion and reform of the papacy were more important than the issue of heresy. And as we will see, attempts to deal with reform and reunion seemed in the eyes of the popes to threaten the political independence and the moral leadership of the papacy itself. This too would remain a problem well into the sixteenth century.

The council deposed two claimants and forced the third to resign. Then, in 1417, the council elected a Roman nobleman as Pope Martin V (r. 1417–1431).

The council justified its actions in what was perhaps its most important decree, *Haec sancta synodus* ("This sacred synod"): "This sacred synod of Constance … declares … that it has its power immediately from Christ, and that all men, of every rank and position, including even the pope himself are bound to obey it in those matters that pertain to the faith."[3] Popes could no longer expect to remain unchallenged if they made claims of absolute dominion, and ecclesiastical rights and jurisdictions increasingly were matters for negotiation.

Reform was more difficult. Both the cardinals and the popes viewed any reforms to the present system as potential threats to their ability to function. The council, however, recognized the need for further reforms. A second reform council met at Basel from 1431 to 1449, but with modest results. The council again tried to reduce papal power, but this time, it received little support from European governments.

Because of the continuing conciliarist threat, the papacy needed the support of the secular rulers of Europe. Thus, the papacy was forced to accept compromises on the issues of reform, on ecclesiastical jurisdictions and immunities, and on papal revenues. Various governments argued that it was they, and not the pope, who should be responsible for ecclesiastical institutions and jurisdictions within their territories.

Lay rulers wanted church officials in their territories to belong to local families. They wanted ecclesiastical institutions to be subject to local laws and administration. By the 1470s, it was clear that they wanted to have local prelates named as cardinal-protectors. These were not churchmen who could serve the church administration in Rome; rather they functioned as mediators between local governments and the papacy.

The reunited papacy had to accept claims it would have staunchly opposed a century earlier. One of the most important of these was the Pragmatic Sanction of Bourges of 1438. The papacy was unable to protest when the French clergy, at the urging of the king, abolished papal rights to annates, limited appeals to the papal court, and reduced papal rights to appoint clergy within France without the approval of the local clergy or the Crown. Similar concessions diminished church authority throughout Europe.

With reduced revenues from legal fees, annates, and appointments, the popes of the fifteenth century were forced to derive more and more of their revenue and influence from the Papal States. By 1430, the Papal States accounted for about half of the annual income of the papacy. Papal interests increasingly centered on protecting the papacy's influence as a secular ruler of a large territory in central Italy. Further, it saw political independence as essential to its continued moral leadership. Thus, the papacy had to deal with many of the same jurisdictional, diplomatic, and military challenges that faced other medieval governments.

SECTION SUMMARY

- A political crisis forced the papacy to abandon central Italy and move to the south of France.

- A disputed papal election left two claimants—one French, the other Italian—and no clear way to resolve the issue.

- The religious beliefs of John Wyclif and Jan Hus challenged the basis of papal authority.

- In addition to resolving the disputed election, conciliarists claimed authority to correct and reform the papacy.

- By 1450, the papacy was reunited but weakened in relation to the European kingdoms.

WAR AND THE STRUGGLE OVER POLITICAL POWER, 1300–1450

What forces limited the political power of rulers in England, France, and Italy?

A lawyer who served King Philip IV of France (r. 1285–1314) observed that "everything within the limits of his kingdom belongs to the lord king, especially protection, high justice and dominion."[4] Royal officials in England and France generally believed that "liberties"—that is, individual rights to local jurisdictions—originated with the king. These ideas were the result of several centuries of centralization of political power in royal hands. At almost the same time, however, an English noble challenged royal claims on his lands, saying, "Here, my lords, is my warrant," as he brandished a rusty long sword. "My ancestors came with William the Bastard [that is, William the Conqueror, in 1066] and conquered their lands with the sword, and by the sword I will defend them against anyone who tries to usurp them."[5] The views of the royal lawyer and the feisty earl exemplify the central tension over power in the late Middle Ages. The struggle over political power was played out in the context of the **Hundred Years' War**, which affected not just England and France but also most of western Europe, especially Italy, as mercenary soldiers traveled south during temporary lulls in the fighting. In England and France, the crisis led to strengthened monarchies. In Italy, however, local and regional entities exercised many of those liberties the old Englishman wanted to protect with his sword.

The Hundred Years' War, 1337–1453

In the twelfth and thirteenth centuries, centralization of royal power in England and France had proceeded almost without interruption. In the fourteenth century, matters changed in both countries. Questions of the nature of royal power, common responsibility, and hereditary rights to rule challenged the power of the English and French monarchs. In both countries, competition began largely over dynastic issues, but by the mid-fifteenth century, resolution of the wars led to governments with a more distinctly national tone to them.

ENGLAND

In England, fears arising from the growing power of the English crown and the weakness of a gullible king brought issues to a head during the reign of Edward II (r. 1307–1327). By the early fourteenth century, resident justices of the peace (JPs) were replacing the expensive and inefficient system of traveling justices. In theory, the JPs were royal officials doing the king's bidding, but this was often not the case in reality. These unpaid local officials were modestly well-to-do gentry, who were often clients of local magnates. When the king was not vigilant, justices were prone to use their offices to carry out local vendettas and feuds and to protect the interests of the wealthy and powerful.

The barons, the titled lords of England, were interested in controlling more than just local justices. Fearing that Edward II would continue many of the centralizing policies of his father, the barons passed reform ordinances in 1311, limiting the king's right to wage war, leave the realm, grant lands or castles, or appoint chief justices and chancellors without the approval of Parliament, which they dominated. Special taxes or subsidies were to be paid to the public Exchequer rather than into the king's private treasury. Some of these ordinances were later voided, but the tradition of parliamentary consent remained a key principle of English constitutional history.

The baronial influence grew because Edward II was a weak and naive king, easily influenced by court favorites. After a humiliating defeat at the hands of the Scots at the Battle of Bannockburn (1314), his position steadily deteriorated until he was deposed in 1327 by a coalition of barons led by his wife, Queen Isabella. After a short regency, their son, Edward III (r. 1327–1377), assumed the throne. He was a cautious king, ever aware of the violence and rebelliousness of the baronage.

FRANCE

French kings seemed significantly more powerful in the early fourteenth century. A complex succession crisis, however, made clear the limits of French kingship. In 1328, the direct Capetian line, which had sired the kings of France since the election of Hugh Capet in 987, finally died out. The last Capetians did produce daughters, but by the fourteenth century, many argued that according to custom the French crown should pass through the male line only. Thus, the French nobility selected as king Philip of Valois (Philip VI; r. 1328–1350), a cousin of the last king through the male line (Charles IV; r. 1322–1328). He was chosen in preference to the daughters of the last Capetian kings and, more significantly, in preference to King Edward III of England, whose mother, Isabella, was the daughter of King Philip IV (r. 1285–1314).

Controversy over succession was just one of the disputes between the French and English. An even longer-standing issue was the status of lands within France that belonged to the English kings. In 1340, climaxing a century of tensions over English possessions in France, Edward III of England formally claimed the title "King of France," and the Hundred Years' War was on.

The war was marked by quick English raids and only occasional pitched battles. With a population of about 16 million, France was far richer and more populous than England. On at least one occasion, the French managed to field an army of over 50,000; the English mustered only 32,000

Hundred Years' War
Series of conflicts, 1337–1453, fought over English claims within the French monarchy. It ended with the nearly complete expulsion of the English from French lands.

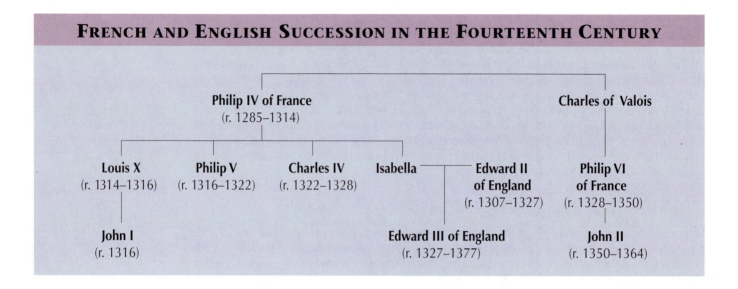

FRENCH AND ENGLISH SUCCESSION IN THE FOURTEENTH CENTURY

Philip IV of France (r. 1285–1314) — Charles of Valois

Louis X (r. 1314–1316) · Philip V (r. 1316–1322) · Charles IV (r. 1322–1328) · Isabella — Edward II of England (r. 1307–1327) · Philip VI of France (r. 1328–1350)

John I (r. 1316) · Edward III of England (r. 1327–1377) · John II (r. 1350–1364)

at most. These armies were easily the largest ever assembled by a medieval European kingdom. In almost every engagement, the English were outnumbered. Their strategy, therefore, was to avoid pitched battles except on the most advantageous terms. Edward III engaged in extremely destructive raids, hoping to lure the French into ill-considered attacks. The English stole what they could, destroyed what they could not steal, and captured enemy knights to hold for ransom.

STAGES OF THE WAR The war can be divided into four stages. The first stage (1337–1360) was characterized by a rapid series of English assaults and victories. The few pitched battles, including Crécy (1346) and Poitiers (1356), show how Edward's strategy worked (see **MAP 11.1**). In these cases, the English gathered their forces in careful defensive positions and took advantage of an individualistic French chivalric ethos according to which, in the words of one knight, "who does the most is worth the most." The key to the English defensive position was the use of longbowmen and cannon. Arrows from the longbow had more penetrating power than a bolt from a crossbow, and the longbow could be fired much more rapidly. By 1300, Europeans had forged cannon for use in siege warfare and to protect defensive positions. Although there is a debate over how effective they were, when used in combination with the longbow, they effectively disrupted and scattered advancing troops.

In the second stage of the war (1360–1396), French forces responded more cautiously to the English tactics and slowly regained much of the territory they had lost. However, during this stage, the disruptions and expenses of war placed a huge burden on both French and English society. First, in the wake of the French defeat at Poitiers in 1356, France was rocked by a series of urban and rural revolts and protests. Later, in 1381, the English faced a similar series of protests over taxes and the costs of war. Finally, because of stress over the war and general noble dissatisfaction, Richard II was forced to abdicate the English throne. Parliament then elected as king Henry IV (r. 1399–1413), the first ruler from the House of Lancaster. Richard died in prison under mysterious circumstances in 1400.

A fateful shift occurred in the third stage of the war (1396–1422). King Charles VI (r. 1380–1422) of France suffered bouts of insanity throughout his long reign, which made effective French government almost impossible. The English king Henry V (r. 1413–1422) renewed his family's claim to the French throne.

The Battle at Agincourt The English victory at Agincourt marked the high point of English influence in France. Once again English archers defeated a larger, mounted force. (The Granger Collection, New York)

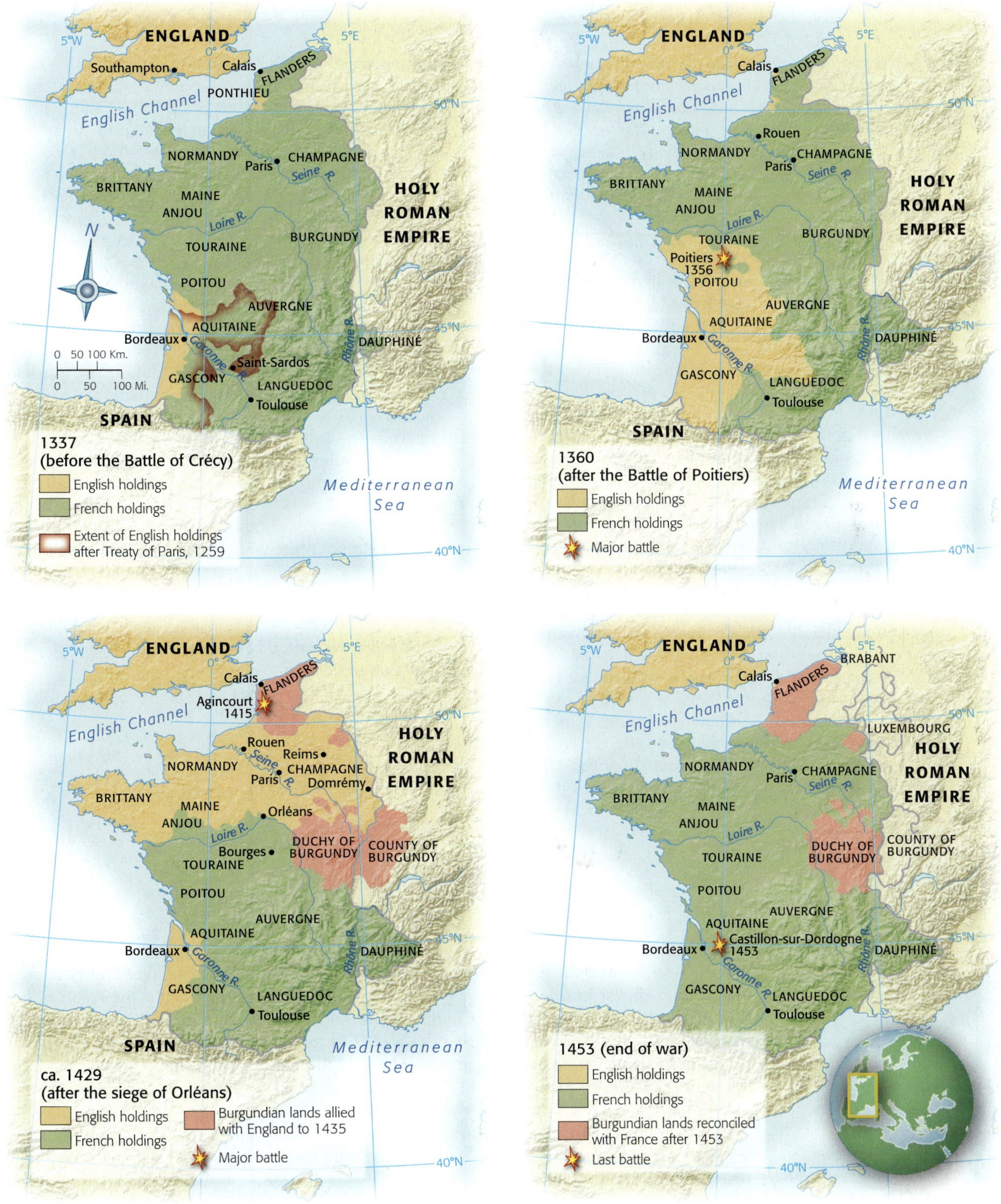

Map 1 — 1337 (before the Battle of Crécy)

ENGLAND
Southampton
Calais
FLANDERS
PONTHIEU
English Channel
5°W
0°
5°E
50°N
NORMANDY
Paris
CHAMPAGNE
Seine R.
BRITTANY
MAINE
ANJOU
Loire R.
HOLY ROMAN EMPIRE
TOURAINE
BURGUNDY
POITOU
AUVERGNE
AQUITAINE
Bordeaux
Garonne R.
DAUPHINÉ
45°N
Saint-Sardos
GASCONY
LANGUEDOC
Toulouse
Rhône R.
SPAIN
Mediterranean Sea
40°N
N
0   50 100 Km.
0   50   100 Mi.

1337
(before the Battle of Crécy)
- English holdings
- French holdings
- Extent of English holdings after Treaty of Paris, 1259

Map 2 — 1360 (after the Battle of Poitiers)

ENGLAND
Calais
FLANDERS
English Channel
5°W
0°
5°E
50°N
Rouen
NORMANDY
Paris
CHAMPAGNE
Seine R.
BRITTANY
MAINE
ANJOU
Loire R.
HOLY ROMAN EMPIRE
TOURAINE
BURGUNDY
Poitiers 1356
POITOU
AUVERGNE
AQUITAINE
Bordeaux
Garonne R.
DAUPHINÉ
45°N
GASCONY
LANGUEDOC
Toulouse
Rhône R.
SPAIN
Mediterranean Sea
40°N

1360
(after the Battle of Poitiers)
- English holdings
- French holdings
- ★ Major battle

Map 3 — ca. 1429 (after the siege of Orléans)

ENGLAND
Calais
FLANDERS
Agincourt 1415
English Channel
5°W
0°
5°E
50°N
Rouen
Reims
Seine R.
NORMANDY
CHAMPAGNE
Paris
Domrémy
HOLY ROMAN EMPIRE
BRITTANY
MAINE
ANJOU
Orléans
Loire R.
Bourges
DUCHY OF BURGUNDY
COUNTY OF BURGUNDY
TOURAINE
POITOU
AUVERGNE
AQUITAINE
Bordeaux
Garonne R.
DAUPHINÉ
45°N
GASCONY
LANGUEDOC
Toulouse
Rhône R.
SPAIN
Mediterranean Sea
40°N

ca. 1429
(after the siege of Orléans)
- English holdings
- French holdings
- Burgundian lands allied with England to 1435
- ★ Major battle

Map 4 — 1453 (end of war)

ENGLAND
Calais
FLANDERS
BRABANT
English Channel
5°W
0°
5°E
50°N
LUXEMBOURG
NORMANDY
Paris
CHAMPAGNE
Seine R.
HOLY ROMAN EMPIRE
BRITTANY
MAINE
ANJOU
Loire R.
DUCHY OF BURGUNDY
COUNTY OF BURGUNDY
TOURAINE
POITOU
AUVERGNE
AQUITAINE
Castillon-sur-Dordogne 1453
Bordeaux
Garonne R.
DAUPHINÉ
45°N
GASCONY
LANGUEDOC
Toulouse
Rhône R.
Mediterranean Sea
40°N

1453 (end of war)
- English holdings
- French holdings
- Burgundian lands reconciled with France after 1453
- ★ Last battle

🌐 **Map 11.1—England and France in the Hundred Years' War**

The succession of maps suggests both why hit-and-run tactics worked for the English early in the war and why the English were ultimately unable to defeat the French and take control of all of France.

The Inquisition of Joan of Arc

An important question at the trial of Joan of Arc was whether her acts had any authoritative value: Did the voices she heard originate with God or the Devil? The judges wanted to demonstrate to their own satisfaction that Joan was one of "the sowers of deceitful inventions" of which the Gospels warned. They fully expected that external signs could reveal hidden truths. The following memorandum is a summation of the commission's case against the maid.

You said that your king received a sign by which he knew you were sent from God, that it was St. Michael, in the company of a host of angels. ... You have said that you are certain of future and contingent events that you recognized men you had never seen, through the voices of St. Catherine and St. Margaret. ... Regarding this article, the clergy find superstition, divination, ... and vain boasting.

You said that you wore and still wear man's dress at God's command and to His good pleasure, for you had instruction from God to wear this dress, and so you put on a short tunic, jerkin, and hose with many points. You even wear your hair cut above the ears, without keeping about you anything to denote your sex, save what nature has given you. ... The clergy declare that you blaspheme against God, despising Him and His sacraments, that you transgress divine law, Holy Scripture and the canons of the Church, ... that you are given to idolatry and worship of yourself and your clothes, according to the customs of the heathen.

You have declared that you know well that God loves certain living persons better than you, and that you learned this by revelation from St. Catherine and St. Margaret; also that those saints speak French, not English, as they are not on the side of the English. And since you knew that your voices were for your king, you began to dislike the Burgundians. ... Such matters the clergy pronounce to be a rash and presumptuous assertion, a superstitious divination, a blasphemy uttered against St. Catherine and St. Margaret, and a transgression of the commandment to love our neighbors. ...

You declared that to those whom you call St. Michael, St. Catherine and St. Margaret, you did reverence, bending the knee ... vowing them your virginity ... now touching these matters, the clergy affirm. ... You are an idolatress, an invoker of demons, an apostate from the faith, a maker of rash statements, a swearer of an unlawful oath.

And you have said ... that you know that all the deeds of which you have been accused in your trial were wrought according to the command of God and that it was impossible for you to do otherwise. ... Wherefore the clergy declare you to be schismatic, an unbeliever in the unity and authority of the Church, apostate and obstinately erring from the faith. ... [The inquisitor admonished her,] "You have believed in apparitions lightly, instead of turning to God in devout prayer to grant you certainty; and you have not consulted prelates or learned ecclesiastics to enlighten yourself: although, considering your condition and the simplicity of your knowledge, you ought to have done so."

QUESTIONS

1. What are the signs that indicated to the judges that Joan was a heretic?
2. Why do the judges believe that Joan's "voices" are false?

Source: "The Inquisition of Joan of Arc" from *The Trial of Jeanne d'Arc*, trans. W.P. Barrett, 1932. Reprinted by permission of Gotham House.

At Agincourt in 1415, the English (led by Henry himself) again enticed a larger French army into attacking an English position fortified by longbows and cannon. By the terms of the Treaty of Troyes (1420), Charles VI's son (the future Charles VII) was declared illegitimate and disinherited; Henry married Catherine, the daughter of Charles VI, and he was declared the legitimate heir to the French throne. A final English victory seemed assured, but both Charles VI and Henry V died in 1422, leaving Henry's infant son, Henry VI (r. 1422–1461), to inherit both thrones.

The kings' deaths ushered in the final stage of the Hundred Years' War (1422–1453), the French reconquest. In 1428, military and political power seemed firmly in the hands of the English and the great aristocrats. Yet, in a stunning series of events, the French were able to reverse the situation.

JOAN OF ARC In 1429, with the aid of the mysterious **Joan of Arc** (d. 1431), the French king, Charles VII, was able to raise the English siege of Orléans (or-lay-OHN) and begin the reconquest of the north of France. Joan was the daughter of prosperous peasants from an area of Burgundy that had suffered under the English and their Burgundian allies. Her "voices" told her to go to the king and assist him in driving out the English. Like many late medieval mystics, she reported regular visions of divine revelation. Even politically or militarily important female leaders depended initially on religious charisma. One of the tests that supported Joan's claim to divine direction was her identification of Charles, who had disguised himself among his courtiers. Dressed as a man, she was Charles's most famed and feared military leader. With Joan's aid, the king was crowned in the cathedral at Reims, the traditional site of French coronations. Joan was captured during an audacious attack on Paris itself and eventually fell into English hands. Because of her "unnatural dress" and her claim to divine guidance, she was condemned and burned as a heretic in 1431. (See the feature, "The Written Record: The Inquisition of Joan of Arc.") A heretic only to the English and their supporters, Joan almost instantly became a symbol of French resistance. Pope Calixtus III reversed the condemnation in 1456, and Joan was canonized in 1920. The heretic became Saint Joan, patron of France.

> **Joan of Arc** Charismatic peasant who heard voices telling her to assist the French crown in its war against England. She was captured and eventually executed as a heretic.

Despite Joan's capture, the French advance continued. By 1450, the English had lost all their major centers except Calais (ca-LAY). In 1453, the French armies captured the fortress of Castillon-sur-Dordogne (kasti-YON sir dor-DON-ya) in what was to be the last battle of the war (see **Map 11.1**). There was no treaty, only a cessation of hostilities.

The war touched almost every aspect of life in western Europe: political, religious, economic, and social. It ranged beyond the borders of France, as Scotland, Castile, Aragon, and German principalities were, at various times, drawn into the struggle. French and English support for rival popes prevented early settlement of the Great Schism in the papacy (see page 291). Further, the war caused a general rise in the level of violence in society. As Henry V casually observed, "War without fire is as bland as sausages without mustard."[6] Because of the highly profitable lightning raids, this war was never bland. During periods of truce, many soldiers simply ranged through France, pillaging small towns and ravaging the countryside. Others went in search of work as mercenaries, especially in Germany, Poland, and Italy. Truces in France did not necessarily mean peace in Europe.

Italy

Compared with France and England, fourteenth- and fifteenth-century Italy was a land of cities. In northern Europe, a town of over 20,000 or 30,000 people was unusual; only Paris and London boasted more than 100,000 people in the fourteenth century. Yet, at one time or another, in the late Middle Ages, Milan, Venice, Florence, and Naples all had populations near or exceeding 100,000, and countless other Italian towns boasted populations of well over 30,000. Unlike northern European states with their kings or emperors, however, the Italian peninsula lacked a unifying force. The centers of power were in Italy's flourishing cities. Political life revolved around the twin issues of who should dominate city governments and how cities could learn to coexist peacefully.

By the late thirteenth century, political power in most Italian towns was divided among three major groups. First was the old urban nobility that could trace its wealth back to grants of property and rights from kings, emperors, and bishops in the tenth and eleventh centuries. Second was the merchant families who had grown wealthy in the twelfth and thirteenth centuries, as Italians led the European economic expansion into the Mediterranean. Third, challenging these entrenched urban groups were the modest artisans and merchants who had organized trade, neighborhood, or militia groups and referred to themselves as the *popolo*, or "people." Townspeople gathered together in factions based on wealth, family, profession, neighborhood, and even systems of clientage that reached back into the villages from which many of them had come. "War and hatred have so multiplied among the Italians," observed one Florentine, "that in every town there is a division and enmity between two parties of citizens."

> **City-States**

Riven with factions, townspeople often would turn control of their government over to a *signor* (sin-YOUR), a "lord" or "tyrant," often a local noble with a private army. Once firmly in power, the tyrant often allowed the government to continue to function as it had, requiring only that he control all major political appointments. The process might appear democratic, but it represented a profound shift in power. In the case of Milan, the noble Viscontis (vis-KON-tees) used support from the emperor Henry VII (r. 1308–1313) to drive their opponents out of the city. Eventually granting Milan and its territories as a duchy, the Viscontis, and later their Sforza successors, made marriage alliances with the French crown and created a splendid court culture. In a series of wars between the 1370s and 1450s, the dukes of Milan expanded their political control throughout most of Lombardy, Liguria, and, temporarily, Tuscany. The Viscontis maintained control of the city and much of the region of Lombardy until the last scion of the family died in 1447.

THE REPUBLICS   The great republics of Venice and Florence escaped domination by signori, but only by undertaking significant constitutional change. In both republics, political life had been disrupted by the arrival of immigrants and by the demands of recently enriched merchants and speculators for a voice in government. In 1297, reacting to increased competition for influence, the Venetian government began a series of reforms that would come to be known as the "Closing of the Grand Council." This enlarged the council to about eleven hundred members from those families eligible for public office, but its eventual effect was to freeze out subsequent arrivals from ever rising to elite status. The Venetian patriciate became a closed urban nobility. Political, factional, and economic tensions were hidden beneath a veneer of serenity as Venetians developed a myth of public-spirited patricians who governed in the interests of all the people, leaving others free to enrich themselves in trade and manufacture.

In Florence, the arguments over citizenship and the right of civic participation disrupted public life. Violent wealthy families, immigrants, and artisans of modest background were cut off from civic participation. A series of reforms, culminating in the Ordinances of Justice of 1293 to 1295, restricted political participation in Florence to members in good standing of certain merchant and artisan guilds. Members of violence-prone families were defined as *Magnate* (literally, "the powerful") and disqualified from holding public office. In spite of the reforms, political power remained concentrated in the hands of the great families, whose wealth was based primarily on banking and mercantile investments. These families used their political influence and economic power to dominate Florentine life.

There were short-lived attempts to reform the system and extend the rights of political participation to include the more modest artisans and laborers. The most dramatic was in 1378, when the Ciompi (CHOMP-ee), unskilled workers in Florence's woolen industry, led a popular revolution hoping to expand participation in government and limit the authority of the guild masters over semiskilled artisans and day laborers. They created new guilds to represent the laborers who had no voice in government. Barely six weeks after the Ciompi insurrection, however, wealthy conservatives began a reaction suppressing, exiling, or executing the leaders of the movement and eventually suppressing the new guilds. Political and economic power was now even more firmly in the grip of influential patricians.

Following a crisis in 1434, brought on by war and high taxes, virtual control of Florentine politics fell into the hands of Cosimo de' Medici (day-MAY-di-chi), the wealthiest banker in the city. From 1434 to 1494, Cosimo, his son Piero, his grandson Lorenzo, and Lorenzo's son dominated the government in Florence. Although the Medicis were always careful to pay homage to Florentine republican traditions, their control was virtually as complete as that of the lords of towns such as Ferrara and Milan.

Indeed, by the middle of the fifteenth century, little differentiated the republics—Florence and Venice—from cities, such as Milan and Mantua, where lords held sway. Although Florentines maintained that they intervened to protect Florentine and Tuscan "liberty" when the Viscontis of Milan threatened Tuscany and central Italy, their interests went beyond simple defense. Relations among the great cities of Milan, Venice, Florence, Rome, and Naples were stabilized by the Peace of Lodi and the creation of the Italian League in 1454. In response to endemic warfare in Italy and the looming threat of the Ottoman Turks in the eastern Mediterranean (see pages 312–314), the five powers agreed to the creation of spheres of influence that would prevent any one of them from expanding at the expense of the others.

The Journey of the Magi   The story of the journey of the Magi to Bethlehem to find the baby Jesus seemed a perfect image of the power and wisdom of rulers. This painting (a detail) of the Magi was commissioned for the private chapel of Cosimo de' Medici, the de facto ruler of Florence.   (Palazzo Medici Riccardi, Florence/Scala/Art Resource, NY)

THE ITALIAN WARS

The limits of these territorial states became clear when King Charles VIII of France invaded Italy in 1494 to assert his hereditary claim to the kingdom of Naples. The French invasion touched off a devastating series of wars called the Habsburg-Valois Wars (1496–1559). French claims were challenged by the Habsburg emperors and also by the Spanish, who themselves made claims on southern Italy and much of Lombardy. The cost of prolonged warfare kept almost all governments in a state of crisis.

In Florence, the wars destroyed the old Medici-dominated regime and brought in a new republican government. Anti-Medici efforts were initially led by the popular Dominican preacher Girolamo Savonarola (1452–1498). In the constitutional debates after 1494, Savonarola argued that true political reform required a sweeping purge of the evils of society. Gangs of youth flocked to his cause, attacking prostitutes and homosexuals. Many of his followers held "bonfires of vanities," burning wigs, silks, and other luxuries. In 1498, when his followers had lost influence in the government, Savonarola was arrested, tortured, and executed.

In spite of republican reforms, new fortresses, and a citizen militia, the Florentine government was unable to defend itself from papal and imperial armies. In 1512, the Habsburg emperor restored Medici control of Florence. The Medicis later became dukes and then grand dukes of Tuscany. The grand duchy of Tuscany remained an independent, integrated, and well-governed state until the French Revolution of 1789. Venice also managed to maintain its republican form of government and its territorial state until the French Revolution, but like the grand dukes of Tuscany, the governors of Venice were no longer able to act independently of the larger European powers.

The Habsburg-Valois Wars ended with the Treaty of Cateau-Cambrésis (kah-toe kam-bray-SEE) in 1559, which left the Spanish kings in control of Milan, Naples, Sardinia, and Sicily. Thus, the Spanish dominated Italy, but without the centralizing control typical of England and France. Venice, Tuscany, the Papal States, and even lesser republics and principalities retained significant influence, as Italy remained a land of regional governments.

CRISIS IN ECONOMY AND SOCIETY

How were economic and social structures changed by plague and economic crisis?

After nearly three centuries of dramatic growth, Europe, in 1300, was seriously overpopulated, with estimates ranging from about 80 million to as high as 100 million. In some parts of Europe, population would not be this dense again until the late eighteenth century. Opportunities dwindled because of overpopulation, famine, war, and epidemic, which also brought changes in trade and commerce. As the population began to decline, this trend, along with deflation and transformed patterns of consumption, affected agriculture, which was still the foundation of the European economy. Recovery from all these crises altered the structure and dynamics of families, the organization of work, and the culture in many parts of Europe. As a result of the crises, there had been a relative shift in economic and demographic vitality from Italy to England, France, and central Europe.

Famine and Declining Births

People in many parts of Europe were living on the edge of disaster in 1300. Given the low level of agricultural technology and the limited amount of land available for cultivation, it became increasingly difficult for the towns and countryside to feed and support the expanding population.

Growing numbers of people competed for land to farm and for jobs. Farm sizes declined throughout Europe, as parents tended to divide their land among their children. Rents for farmland increased, as landlords found that they could play one land-hungry farmer against another. Competition for jobs kept urban wages low, and when taxes were added to high rents and low wages, many peasants and artisans found it difficult to marry and raise families. Thus, because of reduced opportunities brought on by overpopulation, poor townspeople and peasants tended to marry late and have smaller families.

More dramatic than this crisis of births were the deadly famines that occurred in years of bad harvests. The great famine of 1315 to 1322 marks a turning point in the economic history of Europe. Wet and cold weather repeatedly ruined crops in much of northern Europe. Food stocks were quickly exhausted, and mass starvation followed. At Ypres, in Flanders, 2,800 people (about 10 percent of the population) died in just six months and shortages continued. Seven other severe famines were reported in the south of France or Italy during the fourteenth century.

Black Death An epidemic, possibly of bubonic plague, that wiped out one-third or more of Europe's population between 1348 and 1351. It initiated almost three centuries of epidemics.

If Europe's problem had merely been one of famine brought on by overpopulation, rapid recovery should have been possible. However, the difficulties of overpopulation were exacerbated by war and plague. As noted previously, the devastation of cities and the countryside was a common tactic in the Hundred Years' War. It was also typical of the local wars in parts of Spain, Germany, and especially Italy. The destruction of trees and vineyards and the theft of livestock made it difficult for rural populations to survive. Then, in 1348, the **Black Death** or "the great Mortality," as contemporaries called it, struck Europe.

The Black Death

Today there is no consensus as to what caused the Black Death. In the early twentieth century, after the bacillus that causes bubonic plague was identified by French and Japanese physicians in Hong Kong, it was assumed that bubonic plague was the cause. Subsequently, there have been controversial claims that DNA fragments of bubonic plague have been found in mass graves. Yet, bubonic plague usually travels slowly and infects a relatively small portion of a given population. By contrast, the Black Death seemed to race across Europe, wiping out entire families and infecting whole cities. Because of this evidence, some historical epidemiologists have speculated that the cause may actually have been anthrax or even a "hemorrhagic plague" similar to the Ebola virus.

THE SPREAD OF THE DISEASE

Although the historical identification of the Black Death remains controversial, contemporaries had little doubt about the source of the disease. Genoese traders, they believed, contracted the plague in Caffa, on the Black Sea coast. Infected sailors carried the disease south into Egypt and west into Sicily, then on to Genoa and Venice. From there, it followed established trade routes first into central Italy; later to the south of France, the Low Countries, and England; and finally, through the North and Baltic Seas, into Germany and the Slavic lands to the east (see **MAP 11.2**).

Mortality rates varied, but generally 60 percent or more of those infected died. In the initial infestation of 1348 to 1351, 25 to 35 percent of Europe's population may have died. In some of Europe's larger cities, the death rate may have been as high as 60 percent. In Florence, for example, the population probably declined from about 90,000 to about 50,000 or even less. The shock and disruption were immense. Governments in some towns simply ceased to function at the height of the epidemic. Chroniclers reported that no one could be found to care for the sick or bury the dead. Although abandonment of the sick was probably more a fear than a reality, the epidemic nonetheless significantly disrupted daily life.

Just as areas were rebounding from the initial outbreak of the plague, it returned between 1360 and 1363, and then, for three centuries thereafter, almost no generation could avoid it. It has been calculated that in central Italy, where the best records are available, the plague returned on average every eleven years between 1350 and 1400. Less is known about the plague in Muslim lands and in the eastern Mediterranean, but the situation seems to have been similar to the European experience. Because the plague tended to carry off the young, the almost generational return of the disease accounts for the depressed population levels found in many parts of Europe until the late fifteenth century and in western Asia until the late seventeenth or eighteenth century.

Lacking an understanding of either contagion or infection, fourteenth-century doctors depended on traditional theories inherited from the Greeks, especially the work of Galen (GAY-len), to treat the plague. In Galenic medicine, good health depended on the proper balance of bodily and environmental forces; it could be upset by corrupt air, the movement of planets, and even violent

🌐 **MAP 11.2—The Progress of the Black Death**

The Black Death did not advance evenly across Europe; rather, as is clear from the dates at which it struck various regions, it followed the main lines of trade and communication.

shifts in emotions. Yet, in the fifteenth and sixteenth centuries, as the rhythms of the infestations became clearer, towns and, later, territorial governments perceived the contagious nature of the disease. Officials instituted increasingly effective quarantines and embargoes to restrict the movement of goods and people from areas where the plague was raging. Some argue that it was the eventual extension of these efforts throughout Europe that led to the gradual reduction and then disappearance of the plague from western Europe by the early eighteenth century.

Alongside medical theory, however, another class of explanations developed. Taking a lead from miracle stories in which Jesus linked illness and sin, many Christians considered the Black Death a signal of the Last Judgment, or at least a sign of the severe judgment of God on a sinful world. Given that view, a traditional, and logical, religious response was to urge various moral reforms and penitential acts, such as charitable gifts, special prayers, and holy processions. (See the feature, "The Visual Record: A Painting of the Plague.") Many Muslim theologians also concluded that "the plague is part of Allah's punishment." Women were often thought to be a source of moral pollution and hence one of the causes of God's wrath. In Muslim Egypt, women were ordered off the streets; in Christian Europe prostitutes were driven out of towns.

A movement of penitents called "flagellants" arose in Hungary and spread quickly into Germany and across France and the Low Countries. In an imitation of Christ's life and sufferings, they sought to atone in their own bodies for the sins of the world. Following an ancient Christian tradition, they ritually beat (flagellated) themselves between the shoulders with metal-tipped whips. Through their

SOCIAL AND CULTURAL RESPONSES

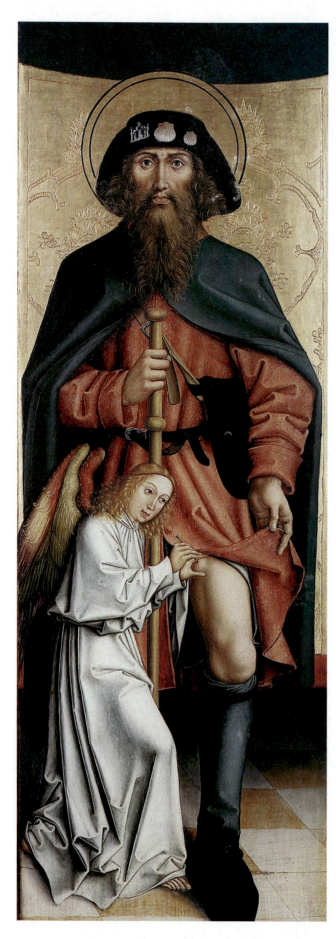

processions and sufferings, these pilgrims hoped to bring about a moral and religious transformation of society. The arrival of flagellants was often an occasion for an end of feuds and political violence within a community. But their arrival, just as often, was an occasion for political and even religious unrest. Authorities recognized the flagellants and the leaders of the religious riots as dangerous and drove them from towns.

In a quest for a purer, truly Christian society, the flagellants brought suspicion on all those who were not Christian or who were otherwise suspect. Some parts of Europe witnessed murderous attacks on outsiders, especially lepers and Jews, who were suspected of spreading the contagion in an attempt to bring down Latin Christendom. These attacks probably have more to do with tensions and fears already existing in parts of Europe than with the provocations of the flagellants. Like many other anti-Semitic myths, the rumors of wells poisoned by lepers and Jews seemed to arise in the south of France and spread in their most virulent forms to German towns along the Rhine. In Strasbourg attacks on Jews preceded the arrival of the plague. Except in a few districts, officials opposed attacks on Jews, lepers, and heretics. Doctors and churchmen often observed that Jews were unlikely culprits, since the plague claimed Jewish as well as Christian victims. Despite official rejection of popular rumors and fears, from the mid-fourteenth century, life became more difficult for the Jews of Christian Europe.

It was a commonplace among contemporary chroniclers that "so many did die that everyone thought it was the end of the world." Yet it was the very young, the elderly, and the poor—those least likely to pay taxes, own shops, or produce children—who were the most common victims. And even in towns, such as Florence, where mortality rates were extraordinarily high, recovery from the initial epidemic was rapid. Government offices were closed at most for only a few weeks; markets reopened as soon as the death rate began to decline; and within two years, tax receipts were back at preplague levels. Yet plague, fear of plague, and social and economic disruption caused by epidemic disease became a regular feature of European life. Thus, famine, warfare, plague, and population decline fueled the economic and social transformations of the late Middle Ages.

Trade and Agriculture

In the aftermath of plague, the economy of Europe changed in a number of profound ways. Disruptions brought on by population decline were accompanied by changes in the basic structure of economic life. In particular, Italy's domination of the European economy was challenged by the growth of trade and manufacturing in many other parts of Europe. Further, by 1500, the relative power of Italian bankers declined as they came to face competition from equally astute northern bankers.

Saint Roch Cured by an Angel Saint Roch is often shown with an exposed plague bubo. The image offered Christians comfort since he was cured because of his faith and charity. It offers modern historians evidence that bubonic plague was responsible for at least some of the mortality. (Courtesy, Bayerisches Nationalmuseum)

Discussions of the economy must begin with Italy because it was the key point of contact between Europe and the international economy. In 1300, Italian merchants sold woolens produced in Flanders and Italy to Arab traders in North Africa, who sold them along the African coast and as far south as the Niger Delta. The Italians used the gold that they collected in payment to buy spices and raw materials in Byzantium, Egypt, and even China. They resold these highly prized goods in the cities and at regional fairs of northern Europe. Italian traders also sold spices, silks, and other luxuries throughout Europe, from England to Poland.

Because of their expertise in moving bullion and goods and their ready sources of capital, Italian merchants, such as the Ricciardis of Lucca who flourished in England, were ideal bankers and financial advisers to the popes and European rulers, who appreciated sources of ready capital. In times of war, rulers tended to trade the rights to various revenues to Italian bankers, who had cash at hand. Merchants from Cremona, Genoa, Florence, and Siena forged commercial agreements with the kings of France, Aragon, and Castile, and with the papacy. The most powerful bank in fifteenth-century Europe was the Medici bank of Florence. Founded in 1397 by Giovanni de' Medici (1360–1429), the bank grew quickly because of its role as papal banker. Medici agents transferred papal revenues from all parts of Europe to Rome and managed papal alum mines, which provided an essential mineral to the growing cloth industry.

The dramatic career of the Frenchman Jacques Coeur (1395?–1456) demonstrates that by the mid-fifteenth century, Italian merchants were not the only Europeans who understood international trade. After making a fortune trading in southern France, Coeur managed the French royal mint and became the financial adviser of King Charles VII (r. 1422–1461). He put the French monarchy back on a solid financial footing after the Hundred Years' War, in the process, becoming the wealthiest individual in France.

By 1500, Italians faced increased competition from local merchants throughout Europe. From as early as the late thirteenth century, trade along the North and Baltic Seas in northern Europe was dominated by the **Hanseatic League**, an association of over a hundred trading cities centered on the German city of Lübeck. By the late fourteenth and early fifteenth centuries, the Hansa towns controlled grain shipments from eastern Europe to England and Scandinavia. The league's domination waned in the second half of the fifteenth century, however, as Dutch, English, and even southern German merchants gained shares of the wool, grain, and fur trades.

Hanseatic League An association of over a hundred German trading towns, which dominated trade in the North Sea and Baltic Sea regions during the fourteenth and fifteenth centuries.

In contrast to the Hanseatic League of towns, merchants in southern Germany adopted Italian techniques of trade, manufacture, and finance to expand their influence throughout central Europe. German merchants regularly bought spices in the markets of Venice and distributed them in central and eastern Europe. By the fifteenth century, the townspeople of southern Germany also produced linen and cotton cloth, which found ready markets in central and eastern Europe.

The Fugger (FOO-ger) family of Augsburg in southern Germany was the most prosperous of the German commercial families. Jacob Fugger (1459–1525) was a dominant figure in the spice trade and also participated in a number of unusually large loans to a succession of German princes. Jacob Fugger's wealth increased fourfold between 1470 and 1500. The Fuggers were indispensable allies of the German emperors. Jacob himself ensured the election of Charles V as Holy Roman emperor in 1519, making a series of loans that allowed Charles to buy the influence that he needed to win election.

As wealthy as the great merchants were, in most parts of Europe, prosperity was still tied to agriculture and the production of food grains. In northern and western Europe, foodstuffs were produced on the manorial estates of great churchmen and nobles. These estates were worked by a combination of farmers paying rents, serfs who owed a variety of labor services, and day laborers who were hired during planting and harvesting. In the face of a decimated population, landlords and employers found themselves competing for the reduced number of laborers who had survived the plague.

Cloth manufacture, not agriculture, was the part of the European economy that changed most dramatically in the late Middle Ages. First in Flanders, then later in England, Germany, and the rest of Europe, production shifted from urban workshops to the countryside. Industries in rural areas tended to be free of controls on quality or techniques. Rural production, whether in Flanders, England, or Lombardy, became the most dynamic part of the industry.

Rural cloth production was least expensive because it could be done as occasional or part-time labor by farmers, or by their wives or children, during slack times of the day or season.

Writers who survived the coming of pestilential disease in 1348 described a world of terror in which things seemed changed forever. Look at this painting, St. Sebastian Interceding for the Plague-Stricken, created by the Flemish artist Josse Lieferinxe between 1497 and 1499. One dying man seems to be falling terrified to the ground, while a female bystander in the background screams in alarm. Images of Christ, Saint Sebastian (pierced by arrows), a devil, and a priest seem to indicate that something terrifying and undreamed-of is happening. But what exactly was the terror, and what had changed?

The art of the later Middle Ages is an extremely valuable source for understanding social and religious values. As you look at *St. Sebastian Interceding for the Plague-Stricken*, the first step is to understand what men and women in the fourteenth and fifteenth centuries thought about death. After 1400 European Christians often depicted the universality of death in paintings showing the Dance of Death. The motif varies, but typically Death grasps the hands of men and women, rich and poor, noble and peasant, and leads them away. Deathbed scenes were another popular motif. In the late Middle Ages most people believed that at death the good and evil acts committed by an individual were tallied in the Book of Life and the person was either granted eternal life, first in Purgatory and then Paradise, or consigned to eternal suffering in Hell. Judgment scenes often depict the Virgin Mary or another saint pleading before God or contending with the Devil or demons over the souls of the dying.

It was essential for people to prepare for a good death. Individuals studied the *artes moriendi*, or "arts of dying." A lingering, painful illness was often interpreted as an opportunity for penitential suffering that would benefit the soul. At the point of death, the dying person could confess and receive absolution for sins and the last sacraments of the church. From that moment on, he or she needed to maintain a calm faith, free from fear. Salvation and eternal life depended on avoiding further sin, especially the questioning of God's forgiveness and mercy. Death was a public event. Clergy, family, religious societies, even neighbors helped the dying person to avoid losing faith at the end. The person might pray, "Virgin Mary, Mother of God, I have placed my hope in you. Free my soul from care, and from Hell, and bitter death."*

The concept of a good death is critical to understanding the European response to the plague. To be sure, individuals rarely look forward to death, then or now. Numerous writers and chroniclers lamented the suddenness of death and the lack of priests to hear confessions. Individuals who were healthy in the morning might be dead by nightfall. The suddenness, the lack of time to prepare for a good death, heightened the dread that accompanied the onset of the illness.

Medieval Christians turned to saints to represent them before God at the point of death and to stop the onslaught of the plague. Three patron saints were especially popular. The Virgin Mary was often shown using her cloak to shelter towns and individuals from arrows carrying pestilence. Saint Roch, himself a victim of the plague, was thought to intercede and protect those who prayed in his name. And Saint Sebastian, an early Christian who as part of his elaborate martyrdom survived being shot with arrows (later understood as symbols of death caused by the plague), was thought to be an especially effective patron during epidemics. In times of plague, people went on pilgrimages to local shrines dedicated to these or local saints, carried images of the saints in processions, and built churches and chapels in honor of the saints in thanks for deliverance from the plague.

With these issues in mind, what do we see in Lieferinxe's painting? The painting portrays an outbreak of the plague. We note first the body of the dead person, carefully shrouded.

Because production was likely to be finished in the countryside (beyond guild supervision), the merchant was free to move the cloth to wherever it could be sold most easily and profitably; guild masters had no control over price or quality.

Two other developments also changed the woolen trade of the fifteenth century: the rise of Spain as an exporter of unprocessed wool and the emergence of England, long recognized as a source of prime wool, as a significant producer of finished cloth. Spain was an ideal region for the pasturing of livestock. By the fifteenth century, highly prized Spanish wool from merino sheep was regularly exported to Italy, Flanders, and England. By 1500, over three million sheep grazed in Castile alone, and revenues from duties on wool formed the backbone of royal finance.

In England, in contrast, economic transformation was tied to cloth production. During the fifteenth century, England reduced its export of its high-quality raw wool and began instead to export its own finished cloth. In 1350, the English exported just over 5,000 bolts of cloth. By the 1470s, exports had risen to 63,000 bolts, and they doubled again by the 1520s. The growth of cloth exports contributed enormously to the expansion of London. During the fourteenth and fifteenth centuries, English commerce became increasingly controlled by London merchant-adventurers. Soon after 1500, over 80 percent of the cloth for export passed through the hands

Ideally the dead, like the corpse here, were taken to a church by friends and relatives and given a Christian burial. This was an important part of the ritual meant to ease the suffering of the soul in Purgatory. But chroniclers often reported that so many died, and died so quickly, that no one could be found to bury them properly. In many towns the dead were gathered on carts and hauled to gaping common graves outside the towns. We can see one such cart leaving the castle in the background. In a series of images, then, Lieferinxe shows what mattered most to people. In the foreground is the shrouded body attended by a priest and other clerics bearing a cross. This person experienced a good death. In contrast, the man who has fallen behind the body is suffering a bad death, one that caught him unaware. He is the object of the concern and grief of those near him. In the sky just above the castle walls, a white-robed angel and a horned, ax-wielding demon contend over the souls of the dead and dying. At the top of the painting Christ listens to the prayers of Saint Sebastian. The painting thus portrays the impact and horror of plague and also the way Christians were expected to respond to it.

Returning to our original question, we can conclude that the terror of epidemic plague was not entirely like a modern panic. Medieval people saw the Black Death, its ghastly devastation, and its only possible solution or meaning in terms of traditional religious values: The true terror was to be caught unaware.

QUESTIONS

1. What is a good death?

2. What responses to epidemic diseases can you find in this image?

3. Which parts of the image illustrate panic and which do not?

Lieferinxe: St. Sebastian Interceding for the Plague-Stricken (Collection of The Walters Art Museum. Photo © The Walters Art Museum, Baltimore)

*Quoted in Philippe Ariès, *The Hour of Our Death* (New York: Knopf, 1981), p. 108.

---

of the Londoners. This development, coupled with the rise of London as a center of administration and consumption, laid the foundation for the economic and demographic growth that would make London the largest and most prosperous city in western Europe by the eighteenth century.

The new structures of agriculture, manufacture, and trade in the fifteenth century challenged customs and institutions by admitting new entrepreneurs into the marketplace. However, Europe was still a conservative society in which social and political influence was more prized than economic wealth. Patricians in many European towns acted to dampen competition and preserve traditional values. Great banking families, such as the Medicis of Florence, tended to avoid competition and concentrations of capital. They did not try to drive their competitors out of business because the leaders of rival banks were their political and social peers. In northern Europe, governments in towns, such as Leiden, restricted the concentration of resources in the hands of the town's leading cloth merchants. Their aim was to ensure full employment for the town's laborers, political power for the guild masters, and social stability in the town.

In the wake of plague, the patricians' role, literally as "city fathers," was challenged by artisans and laborers. As wages rose because of population decline, workers demanded more voice in public life. Famed revolts, like the English Rising of 1381 (see page 296) or the Ciompi Revolt in

PATTERNS OF ECONOMIC LIFE

Street Life in Medieval Towns In a world dependent on natural lighting, shops were entirely open to the street. It made social and economic life much more public than it is in the modern world. (Bibliothèque nationale de France)

Italy (see page 300) are only the tip of the iceberg. Numerous other rebellions are recorded across Europe in the second half of the fourteenth century. Laborers attempted to use demand for labor to social and political advantage.

Full employment was not just for men. Although men had controlled the guilds and most crafts in the thirteenth and early fourteenth centuries, women's guilds existed in several European cities, including Paris and Cologne. In Italy, some women could be found among the more prosperous crafts. Women often practiced their trades in the context of the family. In Cologne, for instance, women produced the linen yarn and silk cloths that their husbands sold throughout Europe. Speaking of the silkmakers of Cologne, a report noted that "the women are much more knowledgeable about the trade than are the men." Unlike southern Europe, where women had no public roles, some northern towns apparently allowed women's guilds to protect their members' activities as artisans and even peddlers. Because they often worked before marriage, townswomen in northern Europe tended to marry at a later age than did women in Italy. Many women earned their own marriage dowries. Since they had their own sources of income and often managed the shop of a deceased husband, women could be surprisingly independent. They were consequently under less pressure to remarry at the death of a spouse. Although their economic circumstances varied considerably, up to a quarter of the households in northern towns such as Bern and Zurich were headed by women. Many of them were widows, but many others, perhaps a third, were women who had never married.

If plague and population decline created new opportunities for women, the fifteenth century brought new restrictions to women's lives. In England, brewing ale had been a highly profitable

part-time activity that women often combined with the running of a household. Ale was usually produced in small batches for household use and whatever went unconsumed would be sold. The introduction of beer changed matters. Because hops were added as a preservative during brewing, beer was easier to produce, store, and transport in large batches. Beer brewing became a lucrative full-time trade, reducing the demand for the alewife's product and providing work for men as brewers. At the same time, the rights of women to work in urban crafts and industries were reduced. Wealthy fathers became less inclined to allow wives and daughters to work outside the home. Guilds banned the use of female laborers in many trades and severely limited the rights of widows to supervise their spouses' shops.

Despite the narrowing of economic opportunities for women, the overall economic prospects of peasants and laborers improved. Lower rents and increased wages in the wake of the plague meant a higher standard of living for small farmers and laborers. Before the plague struck in 1348, most poor Europeans had subsisted on bread or grain-based gruel, consuming meat, fish, and cheese only a few times a week. A well-off peasant in England had lived on a daily ration of about two pounds of bread and a cup or two of oatmeal porridge washed down with three or four pints of ale. Poorer peasants generally drank water except on very special occasions. After the plague, laborers were more prosperous. Adults in parts of Germany may have consumed nearly a liter of wine, a third of a pound of meat, and a pound or more of bread each day. Elsewhere, people could substitute an equivalent portion of beer, ale, or cider for the wine. Hard times for landlords were good times for peasants and day laborers.

Landlords in England responded to the shortage of labor by converting their lands to grazing in order to produce wool for the growing textile market. In parts of Italy, landlords invested in canals, irrigation, and new crops in order to increase profits. In eastern Germany and Poland, landlords were able to take advantage of political and social unrest to force tenants into semi-free servile status. This so-called second serfdom created an impoverished workforce whose primary economic activity was in the lord's fields, establishing commercial grain farming. Increasingly in the second half of the century, grains cultivated in Poland and Prussia found their way to markets in England and the Low Countries. Europe east of the Elbe River became a major producer of grain, but at a heavy social cost.

The loss of perhaps a third of the urban population to the plague had serious consequences in the towns of Europe. Because of lower birthrates and higher death rates, late medieval towns needed a constant influx of immigrants to expand or even to maintain their populations. These immigrants did not find life in the cities easy, however. Citizenship in most towns was restricted to masters in the most important guilds, and local governments were in their hands, if not under their thumbs. In many towns, citizens constructed a system of taxation that worked to their own economic advantage and fell heavily on artisans and peasants living in territories controlled by the towns. Unskilled laborers and members of craft guilds depended for their economic well-being on personal relationships with powerful citizens who controlled the government and the markets. Peace and order in towns and in the countryside required a delicate balance of the interests of the well-to-do and the more humble. When that balance was shattered by war, plague, and economic depression, the result was often a popular revolt, such as the Ciompi insurrection of 1378 in Florence and the Rising of 1381 in England.

SECTION SUMMARY

- The Black Death may have killed one-third or more of Europe's population.
- In response to the epidemics many groups attacked outsiders, lepers, and Jews.
- Italy's medieval bankers and merchants dominated trade between Europe, North Africa, and the eastern Mediterranean.
- By the late fifteenth century, north European merchants challenged Italian economic leadership.
- Cloth production, arranged by a putting-out system, was Europe's most important industry.
- By the end of the fifteenth century, women found it increasingly difficult to maintain a significant role in Europe's craft industries.

THE CONSOLIDATION OF POLITICAL POWER, 1450–1500

How did the political makeup of Europe in 1500 differ from that in 1300?

By 1500, it seemed that the French royal lawyer's claim that all within the kingdom belonged to the king was finally accepted. With the exception of Italy and Germany, strong central governments recovered from the crises of war and civil unrest that wracked the fourteenth and fifteenth centuries. The Hundred Years' War and the resulting disorganization in France and England seemed to strike at the heart of the monarchies. However, through the foundation of standing armies and the careful consolidation of power in the royal court, both countries seemed stronger and more able to defend themselves in the second half of the century. And as the Italians learned in the wars following the French invasion of 1494, small regional powers were no match for the mighty monarchies.

France, England, and Scandinavia

In France, recovery from a century of war was based on a consolidation of the monarchy's power. A key to French military successes had been the creation of a paid professional army, which replaced the feudal host and mercenary companies of the fourteenth century. Charles VII created Europe's first standing army, a cavalry of about eight thousand nobles under the direct control of royal commanders. Charles also expanded his judicial claims. He and his son, Louis XI (r. 1461–1483), created new provincial *parlements*, or law courts, at Toulouse, Grenoble, Bordeaux, and Dijon. They also required that local laws and customs be registered and approved by the parlements.

A second key to maintaining royal influence was the rise of the French court as a political and financial center. Through careful appointments and judicious offers of annuities and honors, Charles VII and Louis XI drew the nobility to the royal court and made the nobles dependent on it. "The court," complained a frustrated noble, "is an assembly of people who, under the pretense of acting for the good of all, come together to diddle each other; for there's scarcely anyone who isn't engaged in buying and selling and exchanging ... and sometimes for their money we sell them our ... humanity."[7] By 1500, France had fully recovered from the crisis of war and was once again a strong and influential state.

The fate of the English monarchy was quite different. Henry VI (r. 1422–1461) turned out to be weak-willed, immature, and prone to bouts of insanity—inherited, perhaps, from his French grandfather, Charles VI (see pages 296–298). The infirmity of Henry VI and the loss of virtually all French territories in 1453 led to factional battles known as the Wars of the Roses—the red rose symbolized Henry's House of Lancaster, the white the rival House of York. Edward of York eventually deposed Henry and claimed the Crown for himself as Edward IV (r. 1461–1483). He faced little opposition because few alternatives existed. English public life was again thrown into confusion, however, at Edward's death. The late king's brother, Richard, duke of Gloucester, claimed the protectorship over the 13-year-old king, Edward V (r. April–June 1483), and his younger brother. Richard seized the boys, who were placed in the Tower of London and never seen again. He proclaimed himself king and was crowned Richard III (r. 1483–1485). He withstood early challenges to his authority but in 1485 was killed in the Battle of Bosworth Field, near Coventry, by Henry Tudor, a leader of the Lancastrian faction. Henry married Elizabeth, the surviving child of Edward IV. Symbolically at least, the struggle between the rival claimants to the Crown appeared over.

Henry VII (r. 1485–1509), like Edward IV who preceded him, recognized the importance of avoiding war and taxation. Following Edward's example, Henry controlled local affairs through the traditional system of royal patronage. He also imitated Edward in emphasizing the dignity of the royal office. Henry solidified ties with Scotland and Spain by marrying his daughter, Margaret Tudor, to James IV of Scotland and his sons, Arthur and (after Arthur's death) Henry, to Catherine of Aragon, daughter of the Spanish rulers Ferdinand and Isabella. The English monarchy of the late fifteenth century departed little from previous governments. The success of Henry VII was based on several factors: the absence of powerful opponents; lower taxation thanks to twenty-five years of peace; and the desire, shared by ruler and ruled alike, for an orderly realm built on the assured succession of a single dynasty.

Public authority varied greatly across Scandinavia. In Norway, Denmark, and Sweden the power of the king was always mediated by the influence of the council, made up of the country's leading landowners. Power was based on ownership or control of lands and rents. All the Scandinavian countries were home to a significant class of free peasants, and they were traditionally represented in the popular assemblies that had the right to elect kings, authorize taxes, and make laws. Scandinavians spoke similar Germanic languages and were linked by close social and economic ties. Thus, it is not surprising that the crowns of the three kingdoms were joined during periods of crisis. In 1397, the dowager queen Margaret of Denmark was able to unite the Scandinavian crowns by the Union of Kalmar, which would nominally endure until 1523.

Eastern Europe and Russia

Two phenomena had an especially profound effect on the governments of eastern Europe. One was the emergence of a newly important ruling dynasty. The other was the decline of Mongol, or Tatar, influence in the region. Since the thirteenth century, much of eastern Europe had been forced to acknowledge Tatar dominion and pay annual tribute. Now, the Tatar subjugation was challenged and finally ended.

As in much of Europe, political power was segmented and based on personal relationships between family members, communities, clients, and friends. Life in the East was further complicated by the mix of languages, cultures, and religions. Native Catholic and Orthodox Christian populations were further diversified in the fourteenth century by the arrival of Muslims in the Balkans and Ashkenazi Jews throughout most of the region. Escaping growing persecution in their traditional homelands in France and western Germany, the Ashkenazim migrated to Poland, Lithuania, and Ruthenian lands (parts of modern Russia), where they lived under their own leaders and followed their own laws.

This mix of cultures and religions played a role in the growth of new states. Under the pretext of converting their pagan neighbors to Christianity, the mostly German Teutonic knights sought to expand eastward against the kingdom of Poland and the Lithuanian state. They were

POLAND AND LITHUANIA

thwarted, however, by a profound dynastic shift. In 1386, Grand Duke Jagiello (yahg-YELL-loh) of Lithuania, who reigned from 1377 to 1434, converted to Catholic Christianity and married Hedwig, the daughter and heir of King Louis of Poland (r. 1370–1382). The resulting dynastic union created a state with a population of perhaps six million that reached from the Baltic nearly to the Black Sea. Polish-Lithuanian power slowed and finally halted the German advance to the east. The descendants of Jagiello, called Jagiellonians, had no hereditary right to rule Poland, and the Lithuanians opposed any Polish administrative influence in their lands. Yet, because of Jagiellonian power, the Poles continued to select them as kings. At various times, Jagiellonians also sat on the thrones of Bohemia and Hungary.

Poland and Lithuania remained more closely tied to western Europe than to the Russian East. They tended to be Catholic rather than Orthodox Christians. They wrote in a Roman rather than a Cyrillic script, and their political institutions resembled those of western Europe. Polish nobles managed to win a number of important concessions, the most significant being freedom from arbitrary arrest and confinement. This civil right was secured in Poland well before the more famous English right of habeas corpus. It was during this period, and under the influence of the Polish kings, that Cracow emerged as the economic and cultural center of Poland. Cracow University was founded in 1364, in response to the foundation of Prague University by the emperor Charles IV in 1348. After the dynastic union of Poland and Lithuania, Polish language and culture increasingly influenced the Lithuanian nobility. This union laid the foundation for the great Polish-Lithuanian commonwealth of the early modern period.

THE RISE OF MOSCOW   Lithuania had never been conquered by the Tatars, and its expansion contributed to the decline of Tatar power. The rise of Moscow, however, owed much to the continuing Tatar domination. Since the Mongol invasions in the thirteenth century, various towns and principalities of Kievan Rus had been part of a Tatar sphere of influence. This primarily meant homage and payment of an annual tribute.

A key to the emergence of Moscow occurred when Ivan I (r. 1328–1341), Prince of Moscow, was named Grand Prince and collector of tribute from the other Russian princes. It was not for nothing that he was called "the Moneybag." It was during this same period that the head of the Russian Orthodox Church was persuaded to make his home in Moscow, and in 1367, the princes began to rebuild the Kremlin walls in stone.

The decisive change for Moscow, however, was the reign of Ivan III (r. 1462–1505). By 1478, Ivan III, called "Ivan the Great," had seized the famed trading center of Novgorod. Two years later, he was powerful enough to renounce Mongol overlordship and refuse further payments of tribute. After his marriage to an émigré Byzantine princess living in Rome, Ivan began to call himself "Tsar" (Russian for "Caesar"), implying that in the wake of the Muslim conquest of Constantinople, Moscow had become the new Rome.

The Ottoman Empire

The most profound political and cultural transformation of the late Middle Ages took place in the Balkans with the conquest of Constantinople (1453) and the emergence of the Ottoman Turks as a major European power (see **MAP 11.3**). They solidified a fragmented and unstable area and from their base spread their influence throughout the Mediterranean and Europe.

The eastern Mediterranean region was a politically tumultuous area in the fourteenth century, when the Ottoman Turks were first invited into the Balkans by the hard-pressed Byzantine emperor. In the 1420s, as the Turks and the Hungarians fought for influence in Serbia, the Serbian king moved easily from alliance with one to alliance with the other. Elites often retained their political and economic influence by changing religion.

An Ottoman victory over a Christian crusading army at Varna, on the Black Sea coast, in 1444 changed the dynamics and virtually sealed the fate of Constantinople. It was only a matter of time before the Turks took the city. When Mehmed (MEH-met) II (r. 1451–1481) finally turned his attention to Constantinople in 1453, the siege of the city lasted only fifty-three days. The destruction of the last vestiges of the Roman imperial tradition that reached back to the emperor Augustus sent shock waves through Christian Europe and brought forth calls for new crusades to liberate the East from the evils of Islam. It also stirred anti-Christian feelings among the Turks. The rise of the Ottoman Turks transformed eastern Europe and led to a profound clash between Christian and Muslim civilizations.

🌐 **MAP 11.3—Turkey and Eastern Europe**

With the conquest of Constantinople, Syria, and Palestine, the Ottoman Turks controlled the eastern Mediterranean and dominated Europe below the Danube River. The Holy Roman emperors, rulers of Italy, and kings of Spain had to be concerned about potential invasions by land or by sea.

After the fall of Constantinople, the Turks worked to consolidate their new territories. Through alliance and conquest, Ottoman hegemony extended through Syria and Palestine, and by 1517, to Egypt. Even the Muslim powers of North Africa were nominally under Turkish control. In short order, they expanded to the west and north, seizing Croatia, Bosnia, Dalmatia, Albania, eastern Hungary, Moldavia, Bulgaria, and Greece. Turkish strength was based on a number of factors. The first was the loyalty and efficiency of the sultan's crack troops, the Janissaries. These troops were young boys forcibly taken from the subject Christian populations, trained in the Turkish language and customs, and converted to Islam. Although they functioned as special protectors of the Christian community from which they were drawn, they were separated from it by their new faith. Because the Turkish population viewed them as outsiders, they were particularly loyal to the sultan.

The situation of the Janissaries underlines a secondary explanation for Ottoman strength: the unusually tolerant attitudes of Mehmed, who saw himself not only as the greatest of the *ghazi* (crusading warriors who were considered the "instruments of Allah"), but also as emperor, heir to Byzantine and ancient imperial traditions. Immediately after the conquest of Constantinople, he repopulated the city with Greeks, Armenians, Jews, and Muslims. Mehmed especially welcomed Sephardic Jews from Spain and Portugal to parts of his empire. Thessalonica (Salonika), for example, was second only to Amsterdam as a Sephardic Jewish center until the community was destroyed in World War II. Religious groups in the cities lived in separate districts centered on a church or synagogue, and each religious community retained the right to select its own leaders. (See the feature, "The Global Record: A Disputation.") Mehmed made Constantinople the capital of the new Ottoman Empire, and by building mosques, hospitals, hostels, and bridges, he breathed new life into the city, which he referred to as Istanbul—that is, "the city." In the

The Siege of Constantinople The siege of Constantinople by the Turks required the attackers to isolate the city both by sea and by land. This miniature from the fifteenth century shows the Turkish camps, as well as the movements of Turkish boats, completing the isolation of the city. (Bibliothèque nationale de France)

fifty years following the conquest, the population of the city grew an extraordinary 500 percent, from about 40,000 to over 200,000, making it the largest city in Europe, as it had been in Late Antiquity.

At a time when Christian Europe seemed less and less willing to tolerate non-Christian minorities, the Ottoman Empire's liberal attitude toward outsiders seemed striking. Muslims and non-Muslims belonged to the same trade associations and traveled throughout the empire. Mehmed had no qualms about making trade agreements with the Italian powers in an attempt to consolidate his control. In Serbia, Bulgaria, Macedonia, and Albania, he left in place previous social and political institutions, requiring only loyalty to his empire.

The Union of Crowns in Spain

While expanding across the Mediterranean, the Turks came in contact with the other new state of the fifteenth century, the newly unified kingdom of Spain. As in Poland-Lithuania, the Spanish monarchy was only a dynastic union. In 1469, Ferdinand, heir to the kingdom of Aragon and Catalonia, married Isabella, daughter of the king of Castile. Five years later, Isabella became queen of Castile, and in 1479, Ferdinand took control of the kingdom of Aragon. This union of Crowns eventually would lead to the creation of a united Spain, but true integration was still a distant dream in 1469.

CASTILE AND ARAGON The permanence of the union was remarkable because the two kingdoms were so different. Castile was a much larger and more populous state. It had taken the lead in the Reconquista, the fight begun in the eleventh century to reclaim Iberia from Muslim rule. As a result, economic power within Castile was divided among the groups most responsible for the Reconquista: military orders and nobles. The military orders of Calatrava, Santiago, and Alcantara were militias formed by men who had taken a religious vow similar to that taken by a monk, with an added commitment to fight against the enemies of Christianity. In the course of the Reconquista, the military orders assumed control of vast districts. Lay nobles who aided in the Reconquista also held large tracts of land and proudly guarded their independence.

Castile's power stemmed from its agrarian wealth. During the Reconquista, Castilians took control of large regions and turned them into ranges for grazing merino sheep, producers of the prized merino wool exported to the markets of Flanders and Italy (see page 306). To maximize the profits from wool production, the kings authorized the creation of the Mesta, a brotherhood of sheep producers. The pastoral economy grew to the point that, by the early sixteenth century, Castilians owned over three million sheep.

Economic power in Castile lay with the nobility, but political power rested with the monarch. Because the nobility was largely exempt from taxation, nobles ignored the Cortes (cor-TEZ), the popular assembly, which could do little more than approve royal demands. The towns of Castile were important only as fortresses and staging points for militias, rather than as centers of trade and commerce.

The kingdom of Aragon was dramatically different. The center of the kingdom was Barcelona, an important trading center in the Mediterranean. In the fourteenth and fifteenth centuries, the kings of Aragon concentrated their efforts on expanding their influence in the

A Disputation

Konstantin Mihailovic, a Serb by birth, was captured by the Turks during the conquest of Constantinople in 1453. He later served with the Turks until he returned to the Christian forces in 1463. His description of a typical Turkish disputation, or debate, taking place in the presence of the sultan or another dignitary is an interesting example of how the Muslim, Jewish, and Christian peoples of the Balkans tried to understand one another.

The masters and scribes have among themselves this custom: they arrange their deliberations before the highest lord after the emperor. … And then they begin to argue one against the other, speaking mostly about the prophets. Some [of these Turkish scribes] recognize Our Lord Jesus Christ as a prophet, and others as an archprophet, alongside God the Creator of Heaven and earth. And also the Lord, from the time when the Mohammedan faith began, created eight hundred camels, like invisible spirits, which go around every night and gather evil *Busromane* [i.e., the Muslim, or the Chosen People of God] from our [Muslim] graves and carry them to *kaur* graves [the Kaury are "the Confused People," i.e., the Christians]; and then gather good kaury and carry them to our graves. And now the good kaury will stand with our Busroman council and the evil Busromane will stand with the kaur council on Judgment Day before God. For [a pious one] says … , "The Christians have a faith but have no works." Therefore Mohammed will lead the Busromane to Paradise and Jesus will order the Christians to hell. Moses will sorrow for the Jews that they have not been obedient to him. … He [one of the scribes] spoke in this way: "Elias and Enoch are both in body and soul in paradise; but before Judgment Day they must die. But Jesus both in body and in soul is in heaven. He is the only one who will not die a death but will be alive forever and ever. Mohammed both in body and soul was in heaven, but remained with us on earth." And then the masters began to dispute, one in one way and one in another, and there were many words among them. And having raised a cry one against another, they began to throw books at one another. [Then the official in charge of the disputation] … told them to cease this disputation and he ordered that food be brought them according to their custom and they gave them water to drink, since they do not drink wine. And then, having eaten their fill, they gave thanks to God, praying for the souls of the living and the dead and for those who fight against the kaury or Christians.

QUESTIONS

1. Like many people, the scribes in the debate are aware that good and evil behavior is not the special preserve of one people. How do they explain that individuals will be punished or rewarded for their deeds?

2. Christian theologians traditionally considered Muslims to be heretics who could not be saved. How do these debaters evaluate Christians?

Source: Konstantin Mihailovic, *Memoirs of a Janissary*, translated by Benjamin Stolz. Copyright © 1975. Reprinted by permission of Michigan Slavic Publications.

Mediterranean, especially south of France and Italy. By the middle of the fifteenth century, the Aragonese empire included the kingdom of Naples, Sicily, the Balearic (ba-LEER-ik) Islands, and Sardinia.

The power of the Aragonese king, in sharp contrast to the Castilian monarchy, was limited because the Crown was not unified. The ruler was king in Aragon and Navarre but only count in Catalonia. Aragon, Catalonia, and Valencia each maintained its own Cortes. In each area, the traditional nobility and the towns had a great deal more influence than did their counterparts in Castile. The power of the Cortes is clear in the coronation oath taken by the Aragonese nobility: "We who are as good as you and together are more powerful than you, make you our king and lord, provided that you observe our laws and liberties, and if not, not."[8] The distinction between Aragon and Castile could not be stronger.

Initially, the union of the crowns of Aragon and Castile did little to unify the two monarchies. Nobles fought over disputed boundaries, and Castilian nobles felt exploited by Aragonese merchants. Trade duties and internal boundaries continued to be disputed. The two realms even lacked a treaty to allow for the extradition of criminals from one kingdom to the other. Castilians never accepted Ferdinand as more than their queen's consort. After the death of Isabella in 1504, he ruled in Castile only as regent for his infant grandson, Charles I (r. 1516–1556). "Spain" would not emerge in an institutional sense until the late sixteenth century.

Nonetheless, the reign of Isabella and Ferdinand marked a profound change in politics and society in the Iberian kingdoms and in Europe in general. Ferdinand and Isabella married their daughter Joanna to Philip of Habsburg in 1496 to draw the Holy Roman Empire into the Italian wars brought on by the French invasion (see page 301). The marriage of their daughter Catherine of Aragon to Prince Arthur of England in 1501 was designed to obtain yet another ally against the

French. Those two marriages would have momentous consequences for European history in the sixteenth century.

1492: MUSLIMS AND JEWS

The reign of Ferdinand and Isabella is especially memorable because of the events of 1492. In January of that year, a crusading army conquered Granada, the last Muslim stronghold in Iberia. In March, Ferdinand and Isabella ordered the Jews of Castile and Aragon to convert or leave the kingdom within four months. In April, Isabella issued her commission authorizing Christopher Columbus "to discover and acquire islands and mainland in the Ocean Sea" (see pages 362–364).

The conquest of Granada and the expulsion of the Jews represented a radical shift in the Spanish mentality. Until the beginning of the fifteenth century, Spain maintained a level of religious tolerance unusual in Christendom. In the fourteenth century, perhaps 2 percent of the population of Iberia was Jewish, and the Muslim population may have been as high as 50 percent. The various groups were inextricably mixed. The statutes of the Jewish community in Barcelona were written in Catalan, a Spanish dialect, rather than in Hebrew. *Maranos*, Jewish converts to Christianity, and *moriscos*, Muslim converts, mixed continuously with Christians and with members of their former religions. It was difficult at times to know which religion these converts, or *conversos*, actually practiced. One surprised northern visitor to Spain remarked that one noble's circle was filled with "Christians, Moors, and Jews and he lets them live in peace in their faith."

This tolerant mingling of Christians, Muslims, and Jews had periodically occasioned violence. All three communities, in fact, preferred clear boundaries between the groups. In 1391, however, a series of violent attacks had long-lasting and unfortunate effects on Iberian society. An attack on the Jews of Seville led to murders, forced conversions, and suppression of synagogues throughout Spain. In the wake of the assault, large portions of the urban Jewish population either converted to Christianity or moved into villages away from the large commercial cities. The Jewish population in Castile may have declined by a fourth. Although the anti-Jewish feelings were expressed in religious terms, the underlying cause was anger over the economic prominence of some Jewish or converso families. After 1391, anti-Jewish feeling increasingly became racial. As one rebel said, "The converso remains a Jew and therefore should be barred from public office."[9]

Hostility and suspicion toward Jews grew throughout the fifteenth century, until Ferdinand and Isabella concluded that the only safe course was to order all Jews to accept baptism. Jews who would not convert would have to leave the kingdom within four months. The order was signed on March 31, 1492, and published in late April, after an unsuccessful attempt by converso and Jewish leaders to dissuade the monarchs from implementing it.

Many Jews could not dispose of their possessions in the four months allowed and so chose to convert and remain. But it is estimated that about ten thousand Jews left Aragon and that even more left Castile. Many moved to Portugal and then to North Africa. Some went east to Istanbul or north to the Low Countries. A number of others moved to the colonies being established in the New World in the vain hope of avoiding the Inquisition, which was already underway when the expulsion order was issued (see below). In 1504, the expulsion order was extended to include all Muslims.

The economic and social costs of the expulsion were profound. Not every Muslim or Jew was wealthy and cultured, but the exiles did include many doctors, bankers, and merchants. Spanish culture, long open to influences from Muslim and

Alfonso de Espina's Fortress of Faith (1474)   The diatribe against heretics, Muslims, and Jews fanned religious tensions in Spain. In this image from the book, Jews, Muslims, heretics, and demons are depicted as related threats to Christianity. Blindfolded Jews (blind to Christian Truth), Muslim warriors, and the Devil himself are seen assaulting the fortress of faith.   (© Topham/The Image Works)

Jewish sources, became narrower and less willing to accept new ideas. After the expulsion, a chasm of distrust opened between the "Old Christians" and the "New Christians"—that is, those newly converted. As early as the first decades of the fifteenth century, some religious orders had refused to accept "New Christians." They required that their members demonstrate *limpieza de sangre*, a purity of blood. By 1500, the same tests of blood purity became prerequisites for holding most religious and public offices. Thus, by the end of the fifteenth century, the Iberian kingdoms had created more powerful, unified governments, but at a terrible cost to the only portion of Christendom that had ever practiced religious tolerance.

Complaints that led to the expulsion arose from a variety of sources. The fact that many of the most important financiers and courtiers were Jews or conversos bred jealousies and tensions among the communities. All three religious communities favored distinct dress and identifying behaviors. Old Christians seemed concerned that many of the conversos might reconvert to Judaism, and the fear of reconversion, or "judaizing," led many to advocate the institution of the **Spanish Inquisition**.

Inquisitions were well known in many parts of Europe, but the Spanish Inquisition was unique because in 1478, Pope Sixtus IV placed the grand inquisitor under the direct control of the monarchs. Like most Christian rulers, Ferdinand and Isabella believed that uniform Christian orthodoxy was the only firm basis for a strong kingdom. Inquisitors attacked those aspects of converso tradition that seemed to make the conversos less than fully Christian. They were concerned that many conversos and maranos had converted falsely and were secretly continuing to follow Jewish or Muslim rituals—a fear that some recent scholars have argued was unfounded.

Because its administration, finances, and appointments were in Spanish, not papal, hands, the Spanish Inquisition quickly became an important instrument for the expansion of state power. Many inquisitors used their offices to attack wealthy or politically important converso families not just to drive them from public life but also to fill the royal treasury, which was where the estates of those judged guilty wound up. "This inquisition is as much to take the conversos' estates as to exalt the faith," concluded one despairing conversa woman.[10]

> **Spanish Inquisition**
> A church court under monarchical control established in 1478 to look for "false Christians" among the newly converted Muslims and Jews.

The Limits of Consolidation: Germany

The issue of central versus local control played a key role in German affairs as well. The Holy Roman Empire of the late Middle Ages was dramatically different from the empire of the early thirteenth century. Emperors generally were unable to claim lands and preside over jurisdictions outside Germany, and within Germany, power shifted eastward. Imperial power had previously rested on lands and castles in southwestern Germany. These strongholds melted away, as emperors willingly pawned and sold traditional crown lands in order to build up the holdings of their own families. Emperor Henry VII (r. 1308–1313) and his grandson, Charles IV (r. 1347–1378), for example, liquidated imperial lands west of the Rhine in order to secure the House of Luxemburg's claims to the crown of Bohemia and other lands in the east. The Habsburgs in Austria, the Wittelsbachs in Bavaria, and a host of lesser families staked out power bases in separate parts of the empire. As a result, Germany unraveled into a loose collection of territories. More seriously, the power of each emperor depended almost entirely on the wealth and power of his dynastic lands.

The power of regional authorities in the empire was further cemented by the so-called **Golden Bull** of 1356, the most important constitutional document of late medieval German history. In it, Charles IV declared that henceforth the archbishops of Cologne, Mainz, and Trier, plus the secular rulers of Bohemia, the Rhenish Palatinate, Saxony, and Brandenburg, would be the seven electors responsible for the choice of a new emperor. He further established that the rulers of these seven principalities should have full jurisdictional rights within their territories. The Golden Bull acknowledged the power of regional princes, but it did nothing to solve the inherent weakness of an electoral monarchy. Between 1273 and 1519, Germany elected fourteen emperors from six different dynasties, and only once, in 1378, did a son follow his father. The contrast between Germany and the monarchies of Iberia, France, and England is striking. By 1350, Germany had no hereditary monarchy, no common legal system, no common coinage, and no representative assembly. Political power rested in the hands of the territorial princes.

> **Golden Bull**　Edict of Holy Roman Emperor Charles IV establishing the method of electing a new emperor. It acknowledged the political autonomy of Germany's seven regional princes.

SECTION SUMMARY

- By the end of the fifteenth century, both England and France had stronger, more centralized governments.

- By the fifteenth century a strong Polish-Lithuanian state had emerged to halt German expansion to the east.

- The rise of Moscow marked the end of Tatar domination in eastern Europe.

- Ottoman Turks established a strong empire that came to dominate the eastern Mediterranean and the Balkans.

- The union of the Aragonese and Castilian crowns created a Spanish monarchy intent on enforcing political unity and religious uniformity.

- In German lands, regional powers emerged to challenge and limit the power of the empire.

Territorial integration was least effective in what is now Switzerland, where a league of towns, provincial knights, and peasant villages successfully resisted a territorial prince. The Swiss Confederation began modestly enough in 1291, as a voluntary association to promote regional peace. By 1410, the confederation had conquered most of the traditionally Habsburg lands in the Swiss areas. Though still citizens of the Holy Roman Empire, the Swiss maintained an independence similar to that of the princes. Their expansion culminated with the Battle of Nancy in Lorraine in 1477, when the Swiss infantry defeated a Burgundian army and killed Charles the Bold, the duke of Burgundy. From then on "turning Swiss" was a common threat made by German towns and individuals who hoped to slow territorial centralization.

CHAPTER SUMMARY

The Europe of 1500 was profoundly different from the Europe of two centuries earlier. The religious, political, and economic crises of the fourteenth and early fifteenth centuries seemed about to destroy the progress of the previous centuries. But the recovery of the second half of the fifteenth century was nearly as dramatic as the preceding disasters.

FOCUS QUESTIONS

- How did the Great Schism change the church and the papacy?

- What forces limited the political power of rulers in England, France, and Italy?

- How were economic and social structures changed by plague and economic crisis?

- How did the political makeup of Europe in 1500 differ from that in 1300?

In the aftermath of schism and conciliar reform, the church also was transformed. Because of conciliar challenges to papal authority, popes had to deal much more carefully with the governments of Europe. They found themselves vulnerable to pressures from the other European powers. Recognizing that, in the end, popes could count on support only from those areas they controlled politically, the papacy became an Italian regional power.

The Hundred Years' War between England and France was a continuation of a long struggle between two royal houses. The English won dramatic battles, but they could not control the territory. As a result, by the end the English lost all their significant possessions in France. The result contributed to the eventual centralization and growth of royal power in the two kingdoms.

The economy had grown more complex in the wake of the epidemic disease and dramatic population decline. Changes included the relative decline of the Italian economy as new patterns of trade and banking and new manufacturing techniques spread throughout Europe. Commerce and manufacture were now more firmly rooted in northern Europe. Italian merchants and bankers faced stiff competition from local counterparts throughout Europe.

Recovery was equally dramatic for the governments of Europe. After the Hundred Years' War and challenges from aristocrats, townsmen, and peasants, governments grew stronger as kings, princes, and town patricians used royal courts and patronage to extend their control. Military advances in the fifteenth century, such as the institution of standing armies, gave the advantage to larger governments. This was as true in Hungary as it was in France. Yet recovery among the traditional Western powers was largely overshadowed by the emergence of the tsars in Moscow and the rise of the Ottoman and Spanish Empires. These three emergent powers upset the political and diplomatic balance in Europe and would dominate politics and diplomacy in the next century.

KEY TERMS

Babylonian Captivity of the Papacy   (p. 290)

Great Schism   (p. 291)

conciliarists   (p. 291)

Jan Hus   (p. 292)

Council of Constance   (p. 293)

Hundred Years' War   (p. 295)

Joan of Arc   (p. 299)

Black Death   (p. 302)

Hanseatic League   (p. 305)

Spanish Inquisition   (p. 317)

Golden Bull   (p. 317)

 This icon will direct you to additional materials on the website: www .cengage.com/history/ noble/westciv6e.

NOTES

1. Quoted in Guillaume Mollat, *The Popes at Avignon, 1305–1378* (London: Thomas Nelson, 1963), p. 112.

2. Quoted in Mary Aston, *Lollards and Reformers: Images and Literacy in Late Medieval Religion* (Ronceverte, W.V.: Hambledon, 1984), p. 60.

3. Quoted in Francis Oakley, *The Western Church in the Later Middle Ages* (Ithaca, N.Y.: Cornell University Press, 1979), pp. 65–66.

4. Quoted in Charles T. Wood, *Joan of Arc and Richard III* (New York: Oxford University Press, 1988), pp. 56–57.

5. Quoted in Michael T. Clanchy, "Law, Government, and Society in Medieval England," *History* 59 (1974): 75.

6. A. Buchon, *Choix des Chroniques* (Paris, 1875), p. 565, as quoted in John Gillingham and J. C. Holt, eds., *War and Government in the Middle Ages* (Totowa, N.J.: Barnes & Noble, 1984), p. 85.

7. Quoted in Peter Shervey Lewis, *Later Medieval France: The Polity* (New York: Macmillan, 1968), p. 15.

8. Quoted in Angus MacKay, *Spain in the Middle Ages: From Frontier to Empire, 1000–1500* (London: Macmillan, 1977), p. 105.

9. Quoted in Angus MacKay, "Popular Movements and Pogroms in Fifteenth-Century Spain," *Past & Present* 55 (1972): 52.

10. Haim Beinart, ed., *Records of the Trials of the Spanish Inquisition in Ciudad Real*, vol. 1 (Jerusalem: Israel Academy of Sciences and Humanities, 1974), p. 391, trans. Duane Osheim.

e See our interactive eBook for map and primary source activities.

12

Raphael: School of Athens (detail)
Raphael created this classical setting by using the technique of linear perspective. (Scala/Art Resource, NY)

The Renaissance

The painting on the left, *School of Athens* by Raphael (1483–1520), was commissioned for the Stanze (STAN-zay), the papal apartments in the Vatican. At the center, Plato and Aristotle advance through a church-like hall, surrounded by the great thinkers and writers of the ancient world. But Raphael portrayed more than just ancient wisdom. The figure of Plato is, in fact, a portrait of Leonardo da Vinci. A brooding Michelangelo leans on a marble block in the foreground. In a companion painting on the opposite wall, Raphael depicted a gathering of the greatest scholars of Christendom. In this way, he brought together Christian and classical, writers and artists, and captured the entire cultural reform plan of the **Renaissance**.

FOCUS QUESTIONS

- How did Italians use classical values to deal with cultural and political issues?

- What was "new" about Renaissance art?

- In what ways did humanism outside Italy differ from Italian humanism?

- How did European rulers use Renaissance art and culture?

The revival these paintings celebrate was a response to the religious, social, economic, and political crises discussed in the previous chapter. Italians, and later Europeans, generally found themselves drawn to imitate Roman literature, ethics, and politics. The wisdom of antiquity seemed to offer an opportunity to perfect the theological ideas about moral and political life current in the earlier Middle Ages. Further, Renaissance writers were convinced that all knowledge, pagan and Christian, ancient and modern, could be combined into a single, uniform view of the world.

Renaissance Italians wrote of themselves and their contemporaries as having "revived" arts, "rescued" painting, and "rediscovered" classical authors. They even coined the phrases "Dark Ages" and "Middle Ages" to describe the period that separated the Roman Empire from their own times. They believed that their society saw a new age, a rebirth of culture. And, to this day, we use the French word for "rebirth," *renaissance*, to describe the period of intense creativity and change that began in Italy in the fourteenth century and then extended to all of Europe.

This view comes to us primarily from the work of the nineteenth-century Swiss historian Jacob Burckhardt. In his book, *The Civilization of the Renaissance in Italy* (1860), he argued that Italians were the first individuals to recognize the state as a moral structure free from the restraints of religious or philosophical traditions. Burckhardt believed that people are entirely free. Their success or failure depends on personal qualities of creative brilliance, rather than on family status, religion, or guild membership. Burckhardt thought he saw, in Renaissance Italy, the first signs of the romantic individualism and nationalism that characterized the modern world.

In fact, as brilliant as Renaissance writers and artists were, they do not represent a radical shift from the ideas or values of medieval culture. As we have seen, there were no "Dark Ages." Although the culture of Renaissance Europe was in many aspects new and innovative, it had close ties both to the ideas of the High Middle Ages and to traditional Christian values.

How, then, should we characterize the Renaissance in Europe? The Renaissance was an important cultural movement that aimed to reform and renew by imitating what the

This icon will direct you to additional materials on the website: www.cengage.com/history/noble/westciv6e.

See our interactive eBook for map and primary source activities.

Renaissance A word that has come to define any period of intense creativity. In this case, it refers specifically to a cultural movement based on imitating classical culture.

reformers believed were classical and early Christian traditions in art, education, religion, and political life. Italians, and then other Europeans, came to believe that the social and moral values, as well as the literature, of classical Greece and Rome offered the best formula for changing their own society for the better. This enthusiasm for a past culture became the vehicle for changes in literature, education, and art that established cultural standards that were to hold for the next five hundred years.

HUMANISM AND CULTURE IN ITALY, 1300–1500

How did Italians use classical values to deal with cultural and political issues?

Italians turned to models from classical antiquity in their attempts to deal with current issues of cultural, political, and educational reform. A group of scholars, who came to be known as humanists, began to argue the superiority of the literature, history, and politics of the past. As humanists discovered more about ancient culture, they were able to understand more clearly the historical context in which Roman and Greek writers and thinkers lived. And by the early sixteenth century, their debates on learning, civic duty, and the classical legacy had led them to a new vision of the past and a new appreciation of the nature of politics.

The Emergence of Humanism

humanism Western European literary and cultural movement, which emphasized the superiority of Greek and Roman literature and especially its values of personal and public morality.

Humanism initially held greater appeal in Italy than elsewhere in Europe because the culture in central and northern Italy was significantly more secular and more urban than the culture of much of the rest of Europe. Members of the clergy were less likely to dominate government and education in Italy. Quite the reverse: Boards dominated by laymen had built and were administering the great urban churches of Italy. Religious hospitals and charities were often reorganized and centralized under government control. Italy was the most urbanized region of Europe. Even the powerful Italian aristocracy tended to live at least part of the year in towns and conform to urban social and legal practices.

Differences between Italy and northern Europe are also apparent in the structure of local education. In northern Europe, education was organized to provide clergy for local churches. In the towns of Italy, education was much more likely to be supervised by town governments to provide training in accounting, arithmetic, and the composition of business letters. Public grammar masters taught these basics, and numerous private masters and individual tutors were prepared to teach all subjects. Giovanni Villani, a fourteenth-century merchant and historian, described Florence in 1338 as a city of nearly 100,000 people, in which perhaps as many as 10,000 young girls and boys were completing elementary education and 1,000 were continuing their studies to prepare for careers in commerce. Compared with education in the towns of northern Europe, education in Villani's Florence seems broad-based and practical.

Logic and Scholastic philosophy (see page 275) dominated university education in northern Europe in the fourteenth and fifteenth centuries but had less influence in Italy, where education focused on the practical issues of town life rather than on theological speculation. Educated Italians of this period were interested in the *studia humanitatis*, which we now call humanism. By *humanism*, Italians meant rhetoric and literature—the arts of persuasion. Poetry, history, letter writing, and oratory, based on standardized forms and aesthetic values, consciously borrowed from ancient Greece and Rome were the center of intellectual life. In general, fourteenth-century Italians were suspicious of ideological or moral programs based on philosophical arguments or religious assumptions about human nature.

By 1300, it was usual for towns to celebrate the feast days of their patron saints as major political, as well as religious, festivals. And town governments often supervised the construction and expansion of cathedrals, churches, and hospitals as signs of their wealth and prestige.

Literature of the early fourteenth century tended to emphasize the culture of towns. The most famous and most innovative work of the fourteenth century, *The Decameron* by Giovanni Boccaccio (1313–1375), pondered moral and ethical issues, but in the lively context of Italian town life. Boccaccio (bo-KAH-cho) hoped the colorful and irreverent descriptions of contemporary

Italians, which make his *Decameron* a classic of European literature, would also lead individuals to understand both the essence of human nature and the folly of human desires. The plot involves a group of privileged young people who abandon friends and family during the plague of 1348 to go into the country. There, on successive days, they mixed feasting, dancing, and song with one hundred tales of love, intrigue, and gaiety. With its mix of traditional and contemporary images, Boccaccio's book spawned numerous imitators in Italy and elsewhere.

Like Boccaccio, the majority of educated Italians in the early fourteenth century were not particularly captivated by thoughts of ancient Rome. Italian historians chose to write the histories of their hometowns. Most, including Giovanni Villani of Florence, were convinced that their towns could rival ancient Rome. Theirs was a practical world in which most intellectuals were men trained in notarial arts—the everyday skills of oratory, letter writing, and the recording of legal documents.

Petrarch and Early Humanism

The first Italians who looked back consciously to the literary and historical examples of ancient Rome were a group of northern Italian lawyers and notaries who imitated Roman authors. These practical men found Roman history and literature more stimulating and useful than medieval philosophy. Writers, such as Albertino Mussato of Padua (1262–1329), adopted classical styles in their poetry and histories. Mussato used his play *The Ecerinis* (1315) to tell of the fall of Can Grande della Scala, the tyrannical ruler of Verona (d. 1329), and to warn his neighbors of the dangers of tyranny. From its earliest, the classical revival in Italy was tied to issues of moral and political reform.

This largely emotional fascination for the ancient world was transformed into a literary movement for reform by **Francesco Petrarch** (1304–1374), who popularized the idea of mixing classical moral and literary ideas with the concerns of the fourteenth century. Petrarch was the son of an exiled Florentine notary living at the papal court in Avignon. Repelled by the urban violence and wars he had experienced on his return to Italy, Petrarch was highly critical of his contemporaries: "I never liked this age," he once confessed. He criticized the papacy in Avignon, calling it the "Babylonian Captivity" (see pages 290–291); he supported an attempt to resurrect a republican government in Rome; and he believed that imitation of the actions, values, and culture of the ancient Romans was the only way to reform his sorry world.

Petrarch believed that an age of darkness—he coined the expression "Dark Ages"—separated the Roman world from his own time and that the separation could be overcome only through a study and reconstruction of classical values: "Once the darkness has been broken, our descendants will perhaps be able to return to the pure, pristine radiance."[1] Petrarch's program, and, in many respects, the entire Renaissance, involved, first of all, a reconstruction of classical culture; then, a careful study and imitation of the classical heritage; and finally, a series of moral and cultural changes that went beyond the mere copying of ancient values and styles.

Petrarch labored throughout his life to reconstruct the history and literature of Rome. He learned to read and write classical Latin. In the 1330s, he discovered a number of classical works, including orations and letters by Cicero, the great philosopher, statesman, and opponent of Julius Caesar (see pages 134–135). Cicero's letters to his friend Atticus were filled with gossip, questions about politics in Rome, and complaints about his forced withdrawal from public life. They create the portrait of an individual who was much more complex than the austere philosopher of medieval legend.

Petrarch's humanism was not worldly or secular; he was and remained a committed Christian. He recognized the tension between the Christian present and pagan antiquity. He wrote a dialogue,

CHRONOLOGY

1304–1314	Giotto paints Arena Chapel in Padua
1345	Petrarch discovers Cicero's letters to Atticus
1348–1350	Boccaccio, *The Decameron*
1393–1400	Chaucer, *The Canterbury Tales*
1401	Ghiberti wins competition to cast baptistery doors, Florence
1405	Christine de Pizan, *The Book of the City of the Ladies*
1427	Unveiling of Masaccio's *Trinity*
1434	Van Eyck, *The Arnolfini Wedding*
1440	Valla, *On the Donation of Constantine*
1440s	Vitterino establishes Villa Giocosa in Mantua
1450s	Gutenberg begins printing with movable metal type
1460	Gonzaga invites Mantegna to Mantua
1475	Pope Sixtus IV orders construction of Sistine Chapel
1494	Dürer begins first trip to Venice
1501	Michelangelo, *David*
1511	Erasmus, *The Praise of Folly*
1513	Machiavelli, *The Prince*
1516	More, *Utopia*
1528	Castiglione, *The Book of the Courtier*

Francesco Petrarch Influential poet, biographer, and humanist who strongly advocated imitation of the literary and moral values of the leading Greek and Roman writers.

THE WRITTEN RECORD

Petrarch Responds to His Critics

Many traditional philosophers and theologians criticized humanists as "pagans" because of their lack of interest in logic and theology and their love of non-Christian writers. In this letter defending humanistic studies, Petrarch explains the value of Cicero's work to Christians.

[Cicero] points out the miraculously coherent structure and disposition of the body, sense and limbs, and finally reason and sedulous activity.... And all this he does merely to lead us to this conclusion: whatever we behold with our eyes or perceive with our intellect is made by God for the well-being of man and governed by divine providence and counsel.... [In response to his critics who argued for the superiority of philosophy he adds:] I have read all of Aristotle's moral books. Some of them I have also heard commented on.... Sometimes I have become more learned through them when I went home, but not better, not so good as I ought to be; and I often complained to myself, occasionally to others too, that by no facts was the promise fulfilled which the philosopher makes at the beginning of the first book of his *Ethics*, namely, that "we learn this part of philosophy not with the purpose of gaining knowledge but of becoming better." I see virtue, and all that is peculiar to vice as well as to virtue, egregiously defined and distinguished by him and treated with penetrating insight. When I learn all this, I know a little bit more than I knew before, but mind and will remain the same as they were, and I myself remain the same.... However, what is the use of knowing what virtue is if it is not loved when known? What is the use of knowing sin if it is not abhorred when it is known? However,

everyone who has become thoroughly familiar with our Latin authors knows that they stamp and drive deep into the heart the sharpest and most ardent stings of speech by which those who stick to the ground [are] lifted up to the highest thoughts and to honest desire....

Cicero, read with a pious and modest attitude, ... was profitable to everybody, so far as eloquence is concerned, to many others as regards living. This was especially true in [Saint] Augustine's case.... I confess, I admire Cicero as much or even more than all whoever wrote a line in any nation. ... If to admire Cicero means to be a Ciceronian, I am a Ciceronian. I admire him so much that I wonder at people who do not admire him.... However, when we come to think or speak of religion, that is, of supreme truth and true happiness, and of eternal salvation, then I am certainly not a Ciceronian, or a Platonist, but a Christian. I even feel sure that Cicero himself would have been a Christian if he had been able to see Christ and to comprehend His doctrine.

QUESTIONS

1. Why is Cicero a valuable author to study?
2. Why does Petrarch believe Cicero is superior to Aristotle?
3. Does it seem that Petrarch sees any limits to the moral value of Cicero?

Source: From *The Renaissance Philosophy of Man,* ed. Ernst Cassirer, Paul Oskar Kristeller and John H. Randall, pp. 86, 103-04, 114-115. Reprinted by permission of the publisher, the University of Chicago Press.

The Secret, reflecting his own ambivalence. Did his devotion to reading and imitating classical authors involve a rejection of traditional Christian values? "My wishes fluctuate and my desires conflict, and in their struggle they tear me apart," he confessed.[2] Yet, he prized the beauty and moral value of ancient learning. He wrote *The Lives of Illustrious Men*, biographies of men from antiquity whose thoughts and actions he deemed worthy of emulation. To spread humanistic values, he issued collections of his poems, written in Italian, and his letters, written in classically inspired Latin. He believed that study and memorization of the writings of classical authors could lead to the internalization of the ideas and values expressed in those works, just as a honeybee drinks nectar to create honey. He argued that ancient moralists were superior to Scholastic philosophers, whose work ended with the determination of truth, or correct responses. "The true moral philosophers and useful teachers of the virtues," he concluded, "are those whose first and last intention is to make hearer and reader good, those who do not merely teach what virtue and vice are but sow into our hearts love of the best ... and hatred of the worst."[3] (See the feature, "The Written Record: Petrarch Responds to His Critics.")

Humanistic Studies

Petrarch's program of humanistic studies became especially popular with the wealthy oligarchy who dominated political life in Florence. The Florentine chancellor Coluccio Salutati (1331–1406), and a generation of young intellectuals who formed his circle, evolved an ideology of **civic humanism**.

civic humanism
An ideology, popular with the political leaders of Florence, that emphasized Rome's classical republican virtues of duty and public service.

Civic humanists wrote letters, orations, and histories praising their city's classical virtues and history. In the process, they gave a practical and public meaning to the Petrarchan program. Civic humanists argued, as had Cicero, that there was a moral and ethical value intrinsic to public life. In a letter to a friend, Salutati wrote that public life is "something holy and holier than idleness in [religious] solitude." To another he added, "The active life you flee is to be followed both as an exercise in virtue and because of the necessity of brotherly love."[4]

More than Petrarch himself, civic humanists desired to create and inspire men of virtue who could take the lead in government and protect their fellow citizens from lawlessness and tyranny. In the early years of the fifteenth century, civic humanists applauded Florence for remaining a republic of free citizens. Florence remained free of a lord, unlike Milan whose government was dominated by the Viscontis (see page 345). In his *Panegyric on the City of Florence* (ca. 1405), Leonardo Bruni (ca. 1370–1444) recalled the history of the Roman Republic and suggested that Florence could re-create the best qualities of the Roman state. To civic humanists, the study of Rome and its virtues was the key to the continued prosperity of Florence and similar Italian republics.

One of Petrarch's most enthusiastic followers was Guarino of Verona (1374–1460), who became the leading advocate of educational reform in Renaissance Italy. After spending five years in Constantinople learning Greek and collecting classical manuscripts, he became the most successful teacher and translator of Greek literature in Italy. Greek studies had been advanced by Manuel Chrysoloras (1350–1415), who, after his arrival from Constantinople in 1397, taught Greek for three years in Florence. Chrysoloras was later joined by other Greek intellectuals, especially after the fall of Constantinople to the Turks in 1453. Guarino built on this interest in Greek culture.

EDUCATIONAL REFORM

Guarino emphasized careful study of grammar and memorization of large bodies of classical history and poetry. He was convinced that through a profound understanding of Greek and Latin literature and a careful imitation of the style of the great authors, a person could come to exhibit the moral and ethical values for which Cicero, Seneca, and Plutarch were justly famous. Although it is unclear whether Guarino's style of education produced such results, it did provide a thorough training in literature and oratory. In an age that admired the ability to speak and write persuasively, the new style of humanistic education pioneered by Guarino spread quickly throughout Europe. The elegy spoken at Guarino's funeral sums up Italian views of humanistic education, as well as the contribution of Guarino himself: "No one was considered noble, as leading a blameless life, unless he had followed Guarino's courses."

Guarino's example was widely followed. One of his early students, Vittorino da Feltre (1378–1446), was appointed tutor at the Gonzaga court of Mantua. Like Guarino, he emphasized close literary study and careful imitation of classical authors. But the school he founded, the Villa Giocosa (jo-KO-sa), was innovative because he advocated games and exercises, as well as formal study. In addition, Vittorino required that bright young boys from poor families be included among the seventy affluent students normally resident in his school. Vittorino was so renowned that noblemen from across Italy sent their sons to be educated at the Villa Giocosa.

Since Italians viewed humanistic education as a preparation for public life, it was not necessary for laborers, women, or others without political power. Leonardo Bruni of Florence once composed a curriculum for a young woman to follow. He emphasized literature and moral philosophy, but, he cautioned, there was no reason to study rhetoric: "For why should the subtleties of … rhetorical conundrums consume the powers of a woman, who never sees the forum? … The contests of the forum, like those of warfare and battle, are the sphere of men."[5] To what extent did women participate in the cultural and artistic movements of the fourteenth and fifteenth centuries? Many assumed that women were intellectually and morally weaker than men. And Bruni saw a limited value to humanistic education for women, but his views were not unopposed.

THE LIMITS OF HUMANISM

During the fifteenth century, many women did learn to read and even to write. Religious women and wives of merchants read educational and spiritual literature. Some women needed to write in order to manage the economic and political interests of their families. Alessandra Macinghi-Strozzi (ma-CHIN-ghee STROT-zi) of Florence (1407–1471), for example, wrote numerous letters to her sons in exile, describing her efforts to find spouses for her children and to influence the government to end their banishments. Her letters, in fact, demonstrate the subtle, indirect power women used to influence politics.

Private Reading Robert Campin's painting of Saint Barbara of 1438 shows a typical Flemish interior with a woman reading. It was not unusual for well-to-do women to read even if they could not write. (Museo de Prado/Institut Amatller d'Art Hispanic)

Women acted with care because many men were suspicious of literate women. Just how suspicious is evident in the career of Isotta Nogarola of Verona (b. 1418), one of a number of fifteenth- and sixteenth-century Italian women whose literary abilities equaled those of male humanists. Isotta quickly became known as a gifted writer, but men's response to her work was mixed. One anonymous critic suggested that it was unnatural for a woman to have such scholarly interests and accused her of equally unnatural sexual interests. Guarino of Verona himself wrote warning her that if she was truly to be educated, she must put off female sensibilities and find "a man within the woman."[6]

The problem for humanistically educated women was that, as Bruni observed, society provided no acceptable public role for them. A noblewoman, such as Isabella d'Este (DES-tay) (see page 345), wife of the duke of Mantua, might gather humanists and painters around her at court, but it was not generally believed that women themselves could create literary works of true merit. When women tried, they were usually rebuffed and urged to reject the values of civic humanism and to hold instead to traditional Christian virtues of rejection of the world. In other words, a woman who had literary or cultural interests was expected to enter a convent. That was a friend's advice to Isotta Nogarola. It was wrong, he said, "that a virgin should consider marriage, or even think about that liberty of lascivious morals."[7] Throughout the fifteenth and early sixteenth centuries, some women in Italy and elsewhere in Europe learned classical languages and philosophy, but they became rarer as time passed. The virtues of humanism were public virtues, and Europeans of the Renaissance remained uncomfortable with the idea that women might act directly and publicly.

The Transformation of Humanism

The fascination with education based on ancient authorities was heightened by the discovery in 1416, in the Monastery of Saint Gall in Switzerland, of a complete manuscript of Quintilian's *Institutes of Oratory*, a first-century treatise on the proper education for a young Roman patrician. The document was found by Poggio Bracciolini (PO-joe bra-cho-LEE-nee) (1380–1459), who had been part of the humanist circle in Florence. The discovery was hardly accidental. Like Petrarch, the humanists of the fifteenth century scoured Europe for ancient texts to read and study. In searching out the knowledge of the past, these fifteenth-century humanists made a series of discoveries that changed their understanding of language, philosophy, and religion. Their desire to imitate led to a profound transformation of knowledge.

A Florentine antiquary, Niccolò Niccoli (1364–1437), coordinated and paid for much of this pursuit of "lost" manuscripts. A wealthy bachelor, Niccolò spent the fortune he had inherited from his father by acquiring ancient statuary, reliefs, and, most of all, books. When he died, his collection of more than eight hundred volumes of Latin and Greek texts became the foundation of the humanist library housed in the Monastery of San Marco in Florence. Niccolò had specified that all his books "should be accessible to everyone," and humanists from across Italy and the rest of Europe came to Florence to study his literary treasures. Niccolò's library prompted Pope Nicholas V (r. 1447–1455) to begin the collection that is now the Apostolic Library of the Vatican in Rome. The Vatican library became a lending library, serving the humanist community in Rome. Similar collections were assembled in Venice, Milan, and Urbino. The Greek and Latin sources preserved in these libraries allowed humanists to study classical languages in a way not possible before.

The career of Lorenzo Valla (1407–1457) illustrates the transformation that took place in the fifteenth century, as humanism swept Europe. Valla was born near Rome and received a traditional human- istic education in Greek and Latin studies. He spent the rest of his life at universities and courts lecturing on philosophy and literature. Valla's studies had led him to understand that languages change with time—that they, too, have a life and a history. In 1440, he published a work called ***On the Falsely Believed and Forged Donation of Constantine***.

The donation purported to record the gift by the emperor Constantine (r. 311–337) of juris- diction over Rome and the western half of the empire to the pope when the imperial capital was moved to Constantinople (see pages 170–172). In the High and late Middle Ages, the papacy used the document to defend its right to political dominion in central Italy. The donation had long been criticized by legal theorists, who argued that Constantine had no right to make it. Valla went further and attacked the legitimacy of the document itself. Because of its language and form, he argued, it could not have been written at the time of Constantine: Valla was correct; the *Donation* was an eighth-century forgery.

> Through his [the writer's] babbling, he reveals his most impudent forgery himself.... Where he deals with the gifts he says "a diadem ... made of pure gold and precious jew- els." The ignoramus did not know that the diadem was [like a turban and] made of cloth, probably silk. ... He thinks it had to be made of gold, since nowadays kings usually wear a circle of gold set with jewels.[8]

Valla later turned his attention to the New Testament. Jerome (331–420) had put together the Vulgate edition of the Bible in an attempt to create a single accepted Latin version of the Hebrew Bible and the New Testament (see page 193). In 1444, Valla completed his *Annotations on the New Testament*. In this work, he used his training in classical languages to correct Jerome's stan- dard Latin text and to show numerous instances of mistranslations. His annotations on the New

LORENZO VALLA AND HISTORICAL PERSPECTIVE

On the Falsely Believed and Forged Donation of Constantine This work demonstrated that an important papal claim to political rule of central Italy was based on an eighth-century forgery.

The Donation of Constantine Pope Julius II commissioned Raphael to include this painting of Constantine's purported gift in the Stanze, the papal apartments in the Vatican. The classical and imperial images were meant to emphasize that the Church was the heir to Roman imperial authority. (Scala/Art Resource, NY)

Testament were of critical importance to humanists outside Italy and were highly influential during the Protestant Reformation.

RENAISSANCE PHILOSOPHY

Like Valla, many other humanists anticipated that literary studies would lead eventually to philosophy. In 1456, a young Florentine began studying Greek with just such a change in mind. Supported by the Medici rulers of Florence, Marsilio Ficino (1433–1499) began a daunting project: to translate the works of Plato into Latin and to interpret Plato in light of Christian doctrine and tradition.

Ficino believed that Platonism, like Christianity, demonstrated the dignity of humanity. He wrote that everything in creation was connected along a continuum ranging from the lowliest matter to the person of God. The human soul was located at the midpoint of this hierarchy and was a bridge between the material world and God. True wisdom, and especially experience of the divine, could be gained only through contemplation and love. According to Ficino, logic and scientific observation did not lead to true understanding. Humans, he observed, know logically only what they can define in human language; individuals can, however, love things, such as God, that they are not fully able to comprehend.

Ficino's belief in the dignity of man was shared by Giovanni Pico della Mirandola (mi-RAHN-do-la) (1463–1494), who proposed to debate, with other philosophers, nine hundred theses dealing with the nature of man, the origins of knowledge, and the uses of philosophy. Pico extended Ficino's idea of the hierarchy of being, arguing that humans surpassed even the angels in dignity. Angels held a fixed position in the hierarchy, just below God. In contrast, humans could move either up or down in the hierarchy, depending on the extent to which they embraced spiritual or worldly interests. Pico further believed that he had proved that all philosophies contain at least some truth. He was one of the first humanists to learn Hebrew and to argue that divine wisdom could be found in Jewish as well as Christian and pagan mystical literature.

THE UNITY OF KNOWLEDGE

Pico's ideas were shared by other humanists, who contended that an original, unified, divine illumination—a "Pristine Theology," they called it—preceded even Plato and Aristotle. These humanists found theological truth in what they believed was ancient Egyptian, Greek, and Jewish magic. Ficino himself popularized the *Corpus Hermeticum* (the Hermetic collection), an amalgam of magical texts of the first century A.D. that was thought mistakenly to be the work of an Egyptian magician, Hermes Trismegistos. Humanists assumed Hermes wrote during the age of Moses and Pythagoras. Like many mystical writings of the first and second centuries, Hermetic texts explained how the mind could influence and be influenced by the material and celestial worlds.

Along with exploring Hermetic magic, many humanists of the fifteenth and sixteenth centuries investigated astrology and alchemy. All three systems posit the existence of a direct, reciprocal connection between the cosmos and the natural world. In the late medieval and Renaissance world, astrological and alchemical theories seemed reasonable. By the late fifteenth century, many humanists assumed that personality was profoundly affected by the stars and that the heavens were not silent regarding human affairs. It was not by accident that, for a century or more after 1500, astrologers were official or unofficial members of most European courts.

Interest in alchemy was equally widespread, though more controversial. Alchemists believed that everything was made of a primary material and that, therefore, it was possible to transmute one substance into another. The most popular variation, and the one most exploited by hucksters and frauds, was the belief that base metals could be turned into gold. The hopes of most alchemists, however, were more profound. They were convinced that they could unlock the secrets of the entire cosmos. On a personal and religious, as well as on a material level, practitioners hoped to make the impure pure. The interest in understanding and manipulating nature that lay at the heart of Hermetic magic, astrology, and alchemy was an important stimulus to scientific investigations and, ultimately, to the rise of modern scientific thought.

Humanism and Political Thought

The humanists' plan to rediscover classical sources meshed well with their political interests. Petrarch and the civic humanists believed that rulers, whether in a republic or a principality, should exhibit all the classical and Christian virtues of faith, hope, love, prudence, temperance, fortitude, and justice. A virtuous ruler would be loved as well as obeyed. The civic humanists viewed governments and laws as essentially unchanging and static. They believed that when change does occur, it most likely happens by chance—that is, because of fortune (the Roman goddess Fortuna). Humanists believed that the only protection against chance is true virtue, for the virtuous would never be dominated by fortune. Thus, beginning with Petrarch, humanists advised rulers to love their subjects, to be generous with their possessions, and to maintain the rule of law. Humanistic tracts of the fourteenth and fifteenth centuries were full of classical and Christian examples of virtuous actions by moral rulers.

The French invasions of Italy in 1494 (see page 301), and the warfare that followed, called into question many of the humanists' assumptions about the lessons and virtues of classical civilization. Francesco Guicciardini (gwih-char-DEE-nee) (1483–1540), a Florentine patrician who had served in papal armies, suggested that, contrary to humanistic hopes, history held no clear lessons. Unless the causes of separate events were identical down to the smallest detail, he said, the results could be radically different. An even more thorough critique was offered by Guicciardini's friend and fellow Florentine, **Niccolò Machiavelli** (1469–1527). In a series of writings, Machiavelli developed what he believed was a new science of politics. He wrote *Discourses on Livy*, a treatise on military organization, a history of Florence, and even a Renaissance play titled *The Mandrake Root*. He is best remembered, however, for *The Prince* (1513), a small tract numbering fewer than a hundred pages.

Niccolò Machiavelli
A government functionary and political theorist in Florence, whose most famous work, *The Prince*, emphasized that the successful ruler must anticipate and adapt to change.

Machiavelli felt that his contemporaries paid too little heed to the lessons to be learned from history. Thus, in his discourses on Livy he comments on Roman government, the role of religion, and the nature of political virtue, emphasizing the sophisticated Roman analysis of political and military situations. A shortcoming more serious than ignorance of history, Machiavelli believed, was his contemporaries' ignorance of the true motivations for people's actions. His play, *The Mandrake Root*, is a comedy about the ruses used to seduce a young woman. In truth, however, none of the characters is fooled. All of them, from the wife to her husband, realize what is happening but use the seduction to their own advantage. In the play, Machiavelli implicitly challenges the humanistic assumption that educated individuals will naturally choose virtue over vice. He explicitly criticizes these same assumptions in *The Prince*. Machiavelli holds the contrary view: that individuals are much more likely to respond to fear and that power rather than morality makes for good government.

Machiavelli's use of the Italian word *virtù* led him to be vilified as amoral. Machiavelli deliberately chose a word that meant both "manliness" or "ability" and "virtue as a moral quality." Earlier humanists had restricted *virtù* to the second meaning, using the word to refer to upright qualities such as prudence, generosity, and bravery. Machiavelli tried to show that, in some situations, these "virtues" could have violent, even evil, consequences. If, for example, a prince was so magnanimous in giving away his wealth that he was forced to raise taxes, his subjects might come to hate him. Conversely, a prince who, through cruelty to the enemies of his state, brought peace and stability to his subjects might be obeyed and perhaps even loved. A virtuous ruler must be mindful of the goals to be achieved—that is what Machiavelli really meant by the phrase often translated as "the ends justify the means."

Like Guicciardini, Machiavelli rejected earlier humanistic assumptions that one needed merely to imitate the great leaders of the past. Governing is a process that requires different skills at different times, he warned: "The man who adapts his course of action to the nature of the times will succeed and, likewise, the man who sets his course of action out of tune with the times will come to grief."[9] The abilities that enable a prince to gain power may not be the abilities that will allow him to maintain it.

With the writings of Machiavelli, humanistic ideas of intellectual, moral, and political reform came to maturation. Petrarch and the early humanists believed fully in the powers of classical wisdom to transform society. Machiavelli and his contemporaries admitted the importance of classical wisdom, but also recognized the ambiguity of any simplistic application of classical learning to contemporary life.

SECTION SUMMARY

- The culture of Italy was more urban and less clerical than the rest of Europe.
- Francesco Petrarch popularized cultural movements that attempted to use Roman learning to change moral values and public behavior in Europe.
- Because women lacked a role in public life, their relationship to the humanistic movement was limited.
- By the end of the fifteenth century, humanists had developed a sense of historical change.
- Political crisis in Italy led Machiavelli to challenge the assumptions about morality and public life.

PAINTING AND THE ARTS, 1250–1550

What was "new" about Renaissance art?

Townspeople and artists in Renaissance Italy shared the humanists' perception of the importance of classical antiquity. Filippo Villani (d. 1405), a wealthy Florentine from an important business family, wrote that artists had recently "reawakened a lifeless and almost extinct art." In the middle of the fifteenth century, the sculptor Lorenzo Ghiberti concluded that, with the rise of Christianity, "not only statues and paintings [were destroyed], but the books and commentaries and handbooks and rules on which men relied for their training." Italian writers and painters themselves believed that the recovery of past literary and artistic practices was essential if society was to recover from the "barbarism" that they believed characterized the recent past.

The Renaissance of the arts is traditionally divided into three periods. In the early Renaissance, artists imitated nature; in the middle period, they rediscovered classical ideas of proportion; in the High Renaissance, artists were "superior to nature but also to the artists of the ancient world," according to the artist and architect Giorgio Vasari (1511–1574), who wrote a famous history of the eminent artists of his day.

Early Renaissance Art

The first stirrings of the new styles can be found in the late thirteenth century. The greatest innovator of that era was Giotto di Bondone of Florence (ca. 1266–1337). Although Giotto's background was modest, his fellow citizens, popes, and patrons throughout Italy quickly recognized his skill. He

Giotto's Naturalism Later painters praised the naturalistic emotion of Giotto's painting. In this detail from the Arena Chapel, Giotto portrays the kiss of Judas, one of the most dramatic moments in Christian history. (Scala/Art Resource, NY)

traveled as far south as Rome and as far north as Padua, painting churches and chapels. According to later artists and commentators, Giotto broke with the prevailing stiff, highly symbolic style and introduced lifelike portrayals of living persons. He produced paintings of dramatic situations, showing events located in specific times and places. The frescoes of the Arena Chapel in Padua (1304–1314), for example, recount episodes in the life of Christ. In a series of scenes leading from Christ's birth to his crucifixion, Giotto situates his actors in towns and countryside in what appears to be actual space. Even Michelangelo, the master of the High Renaissance, studied Giotto's painting. Giotto was in such demand throughout Italy that his native Florence gave him a public appointment, so that he would be required by law to remain in the city.

Early in the fifteenth century, Florentine artists devised new ways to represent nature that surpassed even the innovations of Giotto. The revolutionary nature of these artistic developments is evident from the careers of Lorenzo Ghiberti (gi-BER-tee) (1378–1455), Filippo Brunelleschi (broon-eh-LES-key) (1377–1446), and Masaccio (1401–ca. 1428). Their sculpture, architecture, and painting began an ongoing series of experiments with the representation of space through **linear perspective**. Perspective is a system for representing three-dimensional objects on a two-dimensional plane. It is based on two observations: (1) as parallel lines recede into the distance, they seem to converge; and (2) a geometric relationship regulates the relative sizes of objects at various distances from the viewer. Painters of the Renaissance literally found themselves looking at their world from a new perspective.

In 1401, Ghiberti won a commission to design door panels for the baptistery of San Giovanni in Florence. He was to spend much of the rest of his life working on two sets of bronze doors on which were recorded the stories of the New Testament (the north doors) and the Old Testament (the east doors). Ghiberti used the new techniques of linear perspective to create a sense of space into which he placed his classically inspired figures. Later, in the sixteenth century, Michelangelo remarked that the east doors were worthy to be the "Doors of Paradise," and so they have been known ever since.

In the competition for the baptistery commission, Ghiberti had beaten the young Filippo Brunelleschi, who, as a result, gave up sculpture for architecture and later left Florence to study in Rome. While in Rome, he is said to have visited and measured surviving examples of classical architecture—the artistic equivalent of humanistic literary research. According to Vasari, he was capable of "visualizing Rome as it was before the fall." Brunelleschi's debt to Rome is evident in his masterpiece, Florence's foundling hospital. Built as a combination of hemispheres and cubes and resembling a Greek stoa or an arcaded Roman basilica, the long, low structure is an example of how profoundly different Renaissance architecture was from the towering Gothic of the Middle Ages. But his experience in Rome was also critical to his famous plan for constructing a dome over the Cathedral of Santa Maria del Fiore in Florence. The Florentines were replacing their old cathedral with a vast new one. But until Brunelleschi, no one had been able to design a dome to cover the 180-foot space created by the vast new nave. He designed mutually supporting internal and external domes that were stronger and lighter than a single dome would have been.

In the first decade of the fifteenth century, many commentators believed that painting would never be as innovative as either sculpture or architecture. They knew of no classical models that had survived for imitation. Yet, the possibilities in painting became apparent in 1427 with the unveiling of Masaccio's *Trinity* in the Florentine Church of Santa Maria Novella. Masaccio (ma-SAH-cho) built on revolutionary experiments in linear perspective to create a painting in which a flat wall seems to become a recessed chapel. The space created is filled with the images of Christ crucified, the Father, and the Holy Spirit.

The Doors of Paradise   Ghiberti worked on panels for the baptistery from 1401 to 1453. In his representations of scenes from the Old Testament, he combined a love of ancient statuary with the new Florentine interest in linear perspective.   (Baptistery of San Giovanni, Florence/ Scala/Art Resource, NY)

linear perspective
A revolutionary technique developed by early-fifteenth-century Florentine painters for representing three-dimensional objects on a two-dimensional plane.

In the middle years of the fifteenth century, artists came to terms with the innovations of the earlier period. In the second half of the fifteenth century, however, artists such as the Florentine Sandro Botticelli (bot-ti-CHEL-ee) (1445–1510) added a profound understanding of classical symbolism to the technical innovations of Masaccio and Brunelleschi. Botticelli's famous *Primavera* (*Spring*, 1478), painted for a member of the Medici family, is filled with Neo-Platonic symbolism concerning truth, beauty, and the virtues of humanity.

High Renaissance Art

Leonardo da Vinci
A famous painter, engineer, and scientist who rejected arguments and ideas based on imitation of the ancients. Rather, he advocated careful study of the natural world.

Sistine Chapel The chapel at the Vatican Palace, containing Michelangelo's magnificent paintings of the Creation and Last Judgment; it captures the cultural, religious, and ideological program of the papacy.

The high point in the development of Renaissance art came at the beginning of the sixteenth century. Artists in Venice learned perspective from the Florentines and added their own tradition of subtle coloring in oils. The works of Italian artists were admired well beyond the borders of Italy. Even Sultan Mehmed II of Constantinople valued Italian painters. (See the feature, "The Global Record: Gentile Bellini Travels to Meet the Turkish Sultan.") Italian painters, goldsmiths, and architects continued to work in the Ottoman Empire through the sixteenth century.

The work of two Florentines, **Leonardo da Vinci** (1452–1519) and Michelangelo Buonarroti (1475–1564), best exemplifies the sophisticated heights that art achieved early in the sixteenth century. Leonardo, the bastard son of a notary, was raised in the village of Vinci outside of Florence. Cut off from the humanistic milieu of the city, he desired, above all else, to prove that his artistry was the equal of his formally schooled social superiors. In his notebooks, he confessed, "I am fully conscious that, not being a literary man, certain presumptuous persons will think they may reasonably blame me, alleging that I am not a man of letters."[10] But he defended his lack of classical education by arguing that all the best writing, like the best painting and invention, is based on the close observation of nature. Close observation and scientific analysis made Leonardo's work uniquely creative in all these fields. Leonardo is famous for his plans, sometimes prophetic, for bridges, fortresses, submarines, and airships. In painting, he developed chiaroscuro, a technique for using light and dark in pictorial representation, and showed aerial perspective. He painted horizons as muted, shaded zones rather than with sharp lines. It was Leonardo's analytical observation that had the greatest influence on his contemporaries.

The Pietà Michelangelo sculpted three versions of Mary holding the crucified Jesus. This late, unfinished work reveals Michelangelo's desire to show the suffering of Christ. (Scala/ Art Resource, NY)

Michelangelo, however, was widely hailed as the capstone of Renaissance art. In the words of a contemporary, "He alone has triumphed over ancient artists, modern artists and over Nature itself."

In his career, we can follow the rise of Renaissance artists from the ranks of mere craftsmen to honored creators, courtiers who were the equals of the humanists—in fact, Michelangelo shared Petrarch's concern for reform and renewal in Italian society. We can also discern the synthesis of the artistic and intellectual transformations of the Renaissance with a profound religious sensitivity.

The importance of Michelangelo's contribution is obvious in two of his most important works: the statue *David* in Florence and his commissions in the **Sistine Chapel** of the Vatican in Rome. From his youth, Michelangelo had studied and imitated antique sculpture, to the point that some of his creations were thought by many actually to be antiquities. He used his understanding of classical art in *David* (1501). Florentines recalled David's defeat of the giant Goliath, saving Israel from almost certain conquest by the Philistines. *David* thus became a symbol of the youthful Florentine republic struggling to maintain its freedom against great odds. As Vasari noted, "Just as David had protected his people and governed them justly, so who ever ruled Florence should vigorously defend the city and govern it with justice."[11]

Michelangelo was a committed republican and Florentine, but he spent much of his life working in Rome on a series of papal commissions. In 1508, he was called by Pope Julius II (r. 1503–1513) to work on the ceiling of the Sistine Chapel. Michelangelo spent four years decorating the ceiling with hundreds of figures and with nine scenes from the Book of

Gentile Bellini Travels to Meet the Turkish Sultan

Giovanni and Gentile Bellini were two of the leading Renaissance artists in Venice. Their fame spread throughout the Mediterranean and resulted in this unusual cultural meeting in 1479. A portrait of the emperor Mehmed II by Gentile now hangs in the National Gallery in London.

Some portraits having been taken to Turkey to the Grand Turk [the sultan] by an ambassador, that emperor was so struck with astonishment that, although the Mohammedan laws prohibit pictures, he accepted them with great goodwill, praising the work without end, and what is more, requesting that the master himself be sent to him. But the Senate, considering that Giovanni could ill support the hardships, resolved to send Gentile his brother, and he was conveyed safely in their galleys to Constantinople, where being presented to Mehmed [II], he was received with much kindness as an unusual visitor. He presented a beautiful picture to the prince, who admired it much, and could not persuade himself to believe that a mortal man had in him so much of the divinity as to be able to express the things of nature in such a lively manner. Gentile painted the Emperor Mehmed himself from life so well that it was considered a miracle, and the emperor, having seen many specimens of his art, asked Gentile if he had the courage to paint himself; and Gentile having answered "Yes," before many days were over he finished a lifelike portrait by means of a mirror, and brought it to the monarch, whose astonishment was so great that he would have it a divine spirit dwelt in him. And had not this art been forbidden by the law of the Turks, the emperor would never have let him go. But either from fear that people would murmur, or from some other cause, he sent for him one day, and having thanked him, and given him great praise, he bade him to ask whatever he would and it should be granted him without fail. Gentile modestly asked for nothing more than that he would graciously give him a letter of recommendation to the Senate and Lords of Venice. His request was granted in as fervent words as possible, and then, loaded with gifts and honors, and with the dignity of a cavalier, he was sent away. Among the other gifts was a chain of gold of two hundred and fifty crowns weight, worked in the Turkish manner. So, leaving Constantinople, he came safely to Venice, where he was received by his brother Giovanni and the whole city with joy, every one rejoicing in the honors which Mehmed had paid him. When the Doge and Lords [of Venice] saw the letters of the emperor, they ordered that a provision of two hundred crowns a year should be paid him all the rest of his life.

QUESTIONS

1. What seems to be the role of Renaissance art and artists in Venetian and Turkish diplomacy?
2. What does Bellini's trip to Constantinople suggest about relations between the Turks and Christians?

Source: *Stories of the Italian Renaissance from Vasari*, arranged and translated by E. L. Seeley (London and New York, 1908), pp. 135–137.

Genesis, including the famous *Creation of Adam*. In the late 1530s, at the request of Pope Clement VII (r. 1523–1534), he completed *The Last Judgment*, which covers the wall above the altar. In that painting, the techniques of perspective and the conscious recognition of debts to classical culture recede into the background as the artist surrounds Christ in judgment with saints and sinners. In the hollow, hanging skin of flayed Saint Bartholomew we can detect a psychological self-portrait of an artist increasingly concerned with his own spiritual failings.

Michelangelo's self-portrait reminds us that the intellectual content of the artist's work is one of its most enduring traits. He was a Platonist who believed that the form and beauty of a statue are contained, buried, in the stone itself. The artist's job is to peel away excess material and reveal the beauty within. As he noted in one of his poems, sculpting is a process not unlike religious salvation:

> Just as by carving . . . we set
> Into hard mountain rock
> A living figure
> Which grows most where the stone is most removed;
> In like manner, some good works . . .
> Are concealed by the excess of my very flesh.[12]

Renaissance Art in the North

In the early fifteenth century, while Brunelleschi and Masaccio were revolutionizing the ways in which Italian artists viewed their world, artists north of the Alps, especially in Flanders, were making equally striking advances in the ways they painted and sculpted. Artistic innovation in northern Europe began with changes tied closely to the world of northern courts; only later did artists take up the styles of the Italian Renaissance. Northerners took Italian Renaissance art and fit it to a new environment.

Northern art of the late fourteenth and fifteenth centuries changed in two significant ways. In sculpture, the long, austere, unbroken vertical lines typical of Gothic sculpture gave way to a much more complex and emotional style. In painting, Flemish artists moved from ornate, vividly colored paintings to experiments with ways to create a sense of depth. Artists strove to paint and sculpt works that more faithfully represented reality. The sculptures of Claus Sluter (1350–1406), carved for a family chapel of the Burgundian dukes at Champmol, captured a lifelike drama unlike the previous Gothic sculpture. Court painters, such as Jan van Eyck (ca. 1390–1441), in miniatures, portraits, and altar paintings, also moved away from a highly formalized style to a careful representation of specific places. In van Eyck's portrait of the Italian banker and courtier Giovanni Arnolfini and his bride, the image of the painter is reflected in a small mirror behind the couple, and above the mirror is written, "Jan van Eyck was here, 1434." Whereas Italians of the early fifteenth century tried to re-create space through linear perspective, the Flemish used aerial perspective, softening colors and tones to give the illusion of depth.

The influence of Renaissance styles in the north of Europe dates from the reign of the French king Francis I (r. 1515–1547), when Italian artists in significant numbers traveled north. Francis invited Italian artists to his court—most notably Leonardo da Vinci, who spent his last years in France. The most influential of the Italian style creations in France was doubtless Francis's château Fontainebleau, whose decorations contained mythologies, histories, and allegories of the kind found in the Italian courts. Throughout the sixteenth century, Italianate buildings and paintings sprang up throughout Europe.

Perhaps the most famous artist who traveled to Italy, learned Italian techniques, and then transformed them to suit the environment of northern Europe was Albrecht Dürer of Nuremberg (1471–1528). Son of a well-known goldsmith, Dürer became a painter and toured France and Flanders, learning the techniques popular in northern Europe. Then, in 1494, he left Nuremberg on the first of two trips to Italy, during which he sketched Italian landscapes and studied the work of Italian artists, especially in Venice. What he learned in Italy, combined with the friendship of some of Germany's leading humanists, formed the basis of Dürer's works, which blended northern humanistic interests with the Italian techniques of composition and linear perspective. Dürer worked in charcoal, watercolors, and paints, but his influence was most widely spread through his numerous woodcuts covering classical and contemporary themes. His woodcut, *Whore of Babylon*, prepared in the context of the debate over the reform of the church, is based on sketches of Venetian prostitutes completed during his first visit to Italy.

Numerous other artists and engravers traveled south to admire and learn from the great works of Italian artists. The engravings they produced and distributed back home made the southern innovations available to those who would never set foot in Italy. In fact, some now lost or destroyed creations are known only through the copies engraved by northern artists eager to absorb Italian techniques.

Van Eyck: The Arnolfini Wedding Careful observation of people and places was typical of the new art of both northern and southern Europe. Van Eyck seems to have re-created this scene to the smallest detail. His own image appears in the mirror on the wall. (The National Gallery, London/Art Resource, NY)

Art and Patronage

The variety and vitality of art in the Renaissance depended, in large measure, on the economic prosperity of Europe's cities and towns. Because of banking, international trade, and even service as mercenaries, Italians, and particularly Florentines, had money to spend on arts and luxuries. Thus, the Italians of the Renaissance, whether as public or private patrons, could afford to use consumption of art as a form of competition for social and political status.

It was not just the elite who could afford art. Surprisingly, modest families bought small religious paintings, painted storage chests, and decorative arts. Moralists advised families to buy small paintings of the Virgin Mary or the baby Jesus. Families also bought small paintings of saints considered special to their town or family. Wealthy and modest families alike bought brightly decorated terra-cotta pitchers, platters, and plates. Decorative arts were a critical social marker for families at all levels. (See the feature, "The Visual Record: Renaissance Marriage Chests.") Thus, the market for art steadily increased in the fourteenth and fifteenth centuries, as did the number of shops and studios in which artists could be trained.

Artists in the modern world are accustomed to standing outside society as critics of conventional ideas. In the late Middle Ages and Renaissance, artists were not alienated commentators. In 1300, most art was religious in subject, and public display was its purpose. Throughout Europe, art fulfilled a devotional function. Painted crucifixes, altarpieces, and banners were often endowed as devotional or penitential objects. The Arena Chapel in Padua, with its frescoes by Giotto, was funded by a merchant anxious to pay for some of his sins.

In the late Middle Ages and Renaissance, numerous paintings and statues throughout Italy (and much of the rest of Europe) were revered for their miraculous powers. During plague, drought, and times of war people had recourse to the sacred power of the saints represented in these works of art. (See the feature, "The Visual Record: A Painting of the Plague" in Chapter 11, pages 306–307.) The construction of the great churches of the period was often a community project that lasted for decades, even centuries. The city council of Siena, for example, voted to rebuild its Gothic Cathedral of Saint Mary, saying that the Blessed Virgin "was, is and will be in the future the head of this city" and that through veneration of her "Siena may be protected from harm." Accordingly, although the subject of art was clearly and primarily religious, the message was bound up in civic values.

Portrait of a Black Man Albrecht Dürer sketched this portrait in the early sixteenth century, most likely in a commercial center such as Venice or Nuremberg. By that time, it was common to show one of the three Magi as black, but such depictions, unlike Dürer's drawing here, were rarely based on portrait studies. (Graphische Sammlung, Albertina, Vienna)

ART AND THE COMMUNE

The first burst of artistic creativity in the fourteenth century was paid for by public institutions. Communal governments built and decorated city halls to house government functionaries and to promote civic pride. Most towns placed a remarkable emphasis on the beauty of the work. Civic officials often named special commissions to consult with a variety of artists and architects before approving building projects. Governments, with an eye to the appearance of public areas, legislated the width of streets, height limits, and even the styles of dwelling façades.

Public art in Florence was often organized and supported by various guild organizations. Guild membership was a prerequisite for citizenship, so guildsmen set the tone in politics, as well as in the commercial life of the city. Most major guilds commissioned sculpture for the Chapel of Or San Michele. This was a famous shrine in the grain market (its painting of the Virgin Mary was popularly thought to have wonder-working powers). The room above the chapel eventually became the seat of the Guelf Party, the city's most powerful political organization. Guilds took responsibility for building and maintaining other structures in the city as well. Guildsmen took pride in creating a beautiful environment that would reflect not only on the city and its patron saint, but also on the power and influence of the guild itself.

INDIVIDUAL PATRONS

The princes who ruled outside the republics of Italy often had similarly precise messages that they wished to communicate. Renaissance popes embarked on a quite specific ideological program in the late fifteenth century to assert their dual roles as spiritual leaders of Christendom and temporal lords of a central Italian state (see pages 346–347). Rulers, such as the Este dukes of

Men and Women Playing Cards This fresco painted in the early fifteenth century in Milan is typical of the art used to decorate the homes of the wealthy. It depicts one of the pastimes of noble families. (Scala/Art Resource, NY)

Ferrara and the Sforza dukes of Milan, constructed castles within their cities or hunting lodges and villas in the countryside and adorned them with pictures of the hunt or murals of knights in combat—scenes that emphasized their noble virtues and their natural right to rule.

By the mid-fifteenth century, patrons of artworks in Florence and most other regions of Italy were more and more likely to be wealthy individuals. Many of the patrons who commissioned and oversaw artists were women. Women paid for the construction of convents and chapels. In many cases, their patronage can simply be understood as an extension of their families, but in many other cases, it was not. One woman who had lived for years as a concubine of a merchant in Florence used her dead lover's bequest to commission a painting titled *Christ and the Adulteress*, making clear that even women in her situation could hope for God's mercy.

Republics, in which all families were in principle equal, initially distrusted the pride and ambition implied by elaborate city palaces and rural villas. By the middle of the fifteenth century, however, such reserve was found in none but the most conservative republics, such as Venice and Lucca. Palaces, gardens, and villas became the settings in which the wealthy could entertain their peers, receive clients, and debate the political issues of the day. The public rooms of these palaces were decorated with portraits, gem collections, rare books, ceramics, and statuary. Many villas and palaces included private chapels. In the Medici palace in Florence, for example, the chapel is the setting for a painting of the Magi (the three wise men who came to worship the infant Jesus), in which the artist, Benozzo Gozzoli (1420–1498), used members of the Medici family as models for the portraits of the Magi and their entourage (see the painting on page 300). The Magi, known to be wise and virtuous rulers, were an apt symbol for the family that had come to dominate the city.

Artists at princely courts were expected to work for the glory of their lord. Often the genre of choice was the portrait. One of the most successful portraitists of the sixteenth century was Sofonisba Anguissola (1532–1625). Anguissola won renown as a prodigy because she was female and from a patrician family; one of her paintings was sent to Michelangelo, who forwarded it to the Medici in Florence. Since women would never be allowed to study anatomy, Anguissola concentrated her talents on portraits and detailed paintings of domestic life. Later, she was called to the Spanish court, where the king, queen, and their daughter sat for her. She continued to paint after her marriage and return to Italy. Even in her nineties, she welcomed painters from all parts of Europe to visit and discuss techniques of portraiture.

SECTION SUMMARY

- Renaissance painters were especially prized for their ability to depict particular events in realistic, natural seeming settings.

- Beginning with Brunelleschi, artists consciously searched for ancient models for their work.

- Northern artists were keenly aware of Italian art, but they contributed a realism based on contrasts of dramatic colors.

- The work of Michelangelo shows the combination of artistic skill with humanistic moral and philosophical values.

THE SPREAD OF THE RENAISSANCE, 1350–1536

In what ways did humanism outside Italy differ from Italian humanism?

By 1500, the Renaissance had spread from Italy to the rest of Europe. Well beyond the borders of the old Roman Empire, in Prague and Cracow, for example, one could find a renewed interest in classical ideas about art and literature. As information about the past and its relevance to contemporary life spread, however, the message was transformed in several important ways. Outside Italy, Rome and its history played a much less pivotal role. Humanists elsewhere in the West were interested more in religious than in political reform, and they responded to a number of important local interests. Yet, the Renaissance notion of renewal based on a deep understanding and imitation of the past remained at the center of the movement. The nature of the transformation will be clearer if we begin by considering the nature of vernacular literatures before the emergence of Renaissance humanism.

Vernacular Literatures

The humanistic movement was not simply a continuation of practical and literary movements. The extent of its innovation will be clearer if we look briefly at the vernacular literatures (that is, written in native languages, rather than Latin) of the fourteenth and fifteenth centuries.

As in Italy, fourteenth-century writers elsewhere were not immediately drawn to classical sources. Boccaccio's work, for example, influenced another vernacular writer, Geoffrey Chaucer (ca. 1343–1400), the son of a London burgher, who served as a diplomat, courtier, and member of Parliament. Chaucer's most famous work, *The Canterbury Tales*, consists of stories told by a group of thirty pilgrims who left the London suburbs on a pilgrimage to the shrine of Saint Thomas Becket at Canterbury Cathedral. The narrators and the stories themselves describe a variety of moral and social types, creating an acute, sometimes comic, portrait of English life. The Wife of Bath is typical of Chaucer's pilgrims: "She was a worthy woman all her life, husbands at the churchdoor she had five." After describing her own marriages she observes that marriage is a proper way to achieve moral perfection, but it can be so only, she asserts, if the woman is master!

Although Chaucer's characters present an ironic view of the good and evil that characterize society, Chaucer's contemporary, William Langland (ca. 1330–1400), took a decidedly more serious view of the ills of English life. Whereas Boccaccio and Chaucer all told realistic tales about life as it truly seemed to be, Langland used the traditional allegorical language (that is, symbolic language in which a place or person represents an idea) of medieval Europe. In *Piers Plowman*, Langland writes of people caught between the "Valley of Death" and the "Tower of Truth." He describes the seven deadly sins that threaten all of society and follows with an exhortation to do

Renaissance Marriage Chests

The image here shows a marriage procession, including a servant carrying a large chest, or cassone. The picture is self-referential, since it was painted on the front of just such a cassone. We know that the painter of this image was Lo Scheggia (lo-SKED-ja) (1406–1486), the younger brother of Masaccio, and that he was recording a popular story of a marriage between the Bardi and Buondelmonte families of Florence. Lo Scheggia's work exhibits many of the characteristics we associate with Renaissance style. But historians often want to evaluate more than just painting technique. Historians of material culture are interested in the objects themselves and in the meanings that contemporaries gave to the possession and exhibition of them. To understand this, we need to know when and where cassoni were produced, why individuals prized them, and what the study of this image from a cassone can tell us about life in Renaissance Italy.

These highly practical chests were used by all but the poorest members of society. In houses that lacked closets, cabinets, and other kinds of storage space, everything was kept in wooden chests. Larger chests were used to store clothing, bedding, jewelry, and even weapons. Smaller chests were used for money, account books, and documents. Many of these chests had secret compartments where, for example, a businessman might keep his most sensitive papers. The most important chests made up the furnishings of the master of the house's bedroom. In a Renaissance palace the master's bedroom was also the room where he met with important allies and family members and conducted his most private business.

Cassoni took on new meaning between the late fourteenth and early sixteenth centuries. During that time, it was common for a groom to commission a matched set of chests: one for himself and the second to hold the fine clothes and jewelry that were part of his wife's dowry. These chests were decorated inside and out with scenes from classical mythology, medieval romances, and other popular stories. Classical Roman figures, such as Lucretia, who sacrificed her life to maintain her virtue, were common subjects. Some chests celebrated the virtues of chastity or fortitude—virtues thought to be essential in a proper wife. Thus, cassoni came to represent the taste, wealth, and social status of the families involved.

With these thoughts in mind, let us look closely at Lo Scheggia's cassone painting. The first thing we should notice is the procession at the left of the picture. We see a man accompanying a woman dressed in black into a house. The two are followed by others leading a horse (a sign of nobility) and carrying bedclothes and the chest. The procession testifies to the very public completion of the marriage process, which often stretched over months, if not years. It began with an engagement, followed by a promise of marriage, then a symbolic exchange of rings and physical consummation of the marriage, usually at the bride's home. The marriage was finalized by a procession to the groom's home. This procession celebrated publicly the alliance between the two families, as well as their standing in the community. Everyone noted carefully what and how much was carried in the procession, which was an indication of the size of the bride's dowry. The decoration of the marriage chest(s) in some way reflected the families involved.

What does the cassone image by Lo Scheggia indicate? The bride is the key to the story. Typically, a wealthy bride wore bright new clothes and jewelry, but this bride is dressed in black. The image tells a story not unlike that of Romeo and Juliet. The families of the bride and groom, Lionora de' Bardi and Ippolito Buondelmonte, had been

---

better. Both Chaucer and Langland expected that their audiences would immediately recognize commonly held ideas and values.

Despite the persistence of old forms of literature, new vernacular styles arose, although they still dealt with traditional values and ideas. Letters like those of the Paston family in England or Alessandra Macinghi-Strozzi in Italy described day-to-day affairs of business, politics, and family life. Letters dictated and sent by Saint Catherine of Siena and Angela of Foligno offered advice to the troubled. Small books of moral or spiritual writings were especially popular among women readers in the fourteenth and fifteenth centuries, among them *The Mirror for Simple Souls* by Marguerite of Porete (d. 1310). Though Marguerite was ultimately executed as a heretic, her work continued to circulate anonymously. Her frank descriptions of love, including God's love for humans, inspired many other writers in the fourteenth and fifteenth centuries. Less erotic, but equally riveting, was the memoir of Margery Kempe, an alewife from England, who left her husband and family, dressed in white (symbolic of virginity), and joined other pilgrims on trips to Spain, Italy, and Jerusalem.

One of the most unusual of the new vernacular writers was Christine de Pizan (1369–1430), the daughter of an Italian physician at the court of Charles V of France. When the deaths of her father and husband left her with responsibility for her children and little money, she turned to writing. From 1389 until her death, she lived and wrote at the French court. She is perhaps best known for *The Book of the City of the Ladies* (1405). In it, she added her own voice to what is known

Lo Scheggia: The Bardi-Buondelmonte Wedding (Alberto Bruschi di Grassina Collection, Florence/Bridgeman Art Library International)

enemies for generations. Despite this fact, the two were in love. We can read the tale of their love in three scenes from right to left. In the first scene on the right, Ippolito is caught in Lionora's house. He refuses to declare his love for her because he wants to protect her reputation. In the middle scene, Lionora, dressed as a widow, interrupts Ippolito's trial and declares her love for him. By dressing as a widow, she symbolically declares that they have already made their wedding vows and are, in fact, married. The authorities accept her declaration, and in the final scene on the left, the marriage is made public. Ippolito leads Lionora in a marriage procession, complete with wedding chest, to their new home. According to tradition, their marriage ended the feud between the two families.

We do not know who commissioned this chest. Nonetheless, we can now step back and speculate a bit about what Florentines might have noticed when they viewed the procession in which this cassone was carried through the streets of Florence. The image of the wedding couple and the servants carrying expensive dowry items, as well as the chest itself, testifies to the importance of the families involved. In a community such as Florence, where certain families were at the center of politics and public life, this image no doubt reminded those watching the procession of the power of prominent families and the critical role of marriage alliances in maintaining civic peace.

QUESTIONS

1. Look carefully at the image. Can you identify what seems most significant in the procession of the bride and groom?

2. How would this particular image influence the meaning that observers might give to the procession of the bride and groom?

as the *querelle des femmes*, the "argument over women." Christine wrote to counter the prevalent opinions of women as inherently inferior to men and incapable of learning or moral judgments. She argued that the problem was education: "If it were customary to send daughters to school like sons, and if they were then taught the natural sciences, they would learn as thoroughly and understand the subtleties of all the arts and sciences as well as sons." Christine described, in her book, an ideal city of ladies in which prudence, justice, and reason would protect women from ignorant male critics.

All these vernacular writings built on popular tales and sayings as well as on traditional moral and religious writings. Unlike the early humanists, the vernacular writers saw little need for new cultural and intellectual models.

The Impact of Printing

The spread of humanism beyond Italy was aided greatly by the invention of printing. In the fifteenth century, the desire to own and to read complete texts of classical works was widespread, but the number of copies was severely limited. Manuscripts required time and money to hand-copy, collate, and check each new copy. Poggio Bracciolini's letters are filled with complaints about the time and expense of reproducing the classical manuscripts he had discovered. One copy he had commissioned was so inaccurate and illegible as to be nearly unusable. Traveling to repositories and libraries was often easier than creating a personal library. It was rarely possible for someone who read a manuscript once to obtain a complete copy to compare with other works.

The invention of printing with movable lead type changed things dramatically. Although block printing had long been known in China, it was only in the late fourteenth century that it became a popular way to produce playing cards and small woodcuts in Europe. In China, an entire page would be carved on a single wooden block. **Johann Gutenberg** developed molds by which single letters or individual words could be cast in metal. Metal fonts could produce many more copies before they had to be recast. And further, they could be reused to print different pages. Between 180 and 200 copies of the so-called Gutenberg Bible were printed in 1452 and 1453. It was followed shortly by editions of the Psalms. By 1470, German printing techniques had spread to Italy, the Low Countries, France, and England. It has been estimated that, by 1500, a thousand presses were operating in 265 towns (see **Map 12.1**). The output of the early presses was extremely varied, ranging from small devotional books and other popular and profitable literature to complete editions of classical authors and their humanistic and theological texts.

Johann Gutenberg
German inventor of movable metal type. His innovations led to the publication of the first printed book in Europe, the Gutenberg Bible, in the 1450s.

🌐 **Map 12.1—The Spread of Printing**
Printing technology moved rapidly along major trade routes to the most populous and prosperous areas of Europe. The technology was rapidly adopted in peripheral areas as well as in highly literate centers such as the Low Countries, the Rhine Valley, and northern Italy.

Printing allowed for a dramatic expansion of libraries. Early humanists had to strive to create a library of several hundred volumes. The Venetian printer Aldus Manutius (1450–1515) himself printed and distributed over 120,000 volumes!

Printing allowed for the creation of agreed-upon standard editions of works in law, theology, philosophy, and science. Scholars in different parts of the European world could feel fairly confident that they and their colleagues were analyzing identical texts. Similarly, producing accurate medical and herbal diagrams, maps, and even reproductions of art and architecture was easier. Multiple copies of texts also made possible the study of rare and esoteric literary, philosophical, and scientific works. An unexpected result of the print revolution was the rise of the printshop as a center of culture and communication. The printers Aldus Manutius in Venice and Johannes Froben (d. 1527) in Basel were humanists. Both invited humanists to work in their shops editing their texts and correcting the proofs before printing. Printshops became a natural gathering place for clerics and laymen. Thus, they were natural sources of humanist ideas and later, in the sixteenth century, of Protestant religious programs.

Humanism Outside Italy

As the influence of the humanist movement extended beyond Italy, the interests of the humanists changed. Although a strong religious strain infused Italian humanism, public life lay at the center of Italian programs of education and reform. Outside Italy, however, moral and religious reform formed the heart of the movement. Northern humanists wanted to renew Christian life and reinvigorate the church. Critics of the church complained that the clergy were wealthy and ignorant and that the laity were uneducated and superstitious. To amend those failings, northern humanists were involved in building educational institutions, in unearthing and publishing texts by Church Fathers, and in chronicling local customs and history. The works of the two best-known humanists, Thomas More and Desiderius Erasmus, present a sharp critique of contemporary behavior and, in the case of Erasmus, a call to a new sense of piety. The religious views of Erasmus were so influential that northern humanism has generally come to be known as "Christian humanism."

The intellectual environment into which humanism spread from Italy had changed significantly since the thirteenth century. The universities of Paris and Oxford retained the status they had acquired earlier but found themselves competing with a host of new foundations. Like Paris, almost all had theological faculties dominated by scholastically trained theologians. Nevertheless, the new foundations often had chairs of rhetoric, or "eloquence," which left considerable scope for those who advocated humanistic learning. These new universities, from Cracow (1367) to Uppsala in Sweden (1477), also reflected the increased national feeling in various regions of Europe. The earliest university in the lands of the German Empire, the Charles University in Prague (1348), was founded at the request of Emperor Charles IV, whose court was in Prague. The foundation of a new university at Poszony (1465) by Johannes Vitéz was part of a cultural flowering of the Hungarian court at Buda. A supporter of King Matthias Corvinus, Vitéz corresponded with Italian humanists, collected manuscripts, and tried to recruit humanist teachers to come to Buda. The universities in Vienna (1365), Aix (1409), Louvain (1425), and numerous other cities owed their foundations to the pride and ambition of local leaders.

The humanists associated with the new universities were often educated in Italy, but they brought a new perspective to their work. Humanists in Sweden wrote histories of the Goths, celebrating the contributions of Germans to European culture. Polish humanists wrote similarly, in one case trying to define where in eastern Europe one could draw the line between Europe and Asia.

Humanists on faculties of law at French universities used humanistic techniques of historical and linguistic study. Italian-trained French lawyers introduced what came to be called the "Gallican style" of jurisprudence. Because legal ideas, like language, changed over time, they argued that Roman law had to be studied as a historically created system and not as an abstract and unchanging structure. Humanists, like Guillaume Budé (1468–1540), moved from the study of law to considerations of Roman coinage, religion, and economic life in order to better understand the formation of Roman law. The desire to understand the law led other humanist-legists to add the study of society in ancient Gaul to their work on Rome, and then to examine the law of other societies as well.

HUMANISM AND UNIVERSITIES

**HUMANISM
AND RELIGION**

The new universities often became centers of linguistic studies. Humanistic interest in language inspired the foundation of "trilingual" colleges in Spain, France, and the Low Countries to foster serious study of Hebrew, Greek, and Latin. Like Italian humanists, other humanists believed that knowledge of languages would allow students to understand more clearly the truths of Christianity. Typical of this movement was the archbishop of Toledo, Francisco Jiménez de Cisneros (1436–1517), who founded the University of Alcalá in 1508 with chairs of Latin, Greek, and Hebrew. He began the publication of a vast new edition of the Bible, called the "Polyglot ('many tongued') Bible" (1522) because it had parallel columns in Latin, Greek, and, where appropriate, Hebrew. Unlike Valla, Jiménez intended his translations not to challenge the Vulgate but merely to clarify its meaning. The university and the Bible were part of an effort to complete the conversion of Muslims and Jews and to reform religious practices among the old Christians.

To these humanists, the discovery and publication of early Christian authors seemed critical to any reform within the church. Jacques Lefèvre d'Étaples (le-FEV-ra du-TAHP-le) (1455–1536) of France was one of the most famous and influential of these humanistic editors of early Christian texts. After 1500, he concentrated on editing the texts of the early Church Fathers. The true spirit of Christianity, he believed, would be most clear in the works and lives of those who had lived closest to the age of the apostles. Christian humanists, inspired by Lefèvre, became key players in the later Reformation movements in France.

Tensions between the humanists and the advocates of Scholastic methods broke out over the cultural and linguistic studies that formed the heart of the humanist program. Taking to heart the humanistic belief that all philosophies and religions, not just Christianity, contained universal moral and spiritual truths, Johannes Reuchlin (RYE-klin) (1455–1522) of Württemberg embarked on a study of the Jewish Cabala. Johannes Pfefferkorn, a Dominican priest and recent convert from Judaism, attacked Reuchlin's use of Jewish traditions in the study of Christian theology. Sides were quickly drawn. The theological faculties of the German universities generally supported Pfefferkorn. The humanists supported Reuchlin. In his own defense, Reuchlin issued *The Letters of Illustrious Men*, a volume of correspondence he had received in support of his position. This work gave rise to one of the great satires of the Renaissance, *The Letters of Obscure Men* (1516), written by anonymous authors and purporting to be letters from various narrow-minded Scholastics in defense of Pfefferkorn. Although the debate arose over the validity of Hebraic studies for Christian theology, and not over humanistic ideas of reform or wisdom, it indicates the division between the humanists and much of the Scholastic community. Many people initially misunderstood the early controversies of the Protestant Reformation as a continuation of the conflicts between humanists and Scholastic theologians over the uses of Hebrew learning.

Thomas More Well-known humanist and chancellor of England under Henry VIII. His best-known work, *Utopia*, describes a fictional land of peace and harmony that has outlawed private property.

Desiderius Erasmus Prominent Dutch humanist who is best known for his satire *The Praise of Folly*.

Humanists as Critics

The careers of two humanists in particular exemplify the strength—and the limits—of the humanistic movement outside Italy: Sir **Thomas More** (1478–1535) of London and **Desiderius Erasmus** (1466–1536) of Rotterdam. Their careers developed along very different paths. More was educated at St. Anthony's School in London and became a lawyer. He translated Lucan and wrote a humanistic history of Richard III while pursuing his public career. Erasmus, on the other hand, was born the illegitimate son of a priest in the Low Countries. Forced by relatives into a monastery, he disliked the conservative piety and authoritarian discipline of traditional monastic life. Once allowed out of the monastery to serve as an episcopal secretary, he never returned. He made his way as an author and editor.

THOMAS MORE

More is most famous for his work *Utopia* (1516), the description of an ideal society located on the island of Utopia (literally, "nowhere") in the newly explored oceans. This powerful and contradictory work is written in two parts. Book I is a debate over the moral value of public service between Morus, a well-intentioned but practical politician, and Hythloday, a widely traveled idealist. Morus tries to make the bureaucrat's argument about working for change from within the system. Hythloday rejects the argument out of hand. Thomas More himself seems to have been unsure, at that time, about the virtues of public service. He was of two minds, and the debate between Morus and Hythloday reflects his indecision. As part of his critique of injustice and immoral governments in Europe, Hythloday describes in Book II the commonwealth of Utopia, in which there is no private property but strict equality of possessions, and, as a result, harmony, tolerance, and little or no violence.

Since the publication of *Utopia*, debates have raged about whether More, or anyone, could ever really hope to live in such a society. Some scholars have questioned how seriously More took this work—he seems to have written the initial sections merely to amuse friends. Yet, whatever More's intentions, Utopia's society of equality, cooperation, and acceptance continues to inspire social commentators.

Ironically, More, like his creation Morus, soon found himself trying to work for justice within precisely the sort of autocratic court that Hythloday criticized. Not long after the completion of *Utopia*, More entered the service of King Henry VIII (r. 1509–1547), eventually serving as chancellor of England. As a staunch Catholic and royal official, More never acted on utopian principles of peace and toleration. He was, in fact, responsible for the persecution of English Protestants in the years before the king's break with Rome (see pages 395–396). He implied that society could be reformed, yet, in the period after 1521, his humanism and his vision of utopian justice and tolerance had no influence on his own public life.

DESIDERIUS ERASMUS

Unlike More, who was drawn to the power of king and pope, Erasmus always avoided working for authorities. Often called the "Prince of Humanists," he was easily the best-known humanist of the early sixteenth century. He lived and taught in France, England, Italy, and Switzerland. Of all the humanists, it was Erasmus who most benefited from the printing revolution. The printer Aldus Manutius invited him to live and work in Venice, and he spent the last productive years of his life at Johannes Froben's press in Basel.

Over a long career, Erasmus brought out repeated editions of works designed to educate Christians. His *Adages*, first published in 1500, was a collection of proverbs from Greek and Roman sources. The work was immensely popular, and Erasmus repeatedly issued expanded editions. He tried to present Greek and Roman wisdom that would illuminate everyday problems. *The Colloquies* was a collection of popular stories. Designed as primers for students, they presented moral lessons, even as they taught good language. His ironic *The Praise of Folly* (1511) was dedicated to Thomas More. An oration by Folly in praise of folly, it is satire of a type unknown since antiquity. Folly's catalog of vices includes everyone from the ignoramus to the scholar. But more seriously, Erasmus believed, as Saint Paul had said, that Christians must be "fools for Christ." In effect, human existence is folly. Erasmus's *Folly* first made an observation that Shakespeare would refine and make famous: "Now the whole life of mortal men, what is it but a sort of play in which … [each person] plays his own part until the director gives him his cue to leave the stage."[13]

Erasmus's greatest contributions to European intellectual life were his edition of and commentaries on the New Testament. His was a critical edition of the Greek text and a Latin translation independent of the fourth-century Latin Vulgate of Jerome. Unlike Jiménez, Erasmus corrected parts of the Vulgate. He rejected the authority of tradition, saying, "The sin of corruption is greater, and the need for careful revision by scholars is greater also, where the source of corruption was ignorance."[14] What was revolutionary in his edition was his commentary, which emphasized the literal and historical recounting of human experiences. Erasmus's Bible was the basis of later vernacular translations of Scripture during the Reformation.

Underlying Erasmus's scholarly output was what he called his "Philosophy of Christ." Erasmus was convinced that the true essence of Christianity was to be found in the life and actions of Christ. Reasonable, self-reliant, truly Christian people did not need superstitious rituals or magic. In his *Colloquies*, he tells of a terrified priest who, during a shipwreck, promised everything to the Virgin Mary if only she would save him from drowning. But, Erasmus observed, it would have been more practical to start swimming!

Erasmus believed that a humanistic combination of classical and Christian wisdom could wipe away violence, superstition, and ignorance. Yet, his philosophy of Christ, based on faith in the goodness and educability of the individual, was swamped in the 1520s and 1530s by the sectarian claims of both Protestants and Catholics. Although Erasmus's New Testament was influential in the Reformation, his calls for reforms based on tolerance and reason were not.

SECTION SUMMARY

- Vernacular literatures of northern Europe emphasized religious and moral themes drawn from daily life.

- The development of printing using movable type made books more widely available. Humanists in northern Europe were more closely linked to university life and less tied to ideas of Roman public life.

- Thomas More and Desiderius Erasmus used their humanistic learning to develop a sophisticated critique of contemporary life.

POLITICS AND RENAISSANCE CULTURE

How did European rulers use Renaissance art and culture?

The educational reforms of the humanists and the innovations in the arts between 1300 and 1550 provided an opportunity for rulers and popes alike to use culture to define and celebrate their authority. Art, literature, and politics merged in the brilliant life of the Renaissance Italian courts, both secular and papal. To understand fully the Renaissance and its importance in the history of Europe, we need to examine the uses of culture by governments, specifically investigating the transformation of European ideas about service at court. We will take as a model the politics and cultural life at one noble court: the court of the Gonzaga family of Mantua. Then, we will see how the Renaissance papacy melded the secular and religious aspects of art, culture, and politics in its glittering court in Rome. Finally, we will discuss the development of the idea of the Renaissance gentleman and courtier made famous by Baldassare Castiglione (ka-stee-lee-OH-nay), who was reared at the Gonzaga court.

The Elaboration of the Court

The courts of northern Italy recruited artists and humanists inspired by classical civilization, and they closely imitated many of the values and new styles that were developing in the courts of northern Europe, such as the court of Burgundy. Throughout Europe, attendance at court became increasingly important to members of the nobility as a source of revenue and influence. Kings and the great territorial lords were equally interested in drawing people to their courts as a way to influence and control the noble and the powerful.

Rulers in most parts of Europe instituted monarchical orders of knighthood to reward allies and followers. The most famous in the English-speaking world was the Order of the Garter, founded in 1349 by King Edward III. The orders were but one of the innovations in the organization of the court during the fourteenth and fifteenth centuries. The numbers of cooks, servants, huntsmen, musicians, and artists employed at court jumped dramatically in the late Middle Ages. In this expansion, the papal court was a model for the rest of Europe. The popes at Avignon, in the fourteenth century, already had households of nearly six hundred persons. If all the bureaucrats, merchants, local officials, and visitors who continually swarmed around the elaborate papal court were also counted, the number grew even larger.

Courts were becoming theaters built around a series of widely understood signs and images that the ruler could manipulate. Culture was meant to reflect the reputation of the ruler. On important political or personal occasions, rulers organized jousts or tournaments around themes drawn from mythology. The dukes of Milan indicated the relative status of courtiers by inviting them to participate in particular hunts or jousts. They similarly organized their courtiers during feasts or elaborate entries into the towns and cities of their realms.

The late fourteenth and fifteenth centuries were periods of growth in the political and bureaucratic power of European rulers. The increasingly elaborate and sumptuous courts were one of the tools that rulers used to create a unified culture and ideology. At the court of the Gonzagas in Mantua, one of the most widely known of the fifteenth-century courts, the manipulation of Renaissance culture for political purposes was most complete.

The Court of Mantua

The city of Mantua, with perhaps 25,000 inhabitants in 1500, was small compared with Milan or Venice—the two cities with which it was most commonly allied. Located in a rich farming region near the Po River, Mantua did not have a large merchant or manufacturing class. Most Mantuans were involved in agriculture and regional trade in foodstuffs. The town had been a typical medieval Italian city-state until its government was overthrown by the noble Bonacolsi family in the thirteenth century. The Bonacolsis, in turn, were ousted in a palace coup in 1328 by their former comrades, the Gonzagas, who ruled the city until 1627.

The Gonzagas faced problems typical of many of the ruling families in northern Italy. The state they were creating was relatively small, their right to rule was not very widely recognized, and their control over the area was weak. The first step for the Gonzagas was to construct fortresses and fortified towns that could withstand foreign enemies. The second step was to gain recognition of their right to rule. In 1329, they were named imperial vicars, or representatives in the region. Later, in 1432, they bought the title "marquis" from the emperor Sigismund for the relatively low price of £12,000—equivalent to a year's pay for their courtiers. By 1500, they had exchanged that title for the more prestigious "duke."

Presiding over a strategic area between the Milanese and Venetian states, the Gonzagas maintained themselves through astute diplomatic connections with other Italian and European courts and through service as well-paid mercenaries in the Italian wars of the fifteenth and sixteenth centuries.

The family's reputation was enhanced by Gianfrancesco (jan-fran-CHES-ko) (d. 1444) and Lodovico, who brought the Renaissance and the new court style to Mantua. By 1500, as many as eight hundred or more nobles, cooks, maids, and horsemen may have gathered in the court. Critics called them idlers, "who have no other function but to cater to the tastes of the Duke." It was under the tutelage of the Gonzagas that Vittorino da Feltre created his educational experiment in Villa Giocosa, which drew noble pupils from throughout Italy. It would be hard to overestimate the value for the Gonzagas of a school that attracted sons of the dukes of Urbino, Ferrara, and Milan and of numerous lesser nobles. The family also called many artists to Mantua. Lodovico invited Antonio Pisano, called Pisanello (ca. 1415–1456), probably the most famous court artist of the fifteenth century. Pisanello created a series of frescoes on Arthurian themes for the Gonzaga palace. In these frescoes, Lodovico is portrayed as a hero of King Arthur's Round Table.

The Gonzagas are best known for their patronage of art with classical themes. The Florentine writer and architect Leon Battista Alberti (1404–1472) redesigned the façade of the Church of Sant'Andrea for the Gonzagas, in the form of a Roman triumphal arch. The church, which long had been associated with the family, became a monument to the Gonzaga court, just as the Arch of Constantine in Rome had celebrated imperial power a thousand years earlier. In the 1460s, Lodovico summoned Andrea Mantegna (1441–1506) to his court. Trained in Padua and Venice, Mantegna was, at that time, the leading painter in northern Italy. His masterwork is the *Camera degli Sposi* (literally, "the room of the spouses"), completed in 1474. It features family portraits of Lodovico Gonzaga and his family, framed in imitations of Roman imperial portrait medallions. One scene shows Lodovico welcoming his son, a newly appointed cardinal, back from Rome. Lodovico even included the portrait of the Holy Roman emperor who had never been to Mantua but was related to Lodovico's wife, Barbara of Brandenburg. As Mantegna finished the work, diplomats and rulers throughout Italy carefully monitored it—proof to all of the new status of the Gonzagas.

The Gonzaga court, like most others, was both public and private. On the one hand, finances for the city, appointments to public offices, and important political decisions were made by the men who dominated the court. On the other hand, as the prince's domestic setting, it was a place where women were expected to be seen and could exert their influence. Women were thus actively involved in creating the ideology of the court. Through the patronage of classical paintings, often with moral and political messages, wives of princes helped make the court better known and more widely accepted throughout Italy and Europe.

The arrival at court of Isabella d'Este (1494–1539), as the wife of Francesco Gonzaga, marked the high point of the Renaissance in Mantua. Isabella had received a classical education at Ferrara and maintained an interest in art, architecture, and music all her life. Isabella was also an accomplished musician, playing a variety of string and keyboard instruments. She and others of the Gonzaga family recruited Flemish and Italian musicians to their court. By the end of the sixteenth century, Mantua was one of the most important musical centers of Europe. As a patron of the arts, she knew what she wanted. Isabella used the general interest in the cultural life of Mantua as a way to increase contacts with the Italian and European powers. She used these informal cultural connections to further the family's political and diplomatic goals.

In the fourteenth century, Petrarch had complained that however enjoyable feasting in Mantua might be, the place was dusty, plagued by mosquitoes, and overrun with frogs. By the end of the fifteenth century, the Gonzagas had transformed their city and secured a prominent place for themselves on the Italian, and the European, stage.

The Renaissance Papacy

The issues of power and how it is displayed had religious as well as secular dimensions. After its fourteenth- and fifteenth-century struggles over jurisdiction, the papacy found itself reduced, in many respects, to the status of an Italian Renaissance court. But popes still needed to defend their primacy within the church from conciliarists, who had argued that all Christians, including the pope, were bound to obey the commands of general councils. The ideological focus of the revived papacy was Rome.

THE TRANSFORMATION OF ROME

The first step in the creation of a new Rome was taken by Pope Nicholas V (r. 1446–1455), a cleric who had spent many years in the cultural environment of Renaissance Florence. Hoping to restore Rome and its church to their former glory, Nicholas and his successors patronized the arts, established a lively court culture, and sponsored numerous building projects. Nicholas was an avid collector of ancient manuscripts that seemed to demonstrate the intellectual and religious primacy of Rome. He invited numerous artists and intellectuals to the papal court, including Leon Battista Alberti. He based his treatise, *On Architecture* (1452), on his research in topography and reading done in Rome. This was the most important work on architecture produced during the Renaissance. It was probably under Alberti's influence that Nicholas embarked on a series of ambitious urban renewal projects in Rome, which included bridges, roads, and a rebuilt Saint Peter's Basilica.

The transformation of Rome had an ideological purpose. As one orator proclaimed, "Illuminated by the light of faith and Christian truth, [Rome] is destined to be the firmament of religion . . . , the secure haven for Christians."[15] Thus, the papal response to critics was to note that Rome and its government were central to political and religious life in Christendom. By reviving

Giving of the Keys to Saint Peter   Pietro Perugino's painting of Saint Peter receiving from Christ the keys to "bind and loose" on earth and in heaven illustrates the basis of papal claims to authority within the Christian church. This is the central message of the decorative plan of the Sistine Chapel. (Scala/Art Resource, NY)

the style and organization of classical antiquity, the church sought to link papal Rome to a magnificent imperial tradition, reaching back to Augustus and even to Alexander the Great. To papal supporters, only one authority could rule the church. Early tradition and the continuity of the city itself, they assumed, demonstrated papal primacy.

One particular monument in Rome captures most vividly the cultural, religious, and ideological program of the papacy: the Sistine Chapel in the Vatican Palace. The chapel is best known for the decoration of the ceiling by the Florentine artist Michelangelo (see pages 332–333) and for the striking images in his painting of the Last Judgment. The chapel, however, was commissioned by Pope Sixtus IV in 1475. It was to be an audience chamber in which an enthroned pope could meet the representatives of other states. In addition, it was expected that the college of cardinals would gather in the chapel for the election of new popes.

THE SISTINE CHAPEL

The decorations done before Michelangelo painted the ceiling reflect the intellectual and ideological values that Sixtus hoped to transmit to the ambassadors and churchmen who entered the chapel. Along the lower sidewalls are portraits of earlier popes, a feature typical of early Roman churches. More ideologically significant, however, are two cycles of paintings of the lives of Moses and Christ, drawing parallels between them. To execute the scenes, Sixtus called to Rome some of the greatest artists of the late fifteenth century: Sandro Botticelli, Domenico Ghirlandaio, Luca Signorelli, and Pietro Perugino. The works illustrate the continuity of the Old Testament and New Testament and emphasize the importance of obedience to the authority of God. The meaning is most obvious in Perugino's painting of Saint Peter receiving the keys to the Kingdom of Heaven from Christ. The allusion is to Matthew 16:18: "Thou art Peter and upon this rock I shall build my church." The keys are the symbol of the claim of the pope, as successor to Saint Peter, to have the power to bind and loose sinners and their punishments. Directly across from Perugino's painting is Botticelli's *The Judgment of Corah*, which portrays the story of the opponent who challenged the leadership of Moses and Aaron while the Israelites wandered in the wilderness. Corah and his supporters, according to Numbers 16:33, fell live into Hell. Various popes recalled the fate of Corah and the rebels. The pope was bound to oppose the council, Pope Eugenius argued, "to save the people entrusted to his care, lest together with those who hold the power of the council above that of the papacy they suffer a punishment even more dire than that which befell Corah."[16] The meaning of the painting and the entire chapel could not be clearer.

The effects of Renaissance revival were profound. Rome grew from a modest population of about 17,000 in 1400 to 35,000 in 1450. By 1517, the city had a population of over 85,000, five times its population at the end of the Great Schism. The papal program was a success. Rome was transformed from a provincial town to a major European capital, perhaps the most important artistic and cultural center of the sixteenth century. Visitors to the Sistine Chapel, like visitors to the papal city itself, were expected to leave with a profound sense of the antiquity of the papal office and of the continuity of papal exercise of religious authority. Because the building and decorating were being completed as the Protestant Reformation was beginning in Germany, some historians have criticized the expense of the political and cultural program undertaken by the Renaissance popes. But to contemporaries on the scene, the work was a logical and necessary attempt to strengthen the church's standing in Christendom.

Castiglione and the European Gentleman

Renaissance ideas did not just spread in intellectual circles. They also were part of the transformation of the medieval knight into the early modern "gentleman." In 1528, Baldassare Castiglione (1478–1529) published *The Book of the Courtier*. The work, which describes the ideal behavior of a courtier, was based on Castiglione's own distinguished career serving in Italian courts. Set at the court of Urbino, the book chronicles a series of fictional discussions over the course of four nights in March 1507. Among the participants are the duchess of Urbino, Elizabeth Gonzaga; Emilia Pia, her lady-in-waiting; and a group of humanists, men of action, and courtiers. In four evenings, members of the circle try to describe the perfect gentleman of court. In the process, they debate the nature of nobility, humor, women, and love.

Castiglione describes, in many respects, a typical gathering at court, and the discourses reflect contemporary views of relations between men and women. The wives of princes were

Federigo da Montefeltro's Studiolo The duchy of Urbino was a showpiece of Renaissance court life and was the eventual locale for Castiglione's *Book of the Courtier*. It owed much of its fame to Duke Federigo da Montefeltro. Federigo's study is decorated with an expensive inlaid wooden design. Its illusion of great space and the expense of its construction were meant to celebrate Federigo's wealth and power. (Scala/Art Resource, NY)

expected to be organizers of life at court but also paragons of domestic virtues. Women were expected to manage the household and even the financial interests if her husband was away. Noble and elite women also played an important, but indirect, role in political and diplomatic negotiations. Women communicated informally ideas and information that could not be passed in public dispatches. But even powerful women had to be careful about public appearances. In Castiglione's book, for example, the women organize the discussion, and the men discuss. Although the women direct and influence the talk by jokes and short interventions, they cannot afford to dominate the debate. As Emilia Pia explains, "[women] must be more circumspect, and more careful not to give occasion for evil being said of them ... for a woman has not so many ways of defending herself against false calumnies as a man has."[17] Thus, in debate, as in politics and diplomacy, the influence of women was most effective when it was indirect.

The topics of such discussions were not randomly chosen. Castiglione explains that he wished "to describe the form of courtiership most appropriate for a gentleman living at the courts of princes." Castiglione's popularity was based on his deliberate joining of humanistic ideas and traditional chivalric values. Although his topic is the court with all its trappings, he tells his readers that his models for the discussion were Latin and Greek dialogues, especially those of Cicero and Plato. As a Platonist, he believed that all truly noble gentlemen have an inborn quality of "grace." It has to be brought out, however, just as Michelangelo freed his figures from stone.

What struck Castiglione's readers most was his advice about behavior. Francesco Guicciardini of Florence once remarked, "When I was young, I used to scoff at knowing how to play, dance, and sing, and other such frivolities. ... I have nevertheless seen from experience that these ornaments and accomplishments lend dignity and reputation even to men of good rank."[18] Guicciardini's comment underlines the value that readers found in Castiglione's work. Grace may be inbred, but it must be brought to the attention of those who control the court. Courtiers should, first of all, study the military arts. They have to fight, but only on occasions when their prowess will be noticed. Castiglione adds practical advice about how to dress, talk, and participate in music and dancing: Never leap about wildly when dancing as peasants might, but dance only with an air of dignity and decorum. Castiglione further urges the courtier to be careful in dress: the French are "overdressed"; the Italians too quickly adopt the most recent and colorful styles. Bowing to the political, as well as social realities of Spanish domination of Italy, Castiglione advises black or dark colors, which "reflect the sobriety of the Spaniards, since external appearances often bear witness to what is within."

According to Castiglione, the courtier must take pains "to earn that universal regard which everyone covets." Too much imitation and obvious study, however, lead to affectation. Castiglione counsels courtiers to carry themselves with a certain diffidence or unstudied naturalness (*sprezzatura*) covering their artifice. Accomplished courtiers should exhibit "that graceful and nonchalant spontaneity (as it is often called) ... so that those who are watching them imagine that they couldn't and wouldn't even know how to make a mistake." Thus, Castiglione's courtier must walk a fine line between clearly imitated and apparently natural grace.

Castiglione's book was an immediate success and widely followed even by those who claimed to have rejected it. By 1561, it was available in Spanish, French, and English translations. The reasons are not difficult to guess. It was critical for the courtier "to win for himself the mind and favour of the prince," and even those who disliked music, dancing, and light conversation learned Castiglione's arts "to open the way to the favour of princes." Many of the courtly arts that Castiglione preached had been traditional for centuries. Yet, Castiglione's humanistic explanations and emphasis on form, control, and fashion had never seemed so essential as they did to the cultured gentlemen of the courts of the Renaissance and early modern Europe.

SECTION SUMMARY

- Rulers found Renaissance art and culture to be convenient vehicles to explain or justify political power.

- The Gonzaga rulers of Mantua followed a conscious policy of recruiting famous artists to work at their court.

- The papacy used art and culture to explain and justify their predominance in Rome and the Christian church.

- Castiglione's dialogue on behavior at court became a European bestseller because of its explanation of how to succeed at court.

CHAPTER SUMMARY

The Renaissance was a broad cultural movement that began in Italy in response to a series of crises in the early fourteenth century. It was a cultural and ideological movement based on the assumption that study and imitation of the past was the best method for reform and innovation in the future. The impulse for change arose from the belief, shared by thinkers from Petrarch to Machiavelli, that a great deal could be learned from study of the Roman past. This was the basis for humanistic innovations in language, history, and politics. Even revolutionary thinkers, such as Lorenzo Valla and Niccolò Machiavelli, began with the study of classical literature and history.

The same transformation is evident among the artists. Early in the fifteenth century, Florentines who experimented with perspective were intent on recovering lost Roman knowledge, and Michelangelo was praised not only for mastering, but also for surpassing, Roman norms. Similar trends were evident in northern Europe, where artists like Albrecht Dürer combined their understanding of Italian art with northern ideas. Throughout Europe, art was an important component of religious and political culture.

FOCUS QUESTIONS

- How did Italians use classical values to deal with cultural and political issues?

- What was "new" about Renaissance art?

- In what ways did humanism outside Italy differ from Italian humanism?

- How did European rulers use Renaissance art and culture?

Humanistic studies outside of Italy were less tied to public life. Moral and spiritual issues were more important. Yet, the same movement from imitation to transformation is evident. Erasmus and More valued humanistic learning from Italy, but in *The Praise of Folly* and *Utopia*, the use of past ideas and models was neither simple nor direct. Both authors, however, shared with Italian humanists the idea that humanistic values could lead to a transformation of individuals and society as a whole.

The integration of art, literature, and public life was most evident in the ways that governments used art. The Gonzaga court and the papacy clearly recognized the value of artistic and literary works as vehicles for explaining and justifying power and influence. The beauty of Mantegna's painting and the power of Michelangelo's frescoes do not obscure their messages about power and authority.

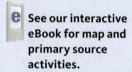

This icon will direct you to additional materials on the website: www.cengage.com/history/noble/westciv6e.

KEY TERMS

Renaissance (p. 321)

humanism (p. 322)

Francesco Petrarch (p. 323)

civic humanism (p. 324)

On the Falsely Believed and Forged Donation of Constantine (p. 327)

Niccolò Machiavelli (p. 329)

linear perspective (p. 331)

Leonardo da Vinci (p. 332)

Sistine Chapel (p. 332)

Johann Gutenberg (p. 340)

Thomas More (p. 342)

Desiderius Erasmus (p. 342)

See our interactive eBook for map and primary source activities.

NOTES

1. Quoted in J. B. Trapp, ed., *Background to the English Renaissance* (London: Gray-Mills Publishing, 1974), p. 11.

2. Quoted in N. Mann, *Petrarch* (Oxford: Oxford University Press), p. 67.

3. Petrarch, "On His Own Ignorance and That of Many Others," in *The Renaissance Philosophy of Man*, ed. Ernst Cassirer, Paul Oskar Kristeller, and John H. Randall (Chicago: University of Chicago Press, 1948), p. 105.

4. Quoted in Benjamin G. Kohl and Ronald G. Witt, *The Earthly Republic* (Philadelphia: University of Pennsylvania Press, 1978), p. 11.

5. Quoted in M. L. King, *Women of the Renaissance* (Chicago: University of Chicago Press, 1991), p. 194.

6. Quoted ibid., p. 222.

7. Quoted ibid., p. 198.

8. K. R. Bartlett, *The Civilization of the Italian Renaissance* (Lexington, Mass.: D. C. Heath, 1992), p. 314.

9. Quoted ibid., p. 160.

10. Quoted in *The Notebooks of Leonardo da Vinci*, ed. J. P. Richter, vol. 1 (New York: Dover, 1883 and 1970), p. 14.

11. Giorgio Vasari, *The Lives of the Artists*, trans. George Bull (Baltimore: Penguin, 1965), p. 338.

12. Julia Bondanella and Mark Musa, eds., *The Italian Renaissance Reader* (New York: Meridian Books, 1987), p. 377.

13. Quoted in A. Rabil, Jr., *Renaissance Humanism: Foundations, Forms, and Legacy*, vol. 2 (Philadelphia: University of Pennsylvania Press, 1988), p. 236.

14. Quoted ibid., p. 229.

15. Raffaele Brandolini, quoted in Charles L. Stinger, *The Renaissance in Rome* (Bloomington: Indiana University Press, 1985), p. 156.

16. Quoted in Leopold D. Ettlinger, *The Sistine Chapel Before Michelangelo* (Oxford: Oxford University Press, 1965), p. 105.

17. Quoted in R. M. San Juan, "The Court Lady's Dilemma: Isabella d'Este and Art Collecting in the Renaissance," *Oxford Art Journal* 14 (1991): 71.

18. Quoted in R. W. Hanning and D. Rosand, eds., *Castiglione: The Ideal and the Real in Renaissance Culture* (New Haven, Conn.: Yale University Press, 1983), p. 17.

INDEX